3.10

0681

history of the

LATER ROMAN EMPIRE

FROM THE DEATH OF
THEODOSIUS I.
TO THE DEATH OF
JUSTINIAN

by J. B. Bury

In two volumes
Volume Two

DOVER PUBLICATIONS, INC., NEW YORK

This new Dover edition first published in 1958 is an unabridged and unaltered republication of the first edition. It is published by special arrangement with St. Martins Press.

International Standard Book Number: 0-486-20399-9
Library of Congress Catalog Card Number: 58-11273

Manufactured in the United States of America

Dover Publications, Inc.
180 Varick Street
New York 14, N. Y.

CONTENTS

VOL. II

CHAPTER XIV

CHAPTER XV

CHAPTER XVI

CHAPTER XX

CHAPTER XXI

CHAPTER XXII

CHAPTER XXIII

CHAPTER XXIV

MAPS

GENEALOGICAL TABLE OF THE HOUSE OF JUSTIN

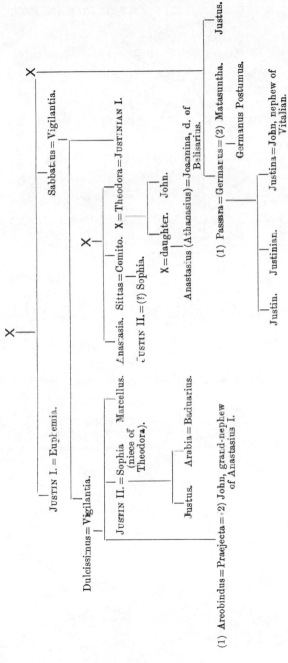

CHAPTER XIV

THE EMPIRE AND PERSIA

§ 1. *Relations with Persia in the Fifth Century*

THE rulers of Constantinople would hardly have steered their section of the Empire with even such success as they achieved through the dangers which beset it in the fifth century, had it not been that from the reign of Arcadius to that of Anastasius their peaceful relations with the Sassanid kings of Persia were only twice interrupted by brief hostilities. The unusually long duration of this period of peace, notwithstanding the fact that the conditions in Armenia constantly supplied provocations or pretexts for war, was in a great measure due to the occupation of Persia with savage and dangerous enemies who threatened her north-eastern frontier, the Ephthalites or White Huns, but there was a contributory cause in the fact that the power of the Sassanid kings at this time was steadily declining. It is significant that when, at the end of the fifth century, a monarch arose who was able to hold his own against the encroachments of the Zoroastrian priesthood and the nobility, grave hostilities immediately ensued which were to last with few and uneasy intervals for a hundred and thirty years.

At the accession of Arcadius, Varahran IV. was on the Persian throne, but was succeeded in A.D. 399 by Yezdegerd I. The policy of this sovran was favourable to his Christian subjects, who had been allowed to recover from the violent persecution which they had suffered at the hands of Sapor, the conqueror of Julian ; and he was an object of veneration to Christian historians,[1] while the Magi and the chroniclers of his own kingdom

---

[1] Compare *e.g.* Socrates, vii. 8; *Chron. Edess.* (ed. Guidi), p. 107. See Labourt, *Le Christianisme dans l'empire perse*, 91-93.

detested his name. After the death of Arcadius there were negotiations between the courts of Constantinople and Ctesiphon, but it is difficult to discover precisely what occurred. There is a record, which can hardly fail to have some foundation, that in his last illness Arcadius was fretted by the fear that the Persians might take advantage of his son's infancy to attack the Empire, and that he drew up a testament in which he requested the Great King to act as guardian of his son.[1] There seems no reason not to accept this statement, provided we do not press the legal sense of guardian,[2] and take the act of Arcadius to have been simply a recommendation of Theodosius to the protection and goodwill of Yezdegerd. The communication of this request would naturally be entrusted to the embassy, which, according to the traditional etiquette, announced the accession of a new Emperor at the Persian court.[3] Yezdegerd took the wish of his " brother " as a compliment and declared that the enemies of Theodosius would have to deal with him.

Whatever be the truth about this record, which is not mentioned by contemporary writers,[4] there is no doubt that there were transactions between the two governments at this juncture, and either a new treaty or some less formal arrangement seems to have been concluded, bearing chiefly on the position of Persian Christians and perhaps also on commerce. The Imperial Government employed the good offices of Maruthas, bishop of Martyropolis,[5] who, partly on account of his medical

---

[1] Procopius, *B.P.* i. 2; Theophanes, A.M. 5900 (a notice evidently drawn from the same source as that in Michael Syrus, viii. 1). Haury's view (*Zur Beurteilung des Procop.* 21) that Arcadius appointed Yezdegerd " guardian " in 402, when he crowned Theodosius, cannot be accepted. Agathias (iv. 26) expresses scepticism about this statement of Procopius, and many modern writers (*e.g.* Tillemont, Gibbon, Nöldeke) have rejected it. (See P. Sauerbrei, *König Jazdegerd, der Sünder*, in *Festschrift Albert v. Bamberg*, Gotha, 1905; on the other hand, Haury, *B.Z.* xv. 291 *sqq.* Cp. Güterbock, *Byzanz und Persien*, 28.) But such a recommendation of a child heir to a foreign monarch is not without parallels. Heraclius, when he went forth against Persia, is said to have placed his son

under the guardianship of the Chagan of the Avars. Kavad proposed that Justin I. should adopt his son Chosroes (see below, p. 79).

[2] Procopius uses the word ἐπίτροπος (=*tutor*), Theophanes (A.M. 5900), κουράτωρ.

[3] According to Skylitzes (Cedrenus, i. 586) Arcadius sent 1000 lbs. of gold to Yezdegerd. This is not improbable; the embassy announcing the Emperor's decease would in any case offer gifts.

[4] Sauerbrei (*op. cit.*) seems to be right in his conclusion that the notice in Theophanes is not taken from Procopius but from a common source. If this is so, the record is not later than the fifth century. Skylitzes seems to have had access to this source or to an independent derivative.

[5] Socrates, *loc. cit.*

knowledge, enjoyed much credit with Yezdegerd, to persuade the king to protect his Christian subjects. Yezdegerd inaugurated a new policy, and for the next twelve years the Christians of Persia possessed complete ecclesiastical freedom.[1] It is possible that at the same time the commercial relations between the two realms were under discussion. It was the policy of both powers alike to restrict the interchange of merchandise to a few places close to the frontier. Persian merchants never came to Constantinople, Roman merchants never went to Ctesiphon. The governments feared espionage under the guise of trade, and everything was done to discourage free intercourse between the two states. Before the treaty of Jovian, Nisibis was the only Roman town in which Persian merchants were allowed to trade.[2] After the loss of Nisibis, Callinicum seems to have become the Roman market for Persian merchandise, but we hear nothing of the new arrangements until the year 408–409, when an Imperial edict was issued for the direction of the governors of the frontier provinces.[3] From it we learn that the two governments had agreed that the Persian towns of Nisibis and Artaxata and the Imperial town of Callinicum should be the only places to which Persian and Roman traders might bring their wares and resort to transact business. Taken in connection with the fact that the two governments had been engaged in negotiations, this promulgation of the edict at this time suggests that if a new compact regarding commercial relations was not concluded, an old agreement, which may have been laxly executed, was confirmed.[4]

---

[1] The important Council of Seleucia held in 410 was the immediate outcome of the new situation. It is stated in the Acts of this Council that Yezdegerd ordained that the churches destroyed by his predecessors should be rebuilt, that all who had been imprisoned for their faith should be set at liberty, and the clergy should be free to move about without fear, *Synodicon orientale*, ed. Chabot, p. 254. See Labourt, *op. cit.* 91 *sqq.*

[2] Peter Patric. *fr.* 3 (*Leg. Rom.* p. 4).

[3] *C.J.* iv. 63. 4. The motive of the restriction of trade to certain places is stated plainly: *ne alieni regni, quod non convenit, scrutentur arcana.*

Artaxata was subsequently replaced by Dubios (Dovin) not far to the north-east; cp. Procopius, *B.P.* ii. 25.
[4] Güterbock (*op. cit.* 74-75) refers the agreement to the treaty of 387, but why not to that of 363 ? The words of the edict are *loca in quibus foederis tempore cum memorata natione nobis convenit.* Sozomen makes the remarkable statement that the Persians prepared for war at this juncture, and then concluded a peace for 100 years (ix. 4 *ad init.*). It is curious that he should have confused the peace of 422 with the transactions of 408. Haury (*loc. cit.* p. 294) suggests that there was actually a movement in Byzantium against the succession of Theodosius and that

At the very end of Yezdegerd's reign the friendly understanding was clouded. All might have gone well if the Christian
clergy had been content to be tolerated and to enjoy their
religious liberty. But they engaged in an active campaign of
proselytism and were so successful in converting Persians to
Christianity that the king became seriously alarmed.[1] It was
perfectly natural that he should not have been disposed to allow
the Zoroastrian religion to be endangered by the propagation
of a hostile creed. It is quite certain that if there had been
fanatical Zoroastrians [2] in the Roman Empire and they had
undertaken to convert Christians, the Christian government
would have stopped at nothing to avert the danger. Given
the ideas which then prevailed on the importance of State
religions, we cannot be surprised that Yezdegerd should have
permitted acts of persecution. Some of the Christians fled to
Roman territory. The Imperial government refused to surrender
them (A.D. 420) and prepared for the event of war.[3] Yezdegerd
died at this juncture, and was succeeded by his son Varahran V.,
who was completely under the influence of the Zoroastrian priests,
and began a general persecution.[4] Some outrages were committed on Roman merchants. The war which resulted lasted
for little more than a year, and the Roman armies were successful.[5] Then a treaty was negotiated by which peace was made

Yezdegerd threatened to intervene.
It may be observed that the appointment of the Persian eunuch Antiochus
to educate Theodosius had nothing to
do with Yezdegerd.

[1] The incident which immediately
provoked the persecution was the
outrageous act of a priest who
destroyed a fire-temple near his
church. Theodoret, v. 38 ; Labourt,
op. cit. 106 sq.

[2] There were some old Zoroastrian
communities in Cappadocia—settlers
from Babylonia—in the time of the
Achaemenids, which still existed in the
fourth and fifth centuries (cp. Basil,
Epp. 258-325) ; they were known
as Magusaeans (Μαγουσαῖοι). Strabo
notices then, xv. 3. 15 ἐν δὲ τῇ Καππα-
δοκίᾳ (πολὺ γὰρ ἐκεῖ τὸ τῶν Μάγων φῦλον,
οἳ καὶ πύραιθοι καλοῦνται· πολλὰ δὲ
καὶ τῶν Περσικῶν θεῶν ἱερά), κτλ. See
Cumont, Les Mystères de Mithra, ed. 3,
pp. 11, 12.

[3] A constitution authorising the
inhabitants of the Eastern and Pontic
provinces to build walls round their
homes (May, 420) is interpreted as
a measure taken in view of impending invasion. C.J. viii. 10. 10. Cp.
Lebeau, v. p. 493.

[4] Labourt, 110 sqq.

[5] The general Ardaburius operated
in Arzanene and gained a victory,
autumn 421, which forced the Persians
to retreat to Nisibis, which Ardaburius
then besieged. He raised the siege
on the arrival of an army under
Varahran, who proceeded to attack
Resaina. Meanwhile the Saracens of
Hira, under Al-Mundhir, were sent
to invade Syria, and were defeated
by Vitianus. During the peace
negotiations the Persians attacked
the Romans and were defeated by
Procopius, son-in-law of Anthemius
(Socrates, vii. 18, 20). The Empress
Eudocia celebrated the war in a poem
in heroic metre (ib. 21).

for a hundred years (A.D. 422). Varahran undertook to stay the persecution; and it was agreed that neither party should receive the Saracen subjects of the other.[1]

The attention of Varahran was soon occupied by the appearance of new enemies beyond the Oxus, who for more than a hundred years were constantly to distract Persian arms from the Roman frontier.[2] The lands between the Oxus and Jaxartes had for some centuries been in the hands of the Kushans. The Kushans were now conquered (c. A.D. 425) by another Tartar people, who were known to the Chinese as the Ye-tha, to Armenian and Arabic writers as the Haithal, and to the Greeks as the Ephthalites.[3] The Greek historians sometimes classify them as Huns, but add the qualification " white," which refers to their fair complexion and distinguishes them from the true Huns (Hiung-nu), who were dark and ugly.[4] The Ephthalites belonged in fact not to the Hiung-nu, but to a different Turanian race, which was known to the Chinese as the Hoa. Their appearance on the Oxus marked a new epoch in the perennial warfare between Iran and Turan. They soon built up a considerable empire extending from the Caspian to the Indus, including Chorasmia, Sogdiana, and part of north-western India.[5] Their chief town was Balkh, and Gurgan [6] (on the river of the same name which flows into the Caspian) was their principal frontier fortress against Persia. The first hostilities against the Ephthalites broke out in A.D. 427 and resulted in a complete victory for Varahran.[7]

The reign of Theodosius II. witnessed a second but less serious disturbance of the peace, soon after the accession of Yezdegerd II. (A.D. 438). The cause is uncertain. It has been conjectured, without sufficient evidence, that the Persian king was in league

---

[1] Malchus (fr. 1 in De leg. gent. p. 568) refers this provision to the peace concluding " the greatest war " in the time of Theodosius. This obviously means that of 422, not that of 442.

[2] The best study of the history of the Ephthalites is the memoir of Ed. Drouin in Le Muséon, xiv. (1895). See also A. Cunningham, Ephthalite or White Huns, in Transactions of Ninth International Oriental Congress, London, 1892.

[3] Theophylactus Simocatta gives the alternative name of 'Αβδελοί (Hist. vii. 7. 8).

[4] See e.g. Proc. B.P. i. 3; Cosmas,

Christ. Top. xi. 11. Procopius states that their habits were not nomad.

[5] Cosmas, l.c.

[6] Γοργώ, Procop. l.c.

[7] The following is a chronological list of the Perso-Ephthalite wars (Drouin, op. cit. p. 288):

A.D. 427 war under Varahran.
,,   442–449 war under Yezdegerd II.
,,   450–451   ,,   ,,
,,   454   ,,   ,,
,,   474–476   ,,   Perozes.
,,   482–484   ,,   ,,
,,   485 war in interregnum.
,,   503–513 war under Kavad.
,,   556–557   ,,   Chosroes.

with Attila and Gaiseric for the destruction of the Empire.[1]
It is possible that Persian suspicions had been provoked by the
erection of a fortress at Erzerum in Roman Armenia, on the
Persarmenian frontier, which was named Theodosiopolis.[2] This
stronghold was to have a long history, reaching down to the
present day, as one of the principal eastern defences of Asia
Minor. Whatever motives may have instigated him to violate
the peace, Yezdegerd raided Roman Armenia (A.D. 440).[3]
Menaced, however, in his rear by an invasion of the Ephthalites he
was easily bought off by Anatolius, the Master of Soldiers in the
East, and Aspar. A new peace was then concluded (A.D. 442),
probably confirming the treaty of A.D. 422, with the additional
stipulations that neither party should build a fortress within
a certain distance of the frontier, and that the Romans should
(as had been agreed by the treaty of A.D. 363) contribute a
fixed sum to keep in repair the defences of the Caspian Gates
against the barbarians beyond the Caucasus. " Caspian Gates "
is a misleading name ; for it was used to designate not, as one
would expect, passes at the eastern extremity of the range, but
passes in the centre, especially that of Dariel, north of Iberia.
These danger-points were guarded by the Romans so long as
they were overlords of Iberia, but now they abandoned Iberia
to Persian influence and were therefore no longer in a position
to keep garrisons in the mountain passes.[4]

The greater part of Yezdegerd's reign was troubled by war
with the Ephthalites. He made energetic efforts to convert
Persian Armenia to the religion of Zoroaster, but the Armenians
were tenacious of their Christianity and offered steady resistance
to his armies. Since A.D. 428, when the last Arsacid king,
Ardashir, had been deposed by the Persian monarch at the

---

[1] Güldenpenning, op. cit. 340.

[2] Moses of Chorene relates its
foundation by Anatolius in his Hist.
Arm. iii. 59. As Book III. ends in
A.D. 433, this seems to be the lower
limit for the date. Procopius, Aed.
iii. 5, p. 255 (cp. p. 210), ascribes the
foundation to Theodosius I. (and so
Chapot, op. cit. p. 361) ; but his
confusion between the two Emperors
of that name is quite clear in iii. 1,
p. 210.

[3] And in Mesopotamia he advanced
as far as Nisibis. See Elisha Vartabed,
Hist. Arm. c. 1, p. 184.

[4] The Persians built the fortress
of Biraparach ('Ιουροειπαάχ Priscus,
fr. 15, De leg. gent. p. 586 ; Βιραπαράχ
John Lydus, De mag. iii. 52) probably
in the pass of Dariel ; and the fortress
Korytzon (Menander, fr. 3, De leg.
Rom. p. 180), which seems to be the
Tzur of Procopius (B.G. iv. 3 ; De
Boor conjectures χώρου Τζόν in
Menander), perhaps farther east. Cp.
P.-W. s.v. Biraparach ; Chapot,
op. cit. p. 369. See also Procopius,
B.P. i. 10. Procopius (ib. 2 ad fin.)
confounds the war of 420-422 with
that of 440-441.

request of the Armenians themselves, the country had been ruled by Persian governors (*marzbans*).[1] In A.D. 450 the Armenians sent a message to Constantinople imploring the Emperor to rescue them and their faith. Marcian, who had just come to the throne and was threatened by Attila, was not in a position to go to war with Persia for the sake of the Persarmenian Christians. He determined to be neutral, and Yezdegerd was informed that he need fear no hostilities from the Empire.[2] The war between the Armenians and their overlord continued after the death of Yezdegerd (A.D. 453) during the reign of Firuz (Perozes), under the leadership of Vahan the Mamigonian.

Firuz perished in a war with the Ephthalites, whose king had devised a cunning stratagem of covered ditches which were fatal to the Persian cavalry (A.D. 484).[3] Valakhesh (Balas), perhaps his brother, followed him, and enjoyed a shorter but more peaceable reign. He made a treaty with the enemy, consenting to pay them a tribute for two years. He pacified Armenia by granting unreserved toleration; Vahan was appointed its governor; and Christianity was reinstated. Valakhesh died in A.D. 488.

During this period—the reigns of Marcian, Leo, and Zeno—there had been no hostilities between the two empires, but there had been diplomatic incidents. About A.D. 464 Perozes had demanded money from Leo for the defence of the Caucasian passes, had complained of the reception of Persian refugees, and of the persecution of the Zoroastrian communities which still existed on Roman territory.[4] Leo sent an ambassador who was received by the king, perhaps on the frontier of the Ephthalites, and the matters seem to have been amicably arranged.[5] Ten years later an incident occurred which illustrates

---

[1] Cp. Lazarus, *Hist. Arm.* c. 15, p. 272. Vramshapu had reigned from 392 to 414, then Chosroes III. for a year, after whose death Yezdegerd appointed his own son Sapor. In 422 Varahran agreed to the accession of Ardashir, Vramshapu's son (Moses Chor. *Hist. Arm.* iii. c. 18).

[2] Elisha Vartabed, *Hist. Arm.* c. 3, pp. 206-207; Lazarus, *op. cit.* c. 36, p. 298. A full and tedious account of the wars in Armenia will be found in these writers who were contemporary. Elisha's history ends in 446,

Lazarus comes down to the accession of Valakhesh.

[3] Procopius, *B.P.* i. 4; Lazarus, *op. cit.* c. 73.

[4] See above, p. 4, *n.* 2.

[5] Priscus, *fr.* 15, *De leg. gent.* p. 586, *frs.* 11, 12, *De leg. Rom.* It is difficult to reconcile the chronology with what is otherwise known of the first campaign of Perozes against the Ephthalites, whom Priscus apparently means by the *Kidarites*. The Kidarites proper seem to have been Huns who had settled in the trans-Caucasian

the danger of the extension of Persian influence to the Red Sea, although the Persian Government was in this case in no way responsible.[1] A Persian adventurer, Amorkesos, who " whether because he was not successful in Persia or for some other reason preferred Roman territory," settled in the province of Arabia. There he lived as a brigand, making raids, not on the Romans but on the Saracens. His power grew and he seized Jotaba, one of the small islands in the mouth of the gulf of Akaba, the eastern inlet formed by the promontory of Sinai. Jotaba belonged to the Romans and was a commercial station of some importance. Driving out the Greek custom-house officers, Amorkesos took possession of it and soon amassed a fortune by collecting the dues. He made himself ruler of some other places in the neighbourhood, and conceived the desire of becoming a phylarch or satrap of the Saracens of Arabia Petraea, who were nominally dependent on the Roman Emperor. He sent an ecclesiastic to Leo to negotiate the matter, and Leo graciously signified his wish to have a personal interview with Amorkesos. When the Persian arrived, he shared the Imperial table, was admitted to assemblies of the Senate, and even honoured with precedence over the patricians. The Byzantines, it appears, were scandalised that these privileges should be accorded to a fire-worshipper, and Leo seems to have been obliged to pretend that his guest intended to become a Christian. On his departure Leo gave him a valuable picture, and compelled the members of the Senate to present him with gifts ; and, what was more important, he transferred to him the possession of Jotaba, and added more villages to those which he already governed, granting him also the coveted title of phylarch.[2] Jotaba, however, was not permanently lost. The Imperial authority there was re-established in the reign of Anastasius.[3]

country and threatened the pass of Dariel, and they are meant in another passage of Priscus (*fr.* 22, *De leg. gent.*) where Perozes announces to Leo that he has defeated them, *c.* A.D. 468. For the Kidarites, and this assumed confusion, see Drouin, *op. cit.* 143-144.

[1] The source is Malchus, *fr.* 1, *De leg. gent.* p. 568. Cp. Khvostov, *Ist. vost. torgovli Egipta*, i. p. 199. Jotaba has been identified with Strabo's Dia (xvi. 4. 18), now Tiran. It was inhabited by a colony of Jews,

once independent, according to Procopius, *B.P.* i. 19. 4.

[2] Leo was criticised for inviting Amorkesos to his court, and for permitting the foreigner to see the towns through which he had to travel, unarmed and defenceless. Malchus, *ib.*

[3] In A.D. 498 by Romanus (see above, Chap. XIII. § 1, p. 432). Theophanes, A.M. 5990. It was arranged that Roman traders should live in the island. Cp. Procopius, *ib.*

Valakhesh was succeeded on the Persian throne by Kavad, the son of Perozes. Kavad was in some ways the ablest of all the Sassanid sovrans. His great achievement was to restore the royal power, which had been gradually declining since the end of the fourth century, and was now well on its way towards the destiny which two hundred years later was to overtake the Merovingian kings of France. The kings had failed to retain their own authority over the Magian priesthood and the official or bureaucratic nobility, and the state was really managed by the principal minister whose title was *wazurg-framadhar*, and whose functions may be compared to those of a Praetorian Prefect.[1] It was one of these ministers to whom Kavad owed his elevation.

Kavad might not have found it easy to emancipate the throne from the tutelage to which it had so long submitted, if there had not been a remarkable popular movement at the time of which he boldly took advantage.[2] A communist had arisen in the person of Mazdak, and was preaching successfully among the lower classes throughout Persia the doctrines that all men are equal, that the present state of society is contrary to nature, and that the acts condemned by society as crimes are, as merely tending to overthrow an unjustifiable institution, blameless. Community of property and wives was another deduction. Kavad embraced and actually helped to promulgate these anarchical doctrines. His conversion to Mazdakism was not, of course, sincere ; his policy was to use the movement as a counterpoise to the power of the nobles and the Zoroastrian priests. There was a struggle for some years of which we do not know the details, but at length the nobles managed to immure the dangerous king in the Castle of "Lethe" (A.D. 497).[3] Mazdak was imprisoned, but forcibly released by his disciples. After a confinement of two or three years Kavad found means to escape, and with the help of the Ephthalites was reinstated on the throne (A.D. 499).

---

[1] See Stein's important study of the reforms of Kavad and Chosroes, *Ein Kapitel vom persischen und vom byzantinischen Staate* (*Byz.-neugr. Jahrbücher*, i., 1920) p. 57.

[2] See Rawlinson, *op. cit.* 342 *sqq.* ; Nöldeke, *Tabari*, 455 *sqq.* Cp. Tabari,

141 *sq.*, Agathias, iv. 27 ; Procopius, *B.P.* i. 5. The Mazdakites are designated as Manichaeans in John Mal. xviii. p. 444, and the fuller account of Theophanes, A.M. 6016. Both these notices are derived from Timotheus, a baptized Persian.

[3] Giligerda, in Susiana.

During his reign Kavad began a number of reforms in the organisation of the state which tended to establish and secure the royal authority. He did not do away with the high office of *wazurg-framadhar*, but he deprived it of its functions and it became little more than a honorific title.[1] He began a new survey of the land, for the purpose of instituting a system of sound finance.[2] Towards the end of his reign his position was so strong that he was able to take measures to suppress the anti-social Mazdakite sect, which he had suffered only because the hostility between these enthusiasts and the nobles and priests helped him to secure and consolidate the royal power.

§ 2. *The Persian War of Anastasius* (A.D. 502–507)

It was some time after the restoration of Kavad that hostilities broke out, after sixty years of peace between Persia and the Empire. In their financial embarrassments the Sassanid kings were accustomed to apply to Constantinople, and to receive payments which were nominally the bargained contribution to the defence of the Caucasian passes. The Emperors Leo and Zeno had extricated Perozes from difficulties by such payments.[3] But in A.D. 483 the Persians repudiated a treaty obligation. It had been agreed by the treaty of Jovian that Persia was to retain Nisibis for 120 years and then restore it to the Romans. This period now terminated and the Persians declined to surrender a fortress which was essential to their position in Mesopotamia. The Emperor Zeno did not go to war, but he refused to make any further payments for the defence of the Caucasus. When king Valakhesh applied to him he said : " You have the taxes of Nisibis, which are due rightfully to us." [4] The Imperial Government cannot have seriously expected Persia to fulfil her obligation in regard to Nisibis, but her refusal to do so gave the Romans the legal right to decline to carry out their contract to supply money. Anastasius followed the policy of Zeno when Kavad renewed the demand with menaces in A.D. 491.[5]

---

[1] See Stein (*ib.* p. 65), who suggests with much probability (p. 52) that the institution of the *astabedh*, a minister whose functions are compared by Greek and Syrian writers to those of the *magister officiorum*, was due to Kavad. The first mention of this official

is in Joshua Styl. c. 59 (A.D. 502) ; see also Procopius, *B.P.* i. 11. 25.

[2] Tabari, p. 241.

[3] Joshua Styl. p. 7.

[4] *Ib.* pp. 7, 12.

[5] *Ib.* p. 13. " As Zeno did not send, so neither will I, until thou

After his restoration Kavad was in great straits for money. He owed the Ephthalites a large sum which he had undertaken to pay them for their services in restoring him to the throne, and he applied to Anastasius. The Emperor had no intention of helping him, as it appeared to be manifestly to the interest of the Empire to promote hostility and not friendship between the Ephthalites and the Persians. It is said that his refusal took the form of a demand for a written acknowledgment (*cautio*), as he knew that Kavad, unfamiliar with the usages of Roman law, would regard such a mercantile transaction as undignified and intolerable.[1] Kavad resolved on war, and the Hundred Years' Peace was broken, not for the first time, after a duration of eighty years (August, A.D. 502).[2]

The Persian monarch began operations with an invasion of Armenia, and Theodosiopolis fell into his hands by treachery. Then he marched southwards, attacked Martyropolis which surrendered, and laid siege to Amida. This city, after a long and laborious winter siege beginning in October, was surprised in January (A.D. 503), chiefly through the negligence of some monks who had undertaken to guard one of the towers, and having drunk too much wine slumbered instead of watching.[3] There was a hideous massacre which was stayed by the persuasions of a priest, the survivors were led away captive, and Amida was left with a garrison of 3000 men.[4]

On the first news of the invasion the Emperor had sent Rufinus as an ambassador to offer money and propose terms of peace.[5] Kavad detained him till Amida fell, and then

restorest to me Nisibis." Kavad applied again during the Isaurian War, and Anastasius offered to send him money as a loan, but not as a matter of custom (*ib.* p. 15).

[1] Procopius, *B.P.* i. 7; Theodorus Lector, ii. 52; Theophanes, *sub* A.M. 5996. John Lydus (*De mag.* iii. 52) attributes the war to a demand for the costs of maintaining the castle of Biraparach, and doubtless the question of the Caucasian defences was mentioned in the negotiations. Kavad refers to the demand for money in his letter to Justinian quoted by John Mal. xviii. p. 450.

[2] Joshua Styl. p. 37.

[3] But whether the monks were to blame is doubtful (Haury, *Zur*

Beurteilung des Proc. 23).

[4] The siege of Amida is described by Joshua Styl. cc. l. liii.; Zacharias Myt. vii. 3; Procopius, *B.P.* i. 7. Eustathius of Epiphania described it in his lost history (Evagrius, iii. 37), and may have been the source of both Procopius and Zacharias; if not, Procopius must have used Zacharias (cp. Haury, *Proleg.* to his ed. of Procopius, pp. 19-20). The stories in the three sources are carefully compared by Merten, *De bello Persico,* 164 *sqq.*

[5] During the siege of Amida, Roman Mesopotamia was invaded and plundered by the Saracens of Hira under Naman (Joshua Styl. p. 39 *sqq*).

despatched him to Constantinople with the news. Anastasius made military preparations, but the forces which he sent were perhaps not more than 15,000 men.[1] And, influenced by the traditions of the Isaurian campaigns, he committed the error of dividing the command, in the same theatre of war, among three generals. These were the Master of Soldiers in the East, Areobindus, great-grandson of Aspar (on the mother's side) and son-in-law of the Emperor Olybrius ; and the two Masters of Soldiers *in praesenti*, Patricius, and the Emperor's nephew Hypatius, whose military inexperience did not deserve such a responsible post.[2]

The campaign opened (May, A.D. 503) with a success for Areobindus, in the neighbourhood of Nisibis, but the enemy soon mustered superior forces and compelled him to withdraw to Constantia. The jealousy of Hypatius and Patricius, who with 40,000 men had encamped [3] against Amida, induced them to keep back the support which they ought to have sent to their colleague. Soon afterwards the Persians fell upon them, their vanguard was cut up, and they fled with the rest of their army across the Euphrates to Samosata (August).[4]

Areobindus meanwhile had shut himself up in Edessa, and Kavad determined to attack it. The Christian legend of Edessa was in itself a certain challenge to the Persian kings. It was related that Abgar, prince of Edessa and friend of the Emperor Augustus, suffered in his old age from severe attacks of gout. Hearing of the miraculous cures which Jesus Christ was performing in Palestine, Abgar wrote to him, inviting him to leave a land of unbelievers and spend the rest of his life at Edessa. Jesus declined, but promised the prince recovery from his disease.

---

[1] So Marcellinus, *sub a*. Joshua Styl. gives 40,000 men to Patricius and Hypatius and 12,000 to Areobindus.

[2] Priscian's Panegyric on Anastasius may perhaps be dated to this year. For he says of Hypatius *quem vidit validum Parthus sensitque timendum* (p. 300) and does not otherwise mention the war. Among the subordinate commanders were Justin (the future Emperor) ; Patriciolus and his son Vitalian ; Romanus. Areobindus was Consul in 506, and his consular diptych is preserved at Zürich, with the inscription Fl(avius) Areob(indus) Dagal(aiphus) Areobindus, V. I., Ex

C. Sac(ri) Sta(buli) et M(agister) M(ilitum) P(er) Or(ientem) Ex C(onsule) C(onsul) Or(dinarius). See *C.I.L.* xiii. 5245; Meyer, *Zwei ant. Elfenb.* p. 65.

[3] At Siphrios, 9 miles from Amida.

[4] John Lydus (*De mag.* iii. 53) attributes the ill-success of the Romans to the incompetence of the generals, Areobindus, who was devoted to dancing and music, Patricius and Hypatius, who were cowardly and inexperienced. This seems borne out by the narratives of Procopius and Joshua. Cp. Haury, *Zur Beurt. des Proc.* 24-25.

The divine letter existed, and the Edessenes afterwards discovered a postscript, containing a pledge that their city would never be taken by an enemy. The text of the precious document was inscribed on one of the gates, as a sort of phylactery, and the inhabitants put implicit confidence in the sacred promise.[1] It is said that the Saracen sheikh Naman urged on Kavad against Edessa, and threatened to do there worse things than had been done at Amida. Thereupon a wound which he had received in his head swelled, and he lingered in pain for two days and died.[2] But notwithstanding this sign Kavad persisted in his evil intention.

Constantia lay in his route, and almost fell into his hands. Here we have a signal example of a secret danger which constantly threatened Roman rule in the Eastern provinces, the disaffection of the Jews. The Jews of Constantia had conspired to deliver the city to the enemy, but the plot was discovered, and the enraged Greeks killed all the Jews they could find. Disappointed of his hope to surprise the fortress, Kavad did not stay to attack it, but moved on to Edessa. He blockaded this city for a few days without success (September 17), and Areobindus sent him a message : " Now thou seest that the city is not thine, nor of Anastasius, but it is the city of Christ who blessed it, and it has withstood thy hosts." [3] But he deemed it prudent to induce the Persians to withdraw by agreeing to pay 2000 lbs. of gold at the end of twelve days and giving them hostages. Kavad withdrew, but demanded part of the payment before the appointed day. When this was refused he returned and renewed the blockade (September 24), but soon abandoned the enterprise in despair.

The operations of the following year were advantageous to the Empire. The evils of a divided command had been realised, Hypatius was recalled, and Celer, the Master of Offices, an Illyrian, was invested with the supreme command.[4] He invaded and devastated Arzanene ; Areobindus invaded Persian Armenia ;

---

[1] Procopius, *B.P.* ii. 12.

[2] Joshua Styl. p. 47.

[3] This idea recurs in Procopius, who describes (*B.P.* ii. 26 *ad init.*) the Mesopotamian campaign of Chosroes, in which he besieged Edessa, as warfare "not with Justinian nor with any other man, but with the God of the Christians."

[4] I infer the superior authority of Celer from Joshua Styl. p. 55. He had arrived, early in 504, with a reinforcement of 2000 according to Marcellinus, but with a very large army according to Joshua.

Patricius undertook the recovery of Amida. The siege of this place lasted throughout the winter till the following year (A.D. 505). The garrison, reduced to the utmost straits by famine, finally surrendered on favourable terms. The sufferings of the inhabitants are illustrated by the unpleasant story that women " used to go forth by stealth into the streets of the city in the evening or in the morning, and whomsoever they met, woman or child or man, for whom they were a match, they used to carry him by force into a house and kill and eat him either boiled or roasted." When this practice was betrayed by the smell of the roasting, the general put some of the women to death, but he gave leave to eat the dead.[1]

The Romans paid the Persians 1000 lbs. of gold for the surrender of Amida. Meanwhile Kavad was at war with the Ephthalites, and he entered into negotiations with Celer, which ended in the conclusion of a truce for seven years (A.D. 505).[2] It appears that the truce was not renewed at the end of that period, but the two empires remained actually at peace for more than twenty years.

It has been justly observed that in these oriental wars the Roman armies would hardly have held their own, but for the devoted loyalty and energy of the civil population of the frontier provinces. It was through their heroic co-operation and patience of hunger that small besieged garrisons were able to hold out. Their labours are written in the remains of the stone fortresses in these regions.[3] And they had to suffer sorely in time of war, not only from the enemy, but from their defenders. The government did what it could by remitting taxes ; but the ill-usage which they experienced from the foreign, especially the German, mercenaries in the Imperial armies was enough to drive them into the arms of the Persians. Here is the vivid description of their sufferings by one of themselves.

" Those who came to our aid under the name of deliverers plundered us almost as much as our enemies. Many poor people they turned out of their beds and slept in them, whilst their owners lay on the ground in cold weather. Others they drove out of their own houses, and went in and dwelt in them. The

---

[1] Joshua Styl. p. 62. Cp. Procopius, *B.P.* i. 9. p. 44, from which it would appear that it was the few Roman inhabitants who were reduced to such straits.

[2] *Ib.* p. 45. John Lydus, *loc. cit.*
[3] Chapot, *op. cit.* p. 376.
[4] Joshua Styl. p. 68. Cp. pp. 71-73.

cattle of some they carried off by force as if it were spoil of war ; the clothes of others they stripped off their persons and took away. Some they beat violently for a mere trifle ; with others they quarrelled in the streets and reviled them for a small cause. They openly plundered every one's little stock of provisions, and the stores that some had laid up in the villages and cities. Before the eyes of every one they ill-used the women in the streets and houses. From old women, widows, and poor they took oil, wood, salt, and other things for their own expenses, and they kept them from their own work to wait upon them. In short they harassed every one both great and small. Even the nobles of the land, who were set to keep them in order and to give them their billets, stretched out their hands for bribes ; and as they took them from every one they spared nobody, but after a few days sent other soldiers to those upon whom they had quartered them in the first instance."

This war taught the Romans the existence of a capital defect in their Mesopotamian frontier. While the Persians had the strong fort of Nisibis against an advance to the Tigris, the Romans had no such defence on their own frontier commanding the high road to Constantia. After the conclusion of the treaty, Anastasius immediately prepared to remedy this weakness. At Daras, close to the frontier and a few miles from Nisibis, he built an imposing fortified town, provided with corn-magazines, cisterns, and two public baths. He named it Anastasiopolis, and it was for the Empire what Nisibis was for Persia. Masons and workmen gathered from all Syria to complete the work while Kavad was still occupied by his Ephthalite war. He protested, for the building of a fort on the frontier was a breach of treaty engagements, but he was not in a position to do more than protest and he was persuaded to acquiesce by the diplomacy and bribes of the Emperor, who at the same time took the opportunity of strengthening the walls of Theodosopolis.[1]

[1] Procopius, *B.P.* ii. 10 ; Joshua Styl. p. 70. The fortifications of Daras will be described below, Chap. XVI. § 3, in connection with the siege of Chosroes.

CHAPTER XV

§ 1. *Election and Reign of Justin I.* (A.D. 518–527)

ANASTASIUS had made no provision for a successor to the throne, and there was no Augusta to influence the election. Everything turned out in a way that no one could have foreseen. The most natural solution might have seemed to be the choice of one of the late Emperor's three nephews, Probus, Pompeius, or Hypatius. They were men of average ability, and one of them, at least, Pompeius, did not share his uncle's sympathy with the Monophysitic creed. But they were not ambitious, and perhaps their claims were not seriously urged.[1]

The High Chamberlain Amantius hoped to play the part which Urbicius had played on the death of Zeno, and he attempted to secure the throne for a certain Theocritus, otherwise unknown, who had probably no qualification but personal devotion to himself. As the attitude of the Palace guards would probably decide the election, he gave money to Justin, the Count of the Excubitors, to bribe the troops.[2]

In the morning (July 9) the people assembled in the Hippodrome and acclaimed the Senate. "Long live the Senate! Senate of the Romans, tu vincas! We demand our Emperor, given by God, for the army; we demand our Emperor, given by God, for the world!" The high officials, the senators, and

---

[1] It is said, indeed, that there were many who wished that one of them should succeed (Evagrius, *H.E.* 4. 2). Anastasius had other relatives too who were eligible ("numerous and very distinguished," Procopius, *B.P.* i. 11).

[2] John Mal. xvii. 410 (cp. *Chr.*

Pasch., sub a.; Cramer, *Excerpta,* ii. 318); Marcellinus, *sub* 519. Theocritus, described by Marcellinus as *Amantii satelles,* is designated as ὁ δομεστικός in John Mal. *fr.* 43, *De ins.* p. 170. It means the "domestic" of Amantius, see Zach. Myt. ix. 1.

the Patriarch had gathered in the Palace, clad most of them
in mouse-coloured garments, and sat in the great hall, the
Triklinos of the Nineteen Akkubita. Celer, the Master of
Offices, urged them to decide quickly on a name and to act
promptly before others (the army or the people) could wrest the
initiative from their hands. But they were unable to agree,
and in the meantime the Excubitors and the Scholarians were
acting in the Hippodrome. The Excubitors proclaimed John,
a tribune and a friend of Justin, and raised him on a shield. But
the Blues would not have him ; they threw stones and some of
them were killed by the Excubitors. Then the Scholarians
put forward an unnamed patrician and Master of Soldiers, but
the Excubitors would not accept him and he was in danger of
his life. He was rescued by the efforts of Justin's nephew, the
candidatus Justinian. The Excubitors then wished to proclaim
Justinian himself, but he refused to accept the diadem. As
each of these persons was proposed, their advocates knocked
at the Ivory Gate, which communicated between the Palace
and the Hippodrome, and called upon the chamberlains to deliver
the Imperial robes. But on the announcement of the name, the
chamberlains refused.

At length, the Senate ended their deliberations by the election
of Justin, and constrained him to accept the purple. He appeared
in the Kathisma of the Hippodrome and was favourably received
by the people ; the Scholarians alone, jealous of the Excubitors,
resented the choice. The coronation rite was immediately
performed in the Kathisma. Arrayed in the Imperial robes,
which the chamberlains at last delivered, he was crowned by
the Patriarch John ; he took the lance and shield, and was
acclaimed Basileus by the assembly. To the troops he promised
a donation of five nomismata (£3 : 7 : 6) and one pound of silver
for each man.

Such is the official description of the circumstances of the
election of Justin.[1] If it is true so far as it goes, it is easy to see
that there was much behind that has been suppressed. The
intrigue of Amantius is ignored. Not a word is said of the
candidature of Theocritus which Justin had undertaken to
support. If Justin had really used his influence with the

---

[1] Preserved in Constantine Porph. *Cer.* i. 93 (taken from the *Katastasis*
of Peter the Patrician).

Excubitors and the money which had been entrusted to him in the interest of Theocritus, it is hardly credible that the name of Theocritus would not have been proposed in the Hippodrome. If, on the other hand, he had worked in his own interest, as was naturally alleged after the event,[1] how was it that other names, but not his, were put forward by the Excubitors ? The data seem to point to the conclusion that the whole *mise en scène* was elaborately planned by Justin and his friends. They knew that he could not count on the support of the Scholarians, and, if he were proclaimed by his own troops alone, the success of his cause would be doubtful. The problem therefore was to manage that the initiation should proceed from the Senate, whose authority, supported by the Excubitors, would rally general consent and overpower the resistance of the Scholarian guards. It was therefore arranged that the Excubitors should propose candidates who had no chance of being chosen, with the design of working on the fears of the Senate. Justin's friends in the Senate could argue with force : " Hasten to agree, or you will be forestalled, and some wholly unsuitable person will be thrust upon us. But you must choose one who will be acceptable to the Excubitors. Justin fulfils this condition. He may not be an ideal candidate for the throne, but he is old and moderate." But, however the affair may have been managed by the wirepullers, Justin ascended the throne with the prestige of having been regularly nominated by the Senate, and he could announce to the Pope that " We have been elected to the Empire by the favour of the indivisible Trinity, by the choice of the highest ministers of the sacred Palace, and of the Senate, and finally by the election of the army." [2]

The new Emperor, who was about sixty-six years of age, was an Illyrian peasant. He was born in the village of Bederiana in the province of Dardania, not far from Scupi, of which the name survives in the town of Usküb, and his native language was Latin.[3] Like hundreds of other country youths,[4] he set forth

---

[1] Evagrius, *loc. cit.* : Zach. Myt. *loc. cit.*

[2] *Coll. Avellana, Ep.* 141.

[3] Born in 452, if he was 75 at his death (John Mal. xvii. 424 ; but 77 acc. to *Chr. Pasch.*). Bederiana is represented by the modern village of Bader. Justinian speaks of Scupi,

which he renamed Justiniana Prima, as *patria nostra* (*Nov.* 11). On the identification, see Evans, *Arch. Researches*, ii. 141 *sqq.*

[4] Cp. in the address of Germanus to his soldiers, in Procopius, *B.V.* ii. 16 ὑμᾶς ἐξ ἀγροῦ ἥκοντας ξίυ τε τῇ πήρᾳ καὶ χιτωνίσκῳ ἑνί.

with a bag of bread on his back and walked to Constantinople
to better his fortune by enlisting in the army. Two friends
accompanied him, and all three, recommended by their physical
qualities, were enrolled in the Palace guards.[1] Justin served
in the Isaurian and Persian wars of Anastasius, rose to be Count
of the Excubitors, distinguished himself in the repulse of Vitalian,
and received senatorial rank.[2] He had no qualifications for the
government of a province, not to say of an Empire ; for he had
no knowledge except of military matters, and he was uneducated.[3]
It is even said that he could not write and was obliged, like
Theoderic the Ostrogoth, to use a mechanical device for signing
documents.

He had married a captive whom he had purchased and who
was at first his concubine. Her name was Lupicina, but she was
crowned Augusta under the more decorous name of Euphemia.[4]
In his successful career the peasant of Bederiana had not forgotten his humble relatives or his native place. His sister,
wife of Sabbatius, lived at the neighbouring village of Tauresium [5]
and had two children, Petrus Sabbatius and Vigilantia. He
adopted his elder nephew, brought him to Constantinople, and
took care that he enjoyed the advantages of an excellent education. The young man discarded the un-Roman names of Peter
and Sabbatius [6] and was known by the adoptive name of
Justinianus. He was enrolled among the candidati. Justin
had other nephews and seems to have cared also for their
fortunes. They were liberally educated and were destined to

---

[1] Procopius, *H.A.* vi. John Mal.
(xvii. 410) describes Justin as good-
looking, with a well-formed nose,
and curly grey hair.

[2] *Ib.* ; John Ant. *De ins., fr.* 100
(p. 142) ; Theodorus Lector, ii. 37.

[3] John Lydus, *De mag.* iii. 51, Procopius, *ib.*, John Mal. *ib.* ἀγράμματος.

[4] Victor Tonn. *s. a.* 518; Theodore
Lector, ii. 37, cp. Cramer, *Anecd.
Par.* ii. 108 ; Procopius, *H.A.* vi., ix.
On a coin supposed to represent
Euphemia, see Wroth, *Imp. Byzantine Coins*, i. p. xiv. *n.* 4. There
are miniature representations of
Justin and Euphemia on the two
extremities of the horizontal bar of a
silver cross preserved in the Treasury
of St. Peter's at Rome. The cross

bears the inscription :

ligno quo Christus humanum subdidit
   hostem
dat Romae Justinus opem et socia
   decorem.

From the style of the headcap of the
Empress, Delbrück (*Porträts byz.
Kais.*) was able to infer that Justin I.
and Euphemia (not Justin II. and
Sophia) are in question.

[5] Now Taor. Justinian built a
rectangular wall round it, with a
tower at each corner, and called it
Tetrapyrgia. Procopius, *Aed.* iv. 1.
18.

[6] His name, however, appeared in
full on his consular diptychs of 521.
C.I.L. v. 8210. 3 : Fl. Petr. Sabbat.
Iustinian., v.i., com(es), mag. eqq.
et p. praes., et c(onsul) o(r)d.

play parts of varying distinction and importance on the political scene.[1]

The first care of Justin was to remove the disaffected; Amantius and Theocritus were executed, and three others were punished by death or exile.[2] His next was to call to Constantinople the influential leader who had shaken the throne of Anastasius. Before he came to the city, Vitalian must have been assured of the religious orthodoxy of the new Emperor, and he came prepared to take part in the reconciliation of Rome with the Eastern Churches. He was immediately created Master of Soldiers *in praesenti*,[3] and in A.D. 520 he was consul for the year. The throne of Justin seemed to be firmly established. The relatives of Anastasius were loyal; Pompeius co-operated with Justinian and Vitalian in the restoration of ecclesiastical unity. Marinus, the trusted counseller of the late sovran, was Praetorian Prefect of the East in A.D. 519.[4]

The reunion with Rome, which involved the abandonment of the Henotikon of Zeno, the restoration of the prestige of the Council of Chalcedon, and the persecution of the Monophysites, was the great inaugural act of the new dynasty.[5] The Emperor's nephew, Justinian, was deeply interested in theological questions, and was active in bringing about the ecclesiastical

---

[1] Vigilantia, who married Dulcissimus, had three children, Justin (afterwards Emperor), Marcellus, and Praejecta. A brother of Justin, or another sister, had three sons, Germanus, Boraides, and Justus (cp. Procopius, *B.P.* i. 24. 53; *B.G.* iii. 31. 12). Germanus, who was to play a considerable part, was thus the cousin of Justinian. He married (1) Passara, by whom he had two sons, Justin and Justinian, and one daughter Justina; (2) the Ostrogothic princess Matasuntha, by whom he had one son Germanus. See the Genealogical Table. Another cousin of Justinian, named Marcian, is mentioned by John Malalas, xviii. 496. I conjecture that he may be identical with Justin, son of Germanus. For this Justin was consul in 540, and on his consular diptych his name runs: Fl. Mar. Petr. Theodor. Valent. Rust. Boraid. Germ. Iust. (Meyer, *Zwei ant. Elf.* p. 10). I take Mar. to be for Marcianus. Germanus was the ἀνεψιός of Justinian (Proc. *locc.*

citt.), and this has generally been taken to mean nephew, so that Justinian would have had a brother or a second sister. But I agree with Kallenberg (*Berl. phil. Wochenschrift*, xxxv. 991) that in *B.G.* iv. 40. 5 'Ἰουστῖνος ὁ Γερμανοῦ θεῖος should be retained (all the editions print the emendation 'Ἰουστινιανός).

[2] Marcellinus, *s.a.* 519, Procopius, *H.A.* 6; John Mal. xvii. 410, and *fr.* 43, *De ins.* Marcellinus describes Amantius as a Manichean; Procopius says that there was no charge against him, except of using insulting language about the Patriarch; Malalas speaks of a demonstration against Amantius and Marinus in St. Sophia.

[3] John Mal. *ib.* 411.

[4] *C.J.* v. 27. 7; ii. 7. 25. John Mal. *ib.* records that Appion, who had been exiled by Anastasius, was recalled and made Pr. pr. Or. Perhaps he held the post in 518-519 and was succeeded by Marinus.

[5] See below, Chap. XXII. § 4.

revolution. His intellectual powers and political capacity must have secured to him from the beginning a preponderant influence over his old uncle, and he would naturally regard himself as the destined successor to the throne. Immediately after Justin's election, he was appointed Count of the Domestics ; and then he was invested with the rank of patrician, and was created a Master of Soldiers *in praesenti*.[1] His detractors said that he was unscrupulous in removing possible competitors for political influence. The execution of Amantius was attributed to his instigation.[2] Vitalian was a more formidable rival, and in the seventh month of his consulship Vitalian was murdered in the Palace. For this crime, rightly or wrongly, Justinian was also held responsible.[3] During the remaining seven years of the reign we may, without hesitation, regard him as the directing power of the Empire.[4] He held the consulship in A.D. 521 and entertained the populace with magnificent spectacles.[5] When he was afterwards elevated to the rank of *nobilissimus*,[6] it was a recognition of his position as the apparent heir to the throne. We may wonder why he did not receive the higher title of Caesar ; perhaps Justin could not overcome some secret jealousy of the brilliant nephew whose fortune he had made.

Justinian's power behind the throne was sustained by the enthusiastic support of the orthodox ecclesiastics, but he is said to have sought another means of securing his position, by attracting the devotion of one of the Factions of the Hippodrome. Anastasius had shown favour to the Greens ; and it followed almost as a matter of course that Justinian should patronise the Blues. In each party there was a turbulent section which was a standing menace to public order, known as the

[1] See *Coll. Avell.* 162, 154, 230 (p. 690). He is *may. eyy. et p. praes.* on his consular diptychs.

[2] Procopius, *H.A.* vi.

[3] *Ib.* Here Procopius is supported by Victor Tonn. *s. a.* 523 (*Iustiniani patricii factione*). Loofs (*Leontius*, 259) does not believe in the guilt of Justinian. John Malalas (*De ins.*, *fr.* 43) seems to connect the murder (which was committed in the Delphax in the Palace) with riotous demonstrations of the Blues and Greens in the Hippodrome and the streets.

[4] In the Secret History Procopius treats the reign of Justin as virtually

part of that of Justinian. That this view of Justinian's influence was generally accepted is shown by passages in the *Public History* and the *De aedificiis. B.V.* i. 9. 5 ; *Aed.* i. 3. 3.

[5] He spent 288,000 (£18,000) on the shows, and exhibited 20 lions and 30 leopards. Marcellinus, *s.a.*

[6] Before 527 ; Marcellinus, *s.a.* Victor Tonn. states that Justinian was created Caesar in 525 (*s.a.*), but his authority is inferior. Cyril, *Vit. Sabae*, p. 386, does not mention either title.

Partisans,[1] and Justinian is alleged to have enlisted the Blue Partisans in his own interest. He procured official posts for them, gave money to those who needed it, and above all protected them against the consequences of their riots. It is certain that during the reign of Justin, both the capital and the cities of the East were frequently troubled by insurrections against the civil authorities and sanguinary fights ; and it was the Blue Faction which bore the chief share of the guilt.[2] The culminating scandal occurred in A.D. 524.[3] On this occasion a man of some repute was murdered by the Partisans in St. Sophia. Justinian happened to be dangerously ill at the time, and the matter was laid before the Emperor. His advisers seized the opportunity to urge upon him the necessity of taking rigorous measures to suppress the intolerable licence of these enemies of society. Justin ordered the Prefect of the City, Theodotus Colocynthius, to deal out merciless justice to the malefactors.[4] There were many executions, and good citizens rejoiced at the spectacle of assassins and plunderers being hanged, burned, or beheaded.[5] Theodotus, however, was immediately afterwards deprived of his office and exiled to Jerusalem, and his disgrace has been attributed to the resentment of Justinian who had unexpectedly recovered from his disease.[6] However this may have been, the

---

[1] Οἱ στασιῶται. Procopius, *H.A.* vii. He says that they affected a peculiar dress, wearing very wide sleeves drawn tight at the wrist, and imitating the costume of the Huns in trousers and shoes. They allowed their beards and moustaches to grow, shaved the head in front and wore the hair long behind. They used to go about in organised bands at night and rob the passers-by. For the connexion of Justinian with the Blues, which rests on the evidence of the Secret History, cp. Panchenko, *O tain. ist. Prok.* 89 *sqq.*

[2] John Mal. xvii. 416 τὸ Βένετον μέρος ἐν πάσαις ταῖς πόλεσιν ἠτάκτει (cp. *H.A.* viii. *ad init.*) καὶ ἐτάρασσον τὰς πόλεις λιθασμοῖς καὶ καταβασίαις καὶ φόνοις. This refers to the first years of the reign. Cp. Mansi, viii. 1106 (relating to Syria Secunda).

[3] The date 524 may be inferred by combining John Mal. (*ib.*), who gives indiction 3 (=524–525) for the fall of Theodotus, with Theophanes (A.M. 6012), who mentions the sixth year

of Justin ; and it is confirmed by *C.J.* ii. 7. 26, which was addressed to Theodotus in 524. Theodore was Prefect of the City in 520 (John Mal. *fr.* 43, *De ins.*) ; Theodotus was appointed in 522–523 (John Mal. xvii. 416) ; and was succeeded by Theodore Têganistes (*ib.*). Hence in *C.J.* ix. 19. 6 (A.D. 526) *Theodoto* is probably an error for *Theodoro.*

[4] *H.A.* ix. The other sources do not mention Justinian's illness.

[5] Marcellinus, whose notice, though dated A.D. 523, must refer to this affair.

[6] Procopius (*ib.*) says that some of the friends of Theodotus were tortured, and confessed that he had spoken disloyally against Justinian, but that the Quaestor Proclus took his part and proved that he had done nothing to deserve death. John Malalas (*ib.*) has a different story. He ascribes Justin's anger to the fact that Theodotus had executed a rich senator without consulting himself. Both accounts may be true. Accord-

Blues had received an effective lesson, and during the last years of the reign not only the capital but the provincial cities also enjoyed tranquillity.[1]

There were few events of capital importance during the reign of Justin. Its chief significance lay in the new orientation of religious policy which was inaugurated at the very beginning, and in the long apprenticeship to statecraft which it imposed on Justinian before the full power and responsibility of government devolved on him. Next to him the most influential minister was Proclus the Quaestor, an incorruptible man who had the reputation of an Aristides.[2] There was some danger of a breach with the Ostrogothic ruler of Italy in A.D. 525-526, but this menace was averted by his death,[3] and the Empire enjoyed peace till the last year of the reign, when war broke out with Persia.

In the spring of A.D. 527 Justin was stricken down by a dangerous illness, and he yielded to the solicitations of the Senate to co-opt Justinian as his colleague. The act of coronation was performed in the great Triklinos in the Palace (on April 4), and it seems that the Patriarch, in the absence of the Emperor, placed the diadem on the head of the new Augustus. The subsequent ceremonies were carried out in the Delphax, where the Imperial guards were assembled, and not, as was usual, in the Hippodrome.[4] Justin recovered, but only to survive for a few months. He died on August 1, from an ulcer in the foot where, in one of his old campaigns, he had been wounded by an arrow.[5]

§ 2. *Justinian*

The Emperor Justinian was about forty-five years old when he ascended the throne.[6] Of his personal appearance we can

ing to John of Nikiu (p. 503) he arrested a nephew of Justin. Procopius and Malalas agree that at Jerusalem Theodotus remained in concealment, believing that his life was in danger.

[1] John Mal. *ib.*, where it is stated the public spectacles were generally prohibited, and that all professional dancers were banished from the East, but that an exception was made in the case of Alexandria.

[2] Procopius, *B.P.* i. 11. 11; *H.A.* vi. 13-14; John Lydus, *De mag.* iii. 20 Πρόκλος ὁ δικαιότατος.

[3] See below, Chap. XVIII. § 1.

[4] Constantine Porph. *Cer.* i. 95 (from the κατάστασις of Peter the Patrician).

[5] John Mal. xvii. 424.

[6] Zonaras, xiv. 5. 40 (we do not know the source).

form some idea from the description of contemporary writers [1]
and from portraits on his coins and in mosaic pictures.[2] He
was of middle height, neither thin nor fat ; his smooth shaven
face was round, he had a straight nose, a firm chin, curly hair
which, as he aged, became thin in front. A slight smile seems
to have been characteristic. The bust which appears on the
coinage issued when he had reached the age of fifty-six, shows
that there was some truth in the resemblance which a hostile
writer detected between his countenance and that of the Emperor
Domitian.

His intellectual talents were far above the ordinary standard
of Roman Emperors, and if fortune had not called him to the
throne, he would have attained eminence in some other career.
For with his natural gifts he possessed an energy which nothing
seemed to tire ; he loved work, and it is not improbable that
he was the most hardworking man in the Empire. Though his
mind was of that order which enjoys occupying itself with
details, it was capable of conceiving large ideas and embracing
many interests. He permitted himself no self-indulgence ; and
his temperance was ascetic. In Lent he used to fast entirely
for two days, and during the rest of the season he abstained

---

[1] Procopius, *H.A.* viii. 12-13 ;
John Mal. xviii. 425.

[2] There are two pictures at Ravenna,
one in the apse of S. Vitale dating
from A.D. 547, the other in the nave
of S. Apollinare Nuovo, about ten
years later. The former is a bad
portrait ; the face is oval, whereas
all the other evidence both literary
and monumental concurs in showing
that it was round. He also wears a
moustache ; perhaps this was true
in 547, though not in 538 or 557
(John Mal. speaks of a beard, but if
this is not simply an error, it must
refer to the very end of his life). The
other picture, truer to life, shows a
round, smooth, shaven face, and con-
veys the impression of a man who
is losing his old energy. The evidence
of the coinage, admirably elucidated
by Wroth (*Byz. Coins*, i. pp. xc.-xcii.),
is more important. The early coins
of the reign display a purely con-
ventional face, but in A.D. 538
changes were introduced. Bronze
money was inscribed with the year
of issue, and a new Imperial bust

appeared both on gold and on bronze
coins, and was not changed again.
The previous bust on the gold of
A.D. 527 had a three-quarters face ;
the new bust showed a full face,
shaven, round, plump, with a slight
smile—unquestionably a genuine portrait of the man whom the picture in
S. Apollinare shows when he was
20 years older. There is also a gold
medallion (perhaps of 534 ; cp.
Wroth, i. p. 25, and Cedrenus, i. p.
649), on which the Emperor's bust
appears with round shaven face.
The fifteenth - century drawing of
Justinian's equestrian statue in the
Augusteum (reproduced in Diehl,
Justinien, p. 27) does not help, nor
the silver disk of Kerch which shows
an Emperor on horseback (Diehl,
p. 30, but the identity of the Emperor
is doubtful). The Barberini ivory
(Diehl, frontispiece) would be useful,
if its date were certain, but some
ascribe it to the age of Constantine
the Great. Compare (as well as
Wroth) Diehl's interesting appreciation of the mosaics.

from wine and lived on wild herbs dressed with oil and vinegar.
He slept little and worked far into the night.[1] His manners
were naturally affable. As Emperor he was easily accessible,
and showed no offence if a bold or tactless subject spoke with
a freedom which others would have resented as disrespectful.
He was master of his temper, and seldom broke out into anger.[2]
He could exhibit, too, the quality of mercy. Probus, the nephew
of Anastasius, accused of reviling him, was tried for treason.
When the report of the trial was laid before the Emperor he
tore it up and said to Probus, " I pardon you for your offence
against me. Pray that God also may pardon you." [3]

The reign of a ruler endowed with these estimable qualities,
animated by a strong and unflagging sense of duty, devoting
himself day and night to the interests of the State [4] for thirty-
eight years, could not fail to be memorable. Memorable
assuredly it was. Justinian wrought not only for his own time
but for posterity. He enhanced the prestige of the Empire and
enlarged its borders. He bequeathed, by his monumental
work in Roman law, an enduring heritage to Europe ; while
the building of the Church of St. Sophia would in itself be an
imperishable title to the gratitude of men. These achievements,
however, are only one side of the picture. The successes and
glories of his reign were to be purchased at a heavy cost, and
the strain which he imposed on the resources of the State was
followed by decline and disaster after his death. Perhaps no
more scathing denunciation of the character, aims, and methods
of a ruler has ever been written than the notorious indictment
which the contemporary historian Procopius committed to the
pages of a Secret History, wherein Justinian is represented as
a malignant demon in human form.[5] Though the exaggerations
of the writer are so gross and manifest that his venomous pen
defeats its own object, there is sufficient evidence from other

---

[1] The statements of Procopius in
H.A. vi. 28-30 and in *Aed.* i. 7. 7-11
are almost identical. In the latter
passage it is said that these excess-
ively abstemious practices caused a
painful disease in the knee, which
was miraculously healed by the relics
of saints which had been discovered
at Melitene.

[2] *H.A.* 13. 1-3.

[3] John Mal. xviii. 438. We shall
meet another instance in the case
of the conspirator Artabanes. Cp.
Procopius, *Aed.* i. 1. 10 and 16.

[4] Cp. John Lydus, *De mag.* iii.
55 τὸν πάντων βασιλέων ἀγρυπνότατον.
Cp. βασιλῆος ἀκοιμήτοιο in the verses
inscribed in the church of SS. Sergius
and Bacchus, which he built (*C.I.G.*
iv. 8639).

[5] The credibility of the *Secret History* is discussed below, Chap. XXIV.

sources to show that the reign of Justinian was, in many ways, far from being a blessing to his subjects.

The capital error of Justinian's policy was due to a theory which, though not explicitly formulated till quite recent times, has misled many eminent and well-meaning sovrans and statesmen in all periods of history. It is the theory that the expansion of a state and the exaltation of its prestige and honour are ends in themselves, and valuable without any regard to the happiness of the men and women of whom the state consists. If this proposition had been presented nakedly either to Justinian or to Louis XIV., he would have indignantly repudiated it, but both these monarchs, like many another, acted on it, with most unhappy consequences for their subjects. Justinian possessed imagination. He had formed a high ideal of the might and majesty of the Empire of which he was the master. It humiliated him to contrast its moderate limits with the vast extent of territory over which the word of Constantine or Theodosius the Great had been law. He was dazzled by the idea of restoring the old boundaries of the Roman Empire. For though he only succeeded in recovering, as we shall see, Africa, Italy, and a small strip of Spain, his designs reached to Gaul, if not to Britain. After he had conquered the African provinces he announced his ambitious policy. " We have good hopes that God will grant us to restore our authority over the remaining countries which the ancient Romans possessed to the limits of both oceans and lost by subsequent neglect." [1] In drawing up this magnificent programme, Justinian did not consider whether such an extension of his government would make his subjects, who had to bear the costs of his campaigns, happier or better. He assumed that whatever increased the power and glory of the state must also increase the well-being of its members. The resources of the state were not more than sufficient to protect the eastern frontier against the Persians and the Danubian against the barbarians of the north ; and if the Emperor had been content to perform these duties more efficiently than his predecessors, he would unquestionably have deserved better of his subjects.

His conception of the greatness of the Empire was indissolubly associated with his conception of the greatness of its sovran,

[1] *Nov.* 30, § 11, published just after the conquest of Sicily, in 536.

and he asserted the absolutism of the autocrat in a degree which
no Emperor had hitherto attempted.[1] This was conspicuously
shown in the dictatorship which he claimed over the Church.
He was the first Emperor who studied dogmatic questions
independently and systematically, and he had all the confidence
of a professional theologian. A theologian on the throne is a
public danger, and the principle of persecuting opinion, which
had been fitfully and mildly pursued in the fifth century, was
applied rigorously and systematically under Justinian. His
determination to be supreme in all departments made him
impatient of advice ; he did not like his commands to be discussed, and he left to his ministers little latitude for decision.
His passion for dealing personally with the minute details of
government had the same unfortunate results as in the case of
Philip II.[2] Like other autocrats, he was jealous and suspicious,
and ready to listen to calumnies against his most loyal servants.
And there was a vein of weakness in his character. He faltered
at one supremely critical moment of his reign, and his consort,
Theodora, had an influence over him which no woman could
have exercised over an Augustus or a Constantine.

§ 3. *Theodora*

It was probably before he had any prospect of the throne
that Justinian formed a violent attachment to a girl of exceptional charms and talents, but of low birth and blemished
reputation. Theodora had already borne at least one child to
a lover [3] when she captured the heart of the future Emperor.
According to a tradition—and perhaps she countenanced this
story herself, for she could not deny the humility of her birth—
she had come from Paphlagonia to the capital, where she was

---

[1] Agathias, v. 14 αὐτοκράτωρ ὀνόματί
τε καὶ πράγματι ἀπεδέδεικτο.

[2] Diehl has noted the resemblance.
Diehl's judgment of the Emperor's
character is that, with many high
qualities, he had " une âme de valeur
plutôt médiocre " (p. 21).

[3] A daughter, whose son Anastasius or Athanasius married Joannina,
daughter of Belisarius. Procopius,
H.A. iv. 37 ; John Eph. Part III. v.
1. (Perhaps the same Athanasius

is meant in John Philoponus, *De
opif. mundi*, i. *Prooem.*, as Reichardt
thinks.) According to *H.A.* 17, 16 *sqq.*
she had also a son John, who was
taken as an infant by his unnamed
father to Arabia because Theodora
wished to destroy her offspring.
When he had grown up, he was
informed by his dying father of the
secret of his birth. He went to
Byzantium and revealed himself
to the Empress, who arranged that
he should never be seen again.

discovered by Justinian, making a scanty living by spinning wool.[1] But contemporary rumours which were circulated by her enemies assigned to her a less respectable origin, and told a circumstantial story of a girlhood spent in singular infamy. She was said to be the daughter of Acacius, who was employed by the Green Faction at Constantinople as keeper of the wild beasts,[2] which they exhibited at public spectacles. When Acacius died his widow married his successor, but this man was soon deprived of the office in favour of another who paid a bribe to obtain it.[3] The woman sent her three little daughters, Comito,[4] Theodora, and Anastasia, in the guise of suppliants with fillets on their heads, to beg the Greens assembled in the Hippodrome to reinstate their stepfather who had been so unjustly treated. The Greens obdurately refused ; but the Blues had compassion and appointed the man to be their own bear-keeper, as the post happened to be vacant. This incident of her childhood was said to be the explanation of the Empress Theodora's implacable hostility towards the Greens. The three sisters, when they were older, went on the stage, and in those days an actress was almost synonymous with a prostitute. According to the scandalous gossip, which is recorded with malicious relish in the *Secret History* of Procopius, Theodora showed exceptional precocity and shamelessness in a career of vice. Her adventures were not confined to Constantinople. She went to the Libyan Pentapolis as the mistress of a new governor, but having quarrelled with him she betook herself to Alexandria, and worked her way back to the capital, where she entrapped Justinian.[5]

This chapter of her biography, which reposes solely on the

---

[1] Πάτρια, p. 248. To commemorate her old abode she founded the church of St. Panteleemon on the site.

[2] Ἀρκτοτρόφος, bear-keeper, was the term.

[3] The official known as ὀρχηστής had these appointments in his hands.

[4] We know from another source than *H.A.* that Theodora had a sister Comito. She married Sittas, Master of Soldiers. John Mal. xviii. 430.

[5] The account of her career in *H.A.* ix. stands alone. Some have thought that it gains some support from a passage in John Eph. *Comm.* p. 68, where

the Empress is described as τὴν ἐκ τοῦ πορνείου (so Panchenko, *op. cit.* 73), but these words are certainly an interpolation, for it is incredible that they were written by John, who was a devoted admirer of the Empress (cp. Diehl, *op. cit.* 42). Was the interpolator acquainted with the *Secret History* ? Perhaps the expression is due to a tradition that Theodora had acted at a theatre at Constantinople which was in a street known by the suggestive name of Πόρναι. See Justinian, *Nov.* 105, § 1 πρόοδον τὴν ἐπὶ τὸ θέατρον ἄγουσαν ἣν δὴ Πόρνας καλοῦσιν.

testimony of enemies, has more value as a picture of contemporary manners than as an indictment of the morals of Theodora. It is difficult to believe that if her girlhood had been so steeped in vice and infamy as this scandalous document asserts, she could have so completely changed as to develop into a matron whose conjugal chastity the same enemies could not seriously impugn, although they were ready to insinuate suspicions.[1] But it would be foolish to argue that the framework of the story is entirely fictitious. Theodora may have been the daughter of a bear-keeper, and she may have appeared on the stage. And her youth may have been stormy; we know that she was the mother of an illegitimate child.

After the rise in his fortunes through the accession of his uncle, Justinian seems to have secured for his mistress the rank of a patrician.[2] He wished to marry her, but the Empress Euphemia resolutely opposed this step, and it was not till after her death [3] that Theodora became the wife of Justinian. When he was raised to the throne, she was, as a matter of course, crowned Augusta.

Her beauty and charm were generally acknowledged. We may imagine her as a small pale brunette, with a delicate oval face and a solemn intense expression in her large black eyes.[4] Portraits of her are preserved in marble, in mosaics, and on ivory. There is a life size bust of her at Milan, which was originally coloured; the tip of the nose is broken off, but the rest is well preserved, and we can see the attractiveness of her face.[5] Then

---

[1] Cp. *H.A.* 16. 11 ὑποψίας δὲ συμπεσούσης αὐτῇ ⟨ἐρωτολήπτῳ εἶναι⟩ εἰς τῶν οἰκετῶν ἕνα Ἀρεόβινδον ὄνομα. The supplement is Haury's. Diehl observes that it is not recorded that any personal taunts were levelled at Theodora during the Nika revolt (p. 44); but this is not quite true (see *Chron. Pasch.*, *sub* 532 τὰς ὑβριστικὰς φωνὰς ἃς ἔλεγον . . . εἰς τὴν αὔγουσταν Θεοδώραν).

[2] *H.A.* 9. 30. If this was so, the law of Justin relaxing the rule which forbade senators to marry actresses (*C.J.* v. 4. 23; 520-523) was not required, as has been supposed, for the purpose of making Justinian's marriage possible. Cp. Panchenko, *op. cit.* 74. John of Ephesus refers to Theodora's activity in the matter of a Monophysite deacon, while she

was still a patrician, but this was probably after her marriage (*Comm.* p. 68).

[3] *H.A.* 9. 47. The year is not known, but she died before Justin.

[4] *H.A.* 10. 11 εὐπρόσωπος καὶ εὔχαρις ἄλλως, cp. *Aed.* 1. 11. 8. Procopius describes her as κολοβός, an uncomplimentary way of saying that she was *petite.*

[5] The identification is due to Delbrück, *Porträts byz. Kais.*, whose arguments have convinced me. He proved in the first place by a very complete examination of the headgear of Empresses in the fifth and sixth centuries that the bust belongs to the sixth; and that it is Theodora's is demonstrated by a comparison with the mosaics and the ivories. It is in the archaeological museum of Castel

we have two ivory tablets representing her in imperial robes.[1]
These three portraits show her probably as she was from the
age of thirty to thirty-five. She is visibly an older woman in
the mosaic picture in the church of S. Vitale at Ravenna
(c. A.D. 547), but the resemblance to the bust can be discerned in
the shape of the face, in the mouth, and in the eyes. But the
dominion which she exercised over Justinian was due more to
her mental qualities than to her physical charms. A contemporary writer praises her as " superior in intelligence to all the
world," [2] and all that we know of her conduct as Empress shows
that she was a woman of exceptional brain and courage. Her
influence in the Emperor's counsels was publicly acknowledged
in a way which had no precedent in the past. In a law which
aimed at suppressing corruption in the appointment of provincial
governors, the Emperor declared that in framing it " we have
taken as partner in our counsels our most pious consort given
to us by God." [3] At the end of the law an oath of allegiance is
prescribed. The official is to swear loyalty to " our divine and
pious despots, Justinian, and Theodora, the consort of his
throne." But although Justinian's devotion to his wife prompted
him to increase her dignity and authority in the eyes of the
Empire in unusual ways, it would be a mistake to suppose that
legally she possessed powers which former Empresses had not
enjoyed or that she was co-regent in the constitutional sense.[4]
Custom was strained to permit her unusual privileges. For
instance, she is said to have received foreign envoys and presented them with gifts " as if the Roman Empire were under

Sforzesco. It is probably eastern
work, and must have been set up at
Milan either in 538, during the few
months in which the town was in
Imperial hands, or before 535.

[1] These tablets (of which one is at
the Bargello in Florence, the other
at Vienna) seem to be leaves of the
same diptych. Gräven thought that
the lady was Amalasuntha, but the
diadem, which Gothic royalties never
wore, disproves this. For comparison
we have a small portrait of Theodora
on the consular diptych of Justin
(A.D. 540) which is preserved at
Berlin. There can be little doubt
that Delbrück is right in his identification. On the Bargello tablet
the Empress is standing with a

sceptre in her left hand and a cruciger
globe in her right. On the segmentum
of her chlamys is a male bust with
a sceptre in his left and the hand-
kerchief (mappa) in his right. This
points to the consular games, so that
the presumption is that the tablet
was associated with a consulship of
Justinian, and this would date it
to 528 or 533 or 534. On the Vienna
tablet the Empress is enthroned,
and on the chlamys is a female bust,
which Delbrück suggests might be
that of her niece Sophia, afterwards
Empress.

[2] John Lydus, De mag. iii. 69.
[3] Nov. 8, A.D. 535.
[4] Compare the remarks of Panchenko, op. cit. 74-76.

her rule." [1] Chosroes was amazed when his minister Zabergan showed him a letter which he had received from Theodora urging him to press his master to make peace.[2] Such incidents might well give the impression that the Empire was ruled by two co-equal sovrans, and some thought that Theodora had greater power than Justinian himself.[3] Such power as she possessed she owed to her personal influence over her husband and to his toleration of her intervention in public affairs.

She was not indeed content to pursue her aims merely by the legitimate means of persuading the monarch. When she knew that he had resolutely determined on a line of policy which was not in accordance with her own wishes, she did not scruple to act independently. The most important matter in which their views diverged was ecclesiastical policy. Theodora was a devoted Monophysite, and one of her constant preoccupations was to promote the Monophysitic doctrine and to protect its adherents from the penal consequences which they incurred under Justinian's laws. Her husband must have been well aware that she had an intelligence department of her own and that secret intrigues were carried on of which he would not have approved. But she was clever enough to calculate just how far she could go.

Her power of engaging in independent political action was due to her economic independence. She had large financial resources at her disposal, for which apparently she had to render no account. The personal expenses of an Emperor's consort and the maintenance of her household were provided by estates in Asia Minor which were managed by a high steward known as the Curator of the House of Augusta,[4] who was responsible to her. Justinian appears to have increased these estates considerably for the benefit of Theodora.[5] He gave her large donations on the occasion of her marriage.[6] The house known

---

[1] Procopius, H.A. 30. 24.

[2] Ib. ii. 32 sqq. Theodora had known Zabergan when he had come as envoy to Constantinople.

[3] The view is expressed by Zonaras, xiv. 6. 5-6. It is highly remarkable that no coins were issued with Theodora's name and face, an honour which had been accorded to all Augustae until Justin's reign (there are no coins of Euphemia, see Wroth, Imp. Byz. Coins, xiv. note 4). In the

reign following, Justin and Sophia appear together in many issues.

[4] Curator divinae domus serenissimae Augustae, C.J. vii. 37. 3.

[5] For her estates in Cappadocia, yielding a revenue of 50 lbs. of gold (over £2250), see Nov. 30. 6; in Helenopontus, Nov. 28. 5; in Paphlagonia, Nov. 29. 4.

[6] C.J. ib. Procopius says that he lavished on her large sums of money before his marriage, H.A. 9. 31.

as the palace of Hormisdas, in which Justinian had resided
before his elevation to the throne, was enlarged and enclosed
within the precincts of the Great Palace, and placed at the disposal
of the Empress.[1]
Theodora did much to deserve the reputation of a beneficent
queen, always ready to use her influence for redressing wrongs,[2]
and particularly solicitous to assist the unhappy of her own sex.[3]
To her initiative are ascribed the stringent laws which were
passed to suppress the traffic in young girls, which flourished
as actively then as in modern Europe, and was conducted by
similar methods, which the legislator graphically describes.
Agents used to travel through the provinces to entice to the
capital poor girls, sometimes under ten years of age, by the bait
of fine clothes and an easy life. Indigent parents were easily
persuaded by a few gold coins to consent to the ruin of their
daughters. The victims, when they came to the city, were fed
and clothed miserably, and kept shut up in the houses of ill-fame,
and they were forced to sign written contracts with their infamous
masters. Sometimes compassionate patrons of these establishments offered to deliver one of these slaves from her misery by
marrying her, but the procurers generally refused to consent.
The new edict forbade the trade and ordered that all procurers
should be banished from Constantinople.[4] The principle of
compensation, however, seems to have been applied. The
patrons were allowed to state on oath how much money they
had given to the parents of each girl ; the average price was five
nomismata, and Theodora paid the total out of her private
purse.[5] To receive unfortunate women who abandoned a life
of shame, a palace on the Asiatic shore of the Bosphorus, not far
from the Black Sea, was converted into a convent which was
known as Metanoia or Repentance.[6]

[1] Procopius, *Aed.* i. 4. 1 and 10. 4 ;
John Eph. *Comm.* c. 42.
[2] John Lydus, *De mag.* iii. 69.
[3] Procopius, *B.G.* iii. 32 ἐπεφύκει
γὰρ ἀεὶ δυστυχούσαις γυναιξὶ προσχωρεῖν.
[4] *Nov.* 14 (A.D. 535), addressed to
the people of Constantinople.
[5] This is related by John Mal. xviii.
440-441, as if it occurred in A.D. 529.
There is no reason to question the
date. The words κελεύσασα (Theodora) τοῦ λοιποῦ μὴ εἶναι πορνοβοσκούς
need not be an anticipatory reference

to *Nov.* 14, but may refer to measures
taken by the Prefect of the City. A
recrudescence of the forbidden practices was inevitable, and may have
necessitated the legislation of 535.
A law of Leo I. against the traffic
will be found in *C.J.* xi. 41. 7.
[6] Procopius, *Aed.* i. 9. 5-10, and
H.A. 17. 5. In the latter passage
the author represents the action of
Theodora as tyrannical. "She collected in the middle of the Forum
more than 500 prostitutes who made

Theodora was perhaps too eager to interfere, as a sort of beneficent providence, in the private affairs of individual persons, and her offices were not always appreciated. She is said to have forced two sisters, who belonged to an old senatorial family and had lost their husbands, to marry against their will vulgar men who were utterly unworthy of them.[1] And her enemies alleged that in her readiness to espouse the cause of women she committed grave acts of injustice and did considerable harm. Wives who were divorced for adultery used to appeal to the Empress and bring accusations against their husbands, and she always took their part and compelled the unfortunate men to pay double the dowry, if she did not cause them to be whipped and thrown into prison. The result was that men put up with the infidelity of their wives rather than run such risks.[2] It is impossible to decide how much truth there may be in these charges, but they illustrate Theodora's desire to be the protectress and champion of her own sex.

There can be little doubt that the Empress used her position to exercise a patronage in appointments to offices, which was not always in the public interest, and that she had few scruples in elevating her favourites and disgracing men who displeased her.[3] It must, however, be confessed that in the two cases in which we have good evidence that she intervened to ruin officials, her intervention was beneficial. Thus she procured the disgrace of an Imperial secretary named Priscus, an unprincipled man who had grown rich at the public expense. He was alleged to have spoken against her, and as she could not prevail on Justinian to take action, she caused the man to be put on board a ship and transported to Cyzicus, where he was tonsured. Justinian acquiesced in the accomplished fact and confiscated his property.[4]

a bare living, and sending them across to the convent called Metanoia she shut them up and forced them to change their way of life. Some of them threw themselves down from a height (the roof or a high window) and in this way escaped the compulsory change."
[1] H.A. 17. 7 sqq. Cp. the case of Saturninus, son of the mag.. off. Hermogenes, ib. 32 sqq. Her interference in the domestic affairs of Belisarius, of which Procopius knows so much, is assuredly not entirely invented. In the case of Artabanes

and Praejecta she had a locus standi, as Praejecta was Justinian's niece (B.G. iii. 31, see below, p. 146).
[2] Ib. 17. 24 sqq.
[3] The case of Peter Barsymes is a notable example, H.A. 22. 22 sqq. She is said to have intended to create Theodosius, the lover of Antonina, a mag. mil., ib. iii. 19. Peter the Patrician may have owed his promotion to the post of mag. off. to her favour (see below, p. 166).
[4] The details are told in H.A. 16. 7-10, but the main fact is confirmed by John Mal. xviii. 449 and De ins.

Procopius, in his *Secret History*, has several stories to tell of cruel punishments which she inflicted privately on persons who had offended her. Lurid tales were whispered of the terrible secret dungeons of her palace in which men disappeared for ever,[1] and the known fact that she had the means of maintaining heretics in concealment for years made gossip of this kind appear credible. Whatever may be the truth about her alleged vengefulness and cruelty, it is certain that she was feared.

There was no disguise in the attitude which she assumed as head of the ecclesiastical opposition to Justinian's policy, and he must have been fully aware that secret intrigues were carried on which he would not have sanctioned. It seemed indeed difficult to believe that a man of his autocratic ideas would have tolerated an independent power beside his own ; and the theory was put forward that this apparent discord between their aims and views was a political artifice deliberately planned to blind their subjects, and to facilitate the transactions which the Emperor could not openly permit.[2] This theory may contain a small measure of truth so far as ecclesiastical policy is concerned. It may have been convenient to the Emperor to allow the severities which his policy forced him to adopt against the Monophysites to be mitigated by the clandestine and illegal protection which the Empress afforded to them. But otherwise the theory can hardly be entertained seriously. We can only regard the latitude which was allowed to Theodora as due to Justinian's weakness. And she was clever enough to know how far she could venture.

Her habits presented a contrast to the temperance and simplicity of Justinian. She spent a long time in her bath. At her meals she indulged in every kind of food and drink. She slept long both at night and in her daily siesta.[3] She spent many months of the year in the suburban palaces on the sea-shore, especially at Hêrion (on the coast of Bithynia, opposite the Islands of the Princes), which Justinian enlarged and

---

fr. 45. The other more important case is that of John of Cappadocia, see below, p. 57. Haury is certainly right in supposing that in describing Priscus as Παφλαγών, Procopius does not mean that he was a Paphlagonian, but is alluding to Cleon, "the Paphlagonian" of the *Knights* of Aristo-

phanes (*B.Z.* ix. 674).

[1] Private prisons were forbidden by law, *C.J.* ix. 5. 2 (529).

[2] *H.A.* 10. 13 *sqq.* Theodora's active partisanship for the Blue Faction, of which Justinian professed to disapprove, is given as an instance.

[3] *H.A.* 15. 6 *sqq.*

improved.[1] Sometimes she visited the hot springs of Pythia (in Bithynia), where Justinian also built an Imperial residence. On these occasions she was attended by an immense retinue of patricians and chamberlains.[2] For Theodora had all a parvenue's love of pomp and show, and she was probably encouraged by the Emperor, who, though simple in his own tastes, thought much of public splendour and elaborate ceremonial as a means of enhancing the Imperial majesty. We are told that new and abasing forms of etiquette were introduced at court. When the Senate appeared in the presence of the Emperor, it had been the custom for one of the patricians to kiss the sovran on the right breast, and the sovran replied to the salutation by kissing the head of the patrician. No corresponding ceremony was practised in the case of the Empress. Under Justinian and Theodora it became obligatory that all persons, of whatever rank, should prostrate themselves on entering the presence of the Emperor and of the Empress alike. The spirit of oriental servility in the Palace was shown by the fact that officials and members of the court who, in talking among themselves used to speak of the sovrans as the " Emperor " and the " Empress " (*Basileus* and *Basilis*), now began to designate them as the " Lord " and the " Lady " (*Despotes* and *Despoina*) and described themselves as their slaves ; and any one who did not adopt these forms was considered to have committed an unpardonable solecism.[3]

It is not improbable that, if Justinian had wedded a daughter of one of the senatorial families, many people would have been happier, and the atmosphere of the Palace would have been less dangerously charged with suspicion and intrigue. But, if Theodora was greedy of power and often unscrupulous in her methods, her energy and determination on one occasion rescued the throne, and on another rendered a signal service to the community. And there is no reason to suppose that in her conduct generally she was not honestly convinced that, if she employed irregular means, she was acting in the true interests of the State.

[1] *Ib.*, where it is said that the court suffered much discomfort at Hêrion. For the reconstruction of the palace see *Aed.* i. 11. 16-22.

[2] Four thousand on the occasion

of her visit in 529, acc. to John Mal. xviii. 441. For the palace see *Aed.* v. 3, 16-20.

[3] *H.A.* 30. 21-26.

§ 4. *John the Cappadocian, Praetorian Prefect of the East*

The brilliancy of Justinian's reign did not bring happiness or contentment to his subjects. His determination to increase the power of the throne and retain the government more completely in his own hands caused dissatisfaction in the senatorial circles and inevitably led to tyranny ; and his ambitious plans of expansion involved expenses that could only be met by increasing the financial burdens which already weighed too heavily on the people.

The frugal policy of Anastasius had bequeathed to his successor a reserve of 320,000 lbs. of gold (about 14½ millions sterling). In the reign of Justin these savings were dissipated, as well as a further amount of 400,000 lbs. which had come into the treasury in addition to the regular revenue.[1] A heavy tax on the exchequer was caused by the terrible earthquake of May A.D. 526, which laid the city of Antioch in ruins and destroyed, it is said, 250,000 people.[2] In the following year war broke out with Persia, and when Justinian came to the throne, the financial position was not such as to justify any extraordinary enterprises. It is asserted by a civil servant who had a long career in the office of the Praetorian Prefect of the East, that the unfavourable financial situation was chiefly caused by the incompetence of those who had held the Prefecture in the reign of Justin.[3] Justinian after some time found a man for the post who knew how to fill the treasury.

John, a native of Caesarea in Cappadocia, began as a clerk in the office of a Master of Soldiers. In this capacity he became, by some chance, known to Justinian, and he was promoted to the post of logothete, a name which had now come into general use for those responsible officials who, under the Praetorian Prefect, controlled the operations of the subordinate assessors and collectors of taxes in the provinces.[4] In the case of Marinus,

---

[1] John Lyd. *De mag.* iii. 51 ; Procopius, *H.A.* 19. 7-8 (οὐδενὶ νόμῳ seems to mean "irregularly ").

[2] John Lyd. *ib.* 54. The details of this disaster are vividly described by the Antiochene writer John Mal. xvii. 419 *sqq.* The Emperor showed his sorrow by appearing in St. Sophia without his diadem. Another serious

earthquake befell Antioch at the end of 529, *ib.* 442.

[3] John Lyd. iii. 51.

[4] The office of logothete is discussed at length by Panchenko, *op. cit.* 106 *sqq.* Stein has shown that it is probably the Greek equivalent of *scriniarius* (cp. above, Vol. I. Chap. xiii. § 3, p. 442).

this post had been a stepping-stone to the Prefecture itself, and John had the same luck. He was first raised to the rank of an illustris, and became Praetorian Prefect before A.D. 531.[1] He had not the qualifications which might have been thought indispensable for the duties of this ministry, for he had not received a liberal education, and could barely read and write ; but he had the qualification which was most essential in the eyes of the Emperor, talent and resourcefulness in raising money. His physical strength and energy were enormous, and in difficulties he was never at a loss.[2] He is described as the boldest and cleverest man of his time.[3] But he was absolutely unscrupulous in his methods, and while he supplied the Emperor with the funds which he required, he also became himself enormously rich and spent his money on gluttony and debauchery. " He did not fear God, nor regard man." The provinces of Lydia and Cilicia were a conspicuous scene of his operations. He procured the appointment of another Cappadocian, also named John, to the governorship of Lydia—a man after his own heart, enormously fat and popularly known as Maxilloplumacius (Flabby-jaw) With the help of this lieutenant, the Prefect ruined Lydia and its capital, Philadelphia. He visited the province himself, and we are told that when he had done with it, he had left not a vessel in a house, nor a wife, a virgin, or a youth unviolated. The exaggeration is pardonable, for our informant was born at Philadelphia. The same writer gives particular instances—some of which had come under his own observation of the violent means to which John the Cappadocian resorted to extort money from rich persons. He had dark dungeons in the Prefect's residence, and he made use of torture and painful fetters.[4]

While contemporary writers agree in painting John as a

---

[1] John Lyd. *ib.* 57. John is Pr. Pr. on April 30, 531 (*C.J.* vi. 27. 5), Julian on Feb. 20 (*ib.* iii. 1. 16).

[2] The sources for John's character are Procopius, *B.P.* i. 24 and John Lyd. *ib.* 57 *sqq.* (where we get the details). The two pictures agree.

[3] Procopius, *B.V.* i. 10. 7.

[4] John Lydus can find no terms too strong to describe the Prefect's cruelty and luxury (Phalaris, Cyclops, Briareus, Sardanapalus, etc.). For his debauchery see cc. 62, 65. As John

Lydus was an official in the Prefecture, his testimony is valuable, though on the other hand he may have had private reasons of animosity (cp. c. 66), and his respect for the traditions of the office made a rude uneducated Prefect, who introduced practical innovations in the conduct of business, repellent to him. It seems certain that Maxilloplumacius was governor of Lydia, for he must be meant by τὸν ὁμόγνιον καὶ ὁμό-ψυχον τῆς αὐτοῦ βδελυρίας ὕπαρχον (that is, ἔπαρχον) c. 61.

coarse monster, without a single redeeming quality, we must make some allowance for exaggeration. It is unlikely that he would have enjoyed so long the confidence of the Emperor if his sole recommendation had been skill in plundering the provinces. As a matter of fact, we shall see that during his second tenure of the Prefecture, which lasted about nine years, a series of provincial reforms was carried through which intimately concerned his own sphere of administration and in some respects diminished his power. This could not have been done without his co-operation, and we cannot fairly withhold from him part of whatever credit the legislation deserves. We may conjecture that he won and retained his influence over the Emperor, not only through his success in replenishing the treasury, but also partly through his independence, which was displayed when he openly opposed the project of conquering Africa, and partly through the fact that he was not hampered by conservative prejudices. It was chiefly his indifference to the traditions of the civil service that made him unpopular among the officials of the Prefecture.

Besides increasing the revenue by fair means and foul, John had recourse to economies which were stigmatised by contemporary opinion as injurious to the public interest. He cut off or reduced the service of the State post, with the exception of the main line to the Persian frontier. The post from Chalcedon to Dakibiza was abolished, and replaced by a service of boats to Helenopolis, while in southern Asia Minor and Syria asses were substituted for horses and the speed of travelling was diminished. The results were twofold. The news of disasters in the provinces, which demanded prompt action, was slow in reaching Constantinople. More serious was the consequence for the farmers in the inland provinces, who, deprived of the public means of transport, were obliged to provide for the transmission of their produce to the ports to be conveyed to the capital. Large quantities of corn rotted in the granaries; the husbandmen were impoverished; and the Prefect's officials pressed for payment of the taxes in gold.[1] Multitudes of destitute people left their homes and went to Constantinople.[2]

---

[1] Procopius, *H.A.* 30. 8-11; John Lyd. *ib.* 61.
[2] John Lyd. *ib.* 70. John had attempted to make a breach between Justinian and Theodora, Procopius, *B.P.* i. 25. 4; *H.A.* 17. 38.

Justinian was well satisfied with the fruits of John's administration, and only too ready to shut his eyes to the methods by which the funds he needed were procured. How far he was really innocent it is impossible to determine, but we are assured that the ministers and courtiers always praised the Prefect to the Emperor, even though they had personal grievances against him. At length Theodora, who disliked the Cappadocian and was well acquainted with his iniquities, endeavoured to open Justinian's eyes and to show him that, if the tyrannical administration were allowed to continue, his own position would be endangered. If her arguments produced any effect on his mind, he wavered and postponed action [1] until action was suddenly forced on him by a revolutionary outbreak which well-nigh cost him his throne.

§ 5. *The Nika Revolt* (A.D. 532)

The famous rising at Constantinople, which occurred in the first month of A.D. 532 and wrecked the city, was the result of widely prevailing discontent with the administration, but it began with a riot of the Hippodrome factions which in ordinary circumstances would have been easily suppressed.[2] We saw

---

[1] John Lydus (*ib.* 69), who says that Justinian was deterred from making a change because John had deliberately, in order to ensure his permanent occupation of the post, introduced such confusion into the book-keeping that a successor would have found it almost impossible to carry on the administration.

[2] The contemporary sources are Procopius, *B.P.* i. 24 ; John Mal. xviii. 473 *sqq.* and *fr.* 46, *De ins.* ; John Lyd. *De mag.* iii. 70 ; Marcellinus, *Chron., sub a.* (also notices, not very important, in Zacharias Myt. ix. 4, Victor Tonn. *sub a,* ; Theodore Lector in Cramer, *Anecd. Par.* ii. 112). The narrative of Malalas was originally much fuller than in the abbreviated text which we possess, but the missing parts can be largely supplied from *Chron. Pasch.* and Theophanes, where we find many details for which it can be shown that Malalas was the source, as well as some derived from elsewhere (cp. the analysis in Bury, *The Nika Riot,* 98 *sqq.*). The short

notice of Marcellinus is important. The Illyrian Marcellinus had been the *cancellarius* in the official staff of Justinian when he was Master of Soldiers. Before 527 he retired and became a priest. His chronicle, in its first form, reached the year 518, but afterwards he brought it down to 534. His personal relations to Justinian make it probable that his account of the revolt represents it in the light in which the court desired it to be viewed. The popular dissatisfaction which made the rising possible is entirely ignored, and the whole movement is explained as a conspiracy organised by the nephews of Anastasius, who appear as the prime movers. It must, of course, be remembered that when Marcellinus wrote, *c.* 534, it was impossible to refer to the oppressions of John the Cappadocian, who was then in office. John Lydus ignores the conspiracy and the elevation of Hypatius, and represents the unpopularity of the Prefect as the sole cause of

how Justinian in his uncle's reign patronised the Blues and made
use of them as a political support. But when he was safely
seated on the throne, he resolved no longer to tolerate the licence
of the factions, from the consequences of which he had formerly
protected the Blues. Immediately after his accession he laid
injunctions on the authorities in every city that the disorders
and crimes of the factions should be punished impartially.[1]

A number of persons belonging to both factions had been
arrested for a riot in which there had been loss of life. Eudaemon,
the Prefect of the City, held an inquiry, and finding seven of
the prisoners guilty of murder, he condemned four to be beheaded
and three to be hanged. But in the case of two the hangman
blundered and twice the bodies fell, still alive, to the ground.
Then the monks of St. Conon, which was close to the place of
execution, interfered, and taking up the two criminals, one of
whom was a Blue, the other a Green, put them in a boat and
rowed them across the Golden Horn to the asylum of the church
of St. Laurentius.[2] The Prefect, on hearing what had occurred,
sent soldiers to guard the church.[3]

The ides of January fell three days later (Tuesday), and,
according to custom, horse races were held in the Hippodrome,
and the Emperor was present. Both the Blues and the Greens
importuned the Emperor with loud prayers to show mercy to
the two culprits who had been rescued by accident from the
gallows. No answer was accorded, and at the twenty-second
race the spectators were amazed to hear the unexpected ex-
clamation, "Long live the humane Greens and Blues!" The
cry announced that the two parties would act in concert to
force the government to grant a pardon, and it is probable that
their leaders had previously arranged to co-operate. When the
races were over, the factions agreed on a watchword, *nika*,
"conquer," and the rising which followed was known as the

the revolt. For modern studies of
the Nika see Bibliography, under
Schmidt, W. A., and Kalligas. Cp.
Hodgkin, *Italy*, iii. 618 *sqq.* ; Ranke,
Weltgeschichte, ii. 2, pp. 23 *sqq.*; Diehl,
Justinien, 462 *sqq.*

[1] John Mal. xvii. 416.

[2] St. Conon was in the 13th Region,
across the Golden Horn. St. Laurentius was close to Blachernae.

[3] Jan. 11 (Sunday). This was

perhaps the day of the curious scene
which occurred between the Emperor
and the Greens, and is recorded by
Theophanes (cp. *Chron. Pasch.*), if
the chronicler is right in associating
it with the Nika riot. But it is
possible that the chronicler is mistaken, and in any case the subject
of the conversation has no apparent
connexion with the sedition. I have
therefore transferred it to an Appendix (below, p. 71).

Nika Revolt. The united factions were known for the time as the Green-Blues (*Prasino-venetoi*).

In the evening the mob of rioters assembled at the Praetorium and demanded from the Prefect of the City what he intended to do with the refugees in St. Laurentius. No answer was given, and the rioters broke into the prison, released the criminals who were confined in it, killed some of the officials, and set fire to the building, which was partly burned. Elated by success they rushed eastward to the Augusteum and committed graver acts of incendiarism. They fired the Chalke, the entrance of the Great Palace, and not only was this consumed, but the flames spread northward to the Senate-house and the church of St. Sophia. These buildings were burned down.[1]

On the following morning (Wednesday, January 14) the Emperor ordered the races to be renewed. But the Blues and Greens were not in the humour for witnessing races. They set on fire the buildings at the northern end of the Hippodrome, and the conflagration destroyed the neighbouring baths of Zeuxippus with the portico of the Augusteum. It is probable that on this occasion Justinian did not appear in the Kathisma, or face the multitudes who were now clamouring in the Hippodrome, no longer interceding for the lives of the two wretches who had escaped the hangman, but demanding that three unpopular ministers should be deprived of their offices. The demonstration was directed against Eudaemon, Prefect of the City, Tribonian the Quaestor, and John of Cappadocia, and the situation had become so serious that the Emperor decided to yield.[2] Tryphon was appointed Prefect of the City, Basilides Quaestor, and Phocas, a man of the highest probity, was persuaded to undertake the office of Praetorian Prefect.

These concessions would probably have satisfied the factions and ended the trouble, like similar concessions in previous reigns, if the decision had depended solely on the leaders of the Blues and Greens. But the movement now wore an aspect totally different from that of the previous day. We saw how the city had been filled by throngs of miserable country folk

---

[1] On the order of the different conflagrations during the sedition see Bury, *op. cit.* 114 *sqq.*

[2] The demands were reported to the Emperor by Basilides, Mundus, and Constantiolus, who had issued from the Palace and addressed the multitude, asking them what they wanted. *Chron. Pasch.*; cp. John Mal. 475.

from the provinces who had been ruined by the fiscal administration of the Praetorian Prefect and were naturally animated by bitter resentment against the Emperor and the government. It was inevitable that they should take part in the disturbances ; [1] it was at least a good opportunity to compass the fall of the detested Cappadocian ; and the riot thus assumed the character and proportions of a popular rising. But there were other forces in the background, forces which aimed not merely at a reform of the administration, but at a change in the dynasty. The policy of Justinian in seeking to make his power completely independent of the Senate and the Imperial Council had caused deep animosity in the senatorial class, and the disaffected senators seized the opportunity to direct the rising against the throne.[2] We must attribute to the secret agitation of these men and their agents the fact that the removal of the obnoxious ministers, especially of John, failed to pacify the people.

The plan was to set on the throne one of the nephews of Anastasius, unfortunate victims of their kinship to an Emperor. For we must acquit them of any ambitious designs of their own. They had been well treated by Justin and Justinian, and their only desire was to live in peace. Pompeius and Hypatius were out of the reach of the insurgents ; they and many other senators were with Justinian in the Palace. It was therefore decided to proclaim Probus Emperor, and the mob rushed to his house. But they did not find him, for, fearing what might happen, he had left the city. In their angry disappointment they burned his house.

It was assuredly high time for the Emperor to employ military force to restore order. But the Palace guards, the Scholarians and Excubitors, were unwilling to do anything to defend the throne. They had no feeling of personal devotion to Justinian, and they decided to do nothing and await events. Fortunately for Justinian there happened to be troops of a more irregular kind in the city, and two loyal and experienced commanders.

---

[1] This is brought out in the account of John Lydus. The agitation against John marks the change from the faction riot to the popular sedition. The quarrel of the Blues was with the Prefect of the City. John had always posed demonstratively as a lover of the Blue party (John Lyd. iii. 62 *ad* *init.* ; cp. Zach. Myt. ix. 14).

[2] Marcellinus, *s.a.* : *iam plerisque nobilium coniuratis,* and the fact comes out in the narrative of Procopius. The conspirators took care that the people should be supplied with arms (*ib.*).

Belisarius, who as Master of Soldiers in the East had been conducting the war against Persia, had recently been recalled, and he had in his service a considerable body of armed retainers, chiefly of Gothic [1] race. Mundus, a general who had done good service in the defence of the Danube, was also in the capital with a force of Heruls. But all the soldiers on whom the Emperor could count can hardly have reached the number of 1500.

It was perhaps on Thursday (January 15) [2] that Belisarius rode forth at the head of Goths and Heruls to suppress the revolution. There was a battle, possibly in the Augusteum ; many were killed ; but the soldiers were too few to win a decisive victory, and the attack only exasperated the people. The clergy, it may be noted, seem to have made some vain attempts to restore order.[3]

During the two following days there was desultory street fighting, and another series of conflagrations. On Friday the mob again set fire to the Praetorium, which had only been partly damaged, but there was a strong north wind which blew the flames away from the building. They also set fire to the baths of Alexander, and the same wind carried the conflagration to the neighbouring hospice of Eubulus and hence to the church of St. Irene and the hospice of Sampson. On Saturday there was a conflict between the soldiers and the insurgents in the street which led northward from Middle Street to the Basilica and the quarter of Chalkoprateia.[4] It would appear that some of the mob had occupied the Octagon, a building close to the Basilica, and the soldiers set it on fire. The same fatal north wind was blowing, and the flames, wafted southwards, spread to the church of St. Theodore Sphoracius and to the palace of Lausus, which was consumed with all its treasures, and thence raged along Middle Street, in the direction of the Forum of Constantine, destroying the colonnades and the church of St. Aquilina.[5] We can imagine how great must have been the alarm

---

[1] John Mal. 475 μετὰ πλήθους Γοτθικοῦ (cp. Procopius, B.P. i. 24. 40). For the practice of keeping private bands of retainers see above, Chap. ii. § 2, p. 43.

[2] Or perhaps on Wednesday. See Bury, op. cit. 107.

[3] This comes from Zonaras, xiv. 6. 14, who also mentions that women took part in the disorders (ib. 16).

On his source cp. Sauerbrei, De font. Zon. quaest. 77.

[4] On the topography see Bury, op. cit. 11 sqq. ; Bieliaev, Khram Bog. Khalk. ; Krasnosel'tsev, Zamietka po voprosu o miestopol. Khalk. Khrama (Lietopis ist.-phil. obshchestva of Odessa, Viz. otd. ii. 1894), 309 sqq.

[5] Theophanes connects the burning of the Praetorium with this conflagration, but see Bury, op. cit. 116-117.

in the Palace, which was almost in a state of siege.[1] Justinian could not trust his guards, and he had strong and not unjustified suspicions that many of the senators who surrounded him were traitors. Fearing their treachery, he ordered them all to leave the Palace on Saturday at nightfall,[2] except a few like John the Cappadocian, whose loyalty was certain or whose interests were bound up with his own. He particularly suspected Hypatius and Pompeius, and when they protested against deserting him, his suspicions only grew stronger, and he committed the blunder of dismissing them.

On Sunday morning (January 18) the Emperor made an effort in person to pacify the people. He appeared in the Kathisma of the Hippodrome with a copy of the Gospels in his hands, and a large crowd assembled. He swore on the holy book that he would grant an amnesty without any reservations and comply with the demands of his subjects. But the great part of the crowd was bitterly hostile. They cried, " You are perjuring yourself," [3] and " You would keep this oath to us as you kept your oath to Vitalian." And there were shouts of " Long live Hypatius ! " Meanwhile it had become known that the nephews of Anastasius had left the Palace. The people thronged to the house of Hypatius, and in spite of his own reluctance and the entreaties of his wife Maria, who cried that he was being taken to his death, carried him to the Forum of Constantine, where he was crowned with a golden chain wreathed like a diadem.

A council was then held by Hypatius and the senators who were supporting his cause.[4] Here we can see clearly that the insurrection was guided and fomented by men of high position who were determined to overthrow Justinian. The question was debated whether the Palace should be attacked immediately. One of the senators, Origen, advised delay. He proposed that the new Emperor should occupy for the moment one of the

---

[1] It may be conjectured that a shortage of food and water was feared in the Palace ; for after the suppression of the revolt Justinian constructed cisterns and a granary close to the Palace, in order to have supplies in emergencies, John Mal. 477.

[2] Procopius, ib. 40. Chron. Pasch. places the dismissal of the senators

after Justinian's appearance in the Hippodrome on Sunday. See Bury, 108.

[3] Chron. Pasch. ἐπιορκεῖς, σγαύδαρι. It has been proposed to read γαύδαρι and explain it as = γάδαρε, " ass."

[4] Procopius, ib. § 25, speaks as if all the senators, who were not in the Palace, were present.

smaller Imperial palaces[1] and prosecute the war against his rival with deliberation, leaving nothing to chance. But his advice did not prevail, and Hypatius, who was himself in favour of prompt action, proceeded to the Hippodrome and was installed in the Kathisma. The insurgents crowded the huge building in dense masses, and reviled Justinian and Theodora.[2] In the meantime, another council was being held in the Palace. The situation seemed desperate. To many, including the Emperor himself, there seemed no resource but escape by sea. John the Cappadocian recommended flight to Heraclea, and Belisarius agreed. This course would have been adopted had it not been for the intervention of the Empress Theodora, whose indomitable courage mastered the wavering spirits of her husband and his councillors. A writer, who may well have heard the scene described by Belisarius himself, professes to reproduce her short speech, and even his sophisticated style hardly spoils the effect of her vigorous words :

The present occasion is, I think, too grave to take regard of the convention that it is not meet for a woman to speak among men. Those whose dearest interests are exposed to extreme danger are justified in thinking only of the wisest course of action. Now in my opinion, on the present occasion, if ever, flight is inexpedient even if it should bring us safety. It is impossible for a man, when he has come into the world, not to die ; but for one who has reigned it is intolerable to be an exile. May I never exist without this purple robe and may I never live to see the day on which those who meet me shall not address me as " Queen." [3] If you wish, O Emperor, to save yourself, there is no difficulty ; we have ample funds. Yonder is the sea, and there are the ships. Yet reflect whether, when you have once escaped to a place of security, you will not prefer death to safety. *I* agree with an old saying that " Empire is a fair winding-sheet." [4]

Theodora's dauntless energy communicated itself to her hearers, and they resolved to remain and fight.

In the Hippodrome it was believed that they had already fled. Hypatius, we are told, still doubtful of his chances of success, had secretly sent a message to the Palace, advising Justinian to attack the people crowded in the Hippodrome. Ephraem, the messenger, gave the message to Thomas, an Imperial

---

[1] Two are mentioned (*ib.* § 30), Placillianae and Helena.

[2] *Chron. Pasch.* ; cp. Cramer, *Anecd. Par.* ii. 320.

[3] Δέσποινα.

[4] Καλὸν ἐντάφιον ἡ βασιλεία ἐστί, *B.P. ib.* 33-38. The phrase comes from Isocrates, *Archidamos*, § 45 καλόν ἐστιν ἐντάφιον ἡ τυραννίς.

secretary, who, ignorantly or designedly, informed him that Justinian had taken to flight.[1] Ephraem proclaimed the news in the Hippodrome, and Hypatius now played the Imperial part with confidence, but the people were soon undeceived. Justinian sent out a trusted eunuch, named Narses, with a well-filled purse to sow dissensions and attempt to detach the Blue faction from the rebellion.[2] He could insinuate that Hypatius, like his uncle, would be sure to protect their rivals the Greens, and remind them of the favour which Justinian had shown them in time past and of the unwavering goodwill of Theodora. While Narses fulfilled this mission, Belisarius and Mundus prepared to attack. At first Belisarius thought it would be feasible to reach the Kathisma directly from the Palace and pluck the tyrant from his throne. But the way lay through a building occupied by a portion of the guards, and they refused to let him pass.[3] The Emperor then ordered him to lead his troops, as best he could, through the ruins of the Chalke into the Augusteum. With great difficulty, climbing through the debris of half-burnt buildings, they made their way round to the western entrance of the Hippodrome and stationed themselves just inside, at the portico of the Blues, which was immediately to the right of the Kathisma.[4] In order

[1] Thomas was a pagan and was possibly disloyal. The episode is related in *Chron. Pasch.* and came from Malalas.

[2] John Mal. 476. Procopius does not mention this incident. Narses, a Persarmenian, was ταμίας τῶν βασιλικῶν χρημάτων since A.D. 530 (Procopius, *B.P.* i. 15. 31, cp. *B.G.* ii. 14. 16). At this time he was not *Praepositus s. cub.*, a post which he afterwards filled (between 540 and 552), see *C.I.L.* vi. 1199. The same financial post was held by Rusticus in 554 (see Agathias, iii. 2), but I cannot agree with Stein that this was an extraordinary post, existent only in time of war, and officially named *comes s. largitionum (Studien,* 163 *sqq.*).

[3] We have no clear knowledge as to the communications between the Palace and the Hippodrome in the sixth century. We have more information about the arrangements existing in the ninth and tenth, but there must have been considerable

changes in the meantime. The Emperors always reached the Kathisma from the Daphne portion of the Palace by a winding stair, *Kochlias* (which must, however, be distinguished from the *Kochlias* leading to a gate by which Mundus left the Palace, Procop. *ib.* § 43). If Belisarius hoped to reach Hypatius by this way, we must suppose that there was a guard-room at the top of the staircase, in the Kathisma structure, for we know that the Daphne buildings, in which there was no room for guards, adjoined the walls of the Hippodrome. But there may have been at this time a direct communication between the part of the Hippodrome north of the Kathisma and the quarters of the guards north of Daphne; and this seems the most probable explanation.

[4] Procopius, *ib.* § 49. See above, Vol. I. Chap. III. p. 81. This passage shows conclusively that there was a western entrance to the Hippodrome, close to the Kathisma. It is possible that the Nekra gate by which Mundus

to gain access to the Kathisma itself, it would have been necessary
to pass through a small gate on the left, which was shut and
guarded. If Belisarius attempted to force this gate, his men
would have been exposed to an attack from the crowd in the
rear. He therefore determined to charge the people. He drew
his sword and gave the word. Though many of the populace
had arms, there was no room in the dense throng to attempt an
orderly resistance, and confronted by the band of disciplined
soldiers the mob was intimidated and gave way. Moreover
there were dissensions among them, for the bribes of Narses had
not been fruitless. They were cut down without mercy, and
then Mundus appeared with his Heruls to help Belisarius in the
work of slaughter. Mundus had left the Palace by another
way, and he now entered the Hippodrome by a gate known as
Nekra. The insurgents were between two fires, and there was
a great carnage. It was said that the number of the slain
exceeded 30,000.[1]

Two nephews of Justinian, Boraides and Justus, then entered
the Kathisma without meeting resistance.[2] They seized Hypatius,
who had witnessed the battle from his throne, and secured
Pompeius, who was with him. The brothers were taken into
the Palace, and, notwithstanding the tears of Pompeius and
the pleadings of Hypatius that he had acted under compulsion,[3]
they were executed on the following day and their bodies were
cast into the sea. The Emperor, suspicious though he was,
probably believed that they were not morally guilty, but feared

---

entered was on the same side, near
the south end, rather than on the
eastern side, as has been generally
supposed. We might infer from
Procopius that when Belisarius and
his troops forced their way into the
Hippodrome, Mundus and his Heruls
stationed themselves just outside the
same (main) entrance (πλησίον που
ἑστηκὼς Μούνδος), and when the
fighting began went to the Nekra. On
the other hand, Mundus seems to have
been awaiting the action of Belisarius
on the eastern side, for he left the
Palace by a gate where there was a
winding descent (Procop. *ib.* § 43)—
evidently an issue on the south of the
Daphne, where there was a fall in
the ground. It is therefore more
natural to suppose that the Nekra,
by which he entered the Hippodrome,

was on the same side.

[1] Procopius, "more than 30,000,"
and John Mal. "35,000 more or less,"
roughly agree. John Lyd. gives an
exaggerated figure, 50,000 ; Zonaras,
40,000.

[2] Procopius, § 53. Acc. to John
Mal. 476, it was Belisarius who
arrested the two brothers.

[3] Procopius contrasts the weakness
of Pompeius with the more dignified
tone of Hypatius. Acc. to John Mal.
ib., they urged that they had deliberately collected the crowd in the
Hippodrome, in order to facilitate
the suppression of the rising. Justinian ironically observed, "If you
had such influence with the insurgents,
why did you not hinder them from
burning down the city ? "

that they would be used as tools in future conspiracies. They were too dangerous to be allowed to live, but their children were spared.

The throne of Justinian was saved through the moral energy of Theodora and the loyal efforts of Belisarius. It was not only saved, but it rested now on firmer foundations, for it gave the Emperor the opportunity of taking vigorous measures to break down the opposition of the senatorial nobles to his autocracy. There were no more executions, but eighteen senators who had taken a leading part in the conspiracy were punished by the confiscation of their property and banishment.[1] At a later time, when he felt quite secure, Justinian pardoned them and restored to them any of their possessions which he had not already bestowed on others, and a similar restitution was even made to the children of Hypatius and Pompeius.

The news of the Emperor's victory over his enemies and the execution of the usurper was proclaimed in the cities throughout the Empire. For a long time after this event the factions of the Hippodrome seem to have been on their good behaviour, if we may judge by the silence of the chroniclers. During the last twenty years of the reign riots and faction fights occurred from time to time, but the rival parties did not combine again and the disorders were easily put down.[2]

§ 6. St. Sophia

After the suppression of this formidable rebellion, one of the first anxieties of the Emperor was to set about rebuilding the edifices which had been destroyed by fire, above all the church of St. Sophia. He was sitting amidst ruin and devastation,

---

[1] The number 18 is in John Mal. *fr.* 46, *De ins.* and *Chron. Pasch.* ; Procopius says generally ἁπάντων (*ib.* § 57). If 18 is correct, Procopius must have exaggerated either here or *ib.* § 25 ; but the latter passage is borne out by Marcellinus (*plerisque nobilium*).

[2] In 547 the factions quarrelled, and the disturbance was suppressed by the Excubitors with some bloodshed (John Mal. xviii. 483). Riots are recorded in 548 and 551 (*ib.* 484). In May 556 there was a more serious popular demonstration against the Prefect of the City, due to a famine which lasted for three months ; the leaders of the Blues were seized and punished (*ib.* 488). In May 559 there were conflicts between the Blues and Greens for two days, and the disorder was accompanied by incendiarism ; the house of Peter Barsymes the Praet. Prefect was burnt, and the intervention of the Excubitors was necessary (*ib.* 490). Other disturbances are recorded in 562 (*ib.* 492) and 563 (Theophanes, A.M. 6055), and (without date) in John Mal. *frs.* 50 and 51, *De ins.*

and it would be natural if he had thought of nothing but restoring the wrecked buildings as rapidly as was possible ; but he saw in the calamity an opportunity for making his capital more magnificent, and constructing a church which would be the wonder of the world. The damage might well have been made good in two years if he had been content to rebuild on the same scale ; the work he designed took five years, and considering what was accomplished the time seems incredibly short.

Forty days after the tumult had subsided, the ruins of the church were cleared away, neighbouring houses were bought up, and space was provided for a new temple of the Divine Wisdom. The plans were prepared by Anthemius of Tralles, an architect and engineer who possessed imagination as well as mastery of his craft, and to him was entrusted the direction of the work, with Isidore of Miletus as his assistant. It is to be noted that both these architects were natives of Asia Minor. We cannot doubt that Anthemius had already given proofs of his skill as a builder, and it is not bold to conjecture that he was the architect of the church of SS. Sergius and Bacchus, which Justinian and Theodora had caused to be erected at the beginning of their reign. Justinian had extended the precincts of the Great Palace to take in the house of Hormisdas—on the seashore, south of the Hippodrome—which had been his residence before he ascended the throne ; and close to it he built two churches side by side with a common court, a basilica of SS. Peter and Paul, which has disappeared,[1] and the octagonal domed church of SS. Sergius and Bacchus, which has survived, converted by the Turks into a mosque which they call the Little St. Sophia. The names of the Emperor and Empress are associated in the metrical inscription which is still to be seen on the frieze and their monograms can be read on the beautiful " melon " capitals. Modern architects have paid tribute to the remarkable skill with which the dome has been buttressed and weighted, and we may divine that it was the skill of Anthemius, of whom a contemporary said that he " designed wonderful works both in the city and in many other places which would suffice to win him everlasting glory in the memory of men so long as they stand and endure." [2]

His plan of St. Sophia was different. It is a Greek cross

---

[1] Van Millingen, *Byz. Churches*, 62 *sqq.* The church was founded in 527.
[2] Agathias, *Hist.* v. 8.

(about 250 by 225 feet) with a dome rising above the quadrilateral space between the arms to the height of 180 feet. He undertook to solve the problem of placing a great aerial cupola, 100 feet in diameter, over this space which was 100 feet square. Hitherto cupolas had been set over round spaces. At each angle of the square Anthemius erected a massive pier, in which the settings of the stones were strengthened by special methods. These piers supported the four arches and pendentives on which the ribbed dome rested, and he calculated on securing stability by the semi-domes on the east and west and buttresses on the north and south. To diminish the weight of the dome very light materials were used, tiles of a white spongy earth manu-factured at Rhodes.[1]

The material of St. Sophia, as of most Byzantine churches, was brick. Its exterior appearance, seen from below, does not give a true impression of its dimensions. The soaring cupola is lost and buried amid the surrounding buttresses that were added to secure it in later ages. From afar one can realise its proportions, lifted high above all the other buildings and dominat-ing the whole city like a watch-tower, as Procopius described it. But in it, as in other Byzantine churches, the contrast between the plainness of the exterior and the richness of the interior decoration is striking. Although the mosaic pictures, including the great cross on a starry heaven at the summit of the dome,

[1] It has been a subject of debate whether the architects of the sixth century, in their dome constructions, derived their inspiration from the East, or were simply working along the lines of Roman architectural tradition and adopting suggestions from Roman models. Rivoira has conjectured that Anthemius (whose brother Alexander was a physician at Rome, Agathias, *loc. cit.*) had visited Rome and picked up ideas there. He calls attention (*Lombardic Arch.* i. p. 79) to the family likeness between the plan of St. Sophia " and the two halls of the Baths of Agrippa and Nero as well as the Basilica Nova of Maxentius and Constantine." He also notes (with Choisy) the resem-blance of SS. Sergius and Bacchus with the Licinian Nymphaeum ; and he thinks the designer of that church derived from the Serapeum of Hadrian's Villa the idea of a dome of which the surface is a rhythmic sequence of flat and concave sections unsupported by pendentives, simply flush with the course of the drum from which they start (p. 81). Further, he holds that the visible radiating ribs with which Isidore provided the dome of St. Sophia, when he restored it, were suggested by the Mausoleum Augustorum, a building (of fifth century) consisting of two rotundas, of one of which (it survived till the sixteenth century) a sketch has been preserved (pp. 82-83). Strzygowski, on the other hand, contends that the origin of domed churches was oriental, and in one of his latest works he particularly connects it with Armenia (*Die Baukunst der Armenier und Europa*, 2 vols., 1918).

are now concealed from the eyes of faithful Moslems by white-
wash, the marbles of the floor, the walls, and the pillars show
us that the rapturous enthusiasm of Justinian's contemporaries
as to the total effect of the decoration was not excessive. The
roof was covered with pure gold, but the beauty of the effect lay,
it was observed, rather in the answering reflexions from the
marbles than from the gold itself. The marbles from which
were hewn the pillars and the slabs that covered the walls and
floor were brought from all quarters of the world. There was
the white stone from the quarries in the Proconnesian islands
near at hand, green cipollino from Carystus in Euboea, verde
antico from Laconia and Thessaly, Numidian marble glinting
with the gold of yellow crocuses, red and white from Caria, white-
misted rose from Phrygia, porphyry from Upper Egypt. To
Procopius the building gave the impression of a flowering meadow.

While the artists of the time showed skill and study in blending
and harmonising colours, the sculptured decoration of the curves
of the arches with acanthus and vine tendrils, and the beauty
of the capitals of white Proconnesian marble, are not less wonderful. The manufacture of capitals for export had long been
an industry at Constantinople, and we can trace the evolution
of their forms. The old Corinthian capital, altered by the
substitution of the thorny for the soft acanthus, had become
what is known as the " Theodosian " capital.[1] But it was found
that this was not suitable for receiving and supporting the arch,
and the device was introduced of placing above it an inter-
mediary " impost," in the form of a truncated and reversed
pyramid, which was usually ornamented with vine or acanthus,
a cross or a monogram. Then, apparently early in the sixth
century, the Theodosian capital and the impost were combined
into a single block, the " capital impost," which assumed many
varieties of form.[2]

The building was completed in A.D. 537, and on December 26
the Emperor and the Patriarch Menas drove together from
St. Anastasia to celebrate the inaugural ceremonies.[3] But
Anthemius had been overbold in the execution of his architectural
design, and had not allowed a sufficient margin of safety for the

---

[1] An example is preserved in the   *Sophia*, 247 *sqq.*; Diehl, *L'Art byz.* 128;
fifth-century church of St. John of   and cp. Rivoira, *op. cit.* i. 128.
Studion.
[2] See Lethaby and Swainson, *S.*   [3] Theophanes, A.M. 6030.

support of the dome. Twenty years later the dome came crashing
down, destroying in its fall the ambo and the altar (May, A.D. 558).[1]
Anthemius was dead, and the restoration was undertaken by
Isidore the Younger. He left the semi-domes on the east and
west as they were, but widened the arches on the north and
south, making " the equilateral symmetry " more perfect, and
raised the height of the dome by more than twenty feet. The
work was finished in A.D. 562, and on Christmas Eve the Emperor
solemnly entered it. The poet Paul, the silentiary, was commanded to celebrate the event in verse, and a few days later [2]
he recited in the Palace the proem of his long poem describing
the beauties of the church. Justinian then proceeded in solemn
procession to St. Sophia, and in the Patriarch's palace, which
adjoined the church, he recited the rest. It was a second in-
auguration, and the effort of Paul was not unworthy of the
occasion.

Terrible, thought a writer of the day, as well as marvellous,
the dome of St. Sophia " seems to float in the air." It was
pierced by forty windows, the half-domes by five, and men were
impressed by the light which flooded the church. " You would
say that sunlight grew in it." Lavish arrangements were made
for artificial illumination for the evening services. A central
chandelier was suspended by chains from the cornice round the
dome over the ambo ; the poet compared it to a circular dance
of lights :

$$\epsilon \dot{v} \sigma \epsilon \lambda \acute{a} \omega \nu \ \delta \grave{\epsilon}$$
$$\kappa \acute{v} \kappa \lambda \iota o \varsigma \ \dot{\epsilon} \kappa \ \phi a \acute{\epsilon} \omega \nu \ \chi o \rho \grave{o} \varsigma \ \emph{ι} \sigma \tau a \tau a \iota.$$

And in other parts of the building there were rows of lamps in
the form of silver bowls and boats.

Justinian did not regard expense in decorating with gold and
precious stones the ambo which stood in the centre under the
dome. Similar sumptuousness distinguished the sanctuary of
the apse—the iconostasis and the altar which was of solid
gold. The Patriarch's throne was of gilded silver and weighed

[1] Agathias, v. 9. John Mal.
xviii. p. 489, " in the 6th indiction."
Theophanes follows Malalas, but
puts the notice under a wrong year,
A.M. 6051, which would mean A.D.
559. The whole dome does not seem
to have collapsed ; as it consisted
of independent sections this was
possible. See Jackson, *Byz. Architecture*, i. 87.

[2] Friedländer (p. 110, Preface to
ed. of Paul) conjectures on Epiphany,
Jan. 6. Paul, son of Cyrus, was of
good family and great wealth.

40,000 lbs. A late record states that the total cost of the building and furnishing of St. Sophia amounted to 320,000 lbs. of
gold, which sent to our mint to-day would mean nearly fourteen
and a half million sterling,[1] a figure which is plainly incredible.
But this, though it was the greatest item in the Emperor's
expenditure on restoring and beautifying the city, was only one.
The neighbouring church of St. Irene also rose from its ashes, as
a great domed basilica, the largest church in Constantinople
except St. Sophia itself.[2] The monograms of Justinian and
Theodora are still to be read on the capitals of its pillars. More
important as a public and Imperial monument was the Church
of the Holy Apostles in the centre of the city, which had not
been injured by fire, but had suffered from earthquakes and
was considered structurally unstable. Justinian pulled it down
and rebuilt it larger and more splendid, as a cruciform church
with four equal arms and five domes. Though it was destroyed
by the Turks to make room for the mosque of Mohammed the
Conqueror, descriptions are preserved which enable us to restore
its plan.[3] San Marco at Venice was built on a very similar design
and gives the best idea of what it was like. It may have been
begun after the completion of St. Sophia, for it was dedicated
in A.D. 546 ; but the mosaic decoration, of which full accounts
have come down to us, was not executed till after Justinian's
death, and it has been shown that these pictures, which may

---

[1] The figure is given in the Διήγησις
περὶ τῆς ἁγ. Σοφίας, c. 25, p. 102 ;
it excludes the cost of the sacred
vessels and the numerous private
gifts. It is a curious coincidence
that the sum is identical with the
reserve saved by Anastasius (see
above, § 4, p. 36). Three hundred and
sixty-five lbs. of gold (c. £1,642,500)
were said to have been spent on the
ambo, ib. This narrative is marked
not only by miracles and obvious
fictions but by curious errors, such
as dating the beginning of the building of the church to A.D. 538. The
fabulous sum which the building is
said to have cost might have been
reached if 10,000 workmen had been
continuously employed and received
the wages de luxe which Justinian is
said to have lavished on them
(Διήγησις, § 9 and § 20). It is
remarkable, however, that the com-

piler believed that his figures were
derived from an account of the
expenses kept by Strategius, who was
Count of the Sacred Largesses (as
we otherwise know) in 536-537 (on
the credibility of the document cp.
Preger, B.Z. x. 455 sqq.). Uspenski,
Ist. viz. imp. i. 532, accepts the figures.
For a more trustworthy figure in
connexion with the building see
below, p. 55, n. 3. I should be
surprised if the total expenses
amounted to a million sterling. If
they were partly paid out of the
Private Estate, the confiscated property of the rich senators concerned
in the rebellion would have gone a
long way.

[2] See George, Church of St. Eirene.

[3] The history, plan, and mosaics of
the church are fully treated in
Heisenberg's work, Die Apostelkirche.

belong to the time of his immediate successors, were designed
and selected with a dogmatic motif. " The two natures of
Christ in one person are the theme of the whole cycle." [1] The
use of pictures for propagating theological doctrine was understood in the sixth century ; we shall see another example at
Ravenna.[2]

The principal secular buildings which had been destroyed by
the fires of the Nika riot and were immediately rebuilt were the
Senate-house, the baths of Zeuxippus, the porticoes of the
Augusteum, and the adjacent parts of the Palace. The Chalke
had been burnt down, and the contiguous quarters behind it—
the portico of the Scholarian guards and the porticoes of the
Protectors and Candidates. All these had to be rebuilt.[3] But
at the same time Justinian seems to have made extensive changes
and improvements throughout the Palace ; we are told that he
renovated it altogether.[4] Of the details we hear nothing, except
as to the Chalke itself. You go through the great gate of the
Chalke from the Augusteum, and then through an inner bronze
gate into a domed rectangular room, decorated by mosaic pictures
showing the Vandal and Italian conquests, with Justinian and
Theodora in the centre, triumphing and surrounded by the
Senate.[5]

If the Emperor spent much on the restoration and improve-
ment of the Great Palace, he appears to have been no less lavish
in enlarging and embellishing his palatial villa at Hêrion, on the
peninsula which to-day bears the name of Phanaraki, to the
south-east of Chalcedon.[6] It was the favourite resort of Theodora
in summer ; she used to transport her court there every year.[7]
Here Justinian created a small town, with a splendid church

---

[1] Heisenberg, *op. cit.* p. 168.

[2] Below, Chap. XVIII. § 12.

[3] Procopius, *Aed.* i. 10. Cp. *Chron.
Pasch.*, *sub* 532.

[4] Procopius, *ib.* 10 νέα μὲν τὰ
βασίλεια σχεδόν τι πάντα. I conjecture that Justinian may have
designed the Chrysotriclinos buildings,
and that Justin II., to whom they
are attributed in our sources, may
have only completed them.

[5] Procopius, *ib.* The central dome
was sustained by four piers, and two
arches on the south and two on the
north, springing from the walls,

formed the vaulted ceilings north and
south of the dome.

[6] The site has been fixed beyond
dispute by Pargoire, *Hiéria.* The
name of the peninsula took many
forms. In the time of Justinian it
was generally called Ἱερόν or Ἥριον,
in the time of Heraclius Ἱέρεια.

[7] Her courtiers did not all like the
change, if we can draw any inference
from the complaint of Procopius
that Theodora inhumanly exposed
them to the perils of the sea and that
they suffered from the lack of the
comforts they enjoyed in the city.
H.A. 15. 36-37.

dedicated to the Mother of God, baths, market-places, and porticoes ; and constructed a sheltered landing-place by building two large moles into the sea.[1]

§ 7. *The Fall of John the Cappadocian* (A.D. 541)

The nine or ten years following the suppression of the Nika revolt were the most glorious period of Justinian's reign. He was at peace with Persia ; Africa and Italy were restored to his dominion. The great legal works which he had undertaken were brought to a successful conclusion ; and Constantinople, as we have just seen, arose from its ashes more magnificent than ever.

But the period was hardly as happy for the subjects as it was satisfactory to their ruler. For a short time the fiscal exactions under which they had groaned may have been alleviated under the milder administration of the popular Phocas, who had succeeded the Cappadocian, and who at least had no thought of using his office to enrich himself.[2] But Phocas was soon removed, probably because his methods failed to meet the financial needs of the Emperor, engaged in preparations for the African expedition and in plans for rebuilding the city on a more splendid scale. In less than a twelvemonth John the Cappadocian was once more installed in the Prefecture, and was permitted for eight or nine years to oppress the provinces of the East.[3] Justinian did not feel himself bound by the promises he had made to the insurgents, seeing that they had been made in vain. He also restored to the post of Quaestor

---

[1] Procopius, *Aed.* i. 11. The historian was perhaps thinking particularly of the construction of this port when he was writing, *H.A.* 8. 7-8, as Pargoire suggests (*op. cit.* p. 58).

[2] Phocas, son of Craterus, was of good family and well off. He began as a silentiary in the Palace. He had been prosecuted as a pagan in 529 (John Mal. xviii. 449, where it is falsely said that he was put to death). See the panegyric of John Lydus (iii. 70 *sqq.*), where his liberality and personal frugality are praised. When he became Prefect he set himself to learn Latin, and John Lydus procured him the services of

an instructor. He is highly spoken of by the Emperor in *Nov.* 82, § 1 (539).

[3] John Mal., *ib.* 477, dates John's restoration to 532. We know from Procopius, *B.V.* i. 10 and 13, that he was Prefect before June 533. He fell in the tenth year of his Prefecture (*B.P.* i. 25. 3), and as his fall can be fixed to May 541 (see below), Procopius seems to count as if his two tenures of office had been continuous. Phocas held the Prefecture long enough to furnish 4000 lbs. of gold (£288,000) towards the building of St. Sophia (John Lyd. *ib.* 76), but for less than a year (Proc. *H.A* 21.7).

the great jurist Tribonian, who, otherwise most fitted to adorn the office, seems to have been somewhat unscrupulous in indulging his leading passion, a love of money. The only person whom John the Cappadocian feared was the Empress. He knew that she was determined to ruin him. He was unable to undermine her influence with Justinian, but that influence did not go far enough to shake Justinian's confidence in him. He dreaded that her emissaries might attempt to assassinate him, and he kept around him a large band of armed retainers, a measure to which no Praetorian Prefect except Rufinus had resorted before. He was exceedingly superstitious, and impostors who professed to foretell the future encouraged him in the hope that he would one day sit on the Imperial throne. In A.D. 538 he enjoyed the expensive honour of the consulship.[1]

If there was one man whom John detested and envied it was the general Belisarius, who in A.D. 540 arrived at Constantinople, bringing the king of the Ostrogoths as a captive in his train. If any man was likely to be a dangerous rival in a contest for the throne, it was the conqueror of Africa and Italy, who was as popular and highly respected as John himself was unpopular and hated. As a matter of fact, thoughts of disloyalty were far from the heart of Belisarius, but he was not always credited with unswerving fidelity to Justinian, even by Justinian himself.

Belisarius, like his master, was born in an Illyrian town,[2] and, like his master, he had married a woman whose parents were associated with the circus and the theatre and who was the mother of children before she married the soldier.[3] Unlike Theodora, she did not mend her morals after her marriage, and her amours led to breaches with her husband. But notwithstanding temporary estrangements she preserved the affection

---

[1] *Fasti cons.* (p. 56): Flavius Johannes. Cp. *C.I.L.* vi. 32,042.

[2] Germania, on the borders of Illyricum and Thrace, Procop. *B.V.* i. 11. 21. Cp. the town of Germae (Γερμαή) in Dardania (*Aed.* iv. 1. 31); Hierocles, *Synecd.* 654. 5).

[3] Her father and grandfather were chariot-drivers, her mother a disreputable actress (τῶν τινος ἐν Θυμέλῃ πεπορνευμένων), Procop. *H.A.*

1. 11. She is said to have been 60 years old in 544 (*ib.* iv. 41). She had borne a daughter to Belisarius, Joannina. An illegitimate daughter married Ildiger, an officer who was prominent in the wars of the time; and by another illegitimate child she had a granddaughter who married Sergius, a nephew of Solomon the eunuch (see below, p. 145). For her son Photius see below, p. 60.

of her husband, who had a weak side to his character, and she faithfully accompanied him on his campaigns and worked energetically in his interests. She often protected him, when he was out of favour with the Emperor, through her influence with Theodora, who found her a useful ally and resourceful agent.

The cunning of this unscrupulous woman compassed the fall of John of Cappadocia. She was interested in destroying him as the enemy both of her husband and of her Imperial mistress. The only hope of damaging him irretrievably in the eyes of the Emperor was to produce clear evidence that he entertained treasonable designs, and for this purpose Antonina resorted to the vile arts of an *agent provocateur*. The Prefect had a daughter, his only child, whom he loved passionately ; it was the one amiable trait in his repulsive character. His enemies could cast no reproach on the virtue of Euphemia, but she was very young and she fell an easy victim to the craft of Antonina. It was in April or May A.D. 541 that the treacherous scheme was executed. Belisarius had set out in the spring to take command in the Persian war, and his wife had remained for a short time at Constantinople before she followed him to the East. She employed herself in cultivating the acquaintance of Euphemia, and having fully won her friendship she persuaded the in-experienced girl that Belisarius was secretly disaffected towards Justinian. It is Belisarius, she said, who has extended the borders of the Empire, and taken captive two kings, and the Emperor has shown little gratitude for his services. Euphemia, who, taught to see things through her father's eyes, feared Theodora and distrusted the government, listened sympathetically to the confidences of her friend. " Why," she asked, " does Belisarius not use his power with the army to set things right ? " " It would be useless," said Antonina, " to attempt a revolution in the camp without the support of civilian ministers in the capital. If your father were willing to help, it would be different." Euphemia eagerly undertook to broach the matter to her father. John, when he heard his daughter's communication, thought that a way was opened for realising the vague dreams of power which he had been cherishing. It was arranged that he should meet Antonina secretly. She was about to start for the East, and she would halt for a night near Chalcedon at the palace

of Rufinianae, which belonged to her husband.[1] Hither John
agreed to come secretly, and the day and hour were arranged.
Antonina then informed the Empress of all she had done and
the details of the scheme. It was essential that the treasonable
conversation should be overheard by witnesses, whose testimony
would convince Justinian. Theodora, who entered eagerly into
the plot, chose for this part the eunuch Narses, and Marcellus,
commander of the Palace guards, a man of the highest integrity,
who stood aloof from all political parties, and never, throughout
a long tenure of his command, forfeited the Emperor's respect.[2]
Theodora did not wait for the execution of the scheme to tell
Justinian of what was on foot, and it was said that he warned
John secretly not to keep the appointment. This may not be
true. In any case, John arrived at Rufinianae at midnight,
only taking the precaution of bringing some of his armed retainers.
Antonina met him outside the house near a wall behind which
she had posted Marcellus and Narses. He spoke, without any
reserve, of plans to attempt the Emperor's life. When he had
fully committed himself, Narses and Marcellus emerged from
their hiding-place to seize him. His men, who were not far off,
rushed up and one of them wounded Marcellus. In the fray
John succeeded in escaping, and reaching the city he sought
refuge in a sanctuary.[3] The historian who tells the tale thought
that if he had gone boldly to the Palace he would have been
pardoned by Justinian. But the Empress now had the Emperor's
ear. John was deprived of the office which he had so terribly
abused and banished to Cyzicus, where he was ordained a deacon
against his will. His large ill-gained possessions were forfeited
as a matter of course, but the Emperor showed his weakness
for the man by letting him retain a considerable portion, which
enabled him to live in great luxury in his retirement.[4]

But he was not long suffered to enjoy his exile in peace. The

[1] At Jadi Bostan (see above, Vol. I.
p. 87). We do not know how this
Imperial residence passed into the possession of Belisarius. At Παντείχιον,
near Chalcedon, evidently to be
identified with Pendik, Belisarius
had also a villa. See Pargoire,
Rufinianes, pp. 459, 477.
[2] It is uncertain whether he was
Count of the Excubitors or Commander of the Scholarians. For his char-

acter see Procopius, *B.G.* iii. 32. 22.
[3] Ἐs τὸ ἱερόν (*B.P.* i. 25. 30), where
Haury conjectures that the words
τοῦ Λαυρεντίου have fallen out.
[4] All the details are derived from
Procopius, *B.P.* i. 25. In the summary notice of John Mal. xviii. 480
(cp. *De ins.* p. 172), the date is given
as August. But Theodotus had succeeded John as Prefect between May 7
and June 1, 541 (*Nov.* 109 and 111).

bishop of Cyzicus, Eusebius, was hated by the inhabitants. They had preferred charges against him at Constantinople, but his influence there was so great that he was able to defy Cyzicus. At last some young men, who belonged to the local circus factions, murdered him in the market-place. As it happened that John and Eusebius were enemies, it was suspected that John was accessory to the crime, and, considering his reputation, the suspicion was not unnatural. Senators were sent to Cyzicus to investigate the murder. John's guilt was not proved ; [1] but the commission of inquiry must have received secret orders to punish him rightly or wrongly, for he was stripped and scourged like a common highwayman, and then put on board ship, clad in a rough cloak. The ship bore him to Egypt, and on the voyage he was obliged to support life by begging in the seaports at which it called. When he reached Egypt he was imprisoned at Antinoopolis. For these illegal proceedings the Emperor, we may be sure, was not responsible, and no private enemy could have ventured to resort to them. The hand of Theodora could plainly be discerned. But she was not yet satisfied with his punishment ; she desired to have him legally done to death.[2] Some years later she got into her power two young men of the Green faction who were said to have been concerned in the murder of the bishop. By promises and threats she sought to extract a confession implicating John the Cappadocian. One of them yielded, but the other, even under torture, refused. Baffled in her design she is said to have cut off the hands of both the youths.[3] John remained in prison till her death, after which he was allowed by the Emperor to return to Constantinople, a free man, but a priest. Yet it was said that he still dreamed of ascending the throne.[4]

[1] Οὐ λίαν ἐξελήλεγκτο, Procop. ib. Theodora's name is not mentioned in the episode as narrated here, but the part which she played comes out in the supplementary story in H.A. 17. 40 sqq. Procopius wrote B.P. i. 25 in the third year of John's imprisonment in Egypt (τρίτον τοῦτο ἔτος αὐτὸν ἐνταῦθα καθείρξαντες τηροῦσιν, § 43), probably in 544–545. For when he says (§ 44) that the retribution for his acts overtook John ten years later, he seems to mean that ten years elapsed between John's reappoint-

ment after the Nika, in 532–533, and the affair at Cyzicus, which would thus have occurred in 542–543.

[2] What follows comes from H.A. 17., where the date given is τέτρασι ἐνιαυτοῖς ὕστερον (i.e. 546–547, see last note).

[3] This was done publicly in the Forum of Constantine. Justinian, according to Haury's very probable emendation of the text (ib., ad fin.), pretended to know nothing about it

[4] Procop. B.P. ii. 30.

It is incontestable that Theodora performed a public service by delivering the eastern provinces from the government of an exceptionally unscrupulous oppressor, and that his sufferings, although they were illegally inflicted, were richly deserved. But the revolting means imagined by her unprincipled satellite Antonina and approved by herself, the employment of the innocent girl to entrap her father,[1] do not raise her high in our estimation. It must be observed, however, that the public opinion of that time found nothing repulsive in a stratagem which to the more delicate feelings of the present age seems unspeakably base and cruel. For the story is told openly in a work which the author could not have ventured to publish if it had contained anything reflecting injuriously on the character of the Empress.[2]

It was not long before the Empress had an opportunity of repaying her friend for her dexterous service. Belisarius and Antonina had adopted a youth named Theodosius, for whom Antonina conceived an ungovernable passion. Their guilty intrigue was discovered by Belisarius in Sicily (A.D. 535–536), and he sent some of his retainers to slay the paramour, who, however, escaped to Ephesus.[3] But Antonina persuaded her uxorious husband that she was not guilty, regained his affection, and induced him to hand over to her the servants who had betrayed her amour. It was reported that having cut out their tongues she chopped their bodies in small pieces and threw them into the sea. Her desire for Theodosius was not cooled by an absence of five years, and while she was preparing her intrigue against John the Cappadocian she was planning to recall her lover to her side when Belisarius departed for the East. But her son Photius, who had always been jealous of the favourite preferred to himself, penetrated her design and revealed the matter to his stepfather, and they bound themselves by solemn oaths to punish Theodosius. They decided, however, that

---

[1] We are not told what became of Euphemia.

[2] One point was indeed omitted, the shameless perjury of Antonina, and in the *Secret History* Procopius holds it up to censure. She had sworn both to John and to his daughter by the most solemn oaths that a Christian can take that no treachery was intended. *H.A.* 2. 61.

[3] The story is told in Procopius, *H.A.* 1. 15 *sqq.* Theodosius was a Thracian ; his parents belonged to the Eunomian sect, and he was baptized into the true faith at his adoption just before the Vandal expedition started. Perhaps he is referred to in *B.V.* i. 12. 2 as " one of the soldiers recently baptized."

nothing could be done immediately ; they must wait till Antonina
followed her husband to the East. Photius accompanied Belisarius in the campaign, and for some months Antonina enjoyed
the society of her paramour at Constantinople. When, in the
summer of the year, she set out for Persia, Theodosius returned
to Ephesus. The general met his wife, showed his anger, but
had not the heart to slay her. Photius hastened to Ephesus,
seized Theodosius, and sent him under a guard of retainers to
be imprisoned in a secret place in Cilicia. He proceeded himself
to Constantinople, in possession of the wealth which Theodosius
had been allowed to appropriate from the spoils of Carthage.[1]
But the danger of her favourite had come to the ears of Theodora. She caused Belisarius and his wife to be summoned to
the capital and she forced a reconciliation upon the reluctant
husband. Then she seized Photius and sought by torture to
make him reveal the place where he had concealed Theodosius.
But her torments were useless ; he was true to his stepfather.
The secret was disclosed, however, through another channel
and Theodosius was rescued ; the Empress concealed him in
the Palace, and presented him to Antonina as a delightful
surprise.

The unhappy Photius, who showed greater force of character
than Belisarius, was kept a captive in the dungeons of Theodora.
He escaped twice, but was dragged back from the sanctuaries
in which he had sought refuge. His third attempt at the end
of three years was successful ; he reached Jerusalem, became a
monk, and escaped the vengeance of the Empress. He survived
Justinian, and in the following reign was appointed, notwithstanding his religious quality, to suppress a revolt of the Samaritans, a task which he carried out, we are told, with the utmost
cruelty, taking advantage of his powers to extort money from
all the Syrian provinces.[2]

---

[1] *H.A.* 1. 17, "it is said that he
had got by plunder 10,000 nomismata from the palaces of Carthage
and Ravenna." He was with Belisarius at Carthage, but was at
Ephesus when Ravenna was taken ;
so that, if the report is true, Belisarius
or Antonina must have sent him a
share of the Italian plunder.

[2] John Eph. *Hist. ecc.* part 3,
book i. cc. 31, 32. This notice
gives a very unfavourable impression
of Photius, with whom Procopius is
sympathetic. They agree in the
statement that he became a monk.

§ 8. The Great Pestilence (A.D. 542–543)

Justinian had been fourteen years on the throne when the Empire was visited by one of those immense but rare calamities in the presence of which human beings could only succumb helpless and resourceless until the science of the nineteenth century began to probe the causes and supply the means of preventing and checking them. The devastating plague, which began its course in the summer of A.D. 542 and seems to have invaded and ransacked nearly every corner of the Empire, was, if not more malignant, far more destructive, through the vast range of its ravages, than the pestilences which visited ancient Athens in the days of Pericles and London in the reign of Charles II. ; and perhaps even than the plague which travelled from the East to Rome in the reign of Marcus Aurelius. It probably caused as large a mortality in the Empire as the Black Death of the fourteenth century in the same countries.[1]

The infection first attacked Pelusium, on the borders of Egypt, with deadly effect, and spread thence to Alexandria and throughout Egypt, and northward to Palestine and Syria. In the following year it reached Constantinople, in the middle of spring,[2] and spread over Asia Minor and through Mesopotamia into the kingdom of Persia.[3] Travelling by sea, whether from Africa or across the Adriatic, it invaded Italy and Sicily.[4]

It was observed that the infection always started from the coast and went up to the interior, and that those who survived

[1] The best and principal authority is Procopius (B.P. ii. 22-23), who was living in Constantinople during the visitation. But we have a second first-hand source in John of Ephesus, who was in Palestine when the plague broke out there, and then, travelling to Mesopotamia and returning to Constantinople through Asia Minor, observed its ravages in Cilicia, Cappadocia, and Bithynia (extracts from his History in Land's ed. of the Commentarii, p. 227 sqq.). The date of the outbreak is fixed to 542 by the order of events in Procopius, and this agrees with the specific date of another contemporary, John Malalas /(xviii. p. 48), who places it in the 5th indiction (541-542), and with that of Evagrius (iv. 29), who places it two years after the Persian capture of

Antioch (June 540). The date of John of Ephesus (year of Alexandria 855 = A.D. 543–544) may be explained by supposing that the year of his journey was 543. The plague was also noticed by Zachariah of Mitylene in the lost portion of book x., but a short extract is preserved in the chronicle of Michael Syrus (ix. 28 ; see Zachariah, p. 313).

[2] Procopius, op. cit. 22, 9.

[3] Zachariah mentions Nubia, Ethiopia, Armenia, Arzanene, and Mesopotamia. For Persia cp. also Procopius, op. cit. 25, 12.

[4] Cont. Marcellini, sub 543, mortalitas magna Italiae solum devastat, Orientem iam et Illyricum peraeque attritos. Zachariah's list of the visited countries includes Italy, Sicily, Africa, and Gaul.

it had become immune. The historian Procopius, who witnessed its course at Constantinople, as Thucydides had studied the plague at Athens, has detailed the nature and effects of the bubonic disease, as it might be called, for the most striking general feature was a swelling in the groin or in the armpit, sometimes behind the ear or on the thighs. Hallucinations occasionally preceded the attack. The victims were seized by a sudden fever, which did not affect the colour of the skin nor make it as hot as might be expected.

The fever was of such a languid sort from its commencement and up till evening that neither to the sick themselves nor to a physician who touched them would it afford any suspicion of danger. . . . But on the same day in some cases, in others on the following day, and in the rest not many days later a bubonic swelling developed. . . . Up to this point everything went in about the same way with all who had taken the disease. But from then on very marked differences developed. . . . There ensued with some a deep coma, with others a violent delirium, and in either case they suffered the characteristic symptoms of the disease. For those who were under the spell of the coma forgot all those who were familiar to them and seemed to be sleeping constantly. And if any one cared for them, they would eat without waking, but some also were neglected and these would die directly through lack of sustenance. But those who were seized with delirium suffered from insomnia and were victims of a distorted imagination, for they suspected that men were coming upon them to destroy them, and they would become excited and rush off in flight, crying out at the top of their voices. And those who were attending them were in a state of constant exhaustion and had a most difficult time. . . . Neither the physicians nor other persons were found to contract this malady through contact with the sick or with the dead, for many who were constantly engaged either in burying or in attending those in no way connected with them held out in the performance of this service beyond all expectation. . . . [The patients] had great difficulty in the matter of eating, for they could not easily take food. And many perished through lack of any man to care for them, for they were either overcome with hunger, or threw themselves down from a height.

And in those cases where neither coma nor delirium came on, the bubonic swelling became mortified and the sufferer, no longer able to endure the pain, died. And we would suppose that in all cases the same thing would have been true, but since they were not at all in their senses, some were quite unable to feel the pain ; for owing to the troubled condition of their minds they lost all sense of feeling.

Now some of the physicians who were at a loss because the symptoms were not understood, supposing that the disease centred in the bubonic swellings, decided to investigate the bodies of the dead. And upon opening some of the swellings they found a strange sort of carbuncle [ἄνθραξ] that had grown inside them.

Death came in some cases immediately, in others after many days; and with some the body broke out with black pustules about as large as a lentil, and these did not survive even one day, but all succumbed immediately. With many also a vomiting of blood ensued without visible cause and straightway brought death. Moreover I am able to declare this, that the most illustrious physicians predicted that many would die, who unexpectedly escaped entirely from suffering shortly afterwards, and that they declared that many would be saved who were destined to be carried off almost immediately. . . . While some were helped by bathing others were harmed in no less degree. And of those who received no care many died, but others, contrary to reason, were saved. And again, methods of treatment showed different results with different patients. . . . And in the case of women who were pregnant death could be certainly foreseen if they were taken with the disease. For some died through miscarriage, but others perished immediately at the time of birth with the infants they bore. However they say that three women survived though their children perished, and that one woman died at the very time of child-birth but that the child was born and survived.

Now in those cases where the swelling rose to an unusual size and a discharge of pus had set in, it came about that they escaped from the disease and survived, for clearly the acute condition of the carbuncle had found relief in this direction, and this proved to be in general an indication of returning health. . . . And with some of them it came about that the thigh was withered, in which case, though the swelling was there, it did not develop the least suppuration. With others who survived the tongue did not remain unaffected, and they lived on either lisping or speaking incoherently and with difficulty.[1]

This description [2] shows that the disease closely resembled in character the terrible oriental plague which devastated Europe and parts of Asia in the fourteenth century. In the case of the Black Death too the chief symptom was the pestboils, but the malady was generally accompanied by inflammation of the lungs and the spitting of blood, which Procopius does not mention.[3]

In Constantinople the visitation lasted for four months altogether, and during three of these the mortality was enormous. At first the deaths were only a little above the usual number, but as the infection spread 5000 died daily, and when it was at its worst 10,000 or upward.[4] These figures are too

---

[1] I have borrowed Dewey's translation.

[2] It agrees generally with the less accurate description of John of Ephesus.

[3] See Hecker, *The Epidemics of the Middle Ages* (transl. Babington, ed. 3), p. 3 *sqq.* The coma in some cases, the

sleeplessness in others, are mentioned.

[4] So Procopius. John of Ephesus (*op. cit.* p. 234) says that 5000, 7000, 12,000, even 16,000 corpses of the poor were removed daily from the streets in the early stage of the plague; and they were counted by men stationed at the harbours, the ferries, and the gates.

vague to enable us to conjecture how many of the population were swept away ; but we may feel sceptical when another writer who witnessed the plague assures us that the number of those who died in the streets and public places exceeded 300,000.[1] If we could trust the recorded statistics of the mortality in some of the large cities which were stricken by the Black Death—in London, for instance, 100,000, in Venice 100,000, in Avignon 60,000—then, considering the much larger population of Constantinople, we might regard 300,000 as not an excessive figure for the total destruction. For the general mortality throughout the Empire we have no data for conjecture ; but it is interesting to note that a physician who made a careful study of all the accounts of the Black Death came to the conclusion that, without exaggeration, Europe (including Russia) lost twenty-five millions of her inhabitants through that calamity.[2]

At first, relatives and domestics attended to the burial of the dead, but as the violence of the plague increased this duty was neglected, and corpses lay forlorn not only in the streets, but even in the houses of notable men whose servants were sick or dead. Aware of this, Justinian placed considerable sums at the disposal of Theodore, one of his private secretaries,[3] to take measures for the disposal of the dead. Huge pits were dug at Sycae, on the other side of the Golden Horn, in which the bodies were laid in rows and tramped down tightly ; but the men who were engaged on this work, unable to keep up with the number of the dying, mounted the towers of the wall of the suburb, tore off their roofs, and threw the bodies in. Virtually all the towers were filled with corpses, and as a result " an evil stench pervaded the city and distressed the inhabitants still more, and especially whenever the wind blew fresh from that quarter." [4] It is particularly noted that the members of the Blue and Green parties laid aside their mutual enmity and co-operated in the labour of burying the dead.

[1] John Eph. ib.

[2] Hecker, op. cit. p. 29.

[3] Referendarii ; there were fourteen (Justinian, Nov. 10). For these officials, not to be confounded with the magistri, see Bury, Magistri scriniorum, ἀντιγραφῆς, and ρεφερενδάριοι.

[4] Procopius, B.P. ii. 23. His account of the measures for the disposal of the corpses agrees with that of John Eph., who, however, does not mention the towers, and says that each of the pits could contain 70,000 bodies. One would have thought that all the arrangements would have been made by the Prefect of the City, but that functionary is not mentioned.

During these months all work ceased ; the artisans abandoned their trades. " Indeed in a city which was simply abounding in all good things starvation almost absolute was running riot. Certainly it seemed a difficult and very notable thing to have a sufficiency of bread or of anything else." [1] All court functions were discontinued, and no one was to be seen in official dress, especially when the Emperor fell ill. For he, too, was stricken by the plague, though the attack did not prove fatal.[2] Our historian observed the moral effects of the visitation. Men whose lives had been base and dissolute changed their habits and punctiliously practised the duties of religion,[3] not from any real change of heart, but from terror and because they supposed they were to die immediately. But their conversion to respectability was only transient. When the pestilence abated and they thought themselves safe they recurred to their old evil ways of life. It may be confidently asserted, adds the cynical writer, that the disease selected precisely the worst men and let them go free.

Fifteen years later there was a second outbreak of the plague in Constantinople (spring A.D. 558), but evidently much less virulent and destructive. It was noticed in the case of this visitation that females suffered less than males.[4]

§ 9. *The Conspiracy of Artabanes* (A.D. 548)

The Empress Theodora died of cancer on June 28, A.D. 548.[5] Her death was a relief to her numerous enemies, but to Justinian it must have been a severe blow. We would give much to have a glimpse into their private life or a record of one of their intimate

---

[1] *Ib.* (Dewey's rendering).

[2] Καὶ αὐτῷ γὰρ ξυνέπεσε βουβῶνα ἐπῆρθαι. Gibbon suggests that Justinian may have owed his safety to his abstemious habits. Another serious illness of Justinian is recorded by Procopius, *Aed.* i. 7. 6 *sqq.*

[3] Cp. Hecker, *op. cit.* p. 31.

[4] Agathias, v. 10. He identifies this disease with that of 543. Of the plagues of the fourteenth century, which were frequent after 1350 until 1383, Hecker says that he does not consider them as the same as the Black Death. " They were rather common pestilences without inflam-

mation of the lungs, such as in former times, and in the following centuries, were excited by the matter of contagion everywhere existing " (p. 27). The plague in Italy and Gaul which Marius Avent. notices, *sub a.* 570, as *morbus validus cum profluvio ventris et variola* seems to be the same as that whose ravages in Liguria Paulus Diac. (*Hist. Lang.* ii. 4) describes. Paul mentions the pestboils.

[5] Date : John Mal. xviii. p. 484, cp. Procopius, *B.G.* iii. 30. 4 (in *Consularia Ital.*, *sub a.*, the day is given as June 27). The disease is named by Victor Tonn. *sub* 549.

conversations. We have no means of lifting even a corner of
the veil. But it is a significant fact that, though they disagreed
on various questions of policy, scandal, which had many evil
things to tell of them both, never found any pretext to suggest
that they quarrelled or were living on bad terms.

Soon after this event a conspiracy was formed against the
Emperor's life, which had little political significance but created
a great sensation because men of his own family were indirectly
involved.[1] A general named Artabanes, of Armenian race,
whom we shall meet as a commander in Africa, had conceived
the ambition of marrying the Emperor's niece Praejecta, but the
plan had been thwarted by Theodora, who compelled him to live
again with the wife whom he had put away.[2] After her death
he repudiated his wife for the second time, but Praejecta, who
had been given to another, was lost to him, and he bore no goodwill towards the Emperor. His disaffected feelings would not
have prompted him to initiate any sinister design, but a kinsman
of his, one Arsaces, was animated by a bitter desire of revenge
upon Justinian, who, when he was found guilty of a treacherous
correspondence with the king of Persia, had ordered him to be
scourged lightly and paraded through the streets on the back
of a camel. Arsaces fanned into flame the smouldering resentment of Artabanes, and showed him how easy it would be to
kill the Emperor, " who is accustomed to sit without guards till
late hours in the night, in the company of old priests, deep in
the study of the holy books of the Christians." But perhaps
what did most to secure the adhesion of Artabanes was the prospect that Germanus, Justinian's cousin, and his two sons [3] would
sanction, if they did not take an active part in, the design.

For Germanus, at this time, had a personal grievance against
the Emperor. His brother Boraides had died, leaving almost
all his property to Germanus, allowing his daughter to receive
only so much as was required by the law. But Justinian, deeming
the arrangement unfair, overrode the will in the daughter's favour.[4]
Relying on the indignation which this arbitrary act had aroused
in the family, Arsaces opened communications with Justin, the
elder son of Germanus. Having bound him by oath not to reveal

---

[1] The source is Procopius, *B.G.* iii. 32. The date seems to be the latter
part of 548.
[2] See below, p. 146.   [3] See above, p. 20.   [4] *B.G.* iii. 31, 17-18.

the conversation to any person except his father, he enlarged on the manner in which the Emperor ill-treated and passed over his relatives, and expressed his conviction that it would go still harder with them when Belisarius returned from Italy. He then revealed the plan of assassination which he had formed in conjunction with Artabanes and Chanaranges, a young and frivolous Armenian who had been admitted to their counsels.

Justin, terrified at this revelation, laid it before his father, who immediately consulted with Marcellus, the Count of the Excubitors, whether it would be wise to inform the Emperor immediately. Marcellus, an honourable, austere, and wary man, dissuaded Germanus from taking that course, on the ground that such a communication, necessitating a private interview with the Emperor, would inevitably become known to the conspirators and lead to the escape of Arsaces. He proposed first to investigate the matter himself, and it was arranged that one of the conspirators should be lured to speak in the presence of a concealed witness. Justin appointed a day and hour for an interview between Germanus and Chanaranges, and the compromising revelations were overheard by Leontius, a friend of Marcellus, who was hidden behind a curtain. The programme of the matured plot was to wait for the arrival of Belisarius and slay the Emperor and his general at the same time ; for if Justinian were slain beforehand, the conspirators might not be able to contend against the soldiers of Belisarius. When the deed was done, Germanus was to be proclaimed Emperor.

Marcellus still hesitated to reveal the plot to the Emperor, through friendship or pity for Artabanes. But when Belisarius was drawing nigh to the capital he could hesitate no longer, and Justinian ordered the conspirators to be arrested. Germanus and Justin were at first not exempted from suspicion, but when the Senate inquired into the case, the testimony of Marcellus and Leontius, and two other officers to whom Germanus had prudently disclosed the affair, completely cleared them. Even then Justinian was still indignant that they had concealed the treason so long, and was not mollified until the candid Marcellus took all the blame of the delay upon himself. The conspirators were treated with clemency, being confined in the Palace and not in the public prison. Artabanes was not only soon pardoned but was created Master of Soldiers in Thrace and sent to take part in the Ostrogothic war.[1] Another plot to assassinate Justinian was organised by a number of obscure persons in November A.D. 562,[2] and would hardly merit to be recorded if it had not injured Belisarius. One of the conspirators talked indiscreetly to Eusebius, Count of the Federates, and they were all arrested. Their confessions involved two followers of Belisarius, who, seized and examined by the Prefect of the City and the Quaestor, asserted that Belisarius was privy to the plot. The Emperor convoked a meeting of the Senate and Imperial Council ; the depositions of the prisoner were read ; and suspicion weighed heavily on the veteran general. He made no resistance when he was ordered to dismiss all his armed retainers, and he remained in disgrace till July A.D. 563, when he was restored to favour.[3] His character and the whole record of his life make it highly improbable that he was guilty of disloyalty in his old age. He died in March A.D. 565.[4] His disgrace, though it was brief, made such an impression on popular imagination in later times that a Belisarius legend was formed, which represented the conqueror of Africa and Italy as ending his days as a blind beggar in the streets of Constantinople.[5]

---

[1] *B.G.* iii. 39. 8.

[2] John Malalas, xviii. 493, and *De ins. fr.* 49 ; Theophanes, A.M. 6055. The conspirators were : Ablabius, son of Miltiades ; Marcellus, Vitus, and Eusebius, bankers ; Sergius, nephew of Aetherius, the *curator domus divinae* ; Isaac, ὁ ἀργυροπράτης ὁ κατὰ Βελισάριον ; and Paul, a retainer of Belisarius. The workshop of Marcellus was near St. Irene, and he is described as ὁ κατὰ Αἰθέριον τὸν κουράτωρα. Marcellus, who was arrested as he entered the Palace with a dagger (βοῦγλιν = *pugio*), killed himself on the spot. Paul the Silentiary refers to this conspiracy in *S. Sophia*, 22 *sqq.*

[3] Theophanes, *ib.* The technical term for political disgrace is ἀγανάκτησις.

[4] Theophanes, A.M. 6057. His property went to the Imperial house of Marina. Antonina survived him according to Πάτρια, p. 254.

[5] The earliest mention of this legend is in Πάτρια, p. 160 (tenth century), cp. Tzetzes, *Chil.* iii. 339 *sqq.* The extant medieval romance on the subject took shape in the age of the Palaeologi. Belisarius, slandered by jealous nobles, is shut up in a tower. The Emperor releases him on the insistent demand of the people that he should be the leader of a military expedition against England (νῆσίν τῆς 'Εγγλητέρας). Belisarius sails thither, takes the English κάστρον, and returns to Constantinople with the king of England as prisoner. He is again accused of treason, and is blinded. The three known versions of the story will be found in Wagner, *Carmina Graeca medii aevi*, p. 304 *sqq.* There is a historical case of disgraced generals (Peganes and Symbatios) being blinded and set to beg in the streets in the ninth century (see Bury, *Eastern Roman Empire*, p. 176), and perhaps this suggested the mythical fate of Belisarius.

§ 10. *The Succession to the Throne*

As Justinian had no children of his own, it was incumbent on him to avert the possibility of a struggle for the throne after his death by designating a successor. So long as Theodora was alive the importance of providing for the future was not so serious, as it might be reasonably supposed that she would be able to control the situation as successfully as Pulcheria and Ariadne. But after her death it was a dereliction of duty on the part of Justinian, as it had been on the part of Anastasius, not to arrange definitely the question of the succession. His failure to do so was probably due partly to his suspicious and jealous temper, and partly to an inability to decide between the two obvious choices.

Of his three cousins, Germanus, Boraides, and Justus,[1] only Germanus survived Theodora, but he, who was an able man and whom the popular wish would have called to the throne, died two years later. His two sons, Justin and Justinian, were competent officers. We have seen them occupying important military posts, and if they were not trusted with the highest commands, it is probable that they did not display ability of the first rank. They were both unreservedly loyal to the sovran, and Justin seems, like his father, to have enjoyed general respect and popularity.[2] If Justinian had decided to create him Caesar or Augustus, the act would have been universally applauded.

The influence of Theodora had rendered it impossible for the Emperor, in her lifetime, to show any special preference for this branch of his kin. Germanus, whose amiable qualities and sense of justice endeared him to others, was hated and suspected by her. She resolved that his family should not multiply. He had children, but he should have no grandchildren. In this design she so far succeeded that neither of his sons married till after her death. All her efforts, however, did not prevent his daughter Justina from espousing the general John, nephew of Vitalian, but she threatened that she would destroy John and he went in fear of his life.[3]

---

[1] See above, p. 20. Germanus died in 550 (Procopius, *B.G.* iii. 40. 9); Boraides *c.* 547–548 (see above, p. 67); Justus in 545 (*B.P.* ii. 28. 1). For the marriage of Germanus see above, p. 20, and for his death, below, p. 254.

[2] Cp. Evagrius, v. 1.

[3] Procopius, *H.A.* 5. 8-15. John, who was in Italy, avoided associating with Belisarius, through fear of Antonina. If we are to connect this with the statement in *B.G.* iii. 18. 25

Justinian had nephews, sons of his sister Vigilantia,[1] and on the eldest of these, Justin, the Empress bestowed her favour. Her desire was that her own blood should be perpetuated in the dynasty, and she married her niece Sophia, a woman who possessed qualities resembling her own, to Justin. After her death, Justinian seems to have been convinced that the conspicuous merits of Germanus entitled him to the succession, but he was unable to bring himself to take a definite decision. When Germanus died the choice lay between the two Justins, the nephew and the cousin, and we may divine that there was a constant conflict between their interests at court. The Emperor's preference inclined, on the whole, to Justin, the husband of Sophia. He created him Curopalates, a new title of rank which raised him above other Patricians, yet did not give him the status of an heir apparent which would have been conferred by the title of Caesar or even Nobilissimus.[2] But Justin enjoyed the great advantage of living in the Palace and having every opportunity to prepare his way to the throne ; while the services of his rival and namesake were employed in distant Colchis.

Not the least of Theodora's triumphs was the posthumous realisation of her plan for the succession. Justinian died on Nov. 14, A.D. 565,[3] and Justin, the son of Vigilantia, supported by the Senate and the Excubitors, secured the throne without a struggle.

APPENDIX

A SCENE IN THE HIPPODROME

THE chronicle of Theophanes contains a remarkable record of a conversation between Justinian and the Green party in the Hippodrome. It is apparently an official record (preserved in the archives of the Greens ?), under the title Ἄκτα διὰ Καλοπόδιον τὸν κουβικου-

---

παρὰ Βελισάριον οὐκέτι ἤει (though a different motive is assigned), the date of the marriage of John and Justina would be A.D. 546.

[1] See above, p. 20.

[2] He was Curopalates in 559, when he repressed a Hippodrome riot. John Mal. xviii. 491. See Evagrius, v. 1. Sophia was perhaps a daughter of Comito and Sittas.

[3] Chron. Pasch., sub a. Theophanes gives Nov. 11 as the day. His funeral is described by Corippus in Laud. Iust. iii. 4 sqq. The Empress Sophia laid over his bier a purple cloth on which were embroidered in gold pictures of his achievements, Iustinianorum series tota laborum, ib. ii. 276 sqq.

λάριον καὶ σπαθάριον, and is inserted after the short summary of the Nika riot which the chronicler has prefixed to his detailed narrative. But it exhibits no connexion whatever with the causes of that event, and may record an incident which occurred at some other period of the reign.[1] It seems likely that Calopodius who had offended the Greens is the same as Calopodius who was *praepositus s. cub.* in A.D. 558 (John Mal. xviii. p. 490).

As we are totally ignorant of the circumstances, a great part of this allusive dialogue is very obscure. Some act on the part of the chamberlain Calopodius had excited the anger of the Greens ; they begin by complaining of this in respectful tones, and obtaining no satisfaction go on to air their grievances as an oppressed party, with violent invective. A mandator or herald speaks for the Emperor, standing in front of the kathisma, and the Greens evidently have a single spokesman.

Greens. Long may you live, Justinian Augustus ! *Tu vincas.* I am oppressed, O best of sovrans, and my grievances, God knows, have become intolerable. I fear to name the oppressor, lest he prosper the more and I endanger my own safety.

Mandator. Who is he ? I know him not.

Greens. My oppressor, O thrice august ! is to be found in the quarter of the shoemakers.[2]

Mandator. No one does you wrong.

Greens. One man and one only does me wrong. Mother of God, may he be humbled (μὴ ἀνακεφαλίσῃ) !

Mandator. Who is he ? We know him not.

Greens. Nay, you know well, O thrice august ! I am oppressed this day.

Mandator. We know not that anyone oppresses you.

Greens. It is Calopodius, the spathar, who wrongs me, O lord of all !

Mandator. Calopodius has no concern with you.[3]

Greens. My oppressor will perish like Judas ; God will requite him quickly.

Mandator. You come, not to see the games, but to insult your rulers.

Greens. If anyone wrongs me, he will perish like Judas.

Mandator. Silence, Jews, Manichaeans, and Samaritans !

Greens. Do you disparage us with the name of Jews and Samaritans ? The Mother of God is with all of us.

Mandator. When will ye cease cursing yourselves ?

Greens. If anyone denies that our lord the Emperor is orthodox, let him be anathema, as Judas.

---

[1] See P. Maas, *Metrische Akklamationen der Byzantiner*, B.Z. xxi. 49-50. He reprints the Greek text so as to bring out the rhythmical character of the conversation. The *Acta* were known to the compiler of the *Chron. Pasch.* (c. A.D. 630), who reproduces the opening words of the Greens. He substitutes plural verbs for singular, but otherwise agrees closely with Theophanes. Both writers probably copied from a sixth-century chronicle.

[2] Εἰς τὰ τζαγγαρεῖα εὑρίσκεται—an allusion to the name of Calo-podius (as Maas points out).

[3] Οὐκ ἔχει πρᾶγμα.

Mandator. I would have you all baptized in the name of one God.

The Greens (tumultuously). I am baptized in One God.[1]

Mandator. Verily, if you refuse to be silent, I shall have you beheaded.

Greens. Every person seeks a post of authority, to secure his personal safety. Your Majesty must not be indignant at what I say in my tribulation, for the Deity listens to all complaints. We have good reason, O Emperor! to mention all things *now*.[2] For we do not even know where tho palaco is, nor whcrc is the government. If I come into the city once, it is sitting on a mule ;[3] and I wish I had not to come then, your Majcsty.[4]

Mandator. Every one is free to move in public, where he wishes, without danger.

Greens. I am told I am free, yet I am not allowed to use my freedom. If a man is free but is suspected as a Green, ho is sure to bo publicly punished.

Mandator. Have ye no care for your lives that ye thus bravo death ?

Greens. Let this (green) colour bo once uplifted [5]—then justice disappears. Put an end to the scenes of murder, and let us be lawfully punished. Behold, an abundant fountain ; punish as many as you like. Verily, human nature cannot tolerate these two (contradictory) things. Would that Sabbatis had ncvcr been born, to have a son who is a murderer. It is the twenty-sixth murder that has been committed in the Zeugma ;[6] the victim was a spectator in the morning, in the afternoon, O lord of all ! he was butchered.

Blues. Yourselves are the only party in the hippodromc that has murderers among their number.

Greens. When ye commit murder ye leave the city in flight.

Blues. Ye shed blood, and debate. Ye are the only party here with murderers among them.

Greens. O lord Justinian ! they challenge us and yet no one slays them. Truth will compel assent.[7] Who slew the woodseller in the Zeugma, O Emporor ?

Mandator. Ye slew him.

Groens. Who slow tho son of Epagathus, Emperor ?

Mandator. Ye slew him too, and ye slander the Blues.

Greens. Now have pity, O Lord God ! The truth is suppressed. I should like to argue with them who say that affairs are managed by God. Whence comes this misery ?

---

[1] Tho Grcons apparontly take up the words of the mandator, εἰς ἕνα βαπτίζεσθαι, in a Monophysitic sense. The preceding words, οἱ δὲ πράσινδι ἐβόησαν ἐπάνω ἀλλήλων καὶ ἔκραζον ὡς ἐκέλευσεν "Αντλας, seem to imply that while the conversation was throughout conducted by a spokesman (Antlas ?), here the whole party shouted together.

[2] Ὀνομάζομεν ἄρτι πάντα. The sense demands that ἄρτι should be the emphatic word.

[3] "Ὅταν εἰς βορδώνιν καθέζομαι. Prisoners were drawn by mules to execution or punishment.

[4] Εἴθοις μηδὲ τότε, τρισαύγουστε.

[5] Ἐπαρθῇ τὸ χρῶμα τοῦτο καὶ ἡ δίκη οὐ χρηματίζει.

[6] De Boor prints εἰκότως ἔκτος. Sabbatius, it will be remembered, was Justinian's father.

[7] Νοήσει ὁ μὴ θέλων.

Mandator. God cannot be tempted with evil.

Greens. God, you say, cannot be tempted with evil ? Who is it then who wrongs me ? Let some philosopher or hermit explain the distinction.

Mandator. Accursed blasphemers, when will ye hold your peace ?

Greens. If it is the pleasure of your Majesty, I hold my peace, albeit unwillingly. I know all—all, but I say nothing. Good-bye, Justice ! you are no longer in fashion. I shall turn and become a Jew. Better to be a " Greek " (pagan) than a Blue, God knows.

Blues. You are detestable, I cannot abide the sight of you. Your enmity dismays me.

Greens. Let the bones of the spectators be exhumed ! [1]

The language of this astonishing dialogue obeys metrical laws, which concern not quantity but the number of the syllables and the accentuation of the last word in each clause. The most frequently occurring form is five syllables with the penultimate accented + four with the antepenultimate (or ultimate ?) accented, *e.g.* :

$$οὐδὲ \ τὸ \ παλάτιν \ τρισαύγουστε.$$

It is evident that to converse in metrical chant both the Imperial mandator and the spokesmen of the demes must have had a special training in the art of improvising.[2]

---

[1] *I.e.* let them be murdered. A customary form of curse in the Hippodrome, cp. Theophanes, A.M. 6187 ἀνασκαφῇ τὰ ὀστέα Ἰουστινιανοῦ (Justinian II.).

[2] An earlier example of metrical cries is preserved in inscriptions on the monument of the famous charioteer Porphyrius (reign of Anastasius). See Woodward's publication in the Appendix to George, *Church of Saint Eirene* ; and his paper in the *Annual of the British School at Athens,* xvii. 88 *sqq.* The dialogue has considerable interest as a sample of the spoken Greek of the sixth century.

CHAPTER XVI

THE PERSIAN WARS

§ 1. *The Roman Army*

Our records of the Persian war conducted by the generals of Anastasius, which was described in a former chapter, give us little information as to the character and composition of the Imperial army. But we may take it as probable that the military establishment was already of much the same kind as we find it a quarter of a century later in the reign of Justinian. In the course of the fifth century the organisation of the army underwent considerable changes which our meagre sources of information do not enable us to trace. During that period, since the early years of Theodosius II., we have no catalogue of the military establishment, no military treatises,[1] no military narratives. When we come to the reign of Justinian, for which we have abundant evidence,[2] we find that the old system of the fourth century has been changed in some important respects.

The great commands of the Masters of Soldiers, and the distinction between the *comitatenses* and the *limitanei*, have not

---

[1] With the exception of that of Vegetius, which does not help much. See above, Vol. I. p. 225.

[2] Besides Procopius, the chief source, we have four tactical documents which supplement and illustrate his information. (1) Fragments of a tactical work by Urbicius, who wrote in the reign of Anastasius. (2) Anonymus Byzantios Περὶ στρατη-γικῆς, and (3) a ἑρμήνεια or glossary of military terms, from the reign of Justinian. (4) Pseudo-Mauricius, *Stratêgikon*, from the end of the sixth century. For editions of these works

see Bibliography In regard to the date of the *Stratêgikon* (falsely ascribed to the Emperor Maurice), it is quite clear that it was composed *after* the reign of Justinian, and *before* the institution of the system of Themes, which is probably to be ascribed to Heraclius. Thus we get as outside limits A.D. 565–c. 615. It it quite perverse to date it (with Vári and others) to the eighth century. For modern studies of the sixth-century armies see Bibliography II. 2, C under Benjamin, Maspéro, Aussaresses, Grosse, Müller.

been altered ; but the legions, the cohorts, and the *alae*, the familiar units of the old Roman armies, have disappeared both in name and in fact, and to the *comitatenses* and *limitanei* has been added a new organisation, the *foederati*, a term which has acquired a different meaning from that which it bore in the fourth century.

The independent military unit is now the *numerus*, a company generally from 200 to 400 strong, but sometimes varying below or above these figures. In old days it was necessary to divide the legion for the purpose of garrisoning towns ; on the new system each town could have a complete, or more than one complete unit. These companies were under the command of tribunes.[1]

Apart from the guard-troops stationed in the capital, the armed forces of the Empire fall into five principal categories. (1) The technical name *comitatenses* is little used. These troops, who are recruited almost exclusively among subjects of the Empire chiefly in the highlands of Thrace, Illyricum and Isauria, are now generally distinguished as *stratiotai*, regular Roman soldiers, from the other sections of the army.[2]

(2) The *limitanei* perform the same duty of protecting exposed frontiers, and on the same conditions as before.

(3) The *foederati*, who must have been organised in the fifth century, are the new and striking feature which is revealed to us by the history of the campaigns of Belisarius. They are the most useful part of the field army, and they consist entirely of

---

[1] The Greek name of the *numerus* is ἀριθμός or τάγμα (Sozomen, *H.E.* i. 8 τὰ ʽΡωμαίων τάγματα ἃ νῦν ἀριθμοὺς καλοῦσι) ; κατάλογος is used in the same sense, *e.g.* Procopius, *B.P.* i. 15. For the evidence as to its strength cp. Maspéro, *op. cit.* 116 *sq.*, who remarks that it was a tactical principle to vary the strength of the *numeri* in order to deceive the enemy (cp. Pseudo-Maurice, *Strat.* i. 4 *ad fin.* χρὴ μηδὲ πάντα τὰ τάγματα ἐπιτηδεύειν πάντως ἴσα ποιεῖν κτλ.). But the theoretical strength of the infantry numerus which Urbicius and the tacticians of Justinian's reign call σύνταγμα was 256 (Ἑρμήνεια 12, cp. Pseudo-Maurice, xii. 8 ; Urbicius says 250). These authorities nearly agree as to the tactical divisions of an army. The chief division, according

to the Ἑρμήνεια, are : phalanx = 4096, meros = 2048, chiliarchia = 1026, pentakosiarchia = 512, syntagma (tagma) = 256, taxis = 128, tetrarchia = 64, lochos = 16 (sometimes 8 or 12 ; Urbicius says 25). Pseudo-Maurice contemplates rather higher figures : the tagma should vary from 300 to 400 as a maximum ; the chiliarchy, which he terms a μοῖρα, should vary from 2000 to 3000 ; the meros, which consists of μοῖραι, should not exceed 6000 or 7000 (*Strat.* i. 4).

[2] It is notable that Procopius sometimes speaks of the Isaurian regiments as if they were distinct from the other Roman troops (κατάλογοι), as in *B.G.* i. 5. 2 ; but they were included among the *stratiôtai.*

cavalry. They were originally recruited exclusively from
barbarians, who volunteered for Imperial service, and were
organised as Roman troops under Roman officers ; [1] but in the
sixth century Roman subjects were not debarred from enlisting
in their companies.[2] The degradation of the term Federates to
designate these forces was not very happy, and it has naturally
misled modern historians into confusing them with (4) the troops
to whom the name was properly applied in the fourth century,
and who are now distinguished as *Allies* : [3] the bands of barbarians, Huns, for instance, or Heruls, who, bound by a treaty
with the Empire, furnished, in return for land or annual subsidies, armed forces which were led by their native chiefs.

To these we must add (5) another class of fighting men, who
were not in the employment of the government, the private
retainers of the military commanders. The rise of the custom
of keeping bands of armed followers has already been noticed.[4]
It was adopted not only by generals and Praetorian Prefects,
but by officers of subordinate rank and wealthy private persons.[5]
The size of the retinues depended upon the wealth of the employer.
Belisarius, who was a rich man, kept at one time as many as
7000.[6]

There were two distinct classes of retainers, the *hypaspistai*,
shield-bearers, who were the rank and file, and the *doryphoroi*,
spear-bearers, who were superior in rank, fewer in number, and
corresponded to officers. Belisarius himself and Sittas had been

---

[1] The position of the Foederati
was misconceived by Mommsen and
by Benjamin (who held that they
were recruited by Roman officers as a
private speculation) and has been
elucidated by J. Maspéro (*Organ. mil.*
and Φοιδερᾶτοι). His arguments
seem to me convincing. The growth
of the Federate troops was gradual,
and appears to have begun in the
reign of Honorius (Olympiodorus, *fr.*
7). Areobindus is a Count of the
Federates under Theodosius II. (John
Mal. xiv. 364) ; in the time of
Anastasius, Patriciolus (Theophanes,
A.M. 6005) and probably Vitalian
held the same post. There was a
special bureau of χαρτουλάριοι φοι-
δεράτων to deal with the payment
of these troops (*C.J.* xii. 37. 19,
probably a law of Anastasius), who
seem to have been considered more

honourable and doubtless received
higher pay than the comitatenses.
For the technical use of Stratiōtai see
Justinian, *Nov.* 116 στρατιῶται καὶ
φοιδερᾶτοι, *Nov.* 117. 11 ; Procopius,
B.P. i. 17. 46 Ῥωμαῖοι στρατιῶται,
B.V. i. 11. 2 ; *B.G.* iv. 26. 10.

[2] Procopius, *B.V.* i. 11.

[3] Σύμμαχοι.

[4] See above, Chap. ii. § 2.

[5] Benjamin (*op. cit.* 24 *sqq.*) has
collected instances from Procopius
and Agathias. Egyptian papyri supply evidence for the employment of
these Bucellarians in Egypt by large
landowners. See the instances cited
by Maspéro, *Organ. milit.* 66 *sqq.*

[6] Procopius, *B.G.* iii. 1. 20.
Valerian, *Mag. mil.* of Armenia, had
more than 1000 retainers (*ib.* xxvii. 3).
Narses had less than 400 (Agathias,
i. 19).

doryphoroi in the retinue of Justinian before he ascended the throne. The doryphoroi on accepting service were obliged to take a solemn oath not only of fidelity to their employer, but also of loyalty to the Emperor,[1] a circumstance which implies an official recognition by the government. They were often employed on confidential missions, they stood in the presence of their master at meals, and attended him closely in battle. Both the doryphoroi and the hypaspistai seem to have been entirely mounted troops. The majority of them were foreigners (Huns and Goths), or mountaineers of Thrace and Asia Minor.

As a rule, in the campaigns of the sixth century, we find the armies composed mainly of comitatenses and foederati, but always reinforced by private retainers and barbarian allies. A single army in the field generally numbered from 15,000 to 25,000 men, a figure which probably it seldom exceeded ; 40,000 was exceptionally large. The total strength of the Imperial army under Justinian was reckoned at 150,000.[2]

The tactics and equipment of the Imperial armies had been considerably altered by the necessity of adapting them to the military habits of their oriental foes. At this time, in establishment and equipments, the Persians differed so little from the Romans that a Roman corps might have appeared in a Persian, or a Persian in a Roman army, with little sense of discrepancy. The long eastern warfare of the third and fourth centuries had been a school in which the Romans transformed in many ways their own military traditions and methods. They adopted from their adversaries elaborate defensive armour, cuirasses, coats of mail, casques and greaves of metal. At the end of the fourth century there were cuirassiers forming *corps d'élite*, and in the sixth these heavily armed " iron cavalry "[3] (*catafractarii*) have become a still larger and more important section of the army. Another result of the eastern wars was the universal practice of archery, which the old Roman legions despised. The heavy cavalry were armed with bow and arrows as well as with lance and sword.

---

[1] *B.V.* ii. 18. 6. The superior position of the doryphoroi is illustrated by the fact that individual hypaspistai are very seldom named by Procopius, whereas he mentions by name 47 doryphoroi. Benjamin,

op. cit. 32-33.

[2] Agathias, v. 13 *ad fin.* The figure is probably very close to the truth.

[3] *Ferreus equitatus*, Amm. Marc. xix. 1. 2.

§ 2. *The First War* (A.D. 527–532)

In his old age king Kavad was troubled and anxious about the succession to his throne, which he desired to secure to Chosroes his favourite son. But Chosroes was not the eldest, and his father feared that when he died the Persian nobles would prefer one of the elder brothers and put Chosroes to death. Accordingly he conceived the idea of placing his favourite under the protection of the Roman Emperor, as Arcadius had recommended Theodosius to the protection of Yezdegerd. But his proposal took a strange form. He asked Justin to adopt Chosroes. Both Justin and Justinian were at first attracted by the proposal, but the influence of the quaestor Proclus induced them to refuse. Proclus, who viewed the matter as a lawyer, represented the request as insidious ; for the adopted son might assert a claim to the father's inheritance ; the Persian king might claim the Roman Empire.

The refusal of his request was deeply resented by Kavad, and there were causes of friction in the Caucasian regions which led to a new breach between the two great powers.[1] Both governments were actively pushing their interests in that part of the world.

The Pontic provinces, as well as Roman Armenia, constantly suffered from the depredations of the Tzani, a heathen people who maintained their independence in an inland district on the borders of Colchis and Armenia, and lived by brigandage. The Imperial government was in the habit of giving them a yearly allowance to purchase immunity, but they paid little regard to the contract. One of the achievements of Justin's peaceful reign was partially to civilise these wild mountaineers. Sittas, the brother-in-law of Theodora, was sent against them. He subdued them, enrolled them in the Roman armies, and they were induced to embrace Christianity.[2]

The reduction of the Tzani proved to be a preliminary to a more active policy in the Caucasian countries. South of the

[1] Legally the two powers seem to have been in a state of war, for the armistice of seven years (A.D. 505) had not been renewed. This may be inferred from the statement of John Malalas (xviii. p. 478) that the peace of 532 terminated a war which had lasted for 31 years, *i.e.* since 502.

[2] Justinian, *Nov.* 28. Proc. *B.P.* i. 15. They returned to their old marauding habits and had to be reduced again in A.D. 558. Agathias, v. 1. 2.

great range, between the Euxine and the Caspian, lay three
kingdoms : in the west, Colchis, the land of the Lazi, whose
name is still preserved in Lazistan ; in the centre, Iberia or
Georgia ; and in the east, almost beyond Roman vision, Albania,

indomitique Dahae et pontem indignatus Araxes.

The importance of Lazica, in Roman eyes, was twofold. It was
a barrier against the barbarians north of the Caucasus, and it
was a barrier against a Persian advance through Iberia to the
coasts of the Black Sea.[1] In the reign of Justin, Tzath, the
king of the Lazi, who had hitherto been friendly to Persia,
visited Constantinople and became a client of the Emperor.[2]
Perhaps this change of policy was caused by the development
of Persian designs in Iberia. This country had long been a
client state of Persia, but it was devoted to the Christian faith.
Kavad either resolved to assimilate it to Persian civilisation
or sought a pretext for invading it, and he issued a command
to the Iberians to abandon the custom of burying their dead.
Gurgenes, the Iberian king, turned to the Roman Emperor for
protection.[3] A force was sent to Lazica, while a Persian army
invaded Iberia, and Gurgenes, with his family, fled within the
Lazic borders and proceeded to Constantinople. Roman garrisons were placed in the Lazic forts on the Iberian frontier,[4] and
Sittas with Belisarius, who now first appears upon the scene, made
a successful incursion into Persarmenia. In a second expedition
the Romans were defeated by two able commanders, Narses and
Aratius, who afterwards deserted and entered Roman service.[5]

Thus the war began before the death of Justin. Perhaps it
might have been averted if his successor had not determined to

[1] For Roman interference in the
domestic affairs of Colchis in the
reign of Marcian see Priscus, *fr.* 8
De leg. Rom., fr. 12 *De leg. gent.* (cp.
also *frs.* 16 and 22).

[2] John Mal. xviii. p. 412. He was
baptized a Christian and married a
Roman lady, Valeriana, daughter of
Nomos a patrician. Justin crowned
him, and the chronicler describes his
royal robes at some length.

[3] Justin sent Probus, the nephew
of Anastasius, with a large sum of
money, to Bosporus, to induce the
Huns of the Crimea to help the
Iberians ; but he was unsuccessful

(Proc. *B.P.* i. 12).

[4] But they soon departed, and the
natives were unable to defend the
forts against the Persians. Proc.
B.P. i. 13, p. 58. Sittas was a *Mag.
mil. in praes.*, and he was now
appointed to the newly created post
of *Mag. mil. per Armeniam.* He
seems to have held the two posts
concurrently. During peace his headquarters were at Constantinople. See
Proc. *B.P.* i. 15, p. 74, ii. 3, p. 154 ;
John Mal. xviii. p. 429.

[5] Procopius, *ib.* i. 12. This is
probably the incursion (noticed by
John Mal. p. 427) under Gilderic and
others.

build a new fortress near Daras. Belisarius, who had been appointed commandant of Daras, was directed to begin the work, and as the building operations were progressing, a Persian army, 30,000 strong, under the prince Xerxes, invaded Mesopotamia (A.D. 528).[1] The Romans, under several leaders who had joined forces, were defeated in a disastrous battle ; two of the commanders were slain and three captured. Belisarius luckily escaped. The foundations of the new fortress were left in the hands of the enemy. But the victors had lost heavily and soon retreated beyond the frontier. Justinian sent more troops and new captains to the fortresses of Amida, Constantia, Edessa, Sura, and Beroea ; and formed a new army (of Illyrians and Thracians, Scythians and Isaurians) which he entrusted to Pompeius, probably the nephew of Anastasius.[2] But no further operations are recorded in this year, which closed with a severe winter.

The hostilities of A.D. 529 began in March with a combined raid of Persian and Saracen forces, under the guidance of Mundhir, king of Hira, who penetrated into Syria, almost to the walls of Antioch, and retreated so swiftly that the Romans could not intercept him. Reprisals were made by a body of Phrygians who plundered Persian and Saracen territory (April). Pompeius seems to have accomplished nothing, and Belisarius was appointed Master of Soldiers in the East.[3] The rest of the year was occupied with ineffectual negotiations.[4]

---

[1] John Mal. p. 441. For the events of 528 we have to combine Procopius (*B.P.* i. 13) and Malalas. The two narratives are carefully compared by Sotiriadis in *Zur Kr. v. Joh. v. Ant.* p. 114 *sq.* It is to be noted that Belisarius held only a subordinate position and was in no way responsible for the defeat. The operations of 529 are entirely omitted by Procopius. For the fortress at Minduos, which the Romans tried to build, see Proc. *ib.* and Zacharias, *Myt.* ix. 2.

[2] John Mal. p. 442. Pompeius was a patrician, and it is not very likely that there were two patricians of this name.

[3] In succession to Hypatius (before June) acc. to John Mal. p. 445. Hypatius (*ib.* 423) had been created *mag. mil. Or.* between April and August 527. It is difficult to reconcile this with the statements of

Procopius, who places both the appointment and the deposition of Hypatius before April 427 (*B.P.* i. 11. p. 53 and p. 55, compared with i. 13. p. 59). It is possible that the notice of the deposition is an anticipation ; the whole section beginning μετὰ δέ, p. 54, to end of chap. ii. may be a chronological digression. But Zacharias, ix. 1, states that Timus (otherwise unknown, perhaps an error for Timostratus) was *mag. mil.* when Justin died, and that Belisarius succeeded him (ix. 2). If this is right, Malalas is wrong.

[4] It is remarkable that in the summer of 529 Justinian should have sent the customary friendly embassy to announce his accession. Hermogenes was the envoy (John Mal. pp. 447-448). He returned with a letter from Kavad, of which the text is given (*ib.* p. 449).

Belisarius was now to win his military laurels at the early age of twenty-five. There was still talk of peace, but Kavad seems not to have really desired it, and the ambassador, Rufinus, waited idle at Hierapolis. Hermogenes, the Master of Offices, was sent out to help the young general with his experience, and they concentrated at Daras an army of 25,000 mixed and undisciplined troops. Perozes, who had been appointed mihran or commander-in-chief of the Persian army, arrived at Nisibis in June [1] (A.D. 530), at the head of 40,000 troops, confident of victory. They advanced within two miles of Daras, and the mihran sent to Belisarius a characteristically oriental message, that, as he intended to bathe in the city on the morrow, a bath should be prepared for his pleasure.

The Romans made preparations for battle, just outside the walls of the town. The Persians arrived punctually as their general signified, and stood for a whole day in line of battle without venturing to attack the Romans, who were drawn up in carefully arranged positions. In the evening they retired to their camp,[2] but returned next morning, resolved not to let another day pass without a decisive action, and found their enemy occupying the same positions as on the preceding day. They were themselves now reinforced by a body of 10,000, which arrived from Nisibis. The Roman dispositions were as follows :

About a stone's throw from the gate of Daras that looks toward Nisibis a deep trench was dug, interrupted by frequent ways for crossing. This trench, however, was not in a continuous right line ; it consisted of five sections. At each end of a short central trench, which was parallel to the opposite wall of the city, a trench ran outwards almost at right angles ; and where each of these perpendicular trenches or " horns " terminated, two long ones were dug in opposite directions at right angles, and consequently almost parallel to the first trench. Between the trenches and the town Belisarius and Hermogenes were posted with the infantry. On the left, behind the main ditch and near the left " horn," was a regiment of cavalry under Buzes, and 300 Heruls under Pharas were stationed on a rising ground, which the Heruls occupied in the morning, at the

---

[1] Theophanes supplies the date.

[2] During the afternoon the armies were diverted by two single combats, in which a Byzantine professor of gymnastics, who had accompanied the army unofficially, slew two Persian champions.

suggestion of Pharas and with the approval of Belisarius. Outside the angle made by the outermost ditch and the horn were
placed 600 Hunnic cavalry, under the Huns Sunicas and Aigan.
The disposition on the right wing was exactly symmetrical.
Cavalry under John (the son of Nicetas), Cyril, and Marcellus
occupied the position corresponding to that occupied by Buzes
on the left, while other squadrons of Hunnic horse, led by Simas
and Ascan, were posted in the angle.

Half of the Persian forces stood in a long line opposite to
the Roman dispositions, the other half was kept in reserve at
some distance in the rear. The mihran commanded the centre,
Baresmanas the left wing, and Pityaxes the right. The corps
of Immortals, the flower of the army, was reserved for a supreme
occasion. The details of the battle have been described by a
competent eye-witness.[1]

As soon as noon was past the barbarians began the action. They had
reserved the engagement for this hour of the day because they are themselves in the habit of eating only in the evening, while the Romans eat
at noontide, so that they counted on their offering a less vigorous resistance if they were attacked fasting. At first each side discharged volleys
of arrows and the air was obscured with them ; the barbarians shot more
darts, but many fell on both sides. Fresh relays of the barbarians were
always coming up to the front, unperceived by their adversaries ; yet the

---

[1] Procopius, *B.P.* i. 14. A diagram will make the arrangement of the
forces clear.

PERSIAN ARMY

Pityaxes   Perozes   Baresmanas

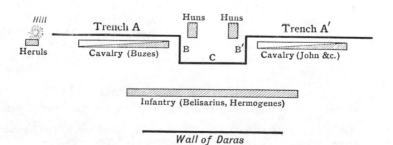

Wall of Daras

Romans had by no means the worst of it. For a wind blew in the faces of the Persians and hindered to a considerable degree their missiles from operating with effect. When both sides had expended all their arrows, they used their spears, hand to hand. The left wing of the Romans was pressed most hardly. For the Cadisenes, who fought at this point with Pityaxes, had advanced suddenly in large numbers, and having routed their opponents, pressed them hard as they fled, and slew many. When Sunicas and Aigan with their Huns saw this they rushed on the Cadisenes at full gallop. But Pharas and his Heruls, who were posted on the hill, were before them (the Huns) in falling on the rear of the enemy and performing marvellous exploits. But when the Cadisenes saw the cavalry of Sunicas also coming against them from the side, they turned and fled. The rout was conspicuous when the Romans joined together and great slaughter was inflicted on the enemy.

The mihran [meanwhile] secretly sent the Immortals with other regiments to the left wing. When Belisarius and Hermogenes saw them, they commanded Sunicas, Aigan, and their Huns, to go to the angle on the right where Simas and Ascan were stationed, and placed behind them many of the retainers of Belisarius. Then the left wing of the Persians, led by Baresmanas, along with the Immortals, attacked the Roman right wing at full speed. And the Romans, unable to withstand the onset, fled. Then those who were stationed in the angle (the Huns, etc.) attacked the pursuers with great ardour. And coming athwart the side of the Persians they cleft their line in two unequal portions, the larger number on the right and a few on the left. Among the latter was the standard-bearer of Baresmanas, whom Sunicas killed with his lance. The foremost of the Persian pursuers, apprehending their danger, turned from their pursuit of the fugitives to oppose the attackers. But this movement placed them between enemies on both sides, for the fugitive party perceived what was occurring and rallied. Then the other Persians and the corps of the Immortals, seeing the standard lowered and on the ground, rushed with Baresmanas against the Romans in that quarter. The Romans met them, and Sunicas slew Baresmanas, hurling him to earth from his horse. Then the barbarians fell into great panic, and forgot their valour and fled in utter disorder. And the Romans closed them in and slew about five thousand. And thus both armies were entirely set in motion ; that of the Persians for retreat and that of the Romans for pursuit. All the infantry of the defeated army threw away their shields, and were caught and slain pell-mell. Yet the Romans pursued only for a short distance, for Belisarius and Hermogenes would not permit them to go further, lest the Persians, compelled by necessity, should turn and rout them if they followed rashly ; and they deemed it sufficient to keep the victory untarnished, this being the first defeat experienced by the Persians for a long time past.[1]

It will be observed that this battle—the first of which we have any full description since the fourth century—was fought and

---

[1] It is curious that Zacharias, ix. 3, in his notice of the battle, does not mention Belisarius. He names Sunicas, Buzes, and Simuth (Simas ?).

won entirely by cavalry. It has been pointed out that the dispositions of Belisarius show his " deliberate purpose to keep his infantry out of the stress of the fight." [1] This was done by throwing forward the wings, and leaving only a comparatively short space between them, so that they drew upon themselves the chief attack of the enemy. We are not told how the Persians disposed their horse and foot. The foot may have been in the centre. But the fighting was evidently done by the cavalry, for the infantry was not efficient. Belisarius, addressing his soldiers before the battle, described the Persian infantry as " a crowd of miserable peasants who only come into battle to dig through walls and strip the slain and generally to act as servants to the soldiers (that is, the cavalry)." We may conjecture that while in mere numbers the Romans were fighting one to two, the great excess of the Persian forces was chiefly in the infantry, and that otherwise they were not so unevenly matched.

About the same time the Roman arms were also successful in Persarmenia, where a victory was gained over an army of Persarmenians and Sabir auxiliaries, which, if it had not been overshadowed by the victory of Daras, would have probably been made more of by the Greek historians [2]

After the conspicuous defeat which his army had experienced, Kavad was not disinclined to resume negotiations, and embassies passed between the Persian and Roman courts ; [3] but at the last moment the persuasions and promises of fifty thousand Samaritans induced him to break off the negotiations on a trifling pretext. The Samaritans had revolted in A.D. 529, and the fifty thousand, who had escaped the massacre which attended the suppression of the rebellion, actuated by the desire of revenge, engaged to betray Jerusalem and Palestine to the foe of the Empire. The plot, however, was discovered and forestalled.

In the following spring (A.D. 531), at the instigation of

---

[1] Oman (*Art of War*, p. 29), who has well elucidated the battle. In one point I disagree with his plan. The central trench (C) was evidently, from the description of Procopius, much shorter than the wing trenches (A, A'), and the lines of infantry must have extended considerably beyond it on either side. But this only brings out and confirms his interpretation of the tactical plan of Belisarius, to force the enemy to attack the wings.

[2] About this time Narses the Persarmenian, with his two brothers, deserted to Rome (Proc. *B.P.* i. 15).

[3] See Proc. *B.P.* i. 16 ; John Mal. p. 454. Sotiriadis (*op. cit.* p. 119) points out the difficulties in the text and gives a probable solution. For the Samaritan rising, *ib.* 445.

Mundhir, in whose advice Kavad had great confidence, fifteen thousand Persian cavalry under Azareth crossed the Euphrates at Circesium with the intention of invading Syria. They marched along the banks of the river to Callinicum, thence by Sura to Barbalissus, whence taking the western road they pitched their camp at Gabbula, twelve miles from Chalcis, and harried the neighbourhood. Meanwhile Belisarius arrived at Chalcis, where he was joined by Saracen auxiliaries under Harith. His army was 22,000 strong, but he did not venture to attack the enemy, who numbered 30,000, and his inactivity aroused considerable discontent among both officers and soldiers.[1] The Hun captain Sunicas set at naught the general's orders, and attacking a party of Persians not only defeated them, but learned from the prisoners whom he took the Persian plan of campaign, and the intention of the foe to strike a blow at Antioch itself. Yet the success of Sunicas did not in the eyes of Belisarius atone for his disobedience, and Hermogenes, who arrived at this moment on the scene of action from Constantinople, arranged with difficulty the quarrel between the general and the captain. At length Belisarius ordered an advance against the enemy, who had meanwhile by their siege engines taken the fortress of Gabbula (near Chalcis) and other places in the neighbourhood. Laden with booty, the Persians retreated and reached the point of the right Euphrates bank opposite to the city of Callinicum, where they were overtaken by the Romans. A battle was unavoidable, and on the 19th of April the armies engaged. What really happened on this unfortunate day was a matter of doubt even for contemporaries ; some cast the blame on Belisarius, others accused the subordinate commanders of cowardice.[2]

At Callinicum the course of the Euphrates is from west to east. The battle was fought on the bank of the river, and as the Persians were stationed to the east of the Romans, their right wing and the Roman left were on the river. Belisarius and his cavalry occupied the centre ; on the left were the infantry and the Hunnic cavalry under Sunicas and Simas ; on the right were Phrygians and Isaurians and the Saracen auxiliaries under

---

[1] Procopius, B.P. p. 92.

[2] Compare the conflicting accounts of Procopius (B.P. i. 18), the secretary of Belisarius, and Malalas. We have no means of determining the source of the latter, but in many cases he furnishes details omitted by the former. The account of Zacharias, ix. 4 throws no light, but he mentions that the wind was blowing in the face of the Romans.

their king Harith.[1] The Persians began the action by a
feigned retreat, which had the effect of drawing from their
position the Huns on the left wing; they then attacked the
Roman infantry, left unprotected, and tried to ride them down
and press them into the river. But they were not as successful
as they hoped, and on this side the battle was drawn. On the
Roman right wing the fall of Apscal, the captain of the Phrygian
troops, was followed by the flight of his soldiers; a panic ensued,
and the Saracens acted like the Phrygians; then the Isaurians
made for the river and swam over to an island. How Belisarius
acted, and what the Hun captains were doing in the meantime,
we cannot determine. It was said that Belisarius dismounted,
rallied his men, and made a long brave stand against the charges
of the Persian cavalry. On the other hand, this valiant behaviour
was attributed to Sunicas and Simas, and the general himself
was accused of fleeing with the cowards and crossing to Callinicum.
There is no clear evidence to prove that the defeat was the fault
of Belisarius; though perhaps an over-confident spirit in his
army prevailed on him to risk a battle against his better judgment.

The Persians retreated, and the remnant of the Roman army
was conveyed across the river to Callinicum. Hermogenes [2]
sent the news of the defeat to Justinian without delay, and the
Emperor despatched Constantiolus to investigate the circumstances of the battle and discover on whom the blame, if any,
rested. The conclusions at which Constantiolus arrived resulted
in the recall of Belisarius and the appointment of Mundus to the
command of the eastern armies.[3] It is significant of the differ-

---

[1] I cannot agree with the plan of
the battle implied by Sotiriadis
(p. 123), which would place the
Persians *west* of the Romans. I
adopt the reverse position, and thus
bring the statements of Malalas into
accordance with those of Procopius.
In the mere fact of the position of
troops there is no reason why the
two accounts should differ. According to Sotiriadis, " the northern part "
(τὸ ἀρκτῷον μέρος) of the Roman
army was the right wing; according
to my explanation, it was the left.

[2] It may be suspected that Hermogenes presented the behaviour of
Belisarius in a suspicious light. He
was a Hun, and sympathised doubtless with Sunicas and Simas.

[3] We cannot, I think, infer from
the recall of Belisarius that the
verdict of Constantiolus was adverse
to him; on the contrary, if it had
been adverse to him, the informant
who furnished Malalas with his
narrative, and who was evidently
unfriendly to Belisarius, would have
certainly stated the fact in distinct
terms. Probably the reason of his
recall was the circumstance that a
bad feeling prevailed between him
and the subordinate commanders;
and Justinian saw that this feeling
was a sure obstacle to success. The
investigation of Constantiolus would
naturally have shown up these
jealousies and quarrels in the clearest
light.

ence between the spirit of the Persian and of the Roman governments that while Belisarius was recalled, with honour, after his
defeat, the victorious Azareth was disgraced. He had been sent
against Antioch and he had not approached it, and his victory
had been bought with great losses.

The arms of Mundus were attended with success. Two
attempts of the Persians to take Martyropolis were thwarted,
and they experienced a considerable defeat. But the death of
the old king Kavad and the accession of his son Chosroes
(September 13, 531) led to the conclusion of a treaty which was
known as " the Endless Peace." The negotiations were conducted on the Roman side by Hermogenes and Rufinus, who was
a *grata persona* with Chosroes, and were protracted during the
winter, because the Persians were unwilling to restore the forts
they had taken in Lazica. They finally yielded and the treaty
was ratified in spring A.D. 532.[1] On their part the Romans
restored two important fortresses in Persarmenia.[2] The other
conditions were that the Emperor should pay 11,000 lbs. of
gold for the defence of the Caucasian passes, that the headquarters of the duke of Mesopotamia were no longer to be at
Daras but at Constantia, and that the Iberian refugees at Constantinople might, as they chose, either remain there or return
to their own country.[3]

This treaty made no change in the frontiers between Roman
and Persian Armenia. In the early years of Chosroes Persian
Armenia was peaceful and contented under a native vassal
prince and the Christians enjoyed full toleration. But at the
same time the Armenian Church was drifting apart from Constantinople and Rome. The decisions of Chalcedon had been
indeed accepted, but the Armenian theologians viewed them
with some suspicion from the first ; the ecclesiastical policy of
Zeno and Anastasius confirmed them in their doubts ; and the
Henotikon of Zeno had been approved in a council held in A.D.
491. On the restoration of the doctrine of Chalcedon by Justin

---

[1] In the sixth year of Justinian,
therefore after April 1. *B.P.* p. 117.

[2] Pharangion and Bôlon.

[3] Procopius, *B.P.* i. 22. John
Mal. xviii. p. 477 states that the two
monarchs agreed, as brothers, to
supply each other with money or
men in case of need. This may seem
improbable, but such an agreement
seems to have been made in a previous
treaty, see .Joshua Styl. c. viii. I
conjecture that this refers to the
treaty of 442 : the stipulated help
consisted of 300 able-bodied men *or*
300 staters.

the Armenians displayed their Monophysitic leanings, and a definite and permanent schism between the Armenian and Greek Churches was the result. This separation was the work of the patriarch Narses, who secured the condemnation of the dogma of the Two Natures,[1] and at the Synod of Duin held just after his death, in A.D. 551, the independence of the Armenian Church was confirmed and a reform of the calendar was inaugurated. The Armenian era began on July 11, A.D. 552. The schism had its political consequences. Chosroes could profit by the fact that Greek influence declined in Persarmenia and Greek political agents were less favourably received.

§ 3. *The Second War* (A.D. 540–545)

The reign of Chosroes Nushirvan [2] extended over nearly half of the sixth century, and may be called the golden or at least the gilded period of the monarchy of the Sassanids. His father Kavad had prepared the way for his brilliant son, as Philip of Macedon had prepared the way for Alexander. It was a period of energetic reforms, in some of which, as in the working out of a new land system, Chosroes was only continuing what his father had begun. This system was found to work so well that after their conquest of Persia the Saracen caliphs adopted it unaltered. In the general organisation some changes were made. The Persian empire was divided into four great circumscriptions each of which was governed by a *marzban* who had the title of " king." The military government of these districts was now transferred to four *spahbedhs*, the civil government to four *pādhospans*, and the marzbans, though allowed to retain the honourable title, were reduced to second-class rank and were subordinate to the spahbedhs.[3] The most anxious pains of Chosroes were spent on the army, and it is said that when he reviewed it he used to inspect each individual soldier. He reduced its cost and in creased its efficiency. But he also encouraged literature and patronised the study of Persian history. Of his personal culture the envy or impartiality of a Greek historian speaks with

---

[1] Perhaps at a synod, *c.* 527. See Tournebize, *Hist. de l'Arménie*, i. 90-91. Le Quien, *Or. Christ.* i. pp. 1381-1384.

[2] Khosru = Hu-srava (fair glory) is etymologically identical with εὔ-κλεια.

The proper form of Nushirvan is Anosha-revan = of immortal soul.

[3] For these changes see Stein, *Ein Kapitel vom pers. Staate*, who (p. 66) would attribute the institution of the 4 pādhospans to Kavad.

contempt as narrow and superficial ;[1] on the other hand, he has received the praises of an ecclesiastical writer. " He was a prudent and wise man, and all his lifetime he assiduously devoted himself to the perusal of philosophical works. And, as was said, he took pains to collect the religious books of all creeds, and read and studied them, that he might learn which were true and wise and which were foolish. . . . He praised the books of the Christians above all others, and said, ' These are true and wise above those of any other religion.' "[2] As a successful and, judged by the standards of his age and country, enlightened ruler, Chosroes stands out in the succession of Sassanid sovrans much as Justinian stands out in the succession of the later Roman emperors.

The Emperor Justinian had, with the energy and thoroughness which distinguished the first half of his long reign, made use of the years of peace to strengthen the defences of the eastern provinces. Sieges were the characteristic feature of the wars on the oriental frontier, and walls were wellnigh as important as men. The fortifications of many of the most important cities and strongholds had fallen into decay, many had weak points, some were ill furnished with water. All the important towns in Mesopotamia and Osrhoene, and not a few of those in northern Syria were restored, repaired, or partly rebuilt in the reign of Justinian under the supervision of expert engineers. An account of these works has been preserved,[3] and most of them were probably executed between A.D. 532 and 539. The fortresses on the Pontic or Armenian border were similarly strengthened.[4] Here, too, an important administrative change was made. Roman Armenia beyond the Euphrates, which had hitherto been governed by native satraps,[5] under the general control of a military officer,[6] was organised as a regular province

---

[1] Agathias (ii. 28), who asks how one brought up in the luxury of an oriental barbarian could be a philosopher or a scholar. For the reception of Greek philosophers at the Persian court see p. 370.

[2] John Eph. vi. 20. John apologises for thus eulogising a Magian and an enemy. What he says about the king's Christian proclivities is more edifying than probable. But Chosroes was not fanatical. He allowed one of his wives and her son to profess

Christianity. In the eyes of Procopius, Chosroes was the typical oriental tyrant, cruel and perfidious.

[3] Procopius, Aed. book ii.

[4] Ib. book iii.

[5] Zeno abolished hereditary succession to the satrapies (except in the case of Belabitene), and vested the nomination in the Emperor (Procop. ib. iii. 1).

[6] The Comes Armeniae, who had been abolished in 528, when the mag. mil. per Arm. was created. See above, p. 80.

under a governor of consular rank, and was officially designated
as the Fourth Armenia. The satraps were abolished. Martyropolis was the chief town and residence of the governor.[1]

When Chosroes concluded the " Endless Peace " with
Justinian, he had little idea that the new Emperor was about
to embark on great enterprises of conquest. Within seven
years from that time (A.D. 532–539) Justinian had overthrown
the Vandal kingdom of Africa, and had reduced the Moors ; the
subjection of the Ostrogothic lords of Italy was in prospect,
Bosporus and the Crimean Goths were included in the circle
of Roman sway, while the Homerites of southern Arabia acknowledged the supremacy of New Rome. Both his friends and
his enemies said, with hate or admiration, " The whole earth
cannot contain him ; he is already scrutinising the aether and
the remote places beyond the ocean, if he may win some new
world." [2] The eastern potentate might well apprehend danger
to his own kingdom in the expansion of the Roman Empire by
the reconquest of its lost provinces. We may consider it natural
enough that Chosroes should have seized or invented a pretext
to renew hostilities, when it seemed but too possible that if
Justinian were allowed to continue his career of conquest undisturbed the Romans might come with larger armies and
increased might to extend their dominions in the East at the
expense of the Sassanid empire.

Hostilities between the Saracens of Hira and their enemies
of Ghassan supplied Chosroes with the pretext he desired. The
Roman provinces had constantly suffered from the inroads of
the Ghassanid tribes who obeyed no common ruler, and one of
the early achievements of Justinian's reign was the creation of
a Ghassanid state under the government of a supreme phylarch,
nominated by the Emperor This client state formed a counterpoise to the Lakhmids of Hira, who were clients of Persia.
Harith was appointed phylarch, and received the title of king
and the dignity of patrician.[3] The cause of contention at this

[1] A.D. 536. Justinian, *Nov.* 31, § 3.
At the same time considerable changes
were made in the East Pontic provinces of 1st, 2nd, and 3rd Armenia,
which will be noticed in another
place (below, p. 344).
[2] Procopius, *B.P.* ii. 3 (p. 160).
[3] See Procopius, *B.P.* i. 17 ;

Theophanes, A.M. 6056. Harith
reigned *c.* A.D. 528–570. Mundhir,
the veteran chief of Hira, was
similarly allowed by the Persians to
bear the title of king (Procop. *ib.*).
He reigned for about 50 years (A.D.
508–554) ; see Tabari, p. 170 (Nol-
deke's note). He was exceptionally

juncture between the two Saracen powers was a tract of waste land called Strata, to the south of Palmyra, a region barren of trees and fruit, scorched dry by the sun, and used as a pasture for sheep. Harith the Ghassanide could appeal to the fact that the name *Strata* was Latin, and could adduce the testimony of the most venerable elders that the sheep-walk belonged to his tribe. Mundhir, the rival sheikh, contented himself with the more practical argument that for years back the shepherds had paid him tribute. Two arbitrators were sent by the Emperor, Strategius, Count of the Sacred Largesses, and Summus, the duke of Palestine. This arbitration supplied Chosroes with a pretext for breaking the peace. He alleged that Summus made treasonable offers to Mundhir, attempting to shake his allegiance to Persia ; and he professed to have in his possession a letter of Justinian to the Ephthalites, urging them to invade his dominions.[1]

About the same time suggestions from without urged the thoughts of Chosroes in the direction which they had already taken. An embassy arrived from Witigis, king of the Ostrogoths, now hard pressed by Belisarius, and pleaded with Chosroes to act against the common enemy (A.D. 539).[2] Another embassy arrived from the Armenians making similar representations, deploring and execrating the Endless Peace, and denouncing the tyranny and exactions of Justinian, against whom they had revolted. The history of Armenia, now a Roman province,[3] had been unfortunate during the years that followed the peace. The first governor, Amazaspes, was accused by one Acacius of treachery, and, with the Emperor's consent, was slain by the accuser, who was himself appointed to succeed his victim. Acacius was relentless in exacting a tribute of unprecedented magnitude (£18,000) ; and some Armenians, intolerant of his cruelty, slew him and fled. The Emperor immediately despatched

---

barbarous. He sacrificed the son of his enemy Harith (Procop. *B.P.* ii. 28) and on another occasion 400 nuns (cp. Noeldeke, *l.c.*) to the goddess Uzza. For these kingdoms see Huart, *Hist. des Arabes*, chap. iv.

[1] Procopius says that he does not know whether these allegations were true or false (*B.P.* ii. 1). The second Book of his *De bello Persico* is our main source for the war which ensued. It comes down to the end of A.D. 549.

[2] See below, chap. xviii. § 9. The reader may ask how the details of this embassy were known. Procopius tells us in another place (*B.P.* ii. 14) that the interpreter, returning from Persia, was captured near Constantia by John, duke of Mesopotamia, and gave an account of the embassy. The pseudo-bishop and his attendant remained in Persia.

[3] See above, p. 90.

Sittas, the Master of Soldiers *per Armeniam*, to recall the people
to a sense of obedience, and, when Sittas showed himself inclined
to use the softer methods of persuasion, insisted that he should
act with sterner vigour. The rebellion became general. Sittas
was accidentally killed soon afterwards, but the rebels found
themselves unequal to coping with the Roman forces, which
were then placed under the command of Buzes, and they decided
to appeal to the Persian monarch. The servitude of their neighbours the Tzani and the imposition of a Roman duke over the
Lazi of Colchis confirmed them in their fear and detestation of
Roman policy.

Accordingly Chosroes, in the autumn of A.D. 539, decided to
begin hostilities in the following spring, and did not deign to
answer a pacific letter from the Roman Emperor, conveyed by
Anastasius, whom he retained an unwilling guest at the Persian
court.[1] The war which thus began lasted five years, and in
each year the king himself took the field. He invaded Syria,
Colchis, and Commagene in successive campaigns ; in A.D. 543
he began but did not carry out an expedition against the northern
provinces ; in the next year he invaded Mesopotamia ; and in
A.D. 545 a peace was concluded.

I. *Invasion of Syria* (A.D. 540) [2]

Avoiding Mesopotamia, Chosroes advanced northwards with
a large army along the left bank of the Euphrates. He passed
the triangular city of Circesium, but did not care to assault it,
because its walls, built by Diocletian, were too strong ; while he
disdained to delay at the town of Zenobia (Halebiya), named
after the queen of Palmyra, because it was too insignificant.
But when he approached Sura his horse neighed and stamped
the ground ; and the magi, who attended the king, seized the
incident as an omen that the city would be taken. On the
first day of the siege the governor was slain, and on the second
the bishop of the place visited the Persian camp in the name of

---

[1] Theodora also wrote a letter to
Zabergan, whom she knew personally
as he had come to Constantinople
as an envoy, requesting him to urge
Chosroes to preserve peace. But this
letter may have been sent later, in
540 or even 541. Chosroes made use
of it to quell discontent among his
troops, arguing that a state must be
weak in which women intervened in
public affairs. Procopius, *H.A.* 32-36.

[2] Procopius, *B.P.* ii. 5-14.

the dispirited inhabitants, and implored Chosroes with tears to spare the town. He tried to appease the implacable foe with an offering of birds, wine, and bread, and engaged that the men of Sura would pay a sufficient ransom. Chosroes dissembled

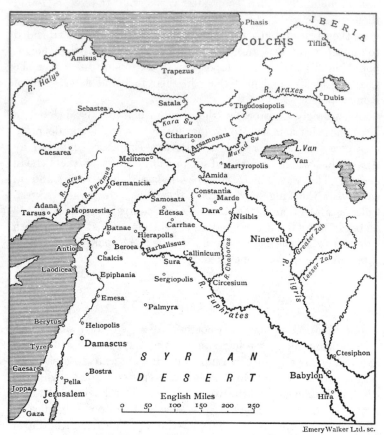

MAP TO ILLUSTRATE THE PERSIAN WARS.

the wrath he felt against the Surenes because they had not submitted immediately ; he received the gifts and said that he would consult the Persian nobles regarding the ransom ; and he dismissed the bishop, who was well pleased with the interview, under the honourable escort of Persian notables, to whom the monarch had given secret instructions.

" Having given his directions to the escort, Chosroes ordered his army to stand in readiness, and to run at full speed to the city when he gave the signal. When they reached the walls the Persians saluted the bishop and stood outside ; but the men of Sura, seeing him in high spirits and observing how he was escorted with great honour by the Persians, put aside all thoughts of suspicion, and, opening the gate wide, received their priest with clapping of hands and acclamation. And when all had passed within, the porters pushed the gate to shut it, but the Persians placed a stone, which they had provided, between the threshold and the gate. The porters pushed harder, but for all their violent exertions they could not succeed in forcing the gate into the threshold-groove. And they did not venture to throw it open again, as they apprehended that it was held by the enemy. Some say that it was a log of wood, not a stone, that was inserted by the Persians. The men of Sura had hardly discovered the guile, ere Chosroes had come with all his army and the Persians had forced open the gate. In a few moments the city was in the power of the enemy." [1] The houses were plundered ; many of the inhabitants were slain, the rest were carried into slavery, and the city was burnt down to the ground. Then the Persian king dismissed Anastasius, bidding him inform the Emperor in what place he had left Chosroes the son of Kavad.

Perhaps it was merely avarice, perhaps it was the prayers of a captive named Euphemia, whose beauty attracted the desires of the conqueror, that induced Chosroes to treat with unexpected leniency the prisoners of Sura. He sent a message to Candidus, the bishop of Sergiopolis, suggesting that he should ransom the 12,000 captives for 200 lbs. of gold (15s. a head). As Candidus had not, and could not immediately obtain, the sum, he was allowed to stipulate in writing that he would pay it within a year's time, under penalty of paying double and resigning his bishopric. Few of the redeemed prisoners survived long the agitations and tortures they had undergone.

Meanwhile the Roman general Buzes was at Hierapolis. Nominally the command in the East was divided between Buzes and Belisarius : the provinces beyond the Euphrates being assigned to the former, Syria and Asia Minor to the latter. But as Belisarius had not yet returned from Italy, the entire army was under the orders of Buzes.

[1] Procopius, *B.P.* ii. 5.

Informed of the presence of Chosroes in the Roman provinces, Justinian despatched his cousin Germanus to Antioch, with a small body of three hundred soldiers.[1] The fortifications of the " Queen of the East " did not satisfy the careful inspection of Germanus, for although the lower parts of the city were adequately protected by the Orontes, which washed the bases of the houses, and the higher regions seemed secure on impregnable heights, there rose outside the walls adjacent to the citadel [2] a broad rock, almost as lofty as the wall, which would inevitably present to the besiegers a fatal point of vantage. Competent engineers said that there would not be sufficient time before the arrival of Chosroes to remedy this defect by removing the rock or enclosing it within the walls. Accordingly Germanus, despairing of resistance, sent Megas, the bishop of Beroea, to divert the Persian advance from Antioch by the influence of money or entreaties. The army had already crossed the Euphrates, and Megas arrived as it was approaching Hierapolis, from which Buzes had withdrawn a large part of the garrison. He was informed by the great king that it was his unalterable intention to subdue Syria and Cilicia. The bishop was constrained or induced to accompany the army to Hierapolis, which was strong enough to defy a siege, and was content to purchase immunity by a payment of 2000 lbs. of silver. Chosroes then consented to retire without assaulting Antioch on the receipt of 1000 lbs. of gold (£45,000), and Megas returned speedily with the good news, while the enemy proceeded more leisurely to Beroea.[3] From this city the avarice of the Sassanid demanded double the amount he had exacted at Hierapolis ; the Beroeans gave him half the sum, affirming that it was all they had ; but the extortioner refused to be satisfied, and proceeded to demolish the city.

From Beroea he advanced to Antioch, and demanded the 1000 lbs. with which Megas had undertaken to redeem it ; and it is said that he would have been contented to receive a smaller sum. Germanus and the Patriarch had already departed to Cilicia, and the Antiochenes would probably have paid the money had not the arrival of six thousand soldiers from Phoenicia Libanensis, led by Theoctistus and Molatzes, infused into their

---

[1] Cp. John Mal. bk. xviii. p. 480. *Contin. Marcell.*, s.a.

[2] The citadel was called Orocasias.

[3] Probably *via* Batnae.

hearts a rash and unfortunate confidence. Julian, an Imperial
secretary, who had arrived at Antioch as an ambassador, bade
the inhabitants resist the extortion ; and Paul, the interpreter
of Chosroes, who approached the walls and counselled them to
pay the money, was almost slain. Not content with defying
the enemy by a refusal, the men of Antioch stood on their walls
and loaded Chosroes with torrents of scurrilous abuse, which
might have inflamed a milder monarch.

The siege which ensued was short. It seems not to have
occurred to the besieged that they should themselves occupy the
dangerous rock outside the citadel, and it was seized by the enemy.
The defence at first was brave. Between the towers, which crowned
the walls at intervals, platforms of wooden beams were suspended
by ropes attached to the towers, that a greater number of
defenders might man the walls at once. But during the fighting
the ropes gave way and the suspended soldiers were precipitated,
some without, some within the walls ; the men in the towers
were seized with panic and left their posts. The confusion was
increased by a rush made to the gates, occasioned by a false
report that Buzes was coming to the rescue ; and a multitude
of women and children were crushed or trampled to death.
But the gate leading to the remote suburb of Daphne was pur-
posely left unblocked by the Persians ; Chosroes seems to have
desired that the Roman soldiers and their officers should be
allowed to leave the city unmolested ; and some of the inhabitants escaped with the departing army. But the young
men of the Hippodrome factions made a valiant and hopeless
stand against superior numbers ; and the city was not
entered without a considerable loss of life, which Chosroes pretended to deplore. It is said that two illustrious ladies cast
themselves into the Orontes, to escape the cruelties of oriental
licentiousness.

It was nearly three hundred years since Antioch had experienced the presence of a human foe, though it suffered
frequently and grievously from the malignity of nature. The
Sassanid Sapor had taken the city in the ill-starred reign of
Valerian, but it was kindly dealt with then in comparison with
its treatment by Chosroes. The cathedral was stripped of its
wealth in gold and silver and its splendid marbles. Orders
were given that the whole **town** should be burnt, except the

cathedral, and the sentence of the relentless conqueror was executed as far as was practicable.

While the work of demolition was being carried out, Chosroes was treating with the ambassadors [1] of Justinian, and expressed himself ready to make peace, on condition that he received 5000 lbs. of gold, paid immediately, and an annual sum of 500 lbs. nominally for the defence of the Caspian Gates. While the ambassadors returned with this answer to Byzantium, Chosroes advanced to Seleucia, the port of Antioch, and looked upon the waters of the Mediterranean ; it is related that he took a solitary bath in the sea and sacrificed to the sun. In returning he visited Daphne, which was not included in the fate of Antioch, and thence proceeded to Apamea, whose gates he was invited to enter with a guard of 200 soldiers. All the gold and silver in the town was collected to satisfy his greed, even to the jewelled case in which a piece of the true cross was reverently preserved. He spared the precious relic itself, which for him was devoid of value. The city of Chalcis purchased its safety by a sum of 200 lbs. of gold ; and having exhausted the provinces to the west of the Euphrates, Chosroes decided to continue his campaign of extortion in Mesopotamia, and crossed the river at Obbane, near Barbalissus, by a bridge of boats. Edessa, the great stronghold of western Mesopotamia, was too strong itself to fear a siege, but paid 200 lbs. of gold for the immunity of the surrounding territory from devastation.[2] At Edessa, ambassadors arrived from Justinian, bearing his consent to the terms proposed by Chosroes ; but in spite of this the Persian did not shrink from making an attempt to take Daras on his homeward march.

The fortress of Daras, which Anastasius had erected to replace the long-lost Nisibis as an outpost in eastern Mesopotamia, was built on three hills, on the highest of which stood the citadel. One of the other heights projecting from higher hills behind and could not be surrounded by the walls, which

[1] Julian, mentioned above, and John, son of Rufinus (doubtless the same Rufinus who had been employed by Anastasius as ambassador to Kavad).

[2] The people of Edessa were generous enough to subscribe to ransom the Antiochene captives ;

farmers who had no money gave a sheep or an ass, prostitutes stripped off their ornaments. But, according to Procopius (*B.P.* ii. 13), Buzes, who happened to be there, seized the money that was collected and allowed the captives to be carried off to Persia.

were built across it. There were two walls between which
stretched a space of fifty feet, used by the inhabitants for the
pasture of domestic animals. The climate of Mesopotamia, the
severe snows of winter followed by the burning heats of summer,
tried the strength of masonry, and Justinian found it necessary
to repair the fortress. He did far more than repair it. He
raised the inner wall by a new story, so that it reached the
unusual height of sixty feet, and he secured the supply of water
by diverting the river, which flowed outside the walls, into the
town by means of a channel worked between the rocks. He
also built barracks for the soldiers, so that the inhabitants were
spared the burden of quartering them.[1]

Chosroes attacked the city on the western side, and burned
the western gates of the outer wall, but no Persian was bold
enough to enter the interspace. He then began operations on
the eastern, the only side of the rock-bound city where digging
was possible, and ran a mine under the outer wall. The vigilance
of the besieged was baffled until the subterranean passage had
reached the foundations of the outer wall ; but then, according
to the story, a human or superhuman form in the guise of a
Persian soldier advanced near the wall under the pretext of
collecting discharged missiles, and while to the besiegers he
seemed to be mocking the men on the battlements, he was really
informing the besieged of the danger that was creeping upon
them unawares. The Romans then, by the counsel of Theodore, a clever engineer, dug a deep transverse trench between
the two walls so as to intersect the line of the enemy's excavation ; the Persian burrowers suddenly ran or fell into the Roman
pit ; those in front were slain, and the rest fled back unpursued
through the dark passage. Disgusted at this failure, Chosroes
raised the siege on receiving from the men of Daras 1000 lbs.
of silver. Justinian, indignant at his enemy's breach of faith,
broke off the negotiations for peace.

When he returned to Ctesiphon the victorious monarch
built a new city near his capital, on the model of Antioch, with
whose spoils it was beautified, and settled therein the captive
inhabitants of the original city, the remainder of whose days

[1] See Procopius, *De aed.* ii. 1 ; *B.P.*
ii. 13. The towers were 100 feet
high. The details of the description of
Procopius have been verified by the
discoveries of Sachau on the site
(*Reise in Syrien und Mesopotamien*,
395 *sqq.*). Cp. Chapot, *op. cit.* 313
sqq.

was perhaps more happily spent than if the generosity of the Edessenes had achieved its intention. The name of the new town, according to Persian writers,[1] was Rumia (Rome) ; according to Procopius it was called by the joint names of Chosroes and Antioch (Chosro-Antiocheia).[2]

II. *The Persian Invasion of Colchis, and the campaign of Belisarius in Mesopotamia* (A.D. 541)

From this time forth the kingdom of Lazica or Colchis began to play a more important part in the wars between the Romans and Persians. This country seems to have been then far poorer than it is to-day ; the Lazi depended for corn, salt, and other necessary articles of consumption on Roman merchants, and gave in exchange skins and slaves ; while " at present Mingrelia, though wretchedly cultivated, produces maize, millet, and barley in abundance ; the trees are everywhere festooned with vines, which grow naturally, and yield a very tolerable wine ; while salt is one of the main products of the neighbouring Georgia." [3] The Lazi were dependent on the Roman Empire, but the dependence consisted not in paying tribute but in committing the choice of their kings to the wisdom of the Roman Emperor. The nobles were in the habit of choosing wives among the Romans ; Gubazes, the king who invited Chosroes to enter his country, was the son of a Roman lady, and had served as a silentiary in the Byzantine palace.[4] The Lazic kingdom was a useful barrier against the trans-Caucasian Scythian races, and the inhabitants defended the mountain passes without causing any outlay of men or money to the Empire.

But when the Persians seized Iberia it was considered necessary to secure the country which barred them from the sea by the

---

[1] See Tabari, pp. 341-342 ; Rawlinson, *Seventh Oriental Monarchy*, p. 395. The new Antioch had one remarkable privilege ; slaves who fled thither, if acknowledged by its citizens as kinsmen, were exempted from the pursuit of their Persian masters.

[2] Procopius, *B.P.* ii. 15-19. Antioch itself was rebuilt by Justinian. The circuit of the wall was contracted, and the high cliffs of Orocasias were not included within the line. The course of the Orontes was diverted

so that it should flow by the new walls. Procop. *De aed.* ii. 10.

[3] Rawlinson, *op. cit.* p. 406, where the facts are quoted from Haxthausen's *Transcaucasia*. Procopius himself mentions (*B.G.* iv. 14) that the district of Muchiresis in Colchis was very fertile, producing wine and various kinds of corn.

[4] See Procop. *B.P.* ii. 29 ; *B.G.* iv. 9. Previous Lazic kings had married Roman ladies of senatorial family.

protection of Roman soldiers, and the unpopular general Peter, originally a Persian captive, was not one to make the natives rejoice at the presence of their defenders. Peter's successor was John Tzibus, a man of obscure station, whose unscrupulous skill in raising money made him a useful tool to the Emperor. He was an able man, for it was by his advice that Justinian built the town of Petra, to the south of the Phasis.[1] Here he established a monopoly and oppressed the natives. It was no longer possible for the Lazi to deal directly with the traders and buy their corn and salt at a reasonable price; John Tzibus, perched in the fortress of Petra, acted as a middleman, to whom both buyers and sellers were obliged to resort, and pay the highest or receive the lowest prices. In justification of this monopoly it may be remarked that it was the only practicable way of imposing a tax on the Lazi; and the imposition of a tax might have been deemed a necessary and just compensation for the defence of the country, notwithstanding the facts that it was garrisoned solely in Roman interests, and that the garrison itself was unwelcome to the natives.

Exasperated by these grievances, Gubazes, the king of Lazica, sent an embassy to Chosroes, inviting him to recover a venerable kingdom, and pointing out that if he expelled the Romans from Lazica he would have access to the Euxine, whose waters could convey his forces against Byzantium, while he would have an opportunity of establishing a connexion with those other enemies of Rome, the barbarians north of the Caucasus.[2] Chosroes consented to the proposals of the ambassadors; and keeping his real intention secret, pretended that pressing affairs required his presence in Iberia.

Under the guidance of the envoys, Chosroes and his army passed into the thick woods and difficult hill-passes of Colchis, cutting down as they went lofty and leafy trees, which hung in dense array on the steep acclivities, and using the trunks to smooth or render passable rugged or dangerous places. When

---

[1] The site of Petra is uncertain. It has been identified with Ujenar (by Dubois de Montpéreux, *Voyage autour du Caucase*, iii. 86), 15 miles S.E. of the mouth of the Phasis and 12 miles from the coast. But the description of Procopius, *B.G.* ii. 17, suggests that it was quite close to the sea.

[2] Another element in the Colchian policy of Chosroes was the circumstance that if Lazica were Persian, the Iberians would have no power in the rear to support them if they revolted. Compare Procopius, *B.P.* ii. 28.

they had penetrated to the middle of the country, they were met by Gubazes, who paid oriental homage to the great king. The chief object was to capture Petra, the stronghold of Roman power, and dislodge the tradesman, as Chosroes contemptuously termed the monopolist, John Tzibus. A detachment of the army under Aniabedes was sent on in advance to attack the fortress ; and when this officer arrived before the walls he found the gates shut, yet the place seemed totally deserted, and not a trace of an inhabitant was visible. A messenger was sent to inform Chosroes of this surprise ; the rest of the army hastened to the spot ; a battering-ram was applied to the gate, while the monarch watched the proceedings from the top of an adjacent hill. Suddenly the gate flew open, and a multitude of Roman soldiers rushing forth overwhelmed those Persians who were applying the engine, and, having killed many others who were drawn up hard by, speedily retreated and closed the gate. The unfortunate Aniabedes (according to others, the officer who was charged with the operation of the battering-ram) was impaled for the crime of being vanquished by a huckster.

A regular siege now began. It was inevitable that Petra should be captured, says our historian Procopius, in the vein of Herodotus,[1] and therefore John, the governor, was slain by an accidental missile, and the garrison, deprived of their commander, became careless and lax. On one side Petra was protected by the sea, landwards inaccessible cliffs defied the skill or bravery of an assailant, save only where one narrow entrance divided the line of steep cliffs and admitted of access from the plain. This gap between the rocks was filled by a long wall, the ends of which were commanded by towers constructed in an unusual manner, for instead of being hollow all the way up, they were made of solid stone to a considerable height, so that they could not be shaken by the most powerful engine. But oriental inventiveness undermined these wonders of solidity. A mine was bored under the base of one of the towers, the lower stones were removed and replaced by wood, the demolishing force of fire loosened the upper layers of stones, and the tower fell. This success was decisive, as the besieged recognised ; they readily capitulated, and the victors did not lay hands on any property in the fortress save the possessions of the defunct governor.

---

[1] Καὶ γὰρ ἔδει Πέτραν Χόσρωι ἁλῶναι.

Having placed a Persian garrison in Petra, Chosroes remained no longer in Lazica, for the news had reached him that Belisarius was about to invade Assyria, and he hurried back to defend his dominions.

Belisarius, accompanied by all the Goths whom he had led in triumph from Italy, except the Gothic king himself, had proceeded in the spring to take command of the eastern army in Mesopotamia.[1] Having found out by spies that no invasion was meditated by Chosroes, whose presence was demanded in Iberia—the design on Lazica was kept effectually concealed— the Roman general determined to lead the whole army, along with the auxiliary Saracens of Harith into Persian territory. It is remarkable that in this campaign although Belisarius was chief in command he never seems to have ventured or cared to execute his strategic plans without consulting the advice of the other officers. It is difficult to say whether this was due to distrust of his own judgment and the reflexion that many of the subordinate generals had more recent experience of Persian warfare than himself,[2] or to a fear that some of the leaders in an army composed of soldiers of many races might prove refractory and impatient of too peremptory orders. At Daras a council of war decided on an immediate advance.

The army marched towards Nisibis, which was too strong to be attacked, and moved forward to the fortress of Sisaurana. where an assault was at first repulsed with loss.[3] Belisarius decided to invest the place, but as the Saracens were useless for siege warfare, he sent Harith and his troops, accompanied by 1200 of his own retainers, to invade and harry Assyria, intending to cross the Tigris himself when he had taken the fort. The garrison was not supplied with provisions, and soon consented to surrender ; all the Christians were dismissed free, the fire-worshippers were sent to Byzantium [4] to await the Emperor's pleasure, and the fort was levelled to the ground.

Meanwhile the plundering expedition of Harith was successful,

---

[1] The Italian generals accompanied Belisarius. One of them, Valerian, succeeded Martin as general in Armenia ; Martin had been transferred to Mesopotamia.

[2] This is dwelt on in one of the speeches which Procopius places in the mouth of Belisarius (*B.P.* ii. 16).

[3] Between Nisibis and the Tigris (the same as Sisara in Amm. Marc. xviii. 10. 1).

[4] These Persians, with their leader Bleschanes, were afterwards sent to Italy against the Goths. It was Roman policy to employ Persian captives against the Goths, Gothic captives against the Persians.

but he played his allies false. Desiring to retain all the spoils for himself, he invented a story to rid himself of the Romans who accompanied him,[1] and he sent no information to Belisarius. This was not the only cause of anxiety that vexed the general's mind. The Roman, especially the Thracian, soldiers were not inured to the intense heat of the dry Mesopotamian climate in midsummer, and disease broke out in the army, demoralised by physical exhaustion. All the soldiers were anxious to return to more clement districts. There was nothing to be done but yield to the prevailing wish, which was shared by all the generals. It cannot be claimed that the campaign of Belisarius accomplished much to set off against the acquisition of Petra by the Persians.

It was indeed whispered by the general's enemies that he had culpably missed a great opportunity. They insinuated that if, after the capture of Sisaurana, he had advanced beyond the Tigris he might have carried the war up to the walls of Ctesiphon. But he sacrificed the interests of the Empire to private motives, and retreated in order to meet his wife who had just arrived in the East and punish her for her infidelity.[2] The scandals may be true, but it is impossible to say how far they affected the military conduct of Belisarius.

III. *The Persian Invasion of Commagene* (A.D. 542) [3]

The first act of Chosroes when he crossed the Euphrates in spring was to send 6000 soldiers to besiege the town of Sergiopolis because the bishop Candidus, who had undertaken to pay the ransom of the Surene captives two years before, was unable to collect the amount, and found Justinian deaf to his appeals for aid. But the town lay in a desert, and the besiegers were soon obliged to abandon their design in consequence of the drought. It was not the Persian's intention to waste his time in despoiling the province of Euphratensis ; he purposed to invade Palestine and plunder the treasures of Jerusalem. But this exploit was reserved for his grandson of the same name, and the invader returned to his kingdom having accomplished

---

[1] Trajan and John the Glutton were in command of these 1200 ὑπασπισταί. When they separated from Harith they proceeded to Theodosiopolis, in order to avoid a hostile army which did not exist.

[2] Procopius, *H.A.* 17-25. For the story see above, p. 60.

[3] Procopius, *B.P.* ii. 20, 21.

almost nothing. This speedy retreat was probably due to the outbreak of the Plague in Persia, though the Roman historian attributes it to the address of Belisarius.

Belisarius travelled by post-horses (*veredi*) from Constantinople to the Euphratesian province, and taking up his quarters at Europus [1] on the Euphrates, he collected there the bulk of the troops who were dispersed throughout the province in its various cities. Chosroes was curious about the personality of Belisarius, of whom he had heard so much, the conqueror of the Vandals, the conqueror of the Goths, who had led two fallen monarchs in triumph to the feet of Justinian. Accordingly he sent Abandanes [2] as an envoy to the Roman general on the pretext of learning why Justinian had not sent ambassadors to negotiate a peace.

Belisarius did not mistake the true nature of this mission, and determined to make an impression. Having sent a body of one thousand cavalry to the left bank of the river, to harass the enemy if they attempted to cross, he selected six thousand tall and comely men from his army and proceeded with them to a place at some distance from his camp, as if on a hunting expedition. He had constructed for himself a pavilion [3] of thick canvas, which he set up, as in a desert spot, and when he knew that the ambassador was approaching, he arranged his soldiers with careful negligence. On either side of him stood Thracians and Illyrians, a little farther off the Goths, then Heruls, Vandals, and Moors ; all were arrayed in close-fitting linen tunics and drawers, without a cloak or *epomis* to disguise the symmetry of their forms, and, like hunters, each carried a whip as well as some weapon, a sword, an axe, or a bow. They did not stand still, as men on duty, but moved carelessly about, glancing idly and indifferently at the Persian envoy, who soon arrived and marvelled.

To the envoy's complaint that the Emperor had not sent an embassy to his master, Belisarius answered, with an air of amusement, " It is not the habit of men to transact their affairs as Chosroes has transacted his. Others, when aggrieved, send an embassy first, and if they fail in obtaining satisfaction, resort

---

[1] Yerabus. Cp. Chapot, *op. cit.* p. 280.

[2] One of the βασιλικοὶ γραμματεῖς (*notarii*).

[3] Παπυλεών, which Procopius introduces with one of his usual apologetic formulae for words that are not Greek.

to war ; but he attacks and then talks of peace." The presence
and bearing of the Roman general, and the appearance of his
followers, hunting indifferently at a short distance from the
Persian camp without any precautions, made a profound impression on Abandanes, and he persuaded his master to abandon
the proposed expedition. Chosroes may have reflected that the
triumph of a king over a general would be no humiliation for
the general, while the triumph of a mere general over a king
would be very humiliating for the king ; such at least is the
colouring that the general's historian puts on the king's retreat.
According to the same authority, Chosroes hesitated to risk
the passage of the Euphrates while the enemy was so near, but
Belisarius, with his smaller numbers, did not attempt to oppose
him.[1] A truce was made, and a rich citizen of Edessa was
delivered, an unwilling hostage, to Chosroes. In their retreat,
the Persians turned aside to take and demolish Callinicum, the
Coblenz of the Euphrates, which fell an easy prey to their assault,
as the walls were in process of renovation at the time. This
retirement of Chosroes, according to Procopius, procured for
Belisarius greater glory than he had won by his victories in
the West. But Belisarius was now recalled to conduct the
war in Italy.

The account of Procopius, which coming from a less able
historian would be rejected on account of internal improbability,
cannot be accepted with confidence. It displays such a marked
tendency to glorify Belisarius, that it can hardly be received as
a candid story of the actual transactions. Besides, there is a
certain inconsistency. If Chosroes retired *for fear of* Belisarius,
as Procopius would have us believe, why was it he who received
the hostage, and how did he venture to take Callinicum ? As
there actually existed a sufficient cause, unconnected with the
Romans, to induce his return to Persia, namely the outbreak
of the Plague, we may suspect that this was its true motive.[2]

---

[1] A Persian army always carried
with it materials for constructing
pontoons (Proc. *B.P.* ii. 21), and they
crossed by such a bridge on this
occasion.

[2] So Rawlinson (*op. cit.* p. 401),
who perhaps is more generous to
Procopius than he deserves. The
Plague broke out in Persia in the
summer of 542.

IV. *The Roman Invasion of Persarmenia* (A.D. 543) [1]

In spite of the Plague Chosroes set forth in the following spring to invade Roman Armenia.   He advanced into the district of Azerbiyan (Atropatene), and halted at the great shrine of Persian fire-worship, where the Magi kept alive an eternal flame, which Procopius wished to identify with the fire of Roman Vesta. Here the Persian monarch waited for some time, having received a message that two Imperial ambassadors [2] were on their way to him.   But the ambassadors did not arrive, because one of them fell ill by the road ; and Chosroes did not pursue his northward journey, because the Plague broke out in his army.   His general Nabedes sent the bishop of Dubios to Valerian, the general in Armenia, with complaints that the expected embassy had not appeared.   The bishop was accompanied by his brother, who secretly communicated to Valerian the valuable information that Chosroes was just then encompassed by perplexities, the spread of the Plague, and the revolt of one of his sons.   It was a favourable opportunity for the Romans, and Justinian directed all the generals stationed in the East to join forces to invade Persarmenia.

Martin was now Master of Soldiers in the East. He does not appear to have possessed much actual authority over the other commanders.   They at first encamped in the same district, but did not unite their forces, which in all amounted to about thirty thousand men.   Martin himself, with Ildiger and Theoctistus, encamped at Kitharizon, a fort about four days' march from Theodosiopolis ; the troops of Peter and Adolius took up their quarters in the vicinity ; while Valerian stationed himself close to Theodosiopolis and was joined there by Narses with a body of Heruls and Armenians.   The Emperor's cousin Justus and some other commanders remained during the campaign far to the south in the neighbourhood of Martyropolis, where they made incursions of no great importance.

At first the various generals made separate inroads, but they ultimately united their regiments in the spacious plain of Dubios, eight days from Theodosiopolis.   This plain, well suited for equestrian exercise, and richly populated, was a famous rendez-

[1] Proc. *ib.* 24, 25.

[2] Constantianus, an Illyrian, and Sergius of Edessa, both rhetors and men of parts.

vous for traders of all nations, Indian, Iberian, Persian, and Roman.[1] About thirteen miles from Dubios there was a steep mountain, on the side of which was perched a village called Anglôn, protected by a strong fortress. Here the Persian general Nabedes, with four thousand soldiers, had taken up an almost impregnable position, blocking the precipitous streets of the village with stones and wagons. The ranks of the Roman army, as it marched to Anglôn, fell into disorder ; the want of union among the generals, who acknowledged no supreme leader, led to confusion in the line of march ; mixed bodies of soldiers and sutlers turned aside to plunder ; and the security which they displayed might have warranted a spectator in prophesying a speedy reverse. As they drew near to the fortress, an attempt was made to marshal the somewhat demoralised troops in the form of two wings and a centre. The centre was commanded by Martin, the right wing by Peter, the left by Valerian ; and all advanced in irregular and wavering line, on account of the roughness of the ground.[2] The best course for the Persians was obviously to act on the defensive. Narses and his Heruls, who were probably on the left wing with Valerian, were the first to attack the foes and to press them back into the fort. Drawn on by the retreating enemy through the narrow village streets, they were suddenly taken in the flank and in the rear by an ambush of Persians who had concealed themselves in the houses. The valiant Narses was wounded in the temple ; his brother succeeded in carrying him from the fray, but the wound proved mortal. This repulse of the foremost spread the alarm to the regiments that were coming up behind ; Nabedes comprehended that the moment had arrived to take the offensive and let loose his soldiers on the panic-stricken ranks of the assailants ; and all the Heruls, who fought according to their wont without helmets or breastplates,[3] fell before the charge of the Persians. The Romans did not tarry ; they cast their arms away and fled in wild confusion, and the mounted soldiers galloped so fast that few horses survived the flight ; but the Persians, apprehensive of an ambush, did not pursue.

Never, says Procopius, did the Romans experience such a

---

[1] Dubios corresponds to Duin.

[2] Procopius assigns as an additional cause the want of discipline or previous marshalling of the troops ; but I feel some suspicions of the whole account of this campaign.

[3] The Herul's only armour was a shield and a cloak of thick stuff.

great disaster. This exaggeration inclines us to be sceptical. We can hardly avoid detecting in his narrative a desire to place the generals in as bad a light as possible, just as in his description of the hostilities of the preceding year we saw reason to suspect him of unduly magnifying the behaviour of his hero Belisarius. In fact his aim seems to be to draw a strong and striking contrast between a brilliant campaign and a miserable failure. We have seen reason to doubt the exceptional brilliancy of the achievement of Belisarius ; and we may wonder whether the defeat at Anglôn was really overwhelming.

V. The Persian Invasion of Mesopotamia ; Siege of Edessa (A.D. 544) [1]

His failure at Edessa in the first year of the war had rankled in the mind of the Sassanid monarch. The confidence of the inhabitants that they enjoyed a special divine protection in virtue of the letter of Jesus to Abgar was a challenge to the superstition of the Fire-worshippers, and the Magi and their king could not bear the thought that they had been defeated by the God of the Christians. Chosroes comforted himself by threatening to enslave the Edessenes, and make the site of their city a pasture for sheep. But the place was strong. Its walls had been ruined again and again by earthquakes, against which the divine promise did not secure it, and again and again rebuilt. It had suffered this calamity recently (A.D. 525) and had been restored by Justin, who honoured it by his own name. But Justinopolis had as little power over the tongues of men as Anastasiopolis or Theupolis. Edessa, the city of Abgar, remained Edessa, as Daras remained Daras and Antioch Antioch. Justinian had reconstructed the fortifications and made it stronger than ever, and installed hydraulic arrangements to prevent the inundations of the river Scyrtus which flowed through the town.[2]

Realising the strength of the place, Chosroes would have been glad to avoid the risk of a second failure, and he proposed to

[1] Procopius, *B.P.* ii. 26-28.
[2] Evagrius, *H.E.* iv. 8 ; Procopius, *De aed.* ii. 7 ; *II.A.* 18. The chief feature of the fortifications of Justinian were the new walls which he built to the crest of a hill overtopping the citadel. For the plan of the castle see Texier and Pullan, *Byzantium Architecture*, p. 183.

the inhabitants that they should pay him an immense sum or allow him to take all the riches in the city. His proposal was refused, though if he had made a reasonable demand it would have been agreed to ; and the Persian army encamped at somewhat less than a mile from the walls. Three experienced generals, Martin, Peter, and Peranius, were stationed in Edessa at this time.

On the eighth day from the beginning of the siege, Chosroes caused a large number of hewn trees to be strewn on the ground in the shape of an immense square, at about a stone's throw from the city ; earth was heaped over the trees, so as to form a flat mound, and stones, not cut smooth and regular as for building, but rough hewn, were piled on the top, additional strength being secured by a layer of wooden beams placed between the stones and the earth. It required many days to raise this mound to a height sufficient to overtop the walls. At first the workmen were harassed by a sally of Huns, one of whom, named Argek, slew twenty-seven with his own hand. This could not be repeated, as henceforward a guard of Persians stood by to protect the builders. As the work went on, the mound seems to have been extended in breadth as well as in height, and to have approached closer to the walls, so that the workmen came within range of the archers who manned the battlements, but they protected themselves by thick and long strips of canvas, woven of goat hair, which were hung on poles, and proved an adequate shield. Foiled in their attempts to obstruct the progress of the threatening pile, which they saw rising daily higher and higher, the besieged sent an embassy to Chosroes. The spokesman of the ambassadors was the physician Stephen, a native of Edessa, who had enjoyed the friendship and favour of Kavad, whom he had healed of a disease, and had superintended the education of Chosroes himself. But even he, influential though he was, could not obtain more than the choice of three alternatives—the surrender of Peter and Peranius, who, originally Persian subjects, had presumed to make war against their master's son ; the payment of 50,000 lbs. of gold (two million and a quarter pounds sterling) ; or the reception of Persian deputies, who should ransack the city for treasures and bring all to the Persian camp. All these proposals were too extravagant to be entertained for an instant ;

the ambassadors returned in dejection, and the erection of the mound advanced. A new embassy was sent, but was not even admitted to an audience ; and when the plan of raising the city wall was tried, the besiegers found no difficulty in elevating their structure also.

At length the Romans resorted to the plan of undermining the mound, but when their excavation had reached the middle of the pile the noise of the subterranean digging was heard by the Persian builders, who immediately dug or hewed a hole in their own structure in order to discover the miners. These, knowing that they were detected, filled up the remotest part of the excavated passage and adopted a new device. Beneath the end of the mound nearest to the city they formed a small subterranean chamber with stones, boards, and earth. Into this room they threw piles of wood of the most inflammable kind, which had been smeared over with sulphur, bitumen, and oil of cedar. As soon as the mound was completed,[1] they kindled the logs, and kept the fire replenished with fresh fuel. A considerable time was required for the fire to penetrate the entire extent of the mound, and smoke began to issue prematurely from that part where the foundations were first inflamed. The besieged adopted an obvious device to mislead the besiegers. They cast burning arrows and hurled vessels filled with burning embers on various parts of the mound ; the Persian soldiers ran to and fro to extinguish them, believing that the smoke, which really came from beneath, was caused by the flaming missiles ; and some thus employed were pierced by arrows from the walls. Next morning Chosroes himself visited the mound and was the first to discover the true cause of the smoke, which now issued in denser volume. The whole army was summoned to the scene amid the jeers of the Romans, who surveyed from the walls the consternation of their foes. The torrents of water with which the stones were flooded increased the vapour instead of quenching it and caused the sulphurous flames to operate more violently. In the evening the volume of smoke was so great that it could be seen as far away to the south as at the city of Carrhae ;[2] and the fire,

---

[1] Just before its completion, Martin made proposals for peace, but the Persians were unwilling to treat.

[2] The distance of Carrhae from Edessa was about thirty miles.

which had been gradually working upwards as well as spreading beneath, at length gained the air and overtopped the surface. Then the Persians desisted from their futile endeavours.

Six days later an attack was made on the walls at early dawn, and but for a farmer who chanced to be awake and gave the alarm, the garrison might have been surprised. The assailants were repulsed ; and another assault on the great gate at mid-day likewise failed.[1]   One final effort was made by the baffled enemy. The ruins of the half-demolished mound were covered with a floor of bricks, and from this elevation a grand attack was made. At first the Persians seemed to be superior, but the enthusiasm which prevailed in the city was ultimately crowned with victory. The peasants, even the women and the children, ascended the walls and took a part in the combat ; cauldrons of oil were kept continually boiling, that the burning liquid might be poured on the heads of the assailants ; and the Persians, unable to endure the fury of their enemies, fell back and confessed to Chosroes that they were vanquished.   The enraged despot drove them back to the encounter ; they made yet one supreme effort, and were yet once more discomfited.   Edessa was saved, and the siege unwillingly abandoned by the disappointed king, who, however, had the satisfaction of receiving 500 lbs. of gold from the weary though victorious Edessenes.

In the following year, A.D. 545, a truce [2] was concluded for five years, Justinian consenting to pay 2000 lbs. of gold.   But Chosroes refused to assent to the Emperor's demand that this truce should apply to operations in Lazica, where he believed that he held a strong position.   Hence during the duration of the truce, there was an " imperfect " war between the two powers in Colchis.   Justinian readily acceded to a request of the king to permit a certain Greek physician, named Tribunus,[3] to remain at the Persian court for a year.   Tribunus of Palestine, the best medical authority of the age, was, we are told, a man of distinguished virtue and piety, and highly valued by Chosroes,

---

[1] At this juncture the Persians desired to treat, and informed the garrison that a Roman ambassador from Constantinople had arrived in their camp. They allowed the ambassador to enter Edessa, but Martin was suspicious of their intentions, and feigning to be ill said that he would send envoys in three days.

[2] Procopius, *B.P.* ii. 28. The 2000 lbs. were calculated at the rate of 400 a year.

[3] Cp. Zacharias Myt. xii. 7, where he is called Tribonian.

whose constitution was delicate and constantly required the services of a physician.   At the end of the year the king permitted him to ask a boon, and instead of proposing remuneration for himself he begged for the freedom of some Roman prisoners. Chosroes not only liberated those whom he named, but others also to the number of three thousand.

§ 4. *The Lazic War* (A.D. 549–557) [1]

The Lazi soon found that the despotism of the Persian fireworshipper was less tolerable than the oppression of the Christian monopolists, and repented that they had taught the armies of the great king to penetrate the defiles of Colchis. It was not long before the Magi attempted to convert the new province to a faith which was odious to the christianised natives, and it became known that Chosroes entertained the intention of removing the inhabitants and colonising the land with Persians. Gubazes, who learned that Chosroes was plotting against his life, hastened to seek the pardon and the protection of Justinian. In A.D. 549, 7000 Romans were sent to Lazica, under the command of Dagisthacus, to recover the fortress of Petra. Their forces were strengthened by the addition of a thousand Tzanic auxiliaries.

The acquisition of Colchis pleased Chosroes so highly, and the province appeared to him of such eminent importance, that he took every precaution to secure it. [2]   A highway was constructed from the Iberian confines through the country's hilly and woody passes, so that not only cavalry but elephants could traverse it.   The fortress of Petra was supplied with sufficient stores of provisions, consisting of salted meat and corn, to last for five years ; no wine was provided, but vinegar and a sort of grain from which a spirituous liquor could be distilled.   The armour and weapons which were stored in the magazines would, as was afterwards found, have accoutred five times the number of the besiegers ; and a cunning device was adopted to supply

---

[1] I have only summarised the military operations in Lazica, recorded by Procopius and Agathias.   Full accounts will be found in the first edition of this work, and in Lebeau, ix. Bks. 47 and 49.

[2] He tried to build a fleet in the Euxine, but the material was destroyed by lightning.

the city with water, while the enemy should delude themselves
with the idea that they had cut off the supply.

When Dagisthaeus laid siege to the town the garrison consisted of 1500 Persians. He committed the mistake of not
occupying the clisurae or passes from Iberia into Colchis, so as
to prevent the arrival of Persian reinforcements. The siege was
protracted for a long time, and the small garrison suffered heavy
losses. At last Mermeroes, allowed to enter Colchis unopposed
with large forces of cavalry and infantry, arrived at the pass
which commands the plain of Petra. Here his progress was
withstood by a hundred Romans, but after a long and bloody
battle the weary guards gave way, and the Persians reached the
summit. When Dagisthaeus learned this he raised the siege.

Mermeroes left 3000 men in Petra and provisioned it for a
short time. Leaving 5000 men under Phabrigus in Colchis, and
instructing them to keep Petra supplied with food, he withdrew
to Persarmenia. Disaster soon befell these troops ; they were
surprised in their camp by Dagisthaeus and Gubazes in the
early morning, and but few escaped. All the provisions brought
from Iberia for the use of Petra were destroyed, and the eastern
passes of Colchis were garrisoned.[1]

In the spring of A.D. 550 Chorianes entered Colchis with a
Persian army, and encamped by the river Hippis, where a battle
was fought in which Dagisthaeus was victorious, and Chorianes
lost his life. Dagisthaeus, however, was accused of misconduct-
ing the siege of Petra, through disloyalty or culpable negligence.
Justinian ordered his arrest, and appointed Bessas, who had
recently returned from Italy, in his stead, Men wondered at this
appointment, and thought that the Emperor was foolish to
entrust the command to a general who was far advanced in
years, and whose career in the West had been inglorious ; but
the choice, as we shall see, was justified by the result.

The first labour that devolved on Bessas was to suppress a
revolt of the Abasgians. The territory of this nation extended
along the lunated eastern coast of the Euxine, and was separated
from Colchis by the country of the Apsilians, who inhabited

---

[1] At this point the two books of
Procopius known as *De bello Persico*
come to an end, but the thread of the
narrative is resumed in the *De bello
Gothico*, Bk. iv., which was written
after the other books had been given
to the world. Procopius apologises
for the necessity which compels him
to abandon his method of *geographical*
divisions (*B.G.* iv. 1).

the district between the western spurs of Caucasus and the sea. The Apsilians had long been Christians, and submitted to the lordship of their Lazic neighbours, who had at one time held sway over the Abasgians. Abasgia was governed by two princes, of whom one ruled in the west and the other in the east. These potentates increased their revenue by the sale of beautiful boys, whom they tore in early childhood from the arms of their reluctant parents and made eunuchs ; for in the Roman Empire these comely and useful slaves were in constant demand, and secured a high price from the opulent nobles. It was the glory of Justinian to bring about the abolition of this unnatural practice ; the people supported the remonstrances which the Emperor's envoy, himself an Abasgian eunuch, made to their kings ; the royal tyranny was abolished, and a people which had worshipped trees embraced Christianity, to enjoy, as they thought, a long period of freedom under the protection of the Roman Augustus. But the mildest protectorate tends insensibly to become domination. Roman soldiers entered the country, and taxes were imposed on the new friends of the Emperor. The Abasgi preferred the despotism of men of their own blood to servitude to a foreign master, and they elected two new kings, Opsites in the east and Sceparnas in the west. But it would have been rash to brave the jealous anger of Justinian without the support of some stronger power, and when Nabedes, after the great defeat of the Persians on the Hippis, visited Lazica, he received sixty noble hostages from the Abasgians, who craved the protection of Chosroes. They had not taken warning from the repentance of the Lazi, that it was a hazardous measure to invoke the Persian. The king, Sceparnas, was soon afterwards summoned to the Sassanid court, and his colleague Opsites prepared to resist the Roman forces which Bessas despatched against him under the command of Wilgang (a Herul) and John the Armenian.

In the southern borders of Abasgia, close to the Apsilian frontier, an extreme mountain of the Caucasian chain descends in the form of a staircase to the waters of the Euxine. Here, on one of the lower spurs, the Abasgi had built a strong and roomy fastness in which they hoped to defy the pursuit of an invader. A rough and difficult glen separated it from the sea, while the ingress was so narrow that two persons could not enter abreast, and so low that it was necessary to crawl. The Romans, who had sailed from the Phasis, or perhaps from Trapezus, landed on the Apsilian borders, and proceeded by land to this glen, where they found the whole Abasgian nation arrayed to defend a pass which it would have been easy to hold against far larger numbers. Wilgang remained with half the army at the foot of the glen, while John and the other half embarked in the boats which had accompanied the coast march of the soldiers. They landed at no great distance, and by a circuitous route were able to approach the unsuspecting foe in the rear. The Abasgians fled in consternation towards their fortress ; fugitives and pursuers, mingled together, strove to penetrate the narrow aperture, and those inside could not prevent enemies from entering with friends. But the Romans when they were within the walls found a new labour awaiting them. The Abasgi fortified themselves in their houses, and vexed their adversaries by showering missiles from above. At length the Romans employed the aid of fire, and the dwellings were soon reduced to ashes. Some of the people were burnt, others, including the wives of the kings, were taken alive, while Opsites escaped to the neighbouring Sabirs.

The truce of five years had now elapsed (April, A.D. 550), and while new negotiations began between the courts of Constantinople and Ctesiphon, Bessas addressed himself to the enterprise in which Dagisthaeus had failed, the capture of Petra. The garrison was brave and resolute, and the siege was long. But the persistency of Bessas achieved success and the stronghold fell in the early spring of A.D. 551. The gallant soldier, John the Armenian, was slain in the final assault. When Mermeroes, who was approaching to relieve Petra, heard the news, he retraced his steps, in order to attack Archaeopolis and other fortresses on the right bank of the Phasis.[1]   His siege of Archaeopolis [2]

---

[1] At this time the total number of Roman soldiers in Lazica amounted to 12,000. Of these 3000 were stationed at Archaeopolis, the remaining 9000, with an auxiliary force of 800 Tzani, were entrenched in a camp near the mouth of the Phasis. A year later the forces amounted to 50,000 (Agathias, iii. 8). A comparison of these numbers with those of the

expeditions to Africa and Italy (see the following chapters) shows the importance of the occupation of Lazica in the eyes of the Imperial government.

[2] Dubois de Montpéreux (*op. cit.* iii. 51) finds Archaeopolis at Nakolakevi, on the Chobos. Mermeroes made another attack on it in 552.

was a failure. He suffered a considerable defeat and was forced to retire. He succeeded in taking some minor fortresses in the course of the following campaigns (A.D. 552–554).[1] His death, which occurred in the autumn of A.D. 554, was a serious loss to Chosroes, for, though old and lame, and unable even to ride, he was not only brave and experienced, but as unwearying and energetic as a youth. Nachoragan was sent to succeed him. Although the operations of the Persians in these years had been attended with no conspicuous success, they had gained one considerable advantage without loss to themselves. The small inland district of Suania, in the hills to the north of Lazica, had hitherto been a dependency on that kingdom. Its princes were nominated by the Lazic kings. The Suanians now (A.D. 552) repudiated this connexion and went over to the Persians, who sent troops to occupy the territory.[2]

In the meantime the question of the renewal of the five years' truce had been engaging the attention of the Roman and Persian courts, and the negotiations had continued for eighteen months. At length it was renewed (A.D. 551, autumn) for another period of five years, the Romans agreeing to pay 2600 lbs. of gold,[3] and, as before, it was not to affect the hostilities in Colchis. A contemporary states that there was much popular indignation that Chosroes should have extorted from the Empire 4600 lbs. of gold in eleven and a half years, and the people of Constantinople murmured at the excessive consideration which the Emperor

---

[1] There has been some difficulty about the chronology of the last years of the Lazic war. The narrative of Procopius ends B.G. iv. 17. He marks the winter 551–552 in c. 16, the spring of 552 in c. 17, and the failure of Mermeroes in that year. The story is continued by Agathias, ii. 18, who refers briefly to the futile attacks of Mermeroes on Archaeopolis, mentioned by Procopius, and then describes the continuation of hostilities, without mentioning that a winter had intervened. In ii. 22 he notices the death of Mermeroes, and ii. 27 places that event in 28th year of Justinian and 25th of Chosroes (but the 24th of Chosroes corresponds to 28 Justin.) = A.D. 554–555. This means that the events related in ii. 19-22 occurred in 553 and 554, and that the author has

omitted to distinguish the years. After this point he invariably marks the years (iii. 15, spring 555 ; 28 and iv. 12, winter 555–556 ; iv. 13, spring and summer 556 ; 15, winter 556–557). This chronology (so Clinton, F.R., sub annis) is borne out by the notice of the earthquake in v. 3, which is dated by John Mal. xviii. p. 488.

[2] We learn this from the negotiations of A.D. 562 ; Menander, De leg. Rom. fr. 3, pp. 178, 186-187. In the reign of Leo, some Suanian forts had been seized by the Persians, and the Suanians had sought help from the Emperor, c. A.D. 468. Priscus, De leg. gent. fr. 22.

[3] At 400 lbs. annually, the rate agreed on in 445. The extra 600 were for the year and a half spent in negotiation. See Proc. B.G. iv. 15.

displayed towards the Persian ambassador Isdigunas [1] and his retinue, who were permitted to move about in the city, without a Roman escort, as if it belonged to them.

Meanwhile king Gubazes, who had been engaged in frequent quarrels with the Roman commanders, sent a complaint to Justinian accusing them of negligence in conducting the war. Bessas, Martin, and Rusticus were specially named. The Emperor deposed Bessas from his post, but assigned the chief command to Martin and did not recall Rusticus. This Rusticus was the Emperor's pursebearer who had been sent to bestow rewards on soldiers for special merit. He and Martin determined to remove Gubazes. To secure themselves from blame, they despatched John, brother of Rusticus, to Justinian with the false message that Gubazes was secretly favouring the Persians. Justinian was surprised, and determined to summon the king to Constantinople. " What," asked John, " is to be done, if he refuses ? " " Compel him," said the Emperor ; " he is our subject." " But if he resist ? " urged the conspirator. " Then treat him as a *tyrant*." " And will he who should slay him have naught to fear ? " " Naught, if he act disobediently and be slain as an enemy." Justinian signed a letter to this effect, and armed with it John returned to Colchis. The conspirators hastened to execute their treacherous design. Gubazes was invited to assist in an attack on the fortress of Onoguris, and with a few attendants he met the Roman army on the banks of the Chobus. An altercation arose between the king and Rusticus, and on the pretext that the gainsayer of a Roman general must necessarily be a friend of the enemy, John drew his dagger and plunged it in the royal breast. The wound was not mortal but it unhorsed the king, and when he attempted to rise from the ground, a blow from the squire of Rusticus killed him outright.[2]

The Lazi silently buried their king according to their customs, and turned away in mute reproach from their Roman protectors. They no longer took part in the military operations, but hid

---

[1] Izedh - Gushnasp ('Ισδεγουσνάφ in Menander). The solemnities observed in the reception and treatment of this embassy were recorded by Peter the Patrician, and are preserved in Constantine Porph. *Cer.* i. 89 and 90. The ambassador is here called 'Ισδεκος (p. 405). He returned to Persia in spring A.D. 552 and the treaty received the seal of Chosroes (Proc. *B.G.* i. 17).

[2] Agathias, iii. 2-4. These events belong to the autumn and winter 554-555.

themselves away as men who had lost their hereditary glory. The other commanders, Buzes and Justin the son of Germanus, concealed the indignation which they felt, supposing that the outrage had the Emperor's authority. Some months later, when winter had begun, the Lazi met in secret council in some remote Caucasian ravine, and debated whether they should throw themselves on the protection of Chosroes. But their attachment to the Christian religion as well as their memory of Persian oppression forbade them to take this step, and they decided to appeal for justice and satisfaction to the Emperor, and at the same time to supplicate him to nominate Tzath, the younger brother of Gubazes, as their new king. Justinian promptly complied with both demands. Athanasius, a senator of high repute, was sent to investigate the circumstances of the assassination, and on his arrival he incarcerated Rusticus and John, pending a trial. In the spring (A.D. 555) Tzath arrived in royal state, and when the Lazi beheld the Roman army saluting him as he rode in royal apparel, a tunic embroidered with gold reaching to his feet, a white mantle with a gold stripe, red shoes, a turban adorned with gold and gems, and a crown, they forgot their sorrow and escorted him in a gay and brilliant procession. It was not till the ensuing autumn [1] that the authors of the death of the late king were brought to justice, and the natives witnessed the solemn procedure of a Roman trial. Rusticus and John were executed. Martin's complicity was not so clear, and the Emperor, to whom his case was referred, deposed him from his command in favour of his own cousin Justin, the son of Germanus.[2] Martin perhaps would not have been acquitted if he had not been popular with the army and a highly competent general.

Immediately after the assassination of Gubazes, the Romans who had assembled in full force before the fortress of Onoguris sustained a severe and inglorious defeat at the hands of 3000 Persians (A.D. 554). In the following spring, Phasis (Poti), at the mouth of the like-named river, was attacked by Nachoragan, and an irregular battle before this town resulted in a victory for Martin which wiped out the disgrace of Onoguris.[3] In the

---

[1] Cp. Agathias, iv. 12 *ad init.*

[2] Justin was created στρατηγὸς αὐτοκράτωρ, Agathias, iv. 21.

[3] In consequence of this failure, Nachoragan was flayed alive by the order of Chosroes.

same year, the Misimians, a people who lived to the north-east
of the Apsilians and like these and the Suanians were dependent
on Lazica, slew a Roman envoy who was travelling through their
country and had treated them with insolence. Knowing that
this outrage would be avenged they went over to Persia. This
incident determined the nature of the unimportant operations
of A.D. 556. A Persian army prevented the Romans from
invading the land of the Misimians. But a punitive expedition
was sent in the ensuing winter and was attended with an inhuman
massacre of the Misimians, who finally yielded and were pardoned.
This expedition was the last episode of the Lazic War.

The truce of five years expired in the autumn of A.D. 556.
Both powers were weary of the war, and the course of the
campaigns had not been encouraging to Chosroes. It is probable,
too, that he was preparing for a final effort to destroy, in conjunction with the Turks, the kingdom of the Ephthalites. Early
in the year he had sent his ambassador Isdigunas to Constantinople [1] to negotiate a renewal of the truce which would
soon expire. It was intended that the arrangement should be
a preliminary to a treaty of permanent peace, and this time it
was not to be imperfect, it was to extend to Lazica as well as
to Armenia and the East. The truce was concluded (A.D. 557)
on the terms of the *status quo* in Lazica, each power retaining
the forts which were in its possession ; there was no limit of
time and there were no money payments.[2]

The historical importance of the Lazic War lay in the fact
that if the Romans had not succeeded in holding the country
and thwarting the design of Chosroes, the great Asiatic power
would have had access to the Euxine and the Empire would have
had a rival on the waters of that sea. The serious menace
involved in this possibility was fully realised by the Imperial
government and explains the comparative magnitude of the
forces which were sent to the defence of the Lazic kingdom.

§ 5. *Conclusion of Peace* (A.D. 562)

It is not clear why five years were allowed to lapse before
this truce of A.D. 557 was converted into a more permanent

---

[1] Malalas, xviii. p. 488, notes the presence of the Persian ambassador in May.
[2] Agathias, iv. 30.

agreement. Perhaps Chosroes could not bring himself to abandon his positions in Lazica, and he knew that the complete evacuation of that country would be insisted on as an indispensable condition by the Emperor. At length, in A.D. 562, Peter the Master of Offices, as the delegate of Justinian, and Isdigunas, as the delegate of Chosroes, met on the frontiers to arrange conditions of peace.[1] The Persian monarch desired that the term of its duration should be long, and that, in return for the surrender of Lazica, the Romans should pay at once a sum of money equivalent to the total amount of large annual payments for thirty or forty years ; the Romans, on the other hand, wished to fix a shorter term. The result of the negotiations was a compromise. A treaty was made for fifty years, the Roman government undertaking to pay the Persians at the rate of 30,000 gold pieces (£18,750) annually. The total amount due during the first seven years was to be paid at once, and at the beginning of the eighth year the Persian claim for the three ensuing years was to be satisfied. From the tenth year forward the payments were to be annual. The inscription of the Persian document, which ratified the compact, was as follows :

" The divine, good, pacific, ancient Chosroes, king of kings, fortunate, pious, beneficent, to whom the gods have given great fortune and great empire, the giant of giants, who is formed in the image of the gods, to Justinian Caesar our brother."

The most important provision of the treaty was that Persia agreed to resign Lazica to the Romans. The other articles were as follows :

(1) The Persians were bound to prevent Huns, Alans, and other barbarians from traversing the central passes of the Caucasus with a view to depredation in Roman territory , while the Romans were bound not to send an army to those regions or to any other parts of the Persian territory. (2) The Saracen allies of both States were included in this peace. (3) Roman and Persian merchants, whatever their wares, were to carry on their traffic at certain prescribed places,[2] where custom-houses were stationed, and at no others. (4) Ambassadors between the two

---

[1] Our source for these transactions is Menander Protector, *fr.* 3, *De leg. Rom.* The provisions have been commented on at length by Güter-

bock, *Byzanz und Persien*, 57 *sqq.*
[2] Doubtless Nisibis, Dubios, and Callinicum. Cp. Güterbock, *op. cit.* 78.

States were to have the privilege of making use of the public posts, and their baggage was not to be liable to custom duties. (5) Provision was made that Saracen or other traders should not smuggle goods into either Empire by out-of-the-way roads ; Daras and Nisibis were named as the two great emporia where these barbarians were to sell their wares.[1] (6) Henceforward the migration of individuals from the territory of one State into that of the other was not to be permitted ; but any who had deserted during the war were allowed to return if they wished. (7) Disputes between Romans and Persians were to be settled— if the accused failed to satisfy the claim of the plaintiff—by a committee of men who were to meet on the frontiers in the presence of both a Roman and a Persian governor. (8) To prevent dissension, both States bound themselves to refrain from fortifying towns in proximity to the frontier. (9) Neither State was to harry or attack any of the subject tribes or nations of its neighbour. (10) The Romans engaged not to place a large garrison in Daras, and also that the *magister militum* of the East [2] should not be stationed there ; if any injury in the neighbourhood of that city were inflicted on Persian soil, the governor of Daras was to pay the costs. (11) In the case of any treacherous dealing, as distinct from open violence, which threatened to disturb the peace, the judges on the frontier were to investigate the matter, and if their decision was insufficient, it was to be referred to the Master of Soldiers in the East ; the final appeal was to be made to the sovran of the injured person. (12) Curses were imprecated on the party that should violate the peace.

A separate agreement provided for the toleration of the Christians and their rites of burial in the Persian kingdom. They were to enjoy immunity from persecution by the Magi, and, on the other hand, they were to refrain from proselytising.

When the sovrans had learned and signified their approbation of the terms on which their representatives had agreed, the two ambassadors drafted the treaty each in his own language. The

---

[1] The word for smuggling is κλεπτο-
τελωνεῖν.

[2] In both these cases the same expression is used, τὸν τῆς ἕω στρατηγόν, and must refer to the same officer. The Latin translation in Müller's edition is misleading, if not positively erroneous ; in the first place the words are rendered *dux orientis*, in the second place *praefectum orientis*, which would naturally mean the Praetorian Prefect of the East. The reference of legal disputes to the Master of Soldiers is noteworthy.

Greek draft was then translated into Persian, and the Persian into Greek, and the two versions were carefully collated. A copy was then made of each. The original versions were sealed by the ambassadors and their interpreters, and Peter took possession of the Persian, and Isdigunas of the Greek, while of the unsealed copies Peter took the Greek and Isdigunas the Persian. It is rarely that we get a glimpse like this into the formal diplomatic procedure of ancient times.

One question remained undecided. The Romans demanded that with the resignation of their pretensions to Lazica the Persians should also evacuate the small adjacent region of Suania. No agreement was reached by the plenipotentiaries, but the question was not allowed to interfere with the conclusion of the treaty, and was reserved for further negotiation. For this purpose Peter went in the following year (A.D. 563) to the court of Chosroes, but Chosroes refused to agree to his argument that Suania was a part of Lazica. In the course of the conversations, the king made the remarkable proposal that the matter should be left to the Suanians themselves to decide. Peter would not entertain this, as Chosroes probably anticipated, and the negotiations fell through.

CHAPTER XVII

§ 1. *The Conquest* (A.D. 533–534)

IT was the claim of the Roman Empire, from its foundation, to be potentially conterminous with the inhabited world and to embrace under its benignant sway the human race. Roman poets often spoke of it simply as the world (*orbis*). This pretentious idea, which was inherited by the Church, might well have been extinguished by the losses which Rome had sustained. Her territory had not been extended since the days of Trajan, and since the beginning of the fourth century her borders had been gradually retreating. All the western provinces were barbarian kingdoms ; Italy itself, with Rome, was no more than a nominal dependency. The idea of restoring the Empire to its ancient limits seems to have floated before the mind of Justinian, but it is difficult to say whether he conceived it from the first as a definite aim of policy. He seized so promptly the opportunities which chance presented to him of recovering lost provinces in the lands of the Mediterranean, that we may suspect that he would have created pretexts, if they had not occurred.

His ambition found its first theatre in Africa. A revolution at Carthage in A.D. 531 gave the desired opportunity for intervention. The perpetual peace which Gaiseric had concluded with the Roman government (A.D. 476) had, under his successors, been faithfully observed on both sides. There appear to have been no hostilities except during the war between Odovacar and Theodoric, when king Gunthamund took advantage of the situation to make descents on Sicily and inflicted a defeat upon the Goths.[1] The Catholic Christians endured more or less cruel

---

[1] Cassiodorus, *Chron.*, *sub* 491 ; Dracontius, *Satisfactio*, vv. 213-214.

persecutions at the hands of Huneric, Gunthamund, and Trasamund,[1] and the Emperors occasionally protested.[2] These kings pursued the policy of Gaiseric and looked with suspicion and jealousy on any relations between their African subjects and Constantinople. The poet Dracontius was thrown into prison by Gunthamund for celebrating the praises of a foreign potentate, and wrote a recantation and apology for his fault. The potentate was undoubtedly Zeno.[3] But there was no breach and the relations between Trasamund and Anastasius were rather friendly.[4] Then Hilderic, the son of Huneric, came to the throne (A.D. 523).[5] The fact that he was the grandson of Valentinian III. was calculated to promote closer intimacy with Constantinople,[6] and under his mild rule persecution ceased. He was the guest-friend of Justinian, and that astute prince probably aimed at making the Vandal state a dependency of the Empire, through his influence on the unwarlike king.[7] Hilderic's complaisance

[1] The contemporary bishop of Vita wrote the story of these persecutions in his *Hist. pers. Afr. prov.*

[2] Huneric allowed the Church of Carthage to ordain a bishop at the request of Zeno and his sister-in-law Placidia Victor, ii. 2, cp. i. 51.

[3] Dracontius, *ib.* 93 :

culpa mihi fuerat dominos reticere modestos
ignotumque mihi scribere vel dominum.

Dracontius was the most considerable of the obscure Latin poets between Sidonius and Corippus. His most ambitious work was the *De laudibus Dei,* but his pagan poems, the *Orestes,* and the ten short pieces collected under the title of *Romulea*

are more interesting. In the reigns of Trasamund, who seems to have encouraged letters, and his successors there was a good deal of literary activity in Africa. We have a verse panegyric on Trasamund by Florentinus (*Anthol. Lat.* No. 376), poems of Felix on the public Thermae which the same king built at Alianae, near Carthage, where the kings had a palace (*ib.* 210-214). We have also the *Book of Epigrams* of Luxorius (*ib.* 287-375), of which the most interesting is that on the death of Damira, the infant daughter of Oageis, a kinsman of king Hilderic.

[4] Procopius, *B.V.* i. 8. 14.

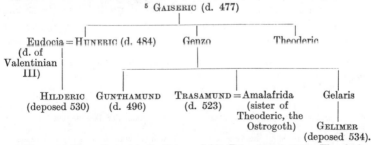

[5] GAISERIC (d. 477)

Eudocia = HUNERIC (d. 484)	Genzo	Theoderic
(d. of Valentinian III)		
HILDERIC GUNTHAMUND	TRASAMUND = Amalafrida	Gelaris
(deposed 530) (d. 496)	(d. 523) (sister of Theoderic, the Ostrogoth)	GELIMER (deposed 534).

[6] The poet Florentinus (*Anth. Lat.* 215) hailed him as

Vandalirice potens, gemini diadematis heres,

and reminded him of the victories of his Roman ancestors, Theodosius and Valentinian III.:

ampla Valentiniani virtus cognita mundo
hostibus addictis ostenditur arce nepotis.

[7] Procopius, *B.V.* i. 9. 8, cp. 19-23.

to Constantinople aroused dissatisfaction ; the opposition was headed by his cousin Gelimer, who usurped the throne in A.D. 530 and threw Hilderic into prison. Justinian at once intervened. He addressed to the usurper a letter of remonstrance, appealing to the testament of Gaiseric and demanding the restoration of the rightful king. Gelimer replied by placing Hilderic under a stricter guard. The Emperor then despatched an ultimatum requiring Gelimer to send the deposed sovran to Constantinople, otherwise he would regard the treaty with Gaiseric as terminated. Gelimer replied defiantly that the matter concerned the Vandals themselves, and that it was not Justinian's business. He probably saw through Justinian's designs and knew that if he yielded he might postpone but would not avert war.[1]

The Emperor decided that the time had come to attempt the conquest of Africa, and as soon as peace had been concluded with Persia in spring of A.D. 532, the preparations were hurried forward. In his eyes it was no war of aggression ; it was the suppression of tyrants in provinces over which the Emperors had always tacitly reserved their rights (*iura imperii*). The ecclesiastics were ardently in favour of an enterprise which would rescue their fellow-Catholics in Africa from the oppression of Arian despots.[2] But from his counsellors and ministers Justinian received no encouragement. The disaster of the great expedition of the Emperor Leo was not forgotten. Their minds were still possessed by the formidable prestige which the Vandal power had attained under Gaiseric both by land and sea. The Empire had not kept up a powerful navy, and without command of the sea the hazard of attempting to transport an army and land it on a hostile coast could not be denied. The Praetorian Prefect, John of Cappadocia, explained to the Emperor the difficulties and risks of the undertaking in the plainest words,

---

[1] Cp. Diehl, *L'Afrique byzantine,* p. 6. The true form of Gelimer's name is Geilamir (so his coins and *C.I.L.* viii. 17. 412). The date of his usurpation 530 follows from length of Hilderic's reign given as 7 years by Procopius, 7 years 3 months by Victor Tonn., and in the shorter edition of the Vandal *Laterculus Regum* as 7 years 14 days. If we take the last figure we get May 19, 530, as the day of Hilderic's defeat. Victor Tonn. places it in 531, and John Mal. places the application of Hilderic to Justinian in the same year (xviii. 459). 531 is the date usually assigned by modern writers (Clinton, Diehl, etc.) ; but Schmidt is right in deciding for 530 (*Gesch. der Wand.* p. 124).

[2] The war was also welcomed by the eastern traders residing at Carthage, who saw in the reunion of Africa with the Empire advantage to their commercial interests. Procopius, *B.V.* i. 20. 5.

and earnestly endeavoured to dissuade him from an adventure which the opinion of experts unreservedly condemned. And this view was justified, although its advocates probably had not realised how far the military strength of the Vandals had decayed since the days of Gaiseric. But notwithstanding this decline, the events of the campaign show that if Gelimer had not committed the most amazing mistakes, which his enemies could not have foreseen, the Roman army would probably have suffered an inglorious defeat. Justinian turned deaf ears to the gloomy anticipations of his counsellors, he believed in the justice of his cause, he believed that Heaven was on his side,[1] and he had confidence in the talents of his general Belisarius, whom he destined to the command of the expedition and invested with the fullest powers, giving him a new title equivalent to *imperator*, which had long been restricted to the Emperors themselves.[2]

The small numbers of the army, deemed sufficient for the conquest of a people who had the military reputation of the Vandals, is surprising. It consisted of not more than 16,000 men. Perhaps this was as much as it was considered possible to transport with safety ; and if it were annihilated, the loss would not be irreparable. There were 10,000 infantry, which were drawn partly from the Comitatenses and partly from the Federates. There were 5000 excellent cavalry, of whom more than 3000 were similarly composed, and the remainder were private retainers of Belisarius.[3] There were two additional bodies of allied troops, both mounted archers, 600 Huns and 400 Heruls. The whole force was transported on 500 vessels, guarded by ninety-two dromons or ships of war.

The hundred years of their rule in Africa had changed the spirit and manners of the Vandals. They had become less

---

[1] For the religious motives cp. Procopius, *ib.* 10. 19-20 ; Diehl, *op. cit.* 7-8.

[2] Procopius (*ib.* 11. 20) does not actually say that he was designated as στρατηγὸς αὐτοκράτωρ, but that all his acts were to be valid ἅτε αὐτοῦ βασιλέως αὐτὰ διαπεπραγμένου. But as he had ceased to be *mag. mil. per Orientem*, and nothing is said of his appointment to another of the regular military commands, we may infer that it was on this occasion that Justinian introduced the new and exceptional post of στρατ.

αὐτοκράτωρ. It is to be remembered that αὐτοκράτωρ is the *official* equivalent of *imperator*. We shall hereafter meet other commanders bearing the same title and authority (Germanus, Narses, Justin).

[3] Procopius, *ib.* 11. 2 *sqq.* The bucellarii (δορυφόροι καὶ ὑπασπισταί) of Belisarius were probably at least 1400 or 1500 (cp. Diehl, *ib.* 17 note). It seems clear from the whole context in Procopius that the Heruls and Huns were not included in the 5000 cavalry (though Diehl hesitates).

warlike ; they had adopted the material civilisation and luxuries of the conquered provincials ; and their military efficiency had declined since Gaiseric's death. It may be doubted whether their army numbered more than 30,000 men.[1] It consisted entirely of cavalry, arrayed in inferior armour, who fought with lance and sword, and were, like other German peoples, unskilled in archery and the use of the javelin. Their king, although he was more martial than his predecessor, was a man of sentimental temperament, who had no military or political talents. The situation required a leader of exceptional ability. For the kingdom was divided against itself. Gelimer's Roman subjects longed for restoration to the Empire and would do all they could to assist the invaders. Even among the Vandals there were the adherents of Hilderic. The Moorish tribes of the interior could not be trusted to remain friendly or neutral if fortune seemed to incline to the Roman cause.

Before the Imperial army set sail from the Bosphorus, two events happened, and Gelimer committed two astounding blunders. The inhabitants of Tripolitana [2] revolted from the Vandals, and Gelimer made no attempt to recover it. This was a fatal policy, for it would enable the Roman army, if it reached the coast of Africa in safety, to land on a friendly soil. Shortly before this the Vandal governor of Sardinia [3] had proclaimed himself independent of Carthage, and when he heard of Justinian's project he offered his submission to the Emperor. Gelimer despatched a force of 5000 men and 120 ships to recover the island. He thus deprived himself of a considerable fraction of his army and virtually of his whole effective naval strength.[4] The Vandal fleet which was reputed so formidable played no part in the war. This curious perversity of Gelimer, in wasting his strength on the recovery of a distant island whose disaffection could hardly have affected the course of events,[5] and

---

[1] Diehl, *op. cit.* p. 9, says less than 40,000 ; cp. Pflugk Harttung, *Hist. Zeitschrift*, lxi. p. 70 (1889). Note that the figure of 80,000 warriors given in Procopius, *H.A.* 18. 6 is merely a repetition of his mistake in *B.V.* i. 5. 18 (see above, Vol. I. p. 246).

[2] Led by a certain Pudentius, who was in correspondence with Justinian and was assisted by a small body of troops sent from Constantinople. Procopius, *ib.* 10. 5.

[3] He was a Goth, named Godas.

[4] Procopius describes the ships as " the best sailers " (*ib.* 11. 24). If they were only part of the fleet, the rest was not strong enough to attempt any action. No inference can be drawn from παντὶ τῷ στόλῳ (*ib.* 25. 17 and 21), which means the whole Sardinian squadron.

[5] Gelimer, no doubt, believed that the Sardinian expedition would return before the enemy landed in Africa.

neglecting to suppress the movement in Tripolitana, whose possession was of the first importance, was perhaps decisive for the whole issue of the war.

If the Sardinian revolt was a piece of luck for Justinian, the attitude of Italy was hardly less fortunate. After the death of Trasamund, his Ostrogothic wife Amalafrida had been imprisoned and afterwards murdered,[1] and this led to an irreconcilable breach between the courts of Carthage and Ravenna. The Ostrogothic government willingly supported the Imperial expedition by placing the harbours of Sicily at its disposal.

The Roman forces set sail from Constantinople in June A.D. 533. Before their departure the ship of the general moored in front of the Imperial palace, and the Patriarch offered prayers for the success of the expedition. Among those who witnessed their sailing perhaps most who were competent to judge believed that they would never return. Belisarius was accompanied by his wife Antonina, and by the historian Procopius, who again acted as his legal assessor, and to whom we owe the story of the war. The *domesticus*, or chief of the general's staff, was the eunuch Solomon, a native of Mesopotamia, one of those able eunuchs whom we frequently meet on the stage of Byzantine history.

The voyage from the Bosphorus to Sicily was marked by many halts,[2] and the shore of Africa was not reached till the beginning of September. Procopius commemorates the practical foresight of Antonina in storing a large number of jars of water, covered with sand, in the hold of the general's ship, and tells how this provision stood them in good stead in the long run from Zacynthus to Catane. Belisarius had been full of misgivings about the voyage from Sicily to Africa, expecting that the enemy would attack him by sea. He now learned for the

---

[1] See next chapter, § 1, p. 158.

[2] Nine days were spent at Heraclea and Abydus, so that, as the expedition sailed "about the summer solstice" (June 21), it left the Dardanelles about July 1. There was a long delay at Methone (Modon, in Messenia), where the army suffered (just as modern armies so often suffer from the dishonesty of contractors) from the greed of the Praetorian Prefect, on whom it devolved to provide the soldiers with the bread necessary for the voyage. It was found that the bread had gone bad, because it had been baked only once, instead of twice. Five hundred soldiers fell victims to dysentery caused by the putrefying dough. The Prefect had saved both fuel and flour. Belisarius was praised for complaining to the Emperor, but no punishment was inflicted on the guilty.

first time (from a man who had just arrived from Carthage) that the Vandal fleet had been sent to Sardinia ; and equally welcome was the news that Gelimer was unaware that the Roman expedition was on its way and had made no preparation to meet it, at Carthage or elsewhere.

The fleet made land at Caputvada (Ras Kapudia) on the African coast, and the army disembarked and fortified a camp. Before landing Belisarius had held a council of war, and some of his generals argued that it would be the better plan to sail straight for Carthage and surprise it, but Belisarius overruled this view ; there was the chance of a hostile fleet appearing, and he knew that the soldiers were ʼafraid of a naval attack. Caputvada is sixty-six Roman miles south of Hadrumetum (Sousse) and one hundred and sixty-two from Carthage,[1] so that if his army marched slightly over eleven miles a day, he was fourteen days' journey from his goal. The road ran close to the coast, and the fleet was instructed to sail slowly and keep within hail of the army. A squadron of 300 horse, under John the Armenian, was sent ahead as an advance guard at a distance of three miles, and the corps of 600 Huns was ordered to march at the same distance to the left of the road, to protect the army from a flank attack. The first town on their route was Syllectum (Selekta), which was seized quietly by a ruse. The overseer of the public post deserted and delivered all the horses to Belisarius, who rewarded him with gold and gave him a copy of a letter addressed by the Emperor to the leading men [2] of the Vandals, to make public. It ran thus :

" It is not our purpose to go to war with the Vandals, nor are we breaking our treaty with Gaiseric. We are only attempting to overthrow your tyrant, who making light of Gaiseric's testament keeps your king a prisoner, and killed those of his kinsmen whom he hated, and having blinded the rest keeps them in prison, not allowing them to end their sufferings by death. Therefore join us in freeing yourselves from a tyranny so wicked, that you may enjoy peace and liberty. We give you pledges in the name of God that we will give you these blessings."

As the man did not venture to publish the letter openly but

---

[1] Procopius reckons the distance as five days' journey for an unencumbered man, *B.V.* i. 14. 17.   [2] Ἄρχοντες.

only showed it secretly to his friends, it produced no effect.
During their march northward the friendliness of the inhabitants
supplied the invaders with provisions, and Belisarius took the
strictest measures to prevent his soldiers from alienating the
sympathies of the population by marauding and looting. It
will be remembered how in England's war with her American
colonies the shameless pillaging of the property of the colonial
loyalists, by the Hessian mercenaries whom George III. had
hired, drove them into the ranks of the rebels, and the English
generals were incapable of keeping a firm hand on their
auxiliaries. Belisarius had a more difficult task. Want of
discipline, as we shall see, was the weak point in his mixed
army. But for the present he succeeded in restraining the
appetites of his barbarian troops, and advanced comfortably
towards the Vandal capital.

Passing Thapsus, Leptis, and Hadrumetum, the army reached
Grasse, where the Vandal kings had a villa and a beautiful park,
full of fruit trees, and as the fruit was ripe the soldiers ate their
fill. This place, now Sidi-Khalifa, is still famous for its fruit
gardens.[1] During the night of the halt at Grasse some of the
Roman scouts met enemy scouts and after exchanging blows
both parties retired to their camps. Thus Belisarius learned
for the first time that the enemy was not far away. It was, in
fact, the king who was following them but keeping out of sight.
Gelimer was at Hermiane [2] when he learned of the Roman
disembarkation. He sent orders immediately to his brother
Ammatas at Carthage to kill Hilderic and the other prisoners,
and, collecting all the troops in the city, to be ready to attack
the Roman army at a given time and place. He marched southward himself at the head of his army to follow and observe the
advance of the invaders without being seen himself. His plan
was to surprise and surround the enemy at a spot near Tunis
and ten miles from Carthage.

Not far from Grasse the high road to Carthage left the coast
and crossed the promontory which runs out into Cape Bon.
Here the army and the ships parted company, and the naval
commander was instructed not to put in at Carthage but to

---

[1] See Tissot, *Géographie*, ii. p. 116. It is close to Fradiz, the ancient
Aphrodisium.
[2] In Byzacena.

remain about three miles out at sea until he should be summoned.
The road rejoined the coast at Ad Aquas, which is now Hammam
el-Enf, twenty-three miles from Carthage.   .By the fourth day [1]
(September 13) the army was approaching Tunis, and it was
perhaps at the northern extremity of the defile of Hammam
el-Enf, on a rocky spur of the Jebel Bu-Kornin—the two-
horned hill—that Belisarius, neglecting no precautions and
hesitating to risk an engagement with his whole army, made a
stockaded camp in which he ordered his infantry to remain
while he rode down into the plain with the cavalry.[2] John the
Armenian had ridden on in advance, as usual, while the Huns
were some miles to the left, west of the Bu-Kornin hills.
Belisarius had no idea of the excellent strategic plan which the
enemy had devised to destroy him.

If we walk out of the modern town of Tunis by the south-
eastern gate, Bab Alleona, we soon reach the railway station of
Jebel Jellud, and near it was the Roman station Ad Decimum,
at the tenth milestone from Carthage.   On the left are a number
of little eminences of which the highest is named Megrin, on
the right the hill of Sidi Fathalla, behind which extends to the
west the Sebkha es-Sejumi or Salt-plain, an arid treeless tract
then as now.[3] This was the place in which Gelimer had planned
to surround the Romans.   Ammatas coming from Carthage was
to confront them in the defile ; when they were engaged with
him, Gibamund, the king's nephew,[4] with 2000 men, advancing
across the Salt-plain, was to descend from the hill on their left,

---

[1] From Grasse. The distance to
Ad Aquas is about 50 miles. The
date was the eve of St. Cyprian's
day, Sept. 13 (*B.V.* i. 21. 23). If
the army landed at Caputvada on
Sept. 2, they reached Syllectum (a
long day's march of 19 miles) on
Sept. 3, Hadrumetum Sept. 5,
Grasse Sept. 9, Ad Aquas Sept. 12.
This would mean much longer
marches between Grasse and Ad
Aquas than the 80 stades (11½ miles)
which Procopius says was the average
day's march.

[2] The position of the camp, at
Darbet es-Sif, is Tissot's plausible
conjecture, *op. cit.* p. 121. Procopius
notes that the place was 7 miles from
Decimum (*ib.* 19. 1).

[3] Πεδίον Ἁλῶν, *B.V.* i. 18. 12. This

indication and the reference to the
hills on either side of the road, *ib.* 19.
19, are the important determinants
in the identification of Ad Decimum,
which is due to Tissot. The fact
that the place was a *mutatio* ten
Roman miles from Carthage is not
enough as we do not know how far the
city of Carthage extended southward
and from what point the distance was
measured. Tissot (*ib.* 114 *sqq.*) has
thrown much light on the topography
of the battle.

[4] Gibamund is mentioned as the
builder of Thermae in a metrical
inscription found at Tunis (*C.I.L.* viii.
25362) :

Gaude operi, Gebamunde, tuo, regalis origo,
    deliciis sospes utere cum populo.

while Gelimer himself with the main army was to come upon them in the rear. The time at which the Romans might be expected to reach Ad Decimum was nicely calculated, and the plan all but succeeded.

Ammatas committed the error of appearing with a few men at Ad Decimum some hours before the appointed time, probably for the purpose of surveying the ground. He arrived at noon and came face to face with the troops of John. He was a brave

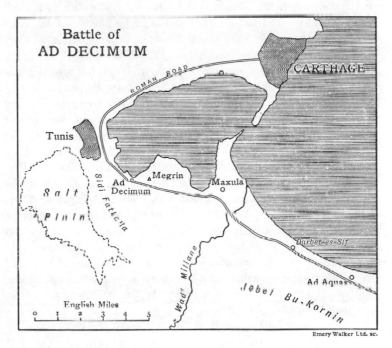

Emery Walker Ltd. sc.

warrior and he killed with his own hand twelve of John's best men before he fell himself. His followers fled and swept back in a hot-foot race to the shelter of Carthage the other troops who were marching negligently in bands of twenty or thirty to the appointed place. John and his riders pursued and slew as far as the city gates.

While this action was in progress, the Huns had reached the Plain of Salt and fell in with the forces of Gibamund who were moving eastward to Sidi Fathalla, and, although in numbers they were less than one to three, utterly annihilated them.

The Huns enjoyed the battle ; the Vandals, they thought, were a feast which God had prepared for them.[1]

Of these two events Belisarius knew nothing as he descended from Hammam el-Enf into the plain of Mornag. His Federate cavalry rode in advance, the regular cavalry and his own retainers at some distance in the rear. Crossing the stream Oued Miliane, the road to Tunis passes Maxula (Rades), which lies between the sea and the southern shore of the lake of Tunis.[2] The Federates, when they reached Ad Decimum, saw the corpses of their comrades and those of Ammatas and some Vandals. The people of the place told them what had happened and they climbed the hills to reconnoitre. Presently they discerned a cloud of dust to the south and then a large force of Vandal cavalry. They sent, at once, a message to Belisarius urging him to hasten. It was Gelimer's army that was coming. Having followed Belisarius at a safe distance along the main road he had doubtless left it at Grombalia, and keeping to the west of the Jebel Bu-Kornin proceeded along a road which is still used by the natives for travelling between Grombalia and Tunis. The hilly nature of the ground did not permit him to see either the movements of Belisarius on his right or the disaster of his nephew on his left. When his vanguard reached Ad Decimum there was a contest with the Roman Federates to win possession of an eminence (possibly Megrin), in which the Vandals were successful. The Federates then fled for a mile along the road to rejoin their own army and met Uliaris with 800 guardsmen, who seeing them galloping in disorder turned themselves and galloped back to Belisarius.

Gelimer now had the victory in his hands, but the gods were determined to destroy him. The historian who tells the tale and who witnessed the cavalry riding back in terror to the commander-in-chief, declares that " Had Gelimer pursued immediately I do not think that even Belisarius would have withstood him, but our cause would have been utterly ruined, so large appeared the multitude of the Vandals and so great the

---

[1] *B.V.* i. 18. 18. From the statement (*ib.* 12.) that the Salt-plain is 40 stades from Decimum, we may infer that the engagement occurred at that distance (5 to 6 miles). The eastern edge of the Salt-plain is much nearer Decimum.

[2] From Maxula the shortest road to Carthage was along the shore, but this way was impracticable on account of the canal connecting the sea with the lake.

fear they inspired ; or if he had made straight for Carthage he would have slain easily all the men with John, and would have preserved the city and its treasures, and would have taken our ships which had approached near, and deprived us not only of victory but of the means of escape." [1]

Gelimer was a man of sentimental temperament. When he reached Ad Decimum and saw the dead body of his brother he was completely unmanned. He set up loud lamentations and could think of nothing but burying the corpse ; and so, as the historian remarks, " he blunted the edge of opportunity," and such an opportunity did not recur.

Meanwhile Belisarius had rallied the fugitives and administered a solemn rebuke. On learning exactly what had happened, he rode at full speed to Decimum and found the barbarians in complete disorder. They did not wait for his attack but fled as fast as they could, not towards Carthage but westward towards Numidia. They lost many, and the fighting ended at night, when John's troops and the Huns arrived on the scene. A considerable victory had been gained, but it was a victory which Gelimer had presented to Belisarius ; it ought to have been a defeat.

The night was passed at Decimum, and on the following day Antonina arrived with the infantry and the whole army marched to Carthage, arriving at nightfall. Its inhabitants opened the gates and welcomed the victor with a brilliant illumination. But Belisarius was cautious, and he would not enter that night, partly because he feared an ambuscade and partly because he was resolved that his soldiers should not plunder the city. The next day (September 15) the army marched in, in formation of battle. Belisarius need not have been afraid ; no snare was set.

He seated himself on the king's throne, and consumed the dinner which Gelimer had confidently ordered to be ready for his own victorious return. The inhabitants welcomed the deliverer, and the Imperial fleet sailed into the lake of Tunis. Belisarius lost no time in repairing the walls of the city and rendering it capable of sustaining a siege. Meanwhile the Moorish tribes of Numidia and Byzacium, learning the issue of the battle, hastened to send friendly embassies to the conqueror.[2]

---

[1] *B.V.* i. 19. 25 *sqq.*

[2] Before the Vandal occupation it had been the custom of the client Moorish chiefs to receive as tokens of office from the Emperor a gilded silver staff and a silver cap in the form of

Gelimer and his vanquished army had fled to the plain of Bulla Regia.[1] His first care was to send the bad news to his brother Tzazo, who commanded the Sardinian expedition, imperatively recalling him. Tzazo, who had succeeded in re-establishing the Vandal authority in Sardinia, returned with his troops, and Gelimer thus reinforced marched towards Carthage. He cut the aqueduct, and he attempted to prevent provisions from arriving in the city, which he hoped to reduce by blockade. He sent secret agents to undermine the loyalty of the inhabitants and the Imperial army. In this he had some success. The auxiliary Huns seem to have determined to stand aloof in the approaching struggle and then rally to the aid of the victorious party.[2]

About the middle of December Belisarius judged that the time had come to bring matters to an issue. Gelimer had pitched his camp at Tricamaron,[3] on the banks of the Mejerda, about twenty miles west of Carthage. Here were collected not only his soldiers but their wives and children and property. The battle of Tricamaron was in some respects a repetition of the battle of Ad Decimum. It was a battle of cavalry. The Roman infantry was again far behind and did not come up till the late afternoon when the issue was virtually decided. It was only after repeated charges that the mailed Roman horsemen succeeded in breaking the enemy's lines. Tzazo and many others of the bravest officers fell. The Vandals fled to their camp, and the Huns who had hitherto refused to join in the combat now joined in the pursuit. As soon as the infantry arrived, the victors fell upon the camp, and Gelimer, seeing that all was lost, fled with a few attendants into the wilds of Numidia. All his soldiers who could escape sought refuge in the churches of the surrounding district. There was no pursuit. The Roman troops thought of nothing but of seizing the rich spoil, women and treasures, which awaited them in the camp.

a crown, a white cloak, a white tunic, and a gilded boot. Belisarius sent these to them now and gave them presents of money. *B.V.* i. 25. 7.

[1] Hammam Daraji, on the borders of the Proconsular province and Numidia.

[2] For the discontent of the Huns, who feared that if the Romans were victorious they would be kept in Africa, see *B.V.* ii. 1. 6. Belisarius swore to them that when the Vandals were defeated he would send them home with all their booty, but notwithstanding this they played a double game at Tricamaron (*ib.* 2. 3).

[3] The place has not been identified.

The general was utterly powerless to restore discipline, and he passed an anxious night.   He feared that some of the enemy, realising the situation, would attack his disorderly troops ; and " if any thing of the kind had happened," says Procopius, " I think that not a Roman would have escaped to enjoy his booty." The victory of Tricamaron (middle of December, A.D. 533) destroyed the Vandal kingdom.   But it was due to the weakness and incompetence of the king.   He had no idea of using to advantage his great numerical preponderance in cavalry.   Even after the defeat, if he had not run away, he might have annihilated the enemy busy with their loot.

It is to be observed that both the actions of the short campaign were fought and won by the Roman cavalry, as in the battle of Daras.   The more numerous infantry might almost as well not have been in Africa.   There is room for wonder whether if Belisarius had been opposed to a commander of some ability and experience in warfare, he would not have been hopelessly defeated.   His secretary, Procopius, expresses amazement at the issue of the war, and does not hesitate to regard it not as a feat of superior strategy but as a paradox of fortune.[1]   But if in this campaign Belisarius did not display signal military talent, there can be no question as to his skill in holding together the undisciplined and heterogeneous troops which he commanded.   The Federates thought of nothing but securing booty ; they were inclined to regard themselves as independent allies ; again and again, but for the general's firmness and tact, their insubordinate spirit might have been disastrous.

The Vandal warriors who had fled to the asylum of sanctuaries surrendered to the Roman general, who promised that they would be well treated and sent to Constantinople in spring. All the treasures belonging to Gelimer were seized in Hippo Regius.[2]   Belisarius then made arrangements to assert the Imperial authority throughout the Vandal dominions, of which he had yet occupied but a small part.   He sent detachments by sea to take possession of Sardinia and Corsica, the Balearic

---

[1] *Ib.* 7. 18 *sqq.* See Diehl, *op. cit.* 30 *sqq.*

[2] A silver basin, found in 1875 not far from Feltre, with the inscription *Geilamir Vandalorum et Alanorum*

rex (C.I.L. viii. 17. 412), must have come from this treasure.   Mommsen (*Hist. Schr.* i. p. 566) conjectures it may have been a gift from Belisarius to a Herul officer, who might have taken it to Italy.

Islands, the fortress of Septum in Tingitana, on the straits of Gibraltar, and Caesarea (Cherchel) on the coast of Mauretania. But the task of establishing Roman administration throughout the African provinces, and especially in the three Mauretanias, was to require several years and far more strenuous military exertions than were needed to destroy the power of the Vandals.

Gelimer had fled to Mount Papua in the wilds of Numidia, where he found among the Moors a miserable but impregnable refuge. Here for three months he and the friends who were with him endured hunger and cold, blockaded by the Herul leader Pharas, whose followers watched the paths at the foot of the mountain. It was a tedious watch during the cold winter months. Pharas sent a friendly message to the king counselling him to surrender. The pride of Gelimer could not yet brook the thought, but he besought Pharas to send him a loaf, a sponge, and a lyre. He had not tasted baked bread since he had come to the mountain ; he wanted a sponge to dry his tears ; and a lyre that he might sing a song which he had composed on his misfortunes. The curious request, which was readily granted, illustrates the temperament of Gelimer, who loved the luxury of grief.[1] At length (in March) pitying the sufferings of his faithful attendants, he surrendered, assured of honourable treatment. He was taken to Constantinople, where he adorned the triumph of Belisarius. When he saw the Emperor sitting in all his splendour in the Kathisma of the Hippodrome, he repeated to himself, " Vanity of vanities, all is vanity." An ample estate in Galatia was granted to him, and the dignity of Patrician would have been conferred on him, if he had not resolutely refused to abandon his Arian religion.[2]

The difficulties of the command of Belisarius were illustrated by the intrigues which the subordinate generals began to spin against him after his final success. They wrote secretly to Constantinople insinuating that he was aiming at the throne. Justinian doubtless knew what these charges were worth. He gave Belisarius the choice of returning to Constantinople or of

---

[1] We saw how he indulged it at an inopportune moment, at the battle of Ad Decimum. His meeting with his brother Tzazo gave him another opportunity.

[2] The progress of bigotry is to be noted. This new condition for the Patriciate was evidently laid down by Justinian. In the fifth century Aspar and Theoderic, both Arians, had been created patricians.

remaining in Africa. Belisarius prudently chose to return, and was rewarded by a triumph, which at this time was an exceptional honour for a private person (A.D. 534). He brought back with him a captive king with the choicest of the Vandal warriors ; [1] an immense treasure ; and what above all appealed to the piety of the Emperor and to the sentiment of orthodox Christians, King Solomon's golden vessels of which Gaiseric had robbed Rome and of which Titus had despoiled Jerusalem.[2] He was soon to be entrusted with the conduct of a longer and more arduous enterprise.

§ 2. *The Settlement and the Moorish Wars* (A.D. 534–548)

The general idea of the Emperor's scheme for the administration of the African provinces was to wipe out all traces of the Vandal conquest, as if it had never been, and to restore the conditions which had existed before the coming of Gaiseric. The ecclesiastical settlement, which lay near Justinian's heart, was easy and drastic.[3] All the churches which the conquered Arians had taken for their own worship were restored to the Catholics, and heretics were treated with the utmost intolerance. Vandals, even those who were converted from their religious errors, were excluded from public offices. The rank and file of the Vandal fighting men became the slaves of the Roman soldiers who married the women. All the estates which had passed into the hands of the barbarians were to be restored to the descendants of the original owners who could establish their claims,—a measure which led to the forgery of titles and endless lawsuits.[4] The ultimate result of the whole policy was the disappearance of the Vandal population in Africa.

When he received the news of the victory of Tricamaron, Justinian must have proceeded immediately, if he had not already begun, to prepare the details of the future government of Africa ; for the whole scheme was published in April A.D.

---

[1] Most of them were formed into five cavalry regiments, known as *Vandali Iustiniani*, and stationed on the Persian frontier, Procopius, *ib.* 14. 17. Some entered the private service of Belisarius (*B.G.* iii. 1). Perhaps there were about 3000 in all.

[2] Also the Imperial ornaments which Gaiseric had taken from Rome, *C.J.* i. 27. 1, § 6. For the mosaics on the walls of the Chalce see above, p. 54.

[3] Justinian, *Nov.* 37.

[4] *Nov.* 36 (A.D. 535) makes provisions to remedy these evils.

534.[1] Its general character was modelled on the system which was in force before the Vandal conquest, but the changed circumstances required some modifications. Formerly Africa had been a diocese of the Prefecture of Italy. This arrangement could not be maintained as Italy was in the hands of the Ostrogoths. Hence the civil governor was invested with the title of Praetorian Prefect of Africa, and enjoyed the corresponding dignity and emoluments. Under him were the governors of the seven provinces : Proconsularis, Byzacena, Tripolitana, Numidia, the two Mauretanias, and Sardinia.[2] But the compass of the Second or Western Mauretania (Caesariensis) was extended so as to include Tingitana, which in old days had belonged to the diocese of Spain.

The military establishment was placed under a Master of Soldiers,[3] a new creation, since in old days the armies of Africa had been under the supreme command of the Master of Soldiers in Italy. The fundamental distinction between the mobile army and the frontier troops was retained. The mobile army consisted of the divisions of the *comitatenses* who had been sent with Belisarius, of *foederati*, and of native African troops (*gentiles*).[4] The frontier troops were distributed in four districts, under dukes, who had authority also over mobile troops stationed in these military provinces.[5] The establishment of this organisation throughout Africa was retarded for some years by wars and mutinies, but it was begun by Belisarius before he departed, and it was gradually carried out, along with an elaborate scheme of fortification against the inroads of the Moorish tribes.

The Moors began hostilities before the Romans had time to make provision for the defence of the country or to organise

---

[1] *C.J.* i. 27. 1 and 2. The total cost of the administration was less than £30,000. Cp. above, Vol. I. p. 33, *n.* 1.

[2] *C.J. ib.* i. § 12. In the text we must read *Zeugi* for *Tingi*, and *Mauritaniae* for *Mauritania*. See Diehl, *op. cit.* 107 *sqq.* Proconsularis Carthage (=Zeugi), Byzacena and Trip. were under *Consulares* ; the other four under *praesides*. On the old system, Numidia had a *consularis*, Trip. a *praeses*. This change may be explained, as Diehl suggests, by the fact that in 534 Tripolitana was regarded as entirely conquered, while most of Numidia had still to be occupied.

[3] *Magister militum Africae*. Under him was a *magister peditum* (Proc. *B.V.* ii. 16. 2).

[4] It included also a small body of guard troops (Excubitores), who were sent with Solomon in 534.

[5] Tripolitana, Byzacena, Numidia, and Mauretania. The chief stations, where the dukes resided, were respectively Leptis Magna, Capsa or Thelepte, Cirta, and Caesarea. A commander of subordinate dignity, with the title of *tribunus*, was stationed at Septum. The military received larger salaries than the civil governors.

the new civil administration. The situation was so grave that Justinian, when he sent Solomon in autumn (A.D. 534) to replace Belisarius, united in his hands the supreme civil as well as military authority. Solomon was Praetorian Prefect as well as Master of Soldiers.[1] This appointment struck the note of a change in the principles of provincial administration which had prevailed since Diocletian. We shall see how elsewhere Justinian departed from the general rule of a strict separation of the civil and military powers. In Africa, although the two offices were seldom united, perhaps only on three occasions,[2] there is a tendency from the beginning to subordinate the Praetorian Prefect to the Master of Soldiers,[3] and before the end of the century the Master of Soldiers will become a real viceroy with the title of Exarch.

The leading feature of the history of North Africa from the Roman reconquest to the Arab invasion in the middle of the seventh century is a continuous struggle with the Moors, broken by short periods of tranquillity. Each province had its own enemies. Tripolitana was always threatened by the Louata, Byzacena by the Frexi ;[4] the townspeople of Numidia lived in dread of the Moors of the Aurasian hills. Mauretania was largely occupied by Berber tribes. The Roman government never succeeded in effecting a complete subjugation of the auto-chthonous peoples. It was not an impossible task, if the right means had been taken. But the Roman army was hardly sufficient in numbers to maintain effectively the defence of a long frontier, against enemies whose forces consisted of light cavalry, immensely more numerous. This numerical inferiority might have mattered little if the troops had been trustworthy. But they were always ready to revolt against discipline, and in war their thoughts were not on protecting the provinces but on

[1] The first Pr. Pr. of Africa had been Archelaus (C.J. i. 27. 1). Solomon was the first *mag. mil. Afr.*

[2] Solomon (534–536); Solomon (539–543) ; Theodore (569 ; John Bicl. *sub a.*, cp. Diehl, *op. cit.* 599). Perhaps Sergius (544) should be added (Marcellinus, *sub* 541).

[3] This seems to be the case with Symmachus under Germanus (536)

and Athanasius under Areobindus (546). Diehl, *op. cit.* 117.

[4] There were other tribes besides the Louata and Frexi, but these were the most prominent. In Justinian's time, Antalas was the chieftain of the Frexi and their confederate tribes ; Cutsina was the chief of other tribes in the same region ; Iabdas was king of the Aurasian Moors ; Mastigas and Masuna were the leading princes of the Mauretanian Moors.

securing booty. They could do work under a commander who
knew how to handle them, but such commanders were rare.
Most of the military governors found their relations with their
own soldiers as difficult a problem as their relations with the
Moors. Here we touch on a second cause of the failure of the
Romans to secure a lasting peace in Africa—the unfitness of
so many of their military governors. A succession of men like
Belisarius, Solomon, and John Troglita would probably have
succeeded, if not in establishing permanent and complete tranquillity, at least in defending the frontiers efficiently. But
when a commander of this type had weathered a crisis or retrieved a disaster, he was too often succeeded by an incompetent
man, who had no control over the soldiers, no skill in dealing
with the Moors, and who undid by his inexperience all that his
predecessor had accomplished. And apart from these weaknesses,
it has been remarked with justice that the general military
policy was not calculated to pacify the restless barbarians
beyond the frontier. It was a policy of strict defence. The
elaborate system of fortresses which were speedily erected
throughout the provinces stood the inhabitants in good stead,
but they did not prevent raids, and the Romans only opposed
raids on Roman soil. Far more would have been effected if
the Romans had taken the offensive whenever there was a sign
of restlessness and sent flying columns beyond the frontier to
attack the Moors on their own ground. Finally the want of
success in dealing with the Moorish danger may have been partly
due to defective and inconsistent diplomacy.[1]

The one fact in the situation which enabled the Romans to
maintain their grip on Africa was the disunion among the Moors.
On more than one occasion they suffered such crushing disasters
that if the Moors had made a determined and united effort
the Imperial armies would easily have been driven into the sea.
But the jealousies and quarrels among the cheftains hindered
common action ; and if one began a hostile movement, the
Romans could generally depend on the quiescence or assistance
of his neighbour.

On his arrival in Africa (A.D. 534) Solomon [2] had immediately

---

[1] Illustrations of all these points
will be found in Diehl, *op. cit.*

[2] Belisarius left most of his cavalry
behind ; Justinian sent new forces ;
and Solomon seems to have disposed
of about 18,000 men (Diehl, 67, note 4).

to take the field against Cutsina and other Moorish leaders
who descended upon Byzacena, while Iabdas was devastating
Numidia.   He defeated the former at Mamma, but not decisively ;
they returned with reinforcements, and were thoroughly beaten
in the important battle of Mount Burgaon (early in A.D. 535).[1]
An expedition against the Numidian Moors in the following
summer was unsuccessful, but Solomon lost no time in setting
about the erection of fortified posts along the main roads in
Numidia and Byzacena. In A.D. 536 the Emperor regarded
peace as established and the Moors as conquered.[2]

The task of keeping the natives in check had at least been
well begun ; but it was interrupted by a dangerous military
revolt.

Various causes contributed to the mutiny. The pay of the
soldiers had fallen into arrears, because the taxes from which it
should have been defrayed had not been paid up. There was
dissatisfaction about the division of booty. There were many
Arians among the barbarian federates in the army who were ill-
pleased at the intolerant religious policy which had been set in
motion.[3] Men who had married Vandal women claimed the
lands which had belonged to their fathers or husbands and
had been confiscated by the State. Above all, Solomon did not
understand the art of tempering discipline by indulgence and
was not a favourite with either officers or men. A conspiracy
was formed to murder him at Easter (A.D. 536). It miscarried
because the courage of those who were chosen to do the deed
failed them, and then a great number of the disaffected, fearing
discovery, left Carthage and assembled in the plain of Bulla
Regia. Those who were left behind soon threw off the pretence
of innocence and the city was a scene of massacre and pillage.
Solomon, having charged his lieutenants Theodore and Martin
to do what they could in his absence, escaped by night, along with
his assessor, the historian Procopius, and sailed for Sicily, to
invoke the aid of Belisarius, who had just completed the conquest
of the island. Belisarius did not lose a moment in setting sail
for Carthage, in which he found Theodore beleaguered by the

---

[1] These localities have not been
certainly identified.

[2] *Nov.* xxx. 11. 2.

[3] Procopius says there were 1000,
some of them Heruls ; and they
were instigated by the Arian clergy
of the Vandals who had lost their
churches and their incomes. *B.V.* ii.
14. 12-13.

rebels. They were about 9000 strong [1] and under the command of Stotzas, who was one of the private retainers of Martin. The design of this upstart was to form an independent kingdom in Africa for himself.

Theodore was on the point of capitulating when Belisarius arrived, and on the news of his appearance the rebels hastily raised the siege and took the road for Numidia. It was a high compliment to the prestige of the conqueror of the Vandals. With the few troops who had remained loyal in Carthage, and a hundred picked men whom he had brought with him, Belisarius overtook Stotzas at Membressa [2] and defeated him. The rebels fled, but they did not submit. Belisarius could not remain ; news from Sicily imperatively recalled him. He arranged that Solomon should withdraw from the scene, and that two officers, Theodore and Ildiger, should assume responsibility until the Emperor appointed Solomon's successor. Soon after his departure the situation became worse, for the troops stationed in Numidia, who had been moved to cut off the retreat of Stotzas, declared in his favour. Two-thirds of the army were now in rebellion.[3]

Justinian was happily inspired at this grave crisis. He sent the right man to deal with it, his cousin Germanus, the patrician, who already had had experience of warfare on the Danube, as Master of Soldiers in Thrace. He was appointed Master of Soldiers of Africa, with extraordinary powers, and it was hoped that his prestige as a member of the Imperial family would have its influence in recalling the rebels to a sense of loyalty. His first act was to proclaim that he had come not to punish the mutineers, but to examine and rectify their grievances. This announcement was at once effective. Many of the soldiers left the camp of the rebels and reported themselves at Carthage. When it was known that they were handsomely treated and that they received arrears of pay even for the weeks during which they were in rebellion, large numbers deserted the cause of Stotzas, and Germanus found himself equal in strength to the

[1] Including about 1000 Vandals, of whom 400 had returned from the east. On the way from Constantinople to Syria—where they were to form part of the frontier forces— they succeeded in seizing a ship at Lesbos and landing in Africa.

[2] Mejez el-Bab, on the river Bagradas (Mejerda).

[3] This was found to be the case by Germanus, who investigated the military register on his arrival. Proc. *B.V.* ii. 16. 3.

insurgents. Stotzas, seeing that his only chance was to strike quickly, advanced on Carthage. A desperate battle was fought at Scalas Veteres (Cellas Vatari) in the spring (A.D. 537), and the rebels were defeated. Moorish forces, under Iabdas and other chiefs, who had promised to support Germanus, were spectators of the combat, but according to their usual practice they took no part till the victory was decided, and then they joined in the pursuit, instead of falling on the exhausted victors.[1]

Germanus remained in Africa for two years and succeeded in re-establishing discipline in the army. Then the experienced Solomon was sent out to replace him (A.D. 539) and to complete the military organisation of the provinces and the system of defence, in which Justinian took a keen personal interest. He began by weeding out of the army all those whom he suspected as doubtful or dangerous, sending them to Italy or the East, and he expelled from Africa the Vandal females who had done much to instigate the mutiny. After successful campaigns against the Aurasian Moors, he established his power solidly in Numidia and Mauretania Sitifensis, and carried out the vast work of strengthening the defences of the towns and building hundreds of forts. Africa enjoyed a brief period of peace to which, amid subsequent troubles, the provincials looked back with regret.

The great pestilence which devastated the Empire in A.D. 542 and 543 visited Africa and took a large toll from the army. At the same time new troubles threatened from the Moors. The Emperor, who gratefully recognised the services and abilities of Solomon, appointed his nephew Sergius [2] duke of Tripolitana. It was a thoroughly bad appointment. Sergius was incompetent, arrogant, and debauched ; he was not even a brave soldier ; and he proved a governor of the well-known type who cannot avoid offending the natives. An insolent outrage committed against a deputation of the Louata provoked that people to arms ; and by an unfortunate coincidence Solomon at the same time succeeded in offending the powerful chief Antalas, who had hitherto been friendly. The Moors joined forces, and in the battle of Cillium [3] (A.D. 544) the Romans were utterly defeated and Solomon was slain.

---

[1] Diehl, *op. cit.* 87.

[2] Sergius was not only nephew of Solomon ; he was also son-in-law of Antonina.

[3] Kasrin, west of Sbeitla. Victor Tonn. *sub* 543 ; Procopius, *B.V.* ii. 21.

The Imperial rule in Africa was again in grave danger. The news of the defeat stirred the Berber tribes all along the frontier ; even the Visigoths seized the occasion to send forces across the straits, and unsuccessfully besieged Septum.[1] The Emperor made the fatal mistake of appointing Sergius, who was at once incapable and unpopular, as Solomon's successor. Stotzas, who since his defeat by Germanus had lived with a handful of followers in the wilds of Mauretania, now reappeared upon the scene and joined the Moors of Antalas, while Sergius quarrelled with his officers. The Emperor, seeing by the tidings from Africa that Sergius was unequal to the situation, committed another blunder. Instead of superseding him, he despatched a second incompetent commander, the patrician Areobindus, who had married his own niece Praejecta. He made Areobindus co-ordinate with Sergius, but he was to command the army of Byzacena, Sergius that of Numidia. The two generals did not agree, and misfortune ensued. The Byzacene forces, relying on the support of Sergius, who left them in the lurch, were severely defeated at Thacia, between Sicca Veneria (el-Kef) and Carthage (end of A.D. 545).[2] After this disaster Sergius was relieved of his post and Areobindus replaced him. He was a man of little merit, and in a few months he was removed by a conspiracy. Guntarith, the duke of Numidia, aspired to play the part of Stotzas, and having come to an understanding with some of the Moorish chiefs, he suddenly seized the palace at Carthage, and Areobindus was assassinated (March A.D. 536). Praejecta fell into the hands of Guntarith, who formed the plan of marrying her. But Guntarith's supremacy lasted little over a month. A portion of the army remained loyal and found a leader in an Armenian officer, Artabanes, who brought about the murder of the rebel at a banquet (May). Justinian appointed Artabanes Master of Soldiers of Africa, and Praejecta offered her hand to her deliverer.[3] But Artabanes was already married and Theodora refused to permit a divorce. He followed Praejecta to Constantinople, and the Emperor tried to console him by creating him Master of Soldiers in praesenti and Count of the Federates.

The situation was deplorable. The ravages of the Moors

---

[1] Isidore, Hist. Goth. 42, p. 284 ; Procop. B.G. ii. 30. 15.

[2] Thacia has been identified with Borj-Messaudi. In this battle, John,

son of Sisinniolus, one of the best officers in the army, fell.

[3] See above, p. 33.

during the last three years had exhausted and depopulated the provinces. At last Justinian made a happy appointment. John Troglita, who had served with distinction under Belisarius and Solomon and was thoroughly acquainted with the conditions of the country, was recalled from the East, where he had given new proofs of military talent, and sent to take command of the armies of Africa (end of A.D. 546). Happily the Moors were divided, and John was a diplomatist as well as a general. He was able to secure the help of Moorish contingents in his campaigns. Early in A.D. 547 he inflicted a decisive defeat on the most dangerous of his opponents, Antalas.[1] But the troubles of Africa were not yet over. A few months later, the Berbers of Tripolitana rose under Carcasan, and won a crushing victory over the Imperial troops in the plain of Gallica.[2] Antalas took the field again and joined his triumphant neighbours. But the Roman cause was retrieved in the great battle of the Fields of Cato,[3] where seventeen Moorish leaders fell, among them Carcasan (early in A.D. 548). This victory secured for Africa complete tranquillity for nearly fourteen years. The relations between the Empire and the dependent Moorish princes were renewed and revised. The administration of the provinces was placed on a normal footing. The inhabitants and the wasted lands had time to recover from the devastations. The military defences of the frontier were re-established and improved.[4] John Troglita, who seems to have governed Africa for about four years after his great victory, stands out, with Belisarius and Solomon, as the third hero of the Imperial reoccupation of Africa. His deeds inspired the African poet Corippus, whose *Johannis* tells us nearly all we know of his campaigns.[5]

Justinian was to have one more war in Africa, and it appears to have been entirely due to the stupid treachery of the military governor. The loyalty of the aged chief Cutsina was secured by an annual pension. In A.D. 563, when he came to Carthage to

---

[1] The scene of this battle is unknown ; probably somewhere south of Sufetula, see Diehl, *op. cit.* 370.
[2] Now Maret, south-east of Gabes. *Ib.* 374.
[3] Unknown locality in Byzacena. Corippus, *Johannis*, viii. 165. On this occasion many Moors, especially the faithful Cutsina, fought for the Romans.
[4] Cp. Diehl, 380.

[5] The full narrative of Procopius, *B.V.*, stops with the arrival of John. But he mentions briefly the three battles of A.D. 547–548, and grimly concludes with words which sum up the terrible sufferings which the provinces had endured : " Thus, at long last, the Libyans who survived, few in number and very poor, won some rest."

receive the money, he was assassinated by order of John Roga-
thinus, the Master of Soldiers.[1] The motive of the crime is
unknown, but the sons of the murdered Moor immediately raised
Numidia in revolt. The forces in the province were insufficient
to cope with the insurrection, and the Emperor was compelled
to send an army under his nephew Marcian, who succeeded,
perhaps by diplomatic means, in re-establishing peace.

§ 3. *The Fortification of the Provinces*

While Solomon was fighting with the Moors, he was at the
same time engaged in carrying out a large scheme of defensive
fortification to protect the African provinces against the incursion of the barbarians in the future ; he was fortifying and
rebuilding old towns and constructing new fortresses. The
building of fortresses was one of the notable features of Justinian's
policy. All the provinces exposed to foes in the East, in the
Balkan peninsula, and in Africa were protected by forts, constructed on principles carefully thought out ; but it is in Africa,
where the soil is covered with their ruins, that the system of
defence which was employed can best be studied. The numerous
walls and citadels dating from the days of Solomon, which are
still to be seen, are the best commentary on the principles and
rules laid down in contemporary military handbooks.[2]

Fortified towns, connected by a chain of small forts, formed
the first frontier defence. Behind this there was a second barrier,
larger towns with larger garrisons, which were all to afford a
refuge to the inhabitants of the neighbourhood in case of an
invasion. When the watchmen in the frontier stations discerned
menacing movements of the tribes, they transmitted the alarm
by the old system of fire signals by night or smoke signals by
day,[3] so that the people of the villages might have time to find

---

[1] The source is John Mal. xviii.
495, transcribed and completed in
Theophanes, A.M. 6055. John is
called simply ἄρχων ; but this, as
Diehl points out (456), certainly
means the *mag. mil.*, not the Praet.
Pref., who at this time was probably
Areobindus.

[2] The whole system of the African
defences has been explained and
illustrated at length by Diehl in
L'Afrique byzantine, to which I may

refer the reader who is interested in
the subject. He has written his
admirable description with the work
of the Anonymus Tacticus beside
him, and refers throughout to its
pages. Here I can only indicate
briefly the general character of the
defensive system. Details would be
useless without illustrations.

[3] See Anon. Tact. viii., and compare the notes of the editors, p.
315.

refuge in the walled towns and the garrisons of the inland places might be prepared.

In many cases the towns were entirely surrounded by walls, and in some had the additional defence of detached forts. In other cases they were open, and protected by the citadel. The neighbouring strongholds of Theveste, Thelepte, and Ammaedera on the frontier of Byzacena present good examples of the three types. The features of a fully fortified town were a wall with towers, an outer wall, and a fosse ; the space between the two walls being large enough to accommodate the refugees who flocked in from the open country in a time of danger. But this scheme is not invariably found ; sometimes there was no outer wall, sometimes there was no ditch. These variations depended upon local circumstances, as the form of the fortress depended on the nature of the ground. A rectangular shape was adopted when it was possible, but very irregular forms were sometimes required by the site. Theveste is a well-preserved example of the large fortress, rectangular, measuring about 350 by 305 yards, with three gates, and frontier towers ; Thamugadi of the smaller castle (about 122 by 75 yards), with a tower at each corner and in the centre of each side. Small forts, like Lemsa, had a tower at each of the four angles.

From Capsa (Gafsa) in the Byzacene province to Zabi Justinia-na and Thamalla in Mauretania Sitifensis the long line of fortresses can be traced round the north foothills of the Aurasian mountains. Thelepte, Theveste, with Ammaedera behind it to the north, Mascula and Bagai, Thamugadi, Lambaesis, Lambiridi, Cellae, and Tubunae [1] were the principal advanced military stations, which were connected and flanked by small castles and redoubts. When invaders from the south had penetrated this line, the inhabitants might seek shelter in Sufes (Sbiba) and Chusira (Kessera) in Byzacena; in Laribus (Lorbeus), Sicca Veneria (Kef), Thubursicum Bure (Tebursuk), Thignica (Aïn Tunga) in the Proconsular Province ; Madaura (Mdaurech), Tipasa (Tifech), Calama (Guelma), Tigisis (Aïn el-Borj) in Numidia, to mention a few of the military posts in the interior.

The Mauretanian provinces were more lightly held. It is interesting to observe that Justinian took special care to

[1] These places are now known as Medinet el-Kedima, Tébessa, Haïdra, Khenchela, Ksar Bagai, Timgad, Lambèse, Ouled Arif, Zerga, Tobna.

strengthen by impregnable walls the fortress of Septum on the straits of Gades. This ultimate outpost of the Empire was to be a post of observation. He gave express directions that it should be entrusted to a loyal and judicious commander, who was to watch the straits, gather information as to political events in Spain and Gaul, and send reports to his superior the duke of Mauretania.[1]

---

[1] *C.J.* i. 27. 2, 2.   Procopius, *Aed.* vi. 7. 14-16.

CHAPTER XVIII

THE RECONQUEST OF ITALY (I.)

§ 1. *The Last Years of King Theoderic* (*died* A.D. 526)

THE ecclesiastical reunion of Rome with the East, accomplished by Justinian and Pope Hormisdas, soon produced political effects. It would be rash to suppose that the idea of abolishing the Gothic viceroyalty and reasserting the immediate power of the Emperor in Italy had assumed a definite shape in the mind of Justinian in the early years of his uncle's reign. His own strong theological convictions may suffice to account for his policy. But the restoration of ecclesiastical unity was evidently the first step that would have been taken by a statesman who nursed the design of overthrowing the Gothic power. The existence of the schism did not indeed reconcile the Italian Catholics to the administration of the Goths, but it tended to render many of them less eager for a close political bond with Constantinople.

The death of Anastasius, with whom Theoderic never had been on terms of amity, was an important event for the Italian government. It can hardly be a coincidence that it was after Justin's succession that arrangements were made for the succession to the Ostrogothic throne. Theoderic had no male children. His daughter Amalasuntha had received a Roman education, and he had selected as her husband Eutharic, an Ostrogoth of royal lineage who was living obscurely in Spain.[1]

---

[1] He was descended from the famous king Hermanric (Jordanes gives the genealogy, *Get.* 81), and was discovered by Theoderic when he assumed the regency of Spain. His full name was Eutharic Cilliga (*C.I.L.* vi. 32003 ; Cassiodorus, *Chron.*, *sub* 518). Rome was surprised and delighted by the magnificent shows of wild beasts procured from Africa and the lavish largesses which signalised his assumption of the consulship in January 519 (*ib.*, *sub a.*). It was probably on the occasion of his consul-

151

The marriage was celebrated in A.D. 515, and a son, Athalaric, was born three years later. This infant Theoderic destined to be his successor. It was the right of the Goths to choose their own king, but the choice could hardly be made without an understanding with the Emperor if the future king was to be also the Emperor's viceroy and Master of Soldiers in Italy. That Justin was consulted, and that he agreed to Theoderic's plan, seems to be clearly shown by the fact that Eutharic was nominated consul for A.D. 519. As Goths were strictly excluded from the consulship, this could only be done by the personal motion of the Emperor, who thus signified his approbation of the settlement of the succession to the Italian throne.

When the reunion of the Churches was accomplished, Justin paid a marked compliment both to Theoderic and to the Senate by resigning the nomination of an eastern consul for A.D. 522 in order that the two sons of the distinguished Roman senator Boethius might fill the consulship as colleagues.[1] It seemed as if cordial relations between Ravenna and Constantinople might now be firmly established, yet within a year the situation became more difficult and dangerous than ever.

We have no precise information as to the views of Eutharic.[2] It appears that he entertained strong national feelings and was devoted to his Arian faith ; and he may have been somewhat impatient of the moderate policy of his father-in-law and the compromises to which it led. We do not know whether he would have been prepared to denounce the capitulations and cut Italy off from the Empire as an independent Gothic state. But he was suspicious of the intentions of the Emperor and of the loyalty of the Roman Senate. He died in the course of A.D. 522, but he may have influenced the situation by propagating these suspicions in Gothic circles. And the suspicions seemed to be confirmed by the edicts which Justin issued against the Arians. The Goths connected these efforts for the extinction of Arianism with the reunion of the Church ; they feared that the Imperial policy would provoke an anti-Arian movement

ship that Cassiodorus eulogised him in the Senate house (*Var.* ix. 25) in an oration of which a fragment is preserved (*Paneg.* pp. 465 *sqq.*, cp. p. 470).

[1] On this occasion Boethius pronounced a panegyric on the king, *De cons. Phil.* ii. 3 ; *Anecd. Holderi.*

[2] See Anon. Val. (the writer hostile to Theoderic) 80.

in Italy ; and the consequence was a growing mistrust of the
Senate, and especially of these senators who had taken a prominent part in terminating the schism. Pope Hormisdas was
trusted by Theoderic, but he died in August A.D. 523, and his
successor, John I., was associated with those who desired a
closer dependency of Italy on the Imperial government, as a
means of attaining greater power and freedom for the Roman
Senate.

It had been a token of Theoderic's goodwill when in autumn,
A.D. 522, he appointed Boethius to the post of Master of Offices.
Anicius Manlius Torquatus Severinus Boethius was a man of
illustrious birth and ample fortune, whose life was dedicated
to philosophy and science.[1] Translated from the society of
his kinsmen and friends at Rome into the court circles of
Ravenna, he did not find himself at home and could not
make himself popular. His severe ethical standards repelled
the pliant and opportune palatine officials who surrounded
the king, and probably he was not very tactful.[2] He had
held office for about a year when a storm suddenly burst over
his head.

An official seized letters which had been despatched by some
Roman senators to the Emperor.[3] In this correspondence
passages occurred which could be interpreted as disloyal to the
government of Theoderic,[4] and the patrician Faustus Albinus
junior was particularly compromised. The matter passed into
the hands of Cyprian, a referendarius whose duty it was to
prepare the case for the king's Consistorium, which was the

---

[1] He had been consul in 510. He
constructed a sun-dial, a water-clock,
and a celestial globe at Theoderic's
request, to be sent as gifts to the
Burgundian king. For his writings
see below, § 11.

[2] He seems to have opposed and
prevented the appointment of a
certain Decoratus to the Quaestorship, because he considered him as
having *mentem nequissimi scurrae
delatorisque* (*De consol. Phil.* iii. 4).
Decoratus became Quaestor after
the fall of Boethius. The epitaph in
Rossi, *Inscr. Chr.* ii. p. 113, may be
his.

[3] Severus was the name of the
official (Suidas, *s.v.* Σεβῆρος). The
sources for the following events are

Boethius, *De cons. Phil.* i. 4 ; Anon.
Val. 85-87 ; *Lib. pont., Vita Johannis*,
pp. 275-276 ; Procopius, *B.G.* i. 1.
The questions relating to the legal
procedure and the exact nature of
the charges have been much discussed, most recently by Cessi in
his introduction to Anon. Val., where
the literature of the subject will
be found, p. cxxv.

[4] *Adversus regnum regis.* The passage in Suidas suggests that Albinus
himself was not the writer of any of
the letters ; they were written by his
friends. He had been consul in
493 and Praet. Pref. of Italy in 513.
He seems to have belonged to the
Decian family (cp. Sundwall, *Abh.*
p. 87).

tribunal for cases of treason.¹ It is important to note that Cyprian was a man of unusual parts, and enjoyed the confidence of Theoderic, whom he used often to accompany on his rides.² The intercepted letters of the friends of Albinus justified an investigation. Boethius was a member of the Consistory *ex officio*, and he spoke in defence of Albinus.³ It was impossible to deny the material facts, and Boethius took the line that Albinus was acting not in his private capacity but as a senator, and therefore was not alone responsible for his act. " The whole Senate, including myself, is responsible ; there can be no action against Albinus as an individual." This defence was construed as a confession, and made the ground of a charge of treason against Boethius himself, and three men who belonged to ministerial circles but were under a cloud came forward to support the charge. He was arrested, and, as a matter of course, deprived of his office. Cassiodorus was appointed in his stead, and it may be ascribed to his influence that no attempt was made to involve other members of the Senate in the crime.⁴

Up to this point there is no reason for thinking that there was anything illegal in the procedure ; but now, instead of completing the process of Albinus and trying Boethius before the

¹ For the duties of the referendarii see Cass. *Var.* vi. 17 (*per eum nobis causarum ordines exponuntur*). Boethius (*loc. cit.*) speaks of Cyprian as a *delator*. Severus was the *delator*, not Cyprian, who only handled the *delatio* ; and Cessi defends him as having simply performed his legal duty. But he may have shown a zeal and partiality in the prosecution which would explain the strong language of Boethius. Cp. Anon. Val. 86.
² See the panegyrics of Cyprian's qualities in the letters conferring on him the office of *Comes s. larg.* and recommending him to the Senate of which this appointment made him a member, A.D. 524. Cassiodorus, *Var.* v. 40 and 41. He knew Gothic as well as Greek and Latin (*trifarii linguis*).
³ I cannot agree with Cessi (p. cxlix.) that it can be inferred from Cass *ib.* vi. 6. 2 that it was a duty of the Master of Offices to defend accused senators. But any member of the Consistory could express his opinion on a case.

⁴ Cp. Sundwall, *Abh.* p. 246. Sundwall thinks that the guilt of Boethius lay not in his defence of Albinus, but in trying to suppress the accusation (p. 243). Cyprian was the subordinate of Boethius, and Boethius appears, on grounds of procedure, to have raised objections to the denunciation of Severus being received (*delatorem ne documenta deferret quibus senatum maiestatis reum faceret impedire criminamur* (*De cons. Phil.* i. 4)). But surely this was only an incidental point, not serious charge. The three witnesses were Basilius, Opilio, and Gaudentius, of whom Opilio was Cyprian's brother and a relative, perhaps son-in-law, of Basilius. Boethius says that Basilius was in debt, and the other two had been condemned to exile *ob multiplices fraudes*. A year or two after Theoderic's death Opilio was appointed *com. sacr. larg.* and eulogised by Cassiodorus (*Var.* viii. 16 and 17) in the usual way.

Consistory, the matter was taken out of the hands of that body, and the two men were thrown into prison at Ticinum (late autumn, A.D. 523). Thither the Prefect of Rome was summoned, and with him the king proceeded with the investigation of the case.[1] Boethius was found guilty and condemned to death. Albinus drops out of the story, his fate is not recorded. Theoderic was determined to teach the Senate a lesson, but perhaps he thought it better to let the course of political events guide him to an ultimate decision as to the fate of the distinguished philosopher. In his dungeon [2] Boethius composed his famous book on the *Consolation of Philosophy*, and probably expected that his sentence would be mitigated. But he was put to death (in the late summer or autumn of A.D. 524),[3] and, it was said, in a cruel manner. A cord was tightened round his head, and he was despatched with a club.[3]

While Boethius was awaiting his trial, the senators had met and debated. They were thoroughly alarmed, and passed decrees designed to exculpate themselves, and therefore repudiating Boethius and Albinus. The only man perhaps who stood by Boethius was his father-in-law Symmachus, the head of the Senate. He may have used strong language ; he declined at least to associate himself with the subservient decrees. Thereby he laid himself open to the charge that he defended treason and sympathised with traitors. He was arrested, taken to Ravenna, and executed. It was a foolish act, the precaution of a tyrant.[4]

---

[1] Boethius speaks of a forged letter which was used against him, *loc. cit.* In ordinary criminal trials of senators the tribunal consisted of the Prefect and five senators (Mommsen, *Strafrecht*, 287), and this procedure may have been adopted as Sundwall suggests (*op. cit.* 248), although, as it was a case of treason, the proper tribunal was the Consistorium. In any case, I am sure that the ordinary view that the Senate tried the case and sentenced Boethius is mistaken (so Cessi, cxlviii.).

[2] Probably at Ticinum. But Boethius himself had been transferred to Calvenzano (Anon. Val. 87) near Melegnano, about seven miles south of Milan.

[3] We do not know when the

sentence was passed. Nine months or more seem to have elapsed between his arrest and execution. October 23 was the date accepted in ecclesiastical tradition for his death, but this tradition only emerges three centuries later and has been questioned (cp. the article on Boethius in *D. Chr. B.*). See Pfeilschifter, *Theod. der Grosse*, p. 164.

[4] The passage in Boethius, i. 4, *an optasse illius ordinis salutem nefas vocabo ? ille quidem suis de me decretis uti hoc nefas esset efficeret*, is important. In my opinion it supplies the key to the arrest of Symmachus, which historians have not explained. It is evident that he did not subscribe to the decree repudiating his son-in-law, for whose wrongs he was mourning

It is probable that these events had some connexion with
an Imperial edict which was issued about this time, threatening
Arians with severe penalties, excluding them from public offices
and from service in the army, and closing their churches. Theoderic was alarmed. He resented the revival of pains and penalties
against his fellow-religionists in the East, and he saw in the
edict an encouragement to the Italians to turn against their
Arian fellow-subjects. But the edict is not preserved, and we
do not know the exact date of its promulgation ; so that we
cannot decide whether it influenced Theoderic's policy before
the execution of Boethius. It may not have been issued till
after his death.[1] We can only say that severe measures against
the Arians had been adopted, and reported in Italy, before the
autumn of A.D. 525. Theoderic determined to bring matters
to an issue at Constantinople by coming forward as the protector
of his fellow-heretics in the East. He selected as his ambassador
John, the bishop of Rome, who was induced to undertake the
distasteful commission of urging the Emperor to relax his policy
and of conveying to him the royal threat that, if he persisted,
reprisals on Italian Catholics would be the consequence. The
Pope set forth, accompanied by several bishops and prominent
senators, some time between the beginning of September and

(Boethius, *op. cit.* ii. 4), and he can
hardly have failed to speak in his
defence. This attitude in the Senate
furnished Theoderic with an excuse
for arresting a man whom he had
reason to fear as a near and dear
relative of Boethius. The sources
say nothing of a trial, but it seems
unlikely that this formality was
dispensed with. The date of the
death of Symmachus fell in 525
(Marius Avent., *sub a.*), probably
in the first half. I cannot agree with
the transposition in the text of Anon.
Val. proposed by Cessi (*op. cit.*
cxxvii.), which, by removing § 88-91
so as to follow § 84, would make the
notice of the death of Symmachus,
§ 92, follow immediately that of the
death of Boethius.

   [1] We possess the edict against
heretics of Justin and Justinian (the
beginning of it is lost) issued in 527
(*C.J.* i. 5. 12 ; we are able to date
it through the reference in i. 5. 18, § 4),
which contains the exception in

favour of the Goths, made after the
negotiations with Pope John. The
date of 523-524 for a measure against
the Arians depends on Theophanes,
A.M. 6016, where the mission of
Pope John is misdated. I cannot
agree with Pfeilschifter (*op. cit.* 168)
that *C.J.* i. 5. 12 was issued in 523,
with its reserve in favour of the
Goths, and that, notwithstanding
that reserve, severe measures were
taken in the winter of 523-524 as a
reprisal for the proceedings against
Albinus and Boethius. It seems
more probable that there was special
legislation against the Arians in 524,
provoked perhaps by the wealth of
the Arian churches (πλοῦτόν τινα
ἀκοῆς κρείττω, Procopius, *H.A.* 11.
16), and that the persecution began
without any reference to Italian
politics. It must be emphasised
that in the prosecution of Boethius
there was no anti-Catholic tendency ;
his opponents (Cyprian, etc.) were
Catholics.

the end of November, A.D. 525.[1] He was received in the eastern
capital with an honourable welcome, and remained there at least
five months. He celebrated Christmas and Easter in St.
Sophia, and successfully vindicated his right to sit on a higher throne
than the Patriarch's. It is recorded, and perhaps we have no
right to question the statement, that Justin, though long since
duly crowned, caused the Pope to crown him again.[2] The mission
succeeded in its principal object. The Emperor agreed to restore
their churches to the Arians and permit them to hold their
services. He refused to allow converted Arians to return to
their old faith, but the main demand of Theoderic was conceded.
Yet when the Pope and his companions returned to Ravenna
in the middle of May[3] their reception was the reverse of that
which successful envoys might expect. They were arrested and
thrown into prison.[4] John, who had been ailing when he started for
the East, died a few days later (May 18, A.D. 526);[5] his body was
taken to Rome and interred in St. Peter's ; there was a popular
demonstration at his funeral and he was regarded as a martyr.

There was a contested election for the succession to the
vacant see. It was probably a contest of strength between the
Italians who were friendly to the Ostrogothic regime and those
who were not. The former succeeded in securing the victory
of their candidate after a struggle of two months, and the election
of Felix IV. (July 12) was a satisfaction to Theoderic, who
had expressly signalised his wishes in the matter to the members
of the Senate.[6]

---

[1] The determination of this date, which is due to Pfeilschifter, depends (1) on the fact that John was in Constantinople at Christmas (so that he could not have started later than the end of November), this is known from the statement of a contemporary priest Procopius, who, when John arrived, was translating a Latin work into Greek (see note to Bonn ed. of *Chron. Pasch.* ii. 120) ; (2) on a letter of Boniface, *primicerius notariorum*, addressed to the Pope before he left Italy in the 4th indiction which began on September 1 (so that he could not have started before September), Pitra, *Analecta novissima*, i. 466, where the addressee is wrongly said to be John IV. Of the senators who were with John, Importunus and

Theodorus, members of the great Decian family, and Agapetus were ex-consuls.

[2] This is mentioned only in *Lib. pont.*

[3] They must have started immediately after Easter day, which fell in 526 on April 19.

[4] *Lib. pont.*, *in custodia eos omnes adflictos cremauit* (tortured). Anon. Val. 93 says only *in offensa sua eum esse iubet*, which Cessi interprets (p. clix.) as pointing to a rigorous surveillance.

[5] *Lib. Pont.* xv. kal. Iun.

[6] This is clear from the letter of Athalaric to the Senate commending that body for having accepted his grandfather's choice. Cass. *Var.* viii. 15.

But the days of Theoderic were numbered. Seven weeks later he was seized by dysentery, and died on August 30. Before his death he called together the Goths of his entourage and, presenting to them his grandson Athalaric as their future king, enjoined upon them to keep on good terms with the Senate and the Roman people, and always to show the becoming respect to the Emperor.[1] Popular legend did not fail to connect his end with his recent acts of tyranny. It was said that a huge fish had been served at the royal table, and that to the king's imagination, tortured by conscience, its head, with long teeth and wild eyes, assumed the appearance of Symmachus. Theoderic took to his bed in terror, and declared to his physician his remorse for the slaughter of the illustrious senators.[2]

During the last year of his life he had been distressed by the fate of his sister Amalafrida, the widow of king Trasamund.[3] She had remained in Africa after her husband's death, and was probably useful to her brother in maintaining the good relations between the courts of Ravenna and Carthage which her marriage had inaugurated. But as king Hilderic leaned more and more towards Constantinople, and fell under the influence of Justinian, he drew away from the Goths, and his friendship with Theoderic cooled. Amalafrida, who had her own Gothic entourage in her adopted country, was accused, rightly or wrongly, of conspiring against the king, and was thrown into prison, where she died, from natural causes it was given out, but it was suspected that her death was violent. All her Goths were killed. Theoderic, if he had lived, would doubtless have attempted to wreak vengeance on Hilderic. After his death his daughter was not in a position to do more than address to the king of the Vandals a strong remonstrance.[4]

---

[1] Jordanes, *Get.* 304. As Justin had agreed to the concession which he demanded, and as he had secured the man he desired as head of the Catholic Church, it is perfectly incredible that four days before his death Theoderic should have drawn up a decree empowering the Arians to take possession of Catholic churches, as Anon. Val. 94 asserts. The statement, which stands alone, has generally been accepted, but Pfeilschifter is assuredly right in rejecting it.

[2] Procopius, *ib.*; Jordanes, *Get.* 59.

[3] In his last years it may be noted that he had experienced a succession of losses, which he must have keenly felt, by the deaths of Ennodius, a trusted friend (in 521), his son-in-law Eutharic (523), his grandson Sigeric of Burgundy (522; see above, chap. xiii. § 5); and the death of Pope Hormisdas, with whom he was always on cordial terms, was also a blow.

[4] The letter was written by Cassiodorus and is preserved (*Var.* ix. 1). The other sources are Procopius, *B.V.* iii. 9. 3-5, and Victor Tonn.

§ 2. *The Regency of Amalasuntha* (A.D. 526–534)

Theoderic was succeeded by a child, his grandson Athalaric, whom his daughter Amalasuntha had borne to Eutharic, and Amalasuntha held the reins of government as regent during her son's minority. She had received a Roman education at Ravenna ; she was brave and intelligent,[1] and perhaps sincerely believed in the ideal of blending the Italians and Goths into a united nation. Even if her convictions and sentiments had been different, the inherent weakness of a regency would have forced her to follow her father's last advice, to keep on good terms with the Emperor and to conciliate the Senate. The restoration of the confiscated properties of Boethius and Symmachus to their children was a pledge of the change. The Roman people was assured that no difference would be made in the treatment of Romans and Goths,[2] and when the Senate and people swore loyalty to the young king, he also took an oath of good government to them. The Senate was invited to express its demands and desires.[3] Ambassadors were sent to the Emperor bearing a letter[4] in which he was requested to aid the youth of Athalaric, and it was suggested that the tomb should be allowed to bury old hatreds : *Claudantur odia cum sepultis.*

Amalasuntha determined to give her son the education of Roman princes, and she confided him to the care of three civilised

---

sub 523 (the year of Trasamund's death). This date has been reasonably questioned by Schmidt (*Gesch. der Wand.* 122). For the letter of Cassiodorus strongly suggests that the queen's death was quite recent. I should be inclined to date it early in 526, and to connect with it (as Schmidt does) Theoderic's urgency in completing his naval armament, and collecting it at Classis on June 13. See *Var.* v. 17. 3 *non habet quod nobis Graecus imputet aut Afer insultet* (also letters 16, 18, and 19).

[1] Compare the laudatory remarks of Procopius, *B.G.* i. 2. p. 10 ; 4. p. 24. There is a miniature representation of Amalasuntha on the consular diptych of Orestes (A.D. 530) which is preserved at South Kensington. She wears earrings and pendants from her head-dress (πρεπενδούλια, like

those worn by Roman Empresses of the time), but no diadem.

[2] Cassiodorus, *Var.* viii. 3.

[3] *Ibid.* 2. A letter was also addressed to the Catholic clergy, requesting their prayers for Athalaric (*ib.* 8).

[4] *Ibid.* 1. This letter is addressed in the MSS. to Justinian. There is a reference in the text to the Emperor's old age, and it is simpler to adopt Mommsen's correction *Iustino* than the explanation attempted by Martroye (p. 158-159). It is to be noted that the Gothic general Tuluin (who had commanded in all Theoderic's campaigns since 504) was created a Patrician soon after Theoderic's death, and thus became a member of the Senate (Cass. *Var.* viii. 9 and 10). This act must have been sanctioned by Justin.

Goths, who shared her own views. But the Goths, as a whole, had no comprehension of the ideal of Italian civilisation at which she, like her father, aimed ; they believed only in the art of war ; and they regarded themselves as victors living in the midst of a vanquished population. It outraged their barbarian sentiments that their king should receive an education in the humanities. Their indignation was aroused when Athalaric, chastised by his mother for some fault, was found in tears. They whispered that the queen wished to do away with her son and marry again. Some of the leaders of this faction then sought an audience of Amalasuntha, and protested against the system of training which she had chosen for the king. A literary education, they urged, promotes effeminacy and cowardice ; children who fear the whip cannot face the sword and spear ; look at Theoderic, he had no idea of letters ; let Athalaric be brought up in manly exercises with companions of his own age. Amalasuntha feigned to be persuaded by arguments with which she profoundly disagreed. She feared that, if she refused, she would be deposed from the regency, for there were but few among the Goths who sympathised with her ideas and policy. Athalaric was released from the discipline of pedagogues, but even the enemies of a liberal education would hardly have contended that the new system was a success. He was of a weak and degenerate nature, and the Gothic youths with whom he associated soon led him into precocious debauchery which ruined his health.

As time went on, the dissatisfaction of the Goths with the rule of Amalasuntha increased, and she became aware that a plot was on foot to overthrow her. She sent three of the most dangerous men who were engaged in the agitation against her to different places on the northern frontier, on the pretext of military duty. Finding that they still carried on their intrigues, she decided on stronger measures. Fully estimating the hazards of her position, she took the precaution of providing herself with a retreat. She wrote to Justinian, asking if he would receive her in case of need. The Emperor, who probably did not view with dissatisfaction the situation in Italy, cordially agreed, and prepared a mansion at Dyrrhachium for the queen's reception on her journey to Constantinople. Thus secured, Amalasuntha proceeded to the commission of murders, which it is common to palliate or justify by the plea of political necessity.

She sent some devoted Goths to assassinate the three arch-conspirators. She stowed 40,000 gold pieces in a vessel, which she sent to Dyrrhachium, directing that it should not be unloaded before her arrival. When she learned that the murders had been duly accomplished she recalled the ship and remained at Ravenna.

It is important to realise that the Ostrogothic kingdom was now politically isolated. The system of friendly understandings, cemented by family alliances, which Theodoric had laboured to build up among the western Teutonic powers was at the best a weak guarantee of peace ; after his death it completely broke down. We have seen how the alliance with the Vandals was ruptured, and how Amalafrida, Theoderic's sister, was put to death by Hilderic,[1] an injury which Amalasuntha was not in a position to avenge. The Thuringians, whose queen was her cousin, were attacked and conquered by the Franks.[2] The Franks were also intent on driving the Visigoths from the corner of Gaul which they still retained ; the young king Amalaric, the grandson of Theoderic, was killed (A.D. 531), and Theudis, who succeeded him, had enough to do to maintain the possession of Septimania. From that quarter the Ostrogoths could look for no support. The power of the Franks became more formidable by their conquest of Burgundy (A.D. 532–534),[3] and there was always the danger that the Ostrogothic provinces in Gaul might be attacked by their insatiable ambition. Thus the Italian regency would have been forced, even if there had been no internal difficulties, to conduct itself demurely and respectfully towards the Imperial power to which constitutionally it owed allegiance.

Amalasuntha had one near relative in Italy, her cousin Theodahad, the son of Amalafrida, queen of the Vandals, by a first marriage. He was the last person to whom she could look for help in her difficulties. Theodahad had none of the soldierly instincts of his race. He had enjoyed a liberal education and was devoted to the study of the philosophy of Plato. But he was far from being free from the passions which philosophy condemns. The ruling trait of his character was cupidity.

---

[1] See above, p. 129.

[2] In 529 and following years. See below, Chap. XVIII. § 13.

[3] Between 529 and 532 Amala- suntha restored to Burgundy districts between the Isère and the Durance, which had been taken by Theoderic in 523. Cass. *Var.* xi. 1. 13 ; cp. viii. 10. 8.

He had estates in Tuscany, and by encroachments on the properties of his neighbours he had gradually acquired a great part
of that province.[1] " He considered it a misfortune to have a
neighbour." The Tuscans had complained of his rapacity, and
Amalasuntha had forced him to make some restitutions, earning
his undying hatred. He was not, however, naturally ambitious
of power. His ideal was to spend the last years of his life in
the luxury and society of Constantinople. When he first appears
on the stage of history he takes a step to realise this desire.
Two eastern bishops had come to Rome on business connected
with theological doctrine.[2] Theodahad entrusted them with a
message to Justinian, proposing to hand over to him his Tuscan
estates in return for a large sum of money, the rank of senator,
and permission to live at Constantinople.

Along with these two bishops, Alexander, an Imperial agent,
had arrived in Italy. His ostensible business was to present
to the regent some trifling complaints of unfriendly conduct.[3]
At a public audience, Amalasuntha replied to the charges, dwelt
on their triviality, and alleged her services to the Emperor in
allowing his fleet to make use of Sicily in the expedition against
the Vandals. But this performance was only intended to deceive
the Goths. Justinian had followed closely events in Italy, and
the real purpose of Alexander's visit was to conclude a secret
arrangement with the regent. Her position was now more critical
than ever. The premature indulgences of Athalaric had brought
on a decline, and he was not expected to live. On his death her
position, unpopular as she was with the Goths, would hardly
be tenable, and she thought of resigning her power into the

---

[1] Theoderic had on more than one
occasion to check and reprove his
nephew's cupidity. Cass. *Var.* iv. 39;
v. 12.

[2] Hypatius of Ephesus and Demetrius of Philippi. Cp. Liberatus,
Brev. xx. They bore a letter from
the Emperor to the Pope, which, with
the Pope's reply, is preserved in
C.J. i. 1. 8. The former is dated
June 6, 533, the latter March 25,
534. Thus the negotiations with
Amalasuntha and Theodahad are
dated to 533 – 534, and we can
infer that Alexander and the bishops
left Italy at the end of March
534.

[3] The three complaints were that
she retained the fortress of Lilybaeum, which belonged to the
Emperor; that she gave refuge to
ten Huns who had deserted from
the Imperial army; and that in a
campaign against the Gepids in the
neighbourhood of Sirmium, the Goths
had committed hostile acts against
Gratiana, a town in Moesia. The
claim of the Emperor to Lilybaeum
was founded on the circumstance
that Theoderic gave it to his sister
when she married Hilderic (see above,
Vol. I. p. 461). Belisarius had demanded its surrender at the end of
the Vandalic war.

hands of the Emperor.[1] She communicated her intention to Alexander, who then returned to Constantinople with the bishops. On receiving the messages of Amalasuntha and of Theodahad, Justinian sent a new agent to Italy, Peter of Thessalonica, an able and persuasive diplomatist.

Meanwhile Athalaric died.[2] But now that the critical moment had come, Amalasuntha, who enjoyed power, could not bear to part with it, and she committed a fatal blunder. She sent for her cousin Theodahad, assured him that, in attempting to curb his rapacity, her intention had been to prevent him from making himself unpopular, and offered him the title of king, on condition that she should retain in her own hands the exercise of government. Dissembling the bitter animosity which he felt towards her and of which she can have had little conception, he consented to her terms, and took a solemn oath to fulfil all she demanded. As soon as he was proclaimed king,[3] formal letters were addressed to the Senate, in which Amalasuntha dwelled upon Theodahad's literary tastes, and Theodahad enlarged on Amalasuntha's wisdom, professing his resolve to imitate her.[4] Letters were also despatched to Justinian, informing him of what had happened.[5]

But after the first hypocritical formalities, Theodahad lost little time in throwing off the mask. He gathered together the relatives of the three Goths who had been murdered by Amalasuntha's orders ; the Gothic notables who were faithful to her were slain, and she was herself seized and imprisoned in an island in Lake Bolsena in Tuscany, which probably belonged to the king.[6] She was then forced to write a letter to Justinian, assuring him that she had suffered no wrong. Theodahad wrote himself

---

[1] If Amalasuntha seriously contemplated this step, it was, though defensible theoretically on constitutional grounds, an act of gross treachery towards her own people.

[2] On October 2, 534, according to *Cons. Ital.* (Agnellus), in *Chron. min.* i. 333. This accords with the statements of Procopius (*B.G.* i. 4) and Jordanes (*Rom.* 367) that Athalaric reigned eight years. For the coins of his reign see Wroth, *Coins of the Vandals*, p. xxxiii. An inscription records that he constructed seats in the amphitheatre of Ticinum in 528-

529 (*d. n. Atalaricus rex gloriosissimus, C.I.L.* v. 6418).

[3] *Cons. Ital. loc. cit.* : *alia die*, which seems to mean October 3, the day after Athalaric's death.

[4] Cassiodorus, *Var.* x. 3 and 4· Cassiodorus had been appointed Praet. Prefect before the end of Athalaric's reign. Cp. *Var.* xi. 7.

[5] *Ib.* 1 and 2.

[6] There are two islands in the lake, Bisentina and Martana ; the latter is supposed to be the scene of the tragedy.

to the same effect, and committed the letters to two senators—Liberius, the Praetorian Prefect of Gaul, and Opilio—to bear to Constantinople.

In the meantime, Peter, the new agent whom the Emperor had selected to continue the secret negotiations, had started. Travelling by the Egnatian Road, Peter met on his way the Goths who bore the news of Athalaric's death and Theodahad's elevation to the throne ; and on reaching the port of Aulon (Valona), he met Liberius and Opilio, who informed him of the queen's captivity. Peter sent a fast messenger to Constantinople and awaited further orders.[1] Justinian immediately wrote a letter to Amalasuntha, assuring her of his protection, and instructed Peter to make it clear to Theodahad and the Goths that he was prepared to support the queen. But the Emperor's authority and his envoy's representations did not avail to save Amalasuntha.[2] She was killed—strangled, it was said, in a bath—in the lonely island by the relatives of the Goths whom she had slain, and who had persuaded Theodahad that her death was necessary to his own safety. Goths and Romans were alike shocked by the fate of Theoderic's daughter, whose private virtues were acknowledged by all. Peter told Theodahad, in the name of Justinian, that the crime which had been perpetrated meant " a war without truce." The king pleaded that it had been committed against his will, but he continued to hold the assassins in honour.[3]

---

[1] That Peter's messenger outstripped the Italian ambassadors is clear from the narrative in Procopius. They arrived after Justinian had forwarded his instructions. Liberius told the whole truth, but Opilio sought to defend Theodahad. Historians have not observed that there is an interesting notice of the Emperor's reception of Liberius in Constantine Porph. *De cerim.* i. 87 (taken doubtless from a work of this same Peter): Λίβερ ὁ πατρίκιος καὶ ἔπαρχος Γαλλιῶν ἐπέμφθη ἐνταῦθα παρὰ Θευδᾶ τοῦ ῥηγὸς Γότθων καὶ τῆς συγκλήτου Ῥωμαίων. Justinian accorded him the same honours as were due to a Praet. Pref. of the East. He afterwards passed into Justinian's service, and was Augustal Prefect of Egypt. We shall meet him again in Sicily and Spain.

[2] Jordanes, *Get.* 306.

[3] The chronology is beset by serious difficulties. The fact that Peter met the envoys of Amalasuntha at Thessalonica and those of Theodahad at Aulon, shows that her captivity began very soon after Theodahad's accession (we cannot infer anything from the vague *post aliquantum tempus* of Jordanes, *Get.* 306). The only evidence for the date of her murder is *Cons. Ital., loc. cit.*, where she is said to have been imprisoned in Lake Bolsena on April 30, 535. It seems probable that this may really be the date of her murder ; it cannot be that of her imprisonment, for she was already confined *in the island* when Theodahad sent his envoys to Justinian (*B.G.* i. 4). In this view, I think, Leuthold (*Untersuchungen zur ostgotischen Gesch.* 26) is right. Peter, who seems to have left Con-

This brief story of Amalasuntha's tragic end, told by Procopius in his *History of the Wars,* raises some perplexing questions, which might compel us, even if we had no other evidence, to suspect the presence of unexplained circumstances in the background. It is difficult to understand Theodahad's motive in permitting the murder, knowing, as he well knew, that such an act would cause the highest displeasure to Justinian and might lead to war, which, as his subsequent policy shows, he desired, almost at any cost, to avoid. Peter was in Italy at the time, and had been there for some months before the event. He had been instructed by the Emperor to champion the cause of Amalasuntha. How was it that he was not only unable to restore her to liberty but could not even save her life ? When we find that Procopius is silent as to any efforts of the ambassador in the queen's behalf, and even, by an ambiguous sentence, allows his readers to believe that Peter arrived too late to interfere, there is ground for suspecting that the tale is only half told.

An explanation is forthcoming from the pen of Procopius himself. In his *Secret History* he has added a sinister supplement, which, he says, " it was impossible for me to publish through fear of the Empress." [1] According to this story, Theodora viewed with alarm the prospect of Amalasuntha seeking refuge at Constantinople. She feared that this handsome and strong-minded woman might gain an influence over the Emperor, and she suborned Peter, by promises of money and office, to procure the death of the queen of the Goths. " On arriving in Italy, Peter persuaded Theodahad to despatch Amalasuntha. And

stantinople in October, and was detained for some time at Aulon to receive instructions, must have reached Italy before the end of the year, or at latest in January. Here the difficulty arises. Procopius says (*ib.*) Πέτρου δὲ ἀφικομένου ἐς ᾽Ιταλίαν ᾽Αμαλασούνθῃ ξυνέβη ἐξ ἀνθρώπων ἀφανισθῆναι. This has been generally interpreted to mean, Peter on his arrival in Italy found that Amalasuntha had already been done away with. We should thus be faced with three alternatives : (1) the rejection of the date April 30 ; (2) the extremely unlikely hypothesis that Peter remained at Aulon till May ; (3) the hypothesis, put forward

by Leuthold (*ib.* 24), that Procopius deliberately falsified facts. But the words of Procopius admit a different interpretation. In fact, they properly mean : After the arrival of Peter in Italy, it occurred that Amalasuntha was done away with (ἀφανισθῆναι is aorist, not pluperfect). My own view is that Procopius designedly made his statement ambiguous. He was treading on delicate ground, and he was afraid to force on the reader's attention the fact that Peter was some time (about four months) in Italy and was unable (or unwilling) to save the queen's life.

[1] *H.A.* 16. *ad init.* Cp. above, p. 34.

in consequence of this he was promoted to the dignity of Master of Offices, and won great power and general detestation." [1] The credibility of this story has been doubted,[2] but the evidence in its favour is considerably stronger than has been realised.

It may be observed, in the first place, that it supplies an adequate explanation of the conduct of Theodahad in consenting to the crime. Relying on the influence of the powerful Empress, he might feel himself safe in complying with the wishes of the Gothic enemies of Amalasuntha and ignoring the Emperor's threats. And, in the second place, there is nothing incredible in Theodora's complicity. There is nothing in her record to make us suppose that she was incapable of such a crime, and the motive was surely sufficient. It must be remembered that, on the scene of public affairs, Amalasuntha was, next to Theodora herself, the most remarkable living woman. She possessed advantages of person and education, which report might magnify, and in her eight years of government she had shown strength of mind and even unscrupulousness. But if in these respects she might compete with the Empress, her unblemished private character and her royal birth were advantages which Theodora could perhaps be hardly expected to forgive. Whatever be the truth about Theodora's early career, her origin was of the lowest, and report, rightly or wrongly, was busy with the licentiousness of her youth. We can well understand that Theodora would have been ready to go far in order to prevent the arrival at Constantinople of a king's daughter who might gain an influence over the Emperor and would in any case inevitably challenge comparisons unfavourable to herself.

The statement of Procopius respecting Theodora's part in the drama must be admitted to be perfectly credible, but, in the absence of corroborative evidence, it would be open to us to dismiss it as the specious invention of malice. We have,

---

[1] Μάλιστα πάντων ἔχθους, Haury's correction of ἐχθρῶν.

[2] Gibbon (c. xli.) accepts it in his text, but throws some doubt on it in his note. Hodgkin rejects it as "a malicious after-thought of the revengeful old age of Procopius" (iii. 720), but does not discuss the evidence. Diehl (*Justinien*, 181) observes: "La chose semble bien douteuse, quoique Théodora entre-tint à ce moment même avec Théodat et sa femme une assez mystérieuse correspondance et que Pierre lui fût tout dévoué." Dahn thought that the story may perhaps be a pure invention (*Prokopius*, 379).

however, independent evidence which corroborates Procopius in one important particular. It is an essential point in his story that Peter was the devoted agent of Theodora, and that she procured his appointment as ambassador to Ravenna. This is fully borne out by letters which Theodahad addressed to the Empress, when Peter returned to Constantinople after the murder. In these letters the ambassador is unambiguously described as her confidential envoy.[1] Here too we learn the significant fact that she enjoined on Theodahad that, if he made any request to the Emperor, he should first submit it to her.[2] Moreover, in a letter of Theodahad's wife Gudeliva to Theodora, there is a mysterious passage which, in the light of what Procopius tells us, can be most easily explained as a veiled reference to the crime. " While it is not seemly," wrote Gudeliva, " that there should be any discord between the Roman realms, an affair has occurred of such a kind as fitly to render us dearer to you." [3] In a letter despatched immediately after the murder, this sentence bears an ominous significance.

The story of Procopius implies that the secret intrigues were known to a wide circle. Even if that were not so, he might have received information from Antonina, who was in Theodora's confidence, or from Peter himself. We must remember too that Theodahad, when he abandoned all thoughts of peace, had no motive to conceal the guilty intervention of Theodora. The conclusion that she did intervene and that Peter, acting by her orders, promoted the murder of Amalasuntha by hints and indirections, while he was ostensibly, in obedience to Justinian, acting in the interests of the queen, seems to be warranted by the evidence considered as a whole. This evidence would, of course, be far from sufficient to procure her conviction in a legal court. No public prosecutor could act on it. But where a jury would not be justified in convicting, public opinion is frequently justified in judging that a charge is true.

---

[1] Cassiodorus, *Var.* x. 20 *additum est etiam gaudio meo quod talem virum vestra serenitas destinavit ; ib.* 23 *legatum vestrum . . . Petrum . . . vestris obsequiis inhaerentem.*

[2] *Ib.* 20 *hortamini eum ut quicquid expetendum a triumphali principe domno iugali vestro credimus, vestris*

ante sensibus ingeramus.

[3] *Ib.* 21 *emersit tamen et qualitas rei, quae nos efficere cariores vestrae debeat aequitati.* It must be remembered that the interests of Gudeliva were also involved. Her position as wife of the king, with Amalasuntha as the queen, would have been intolerable.

§ 3. *The Reign of Theodahad, and Outbreak of Hostilities*
(A.D. 535–536)

Soon after the crime Peter returned to Constantinople. He bore letters from Theodahad and his wife to Justinian and Theodora ; and he was to be followed presently by an Italian ecclesiastic, perhaps Pope Agapetus himself.[1] The object of Theodahad was to avert hostilities, and it is clear that he relied, above all, on the influence of Theodora. It is said that he forced the Roman senators to address Justinian in behalf of peace, by threatening to slay them, with their wives and children, if they refused. And we possess a letter of the Senate, drawn up by the Praetorian Prefect Cassiodorus, professing deep affection for the Amal ruler, nourished at the breasts of Rome, and imploring the Emperor to keep the peace. But the king's hopes of a peaceful settlement were vain. The Emperor immediately prepared for war. The idea of restoring the Imperial power in Italy had probably been long in his mind, his diplomacy had been occupied with it during the past year, and in a law issued six weeks before the murder of the queen he seems to allude to the

---

[1] If we read the six letters in Cass. *Var.* x. 19-24 together, it appears unquestionable that they were despatched about the same time. 19 (Theod. to Justinian), 20 (Theod. to Theodora), 21 (Gudeliva to Theodora) were entrusted to Peter ; 22 (Theod. to Justinian), 23 (Theod. to Theodora), 24 (Gudeliva to Theodora) were to be committed to the unnamed ecclesiastic, who is referred to in the same terms, in five of the letters, as *illum virum venerabilem*. It is obvious from the tenor that hostilities had not yet begun, and that Theodahad's object in writing was to avert them. Further, 19 was the *first* communication addressed by him to the Emperor since Peter's arrival early in 535, as is clear from the first sentence, in which he thanks Justinian for congratulating him on his elevation (*gratias divinitati referimus quod provectum nostrum clementiae vestrae gratissimum esse declarastis*). We may therefore confidently date these documents to summer 535. Another document also belongs here, xi. 13, an appeal of the Roman Senate to preserve peace. The tenor seems to point to a date before the outbreak of war, and the statement that the letter would be delivered *per illum virum venerabilem legatum piissimi regis nostri* seems conclusive. We may naturally connect this letter with the record found only in Liberatus, *Brev.* 21, that Theodahad compelled the Senate by threats to make such an appeal. This *vir venerabilis* is supposed by some to have been Rusticus, who afterwards accompanied Peter to Constantinople in 536 (see below, p. 173 ; cp. Dahn, *Kön. der Germ.* ii. 203). Leuthold, Körbs, and others have attempted to prove that Pope Agapetus is meant, and that the letters were written and sent in February 536. But the tenor of the letters is quite inappropriate to the situation then. The important passage is 19. 4, 5, and I am inclined to think that Theodahad means he will send the Pope, not with Peter, but later on, as his own envoy. The Pope, however, did not start till a much later date (see below. p. 172).

Italian enterprise.[1] If Theodahad were willing to abdicate and give the Emperor peaceful possession, well and good, but the only alternative was war. On this Justinian was fully resolved, and Peter, who returned to Italy during the summer (A.D. 535), must have been the bearer of this ultimatum. In the meantime Justinian pushed on the preparations for war.[2]

The war against the Goths was begun in a very different way from the war against the Vandals. The Emperor had taken his subjects into his confidence when he prepared the African expedition; all the world knew that he was committed to the subjugation of Africa. But the outbreak of hostilities, which was to lead to the subjugation of Italy, was carefully concealed so long as concealment was possible; and the first steps were so contrived as not to commit the government to immediate operations on an extensive scale, if the task should appear too formidable. It is probable that Justinian was still waiting on events in Italy, and calculating that Theodahad, who was devoid of military spirit and capacity, would on the first symptoms of danger yield to all his demands. It was a calculation in which too little account was taken of the feelings of the Ostrogothic people.

The first operations in the war would indeed have been dictated, in any case, by geographical circumstances. To occupy the Gothic province of Dalmatia, which was accessible by land, and that of Sicily, which was the most easily accessible by sea, were obviously, for a power which commanded the sea, the first

---

[1] Justinian, *Nov.* 6 (March 6, 535) *ad init.* : *ea quae sunt firma habebimus et ' quae nondum hactenus venerunt adquirimus.*

[2] Procopius, *B.G.* i. 5. 1, " as soon as he learned what had happened to Amalasuntha, being in the ninth year of his reign, he entered upon war " (the ninth regnal year began April 1, 535). Justinian must have heard the news by the end of May, and Belisarius may have sailed at the end of June. His sailing marked the beginning of the war, and thus we can understand (cp. Körbs, *Untersuchungen,* p. 60) why the years of the war as reckoned by Procopius run from summer solstice to summer solstice. This reckoning

is quite clear; it was pointed out by Eckhardt and Leuthold and has been established by Körbs. Thus year 1 = end of June 535 to end of June 536. The system has been misunderstood because, in noting the end of each year, Procopius uses the formula " the winter was over and the 1st (2nd, etc.) year of the war came to an end," in imitation of Thucydides. The inference that the new year began with the spring equinox was natural, but is inconsistent with the narrative. The end of the winter and the end of the year of war are not coincident, and the former is only introduced to remind the reader of Thucydides (Körbs, 56 *sqq.*).

things to be done. The possession of these two provinces would provide the bases for the conquest of Italy. Mundus, the loyal Gepid, Master of Soldiers in Illyricum, led the forces against Dalmatia. The resistance there seems to have been weak. He defeated the Goths and occupied Salona.[1]

The conqueror of Africa was marked out for the command of the overseas expedition, and the full powers of an *imperator* were again conferred upon him.[2] But the army which was entrusted to him was hardly half as strong as that which he had led against the Vandals. It consisted of 4000 legionaries and Federates ; a special division of 3000 Isaurians under Eunes ; 200 Huns, 300 Moors ; and the armed retainers of Belisarius, who may have amounted to several hundreds. Thus the total strength was about 8000. The principal generals were Constantine and Bessas, both Thracians ; and the Iberian prince Peranius.[3] Belisarius was accompanied by his stepson Photius, still a stripling, but strong and intelligent beyond his age.

The purpose of the expedition was kept secret. It was given out that the destination of the fleet was Carthage, and no one had any idea that its sailing was the first step in a new enterprise. Belisarius was instructed that on landing in Sicily he should still pretend to be on his way to Africa, and should do nothing until he had discovered whether the island could be subjugated without trouble. This would evidently depend on the disposition of the Sicilians and the strength of the Gothic garrisons. If it appeared that he was likely to meet with a serious resistance, he was to proceed to Africa as if no other intention had been entertained. He was to run no risks with his small army. This cautious plan of action shows that the Emperor was not yet prepared to commit himself to an Italian campaign. The operations of Belisarius and Mundus were designed, in the first instance, as auxiliary to the Imperial diplomacy.

If war could not be avoided, Justinian calculated upon obtaining some aid from beyond the Alps. He sent an embassy to the kings of the Franks, urging that it was their interest as a Catholic power to co-operate with him against the Arian Goths,

---

[1] Perhaps in August or September 535.

[2] He is named a στρατηγὸς αὐτο-

κράτωρ (Procopius, *B.G.* i. 5. 4. See above, p. 127).

[3] Son of king Gurgen.

and as he supported his arguments by gold, he secured unreserved promises of assistance.[1]

Belisarius disembarked at Catane and he found his work easier than he could well have anticipated. Having seized Catane, he occupied Syracuse, and from the summary statement which has come down it would almost seem that no resistance was offered anywhere and that no military operations were necessary, except at Panormus. Here the fortifications were strong, and the Gothic garrison, which was probably larger than in the other cities, refused to surrender. The Imperial fleet sailed into the harbour, which was unfortified. The masts of the ships over-topped the walls of the town, and Belisarius conceived the device of hoisting boats, full of soldiers, to the tops of the masts, so that they could shoot down upon the defenders. To this menace the Goths, who must have been half-hearted in their resistance, immediately yielded. The restoration of Roman rule in the island was completed before the end of December. Belisarius was one of the consuls of the year, and on December 31 he was able to enter Syracuse and formally lay down his office. The coincidence seemed to his contemporaries a signal favour of fortune.

The ease with which Sicily was reduced shows that the Sicilians were ready to exchange the yoke of Ravenna for that of New Rome, and that there were not large Gothic forces in the island. It may be observed that it would have been far more difficult for a small garrison, in those days, to hold a town of considerable size against a foe, in spite of the wishes of the inhabitants, than in modern times. A slender force, armed with sword and spear, could not defy a numerous populace, as they might if they were supplied with firearms.

In the meantime communications had passed between Rome and Constantinople.[2] Alarmed by the operations in

---

[1] The Merovingian kingdom was now divided among three rulers, Chlotachar and Childebert, sons of Chlodwig, and their nephew Theodebert. It was Theodebert who was the leading spirit in the Italian policy of the Franks (see below, § 8).

[2] It is highly probable that Theodahad was at Rome during the whole winter 535-536, and directed the negotiations from there (Cassiodorus,

Var. x. 14 and 18, cp. xii. 18 and 19), and that it was then that (as Wroth saw) he issued the fine bronze coins which bear his bust, with *Dn Theodahatus rex* on the obverse, and *Victoria Principum* on the reverse. On these coins the head is "neither bare nor bound with a diadem, but wearing a closed crown ornamented with jewels and two stars. His robe is also richly ornamented with jewels

Dalmatia and Sicily, king Theodahad made a new effort to persuade the Emperor to desist from his purpose. He induced Pope Agapetus to undertake the office of ambassador to Constantinople (early winter, A.D. 535).[1] The appeal did not avail. We are not told how the Pope discharged the duties of a mission which he seems to have undertaken reluctantly, but he soon became absorbed in the ecclesiastical controversies of Constantinople, where he remained till his death (April 22, 536). Meanwhile the successes of Mundus and Belisarius increased the fears of Theodahad, and the fall of Panormus seems to have been decisive. The Imperial envoy Peter, who had returned from Constantinople to Rome, was able to take advantage of the completion of the conquest of Sicily to persuade the vacillating king to attempt to come to terms with his master.[2] Theodahad's fears made him amenable, and he handed to Peter a letter in which he offered to resign Sicily and to submit to a number of capitulations, which would clearly establish and confirm the Emperor's overlordship.[3]   Peter set out, but he had only reached

and a cross. The hair is cut short; the face beardless, but with a moustache such as has been seen already on the portrait coins of Odovacar and Theoderic ": Wroth (*Coins of Vandals, etc.*, p. xxxiv), who sees no reason not to regard it as a true portrait, and suggests that it should be connected with Cassiodorus, *Var.* vi. 7 *ut figura vultus nostri metallis usualibus imprimatur*, etc. The other (Ravennate) coinage of Theodahad is of the ordinary type.

[1] Liberatus, *Brev.* 21, *ipsi papae et senatui Romano interminatur non solum senatores sed et uxores et filios filiasque eorum gladio se interemturum nisi egissent apud imperatorem ut destinatum exercitum suum de Italia submoveret* (Italia is used in its political sense, including Sicily). The date 535 is supplied by *Cont. Marcellini, s.a.* It has generally been supposed that Agapetus was sent in 536, on account of a passage in the life of this Pope in *Lib. pont.* p. 287 *ambulavit Constantinopolim x kl. Mai.*, where Clinton read *x kal. Mart.* = Feb. 21, which is taken to be the date of his arrival at Constantinople, though it would naturally be that of his departure from Rome.

Now as *x kal. Mai.*, April 22, is the date of the Pope's death, Duchesne is certainly right in regarding the date as an interpolation. Against the emendation it may further be urged that Feb. 21–March 13, on which day Agapetus consecrated the Patriarch Menas, is too short a time for the proceedings preliminary to this ecclesiastical victory. Finally, the mission of the Pope *after* the despatch of Peter with the two letters is unintelligible. These objections are conclusive. The view that Agapetus accompanied Peter is quite untenable. Agapetus was in Italy on Sept. 9 (see his letters in Mansi, viii. 848, 850) and as late as Oct. 15, if the date of the letter to Justinian (*ib.* 850) is correct. He may have started in November or December.

[2] From the order of the narrative in Procopius, i. 6 *ad init.*, it is natural to infer that Peter's interviews with the king were later than Dec. 31, 535. The inference, however, is not quite certain, for ταῦτα (ἐπεὶ δὲ ταῦτα Πέτρος ἔμαθεν) might mean loosely the progress of Belisarius in Sicily.

[3] Theodahad undertook (1) to send to the Emperor yearly a gold crown weighing 300 lbs. ; (2) to furnish

Albano when he was recalled. Theodahad's craven spirit was tortured by the fear that his terms would be rejected, and he had decided to seek Peter's advice. The historian Procopius records a curious conversation between the king and the ambassador.[1] " Suppose my terms do not satisfy Justinian, what will happen ? " asked the king. " You will have to fight," said Peter. " Is that fair, my dear ambassador ? " " Why not ? " replied Peter ; " it is fair that every man should be true to his own character." " What do you mean ? " " Your interest is philosophy," said Peter, " while Justinian's is to be a good Roman Emperor. Observe the difference. It could never be seemly for a philosopher to cause death to men, and in such numbers ; especially for a Platonist, whose hands should be pure of blood. Whereas it is natural that an Emperor should seek to recover territory which of old belongs to his dominion." Theodahad then swore, in Peter's presence, and caused queen Gudeliva to swear likewise, that he would deliver Italy over to Justinian, in case his first proposals were rejected. He wrote a letter to this effect, stipulating only that lands producing a yearly revenue of 1200 lbs. of gold should be secured to him ; but he made Peter promise by oath that he would first deliver the previous letter, and only produce the second in case the first proved unacceptable. In agreeing to this arrangement, Peter may seem to have had a strange idea of the duties of an ambassador, but we may take it for granted that he was perfectly certain that the compromise offered in the first communication would be rejected.[2] Rejected it was ; the second letter was presented, and the Emperor was highly pleased. Peter was sent once more to Italy, along with another agent, to confirm the agreement, and to arrange that the estates of the *patrimonium* should be assigned to Theodahad's use.[3] Instructions

---

300 Gothic soldiers, when required ; (3) not to put to death, or confiscate the property of, any senator or cleric, without the Emperor's consent ; (4) not to confer the patrician or the senatorial dignity, except with the same consent ; (5) not to suffer his name to be acclaimed before that of the Emperor, in the circus or theatre ; (6) to allow no statue to be set up to himself alone, without a statue of the Emperor standing on the right.

[1] There seems no reason to suppose that this conversation was invented by the historian. I take it as an important indication that Procopius was personally acquainted with Peter, and that Peter was his source for the diplomatic history of the years 534–536.

[2] Along with Peter, Theodahad sent Rusticus, an ecclesiastic, probably a bishop (cp. Leuthold, *Untersuchungen*, p. 40).

[3] Probably in Tuscany. *B.G.* i. 6. 26, cp. 4. 1.

were sent to Belisarius, who was still in Sicily, to be prepared to take possession of the royal palaces and assume the control of Italy. When the ambassadors arrived they found Theodahad no longer in the same mood. Things in the meantime had been occurring in Dalmatia, where a considerable Gothic army had arrived to recover the province. Maurice, the son of Mundus, went out with a small force to reconnoitre, and fell in a sanguinary skirmish. His father, excited by grief and anger, immediately marched against the Goths, and almost annihilated their forces, but in the heat of a rash pursuit was mortally wounded.[1] His death rendered the victory equivalent to a defeat. The Imperial army, in which it seems that there was none competent to take his place, withdrew from Dalmatia. The field was left to the Goths, but they too had lost their commander, and they did not at first venture to occupy Salona, where the Roman population was not friendly.

The news of these events elated Theodahad, whose unstable mind was vacillating between fear of war and the pleasures of royalty. When the Imperial ambassadors arrived, full of confidence and disregardful of his oath, he refused to fulfil his contract. The Gothic notables, to whom Justinian had sent a conciliatory letter, supported him in his refusal, and he went so far as to detain the ambassadors in close confinement.

On learning what had occurred the Emperor appointed Constantian, his Count of the Stable, to lead the Illyrian army to recover Dalmatia, and sent orders to Belisarius to invade Italy. The task of Constantian was easily enough accomplished. He transported his troops by sea from Dyrrhachium to Epidaurus (Ragusa), and the Goths, who had meanwhile seized Salona, believing that they could not defend it, withdrew towards Scardona. Marching to Salona, Constantian rebuilt parts of

---

[1] The deaths of Mundus and his son seemed to the Italians to supply the interpretation of a Sibylline oracle, which had evidently been in their minds since the conquest of the Vandals. The Latin words, as handed down in the MSS. of Procopius (*B.G.* i. 7, p. 33), present some difficulty. *Africa capta mundus cum nat* is quite clear, but is followed by *uperistal* in one MS., ζρεριστασι in another. The Greek version, given by Procopius, ἡνίκα ἂν 'Αφρικὴ ἔχηται, ὁ κόσμος ξὺν τῷ γόνῳ ὀλεῖται, points to the future of *pereo*. Braun and Haury read *cum nato peribit*, Comparetti *peribunt*. *Periet*, a form which occurs in Corippus, would be nearer (cp. Bury, *B.Z.* xv. 46).

the walls, which were in disrepair, and the Gothic army then
retired to Ravenna.[1]

§ 4. Siege of Naples, and Accession of Witigis
(A.D. 536)

Belisarius was preparing to transport his army to Italy when
he was summoned to Africa to suppress the military mutiny,
with which Solomon was unable to cope (last days of March).[2]
On his return, leaving garrisons in Syracuse and Panormus, he
crossed the straits and landed at Rhegium. The defence of the
straits was in the hands of Evermud, son-in-law of the king.
His forces were probably insignificant ; he deserted to Belisarius, was sent to Constantinople, and rewarded by the patrician
dignity. The general advanced by the coast road to Naples,
accompanied by the fleet, and he met with no opposition.

He encamped before Naples, and received a deputation of
citizens, who implored him not to press them to surrender ;
Naples is a place of no importance, they said, let him pass on
and take Rome. The general, observing that he had not asked
them for advice, promised that the Gothic garrison would be
allowed to depart unharmed, and he privately promised large
rewards to Stephen, the head of the deputation, if he could
prevail upon the citizens to surrender. A meeting was held,
and two influential orators, Pastor and Asclepiodotus, who were
loyal to the Gothic interest, induced the citizens to put forward
demands which they were sure would not be granted. But
Belisarius agreed to everything. Then Pastor and his fellow in
public harangues urged that the general was not in a position
to guarantee their security, and that the city was too strong to
be taken. This view was supported by the Jews, who, favoured
by Theoderic's policy, were deeply attached to Gothic rule, and
it carried the day.

---

[1] The loss of Dalmatia may be
placed in March 536 ; the recovery
in May–June. Peter must have
returned to Italy by the beginning
of April. Procopius notes the end
of the first year of the war, after
the recovery of Dalmatia (i. 7 *ad
fin.*).

[2] See above, p. 143. Belisarius
must have started for Carthage in
the first days of April. He cannot
have been back in Sicily before May,
and he did not cross to Italy before
the end of June (the second year of
the war had already begun, Procopius,
B.G. i. 7. 37 and 8. 1). He did not
reach Naples till October (winter was
approaching, *ib.* 9, 9).

Belisarius decided to besiege the place, but it proved a more difficult operation than he had expected. He cut the aqueduct, but this caused little inconvenience, as the town had good wells. The besiegers had no points of vantage from which they could conduct the attack. Ancient Naples included within its walls only a small portion of the modern city. It corresponded to a rectangular area of about 1000 by 800 yards, in which the church of San Lorenzo would be close to the centre. But the ground must have been distinctly higher than the modern level, to give the besieged the advantages which they possessed.[1] Having wasted some weeks and incurred serious losses in men, Belisarius, impatient to advance against Rome and meet Theodahad, determined to abandon the siege. But the luck which had signally favoured him hitherto was again with him. He had given orders to the army to prepare for departure, when a curious Isaurian, climbing into the broken aqueduct in order to inspect its construction, discovered that, near the walls, the channel had been pierced through solid rock, and that the aperture was still open, too narrow to admit a man in armour, but capable of being enlarged. Belisarius acted promptly. Files were employed to enlarge the opening, so as to make no noise. But before making use of this means of entering the city, the general gave the Neapolitans another chance to avoid bloodshed and the horrors of a sack. He summoned Stephen to his camp, assured him that it was now impossible that the city should not fall into his hands, and implored him to persuade his fellow-citizens to capitulate and avoid the miseries which would befall them. Stephen returned in tears, but the people refused to listen. They were convinced that the appeal of Belisarius was merely a ruse.

Six hundred men crept through the aqueduct at night, slew the sentinels on the northern wall, and enabled the Roman troops who were waiting below with scaling-ladders to ascend on the battlements. The horrors which Belisarius had anticipated ensued, and the Huns particularly distinguished themselves in the work of murder and plunder. At length the general succeeded in gathering the troops together and staying the carnage. Swords were sheathed and captives were released. Eight hundred Goths who were taken were well treated. The Neapolitans turned with anger against the two demagogues

[1] Hodgkin, iv. 49 *sqq.*

whom they held responsible for all that had befallen them.
They slew Asclepiodotus ; they found Pastor already dead,
stricken by apoplexy when he knew that the city was taken.[1]
The people of Naples had confidently expected that king
Theodahad would have sent an army to relieve their city. He
seems to have been paralysed by fear ; he took no measures
for the defence of his kingdom or of any part of it. Disgusted
with his inactivity, the Goths of Rome and the province of
Campania decided, after the fall of Naples, to depose him and
elect a leader of military experience. They met at Regata in
the Pomptine marshes,[2] and, as there was no suitable member
of the royal family of the Amals, their choice fell on Witigis,
a man of undistinguished birth, who had earned some repute
in the campaigns against the Gepids. He was acclaimed king
(November, A.D. 536),[3] and Cassiodorus, whose impartial pen was
prepared to serve him, as it had served Theoderic and Amalasuntha, and as it had served Theodahad, announced to all the
Goths the election of one not chosen, like Theodahad, " in the
recesses of a royal bedchamber, but in the expanse of the bound-
less Campagna ; [4] of one who owed his dignity first to Divine
grace, but secondly to the free judgment of the people ; of one
who knew the brave men in his army by comradeship, having

---

[1] Naples probably fell early in
November. The siege lasted twenty
days. We must allow some time
for the march to Rome, which was
reached on Dec. 9.

[2] Regata (not Regeta) was 280
stades from Rome, near the Decen-
novian canal, which drained the
marshes and reached the sea at
Terracina. The text of Procopius
(i. 11) in this passage equates 19 miles
with 113 stades (τρισκαίδεκα καὶ
ἑκατόν). The reading cannot be
sound. Procopius reckoned 7 stades
to a mile (see above, p. 132). We
should probably read τρεῖς καὶ
τριάκοντα (λγ' instead of ιγ'), $1\frac{33}{7} = 19$.
See Haury, B.Z. xv. 297, who con-
jectures that Regata is a later name
for Forum Appii.

[3] Procopius, ib. Jordanes, Rom.
372, Get. 310. The date of the
accession of Witigis cannot have been
prior to October. For Theodahad, who
was put to death a few days afterwards, was in the third year of his

reign (B.G. i. 11), which began not
earlier than October 3. There is no
reason for rejecting the record in
Cons. Ital. (loc. cit.) that he was
slain mense Decembris, and thus we
obtain the end of November for the
elevation of Witigis. This accords
with the probable date of the siege
of Naples (see above, p. 177, n. 1).
The date usually assigned is August
(so Clinton, Hodgkin, Martroye, etc.),
on the testimony of a passage in Lib.
pont., Silverius, p. 290, where it is
stated that two months after the
ordination of Pope Silverius (June 20)
Theodahad was killed and Witigis
elected. As this contradicts all the
other evidence, we must reject it.
I have little doubt that the text
(post menses vero ii.) offers an instance
of the very common numerical
confusion of ii with u. Leuthold
(op. cit. 48), who is right in his view
of the chronology, makes a subtle
and unsatisfactory attempt to explain
the wrong date in this text.

[4] In campis late patentibus.

stood shoulder to shoulder with them in the day of battle." [1]
The event proved that the choice of the Goths was un-
discerning. Witigis was a respectable soldier, and would
have been a valuable leader of a division under an able
commander, but he possessed none of the higher qualities
demanded in one who was called to lead a nation against a
formidable invader.

Theodahad, who had hitherto been residing at Rome, fled
incontinently to Ravenna. Witigis decided that he must die,
and sent a certain Optaris to bring him alive or dead. Optaris
was selected because he had a personal grudge against Theodahad.
Travelling night and day without a pause, he overtook the
fugitive, flung him on the ground, and butchered him like a
sacrificial victim.

The new king immediately marched to Rome and held a
council. Everything depended on the plan of campaign that
was now formed. The Goths were menaced by two dangers,
the imminent advance of Belisarius from the south, and the
hostile attitude of the Franks in the north. The main forces
of the Goths were stationed in the northern frontier provinces,
in Provence and Venetia. Witigis proposed, and the proposal
was accepted, first of all to deal with the Franks, and then to
take the field against Belisarius with all the forces of the kingdom.
It is safe to say that this plan of postponing the encounter
with the most dangerous enemy was unwise. [2] The best chance
of the Goths would have been to hurry the main part of their
troops from the north, and either join battle with the Imperial
army before it reached Rome, or else hold Rome strongly and
force Belisarius to undertake a siege which would be long and
difficult. In the meantime an envoy could be sent to negotiate
with the Franks. The place of Witigis himself was at Rome,
the threatened point, and he committed a fatal blunder when
he started for Ravenna " to make arrangements for the war."
He left a garrison of 4000 men in Rome, under Leuderis, ex-
tracted an oath of fidelity from Silverius, the Pope, [3] and from

---

[1] Cassiodorus, x. 31 (Hodgkin's
paraphrase, iii. 74).
[2] Compare the remarks of Hodgkin,
iv. 76.
[3] Silverius (son of a previous Pope,
Hormisdas) succeeded Agapetus in

June 536. It is said that he was
imposed on the electors by Theodahad (*Lib. pont., loc. cit.*), but this
may be only an invention. Cp.
Liberatus, *Brev.* c. 22; Hodgkin, iv.
92.

the Senate and people, and took a number of senators with
him as hostages.

At Ravenna, Witigis married, against her will, Matasuntha,
the sister of Athalaric, in order to link himself with the dynasty
of Theoderic ; and the wedding was celebrated in a florid oration
by Cassiodorus.[1] He then proceeded to negotiate with the
Franks. We saw how they had been induced by Justinian to
promise their co-operation. But Theodahad had made them
an attractive offer. He proposed to hand over to them the
Ostrogothic territory in Gaul, along with 2000 lbs. of gold,
in return for their engagement to assist him in the war.
He died before the transaction was concluded. Witigis saw
that the best thing to be done was to carry out this arrangement. The Frank kings consented, but, as they did not wish
openly to break their compact with Justinian, they promised
secretly to send as auxiliaries " not Franks, but men of their
tributary peoples." [2]

At the same time a last attempt was made to come to terms
with the Emperor. It was plausible to argue that, as the
murder of Amalasuntha had been the alleged reason for invading
Italy, the cause for war was removed by the punishment of
Theodahad and the elevation of Matasuntha to the throne.
What more could the Goths do ? Witigis wrote to Justinian
to this effect,[3] and likewise to the Master of Offices urging him
to work for peace.[4] As to these negotiations we possess only
the documents drawn up at Ravenna, and have no information
as to the Emperor's reply. We may conjecture that he offered
Witigis the simple alternative between war and submission.

In the meantime Belisarius had left Naples and was marching

---

[1] Fragments have been preserved
and, edited by Traube, are included
in Mommsen's ed. of the *Variae*, p.
473 *sqq.* The orator refers contemptuously to the effeminate training
of Athalaric by his mother, and
enlarges on the military career and
prowess of Witigis. An elaborate
description of the sumptuous pomp
of the nuptials follows. There are
coins with the monogram of Matasuntha, and they have been generally
attributed to the reign of Witigis, but
for another view see below, p. 254.
The coinage of Witigis is of the
ordinary type.

[2] Procopius says that the three
Frank kings divided the money and
the land (*B.G.* i. 13. 27). But they
did not consider their title secure
until the land was formally ceded by
the Emperor, and Justinian deemed
it wise to agree (iii. 33. 3).

[3] Cassiodorus, *Var.* x. 32. Witigis
at the same time appealed to the
Catholic bishops of Italy to pray for
peace, and wrote to the Praet. Prefect
of Illyricum asking him to help his
ambassadors at Thessalonica on their
journey. *Ib.* 34, 35.

[4] *Ib.* 33.

northward.   The Romans, warned by the experiences of Naples,
and urged by the Pope, who had no scruples in breaking his
oath to Witigis, sent a messenger inviting him to come.   He
had placed small garrisons in Naples and Cumae, the only forts
in Campania, and marching by the Via Latina he entered Rome
on December 9, A.D. 536,[1] by the Porta Asinaria, close to the
Basilica of the Lateran.[2]   On the same day the Gothic garrison
discreetly withdrew by the Porta Flaminia.   Their leader,
Leuderis, remained, and was sent to the Emperor with the keys
of the city gates.

§ 5. *Siege of Rome* (A.D. 537–538)

The Romans soon learned to their deep chagrin that it was
the intention of Belisarius to remain in their city and expose
it to the hardships of a siege.   With the small forces at his
disposal, this was the only prudent course open to him.   Taking
up his quarters in the Domus Pinciana, on the Pincian Hill, in
the extreme north of the city, the general immediately set about
strengthening the fortifications.   The great walls of Aurelian,
which encompassed the city in a circuit of about twelve miles,
had been repaired more than a hundred years ago, in the reign
of Honorius, and recently by Theoderic.   But Belisarius found
many dilapidations to make good, and he added some new
fortifications.   A wide ditch was dug on the outer side.   The
wall, as originally constructed, was well adapted for defence.
A special feature was a covered way running round the inside
of the wall to facilitate the passage of troops from one point
to another.   Some portions of this arched gallery still remain.[3]
Considering the vicissitudes through which Rome subsequently
passed in a period of thirteen hundred years, the walls which the
army of Belisarius defended are wonderfully preserved.[4]

At the same time measures were taken to supply the city
with stores of grain imported from Sicily.   But Belisarius
appears not to have expected that Rome would be attacked by

---

[1] There is a lacuna in the text of
Procopius (i. 14. 14), but it can be
supplied from Evagrius, *H.E.* iv. 19.
See Haury, *ad loc.*

[2] The old gate, which is walled up,
stands beside the Porta San Giovanni.

[3] Near the Porta Asinaria.

[4] A summary enumeration of the
towers, battlements, and loopholes,
from the Porta Flaminia to the Porta
Metrovia, compiled (copied from an
earlier document ?) in the eighth
century, is extant (text in Jordan,
Top. der Stadt Rom, ii. 578).

a formidable army. He diminished his small garrison by fling-
ing out forces northward to seize commanding positions along
the Flaminian Way—Narni, Spoleto, and Perugia, and some lesser
strongholds. In the meantime Witigis had sent a considerable
detachment to Dalmatia. Salona was besieged by land and
sea, but the diversion ended in failure, and the province remained
in Imperial hands.[1] An attempt to recover Perugia was also
defeated. But the confidence of the Goths rose when they
realised the weakness of the forces with which Rome was held,
and heard rumours of the discontent of the inhabitants at the
military occupation of their city. The king decided to throw
all his strength into the recovery of Rome, and he marched
southward at the head of an army, which is thought by some
to have numbered 150,000 warriors, most of them heavily
armed, with horses protected by mail. The figure must be far
in excess of the truth,[2] but there can be no doubt that the Gothic
host was large compared with the army of 5000 against which
it was advancing. Belisarius was now dealing with a very
different problem from that which had faced him in his campaign against the Vandals. He hastily recalled the generals,
Bessas and Constantine, whom he had sent into Tuscany, bidding
them abandon all their positions except Perugia, Spoleto, and
Narni, in which they were to leave small garrisons.

Witigis did not delay to reduce these three places. The
occupation of Narni was important.[3] It forced the Gothic
army, just as, more than a hundred years before, the army of
Alaric had been forced, to diverge from the Flaminian Road
to the east, to march through the Sabine country, and approach
Rome by the Via Salaria, instead of marching by the Via

[1] The end of this expedition is not
related by Procopius.
[2] The figure, nevertheless, was
given by Belisarius in his letter to
Justinian (*B.G.* i. 24); see below, p.
186. 150,000 Gothic warriors would
mean a Gothic population approaching
700,000. When they entered Italy the
number of the Ostrogoths perhaps
hardly reached 100,000, and they
cannot have multiplied seven times in
forty-five years. Moreover, if they had
been so strong, it would have been
out of the question to attempt to
conquer them with the small forces
of Belisarius. The figure is also

disproved by the circumstances of
the siege (see below, pp. 183 *sq.*). I am
inclined to believe that the number
mentioned by Belisarius represents
an estimate of the total Gothic
population of Italy.
[3] Narnia is 54 Roman miles from
Rome. Its situation is described
in some detail by Procopius (i. 17.
8-11), and the description is not
irrelevant, as showing that even with
a small garrison it could bar the
progress of an army. One arch and
some piers of the bridge of Augustus
which Procopius mentions still
remain.

Flaminia.[1] When Witigis reached the Ponte Salario, where the road crosses the Anio, a few miles from the city, he found himself arrested by a fort which Belisarius had built on the bridge with the object of gaining time in order to procure more provisions.

But the garrison of the fort failed him. On the arrival of the Goths they decamped by night, and the enemy secured the bridge. Next day the general, ignorant of the cowardice of his men, rode towards the bridge with a thousand horsemen, and found that the Goths had crossed. A cavalry engagement ensued, in which Belisarius, carried away by the excitement of battle, indiscreetly exposed himself. Deserters knew his dark-grey horse with a white head, and urged the Goths to aim at him. But he escaped unwounded. There were severe losses on both sides, and the small Roman band was in the end forced to flee. They reached the Salarian Gate about sunset, and the sentinels, not recognising the general begrimed with dust of battle, and already informed by fugitives that he was slain, refused to open. Belisarius turned and charged the pursuers, who retreated, thinking that a new army had issued from the gate. He then succeeded in obtaining admission, and spent the

---

[1] The usual view has been that the Goths advanced by the Via Flaminia (regaining it somewhere presumably between Narnia and Ad Tiberim, now Magliano, where there was a bridge), and that the bridge where Belisarius placed the garrison was the Pons Milvius, now Ponte Molle, 2 miles from Rome. This view was held by Gibbon and maintained by Hodgkin. But it is certainly erroneous and inconsistent with the story. If the fighting had been at the Milvian Bridge the Roman fugitives would have returned to the Porta Flaminia, not to the Porta Salaria. The cause of the error is that Procopius does not name the bridge, but calls it simply Τιβέριδος τοῦ ποταμοῦ γεφύρᾳ, "a bridge of the Tiber" (ib. xiii.). Hence, as the Milvian was the only bridge which spanned the Tiber north of the city, it was naturally supposed to be meant. But Τίβερις is ambiguous in Procopius; it means (1) the Tiber, (2) the Anio. That it means the Anio in this passage is shown by the statement in the context (ib. xiv.) that there are bridges over the river in other places (πολλαχόσε τοῦ ποταμοῦ), meaning, of course, in the neighbourhood of Rome. This is not true of the Tiber, which had only the one bridge outside the city; but it is true of the Anio, which is crossed, near Rome, by the Via Nomentana and the Via Tiburtina, as well as by the Via Salaria. In two other passages (B.G. iii. 10. 23, and 24. 31) Τίβερις clearly means the Anio. This was the view of Gregorovius, Rome in the Middle Ages, i. 372 ; is accepted by Hartmann, Gesch. Italiens, i. 295, n. 19 ; and has been defended in a special monograph by L. Fink, Das Verhältnis der Aniobrücken zur Mulvischen Brücke in Prokops Gothenkrieg, 1907. Procopius knew the localities, and the ambiguous use of Τίβερις cannot be due to ignorance. The explanation may be found in the modern name of the Anio, Teverone, and the use in Procopius be taken to show that the old name had passed out of common speech before his time.

night in making arrangements for the defence of the city. Each
gate was assigned to the charge of a different leader. One more
incident occurred before the night was over. Witigis sent an
officer to make a speech outside the Salarian Gate. This man,
whose name was Wacis, reproached the Romans for their
treachery to the Goths and for preferring the protection of
Greeks,[1] people, he said, who had never visited Italy before except
in the capacity of actors or thieving mariners. No one made
any reply to his outburst and he retired.

On the following day the siege began.[2] It was to last a year
and nine days, far longer than either of the belligerents anticipated. The Goths did not attempt to surround the whole circuit
of the city. They constructed seven camps, one on the west
side of the river, in the region of the Vatican, then known as the
Campus Neronis. The other six were east of the Tiber, on the
northern and eastern sides of the city.[3] One of them was under
the command of Witigis himself.[4] Thus from the Porta Maggiore
to the Porta S. Paolo and the river there was no leaguer. The
whole circuit of the Aurelian Wall, including the Transtiberine
region, was less than thirteen miles,[5] so that if Witigis had the

---

[1] Procopius reproduces the Latin
name—Γραικοί (i. 18).

[2] For the chronology of the siege
Procopius supplies the following data.
It ended " about the spring equinox "
in 538, and lasted 1 year and 9 days
(ii. 10, p. 194). It began at the
beginning of March (Μαρτίου ισταμένου,
ii. 24, p. 122). In the *Lib. pont.*
(*Silverius*), Feb. 21 is mentioned as
the first day of the siege. It is not
easy to reconcile this difference.

[3] They can be located as follows:
(1) just north of the Flaminian Gate,
Porta del Popolo; (2) in the grounds
of the Villa Borghese, to command
the Salarian and Pincian Gates; (3)
on the Via Nomentana, to command
the Porta Nomentana; (4) and (5)
on the Via Tiburtina, near San
Lorenzo, and (6) farther south, on
the Via Praenestina, to command the
corresponding gates (P. Tiburtina and
P. Labicana). It is possible that the
Porta Pinciana had been closed and
not used during the fifth century and
was reopened by Belisarius (see Jordan,
Topogr. i. 1, p. 354, cp. ii. p. 578).

[4] Τῶν δὲ δὴ ἄλλων Οὔττιγις ἡγεῖτο
ἔκτος αὐτός. ἄρχων γὰρ ἦν εἰς κατὰ

χαράκωμα ἕκαστον (*B.G.* i. 19).
Hodgkin (iv. 148) says that Procopius
is "rather vague here." Could he
have been more explicit? During the
siege the Goths profaned and damaged
many tombs of Christian martyrs
outside the walls. We know this
from verses which were afterwards
inscribed on the sepulchres when
Pope Vigilius restored them. See
Anth. Lat. Supp. i. Nos. 83, 87, 89, 99.

[5] This includes the wall along the
river from the P. Flaminia to the
Pons Aurelius (Ponte Sisto). See
Jordan, i. 1, 343-344. It must be
remembered that the Transtiberine
portion of the Aurelian Wall enclosed
only the Janiculum and the southern
part of the modern Transtiberine
town, reaching the river just north of
the Ponte Sisto. The Gothic camp
on this side of the river was far from
the walls, and its principal purpose
was to prevent the Romans from
destroying the Milvian Bridge (so
Procopius). It was under the command of Marcias, who had been the
commander of an army in Provence,
and arrived on the scene after the
siege had begun.

huge host which he is supposed to have led against Rome he would have had a man to every foot of the wall and an army of more than 10,000 to spare. He could not have decided that he had too few to blockade the city completely.[1]

The first operation of the Goths was to cut the numerous aqueducts which traversed the Campagna and supplied Rome with water from the Latin hills. The destruction of these magnificent works, although it caused some inconvenience, hardly affected the fortunes of the siege ; but it had far-reaching consequences for the future of Rome.[2] Since the third century B.C. the city had been excellently supplied with pure water, and new conduits had constantly been built to meet the growing needs of the inhabitants. For a thousand years after the act of demolition wrought by the Goths, the Romans were again, as in the early Republic, compelled to draw their water from the Tiber and the wells. The time-honoured habits of luxurious bathing, which had been such a conspicuous feature of their civilisation, came to an end. The aqueducts might easily have been restored at the end of the war, and doubtless this would have been done if Rome had again become an Imperial residence, but the comfort and cleanliness of the people were no object of care to the medieval popes, who regarded the ancient Thermae as part of the unregenerate life of paganism. The long lines of arcades which crossed the Campagna were allowed to fall into ruin.

The cutting of the aqueducts caused an immediate difficulty. There was no water to turn the corn mills which supplied the Romans with bread. The inventive brain of Belisarius devised an expedient. Close to a bridge (probably the Pons Aelius) through whose arch the stream of the Tiber bore down with considerable force, he stretched from bank to bank tense ropes to which he attached two boats, separated by a space of two feet. Two mills were placed on each boat, and between the skiffs was suspended the water-wheel, which the current easily turned. A line of boats was formed, and a series of mills in the bed of the river ground all the corn that was required. The efforts of the

---

[1] Οὐχ οἷοί τε ὄντες ὅλῳ τῷ στρα-τοπέδῳ τὸ τεῖχος περιλαβέσθαι κύκλῳ, B.G. i. 19. 2.

[2] Compare Hodgkin (iv. ch. vi.), who gives an interesting account of the aqueducts, based on Lanciani's monograph Le acque e gli acquedotti di Roma Antica. There were eleven principal aqueducts, including that of Alexander Severus. Procopius says that there were fourteen (i. 19).

enemy to disconcert this ingenious device and break the machines by throwing trees and corpses into the water were easily thwarted by Belisarius ; he stretched across the stream iron chains which formed an impassable barrier against all dangerous obstacles that might harm his boats or wheels.

The Romans chafed under the hardships which the first days of the siege brought upon them and which seemed likely to increase. Witigis, informed of their discontent by deserters, thought that Belisarius, under the influence of public opinion, might be induced to relinquish his plan of defending Rome if a favourable proposal were made. He sent envoys, whom Belisarius received in the presence of his generals and the senators. The Gothic spokesman enlarged on the miseries which the siege must inflict on the Romans, and offered to permit the Imperial army to leave the city unharmed and with all their property. The reply of Belisarius was a stern refusal. " I tell you," he said, " the time will come when you shall be glad to hide your heads under the thorn bushes and shall be unable to do so. Rome belongs to us of old. You have no right to it. It is impossible for Belisarius to surrender it, while he is alive."

A grand attempt to take the city by assault soon followed. The walls were attacked in various places, but everywhere the besiegers were repelled. The fighting was particularly severe near the Aurelian Gate, west of the Tiber, where the Goths attacked the great quadrangular Mausoleum of Hadrian, and the defenders, hard pressed, hurled statues down upon the enemy.[1]

Belisarius, though he openly expressed complete confidence, was well aware of the dangers and difficulties of his situation, and knew that success was hardly possible unless new troops came to his aid. He wrote a letter to Justinian, in which he reported his operations and urged in the strongest language his need of reinforcements. " So far," he wrote, " all has gone well, whether our success be due to valour or to fortune, but in order that this success may continue, it behoves me to declare plainly what it behoves you to do. Though God orders all things as He wills, yet men are praised or blamed according to their success or failure. Let arms and soldiers be sent to us in such numbers that henceforward we may wage the war on terms of equality. Let the conviction penetrate your mind, O Emperor, that if

---

[1] It was supposed that the Gothic losses in dead on this day were 30,000.

the barbarians overcome us now, we shall lose not only your dominion of Italy but the army also, and besides this we shall suffer the immense disgrace of failure, not to speak of the shame of bringing ruin on the Romans who preferred loyalty to your throne to their own safety. Understand that it is not possible to hold Rome long with ever so large a host. It is surrounded by open country and, not being a seaport, it is cut off from supplies. The Romans are now friendly, but if their hardships are protracted the pinch of famine will force them to do many things against their own wishes. For myself, I know that my life belongs to your Majesty, and I shall not be forced out of this place while I live. But consider how such an end to the life of Belisarius would affect your reputation." [1]

The Emperor had despatched reinforcements in December under Valerian and Martin, but they spent the winter months in Greece and had not yet arrived. On receiving the urgent appeal of his general, Justinian ordered them to proceed without delay, and prepared to raise a new armament. Meanwhile, on the day following the Gothic assault, Belisarius sent the women and children and the slaves who were not employed in garrison duties out of the city. Some travelled by boat down the Tiber, others departed by the Appian Way. The enemy made no attempt to hinder their departure. The artisans and tradespeople, whose occupation was almost gone, were drafted into the garrison, mixed with the regular soldiers, and paid a small wage for their services. [2]

Enraged, perhaps, at the failure of his attack, Witigis put to death the senators whom he kept at Ravenna as hostages, except a few who managed to escape. It was an act of barbarity which was seldom practised, and was as useless as it was cruel. At the same time he occupied Portus, at the mouth of the Tiber. This was a serious blow to the besieged, for Portus had for centuries been the port of Rome, with which it was connected by an excellent road and a towpath along the right bank of the

---

[1] I have reproduced a good part of this document because, if not a literal copy of the original letter, there is every reason to believe that Procopius, who may have written it himself, reproduced its actual tenor (*B.G.* i. 24).

[2] A scandal was created at this time by some persons who attempted to open the gates of the temple of Janus in the Forum. Since Rome had become Christian the temple had been kept shut in war as well as in peace. The efforts of the secret pagans (who remained undiscovered) failed to open the bronze doors, but damaged the bolts or hinges so that they would not shut tight.

river, so that heavy barges laden with supplies could be towed up by oxen without the aid of oars or sails. The older harbour of Ostia, over against Portus, remained in the hands of the Romans, but there was no towpath, so that the river traffic from here depended on the wind. Moreover, when the Goths threw a garrison of a thousand men into Portus, boats could not anchor at Ostia, and were forced to put in at Antium, a day's journey distant.[1] The secretary of Belisarius regrets that 300 men could not have been spared to secure Portus, which was so strong that even so few could have held it.

About three weeks later Martin and Valerian arrived with a force of 1600 cavalry, mostly Huns and Slavs, and they succeeded in eluding the Goths and entering Rome. Sorties were carried out after their arrival with uniform success, which Belisarius ascribed to the superiority of his well-trained mounted archers ; and, if he could have had his way, he would have continued to wear down the enemy by constant small sallies, in which little was risked. But the army, rendered confident through their successes and convinced of their superiority to the barbarians, clamoured for a pitched battle, and their leader, wearied by their importunities, reluctantly yielded. A general action was fought in the north of the city, on both sides of the river, and the Romans, routed by sheer weight of numbers, were driven back within the walls.

Towards the end of June the besieged began to feel the pinch of hunger and disease. There was only enough corn to feed the soldiers, and the Goths tightened the blockade, hitherto conducted with remarkable negligence, by constructing a fortress at the junction of two aqueducts commanding the Appian and Latin Ways.[2] The citizens [3] urged Belisarius to risk a battle.

---

[1] On the decline of Ostia and rise of Portus see G. Calza, *Gli scavi recenti nell' abitato di Ostia*, in the *Mon. antich.* of the *Acc. dei Lincei*, xxvi. 1920. Ostia had been a rich and prosperous city, as the excavated ruins show, till the beginning of the fourth century, for the Portus of Claudius across the Tiber had been simply the port of Ostia where all the business was transacted. The policy of Constantine brought Portus directly under the central administration at Rome, and the gradual decline of the old port set in. Cassiodorus (*Var.* vii. 9), in describing the two towns as *duo lumina*, has in mind Ostia's ancient importance.

[2] The medieval tower, known as the Torre Fiscali, about 3½ miles from Rome, marks the place.

[3] Many had looked forward to the month of July as the term of their sufferings, on the faith of a Sibylline oracle which predicted that in that month the Romans would have a new king, and Rome would have nothing more to fear from the Getae.

He refused, but held out promises that large reinforcements and supplies would soon arrive. The prospect of approaching relief was based only on rumour, and he sent his secretary Procopius to Campania to discover whether the report was true, to collect provision ships, and to send to Rome all the troops that could be spared from the garrisons of the Campanian towns. Procopius left Rome at night by the southern gate of St. Paul, and, eluding the Goths, reached Naples and executed his orders. Some time afterwards Belisarius sent Antonina to Naples, where, in a place of safety, she might help, with her considerable capacity for organisation, in the task of sending relief to Rome. She found that Procopius had already raised 500 soldiers and had loaded a large number of vessels with corn. But the reinforcements, so anxiously awaited, had not yet come, though they were on their way. They seem to have arrived in the month of November.[1] 3000 Isaurians disembarked at Naples and 1800 cavalry at Otranto. Of their commanders the most distinguished was John, the nephew of Vitalian, one of the bravest and most skilful officers who served under Belisarius.[2]

In the meantime the army of Witigis was suffering, as well as the Romans, from famine and disease. It was steadily declining in numbers when the discouraging tidings came that new forces were on their way to the relief of Rome. The 3000 Isaurians were sent by sea to Ostia, but John, the nephew of Vitalian, with his 1800 cavalry and the 500 who had been raised by Procopius, marched by the Appian Way, followed by a train of waggons laden with food. To prevent the Goths from intercepting them in force, Belisarius arranged a strong sortie on the

Procopius (i. 24) reproduced the Latin words of the oracle, but they have been corrupted in the MSS. For attempts to restore the original see Bury (*B.Z.* xv. 45), and H. Jackson (*Journal of Philology*, xxxiii. 142), who rightly points out that the word before *mense* (which is quite clear in the MSS.) must have been *quinto*, not *quintili*, as has generally been assumed.

[1] They cannot have arrived sooner, for they must have reached Rome in December, since after their arrival there the Goths *immediately* despaired and sent envoys to Belisarius (εὐθὺς μὲν ἀπεγίνωσκον τὸν πόλεμον (*B.G.* ii. 6 *ad init.*), and this was shortly

before the winter solstice (ii. 7. p. 181). It seems to follow that Procopius cannot have been sent to Naples before September or October, though one would naturally infer from the narrative that he was sent in July (so Hodgkin, iv. 246). But it cannot be supposed that he would have kept back for four months the 500 men whom he collected and who were sorely needed at Rome. Antonina appears to have been back in Rome before November 18, for she took part in the deposition of Pope Silverius (*Lib. pont.* lx. *Silv.* p. 292) ; cp. below, p. 379.

[2] He is called the "Sanguinary" in the *Lib. pont.* (*ib.*).

camp near the Flaminian Gate. It was completely successful; the Goths were utterly routed. This was the turning-point in the siege. Witigis despaired of taking Rome and sent envoys to Belisarius, the chief of whom was a distinguished but unnamed Italian.

The conversation between the general and the spokesman of the Goths is reported by Procopius, and, as we may safely assume that he had returned to Rome and was present at the interview, it is possible that he has given, at least partly, the tenor of the dialogue.

Envoy. We know and you know that the war has gone badly for both of us. It is stupid to persist in suffering with no prospect of relief, and it behoves the leaders of both belligerents to consider the safety of their men instead of their own reputations, and to seek a solution which will be fair both to themselves and to their enemy. We have therefore come with certain proposals. But we request you to interrupt us at once if anything we say appears unreasonable.[1]

Belisarius. I have no objection to the interview taking the form of a conversation. But I hope your proposals will be just and pacific.

Envoy. In coming against us, your friends and allies, with armed force, you Romans have acted unjustly. Remember that the Goths did not wrest Italy from the Romans, but Odovacar overthrew the Emperor and established a tyranny. Then Zeno, wishing to deliver the land,[2] but being himself unable to subdue Odovacar, induced our king Theoderic, who was then threatening Constantinople, to punish Odovacar for the wrong he did to Augustulus and to undertake the government of Italy for the future. It was thus that we Goths were established in Italy, and we have observed the laws and the constitution of the Empire as faithfully as any of the Emperors of the past. Neither Theoderic nor any of his successors has ever enacted a law. We have shown scrupulous respect for the religion of the Romans. No Italian has ever been forcibly converted to Arianism, no Gothic convert has been forced to return to his old creed. We have reserved all the posts in the civil service for Italians, no Goth has ever been appointed. The Romans have had a yearly consul nominated by the Emperor of the East. But you, though for ten years you allowed Odovacar's barbarians to oppress Italy, are now attempting to take it from those who are legally in possession of it. Depart hence, with your property and the plunder you have seized.

Belisarius. You have spoken at length, and disingenuously. Theoderic was sent by Zeno against Odovacar, but not on the condition that he should himself be master of Italy. For what would the Emperor have gained

---

[1] Προσήκει δὲ μὴ ξυνεχεῖ ῥήσει (Braun's correction of ξυνεγχειρήσει) τοὺς λόγους ἀμφοτέρους ποιεῖσθαι, B.G. ii. 6. Procopius is evidently thinking of the dialogue between the Melians and Athenians in Thucydides (v. 85).

[2] Τιμωρεῖν μὲν τῷ ξυμβεβασιλευκότι (*i.e.* Romulus Augustulus) βουλόμενος.

in replacing one tyrant by another ? The object was to restore Italy
to the Imperial authority. Theoderic did well in his dealings with Odovacar, but acted wrongly in refusing to restore the land to its true lord. I
will never hand over the Emperor's territory to any one else.

Envoy. Although all present know perfectly well that what we said
is true, we have not come to bandy arguments. We are willing to surrender the rich island of Sicily, which is so important to you for the
security of Africa.

Belisarius. We thank you. And we on our part are prepared to
surrender to you the whole island of Britain, which belongs to us from
of old and is far larger than Sicily. We cannot accept such a favour
without giving an equivalent.

Envoy. Well, what do you say if we add Campania or Naples ?

Belisarius. I have no powers to dispose of the Emperor's property.

Envoy. We would undertake to pay a yearly tribute to the Emperor.

Belisarius. I am only empowered to keep the land for its legal lord.

Envoy. Then we must send an embassy to the Emperor and negotiate
with him. For this purpose we must ask you to conclude an armistice
for a definite time.

Belisarius. Be it so. It shall never be said that I put obstacles in
the way of a peaceful settlement.

We may take the later part of this conversation as a genuine
report. Nor is it improbable that the Italian delegate of the
Goths raised the question of the constitutional position of Italy
and the legitimacy of the Ostrogothic government. If so, it is
interesting to observe that both his argument and the reply of
Belisarius misrepresented historical facts. On the Gothic side
it was stated that Odovacar's offence, in the eyes of Zeno, lay
in the dethronement of Romulus Augustulus, whereas Zeno
regarded Augustulus as a usurper, and it was out of respect for
the rights of Julius Nepos that he at first refused to recognise
Odovacar. But he did recognise him subsequently, so that
Odovacar, at least during the later years of his reign, was as
little a " tyrant " as Theoderic himself. Belisarius distorted
facts more seriously. He completely ignored the definite agreement concluded between Theoderic and the Emperor Anastasius.
It was on this agreement that the legitimacy of Ostrogothic rule
rested, and its existence invalidated the argument of Belisarius.
It is not too much to read between the lines that Procopius
himself considered that legally the Goths had a good case.

While Belisarius was receiving the envoys the reinforcements
were arriving at Ostia. The same night he rode down to the
port and arranged that the provisions should be transported up

the river and that the troops should march to Rome without delay. His confidence that the enemy would not interfere with the operations was justified by the event. The arrangements for an armistice of three months were then completed. Hostages were interchanged, and a guarantee was given that even if the truce were violated in Italy, the envoys should be allowed to return unharmed from Constantinople.

Rome was revictualled, but the Goths in their camps and fortresses were suffering from want of food. The secretary of Belisarius observes that the cause of this scarcity was the Imperial sea-power, which prevented them from receiving the imports on which Italy depended. The shortage of food decided Witigis to remove his garrisons from Portus, Centumcellae (Cività Vecchia), and Albanum, and these places were promptly occupied by Imperial troops. The Goths complained of this action as a breach of the truce, but Belisarius laughed at them. He certainly put a free interpretation on the meaning of an armistice. He sent John, in command of 2000 troops, to spend the rest of the winter on the borders of Picenum, with instructions that, in case the enemy should break the truce, he was to swoop down on the Picentine territory, plunder it, and make slaves of the Gothic women and children.

About this time the attention of Belisarius was directed to the situation of northern Italy, where the inhabitants were watching the struggle with lively interest. Prominent citizens of Milan, along with Datius the archbishop, succeeded in reaching Rome, and begged him to send a small force to the north, assur ing him that it would be an easy matter not only to hold Milan but also to procure the revolt of the whole province of Liguria. Belisarius consented to the plan, but he could not execute it during the truce, and the Milanese emissaries remained at Rome for the winter.

Soon after this a tragic incident occurred, which, if we may believe the secretary of Belisarius, was connected with domestic scandals in the general's household. When Witigis was preparing to march on Rome, Praesidius, a distinguished citizen of Ravenna, rode with a few servants to Spoletium with the purpose of joining the Imperialist cause. The only valuables he carried with him were two daggers with sheaths richly adorned with gold and gems. He halted at a church outside Spoletium, which was then held by Constantine. This general heard about the precious daggers, and sent one of his followers to the church, who forced Praesidius to surrender his treasure. Praesidius went on to Rome, intent on complaining to Belisarius, but the emergencies and dangers of the siege hindered him from troubling the commander with his private grievance. As soon as the truce had been arranged he made his complaint and demanded redress. Belisarius urged Constantine to restore the weapons, but in vain. Then one day, as he was riding in the Forum, Praesidius seized his bridle, and loudly demanded whether it was permitted by the Imperial laws that when a suppliant arrived from the camp of the enemy he should be robbed of his property. Belisarius was compelled to promise that the daggers should be restored, and summoning Constantine to a private room, in the presence of other generals, told him that he must give up the daggers. Constantine replied that he would rather throw them into the Tiber. Belisarius called his guards. " I suppose they are to slay me," said Constantine. " Certainly not," said Belisarius, " but to force your armour-bearer to restore the daggers." But Constantine, believing that he was to die, drew his dagger and tried to stab Belisarius in the belly. Starting back, Belisarius seized Bessas and sheltered himself behind him, while Valerian and Ildiger dragged Constantine back. Then the guards came in, wrested the weapon from Constantine, and removed him. Some time afterwards he was put to death.

His execution was severely condemned by Procopius, who denounces it as the only impious act ever committed by Belisarius, and an act out of keeping with his character, which was distinguished by fairness and leniency. This verdict is remarkable, for at no time would the capital penalty be considered an unjust severity in the case of an officer who attempted the life of his superior. But in his *Secret History* Procopius supplements the story and thereby explains his condemnation of the act. If we may believe what he there relates, Constantine was sacrificed to the hatred of Antonina. The scandalous anecdote is that when Belisarius had discovered in Sicily his wife's disgraceful intrigue with Theodosius,[1] Constantine expressed his

---

[1] *H.A.* 1, p. 10. It is to be noted that Procopius was not in Sicily when this scandal occurred. He was in Africa. See above, p. 143.

sympathy with the injured husband, and observed, " If it were my case, I would have slain the woman and not the young man." The words were reported to Antonina, who bided her time for revenge. The affair of Praesidius brought her the opportunity to punish Constantine for his offensive words. Her persuasions induced Belisarius to order the execution, and, according to Procopius, the Emperor was seriously displeased at the death of such a capable general.

Soon after this incident the truce was unequivocally broken by repeated endeavours of the Goths to steal secretly into Rome. They planned to gain an entrance through the aqueduct known as the Aqua Virgo, near the Pincian Gate, but their explorations in the tunnel were revealed by the light of their torches. Another device was to drug the guards of a low section of the wall, on the north-western side of the city, with the help of two Romans, who were bribed. But one of them informed Belisarius and the scheme was frustrated. On another occasion the Goths openly attacked and were repelled. In retaliation for these acts Belisarius sent orders to John to descend upon the Picentine provinces. Some preparations for this eventuality had been made by the Goths. John was opposed by a force under Ulitheus, an uncle of the king, but the Romans were victorious, and Ulitheus was slain. This battle must have been fought somewhere in the southern province of Picenum,[1] for John then marched to Auximum (Osimo). Finding that it had strong natural defences, he made no attempt to take it, but marched forward into the northern Picenum and reached Urbinum. He judged that Urbinum, like Auximum, might be difficult to capture, and went on to Ariminum. In leaving two fortresses held by the enemy in his rear, John disobeyed the express injunctions of his commander in chief.[2] But his disobedience had a useful result. He shrewdly foresaw that the seizure of Ariminum, which is only a day's march from Ravenna, would compel Witigis, fearing for the safety of the Gothic capital, to raise the siege of Rome. Ariminum offered no resistance, the garrison fled to Ravenna. John presently received a message from the Gothic queen. Matasuntha hated the husband to

---

[1] Picenum suburbicarium, of which the chief towns were Ancona, Auximum, Firmum, and Asculum.

[2] Belisarius had ordered him to lay siege to any fortress that lay on his route, and if he failed to take it, not to advance farther. Procopius (ii. 10) justifies John's disobedience.

whom she had been united against her will, and now she impetuously proposed to betray Ravenna and to marry John, though he must have been completely a stranger to her.

When the news of the fall of Ariminum reached Rome, the Goths immediately burned the palisades of their camps and prepared to depart. Belisarius did not allow them to go unharmed. He waited till about half of their host had crossed the Milvian Bridge and then attacked them with all his forces. Their losses were considerable. Besides those who were slain in combat many were drowned in the Tiber. Thus the siege of Rome, which had lasted for a year and nine days, came to an end about the middle of March, A.D. 538. It had furnished Witigis with an opportunity to demonstrate his incompetence, and Belisarius to display his resourcefulness.

Small as his forces were, Belisarius seems throughout to have been sanguine that he would be able to overcome the resistance of the Goths. It had been, and was to be, a war of sieges ; if the enemy had met him in the open field, after the arrival of the reinforcements, it is possible that he would have won a decisive victory, and the conquest of Italy might have been achieved almost as rapidly as the conquest of Africa. He was asked during the siege of Rome how it was that he was so confident, seeing the disparity in strength between the army of the enemy and his own. His reply was that he relied on the superiority of his tactics. " Ever since we first met the Goths," he said,[1] " in small engagements, I studied the differences in our tactical methods for the purpose of adapting my tactics so as to make up for the inferiority of my numbers. I found that the chief difference is that almost all our Roman troops and our Hunnic allies are excellent horse-archers, whereas the Goths are totally unpractised in this form of warfare. Their cavalry are accustomed to use only lances and swords, while their bowmen are unmounted and go into battle under the cover of their heavy armed cavalry. And so, except in hand-to-hand fighting, their cavalry have no means of protecting themselves against the missiles of the enemy and can easily be cut up, and their infantry are ineffectual against mounted forces." But no tactics, however able, would have succeeded against the Goths,

[1] Procopius, *B.G.* i. 27. 26.

who were brave and well disciplined, if their army had been as vast as that which the historian alleges Witigis led against Rome.

§ 6. *Siege and Relief of Ariminum* (A.D. 538)

After the raising of the siege of Rome the scene of war shifts northward, to the fortresses along the Flaminian Way, in the lands of Umbria and Picenum, and to the provinces beyond the Po, where fighting was still to go on for two years before Belisarius succeeded in capturing the Gothic capital.

The Flaminian Way, which, traversing the Apennines, connected Rome with Ravenna, reached the Hadriatic at Fanum Fortunae (Fano), whence, following the coast, it led to Ariminum, and was continued to Ravenna. The general disposition of the belligerent forces in these districts is easy to grasp. The principal fortified hill towns to the west of the Flaminian Way, with the exception of Perusia, were held by the Goths, and those to the east, with the exception of Auximum (Osimo), by the Romans.[1] Ariminum, as we saw, had been somewhat audaciously occupied by John, the nephew of Vitalian, with 2000 Isaurians, and Ancona was securely held by Conon.

It appeared to Belisarius that it would be a serious error to keep 2000 excellent cavalry, who would be invaluable in open warfare, shut up in Ariminum, only tempting the Goths to besiege it. Accordingly, as soon as the enemy retired from Rome, his first care was to send forward Martin and Ildiger at the head of 1000 horsemen to order John to withdraw from Ariminum, and replace his Isaurians by a small force of infantry taken from the garrison of Ancona, which could easily spare them. As the retreating army of Witigis had diverged from the Flaminian highroad in order to avoid the forts of Narnia and Spoletium, no obstacle opposed the advance of Martin and Ildiger until they reached Petra Pertusa, " the tunnelled Rock," a pass between Cales (Cagli) and Forum Sempronii (Fossombrone),

---

[1] Cp. Hodgkin, *op. cit.* iv. 288. Urbs Vetus (Orvieto) was held by 1000 Goths, Tuder (Todi) by 400, Clusium (Chiusi) by 1000, Urbinum by 2000, Mons Feletris (Montefeltro) by 500, Caesena by 500, Auximum by 4000. Narnia, Spoletium, and Firmum were in the hands of the Romans. The distance from Rome to Ravenna by the Via Flaminia is 370 kils. ; from Fanum to Ravenna about 96.

about twenty-five miles from the Hadriatic Sea.[1] This pass, now known as the Passo di Furlo, is accurately described by Procopius. The Flaminian Road comes up against a high wall of rock, on the right of which a river descends with such a rapid current that it would be death to attempt to cross it, and on the left the precipitous cliff to which the rock belongs rises so high that men standing on its summit would appear to those below like the smallest birds. The Emperor Vespasian bored a tunnel through this rock, as an inscription on the spot records. It was a natural fortress, well adapted for defence. The Roman troops who now advanced found it held by a Gothic garrison and closed by doors at either end. The Goths, who had their women and children with them, lived in houses outside the tunnel, apparently on the Hadriatic side. When it was found impossible to make any impression on the well-fortified entrance to the passage, some men were sent up to the top of the cliff, and dislodging huge fragments of rock they rolled them down on the Gothic block-houses below. The enemy immediately surrendered, and Martin and Ildiger, leaving a small garrison behind them, continued their journey to Fanum. From here they had to ride southward to Ancona to pick up a detachment of foot-soldiers to replace the Isaurians at Ariminum. Then retracing their steps to Fanum they arrived safely at their destination, and delivered the commands of Belisarius to John. But John declined to obey, and leaving the foot-soldiers with him Martin and Ildiger departed to report the issue of their errand to the commander-in-chief.

The insubordination of John strikes the note of the subsequent course of the Roman conduct of the war. Counsels were divided, and the commander-in-chief could no longer depend on his generals to conform to his plans. Belisarius was slow and cautious, but it is probable that, if he had been able to have his own way and secure the punctual obedience of his subordinates, the war would have been shortened. John was an excellent but sometimes over-confident soldier. He was impatient of the cautious deliberation of Belisarius, and doubtless thought that he was himself more worthy of the post of supreme commander.

---

[1] It is called Intercisa in the Itineraries, and is a little to the east of the modern Acqualagna. The pass is 125 feet long, over 17 feet high, and broad. On either side are the halves of a mountain: on right Monte Paganuccio, 3259 feet high, on left Monte Pietralata, 2960 feet high.

In the present instance, the event speedily showed that Belisarius was right. Witigis had no sooner crossed the Apennines than he addressed himself to the siege of Ariminum. Failing in his assaults, he sat down to take it by hunger, and the besieged were presently reduced to extreme distress (April, A.D. 538).

Belisarius meanwhile had begun to advance northward from Rome, to carry out methodically his plan of reducing, first of all, the Gothic fortresses west of the Apennines. It was about the middle of the year. Clusium and Tuder surrendered on his approach. His next object would have been the reduction of Urbs Vetus, but the execution of his plan was disarranged by the arrival of reinforcements from the East which now reached Picenum under the command of the eunuch Narses, keeper of the Emperor's privy purse.[1] The new army was 7000 strong, consisting of 5000 Roman troops under another Narses and Justin the Master of Soldiers in Illyricum, and 2000 Herul auxiliaries under their own leaders. Such an important addition to the Imperial fighting forces modified the situation, and Belisarius, leaving Urbs Vetus unreduced, marched to Picenum to confer with Narses and arrange the future conduct of the war. They met at Firmum and a council was held which had weighty consequences. The urgent question was the relief of Ariminum, which was hard pressed and might be forced to surrender through hunger. Should the army march to its relief immediately? Belisarius was opposed to this course on military grounds. So long as Auximum was held by the enemy, an advance against the Goths at Ariminum would expose his rear to an attack from the garrison of that fortress. The majority of the generals present agreed, and held that no risks should be taken to save John, whose predicament was due to his own rashness and insubordination. Narses, who was a personal friend of John, opposed this view. He pointed out that the disobedience of John was a side-issue which ought not to affect their decision. After the relief of Ariminum John could be punished for defying the commands of Belisarius. But it would be highly inexpedient, he argued, considering not only the material loss, but also the moral consequences, to allow an important city and a large

---

[1] They probably landed at Ancona. Shortly before this Witigis had sent a force against it. Conon, the commander, gave the Goths battle outside the walls and was severely defeated; but the fortress was not taken.

body of troops—not to speak of a vigorous general—to fall
into the hands of the foe.

While the council was sitting, a soldier from Ariminum who
had eluded the blockade arrived in the camp with a letter from
John. Its purport was : " All our supplies have long since
failed us. Unable to resist the enemy, we cannot hold out
against the pressure of the inhabitants, and within seven days
we shall have reluctantly to surrender ourselves and the city.
Our extreme necessity is, I think, an adequate excuse for an act
which may appear unbeseeming." This message, simply announcing a fact and making no demand for succour, strengthened
whatever effect may have been produced by the arguments of
Narses. Belisarius decided to do all that could be done to save
Ariminum, though he still felt grave scruples whether it was a
wise thing to do.

It would be bold for a modern critic, with the meagre evidence
at his disposal, to assert that the hesitations of the commander-
in-chief were unjustified, but it is difficult to resist the impression
that the course recommended by Narses was the right one. It
required military skill, but when Belisarius set his mind to the
problem he solved it triumphantly. In order to mitigate the
danger from Auximum, he posted a thousand men to the east
of it near the coast. A large force was sent by sea to Ariminum
under the command of Ildiger, who was instructed not to dis-
embark until a second army, which, led by Martin, was to march
along the coast road, approached the city. Martin, when he
arrived, was to light many more fires than were required, in
order to deceive the enemy as to the number of his troops.
Belisarius, accompanied by Narses, led the rest of the army by
an inland mountainous route with the purpose of descending
on Ariminum from the north-west.[1] For the full success of the
plan it was necessary that the arrivals of the three armies on the

---

[1] The only indication that Procopius gives of the route is that they
passed Urbs Salvia (Urbesaglia),
which is half-way between Fermo
and Nocera. They must of course
have crossed the Flaminian Way.
Hodgkin's view that they followed
the Flaminian Way from Nocera, so
that from Fano onward their route
would have coincided with that of
Martin, is entirely incompatible with
the narrative of Procopius. There
can, I think, be little doubt that they
left the Flaminian Way at Scheggia or
at Acqualagna and followed one of
the routes noticed below, pp. 288-89.
Compare the retreat of Garibaldi in
1849, via San Marino to Musano (due
west of Rimini). See G. M. Trevelyan,
*Garibaldi's Defence of the Roman Re-
public*, chaps. xiii., xiv.

scene should be timed to coincide. At a day's journey from
Ariminum a few Goths fell in with the army of Belisarius, and
hardly realised that they were in the presence of an enemy till
Roman arrows began to work havoc among them. Some fell,
others crawled wounded behind the shelter of rocks. From
their concealment they could see the standards of Belisarius,
and they received the impression of an army far in excess of its
actual numbers. In the night they made their way to the camp
of Witigis at Ariminum, and arriving at mid-day reported the
approach of Belisarius with an innumerable host. The Goths
immediately formed in battle order on the northern side of the
city and spent the afternoon looking towards the hills. When
night fell and they were composing themselves to rest, they
suddenly saw to the south-east the blaze of the fires which had
been kindled by the troops of Martin. They realised that they
were in danger of being surrounded, and passed the night in
terror. When morning came and they looked out to sea, they
beheld a great armament of hostile ships approaching. In fear
and confusion they broke up their camp, and no man thought
of anything but reaching the shelter of Ravenna. If the garrison
of the city had rushed out and dealt death among the panic-
stricken fugitives, Procopius thought that the war might have
ended there and then. But the soldiers of John were too
exhausted by their privations to seize the moment.

Ildiger and the troops who had come by sea were the first
to arrive in the abandoned camp of the barbarians. Belisarius
arrived at mid-day. When he met John, pale and gaunt with
hunger, he could not forbear remarking that he ought to thank
Ildiger. John dryly replied that his gratitude was due not to
Ildiger but to Narses.

§ 7. *Dissensions in the Imperial Army*

The relief of Ariminum, accomplished without the loss of a
single life, was a new proof of the military capacity of Belisarius,
but it was a moral triumph for Narses, since but for his influence
it would never have been undertaken. Distrust and division
ensued between the commander-in-chief and the chamberlain,
and the bloodless victory hardly compensated for the injuries
which this dissension inflicted on the Imperial cause. Narses

felt, and his friends convinced him, that it was beneath the dignity of his office to act in subordination to a general, and he determined to use the forces which he had brought to Italy according to his own discretion. In accordance with this resolution he excused himself repeatedly from complying with requests or orders from Belisarius, who at length convoked a military council to clear up the situation.

At this council Belisarius did not at first insist upon his rights as commander-in-chief or rebuke Narses for disobedience. He pointed out that the enemy were far from being defeated ; Witigis had still an army of tens of thousands at Ravenna ; the situation in Liguria was serious ; Auximum with its large and valiant garrison was still uncaptured, as well as other strong places like Urbs Vetus. He proposed that a portion of the army should be sent to Liguria, to the rescue of Milan, which was in grave peril, and that the remaining forces should be employed against the Gothic fortresses south and west of the Flaminian Way, and first of all against Auximum. Narses replied. He contended that it was inexpedient that all the Imperial forces should be concentrated on the two objects of Auximum and Milan. Let Belisarius undertake these enterprises, but he would attempt the conquest of the Aemilian province. This would have the probable advantage of retaining the main army of the Goths at Ravenna, so that they would be unable to send aid to the places attacked by Belisarius. But Belisarius was opposed to any plan which involved a dissipation of forces, and he decided to assert his authority. He produced a letter which the Emperor had recently addressed to the commanders of the troops in Italy. It was conceived in these terms :

" In sending Narses our purser to Italy we do not invest him with the command of the army. It is our wish that Belisarius alone shall lead the whole army as seems good to him, and it behoves you all to obey him *in the interest of our State.*" [1]

In the last phrase there was a possible ambiguity of which Narses at once took advantage, interpreting it as a reservation limiting the duty of obedience. The plan of Belisarius, he said, is not in the interest of the State, and therefore we are not

---

[1] *B.G.* ii. 18. 28 αὐτῷ τε ὑμᾶς ἕπεσθαι ἅπαντας ἐπὶ τῷ συμφέροντι τῇ ἡμετέρᾳ πολιτείᾳ προσήκει.

bound to obey him. It may seem difficult to suppose that
Justinian intended to lay down a principle which logically led
to military anarchy, since it was open to every commander to
take a different view of the wisdom of a strategic plan. Yet
we cannot consider it impossible that the insertion of the words
" in the interest of the State " was designed as a check on the
authority of the commander-in-chief. For if the Emperor had
really meant to enjoin unconditional obedience, the phrase in
question was entirely unnecessary. The fact that the trusted
keeper of his privy purse should have been chosen for a military
mission lends colour to the suspicion that Justinian was dis-
satisfied with the progress of the war, and doubtful whether
Belisarius was conducting it with the necessary energy. It
would be going too far to suggest that he wished to deprive
Belisarius of the undivided glory of conquering Italy, though
we are told that this was the personal object of Narses.

Belisarius was not in a position to enforce his claims, and he
had sufficient self-restraint to avoid an actual breach. Matters
were smoothed over for the time, and the co-operation of the
commanders, though it was far from cordial, continued. A
large force was despatched against Urbs Vetus, and Belisarius,
again postponing his intention of reducing Auximum, marched
to the siege of Urbinum, accompanied by Narses and John. But
the forces of the rival commanders did not mingle; they encamped
separately on the eastern and western sides of the city. The
garrison of Urbinum, which is situated on a high hill at a
strenuous day's journey from Ariminum, refused an invitation
of Belisarius to surrender; they had abundance of provisions and
trusted in the strength of the city. Narses, deeming the place
impregnable, considered it waste of time to remain, and, withdrawing to Ariminum, sent John, at the head of all his forces,
against Caesena. Failing to take this place, John, who was
impatient of sieges, advanced against Forum Cornelii (Imola),
which he captured by surprise, and then easily subjugated the
whole Aemilian province.

Meanwhile fortune played into the hands of Belisarius.
Urbinum was supplied by a single spring. It suddenly ran
dry, and deprived ˙of water the Goths could only capitulate.
Narses is said to have received the news of this success with
deep chagrin.

§ 8. *Siege and Massacre of Milan* (A.D. 539)

It was now December (A.D. 538) [1] and Belisarius decided that it was inopportune then to attempt the siege of Auximum, which promised to prove a difficult enterprise. He left a large force in Firmum to protect the country against the ravages of the garrison, and marched himself to Urbs Vetus, where provisions were already running short. The place could hardly have been taken by assault. It is a natural stronghold, requiring no artificial fortifications,—built on an isolated hill rising out of hollow country. This hill, level at the top, is precipitous below, and is surrounded by cliffs of the same height, between which and the hill itself flows a large and impassable river, according to Procopius, entirely encircling the hill except at one point where the city could be approached from the cliffs. At the present day, Orvieto is not surrounded by water. The river Paglia flows round the northern and eastern sides of the hill, to join the river Chiana, but on the south and west there is no such natural moat. It is supposed that the Paglia may have changed its course.[2] Hunger was the only weapon which could avail against a brave garrison, and the Goths, when they had been reduced to consuming hides softened in water, surrendered at last to Belisarius (spring, A.D. 539).

In the meantime important events had been happening beyond the Po. Immediately after the Goths had raised the siege of Rome, Belisarius, in fulfilment of his promise to Datius, the archbishop of Milan, had sent 1000 Isaurians and Thracians under the command of Mundilas to Liguria (April, A.D. 538). They went by sea from Porto to Genoa, and, crossing the Po, they succeeded in occupying Milan, Bergamum, Comum, Novaria, and all the strong places of inland Liguria except Ticinum (Pavia). On hearing the news Witigis sent his nephew Uraias to recover Milan, and he received powerful aid from abroad.

Theodebert, grandson of Chlodwig, had succeeded his father Theoderic as king of Austrasia in A.D. 533. Besides the Austrasian dominion on both sides of the Rhine, with its capital at Metz, he ruled over a portion of Aquitania and a portion of Burgundy which had recently been conquered by his uncles. We

---

[1] *B.G.* ii. 20. 1.   [2] Cp. Hodgkin, iv. p. 338.

possess a letter which he wrote to Justinian, probably in an early
stage of the war, offering excuses for his failure to send to Italy
a force of 3000 men which he had promised. As he styles
Justinian " father," [1] it may be inferred that the Emperor
formally adopted him as a son when he sought an assurance of
the co-operation of the Franks before the outbreak of the war.
But Theodebert was ambitious and treacherous, and his filial
relation to Justinian was no obstacle to his policy of playing fast
and loose between the two belligerents. At this crisis he resolved
to assist the Goths, and 10,000 Burgundians crossed the Alps
to co-operate with Uraias. He sophistically professed that he
was not violating his convention with the Emperor, because no
Franks were in the army; the Burgundians, forsooth, were
acting as an independent people, without his authority.[2] The
Gothic and Burgundian forces blockaded Milan, which Mundilas
held with only 300 soldiers as the rest of his force had been
distributed in the other Ligurian fortresses.[3] The able-bodied
civilian inhabitants were therefore called upon to take part in
the defence.

After the relief of Ariminum, Belisarius despatched a large
army under Martin and Uliaris to the relief of Milan. These
commanders encamped on the southern bank of the Po ; they
were afraid to face the host of barbarians who were besieging
the city. Mundilas despatched a messenger, who managed to
evade the sentinels of the enemy, to plead the urgent need of
the besieged, and was sent back with promise of speedy aid,
which Martin and Uliaris made no effort to fulfil. At last, after
a delay so long that it amounted to treason to the Imperial cause,
they wrote to Belisarius, representing their forces as hopelessly
inadequate to cope with the enemy and requesting him to send
John and Justin, who were in the neighbouring province of
Aemilia, to reinforce them. Belisarius complied, but John and
Justin refused to move without the authority of Narses. Belisarius wrote to Narses, who gave the requisite order. John
proceeded to collect ships for the purpose of crossing the Po,

---

[1] *D. illustro et praecellentissimo
domno et patri Iustiniano imperatore
Theodebertus rex (Epp. Merow. et
Kar. aevi i. Epp. Austrasicae, 19).*
The soldiers were to have been
sent · to the help of the patrician

Bregantinus (perhaps = Vergentinus,
below, p. 205, *n.* 1).
[2] Procopius, *B.G.* ii. 12. 38.
[3] Marcellinus, *sub* 539, records that
Theodebert devastated the Aemilian
province and plundered Genoa.

but before his preparations were completed he fell ill. Thus delay ensued upon delay, and meanwhile the unhappy inhabitants of Milan were starving. When they were reduced to feeding on dogs and mice, Gothic envoys waited on Mundilas, inviting him to capitulate on the condition that he and all his soldiers should have their lives spared. He was ready to accept these terms if they would agree to spare the inhabitants. But the Goths, who were infuriated against the disloyal Ligurians, did not conceal their determination to wreak a bloody vengeance. Mundilas therefore refused, but his hands were soon forced. He attempted to induce the soldiers to make a desperate sally against the foe, but, worn as they were by the sufferings of the siege, they had not the courage to embrace so forlorn a hope. They compelled their leader to agree to the terms which the Goths had proposed.

Mundilas and the soldiers were placed in honourable captivity, in accordance with the agreement. Milan and its inhabitants felt the full fury of a host of savages. All the adult males, who according to Procopius numbered 300,000, were massacred ; all the women were presented as slaves to the Burgundians. The city itself was razed to the ground. It was the wealthiest and most populous town in Italy then, as now, and if Procopius is near the truth in his estimate of the number of males who were slain, it must have been nearly as populous as it is to-day.[1]

In the long series of deliberate inhumanities recorded in the annals of mankind, the colossal massacre of Milan is one of the most flagrant. Historians have passed it over somewhat lightly. But the career of Attila offers no act of war so savage as this vengeance, carried out by the orders of the nephew of the Gothic king. It gives us the true measure of the instincts of the Ostrogoths, claimed by some to have been the most promising of the German invaders of the Empire.

Reparatus, the Praetorian Prefect of Italy, was found in the city. He was the brother of Pope Vigilius, but this did not save him. He was cut in pieces and thrown to the dogs.

---

[1] *B.G.* ii. 21. 39. The population of modern Milan is between 600,000 and 700,000 (that of Rome is over 500,000). Procopius describes it (*B.G.* ii. 7. 38) as the most populous Italian city next to Rome. It seems probable that he has immensely exaggerated the number of the slain. For the massacre see also *Cont. Marcell.*, *s.a.*, and Marius of Aventicum, *Chron.*, *s.a.* 538 (*senatores et sacerdotes cum reliquis populis etiam in ipsa sacrosancta loca interfecti sunt*). Datius the archbishop escaped.

Cerventinus,[1] another brother, escaped to Dalmatia, and went on to Constantinople to announce the calamity to Justinian. The fall of Milan, which happened towards the end of March [2] (A.D. 539), led to the immediate recovery of all Liguria by the Goths. The news came as a heavy blow to Belisarius, but it was an irresistible proof of the unwisdom of divided military authority by which the Emperor himself could not fail to be impressed. Belisarius wrote to him explaining all the circumstances and showing where the blame rested. Justinian inflicted no punishment on those who were in fault,[3] but he immediately recalled Narses, and in language which was not ambiguous confirmed the supreme authority of Belisarius.[4]

§ 9. *Siege and Capture of Auximum* (A.D. 539, May to November)

In the meanwhile Witigis, while the fate of Liguria still remained undecided, was seriously alarmed for the safety of Ravenna. The Romans were firmly established at Ariminum and Urbinum, and he expected that at any moment Belisarius might advance against his capital. Early in the year he resolved to seek foreign help. He first applied to Wacho, king of the Langobardi, who dwelled beyond the Danube. But no succour was forthcoming from this quarter. Wacho, who was an ally of the Emperor, did not consider it expedient to imitate the double-dealing of the treacherous Franks. The Goths then conceived the idea of appealing to a greater power, the king of Persia himself. They argued, with truth, that Justinian would not have embarked on his enterprises in the West if he had not been secured in the East by the peace which he had concluded with Chosroes. If they could succeed in embroiling him in a war with Persia, it would be impossible for him to continue the war in Italy. As the only practicable route to Persia lay through Imperial territory, it would have been difficult to send Gothic ambassadors. By large bribes two Ligurian priests, who could travel without exciting suspicion, were induced to undertake the mission, and they succeeded in reaching the court of

---

[1] Procopius calls him Vergentinos, *B.G.* ii. 21. 41.

[2] *B.G.* ii. 22. 1 ὁ χειμὼν ἐτελεύτα ἤδη.

[3] Belisarius would not allow Uliaris to appear in his presence, *ib.* ii.

[4] The Heruls, who had come to Italy with Narses, refused to remain when he was recalled.

Chosroes and delivering a letter from Witigis. This appeal was hardly the chief motive which determined Chosroes to reopen hostilities, but undoubtedly it produced its effect. It must have impressed upon him that in considering his foreign policy it would be wise to take account of the situation in the western Mediterranean. He resolved on war, as Witigis hoped, but his operations began too late to rescue Witigis from disaster.

The report that negotiations were passing between Ravenna and Ctesiphon reached Justinian (in June), and inclined him to the idea of ending the Italian war by a compromise as soon as possible, so as to set Belisarius free to take command on the eastern frontier. He accordingly released the Gothic envoys whom he had detained for more than a year,[1] and promised to send ambassadors of his own to discuss peace. When these Goths arrived in Italy, Belisarius would not allow them to proceed to Ravenna till Witigis surrendered the Roman envoys, Peter and Athanasius, who had been held prisoners for four years.[2] The Emperor rewarded these men for their services by creating Peter Master of Offices, and Athanasius Praetorian Prefect of Italy.

Italy indeed needed peace. Agriculture had ceased in the provinces devastated by war, and in Liguria and Aemilia, in Etruria, Umbria, and Picenum the inhabitants were dying of hunger and disease. It was said that in Picenum alone 50,000 tillers of the soil perished. Procopius noted the emaciation, the livid colour, and the wild eyes of the people, suffering either from want of food, or from a surfeit of indigestible substitutes like acorn bread. Cannibalism occurred, and a ghastly story was told of two women who lived in a lonely house near Ariminum where they offered a night's lodging to passers-by. They killed seventeen of these guests in their sleep and devoured their flesh. The eighteenth woke up as the cannibals were about to despatch him ; he forced them to confess, and slew them. Scattered

---

[1] They had been sent to Constantinople during the siege of Rome. See above, p. 191.

[2] We may infer from *B.G.* ii. 22. 25 that this happened at the end of June or beginning of July 539. Körbs (*op. cit.* 31 *sqq.*) calculates that the Gothic embassy to Ctesiphon started in March from Ravenna. They could reach the Bosphorus in about four weeks, if they travelled quickly at the rate of 75 kils. a day. To reach Ctesiphon meant five or six weeks more, so that they might have arrived about the middle of May. Thus Justinian could have heard of their arrival and released the Gothic envoys before the end of June. For the distances of Ravenna from Constantinople via Aquileia see below, p. 225.

over the country-sides were the unburied corpses of those who
had died while they sought with feeble hands to tear blades of
grass from the ground. The Imperial armies suffered little,
for they received a constant supply of provisions by sea from
Calabria and Sicily.

Belisarius in the meantime prosecuted his plans. He considered it essential to capture Auximum and Faesulae before he
advanced upon Ravenna. Placing Martin and John at Dertona
(Tortona) to defend the line of the Po against Uraias, he sent
Justin and Cyprian to blockade Faesulae, and undertook himself
the most important of his tasks, the siege of Auximum. These
two sieges occupied more than six months (April to October or
November, A.D. 539).[1]

The army on the Po succeeded, as Belisarius anticipated, in
hindering Uraias from marching to the aid of Faesulae. The
two hosts, reluctant to risk a trial of strength, remained immobile
on the banks of the river, till a new enemy appeared upon the
scene. The Franks regarded the calamities of Italy as an
opportunity for themselves and were as perfidious towards the
Goths as towards the Empire ; and Theodebert himself, at the
head (it is said) of 100,000 men, descended from the Alps for the
plunder and destruction alike of Goths and Imperialists, with both
of whom they had recently sworn alliance. Procopius describes
their equipment. There were a few mounted spearmen in attendance on the king, the rest were infantry armed with a sword, a
shield, and an axe. The axe (*francisca*), solid and double-edged,
with a very short wooden handle, was a weapon for hurling not for
wielding. At the first onset of battle a shower of axes fell upon
the foe, shattering shields and killing men.

The Goths, fondly imagining that Theodebert was coming to
their aid in fulfilment of his promises, rejoiced to hear of his
approach. At Ticinum, where a bridge spanned the Po, at its
confluence with the stream of Ticinus, the Goths who guarded
it gave the Franks every assistance to cross the river. As soon
as they held the bridge, the invaders threw off the mask. They
seized the women and children of the Goths, slaughtered them,
and threw their bodies into the river. Procopius saw a religious

---

[1] *Cont. Marcell.*, *s.a.*, states that
these cities were taken in 539 *septi-
mo mense*, but erroneously records
their capture before the fall of
Milan. The sieges must have begun
in April or May, cp. *B.G.* xxii. 1,
and so the seventh month would be
October-November.

significance in this act. " These barbarians," he says, " though converted to Christianity retain most of their old beliefs and still practise human sacrifices." Having crossed the Po, the Franks advanced southward towards Dertona, near which Uraias and his army were encamped not far from the Roman camp. The Goths went forth to welcome their allies, and were received by a shower of axes. They turned in headlong flight, rushed wildly through the camp of the astonished Romans, and pursued the road to Ravenna. The Romans imagined that Belisarius must have suddenly arrived and surprised the Gothic camp ; and issuing forth to meet him they found themselves confronted by the immense army of the Franks. They were forced to fight, but were easily routed and retired to Tuscany.

The victors were in possession of two deserted camps, supplied, however, with provisions. The food did not go far among so many, and in the desolated country they found no subsistence but oxen and the water of the Po. It is satisfactory to know that they paid a heavy price for their rapacity. Dysentery broke out, and large numbers—a third of the host, it was reported—died. The survivors were bitter against their king for leading them into a place of desolation to perish of hunger and disease. Then a letter arrived from Belisarius, reproaching Theodebert for his treachery, menacing him with the anger of the Emperor, and advising him to attend to his domestic affairs instead of running into danger by interfering in matters which did not concern him. The barbarians retreated ingloriously across the Alps.[1]

This episode had little influence on the course of the war. All the efforts of the Imperial forces were concentrated on the blockades of Auximum and Faesulae. The flower of the Gothic army was holding Auximum and was resolved to hold it to the end. When the provisions began to give out, the commander of the garrison sent an urgent message to Ravenna, imploring Witigis to send an army to relieve them. Immediate help was promised, but nothing was done. Time wore on, the garrison was sorely pressed by hunger, and too careful a watch was kept to allow any one to steal out of the town. But the Goths managed to bribe a soldier named Burcentius, who was keeping guard at mid-day in an isolated spot near the walls, to carry a

---

[1] The retreat gave Justinian the pretext for assuming the title *Francicus*.

letter to Ravenna. Burcentius executed the errand, and Witigis again sent back good words which were read aloud to the garrison, and encouraged them to hold out. As no help came, they again employed the services of the traitor and informed the king that they would be compelled to surrender within five days. Belisarius meanwhile had repeatedly urged them to surrender on favourable terms, and knowing that they were starving he was puzzled at their refusal to comply. A Slavonic soldier, hidden in a bush for the purpose, succeeded in capturing alive a Goth who had crept out of the city at dawn to gather grass. The prisoner disclosed the treachery of Burcentius, and Belisarius delivered him to his comrades to do with him what they would. They burned him alive in sight of the walls.

The chief water-supply of Auximum was derived from a huge cistern, built in a rocky place outside the walls, so that men had to come out of the city in order to fill their water jars. Belisarius sent some Isaurians to attempt to destroy the cistern, but the masonry resisted all their efforts. Then he poisoned the spring by throwing in quicklime with dead animals and noxious herbs. But there was another small well inside the city, and, though sadly insufficient for their needs, it enabled the loyal Goths to postpone surrender.

The end was brought about by the capitulation of the starving defenders of Faesulae. The captives were brought to Auximum and paraded in front of the walls, and this sight determined the garrison, convinced at last that they had nothing to hope from Ravenna, to follow the example of Faesulae. The terms arranged were that they should give up half of their possessions to be divided among the besiegers, and should pass into the service of the Emperor. They cannot be reproached for having accepted those conditions. Their king had basely left them to their fate. He had professed to regard Auximum as the key of Ravenna, but such was his cowardice that he could not bring himself to send to its relief any portion of the considerable army which was idly protecting his capital.

§ 10. *Fall of Ravenna* (A.D. 540, Spring)

Auximum fell in October or November and Belisarius lost no time in preparing an advance upon Ravenna. New forces had just arrived from Dalmatia, and these he ordered to guard the northern bank of the Po, while another contingent was sent to patrol the southern. The purpose of these dispositions was to prevent food stores from being sent down the river from Liguria. The Imperial command of the sea effectively hindered any attempts to supply the city from elsewhere.

The one thing that Belisarius had now to fear was that the Franks might again descend into Italy and again aid the Goths as they had aided them at Milan. When he learned that a Frank embassy was coming to Ravenna, he sent ambassadors to Witigis. The Frank proposal was that Goths and Franks should make common cause, and, when they had driven the Roman invaders from Italy, should divide the peninsula between them. The Imperial envoys warned the Goths against entertaining the insidious offer of a people whose rapacity was only equalled by their treachery. Their rapacity was proved by the way they had dealt with the Burgundians and Thuringians ; their treachery the Goths knew to their own cost by the events of a few months ago. Witigis and his counsellors decided that it would be wiser to come to terms with the Emperor than to trust such a dangerous ally as Theodebert, and the Frank envoys were sent empty away. Hostilities were suspended, and negotiations opened with Belisarius, who, however, did not relax his precautions against the introduction of provisions into Ravenna. He even bribed some one to set fire to the public corn store in the city—at the secret suggestion, it was said, of the queen Matasuntha. Some of the Goths ascribed the conflagration to treachery, others to lightning ; the one theory suggested enemies among themselves, the other an enemy in heaven.

Uraias in the meantime was preparing to come to the aid of his uncle with 4000 men, most of whom he had taken from the garrisons which held the forts of the Cottian Alps. But John and Martin hurried westward, seized the forts, and captured the wives and children of the Goths. On hearing that their families were in the hands of the Romans, the soldiers of Uraias deserted him and went over to John ; and Uraias was forced to remain inactive in Liguria.

Two senators, Domnicus and Maximin, now arrived from Constantinople, bearing the Emperor's instructions for the

conclusion of peace. The menace of Persia inclined Justinian
to grant more lenient terms than the military situation seemed
to warrant. He proposed a territorial division of Italy. All
the lands north of the Po should be retained by Witigis, all the
lands south of the Po should be retained by the Emperor. The
royal treasury of Ravenna should be divided equally between
the two contracting powers. Witigis and the Goths were surprised by a proposal which was far more favourable than they
had looked for, and they accepted it without hesitation. But it
did not please Belisarius. He saw within his reach a complete
victory to compensate for the toils and anxieties of five weary
years. He had dethroned and led captive the king of the
Vandals ; he was determined to dethrone and lead captive the
king of the Ostrogoths. When the ambassadors returned from
Ravenna to his camp and asked him to ratify by his signature
the treaty of peace, he declined. As his refusal was severely
criticised by some of the generals as an act of disobedience to
the Emperor's decision, he summoned a military council and
asked those present whether they approved of the division of
Italy, or whether they deemed it practicable to conquer it entirely.
All the officers were unanimous in approving the terms which
the Emperor had dictated, and Belisarius required them to
put in writing their opinion that nothing would be gained
by continuing the war, so that he should be exonerated
from blame if future events were to prove that it would have
been wiser to carry to completion the overthrow of the Gothic
kingdom.[1]

But the refusal of the commander-in-chief to sign the treaty
had already produced an unfavourable impression at Ravenna.
Witigis suspected that the negotiations were a trap, and refused
to execute the agreement unless Belisarius signed it and gave
them a sworn guarantee of good faith. Famine meanwhile was
doing its work, and the discontent of the Goths with their
incompetent king reached a climax.

Then a remarkable idea occurred—we do not know from
what quarter the suggestion came—to the men of weight among
the Goths. Why not revert to the political condition of Italy

---

[1] Procopius curiously says that
Belisarius was pleased with the
opinion of the generals (*B.G.* ii. 29. 16
$\dot{\eta}\sigma\theta\epsilon\iota\varsigma$), though he had just recorded
(*ib.* iv.) his vexation at the conditions
prescribed by Justinian.

as it existed before the days of Theoderic, before the days of
Odovacar ?   The regime of Witigis had discredited Ostrogothic
royalty, and they would feel no repugnance to submitting to
the direct authority of a western Emperor [1] residing at Rome
or Ravenna, if that Emperor were Belisarius, whom they deeply
respected both as a soldier and as a just man.   They entertained
no doubts that he would eagerly accept the offer of a throne.
They did not know his uncompromising loyalty or suspect
that there was no rôle that seemed more thoroughly detestable
to him than the rôle of a usurper.   He had once taken an express
and solemn oath that he would never aspire to the throne so
long as Justinian was alive.   But when messengers of the Goths
privately sounded him on the plan he professed to welcome it
with pleasure.   For he saw in it a means of bringing his work
to a speedy and triumphant conclusion.   When these clandestine
negotiations came to the knowledge of Witigis, he resigned
himself to the situation and sent a secret message to Belisarius
urging him to accept the offer.[2]

Belisarius then summoned a meeting of the generals and
invited the presence of the two Imperial ambassadors.   He
asked them whether they would approve if, without striking
another blow, he should succeed in recovering the whole of
Italy, in taking captive Witigis, and seizing all his treasure.
The assembly agreed that it would be a magnificent achievement,
and urged him to accomplish it if he could.   Having in this way
protected himself against misinterpretation of his motive in
pretending to yield to the Gothic proposal, he sent confidential
messengers to Ravenna to announce his definite acceptance.
Official envoys were sent back to the camp, nominally to continue the discussion of peace terms, but privately to receive
from the commander pledges of his good faith.   He gave them
sworn pledges on all matters save his willingness to accept the
purple ; on that point he deferred his oath till he should stand
in the presence of Witigis and the Gothic magnates.   The envoys

---

[1] B.G. ii. 29. 18 βασιλέα τῆς
ἑσπερίας Βελισάριον ἀνειπεῖν ἔγνωσαν.
[2] Martroye (L'Occident, p. 401)
argues that this intrigue had been
arranged in consultation with Chosroes.   His reason is that in autumn
539 the Armenian envoys who urged
Chosroes to declare war pointed out

that Justinian had lost his two best
generals, Sittas who had been killed,
and Belisarius who had left his service
to be the sovran of Italy.   Martroye is
mistaken in supposing that the Gothic
proposal was made to Belisarius at
about the same time; this cannot have
been earlier than Jan. or Feb. 540.

were satisfied ; they could not imagine that he would reject the Imperial diadem.

He then made his arrangements for entering Ravenna. He dispersed a part of his army, under the command of those leaders who were ill-disposed towards himself—John, Aratius, his brother Narses, and Bessas—to various destinations, on the pretext that it was difficult to provide the requisite commissariat for the whole army in one place. He sent his fleet laden with corn and other foods to the port of Classis, to fill the starving mouths at Ravenna. Then he advanced with his army and entered the city in May A.D. 540.[1] It is disappointing that the historian does not describe the scene in which Belisarius undeceived the Gothic king and nobles as to his intentions. We are only told that he kept Witigis in honourable captivity, and that he allowed all the Goths who lived in the cis-Padane provinces to return to their homes. He seized the treasures of the palace, but the Goths were allowed to retain all their private property, and plundering was strictly forbidden.

Most of the garrisons of the strong places north of the Po voluntarily surrendered,[2] apparently under the impression that Italy was to be ruled by Belisarius. Ticinum, which was the head quarters of Uraias, and Verona, which was held by Ildibad, were the chief exceptions. When the Gothic notables of the northern provinces realised that Belisarius had made " the great refusal " and was about to return to Constantinople, they proceeded to Ticinum and urged Uraias to assume the royal insignia and place himself at their head to fight a desperate battle for freedom. Uraias was ready to fight, but he declined to step into the place of Witigis ; the nephew of such an unlucky ruler would not, he declared, have the necessary prestige. He advised them to choose as their king Ildibad, a man of conspicuous energy and valour, and a nephew of Theudis the king of the Visigoths. Accordingly Ildibad, at the request of the Gothic leaders, came from Verona and suffered himself to be proclaimed king. But he persuaded his followers to make one more effort to induce Belisarius to recall his decision. A deputation waited on the commander, who was making his preparations to leave Ravenna.

[1] Agnillus, *Lib. pont.* p. 101.

[2] Tervisium (Treviso) and the forts of Venetia are expressly mentioned. Caesena, west of Ariminum, had held out till the fall of Ravenna.

They upbraided him, with justice, for having broken faith. But reproaches and enticements produced no effect. Belisarius told them definitely that he would never assume the Imperial name in Justinian's lifetime. Soon afterwards he left the shores of Italy, taking with him the dethroned king and queen, many leading Goths, and the royal treasure.[1]

The impregnable fidelity of Belisarius to Justinian's throne, under a temptation which few men in his position would have resisted, is the fact which has been chiefly emphasised by historians in describing these tortuous transactions. But his innocence of criminal disloyalty in thought or deed does not excuse his conduct. He was guilty of a flagrant violation of his promises to the Goths, and he was guilty of gross disobedience to the Emperor's orders. It was not the business of the commander-in-chief to decide the terms of peace ; that was entirely a question for the Emperor. We can understand his unwillingness to allow the complete victory, which seemed within his grasp, to escape him ; but it would be difficult to justify the chicanery which he employed at first in protracting the negotiations, and then in deceiving the enemy by pretended disloyalty to his master. Nor was his policy justified by success. It did not lead automatically to the complete conquest of Italy and the extension of Imperial authority to the Alps. When he sailed for Constantinople, he left behind him in the provinces north of the Po, enemies who had not submitted and a new Ostrogothic king who was bound by no covenant. A resumption of hostilities could not fail to ensue. If the peace which Justinian offered to the Goths had been concluded, and Witigis had remained as the recognised ruler of trans-Padane Italy, bound to the Empire by treaty, the arrangement could not indeed have been final, but the Emperor was justified in calculating that it would ensure for some years to come the tranquillity of Italy, and enable him to throw all his forces into the imminent struggle with Persia.

It is as little surprising then that when the victorious general disembarked at Constantinople with a captive king in his train, the Emperor should have given him a cold reception and denied him the honours of a triumph, as that the people, dazzled by the distinction of his captives and the richness of his spoil,

[1] Probably in June.

and measuring his deserts by these spectacular results,[1] should
have attributed the Imperial attitude to jealousy. Though the
enemies of Belisarius did all they could to poison Justinian's
mind with suspicions, he can hardly have had serious doubts
of his general's loyalty, yet it must have been far from agreeable
to him to know that a subject had been given the opportunity
of rejecting the offer of a throne. But, apart from this, it must
be admitted that he was justified in refusing a triumph to a
general who, whatever his services had been, had deliberately
frustrated his master's policy. That the anxiety of the Emperor
to hasten the departure of Belisarius from Italy was not entirely
due to the urgent need of his services in the East, may be inferred
from the fact that he was not sent against the Persians till the
ensuing spring.

The Gothic prisoners were honourably treated. Witigis
received the title of patrician and an estate on the confines of
Persia.[2] He survived his dethronement for two years.

It is naturally to be assumed that, as the provinces of Italy
were gradually recovered, measures were taken for securing the
civil administration. In some cases probably the Italians who
served under the Goths were allowed to continue in their posts
as governors of provinces, in others new men must have been
appointed. But it was also necessary, perhaps even before the
capture of Rome, to set up a central financial administration.[3]
Sicily had been reorganised after its submission to Belisarius
and committed to the government of a Praetor, who had the

---

[1] The populace indeed were not
permitted to see the treasures. They
were exhibited to the senators in the
Palace. *B.G.* iii. 1. 3. It is possible
that the victory over Witigis was
celebrated in the following year when
Justinian made a triumphal entry
into Constantinople on August 12,
through the Charisian Gate. The
ceremony is briefly described in
Constantine Porphyrog., *App. ad
libr. prim. de Cer.* p. 497, a passage
evidently taken or abridged from
Peter the Patrician. The immediate
motive of the triumph may have
been the success of Belisarius in
Mesopotamia in capturing the fort
of Sisaurana. See Serruys, in *Revue
des études grecques*, xx. 240 *sqq.*
1907. The question has also been

discussed by Martroye, who rejects the
explanation of Serruys, thinks that
the date meant is 540, not 541, and
explains the ceremony as a solemn
entry, distinct from a triumph, in
which Belisarius took part. See
*Mém. de la Soc. des Antiquaires de
France*, 1912, p. 25 (the article is
only known to me through Bréhier's
notice in *Rev. Hist.* ci., Sept.-Déc.
1912, p. 325).

[2] Jordanes, *Get.* § 313 ; *Hist. Misc.*
xvi. p. 107 *administrationem illi
Persarum tribuit terminos.* It is not
quite clear what this means.

[3] *Nov.* 75 (Dec. 537) seems to imply
that a *comes s. patrimonii per Italiam*
had already been appointed. He
dealt with the patrimonial estates
in Sicily as well as in Italy.

responsibility for military as well as for civil affairs.[1] Amid the din of arms these administrative measures occupied little attention, and they were soon to be upset or endangered by the renewal of war throughout the whole peninsula.

§ 11. *Boethius, Cassiodorus, and Benedict*

The power of the Ostrogoths was not yet broken. They were soon to regain much that they had lost, and under a new warrior king to wage a war which was well-nigh fatal to the ambitions of Justinian. But before we proceed to the second chapter of the reconquest of Italy, we may glance at the peaceful work of three eminent Italians who shed lustre on the Ostrogothic period, and secured a higher place in the eyes of posterity than the kings and warriors who in their own lifetime possessed the stage.

It is hardly too much to say that Boethius had a more genuine literary talent than any of his contemporaries, either Latin or Greek. We have seen how he composed in prison the " golden volume "[2] which has immortalised him, the *Consolation of Philosophy*. It was one of the best known and most widely read books throughout the Middle Ages, notwithstanding the fact that it ignores Christianity,[3] though its Platonism has a Christian colouring. It was translated into Anglo-Saxon by King Alfred, and into English by Chaucer.[4]

The *Consolation of Philosophy* has indeed a considerable charm, which is increased by the recollection of the circumstances in which it was composed. A student who, maintaining indeed a lukewarm connection with politics, had spent most of his days in the calm atmosphere of his library, where he expected to end his life, suddenly found himself in the confinement of a dismal

---

[1] *Nov.* 75 (Dec. 537). This law provides that the Quaestor at Constantinople should be the court of appeal for Sicilian lawsuits.

[2] " Not unworthy of the leisure of Plato or Tully," Gibbon, iv. p. 215. On Boethius cp. Ebert, *Gesch. der Litt. des Mittelalters*, i. 485 *sqq.* ; H. F. Stewart, *Boethius*.

[3] Stewart (*op. cit.* 106 *sqq.*) would explain this by the view that the

work " is intensely artificial." The verses, he says, are smooth and cold. There is " nothing that suggests a heart beating itself out against the bars of its prison." Thus the book does not express the personal beliefs of the author, who composed simply as a diversion, to pass the time.

[4] And after the Middle Ages by Queen Elizabeth. There were early translations in the principal European languages.

prison with death impending over him. There is thus in his philosophical meditations an earnestness born of a real need of consolation, while at the same time there is a pervading serenity. Poems, sometimes lyrical, sometimes elegiac, break the discussion at intervals,[1] like organ chants in a religious service. The problem of the treatise [2] is to explain the " unjust confusion " which exists in the world, the eternal question how the fact that the evil win often the rewards of virtue (*pretium sceleris—diadema*) and the good suffer the penalties of crime, can be reconciled with a " deus, rector mundi." If I could believe, says Boethius, that all things were determined by chance and hazard, I should not be so perplexed. In one place he defines the relation of fate to the Deity in the sense that fate is a sort of instrument by which God regulates the world according to fixed rules. In other words, fate is the law of phenomena or nature, under the control of the Supreme Being, which he identifies with the *Summum Bonum* or highest good. His discussion of the subject is not very illuminating—did it really satisfy him ?

But the metaphysical discussion does not interest the student of literature so much as the setting of the piece and things said incidentally.[3] Boethius imagines his couch surrounded by the Muses of poetry, who suggest to him accents of lamentation. Suddenly there appears at his head a strange lady of lofty visage. There was marvellous fluidity in her stature ; she seemed sometimes of ordinary human height, and at the next moment her head touched heaven, or penetrated so far into its recesses that her face was lost to the vision. Her eyes too were unnatural, brilliant and transparent beyond the power of human eyes,

---

[1] This form of mixed verse and prose was originated by the Greek Cynic Menippus, and in later literature had been employed by Varro, Petronius, Seneca, and more recently by Martianus Capella the Neoplatonist (fifth century) in his allegorical work " On the nuptials of Philology and Mercury, and the seven liberal arts." It was probably this work that suggested the form to Boethius.

[2] Book i. contains the story of the writer's personal wrongs, which he relates to Philosophia; Bk. ii. a discussion on Fortune ; Bk. iii.

passes to the *Summum Bonum* ; in Bk. iv. Philosophia justifies God's government ; Bk. v. deals with free will.

[3] It is interesting to notice that Dante's famous verses

Nessun maggior dolore
Che ricordarsi del tempo felice
Nella miseria,

come from Boethius (ii. iv). It has been pointed out that the idea occurs in Synesius, *Ep.* 57 (Sandys, *Hist. of Classical Scholarship*, i. 243, n. 2). Dante assigned to Boethius a place in the Fourth Heaven.

of fresh colour and unquenchable vigour. And yet at the same time she seemed so ancient of days " that she could not be taken for a woman of our age." Her garments were of the finest threads, woven by some secret art into an indissoluble texture, woven, as she told Boethius, by her own hands. And on this robe there was a certain mist of neglected antiquity, the sort of colour that statues have which have been exposed to smoke. On the lower edge of the robe there was the Greek letter Π (the initial of Πρακτική, Practical Philosophy), from which stairs were worked leading upwards to the letter Θ (Θεωρητική, Pure Philosophy). And her garment had the marks of violent usage, as though rough persons had tried to rend it from her and carried away shreds in their hands. The lady was Philosophia ; she bore a sceptre and parchment rolls. She afterwards explained that the violent persons who had rent her robe were the Epicureans, Stoics, and other late schools ; they succeeded in tearing away patches of her dress, fancying severally that they had obtained the whole garment. Philosophia's first act is to drive out the Muses, whom she disdainfully terms " theatrical strumpets," and she remarks that poetry " accustoms the minds of men to the disease but does not set them free." [1]

A striking feature of the *Consolatio* is the interspersion of the prose dialogue with poems at certain intervals, which, like choruses in Greek tragedy, appertain to the preceding argument. Thus the work resembles in form Dante's *Vita Nuova*, where the sonnets gather up in music the feelings occasioned by the narrated events. These poems, which betray the influence of Seneca's plays,[2] have all a charm of their own, and metres of various kinds are gracefully employed.

One poem, constructed with as much care as a sonnet,[3] sings of the " love that moves the sun and stars,"

> hanc rerum series ligat
> terras ac pelagus regens
> et caelo imperitans amor,

an idea familiar to modern readers from the last line of Dante's *Divina Commedia*, but which is as old as Empedocles. As

---

[1] Ed. Peiper, p. 5 : *hominumque mentes* [*musae*] *assuefaciunt morbo, non liberant.*

[2] Peiper in his edition gives a list of passages which contain excerpts from or echoes of Seneca's tragedies.

[3] ii. viii. p. 48 ; it consists of thirty lines thus arranged, $4+4+4+3= 4+4+4+3$.

an example of his metrical devices take two lines of a stanza,
where the author is illustrating the return of nature to itself by
a caged bird, which, when it beholds the greenwood once more,
spurns the sprinkled crumbs—

> silvas tantum maesta requirit,
> silvas tantum voce susurrat.

Immediately after this poem Boethius proceeds : " Ye too, O
creatures of earth ! albeit in a vague image, yet do ye dream of
your origin " (vos quoque, O terrena animalia ! tenui licet imagine
vestrum tamen principium somniatis).

The delicate feeling of Boethius for metrical effect may be
illustrated by the poem on the protracted toils of the siege of
Troy and the labours of Hercules. It is written in Sapphic
metre, but the short fourth lines are omitted until the end. The
effect of this device is that the mind and voice of the reader
continue to travel without relief or metrical resting-place until
all the labours are over and heavenly rest succeeds in the stars
of the concluding and only Adonius—

> superata tellus
> sidera donat.

If the *Consolation* had never been written, Boethius would
still have had his place in the list of men who have done service
to humanity. Possessing the multifarious learning characteristic
of the time, he devoted himself especially to the philosophy of
the great masters, Plato and Aristotle, and at an early age he
conceived the ambitious idea of translating into Latin, and
writing commentaries on, all their works.[1] Of this task of a
lifetime he succeeded only in completing the logical works of
Aristotle, but these translations were of capital importance, in
keeping alive the study of logic throughout the Middle Ages,[2]
and he raised the question as to the nature of *genera* and *species*,
which was to be fought out towards the end of that period in
the debate between the Nominalists and the Realists. His
polymathy carried him into other fields. He translated (perhaps)

---

[1] Περὶ ἑρμηνείας, ii. 2.

[2] We have also his version and
exegesis of the Περὶ ἑρμηνείας, in
two forms (one elementary, the other
for advanced students). His translation of the *Isagoge* of Porphyry to
Aristotle's *Categories* was a vulgar
handbook in the Middle Ages. He
also wrote a commentary on Cicero's
Topica.

the Geometry of Euclid,[1] wrote treatises on arithmetic and music, and even ventured into the region of theological doctrine.[2] Though he was a professing Christian, he did not yield to Symmachus, the illustrious pagan ancestor of his wife, in enthusiasm for the ancients, and his aim was to keep alive in Italy the quickening influence of Greek science.[3] Writing in the year of his consulship (A.D. 510), he said, " The cares of office hinder me from devoting all my time to these studies (in logic), but I think it may be considered of some public utility to instruct my fellow-citizens in the subject." [4]

The other eminent man of letters, who shed a certain lustre on Ostrogothic Italy, Magnus Aurelius Cassiodorus Senator,[5] was of inferior fibre to Boethius in literary taste as well as in personal character, but he was no less genuinely interested in intellectual pursuits, and posterity owes him an even greater debt. The Cassiodori, who seem originally to have come from Syria, acquired an estate at Scyllacium (Squillace) on the eastern coast of Bruttii. The great-grandfather of Cassiodorus successfully defended this province and Sicily against raids of the Vandals.[6] His grand-father, a friend of Aetius, was employed on an embassy to the Huns,[7] and we have seen how his father filled high posts under Odovacar and Theoderic. Born himself not long before Theoderic's invasion, he was a boy when his father became Praetorian Prefect [8] and employed him as a legal assistant in his bureau. He won the king's notice by a panegyric which he pronounced on some public occasion, and was appointed to the high office of Quaestor of the Palace at an unusually early age.[9] In this post he conducted the official correspondence of the

[1] He certainly wrote an original treatise De geometria. It is doubtful whether the extant translation of Euclid ascribed to him is really his.

[2] De trinitate, and one or two other tracts. It has been supposed that they were written for a literary society which met every week to read and discuss papers ; see Stewart, op. cit. p. 132.

[3] Cp. Cass. Var. i. 45 (letter of Theoderic, A.D. 509–510) quascumque disciplinas vel artes fecunda Graecia per singulos viros edidit, te uno auctore patrio sermone Roma suscepit. Here his various literary activities are enumerated. Ennodius addressed Boethius as an indefatigable student

quem in annis puerilibus . . . industria fecit antiquum (Epp. vii. 13).

[4] Comm. in Arist. Cat. ii. Praef. (Migne, P.L. lxiv. 201).

[5] His contemporaries called him Senator. The facts known about his family and the dates of his career are summarised by Mommsen in the Prooemium to his edition. On his literary work see Hodgkin, Letters of Cassiodorus ; Sandys, History of Classical Scholarship, i. 244 sqq.

[6] Var. i. 4. Above, vol. i. p. 258.

[7] Ib.

[8] About A.D. 501.

[9] In his early twenties. His Quaestorship falls between the years 507 and 511.

king, and in the composition of State documents he found
congenial employment for his rhetorical talent. After he laid
down this office (A.D. 511), he seems to have taken no part in
public affairs (except in the year of his consulship, A.D. 514)
till the close of Theoderic's reign, when he was appointed Master
of Offices.[1] He continued to hold this dignity in the first years of
the following reign, and after an interval of retirement [2] he
became Praetorian Prefect, and remained in that post during the
stormy years which followed, content to play the ignoble
rôle of a time-server, apparently as loyal to Theodahad as he
had been to Amalasuntha,[3] and on Theodahad's fall turning
without hesitation to the rising sun of Witigis. But we have
every reason to believe that throughout his career he did not
waver in a sincere conviction that Italy was better off under
Ostrogothic government than she would have been under the
control of Constantinople. It is possible that he retired from
public life before the capture of Ravenna, but while he was still
Prefect, he published (A.D. 537) a collection of the official letters
and State papers, which he had composed during his three
ministries.[4] This collection is a mine of information for the
administration and condition of Ostrogothic Italy, and we have
to thank perhaps the literary vanity of Cassiodorus for the
ample knowledge that we possess of Theoderic's policy; but
it bears all the signs of having been carefully expurgated. As
the work was published when the issue of the war was uncertain,
he consulted his own interests by cutting out anything that
could offend either the Emperor or the Goths,[5] and it is probable
that many documents which would clear up some of our uncer-
tainties as to the relations between Ravenna and Constantinople
have been omitted altogether.

Few rhetorical compositions, and perhaps no public documents,
offer greater difficulties to the reader when he attempts to arrive

---

[1] About A.D. 523–524. In this post
he also fulfilled many of the duties of
Quaestor (cp. ix. 25).

[2] A.D. 527–533.

[3] In his Oration on the marriage
of Witigis, he condemns Amalasuntha
for her education of Athalaric (p.
473): *fas fuit illam sub pietatis
excusatione peccare.*

[4] The *Variae* thus fall into three

chronological groups. (1) *quaestoriae*,
507-511 = Books i.-iv. ; (2) *magisteriae*,
523–527 = Books v. (except last two
letters, A.D. 511), viii., ix. 1–14; (3)
praefectoriae, 533–537 = Books ix., 15–
25, x., xi., xii. Books vi. and vii.
contain *Formulae* for admission to
various offices of state. In 540 he
added to this collection as Book xiii.
a treatise *De anima.*

[5] Cp. Mommsen, *loc. cit.* p. xxii.

at the plain fact which the author intends to convey. " It is ornament alone," he says in his Preface, " that distinguishes the learned from the unlearned," and, true to this maxim of decadent rhetoric, he obscures the simplest and most trivial statements in a cloud of embellishments. But to appreciate his inflated style we must remember that he was, after all, only improving upon what had been, since Diocletian, the traditional style of the Imperial chancery. We have innumerable constitutions of the fourth and fifth centuries, in which the vices of adornment and contorted phraseology make it a laborious task to discover the meaning. Cassiodorus exerted his ingenuity and command of language in elaborating this sublime style, always frigid, but ludicrously inappropriate to legal documents and State papers.

In his later years Cassiodorus betook himself to his ancestral estate at Squillace,[1] and devoted the rest of a long life to religion and literature. He became a monk and founded two monasteries, one, up in the hills at Castellum, a hermitage for those who desired solitary austerity, the other, built beside the fish-ponds of his own domain and hence called *Vivarium*, for monks who were content to live in the less strict conditions of a monastic society. At Vivarium, where he lived himself, Cassiodorus introduced a novelty [2] which led to fruitful results for posterity. He conceived the idea of occupying the abundant leisure of the brethren with the task of multiplying copies of Latin texts. There was a chamber known as the *scriptorium* or " writing-room " in the monastery, in which those monks who had a capacity for intellectual labour, used to copy both pagan and Christian books, working at night by the light of self-filling " mechanical lamps." It is well known that the preservation of our heritage of Latin literature is mainly due to the labours of monastic copyists. The originator of the idea was Cassiodorus. His example was adopted in other religious establishments, and monastic libraries came to be a regular institution.

---

[1] There is a charming description of the situation and amenities of the town of Squillace in *Var.* xii. 15. After the capture of Ravenna in 539 he seems to have gone to Constantinople and lived there for about fifteen years, returning to Italy after the final conquest of Italy by Narses. At least the reference to him in a letter of Vigilius excommunicating two Italian deacons (Mansi, ix. 357) seems to imply that he was at Constantinople about 550. Cp. Sundwall, *Abh.* p. 156.

[2] It had indeed been anticipated in the monastery of St. Martin of Tours, where young monks had practised the copying of MSS. (Sulpicius Severus, *Vita S. Mart.* vii.).

Most of the works of Cassiodorus have come down to us. The great exception is his *History of the Goths*, in which he attempted to reconstruct a historical past for the Gothic race.[1] Starting with the two false assumptions that the Goths were identical on one hand with the Getae and on the other hand with the Scythians, he was able to produce, from the records of Greek and Roman antiquity, a narrative which represented them as playing a great part on the stage of history at a time when they were really living in obscurity on the Lower Vistula, utterly beyond the horizon of Mediterranean civilisation.

The principal works of his later years were intended for the instruction of his monks—the *Institutions* and a treatise on *Orthography*. The *Institutions* consisted of two independent parts, of which the first, *De institutione divinarum litterarum*, was intended as an introduction to the study of the manuscripts of the Bible,[2] and contains an interesting disquisition on the question of correcting the text. The second part is a handbook on the Seven Liberal Arts. The two together offered a general survey of sacred and secular learning.[3] The manual on spelling was composed, for the guidance of copyists, in the ninety-third year of his age (*c.* A.D. 580).[4] Thus he had lived to see great changes. He had witnessed the complete subjugation of Italy by Justinian, and when, at the age of eighty, he saw many of its provinces pass under the yoke of the Lombard barbarians, it may well have occurred to him that if the Ostrogothic rule had

---

[1] On this work (in 12 books), which belongs to the period of leisure between 527 and 533, see his *Praefatio* to the *Variae*, and *Var.* ix. 25 (*originem Gothicam historian fecit esse Romanam*). For the later history of the Goths he drew on their own traditions, and he used the work of Ablabius, who wrote a Roman history in Greek *c.* A.D. 400 (he is *possibly* referred to in *Var.* x. 22). The work of Cassiodorus was liberally used by Jordanes, so that we can form an idea of its scope and contents.

[2] Cassiodorus went to much expense in procuring MSS. (*De ins.* i. 8). He mentions a large codex containing Jerome's version of the Scriptures, and "it has been conjectured that part of it survives in the first and oldest quaternion of the *codex Amiatinus* of the Vulgate, now in the Laurentian Library in Florence" (Sandys, *op. cit.* i. 251).

[3] These books were written before A.D. 555. Of his other works need only be mentioned his Commentary on the Psalms and his Ecclesiastical History (*Hist. Tripartita*).

[4] For this work he had the advantage of using, besides older treatises, that of his elder contemporary Priscian (an African provincial), whose Panegyric on Anastasius has been referred to above, vol. i. p. 467. Priscian's Grammar was a standard text-book in the Middle Ages. It was transcribed at Constantinople by a pupil in 526–527. Sandys, *op. cit.* 258-259.

been allowed to continue this calamity would have been spared to his fellow-countrymen.

While Boethius was immersed in the study of philosophy in his library, with its walls decorated with ivory and glass, and while Cassiodorus was engaged in his political and rhetorical labours in the Palace at Ravenna, another young man, of about the same age as they, who was destined to exert a greater influence over western Europe than any of his Italian contemporaries, was spending his days in austere religious practices in the wild valleys of the upper Anio. St. Benedict, who belonged to the same Anician gens as Boethius, was born at Nursia, in an Apennine valley, about twenty miles east of Spoleto.[1]   Sent to Rome to study, he was so deeply disgusted by the corruption of his school companions and by the vice of the great city, that at the age of fourteen he set out with a faithful nurse for the " desert," and at length took up his abode in a cave at Sublaqueum (Subiaco), near the sources of the Anio, where he lived as a hermit. The temptations which he resisted, the perils which he escaped, and the legends which rapidly gathered round him, may be read in the biography written by his admirer, Pope Gregory the Great.[2]   After his fame had gone abroad, his solitude was interrupted, for men who desired to embrace the monastic life flocked to him from all parts. He founded twelve monasteries in the neighbourhood of Subiaco. In A.D. 528 he left the peaceful region and went into Campania, where, at Monte Cassino, halfway between Rome and Naples, he found a congenial task awaiting him. Here, notwithstanding all the efforts of Christian Emperors and priests to extirpate the old religions, there still stood an altar and statue of Apollo in a sacred grove, and the surrounding inhabitants practised the rites of pagan superstition. Benedict induced them to burn the grove and demolish the altar and image, and on the height above he founded the great monastery where he lived till his death. The Rule which he drew up for his monks avoids the austerities of Egyptian monasticism, and he expressly says that he wished to ordain nothing hard or burdensome.[3]   Within three hundred years this code of laws had superseded all others in western Europe, where it held much the same position as St. Basil's in the East.[4]

---

[1] A.D. 480.
[2] Or in Hodgkin, *Italy and her Invaders,* iv. chap. xvi.

[3] See *Prologue.*
[4] Benedict knew Basil's Rule and refers to it (chap. lxxiii.).

Benedict himself did not anticipate that the order which he founded would ultimately become the learned order in the Church. He ordained that " because idleness is an enemy of the soul," the brethren should occupy themselves " at specified times in manual labour, and at other fixed hours in holy reading," [1] but there is no indication that he included in manual labour the transcription of MSS.[2] Probably this was not introduced at Monte Cassino till after his death, under the influence of Cassiodorus.

APPENDIX

ROUTES FROM ITALY TO THE EAST

It may be convenient to the reader to have before him a table showing some of the distances on the routes between Italy and the East.

1. Rome to Brundusium (Via Appia)   530 kilometres.
   Constantinople to Dyrrhachium
   or Aulon (Via Egnatia) .   .   1120 ,,
   Rome to Constantinople   .   1650 kilometres | sea passage of
   at least 24 hours (total time of
   the journey — 23 to 26 days),
   but messengers in haste could
   do it in between 2 and 3 weeks.

2. Rome to Ravenna (Via Flaminia)   370 kilometres.
   Ravenna to Aquileia (coast road)   245 ,,
   Aquileia to Constantinople (via
   Poetovio) .   .   .   1655 ,,

3. Aquileia to Salona .   .   420 ,,
   Salona to Dyrrhachium .   .   450 ,,

(These numbers are approximate. Note that a Roman mile = nearly 1½ kilometres.)

The usual rate of travelling, on horseback, varied from 60 to 75 kilometres daily. The regular rate of marching for an army was from 15 to 17 kilometres, but might be considerably more if the army was small or when there was a special need for haste.

The average rate of sailing was from 100 to 150 sea miles in 24 hours.

---

[1] *Reg. Ben.* chap. xlviii. (Gasquet's translation).
[2] The rule that no brother is to keep as his own, without the abbot's leave, books or tablets or pens (chap. xxxiii.) proves nothing.

CHAPTER XIX

THE RECONQUEST OF ITALY (II.)

§ 1. *The Reigns of Ildibad and Eraric* (A.D. 540–541)

THE policy of Belisarius had frustrated the conclusion of a peace which would have left the Goths in peaceful possession of Italy north of the Po. Such a peace could hardly have been final, but it would have secured for the Empire a respite of some years from warfare in the west at a time when all its resources were needed against the great enemy in the east. If Belisarius had not been recalled, he would probably have completed the conquest of the peninsula within a few months. This, which would have been the best solution, was defeated by the jealousy of Justinian ; and the peace proposed by the Emperor, which was the next best course, was defeated by the disobedience of his general. Between them they bear the responsibility of inflicting upon Italy twelve more years of war.

The greater blame must be attached to Justinian. He had indeed every reason to be displeased with the behaviour of Belisarius, but the plainest common sense dictated that, if he could no longer trust Belisarius, he should replace him by another commander-in-chief. Of the generals who remained in Italy the most distinguished was John, the nephew of Vitalian. But instead of appointing him or another to the supreme command, the Emperor allowed the generals to exercise co-equal and independent authority each over his own troops. In consequence of this unwise policy there was no effective co-operation ; each commander thought only of his own interests. They plundered the Italians, and allowed the soldiers to follow their example, so that discipline was undermined. In a few months so many **blunders** were committed that the work accomplished by Belisarius in five arduous years was almost undone, the Goths had to be conquered over again, and it took twelve years to do it.[1] The situation was aggravated by the prompt introduction of the Imperial financial machinery in the conquered provinces. The logothete [2] Alexander, an expert in all the cruel methods of enriching the treasury and the tax-collector at the expense of the provincials, arrived, and soon succeeded in making both the Italians and the soldiers thoroughly discontented. Having established his quarters at Ravenna, he required the surviving Italian officials of the Gothic kings to account for all money that had passed through their hands during their years of service, and compelled them to make good deficits out of their own pockets. It cannot be doubted that many of these officials had made illegitimate profits and we need not waste much pity on them ; but Alexander extended his retrospective policy to all private persons who had any dealings with the fisc of Ravenna. In an inquiry into transactions of twenty, thirty, or forty years ago, conducted by a man like Alexander, it is certain that grave injustices were done.

He was acting on the constitutional principle that Italy was, throughout the Gothic régime, subject to the Imperial authority, and that the kings and their servants were responsible to the Emperor for all their acts. But his proceedings were calculated to alienate the sympathies of the Italians and render the government of Justinian unpopular. At the same time, by curtailing the pay of the soldiers on various pretexts, he caused a deep sense of injustice in the army.

After the departure of Belisarius, Vitalius was stationed in Venetia, Constantian commanded the troops in Ravenna, Justin held Florence, Conon Naples, Cyprian Perusia, and Bessas perhaps had his quarters in Spoletium [3] North of the Po, the only important places still held by the Goths were Ticinum,

---

[1] For the second period of the Italian war, our source is still Procopius. But the historian is no longer writing from personal knowledge, for he probably never returned to Italy. Haury indeed is confident that he was in Italy during the twelfth year of the war, 546–547, because he wrote about this year as much as he wrote about the first years of the war (*Procopiana*, i. p. 9), but this is far from decisive. Chance may have supplied him with fuller information for the events connected with the siege of Rome. And as a matter of fact, the events of the last six months of 552 run to as great a length as those of the whole year 546–547.

[2] For the logothetes see below, p. 358.

[3] See *B.G.* iii. 1 § 34 ; 3 § 2 ; 5 § 1 ; 6 § 2 ; 6 § 8 and 5 § 4 ; 6 § 8.

which king Ildibad made his residence, and Verona.[1] The army of Ildibad amounted at first to little more than a thousand men, but he gradually extended his authority over Liguria and Venetia. The Roman generals did nothing to prevent this revival of the enemy's strength, and it was not till he approached Treviso, which appears to have been the headquarters of Vitalius, that Ildibad met any opposition. Vitalius, whose forces included a considerable body of Heruls, gave him battle and was decisively defeated, Vitalius barely escaping, while the Herul leader was slain.

Ildibad did not live long enough to profit by the prestige which his victory procured him. His death was indirectly due to a quarrel with Uraias, to whose influence he had owed his crown. The wife of Uraias was beautiful and wealthy, and one day when she went to the public baths, in rich apparel and attended by a long train of servants, she met the queen, who was clad in a plain dress (for the royal purse was ill-furnished), and treated her with disrespect. The queen implored Ildibad to avenge her outraged dignity, and soon afterwards Uraias was treacherously put to death. This act caused bitter indignation among the Goths, yet none of them was willing to avenge the nephew of Witigis. But a Gepid belonging to the royal guard, who had a personal grudge against the king, murdered Ildibad at a banquet in the palace (A.D. 541, about May). He would not have ventured on the crime if he had not known that it would please the Goths, as a just retribution for the murder of Uraias.

The event came as a surprise, and the Goths could not immediately agree on the choice of a successor to the throne. The matter was decided in an unexpected way. The Rugian subjects of Odovacar, who had submitted after his fall to the rule of Theoderic, had never merged themselves in the Gothic nationality, but had maintained their identity as a separate people in northern Italy. They seized the occasion to proclaim as king Eraric, the most distinguished of their number. The Goths were vexed at the presumption of the Rugians, but nevertheless they recognised Eraric, and endured his rule for five months, presumably because there was none among themselves on whose fitness for the throne they could agree.

---

[1] Procopius, *B.G.* 1 § 27, says only Ticinum; but it is clear from the narrative that Verona had remained in their hands throughout.

Eraric summoned a council and persuaded the Goths to consent to his sending an embassy to Constantinople for the purpose of proposing peace on the same terms which the Emperor had offered to Witigis. But the Rugian was a traitor. He selected as ambassadors creatures of his own, and gave them secret instructions to inform Justinian privately that he was prepared, in return for the Patriciate and a large sum of money, to abdicate and hand over northern Italy to the Empire.

In the meantime he made no pretence of carrying on the war, and the Goths regretted the energy of Ildibad. Looking about for a worthy successor, they bethought them of Totila,[1] Ildibad's nephew, a young man who had not yet reached his thirtieth year and had acquired some repute for energy and intelligence. He had been appointed commander of the garrison of Treviso, and after his uncle's assassination, despairing of the Gothic cause, he had secretly opened negotiations with Ravenna, offering to hand over the town. A day for the surrender was fixed when he received a message from the Gothic nobles who were conspiring against Eraric, inviting him to become their king. Concealing his treacherous intrigue with the enemy, he accepted the proposal on condition that Eraric should be slain before a certain day, and he named the day on which he had undertaken to admit the Romans into the town. Eraric was duly put to death by the conspirators and Totila ascended the throne (A.D. 541, September or October).

§ 2. *The First Successes of Totila* (A.D. 541–543)

Eraric's ambassadors seem to have been still at Constantinople when the news of his murder and Totila's accession arrived. Justinian was incensed at the supine conduct of his generals who had failed to take advantage of Eraric's incapacity, and his indignant messages at last forced them to plan a common

---

[1] So he is always called by Procopius, but on the coins of his reign, both silver and copper, his name is invariably Baduila, which is also found in the *Hist. Miscella*, B. xvi. p. 107. Jordanes (*Rom.* 380) uses both names. The reason of the double designation has not been cleared up. Totila issued at first coins with the head of Justinian, but this recognition of the Emperor was soon abandoned, and the bust of Anastasius was substituted. Finally, in his last years, he issued silver and bronze coins with his own bust (imitated from that of Anastasius), A.D. 549–552. The regal mint was at Ticinum, but coins were afterwards struck at Rome. See Wroth, *Coins of the Vandals*, etc., xxxvii.-xxxviii.

enterprise. They met at Ravenna and decided that Constantian and Alexander should advance upon Verona with 12,000 men. One of the Gothic sentinels was bribed to open a gate, and when the army approached the city, a picked band led by an Armenian, Artabazes, was sent forward at night to enter and take possession. Artabazes did his part, and Verona would have been captured if the commanders had not wasted the night in quarrelling over the division of the expected booty. When they arrived at last, the Gothic garrison had regained possession of the place and barred the gates, and the little band of Artabazes, having no other means of escape, leaped from the walls and all but a few were killed by the fall.[1]

The army retreated across the Po and encamped on the stream of Lamone,[2] near Faventia. Totila marched against them at the head of 5000 men, and in the battle which ensued gained a brilliant victory, all the Imperial standards falling into his hands.[3] Verona and Faventia exhibited the evil of a divided command.

Totila was encouraged by this success to take the offensive in Tuscany. He sent a force against Florence, where Justin, who had helped to capture it three years before, was in command. John, Bessas, and Cyprian hastened to its relief, and on the appearance of their superior forces, the Goths raised the siege and moved up the valley of the Sieve. This locality was then known as Mucellium, and the name survives as Mugello. The Roman army pursued them, and John with a chosen band pushed on to engage the enemy while the rest followed more slowly. The Goths, who had occupied a hill, rushed down upon John's troops. In the hot action which ensued, a false rumour spread that John had fallen, and the Romans retired to join the main army, which had not yet been drawn up in order of battle, and was easily infected with their panic. All the troops fled disgracefully, and the Goths pursued their advantage. The prisoners were well treated by Totila and induced to serve under his banner. The defeated generals abandoned all thought of

---

[1] The attempt on Verona and the battles of Faventia and Mugello are probably to be placed in the spring of 542. See *Cont. Marcell.* §§ 2, 3, *sub a.*

[2] Cp. Hodgkin, *op. cit.* iv. 444.

The Lamone is the ancient Anemo.

[3] The most striking incident in the battle was the single combat between Valaris, a gigantic Goth, and Artabazes, in which the Goth was slain and Artabazes mortally wounded.

further co-operation and hastily retreated, Bessas to Spoletium, Cyprian to Perusia, and John to Rome. The victory of Mugello, however, did not lead to the defection of Tuscany, and Justin remained safely in Florence. Totila captured some places in Umbria—Caesena and Petra Pertusa,[1]— but then instead of pursuing steadily the conquest of central Italy, where the Imperialist forces, concentrated in strong cities, were too formidable for his small army, he decided to transfer his operations to the south of the peninsula. There the success of his arms and policy was swift and sweeping. Avoiding Rome, he marched to Beneventum, which was an easy prey, and razed its walls to the ground. The provinces of Lucania and Bruttii, Apulia, and Calabria acknowledged his authority and paid him the taxes which would otherwise have gone to satisfy the demands of the Imperial soldiers, to whom long arrears were owed. Totila had meanwhile laid siege to Naples, which Conon was holding with a garrison of 1000 Isaurians. He collected considerable treasure from Cumae and other fortresses in the neighbourhood, and created a good impression by his courteous treatment of the wives and daughters of Roman senators whom he found in these places and allowed to go free. This is one instance, and we shall meet others, of the policy which he often followed of winning the sympathy of the Italians by a more generous treatment than they were prepared to expect from an enemy.

The news of the revival of the Gothic power and the danger of Naples alarmed the Emperor, and he took some measures to meet the crisis, but they were far from sufficient. Instead of confiding the supreme command to an experienced general, he appointed a civilian, Maximin, to be Praetorian Prefect of Italy, and gave him powers of general supervision over the conduct of the war, sending with him Thracian and Armonian troops and a few Huns. Maximin, who seems to have been one of the worst choices the Emperor could have made, sailed to Epirus and remained there unable to decide what to do. Soon afterwards Demetrius, an officer who had formerly served under Belisarius, was sent to the west. He appears to have been invested with the office of Master of Soldiers, but we find him acting under the orders of Maximin.[2] He sailed straight to

[1] The Continuer of Marcellinus, *sub* 542, adds Urbinum and Mons Feletris.

[2] *B.G.* iii. 6. 13 Δημήτριον στρατηγόν ; cp. 7. 3.

Sicily, where he learned how severely Naples was suffering from lack of food, and he made prompt preparations to bring help. He had only a handful of men, but collecting as many vessels as he could find in the Sicilian harbours, he loaded them with provisions and set sail in the hope that the enemy would believe that they were conveying a large army. It is thought that if this bold design had been executed the Goths would have withdrawn from Naples and the city might have been saved. But before Demetrius reached his destination, he revised his plan and made for Porto, hoping to obtain some reinforcements from Rome. But the Roman garrison was demoralised and refused to join in an expedition which seemed full of danger. Demetrius then sailed for the bay of Naples. Totila meanwhile had been fully informed of the facts and had a number of war vessels ready to attack the transports when they were close to the shore. Most of the crews were slain or made prisoners ; Demetrius was one of the few who escaped in boats.

Another attempt to relieve Naples was another failure. Maximin and the forces which accompanied him had at last left Epirus and reached Syracuse. Moved by the importunate messages of Conon for help, he consented, although it was now midwinter, to send these troops to Naples, and Demetrius, who had made his way back to Sicily, accompanied this second expedition. It reached the bay of Naples safely, but there a violent gale arose which drove the ships ashore close to the Gothic camp. The crews were easily slain or captured, and Demetrius fell into the hands of Totila.[1]

The Neapolitans were starving, and Totila proposed generous terms. " Surrender," he said, " and I will allow Conon and all his soldiers to depart unhurt and take all their property with them." Still hoping that help might come, Conon promised to surrender on these terms in thirty days. Confident that there was no chance of relief forthcoming, Totila replied, " I will give you three months, and in the meantime will make no attempt to

---

[1] Another Demetrius (originally a Cephallenian sailor who had distinguished himself in the campaigns of Belisarius and had been appointed an overseer of some kind in Naples) had succeeded in leaving the city to communicate with the relief expedition. He, too, fell into the hands of the Goths. He had given dire offence to Totila, whom, on his first appearance before the walls of Naples, he had over whelmed with insolent abuse. The king now punished him by cutting out his tongue and cutting off his hands.

take the city." But before the term had run out, the exhausted garrison and citizens abandoned hope and opened the gates (A.D. 543, March or April).

On this occasion Totila exhibited a considerate humanity which was not to be expected, as the historian Procopius remarks, from an enemy or a barbarian. He knew that if an abundance of food were at once supplied, the famished inhabitants would gorge themselves to death. He posted sentinels at the gates and in the harbour and allowed no one to leave the city. Then he dealt out small rations, gradually increasing the quantity every day until the people had recovered their strength. The terms of the capitulation were more than faithfully observed. Conon and his followers were embarked in ships with which the Goths provided them, and when, deciding to sail for Rome, they were hindered by contrary winds, Totila furnished horses, provisions, and guides so that they could make the journey by land.

The fortifications of Naples were partly razed to the ground.[1]

§ 3. *Return of Belisarius to Italy* (Summer, A.D. 544)

In the meantime the generals of Justinian were making no efforts to stem the tide of Gothic success. They plundered the Italians and spent their time in riotous living. Then Constantian wrote to the Emperor, stating bluntly that it was impossible to cope with the enemy.[2] These messages did not arouse Justinian to action till they were reinforced by news of Totila's next movements.

Totila felt that he was now in a position to attack Rome itself. He began his operations by writing a letter to the Senate, in which he contrasted Gothic with " Greek " rule and attempted to show that it was the interest of the Italians that the old régime of the days of Theoderic and Amalasuntha should be restored. The letter was conveyed to Rome by Italian prisoners,

---

[1] If there is any foundation for the tradition, preserved in Gregory I., *Dial.* ii. cc. 14, 15, that Totila visited St. Benedict at Monte Cassino, the incident must have occurred either before or soon after the siege of Naples. The year of Benedict's death is uncertain, perhaps 544 (so Pagi and Martroye, *L'Occident*, p. 436) ; the traditional date, accepted by the Order, is March 21, 543.

[2] *B.G.* iii. 9. 5 ; the other leaders seem either to have enclosed separate letters to the same effect or to have attached their signatures to Constantian's communication.

but John, who was in command of the garrison, forbade the senators to reply. Totila then contrived that a number of placards, announcing that he bound himself by the most solemn oaths not to harm the Romans, should be smuggled into Rome and posted up. John suspected that the Arian clergy were his agents and expelled them all from the city.

Totila then sent part of his army to besiege Otranto, and with the rest advanced upon Rome (spring, A.D. 544). Thereupon Justinian at last decided to recall Belisarius from Persia and send him to Italy to assume the supreme command, as the only means of retrieving the situation.[1]

The first thing Belisarius had to do was to collect some troops in Europe, for it was impossible to weaken the eastern front by bringing any regiments with him from Asia. At his own cost and with the assistance of Vitalius, who had recently been appointed Master of Soldiers in Illyricum, he recruited 4000 men in the Thracian and Illyrian provinces, and proceeded to Salona. His first care was to send a relief expedition to Otranto (summer, A.D. 544), and this enterprise was completely successful.[2] The siege was raised and the town supplied with provisions for a year. This was a good beginning, but Belisarius then, persuaded by Vitalius,[3] committed a serious mistake. He made Ravenna his base, and he could hardly have chosen a less suitable place for offensive operations of which the most important and pressing objects were to succour Rome and recover Naples and southern Italy.

Some of the fortresses in the province of Aemilia, including Bononia, were occupied, but the Illyrian troops who won these successes, having suddenly received the news that their homes were being devastated by an army of Huns, stole away and marched back to their own country. Bononia could no longer be held, and soon afterwards Auximum surrendered to the Goths, who inflicted a severe defeat on a small force which Belisarius had sent to its relief. At the end of the first year of his command the general had little to show but the saving of

---

[1] It was said that Belisarius persuaded Justinian to send him to Italy, by a promise that the war would be self-supporting and that he would never ask for money (Procopius, *H.A.* 4. 39 ὥς φασι), but we find him writing for money

at the end of the first year (*B.G.* iii. 12. 10; see below, p. 235). He held the office of Comes stabuli.

[2] It was carried out by Valentine, who had won distinction in the siege of Rome by Witigis.

[3] *B.G.* iii. 13. 14.

Otranto.[1] Meanwhile Totila was blockading Rome, now under
the command of Bessas, and he had taken Tibur. The fall of
this place was due to a dispute between the inhabitants and the
Isaurian garrison. The Isaurians betrayed it to the enemy,
and all the inhabitants, including the bishop, were put to death in
a way which the historian declines to describe on the ground that
he is unwilling to " leave to future times memorials of atrocity."

Belisarius saw that the Imperial cause in Italy was lost
unless he received powerful reinforcements and money to pay
them. In the early summer of A.D. 545 he wrote to the
Emperor setting forth the difficulties of the war. " I arrived in
Italy without men, horses, arms, or money. The provinces
cannot supply me with revenue, for they are occupied by the
enemy ; and the numbers of our troops have been reduced by
large desertions to the Goths. No general could succeed in
these circumstances. Send me my own armed retainers and a
large host of Huns and other barbarians, and send me money."
With a letter to this effect, he sent John to Constantinople under
a solemn pledge that he would return immediately. But John,
instead of pressing the urgent needs of his commander, delayed
in the capital and advanced his own fortunes by marrying the
daughter of Germanus, the Emperor's cousin.

It was probably late in the year that John came at last with
a new army. Belisarius had gone over to Dyrrhachium to await
his arrival and had sent another importunate message to the
Emperor. Isaac the Armenian accompanied John, and the
Emperor had sent Narses to the land of the Heruls to secure a
host of those barbarians [2] to take part in the operations of the
following spring.

Totila, in the meantime, had been taking town after town
in Picenum and Tuscany. Fermo and Ascoli, Spoleto and
Assisi, were compelled to capitulate.[3] He offered large bribes
to Cyprian to surrender Perusia, and, finding him incorruptible,
suborned one of his retainers to assassinate him. But the foul
murder did not effect its purpose, as the garrison remained loyal
to the Emperor. The Goths had now secured effective command
of the Flaminian Way, and it was impossible for Imperial troops

---

[1] He rebuilt indeed the walls and
defences of Pisaurum (Pesaro), which
had been, like those of Fano, dis-
mantled by Witigis.

[2] Procopius does not record their
numbers ; evidently he had no
accurate information (*B.G.* iii. 13. 21).

[3] Cp. *Contin. Marcell., sub* 545.

to march from Ravenna overland to the relief of Rome. The only place which the Imperialists still held in the Aemilian province was Placentia, an important fortress, because here the Aemilian Way crossed the Po. Totila presently sent an army against it, and captured it at the end of a year, when the inhabitants were so pressed by hunger that they were driven to cannibalism (May A.D. 545 to May 546).[1]

§ 4. *Second Siege of Rome* (A.D. 546)

It was towards the end of A.D. 545 or early in A.D. 546 that Totila began to besiege Rome in person and with vigour. He had already cut off sea-borne supplies by a considerable fleet of light ships stationed at Naples and in the Liparaean Islands. The whole province of Campania seems to have been subject to the Goths, who, we are told, both here and in the rest of Italy, left the land to the Italians to till peaceably, only requiring them to pay the taxes which would otherwise have been exacted by the Emperor.[2] Of the two ports at the mouth of the Tiber, Ostia was in the possession of the Goths, while Portus was held for the Emperor by Innocent. It will be remembered that during the former siege by Witigis, the position was just the reverse ; the Romans were in Ostia, the Goths in Portus.

Belisarius despatched Valentine and Phocas, one of his guards, with 500 men by sea to reinforce the garrison of Portus. The troops in Rome numbered 3000, and if Bessas, their commander, had co-operated actively with the leaders at Portus, it might have been possible to secure the passage of foodships up the Tiber. But he refused to allow any of his men to hazard a sortie. Valentine and Phocas, with their small forces, attempted a surprise attack on the Gothic camp, but they fell into an ambuscade which Totila, informed of their plan by a deserter, had set for them. Most of the Romans, including the two leaders, perished.

Not long afterwards Pope Vigilius, who was staying at Syracuse on his way to Constantinople, sent a flotilla of corn-ships to feed the starving city. The Goths saw them approaching

[1] *B.G.* iii. 13. 8 and 16. 2.

[2] *Ib.* 13. 1 ; this statement, however, is in direct contradiction with 9. 3, where the provincials are said to have been robbed of their lands by the Goths and of their movable property by the Imperial soldiers.

and posted an ambush.[1] The garrison of Portus, who could see the movements of the enemy from the walls, waved garments and signalled to the ships to keep away from the harbour and land elsewhere, but the crews mistook the signals for demonstrations of welcome, and sailing into the trap which had been laid for them were easily captured and slain. A bishop who accompanied the convoy was seized and interrogated by the king. His replies were unsatisfactory, and Totila, convinced that he was lying, punished him by cutting off his hands.

The pressure of hunger in Rome was now so severe that it was decided to ask Totila for a truce of a few days, on the understanding that, if no help arrived before it expired, the city would be surrendered. One of the Roman clergy, the deacon Pelagius, who was afterwards to fill the chair of St. Peter, undertook the mission. As representative of the Roman see at Constantinople he had ingratiated himself in the favour of Justinian, he enjoyed a high reputation in Italy, and had won popularity by employing his considerable wealth to relieve the sufferings of the siege. Totila received him with the courtesy due to a man of his character and influence, but made a speech, if we can trust the historian, which had the effect of preventing any attempt at negotiation.

" The highest compliment I can pay to an ambassador," such was the drift of the king's statement, " is candour. And so I will tell you plainly at the outset that there are three points on which I am resolved and will entertain no parley, but otherwise I will gladly meet any proposals you may make. The three exceptions are : (1) I will show no mercy to the Sicilians ; (2) the walls of Rome shall not be left standing ; (3) I will not give up the slaves who deserted to us from their Roman masters on our promise that we should never surrender them." Pelagius did not conceal his chagrin at these reservations and departed without making any proposals.

---

[1] It is not clear what the 'Ρωμαίων λιμήν was, behind the walls of which (τῶν τειχῶν ἐντός) the Goths concealed themselves (*ib.* 15. 10), and into which the foodships sailed, according to Procopius. Probably he misconceived the topography. The ships were making for the harbour of Porto, and were captured near the mouth of the channel which divides Porto from the Isola Sacra. This appears to be the interpretation of Hodgkin, *op. cit.* iv. 526. It is difficult to see how the Goths could have hidden themselves in the harbour of Porto (which was presumably under the control of the garrison) as Martroye assumes (*op. cit.* 446). As to the presence of Vigilius in Sicily see below, p. 385.

It is difficult to suppose that this interview has been quite correctly recorded. Why should Totila have introduced the subject of Sicily, which had no apparent bearing on the surrender of Rome, unless it had been first introduced by Pelagius ? If the report of Procopius is true so far as it goes, we must suppose that it is incomplete and that he has omitted to say that the ambassador opened the conversation by mentioning certain conditions for eventual surrender among which were the three points as to which Totila said he could make no concessions.

It is intelligible that Pelagius should have availed himself of this opportunity, whether with or without the authorisation of Bessas, to attempt to safeguard the Sicilians. For it is probable that Totila had made no concealment of his intention to punish them for what he regarded as their black ingratitude to the Goths. They had enjoyed a privileged position under Theoderic and his successors ; for no Goths had been settled in the island. But when Belisarius landed they had welcomed him with unanimous enthusiasm, and smoothed the way for his conquest of Italy. Their conduct rankled in the minds of the Goths, and they might well shiver at the thought of the chastisement awaiting them when Totila should have his hands free after the capture of Rome.

The vindictiveness displayed by Totila towards Sicily seems to have been the reason which induced Pelagius to break off the negotiation without pressing for the truce which he had been sent to arrange. His failure drove the citizens to despair. Some of them appeared before Bessas and his officers and implored them either to give them food to keep them alive or to allow them to leave the city or to kill them. They received a cold, unsympathetic reply. " We cannot agree to any of your suggestions. The first is impossible, the second would be dangerous, the third criminal. But Belisarius will soon be here to relieve the city." Throughout the siege Bessas and his subordinate commanders had been profiting by the dire necessity of the inhabitants to fill their own purses. At first they had plenty of corn in their magazines, and they sold it to the richer people at an exorbitant price.[1] Those who could not afford to buy had

---

[1] About 58 shillings a bushel (7 solidi for a medimnus, *i.e.* 6 modii or about 1½ bushels). Occasionally a stray ox was captured by the soldiers in the vicinity of the walls and was sold for over £30. Hodgkin (*op. cit.* iv. 532) misunderstands Procopius (iii. 17. 12) and supposes this happened only once.

to content themselves with bran at a quarter of the price. The mass of the populace fed on cooked nettles, and when the supplies of corn and bran ran short, nettles became the food of all. On this fare, occasionally supplemented by the flesh of a dog or a rodent, they died, or, wasting away, moved about like ghosts. At last the heart of Bessas was moved by the offer of a sum of money to allow the civilians to leave the city. Nearly all took advantage of the permission. Many fell into the hands of the Goths and were cut to pieces, and of the rest it is said that the greater number dropped by the wayside exhausted and died where they lay. " The fortunes of the Senate and Roman people had come to this." [1]

The next event was the landing of Belisarius at Portus. It was his intention on the arrival of John with reinforcements at Dyrrhachium to proceed immediately with all the forces he had to the relief of Rome. But John urged that it would be better to drive the Goths first out of Calabria and southern Italy, which they did not hold strongly, and then march on Rome. The result of these deliberations was a compromise.[2] The generals divided their forces. The voyage of Belisarius, who, accompanied by Antonina, first set sail with part of the army, was interrupted by adverse winds which compelled him to put in at Otranto. This port was still being besieged by the Goths, who, on the approach of his fleet, fled to Brundusium, where John presently landed and put them to rout. This victory meant the definite recovery of Calabria. John then marched northwards into Apulia and took Canusium, then southwards into Bruttii, where he defeated the Gothic general who was in command at Rhegium. He appears to have been determined, for other than military reasons,[3] not to join Belisarius, who was impatiently expecting him on the Tiber ; for we cannot suppose that he was deterred from fulfilling his promise by a body of 300 cavalry which Totila had sent to Capua.

Having established himself at Portus, Belisarius decided that his forces were too weak to attack the Gothic camp with any

[1] *B.G.* iii. 17. 25.
[2] Hodgkin's interpretation of what happened is probably right (iv. 535).
[3] In *H.A.* 5. 13. 14, Procopius explains John's conduct as due to the fear that Antonina, acting under the instructions of Theodora, might attempt to compass his death. His marriage with the daughter of Germanus had been opposed by Theodora, and Procopius asserts that she threatened to destroy him.

chance of success, and that the only thing he could attempt was to provision the city. To prevent foodships from ascending the river, Totila had thrown across the stream, some miles above Portus, a wooden boom,[1] with a tower at either end in which guards were stationed, and below it he had stretched an iron chain from bank to bank. To overcome this obstacle, Belisarius bound together two broad boats on which he constructed a wooden tower higher than the towers of the boom, and on the top he placed a boat filled with pitch, sulphur, resin, and other combustibles. He loaded with provisions and manned with the best of his soldiers two hundred dromons or light warships, on the decks of which he had erected high wooden parapets pierced with holes through which his archers could shoot. When all was ready he stationed some troops near the mouth of the Tiber, in case the enemy should attack Portus. He left Isaac the Armenian in charge of Portus, entrusting Antonina to his care, with strict injunctions not to leave the place on any plea, not even if he should hear that Belisarius had been slain. Other troops were ordered to advance along the right bank of the Tiber to co-operate with the ships, and a message had been sent to Bessas bidding him distract the enemy by a sortie. It was the one thing which Bessas was determined not to do.

Belisarius embarked in one of the dromons, and the double barge was slowly urged or hauled upstream.[2] Unhindered by the enemy, who did not appear, they reached the iron chain. Here they had to deal with some Goths who had been set on either bank to guard it. Having killed or put them to flight, they hauled up the chain and advanced against the boom, where they were confronted by more serious resistance, for enemy soldiers rushed from their encampments to help the guards in the towers. The double barge was then guided close to the tower on the right bank,[3] the combustibles were set alight, and the boat was dropped on the tower. The tower was immediately wrapt in flame, and the two hundred Goths inside were consumed. Meanwhile the archers in the dromons rained arrows on the Gothic forces which had assembled on the bank till these, terrified at once by the conflagration and by the deadly shower,

---

[1] γέφυρα.

[2] Procopius does not say how. Hodgkin supposes that it was tugged by some of the dromons.

[3] Evidently this side was chosen by Belisarius because his troops on shore could assist.

turned and fled. The men of Belisarius then set fire to the boom, and the way to Rome was clear.

But in the very moment in which he was rejoicing that his difficult enterprise, so skilfully planned and executed, was crowned with success, horsemen galloped up the road from Portus with the tidings that Isaac the Armenian was in the hands of the enemy. Belisarius lost his presence of mind. He did not wait to ask for details. He leaped to the conclusion that Portus had been captured, that his wife had fallen into the hands of the Goths, that he and his army had lost their base and refuge ; and he decided that the only thing to be done was to return at once with all his forces and attempt to recover Portus before the enemy had time to organise its defence.[1] The dromons sailed down the river, to find Portus unharmed and Antonina safe.

What had happened was this. The news of the breaking of the chain and the conflagration of the tower had come—perhaps it was signalled—to the ears of Isaac. He could not resist the temptation of doing something to win glory for himself, and, in flat disobedience to the express orders of his general, he left the fortress, crossed to the other bank of the channel, and, taking a hundred of the cavalry which Belisarius had posted on the Isola Sacra, attacked a Gothic encampment which was under the command of Roderick.[2] The enemy were taken by surprise and retired ; Roderick himself was wounded. But as Isaac and his men were plundering the camp, they were in turn surprised by the Goths who returned to attack them. Many were slain and Isaac was taken alive. Roderick died of his wound, and Totila, who valued him highly, avenged him by putting Isaac to death.

The misfortune might have been retrieved if Belisarius, on discovering his mistake, had promptly retraced his course upstream, before the enemy had time to replace the boom or construct new obstacles. But he had not the heart to make another attempt. The shock had been so great and the disappointment so grievous that his physical strength collapsed.

---

[1] Ἐπιθησόμενος μὲν ἀτάκτοις ἔτι τοῖς πολεμίοις οὖσι, B.G. iii. 19. 31.

[2] Apparently in the Isola Sacra, probably opposite Ostia. Hodgkin assumes that it was at Ostia (which Procopius does not mention), but this would have involved crossing the river between Isola Sacra and Ostia. Nothing is said of this.

Envious fortune seemed to have snatched the cup from his lips, and he must have felt that, if Isaac's unpardonable disobedience had originated the misfortune, it would have had no serious consequences but for his own precipitate action. He fell ill and a dangerous fever supervened.

It was not long after this that Rome was captured. Bessas as well as the soldiers grew negligent of the routine work on which the safety of a besieged city depends. Sentinels slept at their posts, and the patrols which used to go round the walls to see that watch was kept were discontinued. Four Isaurians, whose nightly post was close to the Asinarian Gate, took advantage of this laxity to betray the city. Letting themselves down from the battlements by a rope, they went in the darkness to the camp of Totila and offered to open the gate. He agreed to pay them well for their treachery and sent two of his followers back with them to report whether the scheme was practicable. But he did not altogether trust them, and it was not till they had twice returned to urge him to the enterprise that he finally decided to make use of their help. On the appointed night four strong Goths were hauled up by the Isaurians, and cleaving the wooden bolts of the gate with axes they admitted their king and the army (December 17, A.D. 546).[1]

Bessas and the greater part of the garrison, with a few senators who still had horses, fled through another gate (perhaps the Flaminian). Bessas in his haste left behind him all the treasure which he had spent a year in wringing from the starving citizens. Of the civilian population there were only about 500 left. These took refuge in churches, and sixty of them were killed by the Gothic soldiery when Totila let his troops loose to slay and plunder. He went himself to pray in St. Peter's, where Pelagius, holding the Bible in his hands, accosted him with the words, "Spare thy people, my lord." Totila, thinking of their last meeting, said, "Now, O Pelagius, thou hast come to supplicate me." "Yes," was the reply, "as God has made me thy servant. But henceforth spare thy servants, my lord." Totila then issued an order to stay the slaughter, but he allowed the Goths to plunder at their will, reserving the most valuable treasures for himself. The fact that no acts of violence to women disgraced the capture of Rome redounded to his glory.

---

[1] *Contin. Marcell.*, *sub* 547. John Mal. xviii. p. 483 says μηνὶ Φεβρουαρίῳ.

Totila hoped that this success would end the war. He despatched Pelagius and another Roman to Constantinople bearing a letter to the Emperor, to the following effect :

" You have already heard what has happened to Rome, and you will learn from these envoys why I have sent them. We are asking you to accept yourself and accord to us the blessings of that peace which was enjoyed in the time of Anastasius and Theoderic. If you consent, I will call you my father and we Goths will be your allies against all your enemies."

It is clear from this letter that Totila's idea was not to establish a completely independent power in Italy, like those of the Germanic kingdoms in Gaul and Spain, but to restore the constitutional system which had been in force under Theoderic and Athalaric. The capitulations of A.D. 497 were to be renewed, the Imperial authority was still to be nominally supreme. The ambassadors were instructed to intimate that, if the offer of peace were rejected, Totila would raze Rome to the ground and invade Illyricum. Justinian did not detain them long. He sent them back with a curt answer that as full powers for conducting the war and concluding peace had been committed to Belisarius, Totila might apply to him.[1]

In the meantime the slow but steady progress of the Imperial cause in southern Italy, where, if John had not taken any risks or achieved any striking success, Lucania had been detached from Gothic rule, demanded Totila's presence in the south. He did not want to lock up a garrison in Rome or to leave it for his enemies to reoccupy, and he decided to demolish it. He began by pulling down various sections of the walls,[2] and was about to burn the principal buildings and monuments when envoys arrived with a letter from Belisarius, who was recovering from his illness at Portus. The tenor of the letter is reported thus :

" As those to whom a city owes the construction of beautiful buildings are reputed wise and civilised, so those who cause their destruction are naturally regarded by posterity as persons devoid of intelligence, true to their own nature. Of all cities under

---

[1] It may be conjectured that Procopius, directly or indirectly, gathered a good deal of his information about the siege of Rome from this embassy. We are not told whether Totila did make overtures to Belisarius. The envoys may have been back in Italy in the first half of February.

[2] Procopius estimates the razed portions as about one-third of the whole circuit—probably an excessive estimate (Hodgkin, iv. 566).

the sun Rome is admitted universally to be the greatest and most important. She attained this pre-eminence not suddenly nor by the genius of one man, but in the course of a long history throughout which emperors and nobles by their vast resources and employing skilful artists from all parts of the world have gradually made her what you see her to-day. Her monuments belong to posterity, and an outrage committed upon them will rightly be regarded as a great injustice to all future generations as well as to the memory of those who created them. Therefore consider well. Should you be victorious in this war, Rome destroyed will be your own loss, preserved it will be your fairest possession. Should it be your fortune to be defeated, the conqueror will owe you gratitude if you spare Rome, whereas if you demolish it, there will be no reason for clemency, while the act itself will have brought you no profit. And remember that your reputation in the eyes of the world is at stake."

This is an interesting document, whether it reproduces closely or not the drift of the actual letter of Belisarius. Totila read that letter again and again ; it gave him a new point of view ; and the remonstrance of civilisation finally defeated in his breast the barbarous instincts of his race. He bade the work of vandalism cease.

§ 5. *Reoccupation of Rome, Siege of Rossano, and Recall of Belisarius* (A.D. 547–549)

The greater part of the Gothic army was left, at a place called Algedon, about eighteen miles west of Rome,[1] to watch Belisarius and prevent him from leaving Portus. With the rest Totila marched southward and soon recovered Lucania, Apulia, and Calabria, except Otranto and Taranto, in which John entrenched himself.[2] Then leaving a detachment of 400 men in the hill-town of Acherontia,[3] on the borders of Apulia and Lucania, he marched northwards. Was his design to surprise Ravenna, as the historian

---

[1] The name Ἀλγηδών (? Alcedum) is otherwise unknown. Martroye (*op. cit.* 466) thinks it may be identified with Castel Malnome, not far from Porto. Mount Algidus, which lies east of Rome, is out of the question.

[2] Tarentum was unwalled, and he fortified only that part of it which

lay on the isthmus. Totila probably departed for the south towards the end of February. We have to allow time for the return of the envoys who were despatched in December to Constantinople.

[3] *Celsae nidum Acherontiae* (Horace); now Acerenza.

intimates, or to re-establish his command of the Flaminian Way, which was threatened by a recent success of the Imperialists ? They had recovered Spoletium.

But grave news from Rome compelled him to postpone his purpose. He had left Rome uninhabited, its walls partly destroyed, and all the gates removed. Belisarius, whose health was now returned, visited the desolate city and decided to occupy it and put it in a state of defence.[1] The plan seemed wild, but it was carried out. He transferred his quarters and his army from Portus to Rome, where he was able to establish an abundant market, as there was no longer any obstacle to the importation of food from Sicily. The market attracted the people of the surrounding districts to come and settle in the deserted houses, and in less than four weeks the portions of the wall which the Goths had pulled down had been roughly reconstructed, though without mortar. New gates, however, could not be made so quickly, for lack of carpenters, and when Totila appeared in front of a gateless fortress he expected to capture it with ease. Belisarius placed in the gateways men of notable valour. For two days the Goths spent themselves in furious attacks, suffering great losses, but failed to carry any of the gates. After an interval of a few days, during which they cared for their wounded and mended their weapons, they renewed their assault. Totila's standard-bearer fell mortally wounded, and there was a fierce fight over the corpse. The Goths recovered the standard, but their whole army presently retreated in disorder. They were soon flying far afield pursued by the victors. Rome for the time was saved.[2] Belisarius furnished it with new gates and sent the keys to the Emperor.

This was the first check that Totila had experienced. While he won battles and captured cities, his followers regarded him as a god, but now in the hour of defeat they forgot all he had done and were immoderate in their criticism. The nobles reproached him bitterly with his blunder in leaving Rome in such a condition that the enemy could occupy it ; he should either have utterly destroyed it or held it himself. But though there was open discontent, there was no thought of revolution. Having demolished the bridges across the Tiber, except the

---

[1] In April. For Totila left Rome towards end of February, and it remained uninhabited for forty days (*Cont. Marcell.*, *s.a.*). [2] Probably in May 547.

Milvian, Totila withdrew to Tibur, which he refortified and made his headquarters.

In the course of summer he went to press the siege of Perusia, which Gothic troops had been blockading for some time past and which was now distressed by shortage of food. But his attention was soon diverted to the south, which was to be the scene of the principal operations of the war during the winter. He had interred in Campania those senators and their families whom he had carried off after the capture of Rome. The general John, who had been engaged in besieging Acherontia, determined to rescue them while Totila was still occupied in the north. Moving rapidly, he defeated a squadron of Gothic cavalry at Capua, and successfully delivered many of the Roman captives,[1] whom he immediately sent by sea to the safety of Sicily. It was a blow to Totila, for he regarded these prisoners as hostages who might be useful hereafter, and he marched hastily and stealthily from Perusia, with 10,000 men, into Lucania, where John was encamped. It was a complete surprise, and few of his enemies would have escaped if he had not committed the blunder of attacking the camp by night, for he outnumbered them by ten to one. But in the darkness about 900, including John, were able to escape, and 100 were slain. The prisoners taken were very few. Among them was an Armenian general, Gilak, who could speak no language but his own, and knew only one Greek word, *stratêgos*, " general." The only intelligible answer which his captors could extract from him was *Gilakios stratêgos*. They put him to death a few days later.

The importance of holding Calabria had been realised by John, and Belisarius appears to have anticipated before the end of the year (A.D. 547) that the main operations in spring would probably be in that region. Justinian, urged by his appeals, sent reinforcements of more than 2000 men at the beginning of the winter.[2] Early in the year, Belisarius committed the charge of Rome to Conon and sailed for Sicily with 900 men. Proceeding thence up the eastern coast of Bruttii he found his voyage impeded by strong north winds, and instead of making for Tarentum, as he had intended, he landed at Croton, an un-

---

[1] From *Cont. Marcell.*, *sub* 548, one would infer that only some of the women were rescued ; *nonnullas liberat senatrices*.

[2] Among these, more than 1000 guards (*doryphoroi* and *hypaspistai*) under Valerian, Master of Soldiers in Armenia, iii. 27. 3.

walled town. As the neighbourhood could not furnish provisions for his army, he sent his cavalry northward into the mountains to forage, expecting that if they met the enemy in the narrow defiles they would be able to repulse them.[1] Totila was there with his army bent on taking the hill-town of Ruscianum—the modern Rossano—in which John had placed a garrison.[2] The disparity in numbers was immense, yet the small body of horse inflicted a severe defeat on the Gothic host, of whom more than 200 fell. But the Goths enjoyed a speedy revenge. The Romans, elated by their victory, neglected their night watches and did not pitch their tents in one place, so that Totila was able to surprise and nearly exterminate them. On hearing the news, Belisarius, his wife, and infantry "leapt" into the ships [3] and reached Messina in one day. Totila laid siege to Rossano (probably in May).

Soon afterwards a new contingent of about 2000 arrived in Sicily from the East. Much larger forces were needed against a leader of Totila's capacity ; Belisarius was weary of conducting a war in which, though he might gain local successes, he was never strong enough to take full advantage of them ; and he

---

[1] In *Itin. Antonini* the distance of Rossano from Thurii is given as 12 Roman miles. Procopius gives its distance from the port of Thurii as 60 stades (nearly 9 miles). The name of the port was Ruscia (iii. 28. 8 'Ρουσκία ἐστὶ τὸ Θουρίων ἐπίνειον, 30. 12 ἐπὶ 'Ρουσκίαν ἀνήγοντο) ; the inland territory behind it was called Rusciana, hence the hill-town situated in this territory was called (castrum) Ruscianum. Procopius designates the fort as τὸ ἐπὶ 'Ρουσκιανῆς φρουρίον (29. 21, and 30. 19), or τῷ 'Ρουσκιανῷ φρουρίῳ (30. 5, so one MS., but the other omits 'P. and it may be a gloss). In 30. 2 εὐθὺ 'Ρουσκιανῆς κατὰ τάχος ἔπλει, the text need not be altered, as "sailed straight to the Ruscian territory" is good sense. Haury, wrongly assuming that Rusciana was the name of the port, has perversely corrected the readings of the MSS. in three places (in 28. 8 he reads 'Ρουσκιανῆ, in 30. 12 'Ρουσκιανὴν, and in 30. 5 ἐν τῷ ⟨ἐπὶ⟩ 'Ρουσκιανῆς φρουρίῳ). Martroye has made the opposite mistake and called the fort Ruscia. The port of

Thurii can hardly have been so far from that town as the sea-board near Ruscia (cp. Nissen, *Ital. Landesk.* ii. 2, p. 923).

[2] Procopius names two passes between Bruttii and Lucania, Labūla, and Petra Sanguinis (Πέτρα Αἵματος, iii. 28. 7). The former may mean the east coast road (cp. Nissen, *op. cit.* p. 926). The latter must be on the inland road coming down from Neruli (= Rotonda, on the Laus) and Muranum (= Morano) to Interamnium, which corresponds to Castrovillari, and is situated on the two brooks which unite to form the Sybaris (now the Coscile). The road went on to Capraria (now Tarsia, east of Spezzano) and Consentia. The boundary between E. Lucania and E. Bruttii was the Crathis ; on the west, I suspect that the division lay along the N.-S. road from Neruli to Interamnium.

[3] 'Ες τὰς ναῦς ἐσεπήδησεν. Procopius gives the distance from Croton to Messina as 700 stades, about 92 English miles, which is virtually correct.

had decided that Antonina should return to Constantinople and implore the Empress to use all her influence to secure the sending of such an army as the situation required. They proceeded together to Otranto, and there she embarked on a journey which was to prove fruitless, for she arrived to find that Theodora was dead.[1]

The garrison of Rossano, in dire need of food but expecting aid from Belisarius, promised Totila that they would surrender on a certain day,[2] if no relief arrived, on condition that they should be allowed to depart in safety. The commanders of the garrison were Chalazar, a Hun, and the Thracian Gudilas. The attempts of Belisarius and John to bring help were frustrated, and they then hit on the plan of forcing Totila to raise the siege by diverting his attention elsewhere. Belisarius sailed to Rome, and John with Valerian—a general who had been sent to Italy six months before [3]—set out to relieve the fortresses in Picenum, which enemy forces were besieging. But Totila was bent upon the capture of the Bruttian fortress, and he contented himself with despatching 2000 cavalry in the rear of John.

The garrison of Rossano, confident that help was approaching, failed to keep their promise ; the appointed day passed ; and then, when they knew that they could no longer hope, they threw themselves on Totila's mercy. He pardoned them all except Chalazar, whom he shamefully mutilated and put to death. Those soldiers who were willing to become Gothic subjects remained in the place ; the rest were deprived of their property and went to Croton.[4]

Rome needed the presence of Belisarius. Some time before, the garrison had mutinied and slain Conon their commander. They had then sent some clergy to Constantinople to demand a free pardon for the murder and the payment of their arrears, with the threat that they would deliver the city to the Goths if these conditions were not accepted. The Emperor accepted them. Belisarius then arrived. He saw to it that the city was

---

[1] She died on June 28 ; see above, p. 66.

[2] Μεσούσης μάλιστα τῆς τοῦ θέρους ὥρας is generally taken with ἐνδώσειν in iii. 30. 5. If so, it cannot mean, as it ought, the summer solstice. I think that it should be taken with ὡμολόγησαν, and that the bargain

was made about the end of June.

[3] See above, p. 246, n. 2.

[4] Eighty in number. The garrison consisted of 300 Illyrian cavalry and 100 foot soldiers. There were also in the place many Italians of good family ; these Totila punished by confiscating their property.

furnished with a good supply of provisions in case it should be
again besieged, and he probably weeded out the garrison. When
he left Italy for ever, early in A.D. 549, Rome was held by 3000
chosen troops, under the command of Diogenes, one of his own
retainers, whose intelligence and military capacity he trusted.
Antonina had procured without difficulty her husband's recall.
Theodora's death meant the ascendancy of the party which was
attached to Germanus, and the enemies and critics of Belisarius
could now make their influence felt. What had this great
general accomplished in five years ? He had simply navigated
about the coasts of Italy, never venturing to land except when
he had the refuge of a fortress. Totila desired nothing so much
as to meet him in battle, but he had never taken the field. He
had lost Rome, he had lost everything.[1] He might vanquish
a general of mediocre capacity like Witigis, but it was a different
story when he had to do with a foe of considerable talent and
unflagging energy like Totila. Belisarius might have much to
say in extenuation of his failure, but the broad fact was that he
had failed. Knowing that there was no chance of his receiving
such reinforcements as might enable him to retrieve his reputation, he was glad to bid farewell to Italy.

Soon after his departure, Perusia fell, after a siege of four years.[2]

§ 6. *Third Siege of Rome* (A.D. 549)

In the summer after the departure of Belisarius, the king
of the Goths appeared for the third time before the walls of
Rome.[3] He was determined to capture it, but he had abandoned
all those thoughts of destroying it which had moved him when
he first laid siege to it. He had laid to heart the letter of the
Imperial general, which other opinions had perhaps reinforced, [4]
he had come to realise—as Theoderic and Alaric had realised—
the meaning of Rome.

The garrison was valiant, and the commander Diogenes had
made provident preparations for an eventual siege. As there
was only a small population now, besides the garrison, there
were large areas of waste land in the city, and these were sown

---

[1] Procopius, *B.G.* iii. 35. 1, 2,
repeated with additions in *H.A.* 5. 1-6
and 17.
[2] A.D. 545-549.

[3] At the beginning of the 15th
year of the war (Proc. *B.G.* iii. 36. 1),
i.e. end of June or early in July, 549.
[4] Cp. below, § 8, p. 258.

with grain. When repeated attempts of the Goths to storm
the walls were foiled by the valour of the soldiers, Totila resigned
himself to the prospect of a long blockade. It was uncertain
whether relief forces would arrive from the East under a new
commander-in-chief, but as he had captured Portus, he was in
a much more favourable position for conducting a blockade than
he had been three years before.

The blockade lasted a long time, but the city fell into his
hands at last. The circumstances of the previous capture were
repeated. Isaurian treachery again delivered Rome to the
Goth. Some Isaurian soldiers, who were keeping watch in the
south of the city at the Porta Ostiensis—which was already known
by its modern designation from the Church of the Apostle Paul
—discontented because they had received no pay for years,
and remembering the large rewards which Totila had bestowed
on their fellow-countrymen, offered to open the gate. On a pre-
arranged night, two barques [1] were launched in the Tiber,
probably to the north of the Porta Flaminia.[2] They were rowed
down as close to the city as possible, and then trumpeters who
had been embarked in them sounded a loud blast. The alarm
was given, and all sections of the garrison rushed to the defence
of the walls in the threatened quarter, in the north-west. Meanwhile the Gothic army had been quietly assembled in front of the
gate of St. Paul ; the Isaurians unlocked it, and the army
marched in (January 16, A.D. 550).[3]

It was easy to anticipate that any of the garrison who succeeded in escaping would make for Centumcellae, the only fortress
that remained to the Imperialists in the neighbourhood of Rome,

---

[1] Μικρὰ πλοῖα, "little boats," is
the reading of L (the Laurentian MS.),
and is probably right, but K (the
Vatican MS.) has π. μακρά (long
boats or war-vessels).

[2] This conjecture seems more likely
than that of Hodgkin, who supposes
that the boats were launched south
of the city and ordered " to creep
up the river and blow a loud blast
from their trumpets as near as
possible to the centre of the City "
(p. 615). In this case the garrison
would have supposed that the attack
was to be made, as Hodgkin says,
near the Aventine. The vague words
of Procopius are consistent with

either interpretation ; but he says
nothing about " the centre of the
city " ; on the contrary, his words
are ἐπειδὰν τοῦ περιβόλου ἄγχιστα
ἥκωσι (iii. 36. 9) and ἐπεὶ τῆς πόλεως
ἄγχι ἐγένοντο (ib. 12). As it was
just as easy for Totila to raise the
false alarm in the north, it seems
highly improbable that he would
have chosen to attract all the soldiers
of the garrison to the Aventine,
which is quite close to the Gàte of
St. Paul.

[3] Cons. Ital. p. 334. The year given
here is 549, but we should doubtless
read p. c. Basilii viiii. = 550 (see
Körbs, op. cit. p. 54).

and Totila had posted some troops along the western road to
intercept fugitives. The precaution was effective ; a few escaped
the ambush, among whom was Diogenes. In Rome itself there
was great slaughter, but a band of four hundred cavalry led by
Paul, who had belonged to the household of Belisarius and was
the right-hand man of Diogenes, occupied the Mausoleum of
Hadrian and the adjacent Aelian Bridge. Here they held out
for two days. Totila expected that the cravings of hunger
would compel them to surrender, and kept troops posted on the
eastern bank. They thought of eating their horses, but could
not make up their minds to taste the unaccustomed food. On
the evening of the second day they resolved to court a heroic
death, to make a dash against the enemy and fall fighting. They
embraced one another, said their last adieux, and prepared for
the charge. Totila was watching them and divined their
intention. He knew that desperate men, who had devoted
themselves to death, would decimate his army. He therefore
sent a messenger offering that if they would lay down their arms
and take an oath never to fight against the Goths again, he would
let them depart unharmed to Constantinople, or if they would
fight for him, he would treat them on a perfect equality with
the Goths. The offer was gladly accepted. At first all elected
to go home, but on further reflexion they changed their minds.
They could not bring themselves to undertake the long journey
without horses or arms, they feared its perils, and if they had
any hesitation about going over to the enemy, they remembered
that the Imperial treasury had withheld their pay for years.
Only Paul himself and one other resisted the lure of the barbarian
and returned to Byzantium.

Totila had no longer any thought of destroying Rome or of
leaving it undefended. His position was much stronger than
it had been three years before, and he had come to realise the
prestige which the possession of the Imperial city conferred
in the eyes of the world.[1] He was now bent on rebuilding
and repopulating it. He sent for the senators and other
Romans who were still kept under guard in the fortresses of
Campania.[2]

He was planning to carry the war into Sicily, but he first made

[1] See below, p. 258.
[2] *B.G.* iii. 36. 29 ; 37. 3. This   shows that all the captives had not
been rescued by John in 547.

a new proposal of peace, just as he had done after his former capture of Rome. On this occasion his envoy was not even admitted to the presence of the Emperor, who had just appointed a new commander-in-chief to succeed Belisarius. He had thought of entrusting the conduct of the war to his cousin, Germanus, but changed his intention and selected Liberius, the Roman senator, who fourteen years before had come to him as an envoy of Theodabad, and since then had remained in his service.[1] It was a curious appointment, for Liberius, who had served in civil capacities under Odovacar and Theoderic, had no military experience, and he was now an octogenarian ; the ground of his nomination must have been that as an Italian he would inspire the Italians with confidence.

Totila meanwhile was making preparations for his next campaign. He collected a fleet of 400 ships of war and some large merchant vessels, which he had recently captured from the enemy, to convey his troops across the Sicilian Straits. It was perhaps about the end of March that, having presided at horse-races in the Circus Maximus, he left Rome. Before marching southwards he turned aside with the hope of reducing Centumcellae, which was now under the command of Diogenes. This valiant officer refused to surrender until he had communicated with Constantinople, but agreed that, if by a certain date no reinforcements should arrive, he would leave the city to the Goths. Totila consented, hostages were interchanged, and the Gothic army marched to Rhegium, which it may have reached early in May.[2]

§ 7. *Proposed Expedition of Germanus* (A.D. 549–550)

On the southern coasts of Italy the most important places still held for the Empire were Hydruntum, Rhegium, Tarentum, and Croton. The Goths now laid siege to Rhegium and captured Tarentum. Without waiting for Rhegium to fall, Totila crossed to Messina, which he failed to take. But he was at last able to gratify one of the dearest desires of his heart and wreak vengeance upon the Sicilians for the welcome they had given

---

[1] See above, c. xviii. p. 164. He was a Patrician, and had been appointed Prefect of Alexandria, c. 541; see below, p. 380.

[2] The distance of Città Vecchia from Rome is about 75 kils. ; from Rome to Rhegium less than 700.

Belisarius fifteen years before. His army ravaged the island without resistance. Meanwhile Rhegium, which was short of provisions, surrendered.

The news of these menacing successes seems to have made a greater impression at Constantinople than the recent capture of Rome. The Emperor reverted to his former plan of sending Germanus to the West as commander-in-chief. But Germanus could not start until he had collected an army sufficiently strong to end the war, and in the meantime Liberius was despatched to defend Sicily. He had hardly set sail before it was recognised that he was too old and inexperienced, and Artabanes,[1] who was appointed Master of Soldiers in Thrace, was sent to supersede him.

Germanus was now regarded as the probable heir to the Imperial throne. The death of Theodora had removed the adverse influence which might have withheld the Emperor from favouring his claim.[2] He had already established his reputation by suppressing the Moorish rebellion of Stutzas, and he was ambitious of enhancing it by recovering Italy and succeeding where Belisarius had failed. As the prestige of the dynasty was involved, the Emperor was prepared to spend money in a less stinting spirit than he had shown hitherto in the conduct of the Italian war ; and Germanus had considerable private resources which he did not hesitate to devote to the collection of troops. The raising of an army for services not connected with the defence of the frontiers had come to be the task of the commander who was to lead it. None of the standing troops in the East could be withdrawn, although some of the cavalry squadrons stationed in Thrace might be spared. Germanus, with his sons, Justin and Justinian, busily recruited volunteers in the highlands of Thrace and Illyricum, and bands of barbarians from the Danubian regions flocked to his standards. The king of the Lombards promised a thousand heavily armed warriors. The private retainers of many generals left their less illustrious masters to attach themselves to the service of Germanus.

But besides these preparations for a vigorous military offensive,

[1] Artabanes had recently been implicated in a conspiracy; see p. 67 above.

[2] He was never formally designated, and Justinian never committed himself. But everything points to the fact that it was generally taken for granted that he would succeed, and that Justinian was contented that this opinion should prevail.

the plan of Germanus included what might be called a moral offensive, on which he counted much and with good reason. He contracted a Gothic marriage. He took as his second wife the queen Matasuntha. As the reluctant consort of Witigis she had been once queen of the Goths, but it was as the grand-daughter of king Theoderic and sister of king Athalaric that she had the strongest claims on their loyalty and affection. If her mother had brought her up in the ways of Roman civilisation, she was of the purest Amal lineage, and Germanus might con-fidently hope that the effect of his coming as her husband, and presumably in her company, would be to undermine the allegiance of many of the Goths to Totila, or at least to embarrass their minds in such a way as to impair their military vigour. They would feel that they were fighting no longer merely against Greeks, but against the granddaughter of their greatest king. And they would calculate that, as Germanus was marked out to succeed to the Empire on Justinian's death, Matasuntha would presently share the Imperial throne.[1]

When the news of the marriage reached Italy it seems to have produced the effect which was anticipated. Many Goths began to ask themselves whether it would be well to continue their resistance. And the reports which arrived of the Imperial preparations for prosecuting the war affected the numerous soldiers who had deserted the Roman cause to serve under Totila. They managed to send messages to Germanus that as soon as he landed in Italy they would go over to him and fight again under the standards they had abandoned. Diogenes, who had agreed to surrender Centumcellae on a certain day, declared himself absolved from the covenant because Germanus was coming.

But Germanus was not to come. He was at Sardica, and his army was ready. It was the autumn of A.D. 550.[2] He had announced that he would start in two days, when he suddenly fell sick, and the disease proved fatal. His death meant much.

---

[1] Wroth has an interesting con-jecture on the coins of Matasuntha (bearing her name in monogram), which are generally assumed to have been issued in 536–540, when she was queen of Witigis. Pointing out that there is nothing Italian about the coins, he conjectures that they may have been minted at Constantinople in 550. The issue of such coins would have been a very natural way of asserting the queen's claim to the Ostrogothic throne.

[2] Perhaps in September. Cp. Körbs, *op. cit.* 48-49.

It meant particularly the destruction of the hopes which were swaying opinion in Italy both among Italians and Goths.[1]

§ 8. *Totila in Sicily. Negotiations with the Franks* (A.D. 550–551)

The plans for the prosecution of the war were disconcerted by the death of the commander-in-chief, and Justinian appointed no one to replace him for some time. But in the meantime it was arranged that John, the nephew of Vitalian, who was now the Master of Soldiers in Illyricum, and was to have served under his father-in-law, Germanus, should, with his brother-in-law, Justinian, lead the army to Italy. John had proved himself an able soldier, and if he and Belisarius had been able to work cordially together, it is probable that the duration of the war would have been considerably curtailed. He was not appointed to the supreme command because it was felt that he did not possess the requisite prestige to command the obedience of the other generals.

When the troops were collected in Dalmatia it was late in the year, and it was thought better to spend the winter there than to march immediately to Venetia. There was no sufficient supply of ships at Salona to transport the army across the Hadriatic.

Meanwhile Totila had been wreaking his vengeance upon Sicily. When he was besieging Syracuse, Liberius arrived, and seeing that he was not strong enough to help the city he sailed on to Panormus. Artabanes, who, as we saw, had been appointed to replace Liberius, was already on his way, but his ships were caught off the coast of Calabria by a storm which drove them

---

[1] Matasuntha bore a posthumous son who was called by the name of his father, and is mentioned in the *Getica* of Jordanes (which seems to have been composed in A.D. 551, or at latest 552, before the issue of the war for Italy was decided). The words of Jordanes are (§ 314) : *post humatum patris Germani natus est filius idem Germanus, in quo coniuncta Aniciorum genus cum Amala stirpe spem adhuc utriusque generi domino praestante promittit.* The exact connexion of Germanus with the Anician gens is unknown ; Mommsen conjectured that his mother might have been a daughter of Juliana Anicia, daughter of the Emperor Olybrius and Placidia. From the fact that Jordanes looked upon this infant as the hope of the Ostrogothic race, Schirren (*De ratione quae inter Iordanem et Cassiodorum intercedit*) drew the hardly justifiable conclusion that the motif of the book was political—to promote the idea of reconciling Goth and Italian under the rule of Germanus.

back to Greece. The Goths succeeded in capturing only four fortresses, probably places of secondary importance, in which they placed garrisons, and having lived in the island for many months,[1] they returned to Italy laden with booty and provisions. During the summer and autumn of this year (A.D. 550) the Imperial generals in Italy were inactive, though the absence of Totila in Sicily was an opportunity for an enterprising leader. Then the news arrived that the Emperor had appointed the Armenian eunuch Narses to the supreme command. The appointment was universally welcomed. Narses, the Grand Chamberlain, appears to have been one of the most popular ministers at Justinian's court. He was celebrated for his generosity, he did not make enemies, and such was his reputation for piety that it was believed that the Virgin Mother herself watched over his actions and suggested the right moment for engaging in battle.[2] He was a friend of John, whom, as it will be remembered, he had forced Belisarius to rescue at Rimini, and of whose loyal co-operation he was assured. This fact, we may conjecture, had a good deal to do with his appointment. Narses had the qualities of a leader, but he had not much military experience ; the advice of John would remedy this deficiency.

John had been ordered to await the arrival of the new commander-in-chief at Salona, but Narses was delayed on his way, at Philippopolis, by an invasion of Kotrigur Huns,[3] and it was probably late in A.D. 551.that he arrived in Dalmatia.

Fortune had steadily favoured the Goths for the last four years. In A.D. 547 the Imperialists held in central Italy Ravenna, Ancona, and Ariminum, Spoletium and Perusia, Rome itself with Portus, Centumcellae ; in the south Otranto, Taranto, the province of Bruttii, and Sicily. In A.D. 551 the only important places they held on the mainland were Ravenna, Ancona, Otranto, and Croton, while in Sicily they had lost four strongholds ; and Totila, on returning from Sicily, had sent an army to besiege Ancona. This tide of success was now about to turn.

---

[1] The dates of Totila's arrival in Sicily and his departure are not marked very clearly by Procopius, but we can deduce from the data that he must have reached the island in May and left it before the end of the year.

[2] Evagrius, *H.E.* iv. 24.
[3] See below, p. 303. Narses had left Constantinople about June acc. to our text of John Malalas, xviii. p. 484; but Theophanes, who was copying Malalas, says April (A.M. 6043).

Ever since Totila had crossed the Po after his accession, the war had been waged entirely to the south of that river, and the conditions which prevailed in northern Italy are obscure. Here the situation was complicated by the intervention of a third power. As all the forces of the Ostrogoths were demanded by the struggle in the south, the Franks had seized the opportunity to extend their power into Italy. Theodebert, who followed the progress of the war attentively, had occupied the province of the Cottian Alps, a part of Liguria, and the greater part of Venetia.[1] The only important cities which the Goths still retained seem to have been Verona and Ticinum. Some time afterwards a treaty was concluded between the Franks and Goths, by which Totila acquiesced in the provisional occupation by the Franks of the territory which had been seized, and the two powers agreed, in case the war ended with a Gothic victory, to make a new permanent arrangement.[2] Far-reaching plans are attributed to Theodebert. He was incensed at Justinian's assumption of the titles *Francicus* and *Alamannicus*, with the implication that the Franks and their subjects the Alamanni had been subjugated and were vassals of the Empire, and he expressed his formal independence by issuing gold coins with his own bust and his own name.[3] He was the first German king to venture on this innovation, which from a commercial point of view was hazardous. It was said that he formed the project of leading the German nations, the Lombards, the Gepids, and others through the Illyrian countries and attacking Constantinople itself.

We possess one diplomatic document, belonging to this period, which records the Italian conquests of the Franks. The Emperor had written to Theodebert requesting information as to the extent of his dominions, and Theodebert's reply has been preserved,[4] in which he enumerates Pannonia and the northern parts of Italy among the countries which he has subjugated.

After his capture and abandonment of Rome in A.D. 547,

[1] Procopius, *B.G.* iii. 33. 7 ; iv. 24. 4 and 6-8. The Romans still held coast places in Venetia.

[2] Procopius, *ib.* 9-10 and 27.

[3] Agathias, i. 4. Procopius, *ib.* iii.

33. Cp. Keary, *Coinages of Western Europe*, p. 22.

[4] *Epp. Mer. aeui*, iii. ; *Epp. Austras.* 20. Theodore and Solomon are mentioned as the Imperial envoys to the Frank court.

Totila had proposed to espouse the daughter of one of the Merovingian kings who is not named, but we are entitled to presume that he was Theodebert. The offer was refused, on the ground that Totila would never succeed in the subjugation of Italy, seeing that he had shown himself so foolish as to let the great capital slip from his hands.[1] This criticism helped to open the Ostrogoth's eyes to the importance of Rome. In the following year, Theodebert died and was succeeded by his son Theodebald.[2] To him Justinian sent an ambassador to complain of the encroachments of his father in northern Italy, to demand the evacuation of the cities, and to request him to fulfil the promises of Theodebert and co-operate in the Italian war.[3] Theodebald promptly sent an embassy to Constantinople.[4] The course of the negotiations is unknown, but the Franks remained in Italy.

§ 9. Battle of Sena Gallica (A.D. 551)

Totila realised that a supreme effort was now to be made to destroy the Ostrogothic power in Italy. The appointment of Narses was hardly less significant than the appointment of Germanus. He had always understood the importance of reconciling the Italians to his rule, and he now urgently pressed forward the rebuilding of Rome in order to ingratiate himself with the Romans. His immediate military objects were the capture of Ancona and Croton, two of the few valuable places that were still left to the Empire. In the autumn of A.D. 551, his forces, as we saw, were besieging Ancona, but it is probable that he had not yet sent an army against Croton. At the same

---

[1] Procopius, iii. 37. 1-2.

[2] Gregory of Tours, *Hist. Fr.* iii. 36 (for date, 37 *ad fin.*), says he died of a long illness ; Agathias, i. 4, says he was killed, hunting, by a wild bull.

[3] The date of this embassy (which Hodgkin assigns to 551) cannot be inferred from the fact that Procopius notices it *after* the embassy of Totila in 551 (iv. 24. 11) ; for here he digresses, *à propos* of the Franks, and goes back to Theodebert. I have little doubt that the embassy was sent in 549–550, when the preparations were afoot for the expedition of

Germanus, and that it bore to Theodebald Justinian's congratulatory letter on his accession, in which the Emperor took occasion to say hard words of his father's conduct, and to which Theodebald's reply is preserved (*Epp. Austras.* 18).

[4] It may be conjectured that it was on this occasion that Theodebald attached some Angles to his embassy, to show the Emperor that his authority extended to Britain. See Procopius, iv. 20. 10. These Angles doubtless supplied Procopius with the material for his curious account of that island.

time, he was employing his fleet. Three hundred vessels sailed to the shores of Greece. The rich island of Corcyra was ravaged, and on the mainland the districts around Nicopolis, Anchialus, and Dodona. Transports conveying supplies to the army of Narses at Salona were intercepted and captured. The garrison of Ancona was hard pressed, for it was blockaded by sea as well as by land. Forty-seven Gothic warships hindered any provisions from reaching it by sea. The general, Valerian, who was stationed at Ravenna and was not strong enough to send relief, wrote to John at Salona an urgent letter on the gravity of the situation. John promptly manned thirty-eight warships with seasoned men,[1] and at Scardona, higher up the Dalmatian coast, they were joined by twelve more which came across from Ravenna with Valerian. The two generals and their fleet sailed to Sena Gallica, of which the distance by sea to Ancona is about seventeen miles. The two squadrons were practically equal in strength, and the Gothic commanders, Indulf and Gibal,[2] immediately determined to risk a naval battle, and sailed to Sena.

The action, as in a land battle, was begun by the archers ; then some of the vessels closed with each other, and the crews fought with sword and lance. But the Goths were at a great disadvantage. They had not the natural aptitude of the Greeks for handling ships, and they can have had very little training in the operations of maritime warfare. They were unable, in the excitement of the action, to maintain a suitable distance between their ships. Some of these were too far from their neighbours and were easily sunk by the enemy, but most of them were too close together and had no room to manœuvre. Their opponents, on the other hand, kept perfect order, and with cool readiness took advantage of all the blunders of the Goths, who at last, weary and helpless, gave up the contest and fled. Thirty-six Gothic ships were sent to the bottom and Gibal was captured ; Indulf escaped with eleven ships, which he burned as soon as he landed, and reached the camp at Ancona. When

---

[1] It is clear that Narses had not yet arrived at Salona, for Procopius says that John took upon himself to disobey the Imperial command that he should not stir till Narses came.

[2] Indulf had formerly been a retainer of Belisarius. The MSS. of Procopius (iii. 35. 23 and 29 ; iv. 12) vary between Ἰλαούφ, Ἰνδούλφ, Ἰλδούφ and Γουνδούλφ. I have followed Haury.

the victorious fleet arrived, they found that the enemy had abandoned the camp and taken refuge in Auximum. The crushing victory meant more than the safety of Ancona, it dealt a heavy blow to the power and prestige of the Goths.[1]

Soon after this Artabanes, who had arrived in Sicily, recovered the four fortresses which the Goths had captured. The tide seemed to have definitely turned, and the Goths were acutely conscious of the change in their prospects. They felt that if the enemy came in strength they would be unable to hold out. Once more Totila sent ambassadors to Constantinople to propose terms of peace, offering to resign the claim to Sicily and Dalmatia, and to pay the taxes to which the tenantless estates in those provinces were liable. But the Emperor refused to listen to the pleadings of the envoys. He was so bitter against the Ostrogoths that he had determined to expunge their name from the map of the Roman world.

One more success was achieved by Totila, though it was perhaps purchased too dearly. He had sent a fleet to Corsica and Sardinia with forces sufficient to overcome the Roman garrisons. As those islands belonged to the African Prefecture, it devolved upon John, the Master of Soldiers in Africa, to defend them, and he sent an army to Sardinia (autumn, A.D. 551). It was defeated near Cagliari, and sailed back to Carthage, to return in the spring in greater strength. Whatever prestige Totila gained by the occupation of the islands can hardly have counterbalanced the disadvantage of reducing the numbers of his fighting forces in Italy, when every man was needed for the approaching struggle with the armies of Narses.

During the spring Croton was hard pressed by the Goths who were blockading it. No one came to its relief until the Emperor, hearing that it would inevitably fall unless speedy help arrived, ordered the troops stationed at Thermopylae to embark immediately and sail thither. The mere appearance of the relief squadron in the harbour sufficed to terrify the besiegers, who hastily broke up their camp and fled. The effect of this bloodless victory was that the commanders of the Gothic garrisons in Tarentum and Acherontia offered to surrender those places on condition that their own safety was secured. Their proposals were referred to the Emperor.

[1] *B.G.* iv. 24. 42.

§ 10. *Battle of Busta Gallorum and Death of Totila* (A.D. 552)

In the spring of A.D. 552 Narses was at length ready to set out for Italy. He had collected large forces in addition to those which had been recruited two years before by Germanus, and

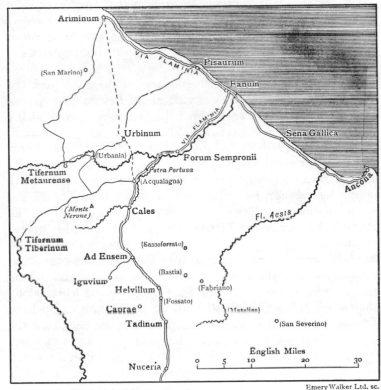

Emery Walker Ltd. sc.

UMBRIA TO ILLUSTRATE THE BATTLE OF BUSTA GALLORUM, A.D. 552.

which had remained at Salona under the command of John. We are not told what was the entire strength of the army, though we know the number of some of the particular contingents. The Lombard King Audoin sent more than 5500 fighting men ; [1] there were more than 3000 Heruls ; [2] there were

---

[1] Two thousand five hundred warriors and a comitatus (θεραπεία) of more than 3000.

[2] More than 3000 under Philemuth and others ; and many others under Aruth, a Romanised Herul.

400 Gepids ; there were Huns,[1] of course, and there was a band of Persian deserters.[2] All these foreign auxiliaries can hardly have amounted to less than 11,000. For the regular Imperial regiments which the Emperor placed at the disposal of Narses, for the Thracian and Illyrian troops which Germanus and Narses had specially recruited at their own expense we have no figures, but it will not be extravagant to suppose that they were more numerous than the foreign contingents, and to conjecture 25,000 as a probable figure for the strength of the whole army which marched with Narses from Salona along the Dalmatian coast road to the head of the Hadriatic.[3]

The towns and forts which commanded the road from the east into Venetia were in possession of the Franks, and Narses, when he approached the Venetian borders, sent envoys to the commanders asking them to permit a friendly army to pass in peace. The request was refused on the pretext that Lombards who were bitter foes of the Franks accompanied the Imperial army. Then Narses learned that, even if the Franks did not oppose his passage, he would be held up when he reached the Adige, inasmuch as Teïas, one of the most capable of Totila's captains, had arrived at Verona with all the best Gothic troops, to hinder and embarrass his march. Every possible measure had been taken to make the road from the Adige to Ravenna impracticable. By the advice of John, who was acquainted with the country, it was decided that the troops should march along the sea coast from Istria, attended by a few ships and a large fleet of small boats to transport them across the mouths of the rivers. Time was lost, but Ravenna was safely reached. But it is curious that an expedition for which long preparations had been made should have been allowed to find itself in such a predicament. One would have thought that an adequate fleet of transports could have been collected at Salona to convey the whole army direct to Classis.[4]

---

[1] Very numerous ($\pi\alpha\mu\pi\lambda\dot\eta\theta\epsilon\iota\varsigma$).

[2] Under Kavad, grandson of king Kavad, and nephew of Chosroes.

[3] Hartmann, *Gesch. Italiens*, i. p. 346, conjectures 30,000.

[4] Totila was aware of the deficiency of transports, and had hoped that if the troops were conveyed in relays to Italian ports he would be easily able to oppose their landing. *B.G.* iv. 26. 23. For the coast route, marked in the *Tabula Peut.*, from Ravenna to Altinum, via Ad Padum, Neronia, and Hadria, see Miller, *Itin.* pp. 309-311. The Goths had probably beset the road and destroyed the bridges of the Meduaco, the Adige, and the Po, and Narses made his way

At Ravenna the army rested for nine days and was reinforced by the troops of Justin and Valerian. Then, leaving Justin in charge of Ravenna, Narses pushed southward along the coast road. He was determined not to spend time or strength in lesser operations, but to come face to face with Totila and decide the issue of the war by a battle involving all the forces of both belligerents. Totila was in the neighbourhood of Rome, and therefore it was on the road to Rome that Narses hastened. When he reached Ariminum he found that the bridge across the river had been destroyed. His engineers bridged it, and he might easily have taken the town, for the commander of the garrison, who had sallied out to see what the Romans were doing, was slain by a Herul. But Narses did not tarry; Ariminum could wait. In ordinary circumstances the quickest route for an army marching from Ariminum to Rome was along the coast as far as Fanum and thence by the Via Flaminia. But this way was not open to Narses, for the eastern end of the Via Flaminia was commanded by the enemy who were in possession of Petra Pertusa, a barrier which might be found insuperable. It was therefore necessary for him to strike the road at some point to the west of that fortress. We do not know whether he left the coast near Ariminum or further on, at Pisaurum. In either case he probably reached the Via Flaminia about five miles on the Romeward side of the gorge of Petra Pertusa, at a place which is now known as Acqualagna.

In the meantime Totila, learning that Narses had reached Ravenna, had recalled Teïas and his army from Venetia, and, as eager for battle as Narses, set out for the north. It is not clear where he expected to encounter the Imperialists,[1] but when the news reached him that the enemy had left Ravenna and passed Ariminum he struck into the Apennines by the Via

through the lagoons with the help of boats from Altinum as far as Ad Padum, which was 24 Roman miles north of Ravenna. The date of his arrival in Ravenna was on a Thursday in June (see Agnellus, c. 62, where the month *July* is a mistake); Körb's (*op. cit.* 84) thinks it was on June 6, and this suits the probable date of the battle of Busta Gallorum, which cannot be placed later than the end

of June or first days of July.

[1] Waiting ἐν τοῖς ἐπὶ ʽΡώμης χωρίοις till the troops of Teïas arrived, he marched intending to choose his own ground for the battle, ὡς τοῖς πολεμίοις ἐν ἐπιτηδείῳ ὑπαντιάσων ᾔει. *B.G.* iv. 29. 2. Procopius does not record the number of his forces, but it is not probable that, even with the 2000 which arrived late, he had many more than 15,000.

Flaminia and encamped near (probably to the north of) Tadinum.[1]
Immediately afterwards the army of Narses reached the neighbourhood and encamped at a place of which the name, Busta
Gallorum, preserved a tradition of the wars of the early Roman
republic with the Celts of the north. The only other clue the
historian gives us as to its position is the statement that it was
about fourteen miles from the camp of Totila. We may conjecture that the place is to be sought to the east of the Flaminian
Way, in the neighbourhood of Fabriano.

As soon as his army had encamped, Narses sent some trusted
officers to Totila, to recommend him to make submission without
attempting to oppose much superior forces, and, if he were
determined to fight, to invite him to name a day for the battle.
Totila would not hear of peace or submission. He said, "Let
us do battle in eight days." But Narses was too shrewd to
trust the Goth's word. He guessed that Totila would attack
him on the next day and made his preparations for battle. So
it fell out. The Goths moved during the night, and at dawn the
Romans saw their army drawn up within two bowshots of their
own line.

Narses placed the Lombards, the Heruls, and the other
barbarian auxiliaries in the centre. They were mounted troops
but he made them dismount and used them as infantry. On
the two wings he posted his regular troops, on the right, under
himself and John, on the left under Valerian, Dagisthaeus, and
John Phagas ; and in front of each wing he stationed 4000
archers. Beyond the extremity of his left, he placed a reserve
of 1500 cavalry. Of these one squadron of 500 was to bring
help to any part of the line that might be hard pressed ;[2] the
other body of 1000 was to attempt, when the Gothic infantry
were engaged, to ride round and take them in the rear.

Narses had chosen a strong defensive position. It was such
that the only way by which the enemy could send a detachment
to circumvent him and attack him from behind was a narrow
path which ran by the slopes of a small hill close to his left wing.

---

[1] Close to the modern village
Gualdo Tadino. Procopius gives the
name as Τάγιναι but the identity
is unquestionable. For the topo-
graphical questions see Appendix to
this chapter.

[2] The natural position for such a
reserve would have been in the centre.
Narses must have placed it on the
left, because he anticipated that it
would be most likely to be needed on
that side.

It was, therefore, important to hold this position, and before daybreak fifty men stationed themselves in the bed of a stream on the slope of the hill facing the Goths. When Totila espied them he sent a squadron of horse to dislodge them, but the Romans held their ground against repeated attacks, performing prodigies of valour. Others were sent, but with the same result, and Totila abandoned the attempt. In the meantime the armies did not join battle. Narses, in his strong position, was determined not to attack first, and Totila had a reason for delaying the action. He was expecting every moment a force of 2000 cavalry under the command of Teïas, who had not arrived in time to march with the main army. Outmatched as he was in numbers by the enemy, this reinforcement was of supreme importance; it might decide the issue of the day. Accordingly he resorted to devices to gain time. Coccas, a horseman of great physical strength, who had deserted from the Imperial to the Gothic side, rode up to the Roman line within speaking distance and challenged the enemy to send out a champion to engage with him in single combat. Anzalas, an Armenian, one of the retainers of Narses, accepted the invitation. Coccas rode hard at him, aiming at his stomach, but Anzalas made his own horse swerve just in time to avoid the lance and at the same moment struck at his opponent's left side. Coccas fell mortally wounded, and cries of triumph rang out from the Roman ranks. After this interlude, Totila himself, caparisoned in shining armour, adorned with gold and purple trimmings, rode out into the space between the armies, on a huge steed, and displayed, for the benefit of the enemy, his equestrian skill, hurling his spear in the air and catching it again as he galloped, and performing other feats of horsemanship. Finally he sent a message to Narses, proposing negotiations, but Narses knew that he was not in earnest.

By these devices Totila wore away the forenoon, and at length in the early afternoon the belated two thousand arrived. The Goths immediately dissolved their array of battle and retired within the precincts of their camp to dine. Apparently Totila was confident that Narses would not attack,[1] and that

---

[1] It may be thought strange that Narses did not attack, but he was determined to avail himself of the strength of his defensive position. Cp. Delbrück, *Kriegskunst,* ii. 372.

the Romans would likewise break their ranks for the purpose of a meal. He thought that he might possibly take them unawares. But their cautious commander did not allow them to move from their places or take off their armour or lie down to rest. They took food as they stood.

In the morning the array of the Goths had been much the same as that of the Imperial army, but when they returned to fight in the afternoon, Totila adopted an entirely different plan. He placed all his cavalry in front and all his infantry

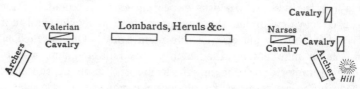

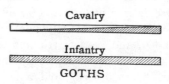

behind. His idea seems to have been that his best chance was to attempt to break the enemy ranks by a concentrated charge of all his horse, and then bring up his infantry (probably few in number) to take advantage of the confusion which his cavalry had wrought. And he issued the extraordinary command that all the troops alike should discard the use of all weapons except their spears.

To meet the tactics of the Goths Narses made a slight change in his dispositions. The two large bodies of archers on the wings,[1] which had faced the enemy full front, were now turned half round so as to form crescents facing each other; and when the Gothic cavalry charged they were assailed from both sides

---

[1] They must have been on elevated ground above the plain, or they would have been swept away by the Gothic cavalry. Delbrück, *Kriegskunst*, ii. 375.

by showers of arrows and suffered considerable losses before they came to grips with the main line. The battle was fierce, but apparently short, and towards evening the Goths gave way and were gradually pressed back on the infantry who had hitherto taken no part in the fighting, and now, instead of opening a way for the cavalry to pass through their ranks and themselves facing the enemy, turned and retreated with them. The retreat soon became a flight. About 6000 were slain ; many were taken alive, to be put to death afterwards ; all the rest fled as they could.

The description of this battle, which we owe to the historian Procopius, and which he doubtless derived from an eyewitness, is so deficient in details that it is difficult to form any definite opinion as to the merits of the combatants. Above all, we do not know the numbers of either army. We are not told how Totila and his ablest general Teïas behaved during the action, nor whether the wings or the centre of the Imperialists were the more heavily engaged. Praise is given to the bravery of the barbarian troops of Narses and of " some of the Romans," but the military critics of the day seem to have ascribed the swift discomfiture of the Goths largely to the strange order of their king that the spear only was to be used. We can, however, divine that Totila's generalship was deficient and that, even if his forces were inferior in number, he might have made better use of them.

But in spite of the slightness of our information as to the course of the battle, it is clear that Narses displayed exceptional military talent and deserves full credit for his victory. His plan was original, differing entirely from the tactics employed by Belisarius in the Persian campaigns. He opposed unmounted troops to the mounted troops of the enemy, and used his bowmen to weaken and disconcert the charge of the cavalry. Thus aided, the barbarian auxiliaries did what the Roman infantry had failed to do on the field of Hadrianople, and resisted the shock of the Gothic horsemen. The battle has been described as " the first experiment in the combination of pike and bow which modern history shows," and reminds us of the battle of Creçy which was won by similar tactics.[1]

Totila himself had fled in the dark and there were various

---

[1] Oman, *Art of War*, p. 35. Tacticians of the time had contemplated battles fought by Roman infantry against enemy cavalry ; cp. the passage of Urbicius quoted in Pseudo-Maurice, *Strat.* xii. 24.

stories as to what befell him. According to one tale, accompanied by four or five of his followers he was pursued by Asbad the Gepid leader, and some others who were unaware of his identity. Overtaking him Asbad was about to strike when a Gothic youth cried, " Dog, will you smite your master ? " The Gepid drove his spear with all his might into Totila's body, but was himself wounded by one of the king's companions. The Goths dragged their wounded lord for about seven miles, not halting till they reached Caprae, a village not far from Tadinum. Here he died and was hastily buried. His fate and place of sepulture were revealed to the Romans by a Gothic woman ; the body was exhumed and identified; the blood-stained garments and the cap adorned with gems which he had worn were taken to Narses, who sent them to Constantinople, where they were laid at the feet of the Emperor as a visible proof that the enemy who had so long defied his power was no more.[1]

A leader who has fought a long fight in a not ignoble cause and failed in the end will always arouse some sympathy and pity, with whatever satisfaction we may view his failure. The sudden reversal of Totila's fortune after an almost unbroken career of success had just the elements of tragedy which appealed even to the imagination of his enemies. He had revived the cause of his nation when it seemed utterly lost and restored their hope, and in a struggle of nine years, in which he displayed untiring energy, unwavering confidence, and some political capacity, had reconquered the whole of Italy except three or four towns. But this long run of success does not argue that he possessed transcendent talents. He owed it to the fact that the Emperor starved his military forces in Italy, refused to send the necessary supplies of money and men, and at first did not even appoint a supreme commander. As soon as Justinian decided, after the return of Belisarius, to make a serious effort to end the war and adopted proper measures for the purpose, the situation began immediately to change, and all that Totila had achieved in nine years was undone in two. But though the weakness and mistakes of his enemies were chiefly responsible for Totila's fame, though he did not possess military genius of a

---

[1] Here John Mal. xviii. p. 486 supplements Procopius. The passage was transcribed by Theophanes, *sub* A.M. 6044, who adds a sentence which evidently belonged to the original text of Malalas but is omitted in ours (καὶ ἐρρίφησαν εἰς τοὺς πόδας τοῦ βασιλέως ἐπὶ σεκρήτου).

high order, and was capable of such a political blunder as the abandonment of Rome when he had captured it, he will always be remembered as one of the great figures in the German heroic age. Some modern writers have idealised him as a romantic hero, distinguished among all his barbarian fellows by chivalrous sentiments and noble behaviour towards his foes, gentle and humane in his instincts. It is difficult to find much in the record of his acts to justify such a conception of the man. He was clear-sighted enough to realise that it was good policy to conciliate the Italians and to attract to his standards deserters from the Imperial army, and for these purposes he often showed a moderation which in time of war was unusual. Perhaps his considerate treatment of the inhabitants of Naples, which the historian Procopius ungrudgingly admired, has won for him a reputation which his conduct on other occasions can hardly be said to bear out. But his friendliness to the Neapolitans was plainly dictated by policy. It was to reward them for the obstinate resistance they had offered to Belisarius eight years before, and Totila intended it to be contrasted with the punishment which he hoped to inflict upon the Sicilians who had received Belisarius with open arms. In the practice of deliberate cruelties can it be said that there is much to choose between this Ostrogoth and other leaders of his race and age ? What instinct of clemency can we attribute to the man who mutilated Demetrius at Naples, who cut off the hands of the bishop from Porto, who put Isaac the Armenian to death, who did not spare his unhappy captive Gilacius, who shamefully mutilated Chalazar ? What are we to say of the assassination of Cyprian at Perusia ? Can we call him humane who suffered the bishop and inhabitants of Tibur to be done to death in such atrocious fashion that the historian declines to describe the treatment ? Did he treat the inhabitants of Rome as leniently as Alaric or Gaiseric ? Narses had no illusions about his character, and it was well for him that, when Totila named a day for the great battle which was to be fought between them, he did not imagine him to be a pure chevalier, but knew him for an ordinary perfidious barbarian and took corresponding precautions.[1]

---

[1] Totila's reputation for cruelty is illustrated by the story told by Pope Gregory I. (*Dial.* 3, c. 11) that he condemned Cerbonius, bishop of Populonium, to be thrown to a bear because he had given shelter to some

§ 11. *Battle of Mons Lactarius* (A.D. 552)

The first act of Narses after his great success, for which he piously ascribed all the credit to the Deity, was to dismiss his savage allies, the Lombards, who, as soon as the victory was won, were devoting themselves to the congenial occupations of arson and rape. He rewarded them with large sums of gold, and committed to Valerian the task of conducting them to the Italian frontier. When Valerian had parted from these undesirable friends, he encamped outside Verona and parleyed with the Gothic garrison. The Goths were willing to capitulate, but the Franks who were firmly stationed in the Venetian province intervened and the negotiations were broken off. Valerian withdrew to the Po, and Narses ordered him to remain there to watch the movements of the Goths, who had not yet given up their cause as lost. The remnant of Totila's army had fled with Teïas northward to Ticinum. There Teïas was elected king,[1] and he hoped with the help of the Franks to restore the fortunes of his people. He had at his disposal the treasures which Totila had prudently left in Ticinum.

In the meantime Narses himself had advanced on Rome. On his way he occupied Narnia and Spoleto, and sent a detachment to take Perusia. The Gothic garrison in Rome was much too small to attempt to defend the great circuit of the city, and Totila had constructed a little fortress round the Mausoleum of Hadrian by building a new wall attached to the external wall. When the army of Narses arrived, the Goths made some attempt to hold the fortifications wherever they were attacked, but the Imperialists soon succeeded in scaling the wall with ladders and opening the gates. The garrison then retreated into the inner fortress; some escaped to Portus. But seeing that further defence was useless they surrendered on condition that their lives were spared. This was the fifth time that Rome had been assaulted and captured during the war.

---

soldiers of the Imperial army. Totila expected to enjoy the spectacle of the execution, but the bear lay down and licked the bishop's feet. Though Gregory appeals to survivors at Rome who witnessed the amazing incident, we can hardly credit this version of Androcles and the lion. But it shows Totila's reputation.

[1] His father's name was Fritigern. He is Theia (also Teia, Thela, Thila) on his coins, which have the head of Anastasius. Wroth, p. 95 *sqq.*

Narses sent the keys to the Emperor. Soon afterwards Portus surrendered.

The Goths now showed themselves, without any reserve, in their true colours. (1) In Campania they put to death the senators who had been sent there by Totila and now proposed to return to Rome. (2) Before Totila went forth to meet Narses he had selected three hundred boys from Roman families of repute and sent them to the north of Italy as hostages. Teïas seized them and slew them all. (3) It will be remembered that Ragnaris, the commander in Tarentum, had agreed to surrender on conditions which Pacurius, the commander of Hydruntum, had gone in person to submit to the Emperor ; in the meantime he had given hostages. Learning that Teïas was resolved to renew the struggle and counted on the help of the Franks, Ragnaris changed his plans. When Pacurius returned from Constantinople,[1] he asked him to send a few Roman soldiers to conduct him safely to Hydruntum and thence by sea to Constantinople. Pacurius sent fifty men. Ragnaris imprisoned them and then informed Pacurius that they would not be released until the Gothic hostages had been restored. The Roman commander lost no time in marching to Tarentum with all his forces. At his approach Ragnaris put the fifty men to death and marched out to meet him. The Goths were defeated and Ragnaris fled to Acherontia. These circumstances of the recovery of Tarentum deserved to be recorded as an illustration of the character of the Ostrogoths.

Narses meanwhile had not been idle. He sent a force to reduce Centumcellae, and another into Campania to lay siege to Cumae. The importance of this fortress lay in the fact that Totila had deposited in it all the Gothic treasure that was not stored at Ticinum, and left it in the custody of his brother Aligern.[2] When the news that this store was in immediate danger reached Teïas, who had been waiting in the vain hope that the Franks would provide an army to help him, he determined to make an attempt to rescue Cumae. It was a long

---

[1] The journey to Constantinople and back need not have taken much more than a month, as the business need have caused no delay.

[2] Agathias, i. 8, records the name, but says he was the youngest brother

of Teïas. Procopius says he was the brother of Totila, *B.G.* iv. 34. 19. Cumae is about 200 kilometres from Rome, so that an army leaving Rome just after the middle of July would have arrived before the end of the month.

march from Ticinum to Campania, and even a small army,
moving more rapidly than usual, could not accomplish it in
much less than a month. The shortest route was through
Etruria, and Narses sent a force under John to watch the Etrurian
roads. But Teïas did not choose the shortest route. His object
was to avoid the enemy, and he went by devious and roundabout
ways, finally following the coast road of the Hadriatic. He
must have crossed the peninsula by Beneventum, where he
could proceed either by Capua or by Salerno to the neighbourhood of Naples.[1]

Narses, when he found that the enemy had eluded both John,
who was guarding the western roads, and Valerian, who had
captured Petra Pertusa[2] and was thus master of the Via Flaminia,
recalled both these generals and proceeded with all his forces
to Campania. When Teïas at last reached the southern foothills of Vesuvius, near Nuceria, he found a Roman army drawn
up on the bank of the Draco.

This river, now the Sarno, runs into the bay of Naples, north of
the Sorrento peninsula. The remnant of the Gothic fleet was
assembled in the bay of Naples. As Teïas might expect that the
land approaches to Cumae, north of Naples, would be guarded,
his plan probably was to embark his troops near Sorrento and
reach Cumae by sea. There was no fleet at hand to oppose
him, and the plan was only foiled by the vigilance and good
intelligence service of the Roman general, who was just in time
to prevent him from reaching the sea.

The armies remained for weeks[3] facing each other on either
bank of the narrow stream, which neither infantry nor cavalry
could ford on account of the steepness of the banks, the archers
carrying on a desultory battle. There was indeed a bridge on

---

[1] The possible route of Teïas is
discussed by Körbs (op. cit. p. 82),
who calculates that he had about
814 kilometres to cover, that he
probably did at least 30 kilometres a
day, that he started soon after the
middle of July and reached Campania
after the middle of August.

[2] B.G. iv. 34. 24; but the Petra
Pertusa which is mentioned (ib. 16)
along with Nepi and Porto seems to
have been another place, also on the
Via Flaminia, but quite close to Rome,

north of Prima Porta. See Tomas-
setti, La Campagna Romana, iii. pp.
138, 260-261.

[3] Two months, acc. to Procopius,
iv. 35. 11. This must be a considerable exaggeration if Agnellus is right
in his dating of the battle to Oct. 1
(in Kal. Octobris, c. 79). Teïas could
not at the earliest have reached
Campania before the middle of
August; it seems more likely that he
arrived at the end of the month. If
Procopius is accurate the date of
Agnellus is wrong.

which the Goths who held it erected towers and assailed their enemies with bolts from *ballistae*. Teïas succeeded in getting into touch with his fleet and it was able to supply him with provisions. The situation was changed when Imperial warships which Narses summoned began to come in great numbers from Sicily and other places. The Gothic naval commander, anticipating their arrival, surrendered his fleet. The food-supply of the army was thus cut off, and at the same time it began to suffer from the play of the engines which Narses installed in wooden towers along his bank of the stream. Teïas broke up his camp and retreated to the shelter of the mountain which overlooks the valley. This mountain, belonging to the St. Angelo range, was known as Mons Lactarius and still retains the name as Monte Lettere. On the slopes of this hill the Goths were safe from attack, which the nature of the ground would have rendered too dangerous an enterprise, but they found themselves worse off for food, and they soon repented their change of ground. At length they resolved to make a surprise attack upon their foes. It was their only chance.

They appeared so unexpectedly in the valley that the Romans had no time to form themselves in the regular array prescribed by military handbooks.[1] The Goths had left their horses behind and advanced as a solid mass of infantry. The Romans received them in the same formation.[2] In the battle there was no room for tactics, it was a sheer trial of personal strength, bravery, and skill. The Gothic king, a few warriors by his side, led the assault, and, the Romans recognising him and thinking that if he fell his followers who were formed in a very deep phalanx would not continue the contest, he became the mark for their most dexterous lancers and javelin-throwers. It was a Homeric combat, and the historian has described it vividly. Teïas stood covered by his shield, which received the spears that were hurled or thrust at him, and then suddenly attacking laid many of his assailants low. When he saw that the shield was full of spears he gave it to one of his squires, who handed him another. He is

[1] According to local tradition the scene of the battle was at Pozzo dei Goti, a kilometre west of Angri at the foot of Monte Lettere.

[2] Procopius does not explain why the Goths should have advanced on foot, or why the Romans should have dismounted. Delbrück (*op. cit.* 382) conjectures that the Romans had constructed fortifications (earthworks and ditch ?) to blockade the Goths, and thus the Goths were obliged to attack on foot, and the Romans to defend the line on foot.

said to have fought thus for a third part of the day, then his strength failed. There were twelve spears sticking in his shield, and he found he could not move it as easily as he would. Without retreating a foot or moving to right or left, smiting his foes with his right hand, he called the name of a squire. A new shield was brought, but in the instant in which he was exchanging it for the old his chest was exposed, and a lucky javelin wounded him mortally.[1]

The head of the fallen hero was at once severed from his body and raised aloft on a pole that all his host might know that he had fallen. But the expectation of the Romans that their enemies would abandon the struggle was not fulfilled. The Goths did not flee like fawns, nor lay down their arms. They were animated by a spirit of desperation, and in a very different temper from that which they had displayed in the last battle of Totila. They fought on till nightfall, and on the next day the fray was resumed, and again lasted till the evening. Then, seeing that they could not win and recognising that God was against them, they sent some of their leaders to Narses to announce that they would yield, not, however, to live in subjection to the Emperor, but to retire somewhere outside the Roman frontiers where they could live independently. They asked to be allowed to retire in peace, and to take with them any money or belongings that they had individually deposited in Italian fortresses.

On the advice of John, who made a strong plea for moderation, these conditions were accepted, on the undertaking of the Goths that they would not again make war on the Empire.[2]

§ 12. The Franco-Alamannic Invasion (A.D. 553-554) : Battle of Capua

The shields of Teïas had not availed to avert the doom of his people. He was their last king. The kingdom of the Ostrogoths went down on the hard-fought field under Mount Lactarius. But there was still fighting to be done. The great defeat did not lead to the immediate surrender of the strongholds which

[1] The whole account of the first part of the battle seems fanciful and improbable. The deep phalanx of the Goths plays no part in the action, and Teïas alone occupies the stage. His heroism is assuredly a fact, but the narrative of Procopius cannot be accepted as a true account of the battle.

[2] The *History of Procopius* ends with the victory of Mons Lactarius, and the story is taken up by Agathias.

were still held by Gothic garrisons. There was Cumae, there was Centumcellae, there were a number of towns in Tuscany, and there was North Italy beyond the Po. Narses had still much strenuous military work before him. He might have hoped to complete the reduction of the land by the following summer, but his plans were disconcerted by the appearance of a new and more barbarous enemy upon the scene.

Teïas had invoked the assistance of the Franks. The answer of the young king Theodebald [1] to the pleadings of his envoys was unfavourable. The Franks had no mind to embark on a war for the sake of the Ostrogoths; they coveted Italy for themselves,[2] but at the moment they judged neutrality to be the best policy. But the neutrality was only official. Two chieftains of their subjects the Alamanni, Leutharis and Buccelin, who were brothers, formed the plan of invading Italy. Ostensibly Theodebald did not approve of this act of aggression, but he took no steps to prevent it.[3] The two adventurers raised a host of 75,000, in which Franks as well as Alamanni served, and descended into Italy in the spring of A.D. 553, confident that they could overwhelm Narses, for whose military talents, eunuch and chamberlain as he was, they professed supreme contempt.[4]

Narses spent the winter months in besieging Cumae, but Aligern and the little fortress held out obstinately. When all his assaults and devices failed, he left a small investing force, and proceeded to Central Italy, where he found the Gothic garrisons ready to make terms. Centumcellae surrendered, and the Tuscan towns, Florence, Volaterrae, Pisa, and Luna did likewise. Lucca alone bargained for a delay; if no help came to them before thirty days expired, surrender was promised, and

---

[1] Theodebald married Vuldetrada, daughter of Wacho, king of the Lombards. Her mother was Austriguna, a Gepid princess. Gregory of Tours, *Hist. Fr.* iv. 9.

[2] Procopius, *B.G.* iv. 34. 18.

[3] Agathias says (i. 6) that the king was opposed to the invasion. On the other hand, the invaders sent him a portion of the treasures which they collected in Italy (Gregory of Tours, *H.F.* iii. 32; Paulus Diac. *II. Lang.* ii. 2). Agathias has much to tell us about the Franks. I conjecture that he gathered his information from

the ambassadors of King Sigebert, who visited Constantinople in A.D. 566. It was their cue to represent the invasion of Italy as not countenanced by Theodebald. Rastia, in which the Alamanni had been settled by Theoderic, had been abandoned by the Goths (Totila ?), and Theodebert had brought it under his rule (Agathias *ib.*).

[4] Agathias is the main source for the invasion, but we have also brief accounts in western sources: Marius of Aventicum, *Chron.*, *sub* 555, 556; Gregory of Tours, *Hist. Fr.* iii. 32, iv. 9; Paulus Diac. *Hist. Lang.* ii. 2.

hostages were given. The help which the Goths of Lucca looked for was the arrival of the Franks, who had already crossed the Alps. It was the imminence of their invasion that had probably decided Narses to march northward, and he had sent the greater part of his army under John and Valerian to guard the passages of the Po.

The thirty days passed and the garrison of Lucca refused to abide by their agreement. Some of his officers, in their indignation at this breach of faith, suggested that the hostages should be put to death. Narses was not a Goth; he would not commit the injustice of executing innocent men. But he led them forth, with their hands bound across their bodies and their heads bowed, within sight of the walls, and proclaimed that they would be slain if the town were not surrendered. Thin pieces of wood, wrapped in pieces of cloth, had been fastened on the backs of the hostages from the neck to the waist, and, when the garrison gave no sign of yielding, guardsmen stepped forward and drawing their swords brought them down on the well-protected necks. The victims, who had been let into the secret, fell forward, as if they had been decapitated, and their bodies feigned the spasms and contortions of death. The spectators on the wall set up howls and wails, for the hostages belonged to the noblest families; mothers and affianced brides rushed along the battlements rending their garments. All cried shame on the bloody cruelty of Narses.

Narses sent a herald to address them.[1] " You have yourselves to blame," he said, " for the shameless violation of your oaths. But if you will come to your senses even now it will be well for you; these men will come to life again and you will suffer no harm." The Goths had no doubt that he was deceiving them, but they readily swore that if he showed them the hostages alive they would at once capitulate. Then at the general's command all the dead stood up together and showed themselves safe and sound to their friends, who were divided between incredulity and joy. But incredulity prevailed, and then Narses, with a magnanimity which was well calculated, set his prisoners free, and allowed them, without imposing any conditions, to return to their people in the town. They went back loud in his

---

[1] Ταῦτα δὲ αὐτῶν ἐπιβοώντων . . . ἔφη ὁ Ναρσῆς (Agathias, i. 43); a herald   is not mentioned but is clearly to be presumed.

praises, but Lucca did not surrender. Oaths and solemn engagements were of no account in the eyes of the Goths, who were elated with new hopes by the successful advance of the Franks. For Buccelin and his Alamanni had won possession of Parma, and had cut to pieces a force of Heruls who, under a brave but rash leader, attempted to recover it. All the Goths in the Ligurian and Aemilian provinces had rallied to the invaders, and it is probable that these were in command at Ticinum itself. John and Valerian, upon whom Narses relied to keep them back from Etruria while he was engaged in reducing Lucca, had withdrawn to Faventia. Lucca, however, he was determined to take, and he prosecuted the siege with vigour. It would have surrendered soon if Frank officers had not succeeded in entering the town and stiffening the defence. But at length the will of the majority prevailed, and the Luccans opened their gates and received the army of Narses, who had agreed not to punish them for their ill-faith.

The siege had lasted three months, and it was now the end of autumn. Narses went to Ravenna to arrange the dispositions of the troops for the winter, and presently Aligern, the Gothic commander of Cumae, which had held out all this time, arrived at Classis and gave him the keys of the town. Aligern had come to the conclusion that the Franks had no intention of restoring the Ostrogothic power, and that whether they succeeded or not in conquering Italy, in neither event had he the least chance of inheriting the throne of Teïas. He therefore decided to resist no longer but to become a subject of the Empire.

Narses spent the winter in Rome, and in the spring (A.D. 554) his army, which had been dispersed among the forts and towns in the Ravennate region for the winter, was collected and reunited at Rome. We do not know his reasons for this retreat, which meant the abandonment of Etruria and the Hadriatic provinces to the enemy. He could rely with some confidence on his garrisons in the great fortresses, but the open country and unwalled towns were at the mercy of the invader.

The host of Buccelin and Leutharis moved southward, without haste, plundering and destroying. When they approached Rome they divided into two separate armies, of which the larger under Buccelin, avoiding Rome itself, marched through Campania, Lucania, and Bruttii to the Straits of

Messina,[1] while Leutharis led the other through Apulia and Calabria as far as Hydruntum. The provinces were systematically plundered, and an enormous booty was collected. In this work of pillage and devastation there was a marked difference between the conduct of the Franks and their Alamannic comrades. The Franks, who were orthodox Christians, showed respect for churches, but the heathen Alamanni were restrained by no scruples from carrying off the ecclesiastical plate and pulling down the roofs of the sacred buildings.[2]

When he had reached the limits of Calabria, Leutharis laden with spoils decided to return home to enjoy them. He had no political ambitions, and his one thought was to get safely away with his wealth and run no further risks. He marched along the coast as far as Fanum, but there his troops suffered considerable losses through an attack by the Roman garrison of Pisaurum, and the greater part of the booty was lost. Leaving the coast he struck into the Apennines and reached the Po safe but dispirited.[3] At the Venetian town of Ceneta,[4] where he took up his quarters to rest, a virulent plague broke out in the army, and Leutharis himself was one of its victims.

His brother Buccelin was more enterprising and ambitious. He had professed to the Goths that his object was to restore their kingdom, and many of them doubtless attached themselves to his army in his southern march. He fell under the influence of their flatteries ; they told him that they would proclaim him king if he drove Narses out of Italy ; and he was finally persuaded to risk everything in a battle with the army which he had hitherto aimed at avoiding.

He returned to Campania and encamped on the banks of the Vulturnus [5] close to Casilinum and Capua, which are only a few

---

[1] Gregory (iii. 32) says that Buccelin defeated Narses in a battle, and then occupied Sicily. These statements may be due to exaggerated rumours derived from Buccelin's report of his successes. It is probable that when he reached Rhegium, he despatched a message to Theodebald.

[2] Agathias (i. 7) describes the nature worship of the Alamanni, their cults of trees, rivers, and hills, but thinks that it will soon disappear through the influence of the Franks.

[3] Οὔτω τε ἰθὺ Αἰμιλείας καὶ ᾿Αλπι-

σκοτίας ἐλθόντες ; here Agathias (ii. 3) betrays his ignorance of Italian geography. He supposed that the district of Alpes Cottiae was adjacent to Venetia.

[4] Paulus, loc. cit., says near lake Garda, between Verona and Trent. Ceneta, now Ceneda, lies between Oderzo and Feltre.

[5] Agathias (ii. 4) calls it the Casulinus. Paulus says the battle was fought at a place called Tannetum (al. Cannetum).

miles apart. Casilinum is the modern Capua, and the ancient
Capua is the modern village of S. Maria di Capua Vetere. On
one side the river formed the wall of his camp, on the other side
he fortified it securely.[1] He had some hopes that he would
soon be reinforced, for his brother had promised that when he
had reached Venetia he would send back his troops. As soon
as Narses learned that Buccelin had occupied this position at
Capua he marched from Rome with his army, numbering about
18,000, and encamped not far from the enemy. The battle
which ensued was probably fought across the Appian Way
which passed through Capua and crossed the river at Casilinum.

The course of the battle was affected by an accident. One
of the Herul captains killed his servant for some delinquency,
and when Narses called him to account asserted that masters
had the power of life and death over their slaves and that he
would do the same thing again. He was put to death by the
command of Narses, to the great indignation of the Heruls,
who withdrew from the camp and said they would not fight.
Narses drew up his line of battle without them. He placed his
cavalry on the two wings and all the infantry in the centre.
There was a wood on the left, and Valerian and Artabanes,
who commanded on that side, were directed to keep a part of
their forces concealed in the wood till the enemy attacked.
Narses himself commanded on the right. The leader of the
Heruls, Sindual, who was burning to fight, implored Narses to
wait until he could persuade his followers to return to the battlefield ; Narses declined, but agreed to reserve a place for them,
where they could fall in, if they arrived late. Accordingly he
left an open space in the middle of the infantry.

Meanwhile two Heruls had deserted to the enemy, and
persuaded Buccelin that his chance was to attack at once, as
the Romans were in consternation at the defection of the Herul
troops. Buccelin had drawn up his army, which consisted
entirely of infantry, in the shape of a deep column, which should
penetrate like a wedge through the hostile lines.[2] In this array

---

[1] Agathias says that his army
amounted to about 30,000, and that
the numbers were considerably
reduced by dysentery, attributed to
the immoderate use of ripe grapes.
The figure of 30,000 is probably
too high.

[2] Agathias (ii. 8) describes the
formation as a triangular ($\delta\epsilon\lambda\tau\omega\tau\hat{\varphi}$)
wedge, with the point towards the
enemy, and compares it to the "head
of a boar." It was simply the cuneus
described by Vegetius (iii. 19):
cuneus dicitur multitudo peditum,

the Franks advanced, armed with missile lances, swords, and axes,[1] confident that they would sweep all before them at the first rush. They penetrated into the central space which was to have been occupied by the Heruls, dislodging the outer ranks of the Roman infantry on either side. Narses quietly issued orders to his wings to face about, and the enemy were caught between the cross fire of the cavalry, who were all armed with bows. The Franks were now facing both ways. The archers on the right wing aimed at the backs of those who were fighting with the infantry on the left, the archers on the left wing at the backs of those who were engaged with the right. The barbarians did not understand what was happening. They saw the foemen just in front of them with whom they were fighting hand to hand, but they could not see the enemies who from far behind were raining arrows upon their backs. Their ranks were gradually mown down, and then Sindual and his Heruls appeared upon the scene. The defeat of the Franks was already certain ; it was now to be annihilation. Buccelin was slain and only a handful escaped alive from the stricken field. The Roman losses were small.[2] It will be noticed that Narses won this, his third victory, by a tactical plan similar to that which he had employed in the battle with Totila.

The Italians had been terror-stricken by the ruthless deeds of the northern barbarians, and they were wild with joy at the news of their utter destruction. Narses and thoughtful people had little hope that the brilliant victory of Capua had dispelled the danger. They reflected that the foes whose corpses were strewn on the banks or floated in the waters of the Vulturnus were such a small fraction of the Frank people and their dependents, that their fate would provoke rather than intimidate. They expected that a greater host would soon come down to

---

quae iuncta cum acie primo angustior deinde latior procedit et aduersariorum ordines rumpit, quia a pluribus in unum locum tela mittuntur. Quam rem milites nominant caput porcinum. There must have been the same number of men in each rank of the column, but in advancing the men of the front ranks drew closer together, and the columns became a trapezium instead of a rectangle, with the smallest side towards the foe.

[1] See Agathias ii. 5 for Frank armour (cp. Sidonius, *Epp.* iv. 20). The axe was called *francisca*, the lance for hurling *angon*. The Franks generally fought naked to the waist, with leather trousers, without breastplate or greaves, and bareheaded, though a few had helmets.

[2] Agathias says only five Franks escaped, and that only eighty Romans were killed ; Marius that Buccelin *cum omni exercitu suo interiit.*

avenge the fallen and restore German prestige.[1] These fears
were not realised, as they might well have been if Theodebert had
been still alive ; his feeble son Theodebald, who suffered from
a congenital disease, died in the following year. Narses was
able to complete in peace the settlement of Italy.

The winter months which followed the battle of Capua were
spent in besieging Campsa, a strong place in the Apennines,
where seven thousand Goths had established themselves under
the leadership of Ragnaris, the man who had behaved so
treacherously at Tarentum.[2] Campsa has been identified with
Conza, about fifty miles east of Naples. Its position defied
assault and Narses sat down to blockade it, but a large stock
of provisions had been laid in. At the beginning of spring
(A.D. 555), Ragnaris proposed to Narses that they should meet
and discuss terms. They met between the fortress and the
camp, and Ragnaris adopted a high tone towards the Roman
general. Narses refused to agree to his proposals, and he retired
in great wrath. When he was near the wall of the fort he
turned round, drew his bow, and aimed an arrow at the general
who was returning to his lines. It missed its mark, but one of
the guardsmen who were with Narses had a surer aim, and
transfixed the treacherous Goth. He fell dead, and the garrison
surrendered immediately and were sent to Constantinople.

All Italy south of the Po was now restored to the Imperial
authority. Of the subjugation of the Transpadane provinces,
where Goths and Franks were still in possession, we have no
record. It was a slow business, and Verona and Brixia were
not recovered till A.D. 562. In November of that year Narses
sent the keys of their gates to Justinian.[3]

§ 13. *The Settlement of Italy*

In the meantime Narses had been engaged in establishing
an ordered administration in Italy, and restoring the life of the

---

[1] See the speech of Narses to his
army in Agathias, ii. 12.

[2] There can hardly be any doubt
as to the identity.

[3] John Mal. xviii. p. 492 – Theophanes, A.M. 6055. With the recovery of Verona and the end of
the warfare in Venetia we may
perhaps connect the defeat of the
Frank Aming and the Goth Widin,
of whom we hear in Paul Diac. (*l.c.*)
and Menander (*De leg. Rom.*, *fr.* 2, p.
171). Aming opposed a Roman army
which was about to cross the Adige.
Narses sent envoys warning him
to depart, as a truce had been con-

provinces and their cities which had suffered so much through the long war. Though officially he held a military post, he acted as viceroy, and was evidently supreme over the civil functionaries as well as over the army. He had at his side a Prefect, Antiochus, at the head of the civil service, but it is significant that the title of Antiochus was not Praetorian Prefect, but simply Prefect of Italy.

The general lines for the reorganisation were laid down by the Emperor in a law which he addressed to Narses and Antiochus in August A.D. 554, and which he described as a Pragmatic Sanction.[1] It was supremely important for the Italians to know immediately how far the Imperial Government would recognise the acts of the Gothic rulers, particularly in regard to property. This law provides that henceforward the enactments of the Imperial Code shall apply to Italy as well as to the other parts of the Empire. All grants that were made to individuals or corporations by Athalaric, Amalasuntha, and Theodahad shall be valid, but all grants made by the tyrant Totila are annulled. All contracts made between Romans in besieged towns during the war shall remain valid.[2] In many cases during the war and the Frank invasion people had been forced to flee from their homes and their property had been occupied by others ; it is enacted that their property must be restored to them. The old regulations allocating funds for the repair of public buildings in Rome, for dredging the bed of the Tiber, for the repair of the aqueducts are confirmed, and doles of food are to be supplied to the Roman populace as of old. A remarkable innovation is made in regard to provincial governors. They are no longer to be appointed from above, but to be elected for each province from among its residents by the bishops and magnates. This change may have had some arguments in its favour, but

---

cluded between the Empire and the Franks. Aming replied that he would not retreat so long as his hand could wield a javelin. He had come to the assistance of a Goth named Widin (possibly the commander in Verona). A battle ensued ; Aming was slain by the sword of Narses, Widin made prisoner and sent to Constantinople.

[1] Considerable extracts are pre-

served, and will be found in editions of the Novellae (e.g. App. vii. in Kroll's ed.). Another law, relating to debts incurred before the Frank invasion, and the rights of creditors, is incompletely preserved (App. viii.). For the title and powers of the Prefect of Italy see Diehl, Études sur l'adm. byz. 157 seq.

[2] § 7 quod enim ritu perfectum est, per fortuitos belli casus subverti subtilitatis non patitur ratio.

it was evidently conceived in the interests of the large landed proprietors and must have increased their local power. In other regulations we see the desire to relieve the burden of taxation so far as was deemed compatible with Imperial needs. The boundaries of the provinces [1] and the general system of the civil service [2] remained as they had been before the war. It is to be observed, however, that Sicily was not included in Italy. It remained under its own Praetor, who was independent of the Imperial authorities at Ravenna, and from whose courts the appeal was to the Quaestor of the Sacred Palace at Constantinople.[3] Sardinia and Corsica were under the viceroy of Africa.

Narses administered Italy for thirteen years after the defeat of the Frank invaders, presiding over the work of reconstruction.[4] The walls and gates of Rome were restored, and one of the few memorials of the time records the rebuilding of a bridge across the Anio, which had been destroyed by the Goths, about two miles from the city on the Via Salaria.[5] Perhaps the most troublesome concern with which the Patrician was called upon to deal was the danger of ecclesiastical strife arising out of the Ecumenical Council of Constantinople in A.D. 553. The circumstances of that assembly will be described in another chapter. The Pope Vigilius who had been forced against his will to subscribe to its decisions died on his way back to Rome on January 7, A.D. 555, and his archdeacon Pelagius was, at the instance of the Emperor, consecrated as his successor on April 13. Pelagius was unpopular in Italy ; he was suspected of having in some way caused the death of Vigilius, and only two Italian bishops could be found willing to consecrate him. Narses was present at the ceremony at St. Peter's, and Pelagius took the Gospels in his hand and swore that he was innocent.[6] His oath

---

[1] A new province, *Alpes Cottiae*, seems to have been cut off from Liguria ; Diehl, *op. cit.* p. 3.

[2] As to the meagre evidence for the *vicarius Italiae* (residing at Milan) and the *vicarius urbis Romae* see Diehl, *op. cit.* p. 161.

[3] Cp. above, p. 216 ; Diehl, p. 169.

[4] His usual title was simply *patricius* (see next note ; Pelagius, *Ep.* 2, *P.L.* lxix. 393 *patricius et dux in Italia*).

[5] It was destroyed in 1798. The inscription (*C.I.L.* vi. 1199) is dated

in 565 and records how Narses *expraeposito sacri palatii, excons. atque patricius* after his Gothic victory, *ipsis eorum regibus celeritate mirabili conflictu publico superatis atque prostratis, libertate urbis Romae ac totius Italiae restituta* restored the bridge *a nefandissimo Totila tyranno destructum*. It concludes with eight verses of which the last two are

qui potuit rigidas Gothorum subdere mentes,
  hic docuit durum flumina ferre iugum.

[6] See his life in *Lib. Pont.*

calmed the popular feeling, but, if he had had his way, he would
soon have created a dangerous schism in the Italian Church.   In
northern Italy particularly, the opinion of the bishops was
against the decisions of the recent Council, while the new Pope
was determined to enforce them and expel from their sees those
who refused to accept them.   He wrote repeatedly to Narses
requesting or rather requiring of him to use the secular arm
against the contumacious bishops.[1] Narses wisely declined to
do anything, and the Imperial government, in the interests of
peace, adopted throughout the Empire the policy of suspending
the anathemas of the Council and allowing time to heal the
discord which the controversy had caused.   This unusual
moderation, which we may probably attribute to the advice
of Narses, was successful.   If the matter had rested with the
Pope, the Church in Italy would have been rent in twain at a
moment when concord and peace were imperatively needed.

The secluded city of the marshes continued to be the seat of
government in Italy under Justinian and his successors until
it was.lost to the Empire in the eighth century.   The Empress
Placidia had lavished money in making it a treasure-house of
art ; the barbarian king Theoderic had lived up to her example ;
and after its recovery by their armies, Justinian and Theodora,
who knew it only by reputation, were eager to associate their
names with the artistic monuments of Ravenna.

The octagonal church of St. Vitalis, close to Placidia's
mausoleum, had been designed and begun under the regency
of Amalasuntha, and the building was continued during the
war, perhaps by the Ostrogoths themselves.   But it was completed and decorated under the auspices of Justinian and
Theodora, who made it peculiarly their own,—a monument of
the Imperial restoration.   It was consecrated by the archbishop
Maximian in A.D. 547, the year before the death of the Empress,
and in the mosaic decoration of the apse the most striking
pictures are those of the two sovrans facing each other offering
their gifts to the church.   But it was not only by their portraits
that they appropriated St. Vitalis.   Justinian gave it his own
impress in the scheme of the Scriptural scenes which are portrayed.
They are not simply, as in the other Ravennate churches, intended
to illustrate sacred history.   The motive is theological, they **are**

---

[1] Pelagius, *Epp.* ii. 4 (*P.G.* lxix. pp. 392, 397).

designed to inculcate doctrine, probably the orthodox view on
the question which was agitating the world, the two natures of
Christ.[1] The effects are fine, but these mosaics are far from
possessing the charm of those which adorn the sepulchral church
of Placidia.

Another church which had been begun by the Goths during
the war and was left to their conquerors to complete was dedicated
two years later (A.D. 549) to St. Apollinaris, not in the city
itself but in the port of Classis. But many of the mosaics of
this basilica, which still stands in the marshes, were executed
at a later period ; among them is the portrait of an Emperor
who ascended the throne a hundred years after Justinian's
death.[2]

The decorations of Theoderic's basilica of St. Martin were
completed under Justinian, and a mosaic representation of the
Emperor's bust was put up on the façade,[3] but was afterwards
transferred to a chapel in the interior where it may still be seen.
In his time the church was still St. Martin's ; it was not till
the ninth century that it received the remains of Apollinaris,
the tutelary saint of Ravenna, and was re dedicated to his
name.[4]

The island city, which was later to become the queen of the
Hadriatic, had not yet been founded. But it is probable that
long before the reign of Justinian inhabitants of the Venetian
mainland had been settling in the islands of the lagoons, Mala-
mocco and Rialto, as a secure retreat where they could escape
such dangers as the invasions of Alaric and Attila. Under
Gothic rule we find the people of this coast in possession of
numerous ships, and they were employed to transport wine and
oil from Istria to Ravenna. The minister Cassiodorus, in a
picturesque despatch, calling upon them to perform this office,
likens them to sea-birds.[5] But though danger from Visigoth
and Hun may have prepared the way for the rise of a city in
the lagoons, it was not till three years after Justinian's death,
when the Lombards descended into the land, that any such

[1] See Dalton, *Byz. Art.* 357-360.

[2] Constantine IV.

[3] During the last years of the reign
(553–566).

[4] Another church of the Justinian-
ean period was St. Michael's (in
Affricisco), A.D. 545. Its mosaics
were sold to the king of Prussia in
1847 and are preserved in the Berlin
Museum.

[5] *Variae*, xii. 24.

large and permanent settlements were made on the islands that
they could properly be described as the foundation of Venice.[1]

§ 14. *Conquests in Southern Spain*

It is impossible to say whether Justinian in the early years of
his reign had formed any definite plan for reconquering Spain,
but we may be sure that it was one of his ambitions, and that
if the fall of Witigis had led immediately to the recovery of
Italy, he would have sought a pretext for carrying his victorious
arms against the Visigoths. But before he had completed the
subjugation of the Ostrogoths he was invited to intervene in
Spain, and, although the issue of the Italian war was still far
from certain, he did not hesitate to take advantage of the
occasion.

Theoderic, who was regent of the Visigothic kingdom during
the minority of his grandson Amalaric, had entrusted the conduct
of affairs to Theudis, a capable general, and after the death of
Theoderic and the end of the regency Theudis continued to be
the virtual ruler. The young king, who had none of the qualities
of either his father or his grandfather, married a Frank princess,
and this mixed marriage proved unfortunate. Amalaric behaved
so brutally to her because she refused to embrace his Arian
faith that she invoked the aid of her brother king Childebert,
and he advanced against Narbonne. Amalaric marched to
defend his Gallic possessions, was defeated in battle, and was
then slain in a mutiny of his own army (A.D. 531).[2] The throne
was seized by Theudis, who reigned for seventeen years, and after
a short intervening reign [3] was succeeded by Agila (A.D. 549).
But Agila was not universally acceptable to the people ; civil
war broke out, and after a struggle of five years he was overthrown by his opponent Athanagild, who ascended the throne
(A.D. 554).

In this struggle Athanagild sought the support of the Emperor,
and the Emperor sent a fleet to the southern coasts of Spain.
The commander of this expedition was the octogenarian patrician

---

[1] See Kretschmayr, *Geschichte von
Venedig*, p. 19. The foundation of
Grado was older, but it was the
Lombard invasion that transformed
it into an important city and made
it definitely the residence of the
Patriarch of Aquileia.

[2] *Chron. Caesarum* (in *Chron. min.*
ii. p. 223).

[3] Thiudigisalus, 548–549.

Liberius, who, it will be remembered, had set out to defend
Sicily against Totila, and had hardly reached the island before
a more experienced general was sent to take his place.[1] As
he appears not to have returned to Constantinople till late in
A.D. 551, it is probable that he received commands to sail directly
to Spain with the troops who had accompanied him to Sicily,
in A.D. 550, for the date of his expedition cannot have been
later than in this year. As the armament must have been small,
it achieved a remarkable success. Many maritime cities and
forts were captured.[2] They were captured professedly in the
interests of Athanagild, but when Athanagild's cause had
triumphed, the Imperialists refused to hand them over and the
Visigoths were unable to expel them. Athanagild recovered
a few places,[3] but Liberius had established an Imperial province
in Baetica which was to remain under the rule of Constantinople
for about seventy years. There can be no doubt that this
change of government was welcomed by the Spanish-Roman
population.

We have very few details as to the extent of this Spanish
province. It comprised districts and towns to the west as well
as to the east of the Straits of Gades ; it included the cities of
New Carthage, Corduba, and Assidonia ;[4] we do not know
whether at any time it included Hispalis. It was placed under
a military governor who had the rank of Master of Soldiers, but
we do not know whether he was independent or subordinate to
the governor of Africa.[5]

It is curious that the two well informed historical writers
who have narrated the fortunes of Justinian's armies in Italy
in these years, Procopius and Agathias, should not have made
even an incidental reference to this far-western extension of
Roman rule. But Agathias was a poet as well as a historian,

[1] See above, p. 255. He died in
Italy (later than 554) ; and was
buried at Ariminum (*C.I.L.* xi. 382).

[2] Jordanes, *Get.* c. 58. As he was
writing in 551, we cannot place the
expedition later than in 550. Isidore,
Chron. 399 ; *Hist. Goth.* p. 286. For
the return of Liberius to Constantinople see Procopius, *B.G.* iv. 24. 1.

[3] Isidore, *ib.* ; Greg. Tur. *H. Fr.*
iv. 8. Athanagild reigned 554 to 567.

[4] John Biclar. *Chron.*, *sub* 570.

Dahn (*Kön. der Germ.* v. p. 178)
defines two groups of towns, (1) eastern
on the Mediterranean, from Colopona
to Sucruna, and (2) western, including
Lacobriga and Ossonoba. See also
Altamira, in *C. Med. H.* ii. p. 164.

[5] An inscription of New Carthage,
of A.D. 589, records that Comentiolus,
sent by the Emperor Maurice to
defend the province, bore the title of
magister militum Spaniae (*C.I.L.* ii.
3420).

and in verses which describe how Justinian has girdled the world with his empire, he alludes to the conquest of which in his History he was silent. Let the Roman traveller, he says, follow the steps of Hercules over the blue western sea and rest on the sands of Spain, he will still be within the borders of the wise Emperor's sovranty.[1]

APPENDIX

ON THE BATTLE OF BUSTA GALLORUM

The route taken by Narses after he crossed the river at Ariminum is not precisely indicated by Procopius. His words are (*B.Ğ.* iv. 28. 13): ὁδοῦ δὲ τῆς Φλαμηνίας ἐνθένδε ἀφέμενος ἐν ἀριστερᾷ ᾔει. The sentence seems to have been misunderstood by Hodgkin, who contended that Narses marched along the coast to a point south of Fanum and north of Sena Gallica, and then turned inland by a road ascending the valley of the Sena (Cesano), and reaching the Via Flaminia at Ad Calem (Cagli). Such a road is noticed in the *Itinerarium Antonini*.[2] But if he had taken this route Narses would have had the Via Flaminia on his right, whereas Procopius plainly says exactly the opposite : " He marched having left the Flaminian Way on his left from this point." [3] In order to have the Flaminian Way on his left he must have turned inland between Ariminum and Fanum.

The word ἐνθένδε " from this point," shows that Procopius supposed that Narses diverged from the coast road close to Ariminum. If this statement is correct, it might imply (1) that Narses passed San Marino, followed a road now well defined to Pieve di S. Stefano, crossed the watershed of the Apennines, reached the town now called Città di Castello : [4] from which point he could proceed

---

[1] In the introduction to the Anthology which he edited (*Anth. Gr.* iv. 3. 82 *sqq.*). The passage ends with:

οὐδὲ γὰρ ὀθνείης σε δεδέξεται ἤθεα γαίης,
ἀλλὰ σοφοῦ κτεάνοισιν ὁμιλήσεις βασιλῆος,
ἔνθα κεν ἀΐξειας, ἐπεὶ κυκλώσατο κόσμον
κοιρανίῃ.

In l. 82 κυανωπὸν ὑπὲρ δύσιν means the waters of the west Mediterranean. There may be an allusion to the Spanish conquest in the poem of Paul the Silentiary on St. Sophia, v. 228 :

ἠρεμέει καὶ Μῆδος ἄναξ καὶ Κελτὶς ὁμοκλή.

Cp. vv. 11-13.

[2] As to this road Nissen observes (*Ital. Landeskunde,* ii. 1. 392 n.): "Das

It. Ant. 315 erwähnt eine Strasse von Helvillum über *ad Calem* und *ad Pirum* nach Sena und Ancona ; jedoch ist dieselbe nicht nachgewiesen und die Entfernungen ganz entstellt." But see on the other hand Cuntz, in *Jahresh. Österr. arch. Inst.* vii. 61. Muratori (*Annali d' Italia,* iii. p. 433) says : " voltò Narsete a man destra per valicar l' Apennino," but does not specify at what point he turned.

[3] The phrase is illustrated *infra,* 34. 23 Τείας ὁδοὺς μὲν ἐν δεξιᾷ τὰς ἐπιτομωτάτας ἐπὶ τὸ πλεῖστον ἀφείς.

[4] Situated on the upper waters of the Tiber, and identified with Tifernum Tiberinum.

XIX

either (a) to Urbania, and thence to Acqualagna, or (b) to Iguvium (Gubbio), and thence to Aesis (Scheggia). But (2) it is not improbable that there was a direct road from Ariminum to Urbinum (by Coriano, Montefiore, Tavoleto, Schieti), and thence to Acqualagna by Fermigiano. The engineer, P Montecchini, found traces of it north of Fermigiano (*La Strada Flaminia dall' Apennino all' Adriatico*, pp. 38 *sqq.*, 1879, published at Pesaro).

The other alternative which was open to Narses was to proceed along the coast road as far as Pisaurum, and there to take the road to Urbinum, and it may be said that we cannot pass ἐνθένδε so strictly as to exclude this possibility from our consideration ; if the informant of Procopius omitted to mention Pisaurum, the historian might easily have received a wrong impression.

It is safer to accept the statement of Procopius as it stands, but the question is not important for the subsequent course of events. By one of three routes the army could reach the Via Flaminia at Acqualagna, about five miles on the Roman side of Petra Pertusa. In any case Gibbon saw the truth as to the general direction taken by Narses : he "traversed in a direct line the hills of Urbino and re-entered the Flaminian Way nine miles beyond the perforated rock."

The situation of the camp of Narses is named by Procopius— Busta Gallorum ; the difficulty is to identify it. The district here east of the Flaminian Way lay in the *ager Sentinas*, the limits of which are unknown ; Sentinum itself was close to Sassoferrato. Somewhere in this district the consuls Fabius and Decius defeated the Gauls (in the *ager Sentinas*, Livy, x. 27) in B.C. 295, and the name—Sepulchres of the Gauls—evidently commemorated that defeat, like the Busta Gallica at Rome which commemorated their repulse from the city nearly a century before (Livy, v. 42).

Cluverius in *Italia antiqua*, lib. ii. c. vi., identified Busta Gallorum with a small " town " in the Apennines called Bosta or Basta :

Extat hodie in Apennino inter Sentinum, Fabrianum, Matilicam et Sigillum oppida . . . oppidum vulgari vocabulo Bosta : quod plerique notiore vulgaris linguae vocabulo, quod Latine valet *sufficit*, seu *satis est*, adpellant Basta.

No town or village of the name seems to exist now ; but Cluver doubtless meant the castle called Bastia, a few miles west of Fabriano, close to the railway connecting that town with Sassoferrato (it will be found marked on maps of the Italian Touring Club). If so, his description of its situation is incorrect, as it does not lie between Matelica and any of the other three towns.

Colucci in his *Antichità Picene*, vol. vii. pp. 42-106, has discussed at great length the two questions where the Romans defeated

the Gauls and where Narses defeated Totila. He identifies Bastia
with Cluver's Basta and with Busta Gallorum, and comes to the
conclusion that the battle of Narses was fought in the plain south
of Sassoferrato (Piano della Croce) and the battle of Fabius
and Decius further south " nella gran pianura in cui ora esiste
Fabriano."

A very different view from these was developed by Hodgkin,[1]
who, having brought Narses from Sena to Cagli, makes him advance
along the Via Flaminia and encamp at Scheggia, " or at some point
south of that place where the valley is somewhat broader." [2] As
Totila encamped at Tadinae, the distance between the two camps
would be about 15 miles. Procopius says that the distance
was 100 stadia, which is about 14 Roman miles. The battle
was fought, according to Hodgkin, somewhere south of Scheggia
and north of Tadino. He thinks it " safe to disregard the Busta
Gallorum of Procopius altogether."

The only other theory he considers is that the battlefield was
near Sassoferrato, and he rules this out on the ground that Totila
could not have marched thither " consistently with the narrative
of Procopius. The best of the roads between Tadino and Sassoferrato is a high mountain pass, somewhat resembling the Pass
of Glencoe. The rest are little more than mountain paths carried
through deep gorges in which no armies could manœuvre."

There are three objections to Hodgkin's reconstruction of the
event. (1) The ground along the Via Flaminia between Tadinae
and Aesis is unsuitable for such a battle as Procopius describes.
(2) It is very difficult to believe that, if this had been the scene,
Aesis or Helvillum, or the Via Flaminia itself, would not have
been mentioned to Procopius by his informants, who knew the place
where Totila encamped and the village to which his body was
carried. (3) No account is taken of the name Busta Gallorum.

The data seem to me to point to the conclusion that the battle
was fought somewhere between the Via Flaminia and the river
Aesis (Esino), and probably in the neighbourhood of Fabriano.
Narses, having reached Acqualagna, marched southward along the
Via Flaminia as far as Cagli, and there diverging to the east proceeded by a road, passing (the village of) Frontone and Sassoferrato,
to the valley of the Bono (a stream which joins the Esino some

---

[1] *Italy and Her Invaders*, iv. 710-
713, and 726-728 ; and a special
memoir (1884) referred to p. 726.

[2] We have several lists of the
stations on the Via Flaminia : *Itin.
Ant.* 125, 310 ; *Itin. Hier.* 613 ; *Tab.
Peut.* ; and *C.I.L.* xi. 3281 - 3284.
They are set out together for the
section we are concerned with in *C.I.L.*
xi. p. 995. The distances are :

Ad Calem to Aesis (Scheggia)
Aesis to Helvillum (Sigillo) . . 6 miles.
Helvillum to Tadinae . . . . 7 miles.

Tadinae is 1½ mile from Gualdo
Tadino, near the church of S. Maria
Tadinae (Nissen, *op. cit.* 392). Above
Tadinae comes in from the west the
road from Iguvium, from the east a
road from the valley of the Aesis
(Esino).

miles east of Fabriano). He expected that Totila would march along the Via Flaminia—probably news of the movements of the Goths reached him at Cagli—and he decided to choose his own battleground.

In order to reach the camping place of Narses, Totila (if his camp was actually at the station of Tadinae) would only have to march a few miles northward along the Via Flaminia to the place which is now Fossato and there diverge to his right and cross the Colle di Fossato, by the same route which leads to-day from Fossato to Fabriano. Assuming that Narses was encamped west of Fabriano, Totila in descending the mountain pass could have turned to the left (a road is marked on modern maps) and reached Melano, which is about halfway between Fabriano and Bastia.

There seems, however, to be a considerable probability in the conjecture that the camp of Totila was not actually at the station of Tadinae, but some kilometres to the north of it, at Fossato, "the Camp"; for if the Gothic camp was pitched here on the occasion of the memorable battle, the origin of the place-name Fossatum is accounted for. As there was no Roman station here, the locality would naturally be associated by the informants of Procopius with the name of one of the nearest stations, either Tadinae or Helvillum.

Procopius gives two indications of distance. He says that (1) the distance between the camps, that is between "Tadinae" and Busta Gallorum, was 100 stades, *i.e.* somewhat more than 14 Roman miles, and that (2) the distance from the place where Totila was wounded to the village of Caprae was 84 stades, *i.e.* 12 Roman miles. Caprae has been identified, no doubt rightly, with the little village of Caprara which lies to the west of the Via Flaminia, about six kilometres to the south-west of Fossato.[1] But as we do not know how far Totila had fled from the battlefield before he was wounded, this second indication does not help us much. The first indication, however, is closely in accordance with my theory if the camp of Totila was at Fossato. For the distance from Fossato, by Melano, to the neighbourhood of Bastia is about 20 kilometres, which is equivalent to about 14 Roman miles, the distance given by Procopius.

I must acknowledge help which I have received from my friend Mr. E. H. Freshfield in investigating this subject. I have had the advantage of seeing in MS. a study (soon to be published) of the Via Flaminia by Mr. Ashby and Mr. Fell, and they introduced me to the book of Montecchini.

---

[1] According to Nissen (*op. cit.* p. 393) the Via Flaminia ran far to the west of the present road: "Die Strasse lief nicht wie jetzt an der östlichen Seite der Einsenkung über Fossato und Gualdo sondern an der entgegengesetzten Seite an Caprara vorbei."

CHAPTER XX

DIPLOMACY AND COMMERCE

JUSTINIAN was not less energetic in increasing the prestige and strengthening the power of the Empire by his diplomacy than by his arms. While his generals went forth to recover lost provinces, he and his agents were incessantly engaged in maintaining the Roman spheres of influence beyond the frontiers and drawing new peoples within the circle of Imperial client states. The methods were traditional and are familiar, but he pursued and developed them more systematically than any of his predecessors. Youths of the dynasties ruling in semi-dependent countries were educated at Constantinople, and sometimes married Roman wives. Barbarian kinglets constantly visited the capital, and Justinian spared no expense in impressing them with the majesty and splendour of the Imperial court. He gave them titles of Roman rank, often with salaries attached ; above all, if they were heathen, he procured their conversion to Christianity. Baptism was virtually equivalent to an acknowledgment of Roman overlordship. He used both merchants and missionaries for the purposes of peaceful penetration. And he understood and applied the art of stirring up one barbarian people against another.[1] Perhaps no Emperor practised all these methods, which are conveniently comprehended under the name of diplomacy, on such a grand scale as Justinian, who was the last to aspire to the Imperial ideal expressed by the Augustan poet:

illa inclyta Roma
imperium terris, animos aequabit Olympo.

The objects aimed at varied in different quarters. On

---

[1] He is praised for his dexterity in this art in the contemporary **anonymous** treatise Περὶ στρατηγικῆς, ii, 4. p. 58.

some frontiers they were mainly political, on others largely commercial. In the north, the problem was to secure the European provinces against invasion by managing the rapacious barbarians who lived within striking distance. In the Caucasian regions, the chief concern was to contend against the influence of Persia. In the neighbourhood of the Red Sea commercial aims were predominant. In a general survey of these multifarious activities it will be convenient to notice the hostile invasions which afflicted the Balkan provinces during this reign and the system of fortifications which was constructed to protect them, and to describe the general conditions of commerce. We have already seen examples of the Emperor's diplomatic methods in his dealings with the Moors and with the Franks.[1]

§ 1. *The Slavs*

The array of barbarous peoples against whom Justinian had to protect his European subjects by diplomacy or arms, from the Middle Danube to the Don, were of three different races. There were Germans and Huns as before, but a third group, the Slavs, were now coming upon the scene. The German group consisted of three East German peoples, the Gepids of Transylvania, and the Heruls and the Langobardi to the north-west of the Gepids. The Huns were represented by the Bulgarians of Bessarabia and Walachia, and the Kotrigurs further east. The Slavs lived in the neighbourhood of the Bulgarians on the banks of the lower Danube in Walachia.

This general disposition of peoples had resulted from the great battle of the Netad which dissolved the empire of Attila. One of the obscure but most important consequences of that event was the westward and southward expansion of the Slavs towards the Elbe and towards the Danube.

It has been made probable by recent research that the prehistoric home of the Slavs was in the marshlands of the river Pripet, which flows into the Dnieper north of Kiev.[2] This unhealthy district, known as Polesia, hardly half as large as England,

---

[1] There is a comprehensive survey of " the diplomatic work " of Justinian in Diehl's monograph, p. 367 *sqq.* Commerce is treated separately (533 *sqq.*).

[2] This theory is based on a combination of botanical and linguistic evidence. It was originated (1908) by Rostafinski and has been developed by Peisker. The Slavs have no

is now inhabited by White Russians. It could produce little corn as it could only be cultivated in spots, and it was so entirely unsuitable for cattle that the Slavs had no native words for *cattle* or *milk*. They may have reared swine, but perhaps their food chiefly consisted of fish and the manna-grass which grows freely in the marshy soil. The nature of the territory, impeding free and constant intercourse, hindered the establishment of political unity. The Slavs of Polesia did not form a state; they had no king; they lived in small isolated village groups, under patriarchal government.

Their history, from the earliest times, was a tragedy. Their proximity to the steppes of Southern Russia exposed them as a prey to the Asiatic mounted nomads who successively invaded and occupied the lands between the Don and the Dniester. Living as they did, they could not combine against these enemies who plundered them and carried them off as slaves. They could only protect themselves by hiding in the forest or in the waters of their lakes and rivers. They built their huts with several doors to facilitate escape when danger threatened; they hid their belongings, which were as few as possible, in the earth. They could elude a foe by diving under water and lying for hours on the bottom, breathing through a long reed, which only the most experienced pursuers could detect.[1]

At a time of which we have no record the Slavs began to spread silently beyond the borders of Polesia, northward, eastward, and southward. In the fourth century they were con-

native words for the beech, the larch, and the yew, but they have a word for the hornbeam; hence their original home must have lain in the hornbeam zone, but outside the zones of the other trees, and this consideration determines it as Polesia. The brief sketch I have given of the primitive Slavs is derived from the writings of Peisker (see Bibliography), especially from *C. Med. H.* ii. chap. xiv. Rostafinski's article, *Les demeures primitives des Slaves*, will be found in *Bull. de l'Acad. des Sciences de Cracovie*, Cl. de phil. 1908.

[1] Pseudo-Maurice, *Strateg.* xi. 5. (It has been conjectured by Kulakovski, *Viz. Vrem.* vii. 108 *sqq.*, that the word πλωταί which occurs in this chapter for rafts or flosses is the Slavonic *plot*.) The accounts of the

manners of the Slavs in this sixth-century treatise and in Procopius, *B.G.* iii. 14, are in general agreement and supplement each other. For their religion (cult of fire, worship of nymphs and rivers) see Peisker, *op. cit.* p. 425; Jireček, *Geschichte der Bulgaren*, 102 *sqq.* The Slavs under this name are, I think, first mentioned in the fourth century by Caesarius (brother of Gregory of Nazianzus), *Quaestiones*, *P.G.* xxxviii. p. 985: οἱ Σκλαυηνοὶ καὶ Φυσωνῖται, οἱ καὶ Δανούβιοι προσαγορευόμενοι, οἱ μὲν γυναικομαστοβορούσιν ἡδέως διὰ τὸ πεπληρῶσθαι τοῦ γάλακτος, μυῶν δίκην τοὺς ὑποτίτθους ταῖς πέτραις ἐπαράττοντες, οἱ δὲ καὶ τῆς νομίμης καὶ ἀδιαβλήτου κρεωβορίας ἀπέχουσιν. See Müllenhoff, *Deutsche Altertumskunde*, ii. p. 367.

quered by Hermanric, king of the Ostrogoths, and included in his extensive realm.[1] They enjoyed a brief interlude of German tyranny instead of nomad raids ; then the Huns appeared and they were exposed once more to the oppression which had been their secular lot. They had probably learned much from the Goths ; but when they emerge at length into the full light of history in the sixth century, they still retained most of the characteristics which their life in Polesia had impressed upon them. They lived far apart from one another in wretched hovels ;[2] though they had learned to act together, they did not abandon their freedom to the authority of a king. Revolting against military discipline, they had no battle array and seldom met a foe in the open field.[3] Their arms were a shield, darts, and poisoned arrows.[4] They were perfidious, for no compact could bind them all ; but they are praised for their hospitality to strangers and for the fidelity of their women.

As we might expect, they had no common name. *Slav*, by which we designate all the various peoples who spread far and wide in Eastern Europe from the original Polesian home, comes from *Slovene*, which appears originally to have been a local name attached to a particular group dwelling at a place called Slovy ; and the fortunes of the name are due to the fact that this group was among the first to come into contact with the Roman Empire. Before the reign of Justinian these Sclavenes, as the historian Procopius calls them,[5] had along with another kindred people, the Antae, settled in the neighbourhood of the Bulgarians,

[1] Jordanes, *Get.* 119, where they are called Veneti (as in Pliny and Tacitus). They attempted to resist, *numerositate pollentes—sed nihil valet multitudo imbellium.* We can put no credence in what Jordanes (after Cassiodorus) tells us of Hermanric's immediate successors (which is at variance with statements of Ammian), and I cannot accept (as Peisker does, *op. cit.* p. 431) his statement that King Vinithar subdued the Antae soon after the Hunnic invasion (*ib.* 247).

[2] Procopius, *ib.* 24.

[3] Pseudo-Maurice, who describes them as ἄναρχα καὶ μισάλληλα (pp. 275-276).

[4] *Ib.*, and Procopius, *ib.* 25, who says that some of them went into battle without tunic or cloak, and wearing only trousers. He describes

them as tall and brave, and in complexion reddish.

[5] Jordanes also has Sclaveni (*e.g. Rom.* 388), distinct from Antae. In Pseudo-Maurice we get as the generic term Σκλάβοι. Procopius says (*ib.* 29) that Antae and Sclavenes had originally a common name Σπόροι, which, according to Dobrovsky and Safarik (*Slav. Altertümer,* i. 95), is a corruption of *Srbi* (Serbs). The thesis maintained by Safarik and Drinov, and defended by Jireček, that Slavs had begun to settle into the Balkan Peninsula already in the third century A.D., and that the Carpi and Kostoboks were Slavonic peoples, must be rejected as resting on insufficient evidence. See Šafarik, *op. cit.* i. 213 *sq.*, Jireček, *op. cit.* ch. iii.

along the banks of the Lower Danube. Antae is not a Slavonic name, and it is not unlikely that they were a Slavonic tribe which had been conquered and organised by a non-Slavonic people—somewhat as in later times the Slavs of Moesia were conquered by the Bulgarians and took their name. However this may be, these new neighbours of the Empire now began to exchange the rôle of victims for that of plunderers. Like the Huns, the Antae and Sclavenes supplied auxiliaries for the Roman army.[1] And along with the Huns they were always watching for an opportunity to cross the Danube and plunder the Roman provinces. In the invasions which are recorded in the reign of Justinian, it is sometimes the Slavs, sometimes the Bulgarians who are mentioned, but it is probable that they often came together. In A.D. 529 the Bulgarians overran Lower Moesia and Scythia. They defeated Justin and Baduarius, the generals who opposed them, and crossing the Balkan passes, invaded Thrace.[2] There they captured another general, Constantiolus, and obtained from the Emperor ten thousand pieces of gold for his release. Another incursion in the following year was repulsed with numerous losses to the invaders by Mundus, the Master of Soldiers in Illyricum ;[3] and Chilbudius, who was appointed Master of Soldiers in Thrace about the same time, not only prevented the barbarians from crossing the Danube for three years, but terrorised them by making raids into their own country. His success made him rash. Venturing to cross the river with too small a force, he was defeated and slain by the Sclavenes. No one of the same ability replaced him, and the provinces were once more at the mercy of the foe.[4] We hear, however, of no serious invasion till A.D. 540, when the Bulgarians, with a host exceptionally huge, devastated the peninsula from sea to sea.[5] They forced

---

[1] See Procopius, B.G. i. 27. 2. They must have supplied recruits already in the fifth century, for in 468 we meet a man of Slavonic name (Anagast) who had risen to be *Mag. mil.* of Thrace. See above vol. i. p. 434.

[2] John Mal. xviii. 437. Theophanes, A.M. 6031. Justin was slain. Baduarius is not to be confused with his namesake, son-in-law of the Emperor Justin II.

[3] *Ib.* 451 Οὖννοι μετὰ πολλοῦ

πλήθους διαφόρων βαρβάρων, Marcellinus, *sub a.* (*Bulgares*).

[4] Procopius, B.G. iii. 14. Chilbudius was appointed in the fourth year of Justinian, A.D. 530–531, and was slain three years later. Here the Οὖννοι, Ἄνται and Σκλαβηνοί are associated as invaders.

[5] Procopius, B.V. ii. 4. John of Ephesus, who was then in Constantinople, speaks of Justinian barricading himself in his Palace, H.E. Part II. p. 485.

their way through the Long Wall and spread terror to the suburbs of the capital. They occupied the Chersonesus, and some of them even crossed the Hellespont and ravaged the opposite coast. They laid waste Thessaly and Northern Greece ; the Peloponnesus was saved by the fortifications of the Isthmus. Many of the castles and walled towns fell into their hands,[1] and their captives were numbered by tens of thousands. This experience moved Justinian to undertake the construction of an extensive system of fortifications which will be described hereafter.

Soon after this invasion a quarrel broke out between the Sclavenes and the Antae, and Justinian seized the opportunity to inflame their rivalry by offering to the Antae a settlement at Turris, an old foundation of Trajan on the further side of the Lower Danube, where as federates of the Empire, in receipt of annual subsidies, they should act as a bulwark against the Bulgarians.[2] We are not told whether this plan was carried out, but we may infer that the proposal was accepted, from the fact that in the subsequent invasions the Antae appear to have taken no part.[3] In A.D. 545 the Sclavenes were thoroughly defeated in Thrace by Narses and a body of Heruls whom he had engaged for service in Italy.[4] Three years later the same marauders devastated Illyricum as far as Dyrrhachium,[5] and in A.D. 549 a band of 3000 penetrated to the Hebrus, where they divided into two parties, of which one ravaged Illyricum and the other Thrace. The maritime city of Topirus was taken, and the cruelties committed by the barbarians exceeded in atrocity all that is recorded of the invasions of the Huns of Attila.[6] In the following summer the Sclavenes came again, intending to attack Thessalonica, but Germanus happened to be

---

[1] Thirty-two fortresses in Illyricum were taken, and the town of Cassandrea was captured by assault.

[2] Procopius, *B.G.* iii. 14. Turris had long been derelict ; Justinian apparently proposed to have it restored at his expense.

[3] The Antae accepted, on condition that a captive, whom they believed to be Chilbudius (the general who was slain in A.D. 533–534), should organise the settlement. The impostor was sent to Constantinople and captured by Narses in Thrace,

and his pretensions were exposed. Procopius does not tell the sequel.

[4] *Ib.* iii. 13.

[5] *Ib.* iii. 29. 1-3.

[6] Procopius relates this invasion under the year 549–550 (iii. 38). I infer that it belongs to 549, from the fact that the next invasion is clearly in the summer of 550 (iii. 40. 1 ; cp. 39. 29). It is often placed in 551 (as by Diehl, *op. cit.* 220). The impalings which the Sclavenes practised may have been learned from the Huns.

at Sardica, making preparations to take reinforcements to Italy. The terror of his name diverted the barbarians from their southward course and they invaded Dalmatia.[1] Later in the year the Sclavenes, reinforced by newcomers, gained a bloody victory over an Imperial army at Hadrianople,[2] penetrated to the Long Wall, but were pursued and forced to give up much of their booty.

Two years later there was another inroad, and on this occasion the Gepids aided and abetted the Sclavenes, helping them, when they were hard pressed by Roman troops, to escape across the river, but exacting high fees from the booty-laden fugitives.[3]

Permanent Slavonic settlements on Imperial soil were not to begin till about twenty years after Justinian's death, but the movements we have been following were the prelude to the territorial occupation which was to determine the future history of south-eastern Europe.

§ 2. The Gepids and Lombards ; Kotrigurs and Utigurs

The most powerful of the barbarous peoples on the Danube frontier, against whom the Emperors had to protect their European subjects, were the Gepids of Transylvania. The old policy of recognising them as federates and paying them yearly subsidies, seems to have been successful until Sirmium was taken from the Ostrogoths by Justinian, and being weakly held was allowed to fall into their hands. Establishing themselves in this stronghold they occupied a portion of Dacia Ripensis and made raids into the southern provinces.[4] Justinian immediately discontinued the payment of subsidies and sought a new method of checking their hostilities. He found it in the rivalry of another East-German nation, the Langobardi, who had recently appeared upon the scene of Danubian politics. Yet another people, the Heruls, who belonged to the same group, played a

---

[1] Germanus had formerly inflicted a great defeat on the Antae, when he was Master of Soldiers in Thrace (*ib.* 40. 6) ; the date is unknown.

[2] The defeated army was under well-known leaders : Constantian (Count of the Stable), Aratius, Nazares (who was or had been *mag. mil. Illyrici, B.G.* iii. 11. 18), Justin, son of

Germanus, and John Phagas, but the supreme command was entrusted to Scholasticus, a Palace eunuch, otherwise unknown. The soldiers forced their leaders to give battle against their· wish.

[3] A piece of gold for every person they ferried into safety. *Ib.* iv. 25. 5.

[4] Procopius, *B.G.* ii. 14.

minor part in the drama, in which the Gepids and Langobardi
were the principal actors, and Justinian the director.

It was more than a century since the Langobardi, or Lombards,
as we may call them in anticipation of the later and more familiar
corruption of their name, had left their ancient homes on the
Lower Elbe, where they were neighbours of the Saxons, whose
customs resembled their own, but the details of their long
migration are obscure.[1] Soon after the conquest of the Rugians
by Odovacar, they took possession of the Rugian lands, to the
north of the province of Noricum, but they remained here only
for a few years and then settled in the plains between the Theiss
and the Danube.[2] At this time, it was in the reign of Anastasius,
they lived as tributary subjects of another East-German people,
more savage than themselves. We have already met the
Heruls taking part in the overthrow of the Hunnic realm and
contributing mercenary troops to the Imperial service. In
the second half of the fifth century they seem to have fixed
their abode somewhere in North-western Hungary, and when
the Ostrogoths left Pannonia they became a considerable and
aggressive power dominating the regions beyond the Upper
Danube. They invaded the provinces of Noricum and Pannonia,
and won overlordship over the Lombards. Theoderic, following
his general policy towards his German neighbours, allied himself
with their king Rodulf, whom he adopted as a son.[3] But soon

---

[1] The original home of the Langobardi was in Scandinavia, but they
had settled in the regions of the Lower
Elbe before the time of Augustus.
Their southward migration is dated
by modern historians as not earlier
than the beginning of the fourth
century. It is probable that the old
interpretation of their name (Long
Beards) is the true one (see Blasel,
Die Wanderzüge der Langobarden, 129
sqq.). The chief sources of their early
history are the *Origo gentis Lango-
bardorum* (c. A.D. 650); Fredegarius,
Chron. iii. 65 (embodying Lombard
tradition); Paulus Diac. *Hist. Lang.*
Book I. (based on the *Origo*). See,
on the difficult geographical and
chronological questions connected with
the movements of the Lombards,
Hodgkin, *Italy and her Invaders*, vol.
v.; Schmidt, *Gesch. der deutschen
Stämme*, i. 427 *sqq.*; Blasel, *op. cit.*

(where a bibliography will be found).
[2] *Campi patentes* = Feld (*Origo* and
Paul, *Hist. Lang.* i. 20); which in
Chron. Gothorum, ch. ii., is called
Tracia.
[3] Cassiodorus, *Var.* iv. 2, a letter
addressed to the king of the Heruls,
whose name comes from the Lombard
sources. Its date is between 507
and 511, so that the battle must be
placed, not c. 505 with Schmidt, but
at earliest 507–508, and at latest 511–
512 (see next note). If it is true that
the Lombards moved from Rugia to
the *Campi patentes* three years before
the battle (Paul, *ib.*), the earliest
date for their change of abode is
504–505. The name of the Lombard
king at this time was Tato. Rodulf,
the Herul, was slain in the battle
(Paul, *ib.*). The best source is Procopius, *B.G.* ii. 14; the fuller story of
Lombard tradition is largely legendary.

afterwards (A.D. 507–512), they attacked the Lombards without provocation and were defeated in a sanguinary battle. This defeat had important results. It led to the dissolution of the Herul nation into two portions, of which one migrated northward and returned to the old home of the people in Scandinavia. The rest moved first into the former territory of the Rugians, but finding the land a desert they begged the Gepids to allow them to settle in their country. The Gepids granted the request, but repaid themselves by carrying off their cattle and violating their women. Then the Heruls sought the protection of the Emperor, who readily granted them land in one of the Illyrian provinces.[1] But their rapacious instincts soon drove them to plunder and maltreat the provincials, and Anastasius was compelled to send an army to chastise them. Many were killed off ; the rest made complete submission, and were suffered to remain. No people quite so barbarous had ever yet been settled on Roman soil. It was their habit to put to death the old and the sick ; and the women were expected to hang themselves when their husbands died. When Justinian came to the throne he effected their conversion to Christianity. Their king with his nobles was invited to Constantinople, where he was baptized with all his party, the Emperor standing sponsor, and was dismissed with handsome gifts. Larger subsidies were granted to them, and better lands in the neighbourhood of Singidunum, with the province of Second Pannonia (A.D. 527–528).[2] Henceforward, for some years, they fulfilled their duties as Federates, and supplied contingents to the Roman army. But though their savagery had been mitigated after they embraced the Christian faith, they were capricious and faithless ; they had not even the merit of chaste manners, for which Tacitus and Salvian praise the Germanic peoples ; they were the worst people in the whole world, in the opinion of a contemporary historian.[3]

Suddenly it occurred to them that they would prefer a republican form of government, though their kings enjoyed only a shadow of authority. Accordingly they slew their king, but

---

[1] Probably Dacia Ripensis. Marcellinus, *s.a.* 512 ; Procopius, *ib.* xv. 1.
[2] Procopius, *B.G.* ii. 14. 33 ; iii. 34. 42 ; John Mal. xviii. 427 ; John Eph., *H.E.* Part II. p. 475 (*sub a.*

844=A.D. 533). Cp. Menander, *fr.* 9 (*F.H.G.* iv.).
[3] Procopius, *ib.* ii. 14. 36 καὶ μίξεις οὐχ ὁσίας τελοῦσιν, ἄλλας τε καὶ ἀνδρῶν καὶ ὄνων.

very soon, for they were unstable as water, they repented, and
decided to choose a ruler among the people of their own race
who had settled in Scandinavia. Some of their leading men
were sent on this distant errand and duly returned with a
candidate for the throne.[1] But in the meantime, during their
long absence, the Heruls, with characteristic indecision, bethought
themselves that they ought not to elect a king from Scandinavia
without the consent of Justinian, and they invited him to choose
a king for them. Justinian selected a certain Suartuas, a Herul
who had long lived at Constantinople. He was welcomed and
acclaimed by the Heruls, but not many days had passed when
the news came that the envoys who had gone to Scandinavia
would soon arrive. Suartuas ordered the Heruls to march forth
and destroy them ; they obeyed cheerfully ; but one night they
all left him and went over to the rival whom they had gone forth
to slay. Suartuas returned alone to Constantinople.

The consequence of this escapade was that the Heruls split
up again into two portions. The greater part attached themselves
to the Gepids ; the rest remained federates of the Empire.[2]
This was the position of affairs when about the middle of the
sixth century war broke out between the Gepids and the
Lombards.

The Lombards are represented as having been Christians
while they were still under the yoke of the Heruls. After they
had won their independence they lived north of the Danube
in the neighbourhood of the Gepids.[3] We hear nothing more of
them until we find their king Wacho, in A.D. 539, refusing to
send help to the Ostrogoths on the ground that he was a friend
and ally of Justinian.[4] Some years later the Emperor assigned
to them settlements in Noricum and Pannonia,[5] and granted
them the subsidies which it was usual to pay to federates. We

---

[1] In his account of this episode
Procopius (ib. 15) designates Scandinavia as Thule and describes it
as ten times larger than Britain.
Among the peoples who inhabit it he
knows of two, the Gauts and the
Skrithifinoi. Of the Gauts in Sweden
we otherwise know, and it is natural
to identify the Skrithifinoi with the
Finns.

[2] Procopius, B.G. iii. 34. 43, who
says that the total fighting strength
of the Heruls was 4500 men, of whom

3000 joined the Gepids. Cp. ii. 15.
37.

[3] This was the period of the linguistic change, which is known as
the second shifting of consonants and
produced the High German language.
It originated in southern Germany,
and the Lombard language was
affected by it.

[4] Proc. B.G. ii. 22. Above, p. 205.

[5] Ib. iii. 33. 10 Νωρικῶν τε πόλει
(Noreia=Neumarkt) καὶ τοῖς ἐπὶ Παν-
νονίας ὀχυρώμασί τε καὶ ἄλλοις χωρίοις.

may take it that he deliberately adopted this policy in order to use the Lombards as a counterpoise to the Gepids, with whom he had recently broken off relations.[1]

It was not long before these two peoples quarrelled and prepared for war. Audoin at this time was king of the Lombards[2] and Thorisin of the Gepids. They both sent ambassadors to Constantinople, the Lombards to beg for military aid,[3] the Gepids hardly hoping to do more than induce the Emperor to remain neutral. Justinian decided to assist the Lombards and sent a body of 10,000 horse, who were directed to proceed to Italy when they had dealt with the Gepids. These troops met an army of hostile Heruls and defeated them severely, but in the meantime the Lombards and Gepids had composed their differences, to the disappointment of Justinian. It was felt, however, by both sides that war was inevitable and was only postponed. The Gepids, fearing that their enemies, supported by Constantinople, would prove too strong for them, concluded an alliance with the Kotrigurs.

The Kotrigurs, who were a branch of the Hunnic race, occupied the steppes of South Russia, from the Don to the Dniester, and were probably closely allied to the Bulgarians[4] or Onogundurs—the descendants of Attila's Huns—who had their homes in Bessarabia and Walachia. They were a formidable people and Justinian had long ago taken precautions to keep them in check, in case they should threaten to attack the Empire, though it was probably for the Roman cities of the Crimea, Cherson and Bosporus, that he feared, rather than for the Danubian provinces. As his policy on the Danube was to

[1] Procopius relates the two events together, under the fourteenth year of the Gothic War, i.e. A.D. 548–549, but in a digression which assigns only the loose date "when Totila had gained the upper hand" (ib. 7). In the following chapter (iii. 34) he anticipates the chronology (χρόνῳ δὲ ὕστερον) and narrates the war of the Gepids and Lombards, which was thus subsequent to A.D. 549.

[2] Audoin (half-brother of Wacho) married the daughter of Hermanfrid, king of the Thuringians. The marriage was arranged by Justinian. For after Hermanfrid's death, his wife Amalaberga (Theoderic's niece) had returned to Italy with her children,

and they were afterwards brought to Constantinople by Belisarius. See B.G. i. 31. 2 ; iv. 12.

[3] Procopius, who puts long speeches into the mouths of the envoys, makes the Lombards urge that they were Catholics, not Arians like the Gepids (iii. 34, 24). Yet when they subsequently conquered Italy, they were Arians. They seem to have been exceptionally indifferent to religion. Cp. Hodgkin, op. cit. v. 158.

[4] The name Kotrigur is to be compared with Kotragos in the genealogy of the Bulgarians. Theophanes describes Κότραγοι near L. Maeotis as ὁμόφυλοι of the Bulgarians (A.M. 6171).

use the Lombards as a check on the Gepids, so his policy in
Scythia was to use another Hunnic people, the Utigurs, as a
check on the Kotrigurs. The Utigurs lived beyond the Don,
on the east of the Sea of Azov, and Justinian cultivated their
friendship by yearly gifts.

When a host of 12,000 Kotrigurs, incited by the Gepids,
crossed the Danube and ravaged the Illyrian lands, Justinian
immediately despatched an envoy to Sandichl, king of the
Utigurs, to bid him prove his friendship to the Empire by
invading the territory of their neighbours. Sandichl, an experienced warrior, fulfilled the Emperor's expectations; he
crossed the Don, routed the enemy, and carried their women
and children into slavery. When the news reached Constantinople, Justinian sent one of his generals [1] to the Kotrigurs who
were still plundering the Balkan provinces, to inform them of
what had happened in their own land, and to offer them a large
sum of money to evacuate Roman territory. They accepted
the proposal, and it was stipulated that if they found their own
country occupied by the Utigurs, they should return and receive
from the Emperor lands in Thrace. Soon afterwards another
party of 2000 Kotrigurs, with their wives and children, arrived
as fugitives on Roman soil. They were led by Sinnion, who
had fought in Africa as a commander of Hunnic auxiliaries
in the Vandal campaign of Belisarius. The Emperor accorded
them a settlement in Thrace. This complacency shown to their
foes excited the jealous indignation of the Utigurs, and king
Sandichl sent envoys to remonstrate with Justinian on the
injustice and impolicy of his action. They were appeased by
large gifts, which it was obviously the purpose of their coming
to obtain.[2]

In the following year (A.D. 559), the war so often threatened
and so often postponed between the Lombards and Gepids broke
out. The Gepids sought to renew their old alliance with the
Empire, and Justinian consented,[3] but when the Lombards
soon afterwards asked him to fulfil his engagements and send

[1] Aratius, the Armenian. The
name of the Kotrigur leader was
Chinialon.
[2] Procopius, B.G. iv. 18 and 19.
The long speech which the author
puts into the mouths of the envoys is,
of course, his own criticism of Justinian's policy. The date of these
events seems to be A.D. 551. Cp. ib.
21, 4.
[3] Ib. 25. 8-9. Procopius obliquely
criticises Justinian by emphasising
the solemnity of the oaths with which
the treaty was confirmed.

troops to help them he denounced his new treaty with the
Gepids on the pretext that they had helped Sclavenes to cross
the Danube. Among the leaders of the forces which marched
to co-operate with the Lombards, were Justin and Justinian,
the Emperor's cousins, but they were detained on their way to
suppress a revolt at Ulpiana, and never arrived at their destination. Only those troops which were commanded by Amala-
fridas, the brother-in-law of the Lombard king,[1] pursued their
march and took part in the campaign. The Lombards won a
complete victory over the Gepids, and Audoin, in announcing
the good news to Justinian, reproached him for failing to furnish
the help which they had a right to expect in consideration of
the large force of Lombards which had recently gone forth to
support Roman arms in Italy.

After this defeat the Gepids concluded treaties of perpetual
peace with the Lombards and with the Empire,[2] and peace
seems to have been preserved so long as Justinian reigned.
After his death the enmity between these two German peoples
broke out again, and the Lombards, aided by other allies,
eliminated the name of the Gepids from the political map of
Europe.

§ 3. *The Invasion of Zabergan* (A.D. 558)

In a few years the Kotrigurs recovered from the chastisement
which had been inflicted upon them by their Utigur neighbours,
and in the winter of A.D. 558-559, under a chieftain whose name
was Zabergan, a host of these barbarians crossed the frozen
Danube, and passing unopposed through Scythia and Moesia,
entered Thrace. These provinces would seem to have been
entirely denuded of troops. In Thrace Zabergan divided his
followers into three armies. One was sent to Greece, to ravage
the unprotected country; the second invaded the Thracian
Chersonese; the third army, consisting of seven thousand cavalry,
rode under Zabergan himself to Constantinople.

The atrocities committed by the third body are thus described by a contemporary writer : [3]

---

[1] He was son of Hermanfrid; see
above, p. 302, *n.* 2.

[2] *Ib.* 27. 21.

[3] Agathias v. 2 ; cp. John Mal.

xviii. p. 490 ; Theophanes, A.M.
6051. The Huns were almost a whole
year in Roman territory. See Clinton, *F.R.*, *sub* A.D. 559.

As no resistance was offered to their course, they overran the country and plundered without mercy, obtaining a great booty and large numbers of captives. Among the rest, well-born women of chaste life were most cruelly carried off to undergo the worst of all misfortunes, and minister to the unbridled lust of the barbarians; some who in early youth had renounced marriage and the cares and pleasures of this life, and had immured themselves in some religious retreat, deeming it of the highest importance to be free from cohabitation with men, were dragged from the chambers of their virginity and violated. Many married women who happened to be pregnant were dragged away, and when their hour was come brought forth children on the march, unable to conceal their throes, or to take up and swaddle the new-born babes; they were hauled along, in spite of all, hardly allowed even time to suffer, and the wretched infants were left where they fell, a prey for dogs and birds, as though this were the purpose of their appearance in the world.

To such a pass had the Roman Empire come that, even within the precincts of the districts surrounding the Imperial city, a *very small* number of barbarians committed such enormities.[1] Their audacity went so far as to pass the Long Walls and approach the inner fortifications. For time and neglect had in many places dilapidated the great wall, and other parts were easily thrown down by the barbarians, as there was no military garrison, no engines of defence. Not even the bark of a dog was to be heard; the wall was less efficiently protected than a pig-sty or a sheep-cot.

The Huns encamped at Melantias, a village on the small river Athyras, which flows into the Propontis. Their proximity created a panic in Constantinople, whose inhabitants saw in imagination the horrors of siege, conflagration, and famine. The terror was not confined to the lower classes; the nobles trembled in their palaces, the Emperor was alarmed on his throne. All the treasures of the churches, in the tract of country between the Euxine and the Golden Horn, were either carted into the city or shipped to the Asiatic side of the Bosphorus. The undisciplined corps of the Scholarian guards, ignorant of real warfare, did not inspire the citizens with much confidence.

On this critical occasion Justinian appealed to his veteran general Belisarius to save the seat of empire. In spite of his years and feebleness Belisarius put on his helmet and cuirass once more. He relied chiefly on a small body of three hundred men who had fought with him in Italy; the other troops that he mustered knew nothing of war, and they were more for appearance than for action. The peasants who had fled before

---

[1] Theophanes, *ib.*, notices that two generals, Sergius and Edermas, were defeated by the Huns before they reached the Long Wall.

the barbarians from their ruined homesteads in Thrace accompanied the little army. He encamped at the village of Chettus, and employed the peasants in digging a wide trench round the camp. Spies were sent out to discover the numbers of the enemy, and at night many beacons were kindled in the plain with the purpose of misleading the Huns as to the number of the forces sent out against them. For a while they were misled, but it was soon known that the Roman army was small, and two thousand cavalry selected by Zabergan rode forth to annihilate it. The spies informed Belisarius of the enemy's approach, and he made a skilful disposition of his troops. He concealed two hundred peltasts and javelin-men in the woods on either side of the plain, close to the place where he expected the attack of the barbarians ; the ambuscaders, at a given signal, were to shower their missiles on the hostile ranks. The object of this was to compel the lines of the enemy to close in, in order to avoid the javelins on the flank, and thus to render their superior numbers useless through inability to deploy. Belisarius himself headed the rest of the army ; in the rear followed the rustics, who were not to engage in the battle, but were to accompany it with loud shouts and cause a clatter with wooden beams, which they carried for that purpose.

All fell out as Belisarius had planned. The Huns, pressed by the peltasts, thronged together, and were hindered both from using their bows and arrows with effect, and from circumventing the Roman wings. The noise of the rustics in the rear, combined with the attack on the flanks, gave the foe the impression that the Roman army was immense, and that they were being surrounded ; clouds of dust obscured the real situation, and the barbarians turned and fled. Four hundred perished before they reached their camp at Melantias, while not a single Roman was mortally wounded. The camp was immediately abandoned, and all the Kotrigurs hurried away, imagining that the victors were still on their track. But by the Emperor's orders Belisarius did not pursue them.

The fortunes of the Hunnic troops who were sent against the Chersonese were not happier. Germanus, a native of Prima Justiniana, had been appointed some time previously commandant in that peninsula, and he now proved himself a capable officer. As the Huns could make no breach in the great wall,

which barred the approach to the peninsula and was skilfully
defended by the dispositions of Germanus, they resorted to the
expedient of manufacturing boats of reeds fastened together in
sheaves ; each boat was large enough to hold four men ; one
hundred and fifty were constructed, and six hundred men
embarked secretly in the bay of Aenus (near the mouth of the
Hebrus), in order to land on the south-western coast of the
Chersonese. Germanus learned the news of their enterprise
with delight, and immediately manned twenty galleys with
armed men. The fleet of reed-built boats was easily annihilated, not a single barbarian escaping. This success was
followed up by an excursion of the Romans from the wall against
the army of the dispirited besiegers, who then abandoned their
enterprise and joined Zabergan, now retreating after the defeat
at Chettus.

The other division of the Huns, which had been sent in
the direction of Greece, also returned without achieving any
signal success. They had not penetrated farther than
Thermopylae, where the garrison of the fortress prevented their
advance.

Thus, although Thrace, Macedonia, and Thessaly suffered
terribly from this invasion, Zabergan was frustrated in all three
points of attack, by the ability of Belisarius, Germanus, and
the garrison of Thermopylae. Justinian redeemed the captives
for a considerable sum of money, and the Kotrigurs retreated
beyond the Danube. But the wily Emperor laid a trap for their
destruction. He despatched a characteristic-letter to Sandichl,
the king of the Utigurs, whose friendship he still cultivated
by periodical presents of money. He informed Sandichl that
the Kotrigurs had invaded Thrace and carried off all the gold
that was destined to enrich the treasury of the Utigurs. " It
would have been easy for us," ran the Imperial letter, " to have
destroyed them utterly, or at least to have sent them empty
away. But we did neither one thing nor the other, because we
wished to test your sentiments. For if you are really valiant
and wise, and not disposed to tolerate the appropriation by
others of what belongs to you, you are not losers ; for you have
nothing to do but punish the enemy and receive from them
your money at the sword's point, as though we had sent it to
you by their hands." The Emperor further threatened that,

if Sandichl proved himself craven enough to let the insult pass,
he would transfer his amity to the Kotrigurs. The letter had
the desired effect. The Utigurs were stirred up against their
neighbours, and ceaseless hostilities wasted the strength of the
two peoples.[1]

The historian who recorded the expedition of Zabergan concludes his story by remarking that these two Hunnic peoples
were soon so weakened by this continual warfare that though they
were not wholly extinguished they were incorporated in larger
empires and lost their individualities and even their names.[2]
The power which threatened them was already at the gates of
Europe at the time of Zabergan's invasion.[3]

§ 4. The Defences of the Balkan Peninsula

Unable to spare military forces adequate to protect the
Balkan provinces against the inroads of the barbarians, Justinian
endeavoured to mitigate the evil by an elaborate system of
fortresses, which must have cost his treasury large sums. In
Thrace, Macedonia, Dardania, Epirus, and Greece, new forts
were built, old forts were restored and improved, about six
hundred in all.[4]

Thrace had always been defended by a line of fortresses on
both sides of the Danube. They were now renovated and their
number was increased. Behind them, in the provinces of Lower
Moesia and Scythia, there were about fifty walled towns and
castles. South of the Balkan range, the regions of Mount
Rhodope and the Thracian plain were protected by 112 fortresses.
The defences of Hadrianople and Philippopolis, Plotinopolis and

---

[1] Agathias, v. 25; John Ant., fr.
217 (F.H.G. iv.); Menander, fr. 1,
De leg. Rom. Another invasion of
Huns is recorded in A.D. 562 (Theophanes, A.M. 6054); Anastasiopolis
was captured.

[2] Agathias, v. 25; while the
Kotrigurs were subjugated by the
Avars, the Utigurs were conquered
by the western Turks about 576 (cp.
Menander, fr. 14, De leg Rom. p. 208).

[3] Below, § 6.

[4] The source is Procopius, Aed. iv.,
where full lists of the forts (of which
few can be identified) will be found.

It seems probable that the fortifications were carried out on a general
plan, after A.D. 540 (we know that
Cassandrea and the Chersonese were
fortified after that date, and Topirus
after 549). The invasion of that
year had displayed the deficiencies
of the existing fortifications. Most
of the old military forts had only one
tower (they were called μονοπύργια).
Justinian's seem to have been larger
and had several towers. Ib. 5. 4.
On the general principles of the
defensive fortifications of the provinces, as illustrated by the remains
in Africa, see above, p. 148.

Beroea (Stara Zagora) were restored, and Topirus, under Mount Rhodope, which the Sclavenes had taken by assault, was carefully fortified. Trajanopolis and Maximianopolis, in the same region, were secured by new walls, and the populous village of Ballurus was converted into a fortified town. On the Aegean coast, the walls of Aenus were raised in height, and Anastasiopolis strengthened by a new sea-wall. The wall, which hedged in the Thracian Chersonese but had proved too weak to keep out the Bulgarians, was demolished, and a new and stronger defence was built, which proved effective against the Kotrigurs. Sestos was made impregnable, and a high tower was erected at Elaeûs. On the Propontis, Justinian built a strong city at Rhaedestus and restored Heraclea. Finally, he repaired and strengthened the Long Wall of Anastasius.

The provinces belonging to the Prefecture of Illyricum were strewn with fortresses proportionate in number to the greater dimensions of the territory. The stations on the Danube from Singidunum to Novae were set in order. In Dardania, the Emperor's native province, eight new castles were built and sixty-one restored. Here he was concerned not only to provide for the defence of the province but to make it worthy of his own greatness by imposing and well-furnished cities. Scupi, near the village where he was born, began a new era in its history under the name of Justiniana Prima, though the old name refused to be displaced, and the town is now Üsküb. It was raised to high dignity as the ecclesiastical metropolis of Illyricum ; the number of its churches, its municipal offices, the size of its porticoes, the beauty of its market-places impressed the visitor. Ulpiana (Lipljan), too, was embellished, and became Justiniana Secunda,[1] and near it the Emperor founded a new town called Justinopolis in honour of his uncle. In the centre of the peninsula the walls of Sardica and Naissus were rebuilt.

The inhabitants of Macedonia were protected by forty-six forts and towns. Cassandrea, which had failed to withstand the Sclavenes, was made impregnable. In the two provinces of Epirus, forty-five new forts were built and fifty rehabilitated. In Thessaly, the decayed walls of Thebes, Pharsalus, Demetrias,

---

[1] For the identification of the two Justinianas see Evans, *Antiquarian Researches in Illyricum*, Part III. 62 *sq.* ; Part IV. 134 *sqq.* Scupi had been ruined by an earthquake in 518 (Marcellinus, *s.a.*).

Larissa, and Diocletianopolis on Lake Castoria, and other towns [1] were restored. The defences of Thermopylae were renewed and improved, and the historic barrier which had hitherto been guarded by the local farmers was entrusted to 2000 soldiers.[2] The Isthmus of Corinth was fortified anew,[3] and the walls of Athens and the Boeotian towns, which were dilapidated by age or earthquakes, were restored.

This immense work of defence did not avail to keep the barbarians out of the land. Writing in A.D. 550 Procopius sums up the situation : " Illyricum and Thrace, from the Ionian Sea to the suburbs of Byzantium, were overrun almost every year since Justinian's accession to the throne by Huns, Sclavenes, and Antae, who dealt atrociously with the inhabitants. In every invasion I suppose that about 200,000 Roman subjects were killed or enslaved ; the whole land became a sort of Scythian desert." [4] The historian's supposition doubtless exaggerates the truth considerably, and he would have been more instructive if he had told us how far the improved fortifications mitigated the evils of the invasions. It is clear, however, that it was a great advantage for the inhabitants to have more numerous and safer refuges when the barbarians approached ; and we may guess that if statistics had been kept they would have shown a decrease in the number of the victims.

§ 5. *The Crimea*

No cities in the Roman Empire deserve greater credit for preserving Greek civilisation in barbarous surroundings than Cherson and Bosporus in the lonely Cimmerian peninsula. They were the great centres for the trade between the Mediterranean and the basins of the Volga and the Don. They were exposed to the attacks of Huns both from the north and from the east, and the subsidies which Justinian paid to the Utigurs must have been chiefly designed to purchase immunity for these

---

[1] Metropolis (near the modern Karditsa), Gomphi, Tricca (now Trikkala), Caesarea, Centauropolis.

[2] Procopius, *Aed.* iv. 2. 14 ; *H.A.* 26, 33, where it is said that, on the pretext of paying the garrison, the municipal rates of all the cities of Greece were appropriated to the treasury ; this change is attributed to the logothete Alexander Psalidios.

[3] The fortress of Megara had been restored apparently under Anastasius, *C.I.G.* iv. 8622. Cp. Hertzberg, *Gesch. Griechenlands*, iii. 469.

[4] *H.A.* 18, 20.

outposts of the Empire. They had always stood outside the
provincial system, and the political position of Bosporus seems
to have been more independent of the central power than that
of Cherson, where the Emperors maintained a company of
artillery (*ballistarii*).[1] In the fifth century the bond between
Bosporus and Constantinople was broken, a change which was
doubtless a result of the Hunnic invasion, and during this period
it was probably tributary to the neighbouring Huns. But in
the reign of Justin the men of Bosporus sought the protection
of the Empire and were restored to its fold.[2] They soon found
that they would have to pay for the privilege. They were not
indeed asked to pay the ordinary provincial taxes, but Cherson
and Bosporus were required to contribute to the maintenance
of a merchant fleet which we may suppose was intended exclusively for use in the Euxine waters. This ship-money was
also imposed on Lazica, when that land was annexed to the
Empire.[3]

The Crimean Huns occupied the territory between the two
cities. It is not clear whether they stood in the definite relation
of federates to the Empire; but in A.D. 528 their king Grod
was induced to come to Constantinople, where he was baptized,
the Emperor acting as sponsor, and he undertook to defend
Roman interests in the Crimea.[4] At the same time Justinian
sent a garrison of soldiers to Bosporus under the command of
a tribune. Grod, on returning home, took the images of his
heathen gods—they were made of silver and electrum,—and
melted them down. But the priests and the people were enraged
by this impiety, and led by his brother, Mugel, they slew Grod,
made Mugel king, and killed the garrison of Bosporus. The
Emperor then sent considerable forces which intimidated the

[1] Cp. Kulakovski, *Proshloe Tavridi*,
c. viii. For the geography of the
peninsula see E. H. Minns, *Scythians
and Greeks* (1913), where a sketch of
the history of Cherson will be found.

[2] Procopius, *B.P.* i. 12. It is a
disputed question whether the inscription of the Caesar Tiberius
Julius Diptunes, "friend of Caesar,
friend of the Romans," belongs to
A.D. 522 (as Kulakovski maintains,
ib. 59). A count and an eparch are
mentioned, raising the presumption
that the stone was inscribed when
Bosporus was subject to the Empire.

The inscription is published in Latyshev, *Sbornik*, ii. 39.

[3] See the *Novel* of Tiberius of A.D.
575 (=Justinian, *Nov.* 163) ἐπὶ τοῖς
λεγομένοις τῶν εἰδῶν πλωίμοις γινομένοις
ἐπί τε τῆς Λάζων χώρας καὶ Βοσπόρου
καὶ Χερσονήσου.

[4] John Mal. xviii. 431. John Eph.
H.E. Part II. p. 475, where the king
is called Gordian. Some time previously, Probus had been sent to
Grod to induce him to send help to
the Iberians against Persia. Procopius, *B.P.* i. 12. 6.

Huns and tranquillity was restored.[1] Bosporus was then strongly fortified, the walls of Cherson, which were old and weak, were rebuilt, and two new forts were erected in the south of the peninsula.[2] In the north of the Crimea there was a small Gothic settlement, apparently a remnant of the Ostrogothic kingdom which in the fourth century extended along the north coast of the Euxine. These Goths are described as few in number, but good soldiers, skilful in agriculture, and a people of hospitable habits. They were under the protection of the Empire and were ready, when the Emperor summoned them, to fight against his foes. Their chief place was Dory on the coast ; they would have no walled towns or forts in their land, but Justinian built long walls at the points where it was most exposed to an invader.[3]

From these genuine Goths of the Crimea we must carefully distinguish another people, who were also described as Goths but perhaps erroneously. These were the Tetraxites (a name of mysterious origin) who lived in the peninsula of Taman over against Bosporus.[4] They too were a small people, and their fate depended on the goodwill of the Utigurs,[5] whose kingdom

---

[1] John Mal. *ib.* ; cp. Theophanes, A.M. 6020. It would be interesting to know more about this expedition. According to John Mal., transports of soldiers were sent by sea, and a large force under Baduarius *by land*, starting from Odessus. The march of a Roman army by the northern coast of the Euxine, through the territory of the Bulgarians and Kotrigurs, was a unique event. John of Ephesus (*ib.*) says that Mugel and his followers fled to another country in fear of the Emperor.

[2] Τὸ ᾿Αλούστου καὶ τὸ ἐν Γορζουβίταις. Procopius, *Aed.* iii. 7. 11. In this passage Procopius clearly alludes to the events of 528. The walls of Cherson had been strengthened in the reign of Zeno, *C.I.G.* iv. 8621. Procopius (*B.G.* iv. 5. 28) curiously describes Phanagoria as near Cherson and still subject to the Romans.

[3] They were Christians, and perhaps they had a bishop at as early a date as the Council of Nicaea (Mansi, ii. 696 *provinciae Gothiae*. *Theophilus Gothiae metropolis*). If this is so, they must have been distinct from the Ostrogoth of Hermanric. The

chief source for this people is Procopius, *Aed.* iii. 7. 13-17. He describes them as ῾Ρωμαίων ἔνσπονδοι. When he says that they numbered about 3000, he perhaps means the men of military age. For these Goths and the Tetraxites see Loewe, *Die Reste der Germanen am Schwarzen Meere*, 22 *sqq.* They are confused by Tomaschek, *Die Goten in Taurien*, 12.

[4] A name for Taman, T'mutarakan, which occurs in old Russian sources and is evidently of Arabic or Turkish origin, supplied Vasil'evski with an ingenious interpretation of Tetraxite, which is approved by Loewe (*op. cit.* 33-34). He explains T'mutarakan as derived from τὰ Μάτραχα*, which he identifies with τὸ Ταμάταρχα (in Constantine Porph. *De adm. imp.* c. 42), from which he gets Τμετραξῖται* as a name of the inhabitants, and hence Τετραξῖται (the corruption being influenced by τετραξός). Loewe thinks that the Tetraxites were Heruls.

[5] They supplied 2000 soldiers to the expedition of the Utigurs against the Kotrigurs in 551. Procopius, *B.G.* iv. 18. 22.

stretched from the Don as far south as the Hypanis. They engaged, however, in secret diplomacy with Justinian. Their bishop had died, and (A.D. 548) they sent envoys to Constantinople to ask the Emperor to provide a successor. This was the ostensible object of the embassy, and nothing else was mentioned in the official audience, for they were afraid of the Utigurs ; but they had a secret interview with the Emperor, at which they gave him useful information for the purpose of stirring up strife among the Huns.[1]

To the south of the Utigurs, in the inland regions north of the Caucasian range, were the lands of the Alans, traditionally friends of the Romans, and further east the Sabirs, whose relations to the Empire have come before us in connexion with the Persian wars. On the coast south of the Hypanis, the Zichs, whose king used in old days to be nominated by the Emperor, were accounted of small importance.[2] But their southern neighbours, the Abasgians and the Apsilians, came, as we have already seen, within the sphere of political intrigue and military operations by which Rome and Persia fought for the control of Colchis. On the Abasgian coast the Romans had two fortresses, Sebastopolis (formerly called Dioscurias) and Pityus. On hearing that Chosroes intended to send an army to seize these places, Justinian ordered the garrisons to demolish the fortifications, burn the houses, and withdraw. But he afterwards rebuilt

---

[1] Procopius, B.G. iv. 4. 9-13. Of their religion he says : "I cannot say whether they were once Arians, like the other Gothic peoples, or held some other creed, for they do not know themselves, but now they adhere with simple sincerity to the (orthodox) religion " (ἀφελείᾳ καὶ ἀπραγμοσύνῃ πολλῇ τιμῶσι τὴν δόξαν). I cannot find in Procopius (ib. iv. 5) the statement, ascribed to him by Loewe, that the Tetraxites lived in the Crimea before they settled in the Taman peninsula. It is to be noticed that the old Greek town of Phanagoria, opposite to Bosporus, was in their hands, and was probably the headquarters of their ecclesiastics. An inscription found at Taman, and doubtless brought there from Phanagoria, relates to the restoration of a church under the auspices of Justinian. It is dated to an eleventh indiction, which gives three possible dates, 533,

548, and 563. This stone is discussed by Latyshev, Viz. Vrem. 1. 657 sqq., who decided for 533; by Kulakovski, ib. 2. 189 sqq., who argued for 548 (but he is now doubtful, Pamiatnik, p. 10, n. 1); and by Semenov, B.Z. vi. 387 sqq., who denies that the year can be fixed.

[2] In his account of these regions in B.G. iv. 4, Procopius places the Saginae apparently to the north of the Zichs, though one might infer from another passage, ib. 2. 16, that they were nearer to Colchis. He also mentions the Bruchoi as dwelling between the Alans and Abasgians. The Sunitae were also neighbours of the Alans, B.P. i. 15. 1. See also B.P. ii. 29. 15. It is difficult to identify all the names of the tribes enumerated as living north of Abasgia in the table of peoples in Zacharias Myt. xii. 7, p. 328 (the Kotrigurs appear as Khorthrigor).

Sebastopolis on a scale worthy of his reputation as a great builder.[1] The fact that he thought it worth while to maintain this outpost shows how considerable were the political and commercial interests of the Empire in this region.

§ 6. *The Avars*

One of the disadvantages of the system of subsidising the barbarians on the frontiers or endowing them with territory was that fresh and formidable enemies were lured to the Roman borders from remote wilds and wastes by the hope of similar benefits. Towards the end of Justinian's reign, a new people of Hunnic race appeared on the frontier of Europe, north of the Caspian, and immediately fixed their covetous desires on the Empire, whose wealth and resources were probably exaggerated far beyond the truth among the barbarian tribes. They called themselves Avars, though it is alleged that they had usurped the name of another people better than themselves;[2] but they were destined to play a part on the European scene similar, if on a smaller scale, to that which had been played by the Huns.

Their westward migration was undoubtedly due to the revolution in Central Asia, which, about the middle of the sixth century, overthrew the power of the Zhu-zhu[3] and set in their place the Turks, who had been their despised vassals. Tu-men was the name of the leader who rose against his masters and founded the empire of the Turks. His successor, Mo-kan (A.D. 553–572), overthrew the kingdom of the Ephthalites and organised the vast Turkish empire which extended from China to the Caspian and southwards to the borders of Persia, dividing it into two khanates, of which the western was subordinate to the eastern.[4]

---

[1] Procopius, *B.G.* iv. 4-6; and *Aed.* iii. 7. 8-9.

[2] Cp. Theophylactus Simocatta, *Hist.* vii. 7 ; Bury, App. 5 to Gibbon, vol. v.

[3] See above, chap. iii. § 3. The Zhu-zhu are supposed to have been the true and original "Avars."

[4] See Bury, Appendix 17 to Gibbon, vol. iv. The scanty information supplied by Greek sources about the early Turkish Empire must be supplemented by Chinese records (cp. E. H. Parker's article in *E.H.R.* xi.

431 *sqq.*, and *A Thousand Years of the Tartars*, 1896 ; Marquart, *Historische Glossen zu den alttürkischen Inschriften*, in *Wiener Zeitschrift f. die Kunde des Morgenlandes*, xii. 157 *sqq.*, 1898). The later history of the Turks and their institutions (seventh and eighth centuries) have been illustrated by the Turkish inscriptions discovered in Eastern Mongolia (Thomsen, *Inscriptions de l'Orkhon déchiffrées*, 1894 ; Radloff, *Die alt-türkischen Inschriften der Mongolei*, 1895 (Neue Folge), 1897 (Zweite Folge),

In A.D. 558 Justin, the son of Germanus, who was commanding the forces in Colchis, received a message from Sarus, king of the Alans, to the effect that Candich, king of the Avars, desired to enter into communications with the Emperor. Justin informed his cousin, who signified his readiness to receive an embassy. The envoys of Candich arrived at Constantinople. They vaunted the invincibility of the Avars and made large demands—land, gifts, annual subsidies. Justinian, having consulted the Imperial Council, gave them handsome gifts, couches, clothes, and gold chains, and sent an ambassador to Candich, who was informed that the Emperor might take his requests into consideration, if the Avars proved their worth by subduing his enemies. The Avars immediately made war upon the Sabirs and destroyed them, and fought with success against the Utigurs. Having cleared the way, they advanced through Kotrigur territory to the regions of the Bug and Seret, subjugated the Antae, and in A.D. 562 they made a great raid through Central Europe, appeared on the Elbe, and threatened the eastern marches of the Frank kingdom of Austrasia. But all these expeditions seem to have been carried out from their headquarters, somewhere between the Caspian and the Black Sea.[1]

In the same year Baian, who had succeeded Candich and was afterwards to prove himself the Attila of the Avars, sent an embassy to Constantinople, demanding land in a Roman province. The ambassadors travelled by Colchis, and Justin, who arranged for their journey to the capital, gained the confidence of one of the party and was secretly informed by him that treachery was intended. He therefore advised Justinian to detain the barbarians as long as possible, since the Avars would not carry out their purpose of crossing the Danube till the envoys had departed. The Emperor acted on this advice, and Bonus, the Quaestor of Moesia and Scythia, was instructed

1899; Marquart, op. cit., and Die Chronologie der alt-türk. Inschriften, 1898. Mokan may almost certainly be identified with Silzibulos in Menander.
    [1] Menander, De leg. gent. frs. 1-13; John Eph. H.E. Part III. vi. 24; Gregory of Tours, Hist. Fr. iv. 23. Cp. also Pseudo-Nestor, Chron. c. 8 (p. 6, ed. Miklovich), on the subjugation of the Slavonic Dudlebians of Volkynia by the Avars (Obre), which

Šafarik (Slaw. Altertümer, ii. 60) and Marquart (Osteur. Streifzüge, 147) refer to the invasion of 562. The comments of Marquart (Chronologie, 78 sqq.) on Menander, fr. 3, based on the theory that the Antae at this time exercised overlordship over the Bulgarians, are very hazardous. John Eph. (ib. cp. iii. 25) says the Avars were so called from wearing their hair long.

to see to the defences of the river.[1] The policy succeeded, though we do not know exactly why ; the Avars did not attempt to invade the Empire ; and the envoys were at last dismissed. They received the usual gifts, which they employed in buying clothes and arms before they left Constantinople. The arms must have been furnished by the Imperial factories, and the Emperor apparently did not consider it politic to refuse to sell them. But he sent secret instructions to Justin to take the arms away from the barbarians when they arrived in Colchis. Justin obeyed, and this act is said to have been the beginning of enmity between the Romans and the Avars. Justinian did not live to see the sequel. But he had not been long in his grave before Baian led his people to the Danube, where they secured a permanent abode and were a scourge to the Balkan provinces for nearly sixty years.

§ 7. *Roman Commerce*

In the efforts of the Imperial government to extend its influence in the Red Sea sphere, the interests of trade were the principal consideration. Before we examine the fragmentary and obscure record of Roman intervention in the affairs of Ethiopia and Southern Arabia, we may survey the commercial activities of the Empire abroad.

The trade of the Mediterranean was almost entirely in the hands of Syrians and Greeks. In Rome and Naples and Carthage, and not only in Marseilles and Bordeaux, but also in the chief inland cities of Gaul, we find settlements of oriental merchants.[2] Their ships conveyed to the west garments of silk and wrought linen from the factories of Tyre and Berytus, purple from Caesarea and Neapolis, pistachios from Damascus, the strong wines of Gaza and Ascalon, papyrus from Egypt, furs from Cappadocia.[3]

---

[1] Menander, *ib. fr.* 4. Bonus is described as πρωτοστάτης τοῦ θητικοῦ καὶ οἰκετικοῦ. He had been appointed *quaestor exercitus* of the Five Provinces (see below, p. 340) in 536 (*Nov.* 41).

[2] Cp. the article of Bréhier, *Les Colonies d'orientaux en occident, B.Z.* xii. 1 *sqq.* (1903). On commerce in general in the sixth century see Heyd, *Hist. du commerce*, i. pp. 1-24.

[3] See the *Expositio totius mundi*,

which was translated from the Greek soon after 345. Sidonius (*Carm.* 17. 15) speaks of the *vina Gazetica*, cp. Cassiodorus, *Var.* 12. 5 ; Greg. of Tours, *Hist. Fr.* vii. 29. Among the exports from Spain, the *Expositio* enumerates oil, bacon, cloth, and mules ; from Africa, oil, cattle, and clothing. On the multitude of Syrian merchants in Gaul *cp.* Salvian, *De gub. Dei*, iv. 14.

There was a large demand for embroidered stuffs, especially for
ecclesiastical use, cloths for altars, curtains for churches.[1] But
the great centre to which the ships from all quarters converged
was the Imperial capital, as the richest and most populous city
of the world.[2] It seems probable that most of the imports
which the Empire received from the countries bordering on the
Euxine came directly across its waters to Constantinople and
were distributed from there : the skins which the Huns exchanged
at Cherson for stuffs and jewels,[3] and the slaves, skins, corn,
salt, wine, which were obtained from Lazica.

For the Empire trade with the East had always been mainly
a trade in imports. The East supplied the Mediterranean
peoples with many products which they could not do without,
while they had themselves less produce to offer that was greatly
desired by the orientals. There had, from of old, been a certain
market in China for glass, enamelled work, and fine stuffs from
Syria ;[4] but whatever exports found their way thither or to
India and Arabia were far from being a set-off to the supplies
of silk, not to speak of spices, precious stones, and other things
which the East sent to the West. The balance of trade was,
therefore, decidedly against the Empire, and there was a constant
drain of gold to the East.[5]

Under the early Roman Empire, the trade with India, the
Persian Gulf, Arabia, and the eastern coast of Africa had been

---

[1] Cp. the document of A.D. 471
given by Duchesne, *Lib. pont.* i.
cxlvii. Wealthy private persons also
obtained from the East the artistic
tapestries which they needed for the
adornment of their houses, like that
embroidered with hunting - scenes
which is described by Sidonius, *Epp.*
ix. 13. On figured textiles see Dalton,
Byz. Art, 577 *sqq.*

[2] Paulus Silentiarius (*S. Sophia*,
232) makes Constantinople say :

εἰς ἐμὲ φορτὶς ἅπασα φερέσβιον ἐλπίδα τείνει
κύκλιον εἰσορόωσα δρόμον διδυμάονος ἄρκτου.

[3] Jordanes, *Get.* 37 ; cp. Procopius,
B.G. iv. 20, 17.

[4] See Hirth, *China and the Roman
Orient.* M. Khvostov's Russian work,
*Istoriia vostochnoi torgovli Greko-
rimskago Egipta*, is indispensable for

eastern trade down to the end of the
third century.

[5] We have no figures bearing on
the amount of the trade except those
furnished by Pliny in the first century.
He says that India received annually
from the Empire 55 million sesterces
(c. £600,000), and that China, India,
and Arabia together took at least 100
million sesterces (c. £1,000,000) ; *Nat.
Hist.* vi. 23, § 101, and xii. 18, § 84.
If these sums represented the whole
value of the imports, the volume of
trade would have been small ; but it
probably only means the balance of
trade—the amount of specie which
was taken from the Empire ; and to
know the value of the imports, we
should have also to know the amount
of the exports which partly paid for
them. So Hirth, *ib.* p. 227, and
Khvostov, *op. cit.* p. 410, inclines to
this view.

in the hands of Roman merchants, who sailed through the Red Sea and the Indian Ocean in their own vessels. Before the end of the third century this direct commerce seems to have ceased almost entirely. The trade between the Mediterranean and the East passed into the hands of intermediaries, the Persians, the Abyssinians, and the Himyarites of Yemen. This change may have been due to the anarchical conditions of the Empire, which followed on the death of Alexander Severus and were unfavourable to commercial enterprise. The energy of Persian merchants, under the orderly rule of the Sassanids, secured a monopoly of the silk trade, and the products of India were conveyed by Abyssinian traders to their own market at Adulis, or even to the Roman ports on the isthmus, Clysma (Suez) [1] and Aila. The Red Sea trade itself seems to have been gradually abandoned, as time went on, to the Abyssinians and Himyarites, who grew more powerful and important as their commercial profits increased. The Abyssinians—as we may conveniently call the Ethiopians of the kingdom of Axum, from which modern Abyssinia descends—also profited by the disuse of the Nile as a trade route with East-Central Africa. The products of those regions (slaves, ivory, ebony, gold, gems, ochre, etc.) had come to Egypt by the Nile, as well as by the Red Sea, in the old days when the Ethiopic kingdom of Meroe flourished. Meroe declined in the second century, and in the third its organisation fell to pieces, and the Upper Nile, under the control of the barbarous Nubians and Blemmyes, became impracticable as a road for trade. With the shifting of power from Meroe to Axum, East African commerce passed entirely into the hands of the Abyssinians.[2]

---

[1] Clysma is Qulzum, a quarter of a mile north of Suez. This is shown by its description in the account of her pilgrimage to Sinai by the Abbess Aetheria (of South Gaul), who travelled in the early years of Justinian's reign (between 533 and 540), according to K. Meister in *Rhein. Mus.*, N.F., lxiv. 337 *sqq.* (1909), and Mommsen, *Hist. Sch.* iii. 610 *sqq.*, but according to others in the last years of the fourth century (see E. Weigand, *B.Z.* xx. 1 *sqq.*, 1912). She saw many large ships there, and mentions that there was a resident *agens in rebus*, known as a logothete, who used to visit India every year by

order of the Emperor. India, of course, must mean Ethiopia. The most important duty of this office was to see that the regulations as to exports were observed (cp. *C. Th.* vi. 29. 8).

[2] Khvostov, *op. cit.* 29 *sqq.* For the early trade of Roman Egypt with the East see also Mommsen, *Röm. Gesch.* v. chap. xii. It is to be observed that the cessation of direct trade with the East was reflected in the decline of geographical knowledge, illustrated by the misuse of India to designate Ethiopia, which is frequent in Greek and Latin writers from the fourth century.

As to the traffic with India, we find much curious information in a remarkable book which was written about the middle of the sixth century, the *Christian Cosmography* of Cosmas.

Cosmas, who is known as Indicopleustes, "sailor of the Indian Sea," was an Egyptian merchant, but when he wrote his book he had probably abandoned his calling and become a monk. The *Cosmography*, which was composed about A.D. 545–550,[1] is unfortunately neither a treatise on geography like Strabo's or Ptolemy's, nor a plain account of his travels, but a theological work, designed to explain the true shape of the universe as proved by Scripture, and especially to refute the error of pagan science that the earth is spherical. His theory as to the shape of the world, which is based on the hypothesis that Moses, "the great cosmographer," intended his tabernacle to be a miniature model of the universe, is not devoid of interest as an example of the fantastic speculations to which the interpretation of the Biblical documents as literally inspired inevitably leads.

The earth, according to Cosmas, is a flat rectangle, and its length is double its breadth. The heavens form a second story, welded to the extremities of the earth by four walls. The dry land which we inhabit is surrounded by the ocean, and beyond it is another land where men lived before the Deluge. The firmament is the ceiling between the two stories, and the earth, the lower story, lies at the bottom of the universe, to which it sank when it was created. There is nothing below it. Hence the pagan theory of the antipodes is a delusion. On its western side the earth rises into a great conical mountain, which hides

<hr>

[1] Books i.-v. appeared first, and vi.-x. were separately added to answer objections and supply additional explanations. The chronological indications are as follows : (1) Timothy, Patriarch of Alexandria, who died in 535, is described as νῦν τετελευτηκώς, x. p. 315. (2) Theodosius of Alexandria is still alive at Constantinople, *ib.* p. 314. Theodosius was confined, after his deposition in 536, in the Thracian fort of Derkos (John Eph. *Comm. de B. Or.*, p. 14), but afterwards lived under Theodora's protection at Constantinople, where he died soon after

Justinian's death (*ib.* p. 159 ; cp. *H.E.* Part II. p. 218). These indications give the limits 536 and 565. (3) It is stated in vi. p. 232 that a solar and a lunar eclipse, which occurred in the same year, on Mecheri 12 and Mesori 14, had been predicted. Two such eclipses did occur on February 6 and August 17 in 547. Hence Book vi. was written after 547. (4) Book ii. was written (p. 72) twenty-five years after the Himyarite expedition of Elesboas, which occurred "at the beginning of the reign of Justin." This implies about 544–545 for Books i.-v.

the sun at night. The sun is not larger than the earth, as the
pagans falsely imagine, but much smaller. The revolutions of
all the celestial bodies are guided by angel pilots.[1]

It would be a mistake to suppose that this strange reconstruction of the world, which contemptuously set aside all that
Greek science had achieved, represented the current views of
orthodox Christians or ever obtained any general credence.
It was not indeed original. Cosmas derived his conceptions
from hints which had been thrown out by theologians of the
Syrian school, especially from Theodore of Mopsuestia.[2] But
for us the value of the work lies in the scraps of information
relating to his own travels which the author introduces incidentally, and in the contents of an appendix, which has no relation
to his theme, and seems to have been part of another work of
Cosmas, and to have been attached to the *Cosmography* by
some injudicious editor.[3]

Cosmas knew the Red Sea well. He visited Ethiopia in the
reign of Justin,[4] and he made at least one voyage to the Persian
Gulf.[5] It is to this voyage that he probably referred when he
wrote : " I sailed along the coast of the island of Dioscorides
(Socotra), but did not land, though in Ethiopia I met some of
its Greek-speaking inhabitants." [6] The Persian Gulf probably
represents the limit of his eastern travel, for in all that he tells
of Ceylon and India we are struck by the absence of any of those
personal touches which could not fail to appear in the descriptions of an eye-witness. It was only a rare Roman merchant

---

[1] The extension of the work of
creation over six days—whereas it
could have been accomplished by a
single fiat—is ingeniously explained
as due to the Creator's wish to give
a series of object-lessons to the
angels, iii. p. 105 *sqq.*

[2] Cosmas was a Nestorian. Cp.
M'Crindle, *Introd.* to his translation,
p. ix.

[3] Books xi. and xii., of which the
latter is a series of fragments. He
had written a general geography
which is lost (*Prologue, ad init.*), but
it has been suggested that Book xi.
formed part of it (Winstedt, *Introd.*
p. 5).

[4] ii. p. 72.

[5] He says that he had sailed in the
Persian, Arabian, and Roman Gulfs

(the Roman means the Mediterranean),
ib. p. 62, where he relates that " once
having sailed to Inner India and
crossed a little towards Barbaria—
where farther on is situated Zingion,
as they call the mouth of the Ocean
—we saw a flight of albatrosses
(suspha)." Inner India is either
South Arabia or Abyssinia, though in
the same passage Ceylon is said to
be in Inner India (if Inner is not an
error for Outer). Barbaria is the
African coast south of Abyssinia, and
Zingion is Zanzibar.

[6] iii. p. 119. There were Christian
clergy here who received ordination
from Persia. Cosmas also mentions
that there were Christian churches in
Ceylon, Mala (Malabar), and Calliana
(near Bombay) under a bishop
ordained in Persia.

who visited the markets of Ceylon.[1] The trade between the Red Sea and India was entirely in the hands of the Abyssinians, and the Roman merchants dealt with them.

Ceylon, which the ancients knew as Taprobane,[2] was the great centre of maritime commerce between the Far East and the West. In its ports congregated Persian, Ethiopian, and Indian merchants. Silk was brought from China to its markets, and continental India sent her products : Malabar, pepper ; Calliana, copper ; Sindu, musk and castor.[3] The islanders exported their own products eastward and westward, and they had a merchant service themselves, but the significance of Ceylon was its position as an emporium for merchandise in transit. The Persians had an advantage over the Romans in that they traded directly with the island, and had a commercial colony there,[4] while the Roman trade, as we have seen, was carried on through the Ethiopians and intermediaries.

While it is probable that most of the Indian commodities which were consumed in the Empire travelled by this route, the Ethiopian traders did not carry silk. The large supplies of silk which reached the Romans were bought from Persian merchants, and most of it was probably conveyed overland from China to Persia, though part of it may also have come by sea, by way of Ceylon and the Persian Gulf. We do not know by what methods the Persians succeeded in establishing this monopoly and preventing the Abyssinians from trading in silk. It was highly inconvenient to the Empire to depend exclusively on a political rival for a product of which the consumption was immense, and in time of war the inconvenience was grave. Justinian deemed it a matter of the first importance to break the Persian monopoly, and for this purpose, during the first Persian War, he entered into negotiations with the king of Abyssinia.

---

[1] Cosmas knew one. See below, p. 332.

[2] Cosmas also calls it Sielediva (from which comes the modern Arabic Serendib). He tells us that there were two kings in the island, and there were many temples, on the top of one of which (perhaps the Buddhist temple of Anarajapura) shone a red stone, large as the cone of a pine, which Cosmas calls a hyacinth. This stone was known by report to Marco Polo (iii. 14), who calls it a ruby. It is supposed by some to be an amethyst. Cosmas, xi. 321 *sqq*.

[3] Sindu has been identified with Diul-Sind, at the mouth of the Indus. China in Cosmas is Τζινίστα. He says that from there and other emporia (probably Further India) Ceylon receives silk, aloes (ἀλοήν), cloves (καρυόφυλλα), sandalwood (τζανδάναν).

[4] xi. p. 322.

§ 8. *The Abyssinians and Himyarites*

The kingdom of the Abyssinians or Ethiopians, who were also known as the Axumites, from the name of their capital city Axum, approached Suakim on the north, stretched westwards to the valley of the Nile, and southwards to the Somali coast. Their port of Adulis was reckoned as a journey of fifteen days from Axum where the king resided.[1] Roman merchants frequented Adulis, where there was a great market of the products of Africa, slaves, spices, papyrus, ivory, and gold from Sasu.[2]

The commercial relations of the Abyssinians with their neighbours across the straits, the Himyarites of Yemen, were naturally close, and from time to time they sought to obtain political control over South-western Arabia. Christian missionaries had been at work in both countries since the reign of Constantius II., when an Arian named Theophilus was appointed bishop of the new churches in Abyssinia, Yemen, and the island of Socotra.[3] He is said to have founded churches at Safar and Aden.[4] After this we lose sight of these countries for about a century and a half, during which Christianity probably made little way in either country, and Judaism established itself firmly in Yemen. Then we learn that in the reign of Anastasius a bishop was sent to the Himyarites.[5] We may conjecture that this step was the consequence of a war between the Himyarites and Abyssinians, which is misdated in our records, but apparently belongs to the reign of Zeno or of Anastasius.[6]

---

[1] So Nonnosus, who had made the journey (*F.H.G.* iv. 179). Procopius says 12. We first hear of this Ethiopian kingdom in the *Periplus maris Erythraei*, § 2 *sqq.* (*Geogr. Gr. Minores*, vol. i.), *i.e.* in the first century A.D. Its history has been elucidated by Dillmann in his articles in *Abh. Berliner Akad.*, 1878 and 1880.

[2] The Ethiopians gave meat, salt, and iron in exchange for the gold they got from Sasu, Cosmas, ii. p. 70. The mention of iron is to be noticed in view of what Procopius says, *B.P.* i. 19. 25 : the Ethiopians have no iron ; they cannot buy it from the Romans, for it is expressly forbidden by law.

[3] Frumentius, ordained by Atha-

nasius, had been the first bishop in Abyssinia. Athanasius (*Apologia ad Constantinum*, 31) quotes a letter from Constantius to the Ethiopian kings, Aizan and Sazan, asking them to send back Frumentius as a heretic. (An inscription of this Aizan is preserved, *C.I.G.* iii. 5128, where he appears as sole king, but his brother Saiazan is mentioned.) The mission of Theophilus is recorded by Philostorgius, iii. 4-6.

[4] Τάφαρον, ’Αδάνη.

[5] Theodore Lector, ii. 58 (his source was John Diakrinomenos).

[6] The events connected with the names of Andas and Dimnos are related by John Mal. (xviii. 433 and 429) to the reign of Justinian (A.D. 529). But we know on unimpeach-

Dimnos, king of the Himyarites, who was probably a convert to Judaism, massacred some Greek merchants, as a measure of reprisal for alleged ill-treatment of Jews in the Roman Empire. Thereupon, presumably at direct instigation from Constantinople, the Abyssinian king Andas invaded Yemen, put Dimnos to death, and doubtless left a viceroy in the country with an Ethiopian garrison. Andas had vowed that, if he were victorious, he would embrace Christianity. He fulfilled his vow, and the Emperor sent him a bishop from Alexandria. Andas was succeeded by Tazena, whose inscriptions describe him as " King of Axum and Homer and Reidan and Saba and Salhen." [1] He also was converted from paganism, and his son Elesboas, who was on the throne at the beginning of Justin's reign, was probably brought up a Christian.[2]

In the meantime a Himyarite leader, Dhu Novas, of Jewish faith, succeeded in overpowering the Ethiopian garrison, proclaimed himself king, and proceeded to persecute the Christians.[3] It is not quite certain whether Elesboas immediately sent an army to re-establish his authority (A.D. 519–520),[4] but if he did so, Dhu Novas recovered his power within the next two years

able authority that at that time the names of the kings were respectively Elesboas and Esimiphaios, and Elesboas had been on the throne since the beginning of Justin's reign. We must therefore suppose that John Malalas, misunderstanding his authority, made a chronological mistake, and refer the episode to an earlier period. Cp. Duchesne, *Les Églises séparées,* 316-317; Nöldeke, *Tabari,* 175; Fell, *Die Christenverfolgung in Südarabien,* in *Z.D.M.G.* xxxv. 19. The name "Ανδας appears as 'Αδάδ in Theophanes (A.M. 6035), and as Aidug in John Eph. *H.E.* Part II., extract in Assemani, *Bibl. Or.* i. p. 359. It is supposed to correspond to Ela-Amida in Ethiopic chronicles.

[1] Homer is Himyar ; Reidan has been explained as=Safar, and Salhen as the fortress of Ma'rib (Fell, *ib.* 27) ; Saba (Sheba) is familiar. For the inscriptions of Tazena see Dillmann, *Z.D.M.G.* vii. 357 *sqq.* Huart (*Hist. des Arabes,* p. 53) suggests that the Ethiopians had no ships and that the Romans must have supplied them with transports for their expeditions to Yemen.

[2] Ela Atzbeha is the Ethiopic name (Nöldeke, *ib.* 188). Of the Greeks, Cosmas gets nearest to it with his 'Ελλατζβάας, ii. p. 72 ; John Mal. has 'Ελευβάας, *Acta mart. Arethae,* p. 721 'Ελεσβάς, Procopius 'Ελλησθεαῖος. On his coins he was also called Chaleb (see Schlumberger in *Rev. numism.* 1886, pl. xix. Χαλὴβ βασιλεὺς υἰὸς θεξενα), and this, his " throne-name," appears in the Ethiopic version of the *Acta mart. Arethae.* Cp. Fell, *ib.* 17 *sqq.*

[3] See the consolatory letter written by Jacob of Sarug (who died November 20, 521) to the Himyarite Christians, edited by Guidi (see Bibliogr. I. 2, B).

[4] Guidi (*op. cit.* pp. 476, 479) argues for two expeditions against Dhu Novas, the earlier in 519. There is a good deal to be said for this. Cosmas witnessed the preparations of Ela Atzbeha " at the beginning of the reign of Justin " (*loc. cit.*), and, as Justin reigned only till 527, it would have been a strange misuse of words to speak of 524 as the beginning of his reign. See above, p. 319, *n.* 1. Cp. Mordtmann, *Z.D.M.G.* xxxv. 698.

and began systematically to exterminate the Christian communities of southern Arabia, if they refused to renounce their errors and embrace Judaism. Having killed all the Ethiopians in the land, he marched with a large army against the fortified town of Nejran, which was the headquarters of the Christians (A.D. 523). The siege was long, but, when the king promised that he would spare all the inhabitants, the place capitulated. Dhu Novas, however, had no intention of keeping faith, and when the Christians refused to apostatise, he massacred them to the number of 280, among whom the most conspicuous was Harith, the emir of the tribe of Harith ibn-Kaab. After having performed this service to the Jewish faith, Dhu Novas despatched envoys to Al-Mundhir of Hira, bearing a letter in which he described his exploits, boasted that he had not left a Christian in his land, and urged the Saracen emir to do likewise. When the envoys arrived at Al-Mundhir's camp at Raṁla (January 20, A.D. 524), Simeon Beth Arsham, the head of the Monophysites of the Persian empire, happened to be there, having come on the part of the Emperor Justin to negotiate peace with the Saracens. Horrified by the news, Simeon immediately transmitted it to Simeon, abbot of Gabula, asking him to arrange that the Monophysites of Antioch, Tarsus, and other cities should be informed of what had happened.[1]

It is possible that Justin and the Patriarch of Alexandria [2] despatched messengers to Axum to incite the Abyssinians to avenge the slaughtered Christians and suppress the tyrant. In any case Ela Atzbeha invaded Yemen with a great army (A.D. 524-525), defeated and killed Dhu Novas, and set up in his

[1] For these events the Syriac letter of Simeon, which has been edited by Guidi, and is generally recognised as genuine, is the most authentic source. Simeon, who was accompanied by Mar Abram and Sergius, bishop of Rosapha, had obtained further information as to the massacre when he returned to Hira from Al-Mundhir's camp. It has been conjectured by Duchesne (*op. cit.* p. 325) that Sergius was the author of the *Martyrium Arethae et sociorum* which has come down in Greek. John Psaltes, in 524-525, composed a Greek hymn on the martyrs, which was immediately translated into Syriac by Paul, bishop of Edessa (died October

30, 526), and his version is preserved (*Z.D.M.G.* xxxi. 400 *sqq.*). He speaks not of 280, but of more than 200 martyrs. A verse in the Koran (Sura 85) is said to refer to the massacre : " Cursed were the contrivers of the pit, of fire supplied with fuel ; when they sat round the same, and were witnesses of what they did against the true believers."

[2] So the Greek version of the *Mart. Arethae*, where a letter from Justin (doubtless an invention) is given. But as the Armenian version contains nothing of these negotiations, we have no guarantee that they were mentioned in the original Syriac work. Cp. Duchesne, *loc. cit.*

stead a Himyarite Christian, whose name was Esimiphaios, as
tributary king.[1]

Such were the political relations of the two Red Sea kingdoms
when, in A.D. 531, Justinian sent Julian, an *agens in rebus*, to
the courts of Ela Atzbeha and Esimiphaios.[2] The purpose of
the embassy was to win their co-operation against Persia in
different ways. Julian travelled to Adulis by sea, and had an
audience of Ela Atzbeha at Axum. The king stood on a four-
wheeled car harnessed to four elephants. He was naked, except
for a linen apron embroidered with gold and straps set with pearls
over his stomach and shoulders.[3] He wore gold bracelets and
held a gilt shield and two gilt lances. His councillors, who stood
round him, were armed, and flute-players were performing. He
kissed the seal of the Emperor's letter, and was amazed by the
rich gifts which Julian brought to him. He readily agreed to
ally himself with the Empire against Persia. The chief service
which the Abyssinians could render was to destroy the Persian
monopoly in the silk trade by acting as carriers of silk between
Ceylon and the Red Sea ports, a service which would also be
highly profitable to themselves.

The consent of Ela Atzbeha, as overlord of Yemen, must also
have been obtained to the proposals which Julian was instructed
to lay before Esimiphaios. The Arabians of Maad (Nejd) were
subject to the Himyarites, and their chieftain, Kais, who was a
notable warrior, had slain a kinsman of the king and had been
forced to flee into the desert. The plan of Justinian was to procure the pardon of Kais, in order that he, at the head of an army
of Himyarites and Maadites, might invade the Persian empire.

---

[1] Procopius, *B.P.* i. 20. 1. (John
Mal. xviii. 457, says that the king of
the Axumites made Anganes, a man
of his own family, king of the
Himyarites.) A Himyarite inscription found at Hisn-Gurab seems to
record these events. It commemorates an Abyssinian invasion, and the
defeat and death of the Himyarite
king. The name of the man who
set it up was read as Es-Samaika,
but Fell has plausibly suggested that
the true reading may be Es-Samaifa,
which would correspond to Ἐσιμιφαῖος.
He does not, however, designate himself as king. The date is 640 of the
Himyarite era, which (if the theory

is correct) would be determined as
640 – 525 = 115. See *Z.D.M.G.* 7, 473,
and 35, 36.

[2] There are two sources for this
embassy, Procopius, *ib.* 20. 9 *sqq.*,
and John Mal. *loc. cit.* (with the
additions of Theophanes, who has
placed it under a wrong year, A.M.
6064 = A.D. 571–572). It can be inferred from the words of John Mal.
(ὡς ἐξηγήσατο ὁ αὐτὸς πρεσβευτής) that
Julian published an account of his
embassy, which was doubtless also
known to Procopius.

[3] Σχιαστὰς διὰ μαργαριτῶν καὶ κλαβία
ἀνὰ πέντε (John Mal. *ib.*).

Although Julian was successful in his negotiations and the kings promised to do what was required, they were unable to perform their promises. For men of Yemen to attack Persia meant long marches through the Arabian deserts, and the Himyarites shrank from such a difficult enterprise. In Ceylon the Abyssinian merchants were out-manœuvred by the Persians, who bought up all the cargoes of silk as soon as they arrived in port.

It must have been soon after Julian's embassy that a revolt broke out in Yemen. Esimiphaios was dethroned and imprisoned, and a certain Abram, who was originally the slave of a Roman resident at Adulis, seized the power.[1] It seems to have been a revolt of the Ethiopian garrison, not of the natives, and it is probable that Abram, who was a Christian, had been appointed commander of the garrison by Ela Atzbeha himself. Two expeditions were sent against Abram, but in both the Abyssinians were decisively defeated, and Ela Atzbeha then resigned himself to the recognition of Abram as viceroy.

Of the subsequent mission of Nonnosus, whom Justinian sent to Abyssinia, Yemen, and Maad, we only know that the ambassador on his journeys incurred many dangers from both men and beasts. The father of Nonnosus, Abram, was employed on similar business, and on two occasions conducted negotiations with Kais, the Arab chief of Nejd. Kais sent his son Muaviah as a hostage to Constantinople, and afterwards, having resigned the chieftaincy to his brother, visited the Imperial capital himself and was appointed phylarch of Palestine.[2]

---

[1] Procopius, *ib.* 3-8, who, as he says, anticipates events subsequent to Julian's embassy. · According to *Mart. Arethae* and the Gregentius documents (see below), which entirely ignore Esimiphaios, Abram was set up as king immediately after the overthrow of Dhu Novas. If Abram was commander of the resident Abyssinian troops, the error is explicable.—The name of Abram or Abraha was remembered in Arabic legend for his expedition against Mecca. His purpose was to destroy the Ka'ba. He was riding an elephant called Mahmud, and when he approached the city the animal knelt down and refused to advance. Then a flock of birds came flying from the sea with stones in their bills which they dropped on the heads of the troops. The legend is commemorated in the Koran (Sura 105) : "Hast thou not seen how the Lord dealt with the masters of the elephant ? "

[2] The fragments of the book of Nonnosus, preserved by Photius, are meagre and disappointing, and there are no chronological indications (*F.H.G.* iv. 179). We may conjecture that Abram was of Saracen race and that both he and Nonnosus could speak Arabic.

Historians and chroniclers tell us nothing of the revival of
the Christian communities in the kingdom of the Himyarites
after the fall of their persecutor Dhu Novas. There are other
documents, however, which record the appointment of a bishop
and describe his activities in Yemen. According to this tradition,
Gregentius of Ulpiana was sent from Alexandria as bishop of
Safar in the reign of Justin. He held a public disputation on
the merits of Judaism and Christianity with a learned Jew and
utterly discomfited him ; and he drew up a Code of laws for
Abram king of the Himyarites. As some of the historical statements in these documents are inconsistent with fact, the story
of Gregentius has been regarded with scepticism and even his
existence has been questioned.[1] But there is no good reason to
suppose that the story does not rest on a genuine tradition which
was improved by legend and was written down when the historical
details were forgotten. The Code of laws bears some internal
marks of genuineness, though we may hope, for the sake of the
Himyarites, that it was never enforced.[2]

[1] All the interesting parts of the
Vita Gregentii, preserved in a Sinaitic
MS., have been published by Vasil'ev
(see Bibliography). The disputation
with the Jew Herbanus, which is
included in the *Vita*, is found by itself
in many MSS., and had already been
edited (see Migne, *P.G.* lxxxvi.). According to the Life, Gregentius was
born at Ulpiana in Dardania. It is
significant that this city, which is
called Μπλιαρές (cp. the Slavonic
name Lipljan), is described as ἐν τοῖς
μεθορίοις 'Αβάρων and τελοῦσα εἰς τὸ
αὐτὸ τῶν 'Αβάρων γένος, suggesting that
the word was composed between 580
and 630. Gregentius travelled in
Sicily, Italy, and Spain (Καρταγένα),
and finally went to Alexandria ἐν
ταῖς ἡμέραις 'Ιουστίνου βασιλέως 'Ρωμαίων καὶ 'Ελεσβοὰμ βασιλέως Αἰθιόπων
καὶ Δουναῦ (Dhu Novas) βασιλέως 'Ομηρι-
τῶν καὶ Προτερίου πάπα 'Αλεξανδρείας.
When the Ethiopian king overthrew
Dhu Novas, he wrote to Proterius
asking him to ordain and send a
bishop to the Himyarites. Proterius
consecrated the deacon Gregentius,
who travels apparently up the Nile and
reaches the capital city of the Ethiopians, which is called 'Αμλέμ. Thence

he proceeds to Safar, where he finds
Ela Atzbeha, and under his auspices
restores and founds churches at
Nejran (Νεγρά), Safar, Akana, and
Legmia. Before Ela Atzbeha returned home (he had remained, ὡς
ἔφασάν τινες, about three years in
Yemen) he and Gregentius elevated
Abram to the throne. In this narrative Abram appears as the successor
of Dhu Novas ; Esimiphaios is
entirely ignored ; and a Patriarch of
Alexandria, Proterius, is introduced
who is never mentioned in any records
except in connexion with Gregentius.
Another suspicious point has been
noticed. Gregentius visits Agrigentum ; the names of his parents are
Agapius and Theodote. Now there
exists the Life of a mysterious saint,
Gregory of · Agrigentum, and his
parents were Chariton (which has
much the same meaning as Agapius)
and Theodote, while the name Gregentius itself suggests Agrigentum
(cp. Vasil'ev, p. 67). In the Greek
and Slavonic Menaea and Synaxaria
Gregentius is noticed, sometimes
under the name of Gregory. See
Synax. eccl. Cplae. (*A.SS. Nov.*), p. 328.

[2] For the Code see below, p. 413.

§ 9. *The Nobadae and Blemyes*

The missionary zeal of Justinian and Theodora did not over-
look the African peoples who lived on the Upper Nile between
Egypt and Abyssinia. We have already seen how the hostility
of the Blemyes, whose seats were above the First Cataract, and
their southern neighbours the Nobadae, whose capital was at
Dongola, constantly troubled the upper provinces of Egypt.
The Nobadae and their king Silko were converted to Christianity
about A.D. 540. The story of their conversion is curious.
Theodora was determined that they should learn the Monophysitic
doctrine ; Justinian desired to make them Chalcedonians. In
this competition for the souls of the Nobadae, Theodora was
successful. The episode is thus related by a Monophysitic historian : [1]

Among the clergy in attendance on the Patriarch Theodosius was a
proselyte named Julianus, an old man of great worth, who conceived an
earnest spiritual desire to christianise the wandering people who dwell on
the eastern borders of the Thebais beyond Egypt, and who are not only not
subject to the authority of the Roman Empire, but even receive a subsidy
on condition that they do not enter nor pillage Egypt. The blessed
Julianus, therefore, being full of anxiety for this people, went and spoke
about them to the late queen Theodora, in the hope of awakening in her
a similar desire for their conversion ; and as the queen was fervent in
zeal for God, she received the proposal with joy, and promised to do everything in her power for the conversion of these tribes from the errors of
idolatry. In her joy, therefore, she informed the victorious King Justinian of the purposed undertaking, and promised and anxiously desired
to send the blessed Julian thither. But when the king [Emperor] heard
that the person she intended to send was opposed to the council of Chalcedon, he was not pleased, and determined to write to the bishops of his
own side in the Thebais, with orders for them to proceed thither and instruct the Nobadae, and plant among them the name of synod. And as
he entered upon the matter with great zeal, he sent thither, without a
moment's delay, ambassadors with gold and baptismal robes, and gifts of
honour for the king of that people, and letters for the duke of the Thebais,
enjoining him to take every care of the embassy and escort them to the
territories of the Nobadae. When, however, the queen learnt these
things, she quickly, with much cunning, wrote letters to the duke of the
Thebais, and sent a mandatory of her court to carry them to him ; and
which were as follows : " Inasmuch as both his majesty and myself have
purposed to send an embassy to the people of the Nobadae, and I am now

---

[1] John Eph. *H.E.* Part III. iv.
6-7. I have borrowed the version of
Payne-Smith. A short account of
the conversion of the Nobadae and
Blemyes will be found in Duchesne,
op. cit. 287 *sqq.*

despatching a blessed man named Julian ; and further my will is that my ambassador should arrive at the aforesaid people before his majesty's ; be warned, that if you permit his ambassador to arrive there before mine, and do not hinder him by various pretexts until mine shall have reached you and shall have passed through your province and arrived at his destination, your life shall answer for it ; for I shall immediately send and take off your head." Soon after the receipt of this letter the king's ambassador also came, and the duke said to him, " You must wait a little while we look out and procure beasts of burden and men who know the deserts, and then you will be able to proceed." And thus he delayed him until the arrival of the merciful queen's embassy, who found horses and guides in waiting, and the same day, without loss of time, under a show of doing it by violence, they laid hands upon him, and were the first to proceed. As for the duke, he made his excuses to the king's ambassador, saying, " Lo ! when I had made my preparations and was desirous of sending you onward, ambassadors from the queen arrived and fell upon me with violence, and took away the beasts of burden I had got ready, and have passed onward ; and I am too well acquainted with the fear in which the queen is held to venture to oppose them. But abide still with me until I can make fresh preparations for you, and then you also shall go in peace." And when he heard these things he rent his garments, and threatened him terribly and reviled him ; and after some time he also was able to proceed, and followed the other's track without being aware of the fraud which had been practised upon him.

The blessed Julian meanwhile and the ambassadors who accompanied him had arrived at the confines of the Nobadae, whence they sent to the king and his princes informing him of their coming ; upon which an armed escort set out, who received them joyfully, and brought them into their land unto the king. And he too received them with pleasure, and her majesty's letter was presented and read to him, and the purport of it explained. They accepted also the magnificent honours sent them, and the numerous baptismal robes, and everything else richly provided for their use. And immediately with joy they yielded themselves up and utterly abjured the errors of their forefathers, and confessed the God of the Christians, saying, " He is the one true God, and there is no other beside Him." And after Julian had given them much instruction, and taught them, he further told them about the council of Chalcedon, saying that " inasmuch as certain disputes had sprung up among Christians touching the faith, and the blessed Theodosius being required to receive the council and having refused was ejected by the king [Emperor] from his throne, whereas the queen received him and rejoiced in him because he stood firm in the right faith and left his throne for its sake, on this account her majesty has sent us to you, that ye also may walk in the ways of Pope Theodosius, and stand in his faith and imitate his constancy. And moreover the king has sent unto you ambassadors, who are already on their way, in our footsteps."

The Emperor's emissaries arrived soon afterwards, and were dismissed by Silko, who informed them that if his people embraced

Christianity at all it would be the doctrine of the holy Theodosius of Alexandria, and not the " wicked faith " of the Emperor. The story, which is told by one who admired the Empress and lived under her protection, illustrates her unscrupulousness and her power. The Nobadae, converted to Christianity, immediately co-operated with the Empire in chastising the Blemyes and forcing them to adopt the same faith. Roman troops under Narses made a demonstration on the frontier of the Thebaid, but the main work was done by Silko, who celebrated his victory by setting up an inscription in the temple of the Blemyes at Talmis (Dodekaschoinos, now Kelabsheh). The boast of this petty potentate might be appropriate in the mouth of Attila or of Tamurlane : " I do not allow my foes to rest in the shade but compel them to remain in the full sunlight, with no one to bring them water to their houses. I am a lion for the lands below, and a bear for the lands above." [1] The conversion of the Blemyes enabled Justinian to abolish the scandal of the pagan worship at Philae, which had been suffered to exist on account of an ancient convention with that people.[2] A Greek agent was appointed to reside at Talmis and represent the Imperial authority.[3]

§ 10. *The Silk Industry*

The efforts of Justinian and his Abyssinian friends to break down the Persian monopoly of the silk trade had been frustrated by the superior organisation of Persian mercantile interests in

[1] Lefebvre, *Recueil*, 628, p. 118 ; *C.I.G.* iii. 5072. He describes himself as ἐγὼ Σιλκὼ βασιλίσκος Νουβάδων καὶ ὅλων τῶν Αἰθιόπων. The Greek who composed the inscription must have smiled to himself when he introduced the diminutive βασιλίσκος, " kinglet." Silko was succeeded by Eirpanomos (or Ergamenes). See Revillout, *Mémoire sur les Blemmyes*, in *Acad. des Inscr.* sér. 1, viii. 2. pp. 371 *sqq.*—References to the hostilities of the Blemyes in the sixth century will be found in *Pap. Cairo* i. 67004, 67007, and 67009. Here we find them plundering Omboi, and a pagan subject of the Empire reopening apparently a heathen temple for them (67004).

[2] See below, p. 371.

[3] Cp. *C.I.G.* iv. 8647-8649 (posterior to Justinian's reign). Three interesting Greek inscriptions, found at Gebeleïn, are discussed by J. Krall, in *Denkschr.* of the Vienna Academy, vol. xlvi. (1900). The princes of the Blemyes, like those of the Nobadae, were styled βασιλίσκοι by their Greek notaries. In the first of these texts (which date probably from the time of Anastasius or Justin) we find Charachen, βασιλείσκος τῶν Βλεμύων, giving orders as to an island in the Nile (perhaps near Gebeleïn), for which the Romans (οἱ Ῥώμεις) paid a συνήθεια. See Wessely, *Gr. Papyrusurk.* No. 132.

the markets of Ceylon. There was one other route by which it might have been possible to import silk direct from China, namely overland through Central Asia and north of the Caspian Sea to Cherson. This possibility was no doubt considered. Justinian, however, does not seem to have made any attempt to realise it, but it was to be one of the political objects of his successor.

After the outbreak of the war with Persia in A.D. 540, the private silk factories of Berytus and Tyre suffered severely.[1] It must be explained that, in order to prevent the Persian traders from taking advantage of competition to raise the price of silk, all the raw material was purchased from them by the *commerciarii* of the fisc, who then sold to private enterprises all that was not required by the public factories (*gynaecia*) which ministered to the needs of the court.[2] Justinian instructed the *commerciarii* not to pay more than 15 gold pieces (£9 : 7 : 6) for a pound of silk, but he could not force the Persians to sell at this price, and they preferred not to sell at all or at least not to sell enough to serve the private as well as the public factories. It is not clear whether hostilities entirely suspended the trade, but at best they seriously embarrassed it, and as the supplies dwindled the industrial houses of Tyre and Berytus raised the prices of their manufactures. The Emperor intervened and fixed 8 gold pieces a pound as the maximum price of silk stuffs. The result was that many manufacturers were ruined. Peter Barsymes, who was Count of the Sacred Largesses in A.D. 542, took advantage of the crisis to make the manufacture of silk a State monopoly, and some of the private industries which had failed were converted into government factories. This change created a new source of revenue for the treasury.[3]

Chance came to the aid of Justinian ten years later and solved the problem more effectively than he could have hoped. Two monks, who had lived long in China or some adjacent

---

[1] Procopius, *H.A.* 25. 13 *sqq.*

[2] *C.J.* iv. 40. 2. The most important study of the silk trade in the sixth century is that of Zachariä von Lingenthal, *Eine Verordnung Justinians über den Seidenhandel* in *Mém. de l'Acad. de St-Pét.*, sér. vii. vol. ix. 6. (See also a paper of Herr-

mann, *Die alten Seidenstrassen*, in Sieglins Forschungen, Heft 21.

[3] Procopius, *ib.* The government sold silk stuffs with ordinary dye at 6 nomismata an ounce, but the Imperial dye, called ὁλόβηρον, at more than 24 nom. an ounce.

country,[1] visited Constantinople (A.D. 552) and explained to the
Emperor the whole process of the cultivation of silkworms.
Though the insect itself was too ephemeral to be carried a long
distance, they suggested that it would be possible to transport
eggs, and were convinced that they could be hatched in dung,
and that the worms could thrive on mulberry leaves in Europe
as successfully as in China. Justinian offered them large rewards
if they procured eggs and smuggled them to Constantinople.
They willingly undertook the adventure, and returned a second
time from the East with the precious eggs concealed in a hollow
cane. The worms were developed under their instructions,
Syria was covered with mulberry trees, and a new industry was
introduced into Europe. Years indeed must elapse before the
home-grown silk sufficed for the needs of the Empire, and in
the meantime importation through Persia continued,[2] and
Justinian's successor attempted to open a new way of supply
with the help of the Turks.

If we regard Roman commerce as a whole, there is no doubt
that it prospered in the sixth century. Significant is the universal
credit and currency which the Imperial gold nomisma enjoyed.
Cosmas Indicopleustes, arguing that the " Roman Empire
participates in the dignity of Christ, transcending every other
power, and will remain unconquered till the final consummation,"
mentions as a proof of its eminent position that all nations from
one end of the earth to the other use the Imperial coinage in
their mercantile transactions.[3] Illustrative anecdotes had been
told of old by merchants who visited Ceylon. Pliny relates that
a freedman who landed there exhibited Roman denarii to the
king, who was deeply impressed by the fact that all were of
equal weight though they bore the busts of different Emperors.[4]
Sopatros, a Roman merchant who went to Ceylon in an Ethiopian
vessel in the reign of Zeno or Anastasius, told Cosmas [5] that he

---

[1] Serinda, supposed by some to be
Khotan. Procopius (*B.G.* iv. 17)
describes it as ὑπὲρ Ἰνδῶν ἔθνη τὰ
πολλά. Possibly Cochin - China is
meant. The sources are Procopius, *ib.*
(the order of whose narrative points
to the year 552), and Theophanes of
Byzantium, *F.H.G.* iv. p. 270, who
ascribes the importation to a Persian.

[2] Compare the treaty of 562 (above,
p. 121).

[3] Cosmas, ii. p. 81. Coins of Arcadius
and Honorius, Theodosius II., Marcian,
Leo I., Zeno, Anastasius and Justin
I. have been found in southern and
western India ; of Marcian and Leo
in northern India. See Sewell, *Roman
Coins found in India, Journal Asiat.
Soc.* xxxvi. 620-635 (1904).

[4] *Nat. Hist.* vi. 22.

[5] xi. p. 323.

had an audience of the king along with a Persian who had arrived
at the same time. The king asked them, " Which of your
monarchs is the greater ? " The Persian promptly replied,
" Ours, he is the king of kings." When Sopatros was silent,
the king said, " And you, Roman, do you say nothing ? "
Sopatros replied, " If you would know the truth, both the kings
are here." " What do you mean ? " asked the king. " Here
you have their coins," said Sopatros, " the nomisma of the one
and the drachm of the other. Examine them." The Persian
silver coin was good enough, but could not be compared to the
bright and shapely gold piece. Though Sopatros was probably
appropriating to himself an ancient traveller's tale,[1] it illustrates
the prestige of the Imperial mint.

The independent German kingdoms of the West still found
it to their interest to preserve the images and superscriptions
of the Emperors on their gold money. In the reign of Justinian
the Gallic coins of the Merovingian Franks have the Emperor's
bust and only the initials of the names of the kings.[2] The
Suevians in Spain continued to reproduce the monetary types of
Honorius and Avitus. The last two Ostrogothic kings struck
Imperial coinage, only showing their hostility to Justinian by
substituting for his image and inscriptions those of Anastasius.[3]

[1] So Winstedt rightly (his ed. of
Cosmas, p. 355).

[2] Only Theodebert, as a sign of
defiance, substituted his own name
for that of Justinian, but left the
title PP *Aug. This is what Procopius refers to, B.G. iii. 33. 5. Here
he makes the curious statement that it
is not lawful (θέμις) for any barbarian
potentates, including the Persian
king, to stamp gold coins with their
own images, because even their own
merchants would not accept such
money.

[3] Wroth, Catalogue of Coins of the
Vandals, etc., Plates x. and xii., cp.
Introd. p. xxxviii. The rule did not
apply to silver and bronze coins.

CHAPTER XXI

ADMINISTRATIVE REFORMS AND FINANCE

§ 1. *Attempts to reform Abuses* (A.D. 533–540)

THE second Prefecture of John the Cappadocian (A.D. 533–540) was marked by a series of reforms in the administration of the Eastern provinces, and it would be interesting to know how far he was responsible for instigating them. Administrative laws affecting the provinces were probably, as a rule, evoked by reports of the Praetorian Prefects calling attention to abuses or anomalies and suggesting changes.[1] If half of what the writers of the time tell us of John's character is true, we should not expect to find him promoting legislation designed to relieve the lot of the provincial taxpayers. But we observe that, while the legislator is earnestly professing his sincere solicitude for the welfare of his subjects, he always has his eye on the interests of the revenue, and does not pretend to disguise it. The removal of abuses which diminished the power of the subjects to pay the taxes was in the interest of the treasury, and it was a capital blunder of the fiscal administration of the later Empire that this obvious truth was not kept steadily in view and made a governing principle of policy. It was fitfully recognised when the excessive burdens of the cultivators of the land led to an accumulation of arrears and the danger of bankruptcy, or when some glaring abuse came to light. John, clever as he was, could not extract money from an empty purse, and there is no reason to suppose that he may not have promoted some of the remedial laws which the Emperor directed him to administer.

---

[1] For instance, *Nov.* 151 (A.D. 533–534), intended to check the practice of senators and officials in the pro- vinces coming to Constantinople on litigation business, was due to a *relatio* of John Capp.

We need not doubt that the Emperor was thoroughly sincere when he asserts his own concern for the welfare of his subjects, nor suspect him of hypocrisy when he expresses indignation at the abuses which he strives to suppress. All the capable Roman Emperors honestly desired a pure administration and a contented people ; but their good intentions were frustrated by defects of the fiscal system which they had inherited, and by the corruption of the vast army of officials who administered it.

We do not know how far Justinian's enactments may have been successful, but they teach us the abuses which existed. There was none perhaps which he himself regarded as more important—if we may judge from his language—than the law which forbade the practice of buying the post of a provincial governor.[1] Theodora, if she did not instigate the measure, had taken a deep interest in it, and the Emperor also expressly acknowledges that he had received some help from the Prefect. It had long been the custom to require the payment of considerable sums (*suffragia*) from those who received appointments as governors of provinces, and these sums went partly to the Emperor, partly to the Praetorian Prefect. Men who aspired to these posts were often obliged to borrow the money. The official salary was not sufficient to recompense them for the expense of obtaining the post, and they calculated on reimbursing themselves by irregular means at the cost of the provincials. The Emperor states that they used to extract from the taxpayers three or even ten times the amount they had paid for the office, and he shows how the system caused loss to the treasury, and led to the sale of justice and to general demoralisation in the provinces. The law abolishes the system of *suffragia*. Henceforward the governor must live on his salary, and when he is appointed he will only have to pay certain fixed fees for the ensigns and diploma of his office.[2] Before he enters on his post he has to swear—the form of oath is prescribed—that he has paid no man any money as a *suffragium* ; and severe penalties

---

[1] *Nov.* 8 (April 15, 535). Procopius refers to this law (*H.A.* 21. 16) and says that before a year had passed Justinian disregarded it and allowed the offices to be sold openly.

[2] The fees (συνήθειαι) for the higher posts (like the comes Orientis, proconsul of Asia) amounted to £122 : 10s., for the posts of consular rank £47 : 10s., for those of praeses or corrector, about £39.

are provided if the Prefect or any of his staff or any other person should be convicted of having received such bribes. The governor who has paid for his appointment or who receives bribes during his administration is liable to exile, confiscation of property, and corporal punishment. Justinian takes the opportunity of exhorting his subjects to pay their taxes loyally, " inasmuch as the military preparations and the offensive measures against the enemy which are now engaging us are urgent and cannot be carried on without money ; for we cannot allow Roman territory to be diminished, and having recovered Africa from the Vandals, we have greater acquisitions in view."

Several other laws were passed in this period to protect the people from mal-administration.[1] The confirmation of the old rule that a governor should remain in his province for fifty days after vacating his office, in order to answer any charges against his actions, may specially be mentioned.[2] The office of *defensor civitatis* had become practically useless as a safeguard against injustice because it had come to be filled by persons of no standing or influence, who could not assume an independent attitude towards the governors. Justinian sought to restore its usefulness by a reform which can hardly have been welcomed by the municipalities. He ordained that the leading citizens in each town should fill the office for two years in rotation ; and he imposed on the *defensor*, in addition to his former functions, the duty of deciding lawsuits not involving more than 300 nomismata and of judging in minor criminal cases. The work of the governor's court was thus lightened. We may suspect that the bishops who were authorised to intervene when a governor was suspected of injustice were more efficacious in defending the rights of the provincials because they were more independent of the governor's goodwill.[3]

Among the restrictions which the Roman autocrats placed upon the liberty of their subjects there is none perhaps that would appear more intolerable to a modern freeman than those which hindered freedom of movement. It was the desire of the Emperors to keep the provincials in their own native places and to discourage their changing their homes or visiting the

---

[1] See *Edicts* 2 and 12.   [2] *Nov.* 95 (539) ; cp. *Nov.* 8, § 9.
[3] *Nov.* 15 (535) ; *Nov.* 86 (539).

capital. This policy was dictated by requirements of the system of taxation, and by the danger and inconvenience of increasing the proletariat of Constantinople. Impoverished provincials had played a great part in the Nika sedition, and the duties of the Prefect of the City were rendered more difficult and onerous by the arrival of multitudes of unemployed persons to seek a living by beggary or crime. Justinian created a new ministry of police for the special purpose of dealing with this problem.[1] The function of the *quaesitor*, as the minister was named, was to inquire into the circumstances and business of all persons who came from the provinces to take up their quarters in the capital, to assist those who came for legitimate reasons to get their business transacted quickly and speed them back to their homes,[2] and to send back to the provinces those who had no valid excuse for having left their native soil. He was also empowered to deal with the unemployed class in the capital, and to force those who were physically fit into the service of some public industry (such as the bakeries), on pain of being expelled from the city if they refused to work. Judicial functions were also entrusted to him, and his court dealt with certain classes of crime, for instance forgery.

The Prefect of the City was further relieved of a part of his large responsibilities by the creation of another minister, who, like the quaesitor, was both a judge and a chief of police. The Praefectus Vigilum,[3] who was subordinate to the Prefect, was abolished, and his place was taken by an independent official

[1] *Nov.* 80 (A.D. 539), addressed to the Pr. Prefect of the East, because it concerned the provincials as well as the capital. The institution of the quaesitor is also mentioned by John Lyd. *De mag.* ii. 29 (τὸν λεγόμενον κυαισίτορα ἀντὶ ⟨τοῦ⟩ τῶν βιωτικῶν ἐγκλημάτων ἐρευνάδα σεμνότατον), by John Mal. xviii. 479 (A.D. 539–540), and by Procopius, *H.A.* 20. 9 and 11. The notice of Procopius ignores the principal functions of the quaesitor, and represents him as concerned with unnatural vice and offences against religion. Nothing is said of such duties in *Nov.* 80, and Panchenko (*O tain. ist.* 213) therefore thinks that the quaesitor of Procopius and John Lydus is a different official from that of *Nov.* 80, whose title he supposes to have been *quaestor*. But

he is wrong in supposing that κοιαισίτωρ has no manuscript authority in the Novel (see Kroll's ed. p. 391). The difficulty may easily be solved, I think, by supposing that the duties mentioned by Procopius were subsequently assigned to the quaesitor, who was already empowered (*Nov.* 80, § 7) to try cases of forgery (πλαστογραφία).

[2] The business affairs, referred to in the law, are chiefly lawsuits (cp. *Nov.* 69), or the affairs of agricultural tenants whose landlords resided in the capital. Persons who have once been dismissed from the city by the quaesitor and return are liable to punishment (§ 9).

[3] The Greek term was νυκτέπαρχος "night - prefect," which Justinian wastes many words in deriding.

who was named the Praetor of the Demes,[1] and whose most important duty was to catch and punish thieves and robbers.

§ 2. *Provincial Reorganisation*

During the fifth century few changes had been made in the details of the provincial system as it was ordered by Diocletian and modified here and there by his successors. Such alterations as had been found advisable were in accordance with the principles which had inspired Diocletian's reform. Provinces were further subdivided, they were not enlarged. Theodosius II., for instance, broke up Epirus, Galatia, and Palestine, each into two provinces.[2] Changes had also been made in Egypt. This diocese had at first consisted of five provinces, Aegyptus, Augustamnica, Thebais, and the two Libyas, but Theodosius I. (after A.D. 486) cut off a part of Augustamnica (including the Oxyrhynchus district) to form the province of Arcadia.[3] At some later period Augustamnica was again divided into two provinces, Prima and Secunda.[4] But the principal innovation was made by Theodosius II., who subdivided the Thebaid into the Upper and the Lower provinces. The Upper or southern Thebaid was constituted under a duke, to whom the civil as well as the military administration was entrusted, along with a general authority over the Lower Thebaid, which had its own civil governor.[5] The motive of this arrangement was to strengthen the hands of the commander who was responsible for protecting the frontier against the Blemyes and Nobadae. Yet another alteration was made, perhaps early in the sixth century ;

---

[1] Πραίτωρ δήμων, *Nov.* 13, A.D. 535 (John Mal. *ib.*, gives a wrong date, 539) ; John Lyd. *ib.* ; Procopius, *ib.* We can infer from the law that at this time crime was particularly prevalent in the capital ; and the Praefectus Vigilum employed agents who were in collusion with the criminals. Procopius complains that the Praetor and the Quaesitor were arbitrary in administering justice, condemning men without evidence, and, in accordance with his thesis, represents them as instituted for the purpose of oppression and extortion.

[2] John Mal. xiii. 347-348.
[3] *Not. dig., Or.* i. 29. See M. Gelzer, *Stud. z. byz. Verw. Agyptens,* 8-9.
[4] Before A.D. 535 (Hierocles, *Synekd.* 726. 3 ; 727. 13 ; Justinian, *Nov.* 8).
[5] We have a contemporary record of this change in an Imperial rescript preserved in a Leiden papyrus (*Archiv für Papyrusforschung,* i. 397), and discussed by Gelzer, *ib.* 10 *sqq.*, who shows that the innovation must be dated between 435 and 450. The Upper Thebaid extended from Ptolemais to Omboi.

the province of Aegyptus was divided into two, Prima and Secunda.[1]

A charge of a different kind, but based on the same principle of dividing responsibility, had been introduced by Anastasius in Thrace. When he constructed the Long Wall he established a new vicariate, at the expense of the vicariate or diocese of Thrace. We do not know its extent, or what powers the new official possessed, but as he was entitled " Vicar of the Long Walls " his diocese evidently stretched northwards from Constantinople.[2]

Justinian did not indeed attempt a complete revision of the existing system, but he made a great number of changes in which he departed from the principles of Diocletian. He combined in some cases small provinces to form larger circumscriptions ; he did away with most of the diocesan governors, who formed the intermediate links in the hierarchical chain between the provincial governors and the Praetorian Prefect ; and he united in many cases the civil and military powers which had been so strictly divorced by Diocletian. The tendency of these changes anticipates to some extent the later system which was to come into being in the seventh century and was characterised by large provinces, the union of civil and military administration in the same hands, and the total disappearance of the dioceses. The reforms of Justinian, which belong to the years 535 and 536, were called forth by particular circumstances. Some of them were designed to avert conflicts between the civil and military authorities.

The Count of the East was deprived of his jurisdiction over the Orient diocese and, retaining his title, rank, and emoluments, became the civil governor of the province of Syria Prima. The Vicariate of Asiana was likewise abolished, and the vicar became the governor of Phrygia Pacatiana, exercising both civil and military powers, and adorned with the new title of *comes Iustinianus*.[3]

Similarly the Vicariate of Pontica was abolished, the vicar becoming the comes Iustinianus of Galatia Prima. But this arrangement was found to work badly, and at the end of thirteen

---

[1] *Nov.* 8 (April 15, 535); in Hierocles Egypt is still one province. The precise date of the *notitia* of Hierocles has not been fixed.
[2] The sources are the *notitiae*

appended to *Nov.* 8, and *Nov.* 26. That the vicariate was created by Anastasius is not stated, but is a natural inference.
[3] *Nov.* 8 (April 15, 535).

years the vicariate was restored. We are told that the Pontic provinces were infested by robbers and assassins, who formed armed bands and escaped the justice which threatened them in one province by moving into another. No governor ventured to transgress the limits of his own province by pursuing them. It seemed that the difficulty could only be met by the appointment of a superior governor with jurisdiction over all the provinces, and the Vicar of Pontica was reinstated, but with powers considerably larger than those which had belonged to him before. He was to have military and financial as well as civil functions. He was to be the vicar not only of the Praetorian Prefect, but also of the Master of Soldiers, and was to have authority over all the troops stationed in his diocese. He was also to represent the Master of Offices and the Counts of the Private Estate and the Sacred Patrimony ; so that none of the officials who served these ministers could defy or evade his authority.[1]

In Thrace discord between the military and civil officials appears to have been incessant, and as the Thracian provinces constantly suffered from the incursions of the barbarians, want of harmony in the administration was more disastrous here than elsewhere. Justinian abolished the Vicar of Thrace and the Vicar of the Long Wall, and committed the civil and military power of the whole diocese to a single governor with the title of Praetor Justinianus of Thrace.[2] Soon afterwards, however, the dominion of the new Praetor was curtailed by the withdrawal from his jurisdiction of the frontier provinces of Lower Moesia and Scythia. These, by a very curious arrangement, were associated with Caria, the Cyclades, and Cyprus, and placed under the control of a governor entitled *Quaestor Iustinianus of the Army*, who enjoyed an authority independent of the Praetorian Prefect as well as of the Masters of Soldiers. He was really a fourth Praetorian Prefect but with military functions, and his institution must have been deliberately intended to diminish the power of the Prefect of the East. The motive of this strange union of provinces so far apart and without any common interest to connect them is unknown ; [3] but we may conjecture that the

[1] *Edict* 8, A.D. 548.
[2] *Nov.* 26, A.D. 535, May 18.
[3] The body of the law (*Nov.* 41)

which created the office, May 18, 536, is lost, but information is supplied by *Nov.* 50 (August 537).

object was to place the financial expenses of administering the Danubian lands, exhausted by invasions, on provinces which were exceptionally rich.[1]

These changes made a considerable breach in the hierarchical system which had been constructed by Diocletian and Constantine. The union of civil and military powers was also introduced in many of the Asiatic provinces, and in every case the new governor received the rank of spectabilis and a new title. Pisidia and Lycaonia were each placed under a Praetor Iustinianus. The Count of Isauria had already possessed the double authority under the old system; Justinian did not change his title, but gave him the rank of spectabilis.[2] In three cases large provinces were created by the union of two smaller. Pontus Polemoniacus was joined to Helenopontus, and formed a new Helenopontus under a Moderator Iustinianus. Paphlagonia and Honorias were reunited as Paphlagonia under a Praetor Iustinianus. The Moderator and the Praetor possessed the double functions.[3]

The third case was the union of the two provinces of Cappadocia under a Proconsul Iustinianus. Cappadocia presented peculiar problems of its own. It had drifted into an almost anarchical condition which demanded special treatment. Here were the large Imperial domains, which were under the management of the Praepositus of the Sacred Bedchamber, and the rest of the land seems to have mainly consisted of large private estates. The wealthy landowners and their stewards kept bodies of armed retainers, and acted as if they were masters of the provinces. They even encroached upon the Imperial domains, and the Emperor complains that " almost all the Imperial Estate has become private property." He declares that every day he and his ministers have to deal with the petitions of Cappadocians who have been deprived of their property, including clergy and especially women. The governors and officials were afraid to

---

[1] This is rather suggested by the words of John Lyd. *De mag.* ii. 29 προάγει ἔπαρχον ἐπόπτην τῶν Σκυθικῶν δυνάμεων, ἀφορίσας αὐτῷ ἐπαρχίας τρεῖς τὰς πασῶν ἐγγὺς εὐπορωτάτας.

[2] Pisidia, *Nov.* 24; Lycaonia, *Nov.* 25; Isauria, *Nov.* 27 (all in May 535).

[3] Helenopontus, *Nov.* 28; Paphlagonia, *Nov.* 29 (July 535). Other changes were the elevation of the

praeses of Phoenicia Libanensis to the rank of *Moderator* (spectabilis), and that of the praeses of Palestine Salutaris to that of proconsul, with authority to supervise the government of Palestine Secunda. See *Edict* 4 and *Nov.* 103 (536). The civil governor of Arabia, whose authority had been reduced to a cipher by that of the duke, was made a moderator, *Nov.* 102 (536).

resist these powerful magnates, who stopped their mouths with gold. " The crimes which are committed in that country," says Justinian, " are so many that even the greatest man would find it difficult to check them." He therefore invested the new governor of united Cappadocia with exceptional powers and prestige. The Proconsul controlled the civil administration and the military forces, but he was also responsible for the revenue and controlled all the officials and agents of the Private Estate, and that not only in Cappadocia, but in other provinces of the Pontic diocese. He received a salary double that of the Moderator of Helenopontus or the Praetor of Paphlagonia.[1]

Some changes were also made in the administration of Egypt.[2] Here perhaps the chief preoccupation of the government was to secure the regular delivery of the grain with which the country of the Nile supplied Constantinople. Justinian found that the wheels of the administrative machinery were out of gear. For some time back, he says, things have been in such confusion in the Egyptian Diocese that the central authorities have not known what was going on there. " The taxpayers asserted that all the legal dues were demanded in a lump, and that they had entirely fulfilled their liabilities, while we received nothing beyond the corn supplies ; and the curials, the pagarchs (mayors of the villages), the tax-collectors, and the governors arranged things in such a way as to obscure the true facts and to make profit for themselves." But there were other considerations, which, though not specially mentioned in the Imperial edict, must have influenced the legislator. In A.D. 536 and 537 Alexandria had been the scene of popular seditions, arising out of a contest between two heretical claimants to the Patriarchal throne. The military forces had been powerless to suppress the disorders.[3]

Justinian here adopted a policy opposite to that which he had pursued in Cappadocia. Instead of making one man responsible for the whole administration, he reduced the responsi-

---

[1] *Nov.* 30. The salary of the Proconsul was 20 lbs. of gold (about £900) ; that of the Moderator and the Praetor was 725 *nom.* (about £450). The Praetors of Thrace, Lycaonia, and Pisidia received 300 *nom.* annually (£187).

[2] *Edict* 13, A.D. 538–539 (there can be little doubt about the date ; it was addressed to John Capp. in a 2nd indiction, see § 15 and § 24. The reasons given by Zachariä von L. for ascribing it to 553–554 are not convincing, and are confuted by papyrus evidence, see Gelzer, p. 23 *sq.*). This long edict throws much light on the arrangements connected with the corn supplies.

[3] Liberatus, *Brev.* 19. Cp. Gelzer, *ib.* 25 *sqq.*

bilities of the Augustal Prefect, who had hitherto governed the Diocese. He made him governor of Alexandria and of the two provinces of Aegyptus Prima and Aegyptus Secunda, with civil and military powers.[1] These provinces were not united ; they still retained their civil governors, subordinate to the Prefect, who now bore the title of duke. The Emperor expressly justified this change by the consideration that the supervision of the whole Diocese was too much for one man. It is not quite clear whether the two provinces of Lower and Upper Libya were united under one civil prefect, or whether they continued to be distinct, but in either case the governors were placed under the control of the military duke of the Libyan frontier.[2] In Upper Egypt the duke of the Thebaid received the Augustal title and was endowed with both civil and military authority over the two Thebaid provinces whose governors were subordinate to him. The general result of these reforms was the completion of the policy of abolishing Diocesan governors in the Eastern Prefecture. In Egypt there were now eight (or nine) provinces grouped in five independent circumscriptions, Egypt, Augustamnica, Arcadia,[3] Thebais, and Libya, of which the governors had each military as well as civil competence and were directly responsible to the Praetorian Prefect of the East.

The law which introduced these changes laid down minute regulations for the collection and transportation of the corn supplies both for Constantinople and for Alexandria, and for the gathering in of all other dues whether for the treasury of the Praetorian Prefect or for that of the Count of the Sacred Largesses. The several duties and responsibilities of all the authorities concerned were carefully distinguished.

---

[1] Mareotes and the city of Menelaites were separated from Aegyptus Prima and added to the province of Libya. The Prefect's staff, both civil (αὐγουσταλιανή) and military (δουκική), was to number 600, and he was to receive the large salary of 40 lbs. of gold (£1800).

[2] The Edict speaks of ἡ Λιβύων ἐπαρχία and τοῦ τῆς Λιβύων πολιτικοῦ (civil) ἄρχοντος, as if there were only one province (cp. the note of Zachariä v. L. in his edition, p. 51). But in the *Descriptio orbis Romani* of Georgius Cyprius (c. A.D. 600) the two provinces appear (ed. Gelzer, p. 40).

Paraetonium in Lower Libya was the seat of the duke of the Libyan frontier. Upper Libya was the Cyrenaica.

[3] Arcadia is not mentioned in the Edict, but there is some evidence from papyri which confirms the reasonable inference that it was independent (Gelzer, *ib.* 29). From the same sources we learn that the governor was known as the count of Arcadia, and afterwards had the rank of Patrician (*ib.* 33), a dignity which was also conferred on the Augustal dukes of Egypt and the Thebaid. For the title δοὺξ καὶ αὐγουστάλιος of the duke of Thebais see *ib.* 23.

The treatment of the Armenian provinces, which embraced the most easterly districts of the Diocese of Pontus, stands apart. Here Justinian's policy was not to increase the size of the governments, but to rearrange. He formed four provinces, partly by readjustments in the two old Armenian provinces, partly by taking districts from Helenopontus, and partly by converting new districts into provincial territory, suppressing the native satraps.

The new First Armenia, which had the privilege of being governed by a proconsul, included four towns of the old First Armenia, namely Theodosiopolis, Satala, Nicopolis, and Colonea, and two towns of the old Pontus Polemoniacus, Trapezus and Cerasus. The once important town of Bazanis or Leontopolis received the name of the Emperor, and was elevated to the rank of the metropolis.

The new Second Armenia, under a *praeses*, corresponded to the old First Armenia, and included its towns Sebastea and Sebastopolis. But in place of the towns which had been handed over to the new First Armenia, it received Comana, Zela, and Brisa from the new province of Helenopontus.

The Third Armenia, governed by a *comes Iustinianus* with military as well as civil authority, corresponded to the old Second Armenia, and included Melitene, Arca, Arabissus, Cucusus, Ariarathea, and Cappadocian Comana.

Fourth Armenia was a province new in fact as well as in name, consisting of the Roman districts beyond the Euphrates [1] (to the east of the Third Armenia), which had hitherto been governed by native satraps. It was placed under a consular, and the metropolis was Martyropolis.

The names appear to have been determined by the geographical order. The new trans-Euphratesian province went naturally with the district of Melitene, and therefore the Second Armenia became the Third, because it was connected with what it was most natural to call the Fourth. For the consular of Fourth Armenia was to be in a certain way dependent on the count of Third Armenia, who was to hear appeals from the less important province. In the same way the new First and Second Armenias naturally went together, and therefore it was con-

---

[1] Sophanene, Anzitene, Sophene, Asthianene, and Belabitene. Cp. Procopius, *Aed.* iii. 1.

venient that the numbers should be consecutive. The *praeses*
of Second was dependent to a certain extent on the proconsul
of First Armenia.[1]

In the case of these provinces, Justinian not only revised the
administrative machinery, but also introduced changes of another
kind. Hitherto the Armenians had lived according to their own
laws and customs, and had not been called upon to regulate their
private dealings according to the civil law of Rome. It was in
the domain of real property that the divergence of Armenian
from Roman law provoked the Emperor's special intervention.
Armenian estates [2] passed undivided from father to son, or in
default of a son to the nearest male agnate. No proprietor could
leave his property by will—wills, in fact, were unknown. No
woman could inherit, nor did she receive a dowry when she
married. Justinian determined to break down this system, which
he professes to consider barbarous ; and in two successive laws [3]
he ordained that henceforward the inheritance of property
should be regulated by Roman law, that women should inherit
their due shares, and should receive dowries. It is not probable
that Justinian was moved to this reform solely by consideration
for the female population of the Armenian provinces. Apart
from the fact that it outraged his ideal of uniformity that Roman
law should not prevail in any quarter of the Empire, we may
suspect that it was his aim to break up the large estates of
Armenia and thereby weaken the power of the princes and
magnates, to force them to give up their national exclusiveness
and draw them into the sphere of general Imperial interests.[4]
The policy was crowned with success. Constantinople and
the Imperial service had already begun to attract many
Armenians, and this movement towards the centre increased.
In Justinian's reign men of this race began to come to the
front in the Imperial service ; Narses and Artabanes are the

---

[1] *Nov.* 31 (March 536). The regulations are discussed at length by
Adonts, *Armeniia v Epokhu Iustiniana,* 157 *sqq.* I cannot think
that he is right in supposing that in
selecting his First and Third Armenia
as provinces of superior rank the
Emperor was influenced by no better
reason than " to reward the Imperial
favourites Acacius and Thomas," who
at the time were governing in those

districts (p. 176) ; for he could easily
have transferred them. Both these
persons were of Armenian origin,
and Procopius gives Acacius a very
bad character (*B.P.* ii. 3).

[2] Γενεαρχικὰ χωρία.

[3] *Edict* 3 (535) : *Nov.* 21 (March
536). These documents are discussed
at length by Adonts, *op. cit.* 184 *sqq.*

[4] Adonts, *ib.* 201.

most eminent examples.   Hereafter they would ascend the
throne itself.[1]

The long list of administrative changes which we have surveyed shows that the Emperor addressed himself earnestly in
A.D. 535 to the task of thoroughly overhauling the system of
provincial government, and, in the appreciation of his work as
a ruler, these reforms have hardly received due attention. He
did not attempt, according to any general preconceived plan, to
organise a new system, like Augustus or Diocletian, but sought
to remedy, in each case according to its own circumstances, the
defects of the existing scheme. It is characteristic of him that
he likes to justify his innovations by appeals to history and
antiquity. For example, when he bestows upon Lycaonia a
governor of higher rank with the title of praetor, he pedantically
recalls the legendary connexion of the country with Lycaon of
Arcadia, who was also said to have colonised in Italy, thereby
anticipating Aeneas the ancestor of Romulus. " On this account,
it would be just to decorate the province with the ancient symbols
of Roman government, and therefore we give the governor the
title of praetor, older even than that of consul." It was probably a consideration of public opinion as well as his own personal
sentiments that made him seek to represent his innovations,
whenever it was possible, as reversions to an older order. He
wished it to be thought, and possibly thought himself, that he
was "reintroducing antiquity with greater splendour." [2] He
frequently speaks with pride of his own native language, Latin ;
yet it was in his reign that it definitely became the practice to
issue the laws in Greek. The contrast between the innovator
and the enthusiast for historical tradition stands out most conspicuously in the abolition of the consulship.

§ 3. *The Lapse of the Consulship* (A.D. 542)

It would be difficult to contend that Justinian in allowing
the consulship to lapse was not thoroughly justified by the

---

[1] In the period after Justinian, and
indirectly as a consequence of his
policy, a westward expansion of the
Armenian population began in two
directions, from the Second Armenia
westward towards Caesarea and north-
westward towards the Black Sea,
and from the Third Armenia south-
westward towards Cilicia and the
Mediterranean. See Adonts, *ib.* 203
sq.

[2] Τὴν παλαιότητα πάλιν μετὰ μείζονος
ἄνθους εἰς τὴν πολιτείαν ἐπαναγαγόντες,
Nov. 24, § 1.

circumstances. Before he finally took this step, he had made an effort to render possible the preservation of an institution " which for nearly a thousand years had grown with the growth of the Roman state." For all political purposes the institution was obsolete. It was a distinction to a man to hold it, to give his name to the year and have it perpetuated in the Fasti Consulares. But the public spectacles, which the new consul exhibited in the first weeks of January, and the largesses which he was expected to distribute to the people, entailed a large outlay, which only the wealthiest could undertake. It became more and more difficult to find private persons ready to incur the expenditure, which amounted at least to 2000 lbs. of gold (£90,000), for the sake of the honour, and the Emperor was sometimes obliged to contribute from the treasury a large part of the money.[1] Belisarius was consul in A.D. 535, and in the two following years no consul was elected, presumably because no one was willing to pay and the treasury could not afford the luxury. We can well imagine that there was much disappointment and discontent among the populace of the capital, and Justinian attempted to rescue the endangered institution by a legal curtailment of the expenses. The Praetorian Prefect, John of Cappadocia, had come forward to fill the consulship for A.D. 538, perhaps on this condition, and a few days before the kalends of January the Emperor subscribed a law [2] which abbreviated the programme of consular spectacles, made it optional for the consul to distribute a largesse or not, but ordained that if there were a distribution it should be of silver not of gold.[3] It is manifest that the permission to withhold the largesse was useless, as no consul could have ventured to face the unpopularity which such an economy would bring upon him. The people ought to be grateful to him, Justinian thinks, and not grumble

---

[1] Procopius, *H.A.* 23. 13.

[2] *Nov.* 105, dated 537, December 28. It is addressed to Strategius, Count of the Sacred Largesses, presumably because the fisc had sometimes contributed to the expenses. Justinian says that the law is intended to secure that the consulship shall be perpetual and not beyond any suitable person's purse (ὅπως ἂν διηνεκὴς μείνῃ 'Ρωμαίοις ἅπασι δὲ τοῖς ἀγαθοῖς ἀνδράσιν ὑπάρχῃ βατή). It provides that the consular festivities shall last for only seven

days : January 1, inaugural procession and ceremony of investiture ; January 2, chariot races ; January 3, *theatrokynêgion* (exhibition of wild beasts) ; January 4, combats of men with wild beasts ; January 5, theatrical representations ; January 6, chariot races ; January 7, the consul lays down his office.

[3] § 2. The silver is to be in the form of miliaresia καὶ μήλοις καὶ καυκίοις (cups) καὶ τετραγωνίοις καὶ τοῖς τοιούτοις.

at this curtailment of the amusements and largesses to which they have been accustomed, for they are threatened with the alternative of enjoying neither one nor the other. He expressly exempted the Emperor from the provisions of the law.

The new regulations postponed the doom of the consulship for just four years. Basilius was consul for A.D. 541,[1] and he was the last private person to hold it. The practice of dating years officially by the consuls was not given up. During the rest of Justinian's reign the year was designated as " such and such a year after the consulship of Basilius." [2] Succeeding Emperors assumed the consular dignity in the first year of their reigns. But Justinian introduced a new system of dating state documents by three distinct indications, the consulate (or post-consulate), the regnal year of the Emperor, and the indiction (A.D. 537).[3] The innovation of using the regnal year as an official mark of time was perhaps suggested by the practice of the Vandal kings.[4]

§ 4. *Financial Policy*

The system of raising revenue in the later Roman Empire was so oppressive that there is perhaps no Emperor whom a hostile critic could not have made out a case for charging with a deliberate design to ruin his subjects. The lot of the provincials might have been tolerable if the ministers and governors and their hosts of subordinate officials had all been men of stainless integrity, but an incorruptible official seems to have been the exception. The laws show how the Emperors were always striving to secure a just and honest administration and imagining new devices to check corruption and oppression. In such endeavours Justinian was indefatigable, as his laws eloquently prove. But it was easy for an enemy to dwell on all the evils and abuses which

---

[1] One leaf of the consular diptych of Anicius Faustus Albinus Basilius is preserved in Florence, and Meyer thinks that the second leaf may be identified with one in the Brera at Milan, with the inscription *Et inl(ustris) ex c. dom(esticorum) pat (ricius) cons. ord.* (*Zwei ant. Elfenb.* pp. 74-75).

[2] A.D. 536 and 537, in which no consul was elected, had been designated as *p.c. Belisarii* and *p.c.*

Bel. ann. ii.

[3] *Nov.* 47 (August 31). (*E.g.* a law of March 545 is dated " in the 18th year of Justinian, the 4th after the consulship of Basilius, the 8th indiction.") Shortly afterwards in 538–539, the practice came in of dating the issue of bronze coins by the number of the regnal year on the reverse.

[4] See Mommsen, *Hist. Schr.* iii. 357.

existed, to represent them as due to his deliberate policy, and
to ignore his remedial legislation or misinterpret its intention.
This is the method of the author of the *Secret History.* His
statements as to the abuses and hardships and misery suffered
by Justinian's subjects are borne out in general by Justinian's
own statements in his laws, but the same laws disprove the
historian's inferences as to the Emperor's intentions. Although,
as has been already observed, his policy of aggrandisement and
the scale of his public expenditure placed a disastrous strain on
the resources of his subjects, he was far from being indifferent
to their welfare, and he fully understood that it was to the interest
of the treasury that they should be protected from injustice
and extortion. We have already seen some of his efforts in
connexion with his reforms in the provincial administration.
The fact remains, however, that he was inflexible in insisting
on the regular exaction of legal dues and was less liberal and
prudent than many of his predecessors in cancelling accumulated
arrears, and remitting the taxation of provinces which had been
devastated by hostile invasions.[1]

If we examine the principal charges of economic oppression
which were preferred against him by his enemies, we shall find
that the abuses which they stigmatise were for the most part
not new inventions of Justinian but legacies from the past.
There was nothing new, for instance, in the fact that the inhabitants of the provinces through which troops passed to the
scene of war were bound to provide food for the soldiers and
fodder for the horses, and to transport these supplies to the
camps. Sometimes a province had not sufficient provisions
and they had to be procured elsewhere. The system, which
was known as coemption,[2] lent itself to intolerable exactions,

[1] Procopius, *H.A.* 23 (where it is,
however, acknowledged that a year's
tribute was remitted to cities actually
taken by an enemy). It is stated
here that there was no remission of
arrears throughout the thirty-two
years of his rule from 518 to 550 (the
author represents Justin's reign as
virtually part of Justinian's). This is
not accurate, as there was a remission
in 522 (*Nov.* 147, § 1). In 553, however, there was a general remission of
all arrears to 554 inclusive (*ib.*).

[2] Συνωνή. There was another form
of coemption of which Procopius
(*H.A.* 22. 17 *sqq.*) complains and
gives one example. One year when
the harvest in Egypt was bad and
the corn supply was insufficient for
the needs of the people, the Praetorian
Prefect bought up immense quantities
in Thrace and Bithynia at low compulsory prices ; the farmers were
obliged to transport the corn to the
capital, and were at a dead loss.
This seems to have occurred in 545–
546, shortly before Peter Barsymes
was deposed from the office of Prefect.

and Justinian in A.D. 545 issued a law to guard the interests of the inhabitants. It provided that they should be paid in full for all they furnished to the troops, and that no contributions in money should be demanded from them, and forbade them to give anything gratuitously or without a written receipt.[1] Another burdensome institution was the *epibole*, which, it will be remembered, when lands fell out of cultivation, made, in certain cases, neighbouring landowners responsible for the taxes. Justinian maintained this principle, but he does not appear to have made it harsher than before, and he sought to guard against its abuse.[2] It is probable, however, that in the oriental provinces during the Second Persian War the invasions of the enemy as well as the pestilence had caused the ruin of many proprietors, and that the application of the *epibole* was a frequent and serious grievance.[3]

One tax is mentioned which seems to have been a novelty, and of which we can find no trace in the Imperial legislation. It was called the air-tax or sky-tax (*aërikon*), a name which suggests that it was a tax on high buildings, such as the *insulae* or apartment houses in cities. It was administered by the Praetorian Prefect and yielded 3000 lbs. of gold (£135,000) a year to the treasury, while it is insinuated that the Prefects made much more out of it.[4]

---

[1] *Nov.* 130. Quartering soldiers in private houses was forbidden (§ 9). Procopius, *H.A.* 23. 11 *sqq.*

[2] *Nov.* 128 (A.D. 545), §§ 7, 8. Here the persons responsible are described as οἱ ὁμόδουλα ἢ ὁμόκηνσα χωρία κεκτημένοι (see above, Chap. XIII. p. 444 *sq.*, where the general nature of the epibole is explained). It is expressly stated that they were not liable for arrears. Justin and Justinian relieved Church lands from liability to the epibole (see Cyril, *Vita Sabae*, 294).

[3] Procopius, *ib.* 9 and 15-16.

[4] The only source is Procopius, *H.A.* 21. 1 *sqq.*, who states that it was an unusual tax and was so called ὥσπερ ἐξ ἀέρος ἀεὶ αὐτὴν φερομένην. In much later times we meet a tax of the same name (Leo VI. *Tactica*, xx. 71 ; Alexius Comnenus, *Nov.* 27, § 4). Kalligas, improbably, explains the ἀερικόν as a hearth-tax (καπνικόν) ; such a tax would have produced a

far larger sum. The discussion of Panchenko (*O tainoi ist.* 149 *sqq.*) throws little light on it, and he misinterprets Procopius, who says καὶ ταῦτα μὲν τῷ αὐτοκράτορι ἀποφέρειν ἠξίουν, αὐτοὶ δὲ πλοῦτον βασιλικὸν περιεβάλλοντο οὐδένι πόνῳ. He curiously refers αὐτοί to the ministry of the *comes larg.*, whereas it is the Praet. Prefects who are in question, and, explaining the words to mean that the proceeds of the tax were paid into the treasury and then paid out to the officials, he infers that the purpose of the tax was to supply the officials with *sportulae* (pp. 151, 153). But περιεβάλλοντο refers to ληστείαις in the preceding sentence, not to legal acquisition. Monnier supposed that the ἀερικόν was a tax on houses (*Étude de droit byz.* 508 *sqq.*), and that it was so called from counting the openings, doors, and windows. But this is a far-fetched derivation and incongruous with the

The decay of municipal life reached a further stage in the
reign of Justinian, who describes its decline ;[1] and increased
interference on the part of the central government in the local
finances seems to have been unavoidable. We saw how Anastasius took the supervision of the collection of taxes out of the
hands of the decurions and appointed *vindices*, whose administration proved a failure. Justinian stigmatises them as pestilential
and appears to have abolished them, though not entirely.[2]
The rates, known as *politika*, which were imposed for municipal
purposes and used to be altogether under the control of the
local authorities, had already in the time of Anastasius been
partly appropriated by the fisc. They were collected along with
the other taxes, and were divided into two portions, of which
one went to the treasury, the other to the cities. The same
Emperor sometimes sent a special inspector to see that the
necessary public works were carried out.[3] In A.D. 530 Justinian
placed the management of the public works, the local expenditure,
and the control of the accounts in the hands of the bishops and
the leading local dignitaries. But he reserved to himself the
right of sending special accountants to exercise supervision.[4]
These accountants (*discussores*) must be sent by his own personal
mandate, and the local authorities are warned to recognise no
one who comes with a mandate of the Praetorian Prefect. It
would appear that the treatment of the *politika* as a due to the
treasury had given the Praetorian Prefects and their officials
additional opportunities of injustice and extortion, for the
Emperor shows great concern to exclude any interference on
the part of this ministry in the local administration. Some
years later he committed to the provincial governors the general
duty of seeing that the most necessary public works, such as
repairs of bridges, roads, walls, harbours, were carried out, that
the cities were properly provisioned with food, and that the

use of ἀήρ ; whereas " aerial house "
would have been a natural Greek
expression for " sky-scraper." Moreover, it is clear from the amount of
the yield that it cannot have been a
tax on *all* houses. Stein (*Hermes*,
lii. 579) discusses it in connexion
with *Nov.* 43, and factories (ἐργαστήρια)
would probably have been liable to
the tax.
[1] *Nov.* 38, *Pref.*

[2] *Ib.* and *Edict* 13.
[3] *C.J.* x. 16. 13. Procopius (*H.A.*
26. 6) ascribes to Justinian the
appropriation of πολιτικά by the
treasury, and although *Nov.* 128
seems inconsistent with this charge,
the evidence of *Edict* 13 virtually
bears it out. Cp. Maspéro in *Archiv
f. Papyrusforschung*, v. 363 *sqq.* (1913).
[4] *C.J.* x. 39. 4 *discussores operum
publicorum.*

accounts were duly audited. But they were to do this in person and not through subordinates.[1]

But the proceeds of the local taxes, diminished by the claims of the treasury, were frequently insufficient to defray the municipal upkeep, especially when exceptional expenses were incurred in consequence of earthquakes, for instance, or hostile invasions. In such cases, the matter was referred to the Emperor, who sometimes advanced large sums from the treasury to assist a city which had been visited by some grave disaster. But as a rule the method was to levy a special tax known as a *description*, which was assessed in proportion to the amount of the land-tax. That this tax gave rise to abuses is shown by the fact that Justinian forbids governors to impose *descriptions* on towns during their progresses through the provinces.[2]

The decline of the municipal resources became more marked from A.D. 543 onwards in consequence of the ravages of the Plague, and it led to the decay of the liberal professions. The cities, forced to economise, withdrew the public salaries which they had hitherto paid to physicians and teachers. Advocates are said to have suffered because people were so impoverished that they could not afford the luxury of litigation. Some towns could not defray the cost of lighting the streets, and public amusements, theatres, and chariot races were curtailed.[3]

On the whole, although he made alterations in detail, which were chiefly designed to check the abuse of their authority by officials and to diminish the power of the Praetorian Prefect, Justinian preserved the existing financial system in all its essential principles. He did not make it worse, and he endeavoured to arrest the progress of municipal decay. The ruin

---

[1] See the *Mandata principis* to governors, *Nov.* 17, § 4, A.D. 535; also *Novv.* 24, § 3; 25, § 4; 26, § 4; 30, § 8. In *Nov.* 128 (A.D. 545), however, the rights of the governor to interfere are carefully limited. He is to see that the portion of the πολιτικά appropriated to the city is duly paid, that it is not diverted to improper purposes by the inhabitants, that the bishop and the curials duly elect a "father of the city," a corn-commissioner (σιτώνης), and other functionaries, and that the accounts are regularly audited (§ 16).

[2] Imperial, senatorial, and church lands were exempt from these διαγραφαί (*C.J.* xii. 1. 7; *Nov.* 131, § 5), which Procopius (*H.A.* 23. 17-19) describes as one of the principal burdens falling on the provincials. They had at one time been imposed on other classes as well as on the curials and landowners (cp. *C.J.* xi. 1. 2). These διαγραφαί *extraordinariae* are to be distinguished from διαγραφαί *lucrativων*, taxes on estates which changed hands. Church lands were exempted from this burden also (*Nov.* 131, *ib.*).

[3] Procopius, *H.A.* 26. 5-11.

wrought by the inroads of the Persians and of the northern
barbarians, and the effects of the Plague made, however, in
many parts of the Empire the burdens more grievous than ever,
and the Emperor may be blamed for not seeing that a fundamental and drastic reform of the whole system of taxation was
demanded in the interest of the public welfare. The retrench-
ments which he might well have made in the early years of his
reign, instead of embarking on large schemes of conquest and
spending exorbitant sums on buildings, were almost impossible
subsequently when he was involved simultaneously in the wars
with Persia and the Ostrogoths. The measure to which he was
forced in A.D. 552 of cancelling all arrears of taxation is an
eloquent indication of the plight of the provinces, for his previous
policy shows that he would not have forgone a fraction of the
treasury's legal dues unless absolute necessity had compelled him.[1]

The conquest of Africa enabled him to make large additions
to the Imperial estates,[2] but in the eastern provinces also the
Private Estate and the crown domains appear to have been
gradually and considerably extended, at the expense of adjacent
private property. We have not much information as to the
methods and pretexts by which this was effected, but about
fifteen years after the death of Justinian complaints reached
the Emperor Tiberius from almost all the provinces as to the
unjust appropriation of private property by the officials of
Imperial estates.[3] That this form of robbery was practised in
Justinian's reign we have other evidence.[4] In some cases on

---

[1] Stein (*Studien*, 143 *sqq.*) has
attempted to prove that the total
revenue of the State in this reign
cannot have much exceeded 7,000,000
solidi (£4,375,000), and that this was
enough to cover the outgoings. He
starts with a fallacious assumption,
and leaves out of account many
departments of expenditure. Even
if Justinian had no more than
21,000,000 subjects, his conclusion
would imply that the taxation only
came to about 4s. 2d. per head of the
population annually. The errors have
been pointed out by Andreades in
Revue des études grecques, xxxiv. No.
156 (1921). The taxation accounts of
Antaeopolis (*Pap. Cairo*, i. 67057)
give information which may ultimately help us to estimate the contribution of Egypt to the revenue.

Cp. the accounts of the village of
Aphrodito (*ib.* 67058) and those of
the rich proprietor Ammonius (ii.
67138-67139).

[2] Procopius, *B.V.* ii. 14. This
policy led to sedition among the
soldiers, who expected that the land
would be distributed among themselves.

[3] Zachariä v. Lingenthal, *Jus
Graeco-Rom.* iii., Nov. 12.

[4] Aetherius, *curator domus divinae*
under Justinian, was brought to
account under Justin II. for his acts
of plunder (τάς τε τῶν ζώντων τῶν τε
τελευτώντων τὰς οὐσίας ληιζόμενος,
Evagrius, v. 3). The appropriations
of Anatolius, another curator, are
described by Agathias, v. 4. Cp.
Procopius, *H.A.* 12. 12.

the death of a proprietor his will or the claims of his legal heirs were set aside and his possessions acquired by the fisc. It is only too likely that many unjust acts were deliberately committed by the help of legal quibbles, but we need not pay serious attention to the allegations that Justinian forged wills or acts of donation in order to acquire the possessions of rich subjects.[1] Nor does the less improbable charge that he misused criminal justice for the purpose of confiscating property seem to be borne out by the facts. For instance, he restored, so far as he was able, to the disloyal senators their properties which had become forfeit to the State after the Nika rebellion. And in the later years of his reign, at a time when fiscal necessities were urgent, he abolished confiscation as a penalty for ordinary crimes.[2]

The treatment of the private estates had varied, as we have seen, from time to time since the days of Septimius Severus. The last innovation had been that of Anastasius who, instead of incorporating recently confiscated lands in the *res privata*, had instituted a new minister, the Count of the Patrimony. This had simply meant a division of administration, for the Patrimony as well as the Private Estate was appropriated to public needs, not to the Emperor's private use. Justinian made yet another change. The Patrimony disappears,[3] and the domains which composed it are placed under the management of Curators (*curatores divinae domus*). We do not know exactly what was involved in this change ; more perhaps than a mere change of

[1] Procopius, *ib.* 1-11, gives six instances with the names of the persons. We can accept them as cases in which the fisc inherited, but the charge of forgery is evidently asserted merely on hearsay, as indeed in one case the writer lets out (διαθήκην ἥνπερ οὐ παρ' ἐκείνου ξυγκεῖσθαι διατεθρύλληται). Against these cases and that of the inheritance of Anatolius (*H.A.* 29. 17 *sqq.*) we may set the generosity of Justinian in dealing with the daughters of Eulalius (John Mal. xviii. 439).

[2] *Nov.* 134, § 13, A.D. 556.

[3] Stein (*Studien*, 174 *sqq.*) has established this, or at least made it highly probable. (1) There is no mention of the *comes patr.* in *C.J.* vii. 37. 3 (A.D. 531), where he ought to appear if he still existed, or in *Nov.*

22 (A.D. 536). (2) In Justinian's laws *sacr. patrimonium* is sometimes used as an equivalent of *s. larg.* ; this would have been confusing if the patrimony existed. (3) While we hear no more of the *comes patr.*, we begin to hear a great deal of the *divinae domus* and *nostri curatores per quos res divinarum domuum aguntur* (*C.J. ib.*). Τὸ πατριμόνιον in Procopius, *H.A.* 22. 12, Stein identifies with the estates in Sicily which were under the *com. patr.* who was instituted by Theoderic, and continued to function under Justinian. The passage in John Lydus, *De mag.* ii. 27, on ὁ λεγόμενος πατριμώνιος of Anastasius, would certainly by itself suggest that the *com. patr.* still existed during Justinian's reign, but it cannot be pressed in view of the other evidence.

name. The *domus divina* was the patrimony,[1] and the Curator, subordinate to whom were the curators of the several domains,[2] discharged the functions of the *comes patrimonii*. But the Curator seems to have been a court official rather than a State official, and Justinian's aim may have been to assert the principle that the administration of the patrimonial domains, consisting of confiscated properties, was the Emperor's own personal affair.

The policy of this reign in regard to trade is not very clear, and it is difficult to say how far it was responsible for the economic crises which arose and compelled the intervention of the government. Some changes were made in the custom-house arrangements at Constantinople. Hitherto the custom duties had been collected when ships reached the harbour of the capital. But there were posts of observation in the Hellespont and the Bosphorus to make sure that the public regulations were not evaded. An officer was stationed at Abydos to see that no vessel with a cargo of arms entered the straits without Imperial orders, and that no vessel passed through to the Aegean without papers duly signed by the Master of Offices. This officer was paid by fees levied on the owners of the ships.[3] Another officer was posted at Hieron, at the northern issue of the Bosphorus, to examine the cargoes of craft sailing into the Euxine and prevent the export of certain wares which it was forbidden to furnish to the peoples of southern Russia and the Caucasian regions.[4] He was paid a fixed salary and received no money from the shipowners. Justinian's innovation was to convert both these stations into custom houses for imports, of which the officials were salaried but also received an additional bonus proportionate to the amount of the duties which they collected.[5]

---

[1] The equation will be found in Procopius, *B.G.* i. 4. 1 and 6. 26.

[2] Stein asserts that the curators of the particular domains were independent and had no superior. This certainly was not the case under Justinian and Justin II. The title *curator dominicae domus*, without any limitation in *C.J. ib.*, and κουράτωρ τῶν οἰκιῶν in *Nov.* 148, § 1, point to a central controller. Anatolius, for instance, held this post (Agathias, v. 3).

[3] The source is Procopius, *H.A.* 25. 2 *sqq.* Cp. the inscription of Abydos (probably belonging to the time of Anastasius) published in the *Mittheilungen des deutschen arch. Inst.* (Athen), iv. 307 *sqq.* (1879).

[4] For *quae res exportari non debeant* see *C.J.* iv. 41 (wine, oil, lard, and arms are mentioned).

[5] The title of the officer at Hieron was in later times at least κόμης τοῦ Ἱεροῦ καὶ τοῦ Πόντου. John Mal. (xviii. 432) describes him as κόμης στενῶν τῆς Ποντικῆς θαλάσσης, and dates his institution to A.D. 528–529. For seals of commerciarii of Abydos see Schlumberger, *Sig. byz.* 196 *sqq.*

But the tolls on exports were still collected at Constantinople, and these charges are said to have been so onerous that they forced the merchants to raise the prices of their wares enormously. But we have no information as to the tariff.[1]

Justinian is accused of having made necessaries as well as luxuries dearer not only by exorbitant duties on merchandise— a charge which we cannot control—but also by establishing " monopolies " for the benefit of the government.[2]   The restrictions which he imposed in the silk trade were considered when we surveyed the commercial relations of the Empire with foreign lands, and we saw that, though his policy in some respects was not happy, he deserves credit for his efforts to solve a difficult problem. It is far from clear how he made an income of 300 lbs. of gold from the sale of bread in the capital, as he is alleged to have done.[3]   Whatever new regulations were introduced cannot be described as a monopoly in the proper sense of the term. It is, however, certain that in the years after the Plague the price of labour rose considerably, and in A.D. 544 the Emperor issued an edict to re-establish the old prices. " We have learned," he says, " that since the visitation of God traders and artisans and husbandmen and sailors have yielded to a spirit of covetousness and are demanding prices and wages two or three times as great as they formerly received. We therefore forbid all such to demand higher wages or prices than before. We also forbid contractors for building and for agricultural and other works to pay the workmen more than was customary in old days." A fine of three times the additional profit was imposed on those who transgressed the edict. Justinian evidently assumes that there was no good reason for the higher rates. Unfortunately we have no information as to the effects of the edict, in which the interests of the customers are solely considered.[4]   That there was a fall of credit even before the Plague

[1] That the customs levied at Abydos and Hieron were only on imports to the capital, and those levied at Constantinople were on the cargoes of outgoing ships is my interpretation of the passage in Procopius, which is not very clear. The supervisor of the latter was probably entitled *comes commerciorum* (cp. Panchenko, *op. cit.* 155), and the office was held by a Syrian named Addaeus (who was afterwards, in 551,

Pr. Prefect of the East, *Nov.* 129).

[2] The motive of the monopoly of the manufacture of arms (*Nov.* 85) was not financial. The sale of arms to private persons was forbidden.

[3] Procopius, *H.A.* 20. 1 *sqq.*, and 26. 19 *sqq.* He says that the bread was not only dearer but of worse quality. His τριπλάσιονα τιμήματα agrees with *Nov.* 122.

[4] *Nov.* 122.

is indicated by measures which were taken to protect the interests of the powerful corporation of bankers against their debtors.[1] It would probably be rash to infer from the tendency of interest on loans to rise since A.D. 472 that trade had been tending to decline.[2] The ordinary commercial rate of interest in Justinian's reign was 8 per cent.[3] On good securities money could be borrowed at 6 or 5 per cent. Justinian paid attention to the question of interest and reduced the maximum 12 per cent, which had hitherto been legal, to 8, except in the case of maritime ventures, where 12 was allowed. But 8 was allowed only in the case of traders, and 6 was fixed as the maximum for loans between private persons. In the case of money advanced to peasants he enacted that only 4 per cent should be charged, and he forbade senators of illustrious or higher rank to exact more than 4 per cent.

The coinage of Justinian's reign, which is exceptionally abundant, may be taken as testifying to a flourishing condition of commerce. The curious statement in the *Secret History* that he depreciated the gold coinage has no confirmation in the evidence of the extant *nomismata*.[4] The number of Imperial mints was increased, not only in consequence of the conquest of Africa and Italy, but also by the establishment of a new centre in the East.[5] The minting of gold was confined to Constantinople, and silver was issued only there and in Carthage.

If Justinian was blamed for his expenditure on wars, for his extravagance in building, for the large sums with which he bought off the hostilities of the northern barbarians, he was blamed no less for his economies. Some of these may have been short-sighted and unwise, for instance the curtailments of the

---

[1] *Nov.* 136 (A.D. 535); *Edict* 9; *Edict* 7 (A.D. 542).

[2] See Billeter, *Gesch. des Zinsfusses* (pp. 219, 317).

[3] This may be illustrated from papyri, *e.g. Pap. Cairo*, ii. No. 67126. Cp. *C.J.* iv. 32. 26 ; and *Nov.* 110, repeating *Nov.* 106.

[4] *H.A.* 22. 38. In 25. 12, the Emperor is blamed for the practice of the money-changers to give only 180

folles for a nomisma instead of the normal 210.

[5] Under Anastasius there were only three mints, Constantinople, Nicomedia, and Antioch ; under Justin I. Thessalonica and Cyzicus were added. Under Justinian money was coined also at Alexandria and Cherson ; and in the west, at Carthage, in Sicily (Catana ?), at Rome and Ravenna. See Wroth, *Imp. Byz. Coins*, i. xv. *sqq.*

public Post, to which attention has already been called, and the reduction of the intelligence department.[1] But much greater dissatisfaction was caused by economies which to an impartial posterity seem unquestionably justified. Such, for instance, were the abolition of the consulship, which had ceased to perform any useful function, the reduction of expenses on public amusements, the discontinuance of the large distribution of corn which, since the time of Diocletian, had pauperised the proletariate of Alexandria.[2] Another economy was the diminution of the pensions of the officials serving in the central bureaux, which had hitherto cost the treasury about 10,000 lbs. of gold (£450,000), a measure which must have been extremely unpopular.[3]

The parsimony of Justinian which seems most open to criticism was in the treatment of the army. He reduced its numbers and tried to reduce the expenses on its upkeep. The names of the dead remained on the lists, new soldiers were not recruited, and there was no promotion. The old practice of Imperial donatives every five years was discontinued. Pay was always in arrears, and was often refused altogether on various pretexts. No sooner had a soldier received his pay than the logothete appeared with a bill for taxes. We are told that Justinian appointed the worst sort of men as logothetes, and they received a commission of one-twelfth on all they managed to collect. After the peace of A.D. 545 there appears to have been a considerable reduction of the frontier forces in the East.[4]

---

[1] Procopius (*H.A.* 30. 12 *sqq.*) says that the secret service ceased to exist, but this is assuredly an exaggeration. These spies (κατάσκοποι) used to penetrate into the palace of the Persian king as merchants or on other pretexts. Procopius ascribes the successes of Chosroes to the fact that he improved his secret service, while Justinian refused to spend money on his.

[2] *Ib.* 26. 40 *sqq.* This was done when Hephaestus was Augustal prefect; he is said to have enriched himself and the treasury by monopolising in his own hands the sale of all provisions in the city. Hephaestus is probably the same person who was Pr. Pref. of the East *c.* A.D. 550–551 (John Lyd. *De mag.* iii. 30).

[3] *H.A.* 24. 30 *sqq.* ἐν Βυζαντίῳ

shows that the provincial bureaux are not included. We have no means of judging whether the pensions were excessive, and the reduction may not have been considerable; for we cannot trust Procopius when he says τούτων αὐτοὺς ἀποστερήσας σχεδόν τι ἁπάντων, as hyperbole is a note of the *Secret History.* But the complaints of John Lydus (*De mag.* iii. 67) bear out the statement.

[4] The decline of the army is the subject of *H.A.* 24. Procopius speaks as if the *limitanei* were finally abolished after A.D. 545, but so far as his criticisms have a foundation they apply only to the East (see Hartmann, *Byz. Verwaltung in Italien,* p. 151; Panchenko, *op. cit.* 117 *sqq.*). Maspéro has made it probable that the total of the forces stationed in Egypt was from 29,000 to 30,000

That the efficiency of Justinian's administration degenerated in the latter part of his reign there is every sign. After the deaths of Theodora and Germanus he concentrated his attention more and more on theology—*in caelum mens omnis erat*—and was inclined to neglect public affairs and postpone decisions. When he died it was probably the general opinion that it was high time for a younger man to take the helm and restore, above all, the financial situation. For the fisc was exhausted.[1]

men, of whom about 5000 were in Libya and Tripolitana. Only two or three thousand of these were καστρησιανοί, *limitanei* (*Org. mil. de l'Égypte*, 117). Maspéro thinks that when Agathias (v. 13) gives the total strength of the army as 150,000, he does not include the *limitanei* (*ib.* 119). Justinian appears to have formed a new corps of Palace guards called Scribones; it is at least in his reign that we first hear of them (Agathias, iii. 14). They were often employed on special missions in the provinces. The Scholarian guards (3500 in number) had now ceased to have any military significance ; they were employed purely for parade purposes. Young men who had a little money and desired to lead an idle life in splendid uniform invested it in purchasing a post in the guards, and the high pay was a satisfactory annuity for their capital (cp. Agathias, v. 15). Procopius says that in Justin's reign 2000 "supernumeraries" were added in order to obtain the entrance fees, and that Justinian on his accession disbanded them without compensation (*ib.* 20).

[1] See Corippus, *In laud. Iust.* ii. 260 *sqq.* :

> plurima sunt vivo nimium neglecta
>   parente
> unde tot exhaustus contraxit debita
>   fiscus
> reddere quae miseris moti pietate
>   paramus.
> quod minus ob senium factumve actumve
>   parentis
> tempore Iustini correctum gaudeat orbis
> nulla fuit iam cura senis, etc.

CHAPTER XXII

ECCLESIASTICAL POLICY

§ 1. *Ecclesiastical Legislation*

THEORETICALLY the Emperors were as completely competent to legislate in all religious as in all secular affairs. How far they made use of this right was a question of tact and policy. No Emperor attempted to order the whole province of sacred concerns. Questions of ritual, for instance, were left entirely to the clergy, and the rulers, however bent they might be on having their own way in questions of doctrine, always recognised that doctrine must be decided by ecclesiastical councils. The theory, which was afterwards to prevail in western Europe, of a trenchant separation between the spiritual and temporal powers was still unborn, and ecclesiastical affairs were ordered as one department of the general civil legislation. In framing laws concerning the organisation of the Church, it was a matter of course that the Patriarch of Constantinople should be consulted, but it is significant that such contributions were often addressed not to the Patriarch or the bishops, but to the Praetorian Prefect of the East, whose duty it was to make them publicly known throughout the Empire.

Justinian took his responsibilities as head of the Church more seriously than any Emperor had hitherto done, and asserted his authority in its internal affairs more constantly and systematically. It was his object to identify the Church and State more intimately, to blend them, as it were, into a single organism, of which he was himself the controlling brain. We must view in this light his important enactment that the Canons of the four great Ecumenical Councils should have the same validity as

360

Imperial laws.[1] And we can see in his legislation against heretics and pagans that he set before himself the ideal of an Empire which should be populated only by orthodox Christians. He determined " to close all the roads which lead to error and to place religion on the firm foundations of a single faith," [2] and for this purpose he made orthodoxy a requisite condition of citizenship. He declared that he considered himself responsible for the welfare of his subjects, and therefore, above all, for securing the salvation of their souls ; from this he deduced the necessity of intolerance towards heterodox opinions.[3] It was the principle of the Inquisition. None of his predecessors had taken such a deep personal interest in theology as Justinian, and he surpassed them all in religious bigotry and in the passion for uniformity.

The numerous ecclesiastical laws of Justinian, which do not concern doctrine or heresy, deal with such topics as the election of bishops, the ordination of priests and deacons, the appointment of the abbots of monasteries, the management of Church property, the administration of charitable institutions, such as orphanages, hostels, and poorhouses, the privileges and duties of the clergy.[4] We learn from this legislation the existence of various abuses, simony,[5] for instance, and illiterate priests and bishops. Little regard was shown for freedom in the restrictive enactments which were intended to prevent bishops from neglecting their sees ; [6] and the clergy were strictly forbidden to indulge in the pastimes of attending horse-races or visiting the theatres.[7]

But the most important feature in this section of Justinian's legislation is the increasing part which the bishops were called upon to play in civil and social administration. They were gradually taking the place of the *defensores civitatis*, and probably served as a more powerful check on unjust or rapacious provincial

---

[1] *C.J.* i. 3. 44 ; *Nov.* 131.

[2] Procopius, *Aed.* i. 1.

[3] *C.J.* i. 5. 18.

[4] *C.J.* i. titles 1-13, and 33 Novels are devoted to ecclesiastical laws.

[5] To remedy bribery at episcopal elections, a definite tariff of fees was fixed, to be paid by the new bishop to those who ordained him and their assistants, according to the income

of the see. *E.g.* if the income was not less than £1350, the total of the fees amounted to £250 (*Nov.* 123, § 3).

[6] *Ib.* § 9. Bishops were forbidden to leave their sees without permission of their metropolitan, and they could only visit Constantinople with leave of the Patriarch or by order of the Emperor.

[7] *C.J.* i. 4. 34.

governors.[1]   In certain matters of business they could act instead of the governor himself.[2]   They were expected to take part in overseeing the execution of public works, to take charge of the rearing of exposed infants, to enforce the laws against gambling. When Justinian issued a law against the constraint of any woman, slave or free, to appear on the stage, it was to the bishops that he addressed it, and they were charged to see that it was enforced, even against a provincial governor.[3]   It was on their vigilance that the government chiefly relied for setting the law in motion against heretics.

On any theory of the relations of Church and State, it would have been reasonable that, as the State granted to the bishops judicial and administrative authority and to the clergy special privileges, it should insist on their fulfilling certain qualifications and should lay down rules binding on the clerical order.   It was not so clear why the Emperor should consider it his business to regulate the conduct of monastic institutions,[4] seeing that they discharged no function in the political organisation and were established only for those who desired to escape the temptations, the troubles, and the labours of social life.   He justifies his action in one of his laws, where he expresses the superstitious belief that the prosperity of the State could be secured by the constant prayers of inmates of monasteries. " If they, with their hands pure and their souls bare, offer to God prayers for the State, it is evident that it will be well with the army, and the cities will prosper and our land will bear fruits and the sea will yield us its products, for their prayers will propitiate God's favour towards the whole State." [5]   The great pestilence and numerous earthquakes were a commentary on the Emperor's faith, which he was not likely to take to heart.

It has been observed that his legislation " became in the Byzantine Empire the true foundation of monastic institutions." [6] During his reign the number of monasteries enormously increased,[7] and in later times the growth of these parasitic institu-

---

[1] *Nov.* 86.   The *defensores* (ἔκδικοι) still existed (*ib.* and *Nov.* 15).

[2] *C.J.* i. 4. 21, and 31.   Other examples of the use which the government made of bishops will be found in this title.

[3] *Ib.* 33.

[4] The chief regulations will be found in *Nov.* 5, 123, 133.

[5] *Nov.* 133, § 5 (A.D. 539).

[6] Diehl, *Justinien,* 503.   For a general picture of monasticism in this age, see the whole chapter (499 *sqq.*).

[7] In A.D. 536 there were sixty-seven monasteries for men in Constantinople and its suburbs (Mansi, viii. 1007 *sqq.*). For the plan of the monastery of Saint Simeon, between Antioch and

tions multiplied more and more. Rich men and women vied with each other in adding to their number.

In Syria and Palestine monastic houses were particularly numerous and powerful, and the oriental monks enjoyed and merited a higher reputation than any others for extreme asceticism. A certain number of cells were reserved in the Syrian convents for those who, not content with the ordinary rule and desiring a more rigorous mortification of the flesh, yet preferred the shelter of a monastery to the life of the recluses who lived isolated in deserts or mountains. The historian, John of Ephesus, has left us a gallery of contemporary eastern monks, who were distinguished by their piety or eccentricities, and his portraits are sufficiently repulsive. They exercised an extraordinary influence not only over the common people, but even at court, and could indulge with impunity in the most audacious language in the Imperial presence. For instance, when proceedings were taken against the Monophysites in Egypt in A.D. 536, Maras, a heretical anchoret of the most savage manners, arrived at Constantinople for the purpose of loading the Emperor and Empress with vituperation. Admitted to an audience he used language which would have been almost incredible if it had been flung at persons of low degree ; his panegyrist declines to reproduce it. But the Emperor and Empress, if astonished, did not resent the insults of the ragged hermit ; they said that he was a truly spiritual philosopher.[1]

One important change in diocesan administration was introduced by Justinian. He divided the ecclesiastical vicariate of Illyricum into two parts for the sake of increasing the prestige and importance of Justiniana Prima, as he had renamed the town of Scupi, which was close to his own birthplace. Having first transferred the seat of the Praetorian Prefect of Illyricum from Thessalonica to Justiniana, he resolved to increase the prestige of his home [2] by making it also a great ecclesiastical centre. The bishop of Justiniana was raised to the rank not only of a metropolitan but of an archbishop, and his diocese

Aleppo, see Vogüé, *Syrie centrale*, Pl. 139-150 ; for that of Tebessa in Byzacena, Diehl, *L'Afrique byzantine*, Pl. xi.

[1] John Eph. *Comm. de b. or.* c. 37. Maras was a native of the region of Amida, but he set up a cell in the Thebaid. Another Monophysite monk, Zooras, about the same time used similarly audacious language to Justinian and made the Emperor very angry (*ib.* c. 2).

[2] *Nostram patriam augere cupientes*, *Nov.* 11 (A.D. 535) ; 131, 3 (A.D. 545).

corresponded to the civil diocese of Dacia, with its seven provinces. He was independent of Thessalonica, but the see of Thessalonica retained its authority over the rest of Illyricum, the diocese of Macedonia. This arrangement, which was carried out with the consent of the Pope, did not change the position of ecclesiastical Illyricum as a vicariate of the Roman see. The only difference was that the Pope was now represented by two vicars.[1]

§ 2. Persecution of Heretics and Samaritans

The measures which Justinian adopted to suppress heresy were marked by a consistency and uniformity which contrast with the somewhat hesitant and vacillating policy of previous Emperors. Laying down the principle that "from those who are not orthodox in their worship of God, earthly goods should also be withheld,"[2] he applied it ruthlessly. Right belief was made a condition for admission to the service of the State, and an attestation of orthodoxy from three witnesses was required.[3] Heretics were debarred from practising the liberal professions of law and teaching.[4] But Justinian went much further in the path of persecution. He deprived heretics of the common rights of citizenship. They were not allowed to inherit property ; their testamentary rights were strictly limited ; they could not appear in court to bear witness against orthodox persons. On the other hand, they were liable to the burdens and obligations of the curiales.[5] The spirit of the Imperial bigot is shown by a law which deprived a woman, if she belonged to a heretical sect, of her legal rights in regard to her dowry and property. The local priests and officials were to decide whether she was orthodox, and attendance at Holy Communion was to be regarded as the test.[6] Here we have a foretaste of the Inquisition.

It is noteworthy that the sect of the Montanists in Phrygia was singled out for particularly severe treatment. But the penalty of death was inflicted only on two classes, the Manichaeans, whom the government had always regarded as the worst enemies of humanity, and heretics who, having been converted to the

---

[1] For details see Zeiller, *Origines chrét.* 385 *sqq.* ; Duchesne, *Églises sép.* Scupi (Üsküb) remained a metropolitan see till 1914.

[2] *C.J.* i. 5. 12, 5 (A.D. 527).

[3] *Ib.* i. 4. 20.

[4] *Ib.* i. 5. 12, and 18.

[5] *Ib.* i. 5. 12 ; *Nov.* 45.

[6] *Nov.* 109 (A.D. 541).

true creed, relapsed into their errors.[1]   Perhaps these severe laws
were not executed thoroughly or consistently, but we have a
contemporary account of a cruel persecution of Manichaeans,
which occurred perhaps about A.D. 545.[2]

Many people adhered to the deadly error of the Manichaeans.   They
used to meet in houses and hear the mysteries of that impure doctrine.
When they were arrested, they were taken into the presence of the Emperor
who hoped to convert them.   He disputed with them but could not convince
them.   With Satanic obstinacy they cried fearlessly that they were ready
to face the stake for the religion of Manes and to suffer every torture.
The Emperor commanded that their desire should be accomplished.   They
were burned on the sea that they might be buried in the waves, and their
property was confiscated.   There were among them illustrious women,
nobles, and senators.

The most important of all the heretical sects, the Monophysites,
were hardly affected by the general laws against heretics.   Their
numbers and influence in Egypt and in Syria would have rendered
it impossible to inflict upon them the disabilities which the laws
imposed on heretics generally, and they were protected by the
favour of the Empress.   Moreover, the Emperor's policy vacil-
lated ; he was engaged throughout his reign with doctrinal
questions arising from the Monophysitic controversy, and the
position of the Monophysites will most conveniently be considered
in that connexion.

The Jews and Samaritans were subject to the same disabilities
as heretics.[3]   This severity was followed by the destruction of
the Samaritan synagogues, and a dangerous revolt broke out in
Samaria in the summer of A.D. 529.[4]   Christians were massacred ;
a brigand named Julian was proclaimed Emperor ; and the
rising was bloodily suppressed.[5]   The desperate remnant of the
people then formed a plan to betray Palestine to the Persians,[6]
but their treachery appears to have had no results.   Twenty
years later, at the intercession of Sergius, bishop of Caesarea, and
his assurance that the Samaritans had been converted from their

---

[1] Cp. esp. *Cod. J.* i. 5. 20, and
Procopius, *H.A.* 11.

[2] John of Ephesus, *H.E.* Part II.
(Nau), p. 481.   The date is uncertain,
but the notice precedes events dated
to the nineteenth year of Justinian.

[3] *C.J.* i. 5. 12, 17, 18.

[4] John Mal. xviii. p. 445 ; Procopius, *ib.*

[5] Malalas says that 20,000 were
slain and 20,000 (of both sexes)
given to the Saracens, who assisted
the duke of Palestine in the war, to
be sold into slavery.   Procopius says
that 100,000 were reported to have
perished.

[6] John Mal. xviii. p. 455, states
that 50,000 fled to Persia and offered
their aid to Kavad.

evil ways and would remain tranquil, the Emperor removed some of the civil disabilities which he had imposed.[1] But the hopes of Sergius were not realised. Samaritans and Jews joined in a sanguinary revolt at Caesarea, and murdered Stephanus, the proconsul of Palestine.[2] Their ringleaders were executed, but the Samaritans were refractory and abandoned the pretence of having been converted to Christianity. The civil disabilities which had been imposed on them by Justinian were renewed by his successor.[3] The Samaritan troubles are a black enough page in the history of persecution.

The Jews were treated less harshly. Though the lawgiver regarded them as " abominable men who sit in darkness," and they were excluded from the State-service, they were not deprived of their civil rights. Justinian recognised their religion as legitimate and respectable so far as to dictate to them how they should conduct the services in their synagogues.[4] He graciously permitted them to read aloud their Scriptures in Greek or Latin or other versions. If Greek was the language they were enjoined to use the Septuagint, " which is more accurate than all others," but they were allowed to use also the translation of Aquila.[5] On the other hand, he strictly forbade the use of the " Deuterosis," which he described as the invention of uninspired mortals.[6] This amazing law is thoroughly characteristic of the Imperial theologian.

§ 3. *The Suppression of Paganism*

We saw in a former chapter how throughout the fifth century the severe laws against paganism were not very strictly enforced.

---

[1] *Nov.* 129 (A.D. 551).

[2] John Mal. *ib.* p. 487.

[3] *Nov.* 144.

[4] *Nov.* 146 (A.D. 553).

[5] Aquila, a native of Pontus, converted to Judaism (hence called by Justinian ἀλλόφυλος), published his translation in the second century A.D. His aim was to produce a version more literal and accurate than the Septuagint ; it was so literal that it was often obscure.

[6] It is uncertain what precisely the Deuterosis means. The term occurs several times in Jerome. In his *Comm. in Matth.* c. 22 (*P.L.* xxvi. p. 165) he explains δευτερώσεις as the traditions and observations of the Pharisees. S. Krauss in an art. on Justinian in the *Jewish Encyclopaedia*, and in his *Studien zur byz.-jüdischen Gesch.* (1914), contended that by Deuterosis must be understood the whole of the oral teaching, and repeated this view in *Jewish Guardian*, March 26, 1920, p. 4 ; but in the same periodical, April 2, 1920, p. 11, J. Abrahams maintains that what Justinian forbade under Deuterosis was " the traditional Rabbinic translation of the Law—the Targum." The words of the legislator certainly seem to imply a book. Mr. F. Colson has suggested to me that the Mishna is meant : *deuterosis* has the same meaning, " repetition."

So long as there was no open scandal, men could still believe in the old religions and disseminate anti-Christian doctrine. This comparatively tolerant attitude of the State terminated with the accession of Justinian, who had firmly resolved to realise the conception of an empire in which there should be no differences of religious opinion. Paganism was already dying slowly, and it seemed no difficult task to extinguish it entirely. There were two distinct forms in which it survived. In a few outlying places, and in some wild districts where the work of conversion had been imperfectly done, the population still indulged with impunity in heathen practices. To suppress these was a matter of administration, reinforced by missionary zeal ; no new laws were required. A more serious problem was presented by the Hellenism which prevailed widely enough among the educated classes, and consequently in the State-service itself. To cope with this Justinian saw that there was need not only of new administrative rigour, but of new legislation. He saw that Hellenism was kept alive by pagan instructors of youth, especially in teaching establishments which had preserved the Greek traditions of education. If the evil thing was to be eradicated, he must strike at these.

Not long after his accession, he reaffirmed the penalties which previous Emperors had enacted against the pagans, and forbade all donations or legacies for the purpose of maintaining "Hellenic impiety," while in the same constitution he enjoined upon all the civil authorities and the bishops, in Constantinople and in the provinces, to inquire into cases of pagan superstition.[1] This law was soon followed by another which made it illegal for any persons "infected with the madness of the unholy Hellenes" to teach any subject, and thereby under the pretext of education corrupt the souls of their pupils.[2]

The persecution began with an inquisition at Constantinople. Many persons of the highest position were accused and condemned.[3] Their property was confiscated, and some may have

---

[1] *C.J.* i. 11. 9, evidently the law of Justinian which preceded the trials at Constantinople, which apparently began (John Mal. xviii. 449) in the last months of 528.

[2] *C.J.* i. 11. 10, probably A.D. 429. One of the provisions is the penalty of death for apostates. The con-

stitution i. 15. 18, seems to be later (cp. § 4 μηδὲ ἐν σχήματι διδασκάλου παιδείας).

[3] John Mal. *ib.*, but Theophanes, A.M. 6022, gives the fuller text of Malalas. Asclepiodotus, ex-prefect, took poison. Malalas says that Thomas, Phocas, and the others

been put to death ; one committed suicide. Among those who
were involved were Thomas the Quaestor and Phocas, son of
Craterus. But Phocas, a patrician of whose estimable character
we have a portrait drawn by a contemporary,[1] was speedily
pardoned, for, as we saw, he was appointed Praetorian Prefect
of the East after the Nika riot.

Some of the accused escaped by pretending to embrace the
Christian faith, but we are told that " not long afterwards they
were convicted of offering libations and sacrifices and other
unholy practices." [2] There was, in fact, a second inquisition in
A.D. 546. On this occasion a heretic was set to catch the pagan.
Through the zeal of John of Ephesus, a Monophysite, who was
head of a Syrian monastery in the suburb of Sycae, a large
number of senators, " with a crowd of grammarians, sophists,
lawyers, and physicians," were denounced, not without the use
of torture, and suffered whippings and imprisonment. Then
" they were given to the churches to be instructed in the Christian
faith." One name is mentioned : Phocas, a rich and powerful
patrician, who, knowing that he had been denounced, took poison.
The Emperor ordered that he should be buried like an ass
without any rites. We may suspect that this was the same
Phocas, son of Craterus, who had been involved in the earlier
inquest and knew that death would be the penalty of his relapse.[3]
There was yet another pagan scandal in the capital in A.D. 559 ;
the condemned were exposed to popular derision in a mock
procession and their books publicly burned.[4]

It may be considered certain that in all cases the condemned
were found guilty of actual heathen practices, for instance of

ἐτελεύτησαν ; but Theophanes has
συνελήφθησαν, evidently the right reading, leaving their fate open. The
fact that Procopius does not mention
executions in the brief passage where
he refers to the persecution of pagans
(*H.A.* 11 αἰκιζόμενός τε τὰ σώματα
καὶ τὰ χρήματα ληιζόμενος) must make
us hesitate to accept the text of
Malalas. Those who were executed
must have been condemned as
apostates. It is to be observed that
Thomas was still Quaestor in April
529, *C.J.*, *De Just. cod. confirmando* ;
this shows that the investigations
lasted a considerable time.

[1] John Lyd. *De mag.* iii. 72 ; cp.

Procopius, *H.A.* 21. This Phocas is
not to be confused with Phocas who
was Praet. Prefect of Illyricum in
529 and took part in compiling the
Code (*C.J. ib.*).

[2] Procopius, *ib.*

[3] John Eph., *H.E.* Part II. (Nau),
p. 481. The date is given as the
nineteenth year of Justinian, which
was 546 ; but as John places the
association of Justinian with Justin
in 531 (p. 474), it may be that 550
is the true date. Against this is the
apparent reference of Procopius (see
last note) in a work written in 550.

[4] John Mal. *ib.* p. 491.

sacrificing or pouring libations in their private houses, on the altars of pagan deities. Men could still cling to pagan beliefs, provided they did not express their faith in any overt act. There were many distinguished people of this kind in the highest circles at Constantinople, many lawyers and literary men, whose infidelity was well known and tolerated. The great jurist Tribonian, who was in high favour with the Emperor, was an eminent example. He seems to have made no pretence at disguising his opinions, but others feigned to conform to the State religion. We are told that John the Cappadocian used sometimes to go to church at night, but he went dressed in a rough cloak like an old pagan priest, and instead of behaving as a Christian worshipper he used to mumble impious words the whole night.[1]

It can hardly be doubted that by making the profession of orthodoxy a necessary condition for public teaching Justinian accelerated the extinction of " Hellenism." Pagan traditions and a pagan atmosphere were still maintained, not only in the schools of philosophy, but in the schools of law, not only at Athens, but at Alexandria, Gaza, and elsewhere. The suppression of all law schools, except those of Constantinople and Berytus, though not intended for this purpose, must have affected the interests of paganism. But philosophical teaching was the great danger, and Athens was the most notorious home of uncompromising Hellenists. After the death of Proclus (A.D. 485) the Athenian university declined, but there were teachers of considerable metaphysical ability, such as Simplicius and Damascius, the last scholarch,[2] whose attainments can still be judged by their works.[3]

The edicts of Justinian sounded the doom of the Athenian schools, which had a continuous tradition since the days of Plato and Aristotle. We do not know exactly what happened in A.D. 429.[4] We may suppose that the teachers were warned that

---

[1] Procopius, B.P. i. 25. 10.

[2] Proclus was succeeded by Marinus his biographer ; then came Isidore, Hegias, Damascius.

[3] The excellent commentaries of Simplicius on Aristotle are well known. Damascius wrote commentaries on Aristotle and a treatise, περὶ πρώτων ἀρχῶν, which are extant. Their colleague, Priscian, also wrote on the

Aristotelian philosophy, and we have in a Latin translation his " Solutions of Questions proposed by King Chosroes."

[4] John Mal. xviii. p. 451 ὁ αὐτὸς βασιλεὺς θεσπίσας πρόσταξιν ἔπεμψεν ἐν Ἀθήναις, κελεύσας μηδένα διδάσκειν φιλοσοφίαν μήτε νόμιμα ἐξηγεῖσθαι. θεσπίσας seems to refer to C.J. i. 11. 10.

unless they were baptized and publicly embraced Christianity, they would no longer be permitted to teach ; and that when they refused, the property of the schools was confiscated and their means of livelihood withdrawn.[1] This event had a curious sequel. Some of the philosophers whose occupation was gone resolved to cast the dust of the Christian Empire from their feet and migrate to Persia. Of these the most illustrious were Damascius, the last scholarch of the Academy, Simplicius, and Priscian. The names of four others are mentioned, but we do not know whether they had taught at Athens or at some other seat of learning.[2] These men had heard that king Chosroes was interested in philosophy, and they hoped, protected by his favour and supported by his generosity, to end their days in a more enlightened country than their own. But they were disappointed. Chosroes was flattered by their arrival and begged them to remain. But they soon found the strange conditions of life intolerable. They fell homesick, and felt that they would prefer death on Roman soil to the highest honours the Persian could confer. And so they returned. But the king did them a great service. In his treaty with Justinian in A.D. 532 he stipulated that they should not be molested or forced to embrace the Christian faith. We are told that they lived comfortably for the rest of their lives, and we know that

---

[1] The provision in *C.J. ib.* § 2 μηδὲ ἐκ τοῦ δημοσίου σιτήσεως ἀπολαύειν αὐτούς would hardly apply, as it refers only to grants from the fisc. But the seizure of the endowments might be covered by i. 11. 9, whereby it is provided that all property bequeathed or given for the maintenance of Hellenic impiety should be seized and handed over to the municipality. In case this law was applied, Athens at least had the benefit of the property which the Academy and the Lyceum had accumulated. Damascius, *Vita Isidori*, § 158, says that in the time of Proclus the revenue of the Academy was 1000 solidi (£625), or somewhat more. The closing of these schools—which was the result of Justinian's general laws, not of any edict aimed specially at Athens—has been discussed by Hertzberg, *Gesch. Griechenlands unter der röm. Herrschaft*, iii. 538 *sqq.* ; Gregorovius, *Gesch. der Stadt Athen,*

i. 54 *sqq.* ; Paparrigopulos, Ἱστ. τοῦ Ἑλλ. ἔθνους, iii. 174-175 ; Diehl, *Justinien*, 562 *sqq.*

[2] It has been generally assumed that they were all Athenian professors, but Agathias, who is our authority, does not say so (ii. 30). The others were Eulamios of Phrygia, Hermeias and Diogenes of Phoenicia, and Isidore of Gaza, all otherwise unknown. Suidas, *s.v.* πρέσβεις, says that they accompanied Areobindus, who was sent as envoy to Persia ; and Clinton (*sub* A.D. 532) accepts this, not perceiving that Suidas transferred to the philosophers what Agathias had said about the impostor Uranius (ii. 29). As Chosroes came to the throne in September 531, Clinton perhaps rightly places their journey after that date. Gregorovius notes that the Pythagorean number of the *seven* philosophers is somewhat suspicious.

Simplicius was still writing philosophical works in the later years of Justinian.[1]

In western Asia Minor, in the provinces of Asia, Phrygia, Lydia, and Caria, there was still a considerable survival of pagan cults, not only in the country regions, but in some of the towns, for instance in Tralles. In A.D. 542 John of Ephesus, the Monophysite whose activity in hunting down the Hellenes at Constantinople has already been noticed, was sent as a missionary to these provinces to convert the heathen and to put an ond to idolatrous practices. He tells us in his *Ecclesiastical History* that he converted 70,000 souls. The temples were destroyed; 96 churches and 12 monasteries were founded. Justinian paid for the baptismal vestments of the converts and gave each a small sum of money (about 4s.).[2]

In Egypt, in the oasis of Augila, the temple dedicated to Zeus Ammon and Alexander the Great still stood, and sacrifices were still offered. Justinian put an end to this worship and built a church to the Mother of God.[3] At Philae the cult of Osiris and Isis had been permitted to continue undisturbed. This toleration was chiefly due to the fact that the Blemyes and Nobadae, the southern neighbours of Egypt, had a vested interest in the temples by virtue of a treaty which they had made with Diocletian. Every year they came down the river to worship Isis in the island of Elephantine; and at fixed times the image of the goddess was taken up the river in a boat to the land of the Blemyes that it might give them oracular answers, and duly brought back to the temple.[4] Justinian would tolerate this indulgence no longer. Early in his reign he sent Narses the Persarmenian to destroy the sanctuaries. The priests were arrested and the divine images sent to Constantinople.[5] Much about the same time the Christian conversion of the Nobadao and Blemyes began.

Justinian was undoubtedly successful in hastening the disappearance of open heathen practices and in suppressing anti-

---

[1] Agathias, ii. 31 ὁ ἐφεξῆς βίος εἰς τὸ θυμῆρές τε καὶ ἥδιστον ἀπετελεύτησεν. For the date of the commentaries of Simplicius on Aristotle's *De caelo* and *Physica* cp. Clinton, *F.R.* ii. pp. 328-329.

[2] Of the new churches 55 were paid for by the treasury, 41 by the proselytes. John Eph., *H.E.* Part II. (Nau), p. 482; Part III. iii. cc. 36-37; *Comm. de b. or.* cc. 40, 43, 51, etc.

[3] Procopius, *Aed.* vi. 2.

[4] Priscus, *De leg. gent., fr.* 11, p. 583.

[5] Procopius, *B.P.* i. 19. The death of Narses in 543 gives a posterior limit of date.

Christian philosophy. Although in some places, like Heliopolis,[1] paganism may have survived for another generation, and although there were inquisitions under his immediate successors, it may be said that by the close of the sixth century the old faiths were virtually extinct throughout the Empire.

§ 4. *Persecution of Monophysites under Justin*

Throughout his reign one of Justinian's chief preoccupations was to find an issue from the dilemma in which the controversy over the natures of Christ had placed the Imperial government. Concord with Rome and the western churches meant discord in the East; toleration in the East meant separation from Rome. The solution of the problem was not rendered easier by the fact that the Emperor was a theologian and took a deep interest in the questions at issue on their own account apart from the political consequences which were involved.

In the abandonment of the ecclesiastical policy of Zeno and Anastasius, in order to heal the schism with Rome, Justinian, co-operating with Vitalian and the Patriarch John, had been a moving spirit. The greater part of the correspondence between Pope Hormisdas and the personages at Constantinople who took part in the negotiations has been preserved.[2] The main question was settled by a synod which met in the capital in 518 and decided that the Monophysite bishops should be expelled from their sees. The only difficulty which occurred in the negotiations with the Pope regarded the removal of the name of Acacius from the diptychs of the Church. There was a desire at Constantinople to spare the memory of the Patriarch, but Hormisdas was firm,[3] and in April A.D. 519 the Patriarch despatched to the Pope a memorandum, in which he anathematised Acacius and all those who had participated with him, and confessed that " the Catholic faith is always kept inviolable in the Apostolic see." [4]

---

[1] The great temple of Baal had been converted into a church; but sacrifices were still performed there in the sixth century. In A.D. 555 it was ruined by lightning. John Eph., *H.E.* Part II. p. 490. See Diehl, *Justinien*, pp. 550-551.

[2] It will be found in the *Collectio Avellana*, *Epp.* 142-181.

[3] See *ib. Ep.* 147. Justinian's

letter of September 7, received December 20, and the Pope's letters, *Epp.* 145, 148, 149.

[4] *Ep.* 159. The Pope had already sent a deputation of bishops to Constantinople (January), and the deacon, Dioscorus, who attended them describes their journey by the Egnatian Way, their reception at the tenth milestone from the capital by

The names of five Patriarchs, Acacius, Fravitta, Euphemius, Macedonius, Timotheus, and of two Emperors, Zeno and Anastasius, were solemnly erased from the diptychs of the Church of Constantinople, and it only remained for the Pope to remind the Emperor that he had still to take measures to " correct " the Churches of Antioch and Alexandria.[1]

" Correction " meant persecution, and the Emperor did not hesitate. The great Monophysite leader Severus had already been expelled from Antioch, and more than fifty other bishops driven into exile, including Julian of Halicarnassus, Peter of Apamea, and Thomas of Daras. The heretical monastic communities in Syria were dispersed and the convents closed. Resistance led to imprisonment and massacres. Such measures did not extirpate the heresy. In Egypt, Palestine, Syria, and the Mesopotamian deserts the Monophysites persisted in their errors, hoping for better days. Severus himself was able to live quietly in Alexandria.[2]

The persecution continued throughout the reign of Justin. But Justinian determined to essay a different policy. He did not despair of finding a theological formula which would reconcile the views of moderate Monophysites with the adherents of the dogma of Chalcedon. For there was after all a common basis in the doctrine of Cyril, which the Monophysites acknowledged and the Dyophysites could not repudiate. For the Council of Chalcedon had approved the views of Cyril, and Severus would hardly have admitted that his own doctrine diverged from Cyril's, if rightly interpreted.

The whole question was being studied anew by a theologian whom modern authorities regard as the ablest interpreter of the Chalcedonian Creed, Leontius of Byzantium.[3]   In his youth he

Vitalian, Pompeius, Justinian, and many other illustrious persons, and their presentation to the Emperor in the presence of the Senate (*Ep.* 167).

[1] *Ep.* 168 (July 9, 519).

[2] For the persecutions see Zacharias Myt. ix. 4, 5 ; John Eph. *H.E.* Part ii. pp. 467-468, and *Comm.* c. 5, p. 35 *sqq*, c. 8, p. 46 *sqq.* (cp. pp. 217-220) ; *Chron. Edess.* p. 124-128.

[3] The study of Loofs, *Leontius von Byzanz* (1887), rescued this theologian from neglect, and was followed in 1894 by a monograph with the same

title by Rügamer, written from the Catholic point of view and traversing successfully some of the conclusions of Loofs. The earliest work of Leontius was probably the Three Books against the Nestorians and Eutychians (*P.G.* lxxxvi. 1267 *sqq.*), which may be dated to A.D. 529-530 (cp. Rügamer, 9 *sqq.*). The *Epilysis of the Syllogisms of Severus* (*ib.* 1915 *sqq.*) and the *Thirty Chapters against Severus* (*P.G.* cxxx. 1068 *sqq.*) may have been composed in the years immediately following. Other works against the Monophysites (*P.G.* lxxxvi.

had been ensnared in the errors of Nestorianism, but, happily, guided into the ways of orthodoxy, he lived to write with equal zeal against Nestorians and Monophysites. He has the distinction of introducing a new technical term into Greek theology, *enhypostasis*, which magically solved the difficulty that had led Nestorians and Monophysites into their opposite heresies. Admitting the axiom that there is no nature without a hypostasis, Leontius said : it does not follow that the subsistence of two natures in Christ involves two hypostaseis (as the Nestorians say), nor yet that to avoid the assumption of two hypostaseis we must assume only one nature with the Monophysites. The truth is that both natures, the human like the divine, subsist in the same hypostasis of the Logos ; and to this relation he gave the name of *enhypostasis*.[1]

Of much greater interest is the fact that in his theological discussions he resorts to a new instrument, the categories and distinctions of the Aristotelian philosophy.[2] Substance, genus, species, qualities, play their parts as in the western scholasticism of a later age. It is not probable that Leontius himself was a student of Aristotle, but at this period there was a revival of Aristotelian thought which influenced Christian as well as secular learning. The ablest exponent of this movement was indeed in the camp of the heretics, John Philoponus of Alexandria, a philosopher, and a Monophysite. His writings are said to have been partly responsible for the development of a theory about the Trinity, known as Tritheism, which had some vogue at this period and was ardently supported by Athanasius, a grandson of the Empress. The Tritheites held the persons of the Trinity to be of the same substance and One God ; but they explained the identity of substance as purely generic, in the Aristotelian sense. Numerically, they said, there are three substances and three natures, though these are one and equal by virtue of the unchangeable identity of the Godhead.[3]

1769 *sqq.*) and the Nestorians (*ib.* 1399 *sqq.*), and the *Scholia*, a treatise on Sects, which bears the marks of later editing (*ib.* 1193 *sqq.*), may be later than A.D. 544.

[1] Cp. *ib.* 1277 *sqq.* ; 1944.

[2] See Loofs, *op. cit.* 60 *sqq.*

[3] John Ascosnaghes is said to have been the founder of the Tritheite sect, to which bishops Conon of

Tarsus and Eugenius of Seleucia belonged. See John Eph. *H.E.* Part III. v. 1-12 ; Timotheus, *De recept. haereticorum* ; Migne, *P.G.* lxxxvi. p. 64. John Philoponus in his Διαιτητής (" Arbiter ") discussed the bases of Tritheism and Monophysitism. We possess a philosophical work by him *On the Eternity of the World* (against Proclus), written in A.D. 529

To return to Leontius, it is a curious fact that notwithstanding the importance and considerable number of his theological works contemporary writers never mention him. Modern writers have indeed proposed to identify him with other persons of the same name who played minor parts in the ecclesiastical history of his time, but these conjectures are extremely doubtful.[1] His works were composed during a period of fifteen or twenty years (about A.D. 530–550), and it is probable that they helped Justinian in his efforts to interpret the creed of Chalcedon in such a way as to win Monophysites of the school of Severus.

The Monophysites were far from being a united body. The ground common to all was the repudiation of the Council of Chalcedon and the reception of the Patriarch Dioscorus. There were ultimately twelve different sections,[2] but the only division of much importance was that between the followers of Severus of Antioch and those of Julian of Halicarnassus. Julian, identifying the substance and qualities of the divinity and humanity of Christ, deduced that his body was indestructible from the moment at which it was assumed by the Logos. This doctrine, which was known as *aphthartodocetism*, called forth the polemic of Leontius ; but no Chalcedonian could have attacked it with more energy than Severus.[3]

§ 5. *Justinian's attempts at Conciliation, and the Second Persecution*

Justinian began his policy of conciliation by allowing the heretical bishops and monks to return from exile, about A.D. 529.[4] His plan was to hold a conference, not a formal synod, at Constantinople, and to have the whole question discussed. Severus himself resisted all the Emperor's efforts to induce him to attend it, but some of his followers came and the conference was held

(cp. xvi. 4), and an *Exegesis of the Cosmogony of Moses*, dedicated to Sergius, Patriarch of Antioch (c. 546–549).

[1] We may decidedly reject the identification, maintained by Loofs (*op. cit.*) with Leontius, the Origenist of Palestine, who visited Constantinople with St. Sabas in A.D. 531 and was repudiated by him. Cp. the criticisms of Rügamer, *op. cit.* 58 *sqq.* The other proposition of Loofs

that Leontius of Byzantium is the same as Leontius, a relative of Vitalian, and one of the Scythian monks who raised the Theopaschite question at the beginning of Justin's reign, can neither be proved nor disproved.

[2] Timotheus, *op. cit.* 52 *sqq.*

[3] Leontius, *Contra Nest. et Eut.* book ii. ; Zach. Myt. ix. 9-13.

[4] John Eph. *H.E.* Part II. p. 469; Zacharias Myt. ix. 15.

in A.D. 531.[1] Leontius, representative of the orthodox monks of Jerusalem, took part in it, and we may possibly identify him with Leontius of Byzantium, the theologian.[2] The conference led to no results.

The failure of his first attempt did not deter Justinian from making a second, and he sought a formula of conciliation in what is known as the Theopaschite doctrine. The thesis that it was orthodox to hold that " one of the Holy Trinity suffered in the flesh " had been defended in A.D. 519 by four Scythian monks, in the presence of John the Patriarch and the Papal legates who had come to restore peace to the Church.[3] The formula was denounced as heretical by the Sleepless monks, who had been so active in opposing the *Trisagion*, to which it had a suspicious resemblance. Justinian was interested in the question, and he wrote to Pope Hormisdas repeatedly, urging him to pronounce a decision.[4] But the Pope evaded a definite reply. Justinian recurred to the subject in A.D. 533, with a political object. He issued an edict which implicitly asserted that one of the Trinity suffered in the flesh, and he procured a confirmation of the edict by Pope John II.[5] The Sleepless monks, who refused to accept the doctrine, were excommunicated.

The recognition of a formula which did not touch the main issue [6] could not deceive Severus and the Monophysites, and

---

[1] Mansi, viii. 817 *sq.* ; John Eph. *Comm.* 203. 245. For the attempt to win Severus cp. Evagrius, iv. 11 ; Zacharias reproduces the letters of Severus, *ib.* 16. The date of the conference, at which Hypatius, bishop of Ephesus, presided, is 531 (not 533), cp. Loofs, *op. cit.* 283.

[2] Mansi, *ib. Leontius vir venerabilis monachus et apocrisiarius patrum in sancta civitate constitutorum.* In the MSS. of some of his works Leontius Byz. is described as μοναχός and Ἱεροσολυμίτης. The same Leontius was present at the Synod of 536.

[3] The sources for the affair of the Scythian monks are their joint letter to some African bishops exiled in Sardinia (*P.L.* lxv. 442 *sqq*), the writings of their patron John Maxentius (*P.G.* lxxxvi. 73 *sqq.*), and the correspondence of Justin, Justinian, and others with Hormisdas concerning them (*Coll. Avellana, Epp.* 187, 188, 196, 216, 232-239). The Papal legates

were unfavourably impressed by them, and their secretary Dioscorus reported to the Pope that the monks, whom he describes as *de domo Vitaliani*, were " adversaries of the prayers of all Christians." The monks went to Rome (summer 519) to submit their views to the Pope and remained there till August 520. It has been already mentioned that Loofs identifies Leontius, one of these monks, with Leontius of Byzantium, but in this theologian's voluminous works he can only find one or two allusions to the Theopaschite dogma (*Contra Nest. et Eut.* 1289, 1377); see Loofs, *op. cit.* 228.

[4] *Coll. Avell.* cxcvi. 235.

[5] *C.J.* i. 1. 6 ; Mansi, viii. 798. Cp. Loofs, *ib.* 260.

[6] Loofs says (255) : " The Theopaschite controversy is an event in the history of the doctrine of the Trinity far more than in that of Christology: it is one of the first signs of the victory of Aristotle over Plato."

having suffered two defeats the Emperor seems to have been persuaded by Theodora to allow her to deal with the situation on other lines. At least it is difficult otherwise to explain what happened. When Epiphanius, the Patriarch of Constantinople, died (June, A.D. 535), she procured the election of Anthimus, bishop of Trapezus, who was secretly a Monophysite. He addressed to Severus a letter containing a Monophysitic confession of faith ; he communicated with Theodosius, the Monophysite Patriarch of Alexandria,[1] and induced the Patriarch of Jerusalem to follow his example. Severus was invited to the capital and Theodora lodged him in the Palace.[2] The Patriarch of Antioch, Ephraim, was a firm adherent of Chalcedon, and he sent a message to Pope Agapetus warning him that heresy was again in the ascendant. Agapetus, arriving at Constantinople early in A.D. 536 and received with great honour by Justinian,[3] refused to communicate with Anthimus, procured his deposition (March 12), and consecrated Menas as his successor.[4] The Pope died suddenly a few weeks later, but in May Menas summoned a synod which anathematised Anthimus, Severus, and others, and condemned their writings.[5] The Emperor then issued a law confirming the acts of the synod, and forbidding Anthimus, Severus, and the others to reside in any large city.[6] Severus spent the last years of his life in the Egyptian desert. Anthimus lived in concealment in Theodora's palace, along with other Monophysites like Theodosius of Alexandria.[7]

A new persecution was now let loose in the East. It was organised by Ephraim of Antioch, who acted as grand inquisitor, and the Monophysite historians have their tale to tell of

---

[1] Theodosius succeeded Timothy IV. on February 9 or 11, 535, but at the same time a rival Patriarch, Gaian (whose views agreed with those of Julian of Halicarnassus), was elected and was Patriarch in possession for 103 days (till May 23 or 25). See Brooks, *B.Z.* xii. 494 *sqq.* For the letter of Anthimus see Zach. Myt. ix. 21.

[2] *Ib.* ix. 15, 19.

[3] *Ib.* 19, where it is said that Justinian was particularly pleased to see Agapetus because he spoke the same language (Latin).

[4] Anthimus had held office for ten months. Menas succeeded on March 13. Cp. Andreev, *Kpl. Patr.* 170-173.

[5] Mansi, viii. 877 *sqq.* Peter of Apamea and Zooras were the others who were condemned.

[6] *Nov.* 42.

[7] See John Eph. *Comm.* pp. 247-248. At the time of the Council Anthimus could not be found anywhere (Mansi, viii. 941). The date of the death of Severus is probably February 8, 538 (Michael Mel. *Chron.* ix. 29). Cp. Brooks, *B.Z.* xii. 497 ; Krüger places it in 543 (art. *Monophysiten* in *Realenc. f. protest. Theologie*).

imprisonments, tortures, and burnings.[1] The Emperor, abandoning his policy of conciliation, was perhaps principally moved by the consideration of his designs on Italy. It was important at this juncture to make it quite clear that his own zeal for orthodoxy was above cavil and to dispel in the minds of the Italians any suspicion that he was inclined to coquette with the Monophysites.[2]

The fall of Anthimus, the ensuing synod, and the Imperial edict which confirmed it, were deeply displeasing to Theodora. But she did not lose heart. She not only protected the heretical leaders, but she formed the bold design of counteracting her husband's policy from Rome itself. The deacon Vigilius was at this time the apocrisiarius or nuncio of the Roman see at Constantinople. He was a man of old senatorial family, the son of a consul, and he had been a favourite of Boniface II., who had desired to secure his succession to the pontifical throne. On the death of Agapetus he saw his chance, and Theodora, who though she knew what manner of man he was, saw her opportunity. An arrangement was made between them. Theodora promised to place at his disposal 200 lbs. of gold (£9000) and provided him with letters to Belisarius and Antonina, and on his part, if he did not definitely promise, he led her to believe that he would repudiate the Council of Chalcedon and re-establish Anthimus in the see of Constantinople.[3] He hastened to Italy, but he arrived too late. King Theodahad had received early notice of the sudden death of Agapetus, and under his auspices Silverius had been elected Pope (in June).[4]

The Empress then wrote to Silverius asking him to procure the restoration of Anthimus, and on his refusal she determined to avail herself of the military occupation of Rome by Belisarius

---

[1] Zacharias Myt. (x. 1) and John Eph. (cp. *Comm.* pp. 111, 134, etc.; 221 *sqq.*) are the chief sources on the persecution. John, bishop of Tella, died in consequence of the tortures which he underwent (John Eph. *Comm.* c. 24).

[2] Dante (*Paradiso*, vi. 13 *sqq.*) represents Justinian as holding Monophysitic opinions and converted by Agapetus :

E prima ch' io all' opra fossi attento,
  Una natura in Cristo esser, non piue
  Credeva, e di tal fede era contento.
Ma il benedetto Agabito, che fue
  Sommo pastore, alla fede sincera
  Mi dirizzò con le parole sue.

[3] Liberatus, *Brev.* 22 ; *Lib. Pont.*, *Vita Silv.* p. 292 ; *Vita Vigil.* p. 297. Victor Tonn. *Chron.*, *sub* 542, says that Vigilius undertook to condemn the Three Chapters *occulto chirographo* which he gave to Theodora ; that he was made Pope by Antonina ; and he quotes a letter of Vigilius (probably spurious) in which Antonina is mentioned. The reference to the Three Chapters here is an anachronism.

[4] June 8. In *Lib. Pont.* p. 290, it is erroneously said that Silverius held the pontifical chair for one year, five months, eleven days, which would give November 18, 537, for his deposition.

to intimidate or, if necessary, to remove him.   She sent secret
instructions to Antonina, probably leaving it to her ingenuity to
concoct a plot against the Pope.   Silverius resided at the Lateran
beside the Asinarian Gate, and a letter was fabricated as evidence
that he was in treacherous communication with the Goths and
proposed to admit them into the city.   Belisarius summoned
him to the Pincian palace, showed him the danger of his position,
and intimated that he could save himself by obeying the wishes
of the Empress.   Silverius refused to yield, and was suffered to
depart, but he took the precaution of withdrawing from the
Lateran to the St. Sabina on the Aventine at a safe distance
from the walls, to prove that he had no desire to communicate
with the enemy.   He was called a second time to the general's
presence and went attended by a numerous retinue, including the
deacon Vigilius, who had come to Rome with Belisarius and was
eagerly awaiting the development of events.   The chief hall in
the Pincian palace was divided by curtains into three apartments.
The Roman clergy remained in the two outer rooms ; only
Silverius and Vigilius were admitted into the presence of Belisarius.
When the Pope again proved inflexible, two subdeacons entered,
removed his pallium, and clothed him in the garb of a monk.
He was banished to Patara in Lycia.   This perfidious act occurred
about the middle of March, and was followed by the election of
Vigilius, who was undoubtedly accessory to it.   He was ordained
bishop of Rome on March 29, A.D. 537.[1]

There is a certain mystery about the subsequent fate of the
unhappy Silverius.   The government of Constantinople deemed
it expedient that he should leave Patara and return to Italy.
It is not clear whether Theodora approved or not, but Pelagius,
the Papal nuncio, protested.   It would be difficult to believe that
Pelagius was not perfectly aware of the scandalous intrigue to
which Vigilius owed his elevation, and it was certainly in the
interest of Vigilius that he desired to keep Silverius far from
Italy.   When Silverius returned, Vigilius appealed to Belisarius
and Antonina.   With their permission, he caused his victim to

<hr>

[1] The story is told in *Lib. Pont.*, *Vita
Silv.* 292-293, and is noticed briefly
by Procopius, *B.G.* i. 25. 13, who only
gives the publicly alleged ground
for the action against Silverius,
namely ὡς δὴ προδοσίαν ἐς Γότθους
πράσσοι, and says that he was immediately sent to Greece.   But in
H.A. (see next note) the hand of
Theodora is recognised.   *Cont. Marcellini*, *sub* 537, gives the official
story : *cui* (*Vitigi*) *tunc faventem
papam Silverium Belisarius ab episco-
patu summovit.*

be conveyed to the island of Palmaria, where according to one account he died of hunger and exhaustion, while there is another record that he was done to death by a creature of Antonina.[1] This intrigue of the Empress did not profit her much. The theological convictions of Pope Vigilius were stronger than his respect for his plighted word, and, when he had attained the goal of his ambition by her help, his robust conscience had no scruples in evading the fulfilment of his promises. By evasions and postponements, and by the assistance of his loyal and tactful nuncio, Pelagius, who had succeeded in ingratiating himself with Theodora as well as with Justinian, he managed to avoid a breach with the Empress, while he addressed to the Emperor and to the Patriarch letters in which he maintained the condemnation of the opponents of the Council of Chalcedon.[2]

§ 6. The Origenistic Heresies in Palestine

Theodosius, the Monophysite Patriarch of Alexandria, who had been deprived of his see in A.D. 536, was succeeded by Paul, a monk of Tabenna, who was ordained by Menas and went to Egypt with full powers to cleanse the sees of the Patriarchate from heretical bishops. Rhodon, the Augustal Prefect, received instructions to support him in all the measures he thought fit to take.[3] The submission seems to have been general; the treatment of Theodosius, who had not been popular, excited little resentment. But a certain deacon, named Psoes, headed an opposition to the new Patriarch, at whose instance he was arrested by Rhodon and died under torture. Theodora was furious and insisted on an investigation; Liberius, the Roman senator who had held high offices in Italy under the Ostrogothic kings and came to Constantinople as ambassador of Theodahad,[4] was appointed to succeed Rhodon, and a clerical commission, in-

---

[1] H.A. 1. 14. Σιλβέριον διαχρησαμένη (Antonina, in the interest of Theodora), and 27 τῶν τινος οἰκετῶν Εὐγενίου ὄνομα ὑπουργήσαντός οἱ ἐς ἅπαν τὸ ἄγος, ᾧ δὴ καὶ τὸ ἐς Σιλβέριον εἴργασται μίασμα. Nothing is said of the motive. In Lib. Pont. 293, the other account will be found.

[2] Coll. Avell., Epp. 92, 93 (also in Migne, P.L. lxix. p. 21 and p. 25).

Pelagius, who was a man of large fortune and high social position, had gone to Constantinople with Agapetus, where he remained for the Council of 536, and was appointed nuncio, in succession to Vigilius, in the same year.

[3] Procopius, H.A. 27. 3 sqq.; and Liberatus, Brev. 22, 23, are the sources.

[4] See above, p. 164.

cluding the nuncio Pelagius, was sent with him to Alexandria to pronounce on the conduct of Paul. The clergy proceeded to Gaza, where they held a synod (about Easter, A.D. 542),[1] at which Pelagius presided, and Paul was found guilty for the death of Psoes and deposed. Rhodon, who fled to Constantinople, was beheaded, though it is said that he produced thirteen letters of the Emperor authorising all that he had done.[2]

Pelagius returned from Gaza through Palestine, where he fell in with some monks of Jerusalem who were on the point of starting for Constantinople for the purpose of inducing Justinian to condemn the opinions of Origen, which were infecting the monasteries of Palestine.

The revival of Origenistic doctrine in the sixth century was closely connected with a mystical movement which seems to have originated in eastern Syria and threatened to taint Christian theology with speculations of a pronounced pantheistic tendency. The teacher who was principally responsible for propagating a Christian pantheism, seductive to many minds, was Stephen bar-Sudaili, of Edessa, who in consequence of his advanced opinions was compelled to leave Edessa and betake himself to Palestine.[3] He seems to have been the author of a book which pretended to have been composed by Hierotheus, an Athenian who was alleged to have been a follower of St. Paul and to have taught Dionysius the Areopagite.[4] If this is so, Stephen was the spiritual father of the famous mystical treatises which, professing to be the works of Dionysius, were given to the world early in the sixth century. The author of these fabrications emphasises his debt to " Hierotheus," but he was also profoundly influenced by the writings of Proclus, the Neoplatonic philosopher, though this was an influence which naturally he

---

[1] See Mansi, viii. 1164. Ephraim, Patriarch of Antioch, attended. For the date see Diekamp, *Die origenistichen Streitigkeiten*, 41 *sqq.*

[2] Procopius, *ib.* 15 and 18. Probably Justinian's letters only instructed the Prefect to obey Paul in all things, though Procopius seems to wish to suggest that they authorised the particular act. Arsenius, a converted Samaritan, who had cooperated with Paul, was hanged by Liberius at the instance of Theodora, *ib.* 19.

[3] A letter of Jacob of Sarug (died 521) to Stephen himself, and another from Philoxenus (Xenaias) the Monophysite bishop of Mabug (485–518) to two priests of Edessa, are the chief sources for the little we know of Stephen. They will be found with English translations in A. L. Frothingham, *Stephen Bar Sudaili.*

[4] A summary of the work (extant in a Syriac MS. of the British Museum) is given by Frothingham, *op. cit.* 91 *sqq.*

could not acknowledge.[1] The learned physician Sergius of
Resaina translated these mystical treatises into Syriac, and it is
noteworthy that Sergius is described as versed in the teaching
of Origen.[2]

Stephen bar-Sudaili, spending the later years of his life in a
convent near Jerusalem, seems to have provoked by his teaching
the return to Origen's speculations, which was to be for half a
century the burning interest in the monasteries of Palestine.
The ablest of the Origenist party and their leading spirit was a
monk named Nonnus. It is not probable that they went so far
in their speculations as Stephen himself, whose views are briefly
summed up in the treatise of " Hierotheus " in the following
words :

" All nature will be confused with the Father ; nothing will
perish, but all will return, be sanctified, united and confused.
Thus God will be all in all. Even hell will pass away and the
damned return. All orders and distinctions will cease. God will
pass away, and Christ will cease to be, and the Spirit will no
longer be called spirit. Essence alone will remain." [3]

Origen could not have endorsed such doctrine, but it is easy
to understand that any one who entertained these ideas would
find his writings more congenial than those of any other Christian
theologian. There was common ground especially in the rejection of eternal damnation.[4] Among the other heterodox opinions
which the Palestinian heretics derived from Origen were the
persistence of the soul, the creation of the world not by the
Trinity but by creative Nous, the similarity of Christ to men in
strength and substance, the doctrines that in the resurrection our
bodies will be of circular form, that ultimately matter will entirely
disappear and that the kingdom of Christ will have an end.[5]

---

[1] See Hugo Koch, *Pseudo-Dionysius
Areopagita in seinen Beziehungen zum
Neuplatonismus und Mysterienwesen*,
1900. The Pseudo-Dionysius works
(of which the chief are entitled *On
the Heavenly Hierarchy* ; *On the
Ecclesiastical Hierarchy* ; *On Divine
Names* ; *On Mystic Theology*) will be
found in *P.G.* 3 and 4. These works
were referred to at the conference
with the Severian Monophysites in
531, when Hypatius, bishop of
Ephesus, pointed out that they could
not be genuine (Mansi, viii. 821).
But they were soon generally accepted

in the Eastern Church. In the ninth
century Michael II. sent a copy to
the Emperor Lewis the Pious, and
soon afterwards they were translated
into Latin by Joannes Erigena. The
strong influence which they exerted
on Thomas Aquinas is well known.

[2] Zach. Myt. ix. 19.

[3] Frothingham, *op. cit.* p. 99.

[4] This view is dealt with mercilessly
in the letter of Philoxenus referred to
above, p. 381, *n.* 3.

[5] See the denunciations of Justinian and of the assembly of bishops
in 553 (below, p. 389, *n.* 2).

After the death of St. Sabas (December 5, A.D. 532), the number and influence of the Origenists grew in the monasteries of Palestine. Two of the most prominent, Theodore Ascidas and Domitian,[1] visited the capital in A.D. 536 to attend the synod which condemned the Monophysites, and gaining the favour of the Emperor they were appointed to fill the sees, Domitian of Ancyra and Theodore of Caesarea in Cappadocia. Both Pelagius and the Patriarch Menas were anxious to break the influence which Theodore Ascidas, a man of considerable astuteness and not over-scrupulous, exerted over Justinian ; and they eagerly took up the cause of the monks who desired to purge Palestine of the heresy. Ephraim, the Patriarch of Antioch, held a synod in summer A.D. 542 to condemn the doctrines of Origen, but the heretics were so powerful that they induced the Patriarch of Jerusalem to strike out Ephraim's name from the diptychs.

Pelagius and Menas convinced Justinian that it was imperative to take action, and in A.D. 543 the Emperor issued an edict condemning ten opinions of Origen.[2] It was subscribed by Menas, and the Pope and the other Patriarchs, including Peter of Jerusalem, signed it also.[3] Theodore Ascidas was in a difficult position. To refuse to accept the edict would have cost him his bishopric and his influence at court. He sacrificed his opinions and affixed his signature,[4] but he had his revenge by raising a new theological question which was to occupy the stage of ecclesiastical politics for more than ten years.[5]

§ 7. *Controversy of the Three Chapters*

There was no theologian whose writings were more offensive to the Monophysites than Theodore of Mopsuestia, who was esteemed the spiritual father of Nestorianism. He had also

---

[1] Theodore was a deacon of the New Laura, Domitian was abbot of the convent of Martyrius. Mansi, viii. 910, 911 ; Cyril, *Vita Sabae* (the principal source for the Origenistic movement in Palestine), p. 518.

[2] The text will be found in Mansi, ix. 488 *sqq.* : and *P.G.* lxxxvi. 945 *sqq.*

[3] Liberatus, 22 ; Cassiodorus, *De inst. div. litt.* c. 1 (*P.L.* lxx. p. 1111).

[4] Domitian of Ancyra also signed

but afterwards retracted.

[5] After the death of Nonnus in 547, a schism arose among the Origenists. The Isochristoi of the New Laura, who held that in the ἀπο-κατάστασις or restitution after the general Resurrection men will be united with God as Christ is, were opposed to the Protoktistai or Tetra-dites (of the Laura of Firminus), whose names and views are obscure. See Diekamp, *op. cit.* 60 *sqq.*

written against Origen and was detested by the Origenists. To
Theodore Ascidas, who was apparently a secret Monophysite as
well as an Origenist, there could hardly be a greater triumph
than to procure his condemnation by the Church.

Ascidas, warmly seconded by Theodora, persuaded the Emperor that he might solve the problem which had hitherto
baffled him of restoring unity to the Church, by anathematising
Theodore of Mopsuestia and his writings. This, he urged, would
remove the chief stumbling-block that the Monophysites found
in the Council of Chalcedon. For their objection to that Council
was based far less on its dogmatic formula than on the countenance which it gave to a Nestorian like Theodore. For if the
formula were consistent with Theodore's opinions, it would not
be consistent with the doctrine of Cyril, and therefore could not
admit of an interpretation that could ever be acceptable to the
Monophysites. What Ascidas proposed was a rectification of the
acts of Chalcedon, so as to make it clear that Chalcedonian
orthodoxy had no leanings to Nestorianism. There were some
other documents which it would be necessary to condemn at the
same time : certain writings of Theodoret against Cyril, and a
letter of Ibas, bishop of Edessa, in which Cyril was censured.
Justinian was impressed by the idea, and acted promptly. In
A.D. 546 he promulgated an Edict of Three Chapters, condemning
(1) Theodore of Mopsuestia and his works ; (2) specified works
of Theodoret ; and (3) the letter of Ibas.[1] In the subsequent
controversy the expression " Three Chapters " was perverted to
mean the condemned opinions, so that those who opposed the
edict were said to defend the Chapters.

The eastern Patriarchs were at first unwilling to subscribe to
this edict. It seemed a dangerous precedent to condemn the
dead who could not speak for themselves. And was there any
prospect that anything short of the repudiation of the Council
of Chalcedon would satisfy the Monophysites ?[2] But the pressure of the Emperor induced the four Patriarchs to sign on the
express condition that the Pope should be consulted.

On November 22, A.D. 545, during Totila's siege of Rome,
Pope Vigilius was in the church of St. Cecilia in Trastevere,
celebrating the anniversary of its dedication. In the middle of

---

[1] The Edict has not been preserved. Diekamp (op. cit. 54) would date it to 543.
[2] Cp. Duchesne, op. cit. 395-396.

the ceremony a body of soldiers arrived, and an officer entered the church and presented Vigilius with a mandate to start immediately for Constantinople. He did not stay to finish the service, but accompanied the soldiers to the Tiber, where a ship was waiting. The congregation followed him and he pronounced the blessing which concluded the liturgy, but when the ship started, the crowd hurled missiles and maledictions. It looked as if the Pope were being carried off against his will, and general rumour ascribed his departure from Rome to the machinations of Theodora. But the sequel does not bear out this explanation. Vigilius was not taken to Constantinople under constraint. He went to Sicily, where he remained for ten months and made arrangements for sending provisions to Rome from the lands belonging to the pontifical patrimony. The truth seems to be that the Emperor wanted Vigilius, that Vigilius was not reluctant to leave the besieged city, and that the scene in St. Cecilia was concerted in order to protect him from the reproach that he was voluntarily abandoning Rome.[1]

In Sicily, the Pope was able to learn the opinion of western ecclesiastics on the Three Chapters of Justinian. They were unanimously opposed to the edict. Dacius, the archbishop of Milan, arrived from Constantinople, where he had lived for some years, and informed him that he had broken off communion with Menas. Supported by western opinion the Pope resolved to oppose the edict, and in autumn A.D. 546 [2] he set sail for Patrae, accompanied by Dacius. He travelled slowly, and when he reached Thessalonica he wrote a letter to Menas explaining his views and threatening to break off communion with him if he continued to support the Three Chapters.[3] On January 25 (A.D. 547) he arrived at the capital, where he was honourably and cordially received by the Emperor. He took up his quarters in the palace of Placidia, the residence of the Roman nuncios.

It was unfortunate for him that Pelagius was no longer at Constantinople. He sorely needed the guidance of a man of ability and tact. He had a learned adviser in Facundus, bishop of Hermiane in Africa, who was well acquainted with Greek, but the disposition and manners of Facundus were far from

---

[1] This is the view of Duchesne.
[2] For the dates see Procopius, B.G. iii. 16. 1 ; Lib. Pont., Vita Vig. 297 ; Cont. Marcellini, s.a. 547 ;

John Mal. xviii. 483.
[3] Facundus, Contra Mocianum, P.L. p. 862 ; Pro def. trium capit. iv. 3 ; ib. p. 623.

conciliating.[1] Vigilius himself was not much of a theologian, and he seems never to have been quite sure as to the merits of the controversy. He was pressed on one side by the Emperor and the Patriarch, on the other by western opinion. His vacillations, due both to intellectual and to moral weakness, presented a pitiable spectacle. In view of his past record, he cannot excite much compassion, but it is not uninteresting to read the story of a Pope trailing in the dust the dignity of the Roman see.

When the Patriarch Menas, who, notwithstanding his first hesitations, had become a warm supporter of the Imperial policy, refused to withdraw his subscription to the Three Chapters, Vigilius excommunicated him and his followers, but a reconciliation was soon effected by the intervention of Theodora,[2] and presently the Pope was assailed with doubts whether the Three Chapters were not justifiable. He read extracts from the works of Theodore of Mopsuestia, which the Greeks translated for him, and came to the conclusion that his doctrines were extremely dangerous. He would not indeed sign the edict; to do so, would concede to the Emperor the right to dogmatise on matters of faith. But he promised to declare an independent judgment, and in the meantime gave the Emperor and Empress written assurances that he intended to pronounce in the sense of the edict.[3] On Easter-eve, A.D. 548, he issued a *Iudicatum* [4] or pronouncement, addressed to Menas, condemning Theodore and the writings condemned in the edict, but carefully protecting the authority of Chalcedon.

The Papal decision created consternation in western Christendom. Facundus, bishop of Hermiane, published a learned treatise against the Three Chapters, on which he had been engaged.[5] The African Church dissolved communion with the Pope, and even Zoilus, Patriarch of Alexandria, who had provisionally subscribed to the edict, withdrew his signature and refused to accept

---

[1] Duchesne, p. 402.

[2] June 9, 547, Theophanes, A.M. 6039 (source, John Mal. cp. xviii. p. 483).

[3] *Acta V. Conc.*, Mansi, ix. 350.

[4] Only some fragments are preserved, Mansi, ix. 104-105, 181.

[5] *Pro defensione trium capitulorum.* In its original form it consisted of two books, which were presented to

the Emperor, but was afterwards expanded into twelve. Facundus returned to Africa, took part in the African Council of 550 which excommunicated Vigilius, and avoided imprisonment by flight. In 571 he wrote the treatise *Contra Mocianum* on the same subject. These two works are important sources for the story of the Three Chapters.

the Iudicatum. The good opinion of the west was of more importance to Vigilius than the Emperor's favour, and, alarmed by the general outcry which his decision had provoked, he sought refuge in the expedient of a General Council. He told the Emperor that this was the only way of averting a schism, and persuaded him to consent to the withdrawal of the Iudicatum. But Justinian, before he agreed, made him swear on the Gospels and the nails of the Cross that he would use all his influence to procure the confirmation of the edict.[1]

Justinian, however, took further measures before the meeting of the Council. He deposed from their sees the Patriarchs of Alexandria and Jerusalem, who refused to approve the Three Chapters, and he issued another edict (A.D. 551) to the same purport as the former one. On the morning of its publication Theodore Ascidas and other Greek clergy visited the Pope in the Placidian palace. He urged them not to commit themselves to any judgment on the Imperial decree, but to await the decision of the Council. When they refused, he declined to receive them or enter their churches, and he excommunicated Menas and Ascidas. The rumour reached him that it was proposed to remove him by force from his residence, and he took refuge, along with the archbishop of Milan, in the sanctuary of SS. Peter and Paul near the palace of Hormisdas. Soldiers were sent to drag them away, and they clung to the altar. Vigilius was seized by his feet and beard, but he was a man of powerful build and in the struggle the altar gave way and fell to the ground crushing him under its weight. There was a cry of horror from the crowd which had gathered in the church, and the soldiers and their commander [2] retreated, abandoning their purpose (August).

The Emperor comprehended that he had gone too far. He sent assurances to the Pope and his clergy that they would be safe if they returned to the Placidian palace. They went back, and though no further violence was offered, the house was guarded like a prison. This became so intolerable that, two days before Christmas, Vigilius resolved to escape and fled under cover of darkness to the church of St. Euphemia in Chalcedon, the scene of the Council which had been the origin of so many

---

[1] *P.L.* lxix. 121-122.
[2] Vigilius calls him *praetor*, and if

this is not a loose term, the Praetor of the Demes must be meant.

troubles. The Emperor then sent Belisarius, chosen doubtless on account of his old relations with the Pope, at the head of a distinguished deputation, to offer him sworn guarantees that he would be honourably treated. The Pope replied that the time for oaths was past ; let the Emperor abstain from holding relations with Menas and Ascidas. His tone enraged Justinian, who wrote him a long unsigned letter full of menaces. Vigilius employed the days of his sojourn at St. Euphemia in composing an Encyclical Epistle, addressed " to the whole people of God," describing the violent treatment he had received, and declaring a profession of faith in which no mention was made of the Three Chapters. At length a new message arrived from the Emperor, again offering guarantees (Feb. 4, A.D. 552), but nothing came of it.[1] Some time afterwards the Pope published his sentence of excommunication against Menas and Ascidas and their followers.

This obstinate attitude wore out Justinian, and, not seeing how he could find any one to put in the place of Vigilius, he agreed with the Patriarch and his clergy that they should make submission to the Pope. They presented to him a declaration, couched in sufficiently humble terms, of their reverence for the Council of Chalcedon and the dogmatic Epistle of Leo, and he then returned to the Placidian palace.

The Emperor had hoped to avoid the convocation of a Council, but he resigned himself to the necessity before the end of the year. Menas died in August (A.D. 552),[2] and his successor Eutychius addressed a letter on the subject to the Pope, who replied favourably.[3] Then the Emperor proceeded to issue notes convoking the bishops. From Gaul and Spain, from Illyricum and Dalmatia none came ; and from Africa only those were allowed to attend on whom the Emperor thought he could count. It was clear that the Council would consist almost entirely of bishops of the Eastern Patriarchates.

The bishops duly arrived, but they were kept waiting at Constantinople for months before the Council met. The delay

---

[1] Vigilius added an account of the interview to his Encyclical, which he signed on the following day. The text of the Encyclical will be found in *P.L.* lxix. 53 *sqq.* ; the condemnation of Ascidas (dated in August 551), *ib.* 59 *sqq.*

[2] John Mal. xviii. 486. This agrees with the Lists of the Patriarchs which assign sixteen years six months to Menas. Eutychius was consecrated immediately after his death. See Andreev, *op. cit.* 175.

[3] *P.L.* lxix. 63 *sq.*, and 65 *sqq.* (January 6, 553).

was due to the Pope, who, though he had originated the proposal of a Council, now declared that he would not take part in it. Afraid, at the last moment, of injuring irrevocably his authority in the eyes of the western churches, he had bethought himself of a *via media*.[1]   He would condemn certain doctrines of Theodore of Mopsuestia without anathematising his person ; but he would refuse to pass any judgment on the writings of Theodoret and Ibas, on the ground that their condemnation would bring discredit on the Council of Chalcedon which had defended them. But he did not imagine that he would be able to induce the Council to adopt this compromise, and he therefore decided not to attend it but to issue his own judgment independently.

The meeting of the Council could not be indefinitely postponed, and at last the first session was held in the Secretariat of St. Sophia, on May 5, A.D. 553.[2]   The proceedings opened by the reading of a letter of the Emperor reviewing the question of the Three Chapters.   The assembly sent many deputations to the Pope requesting him to appear ;   he replied that he would send a written judgment on the question at issue.[3]   On May 14 it was ready, and Belisarius proceeded to the Placidian palace, but only to decline to transmit the document.   A messenger of Vigilius then carried it to the Great Palace, but the Emperor refused to receive it, on the ground that if it confirmed the Three Chapters, it merely repeated what Vigilius had already declared and was therefore superfluous ; and if it was unfavourable, it was inconsistent with his previous utterances and could carry no weight.

At a subsequent session, Justinian presented to the Council documents in which the Pope had approved of the Chapters of his edict, and then laid before the assembly an Imperial decree directing that the name of Vigilius should be struck out of the

[1] Duchesne thinks that this compromise was probably suggested by Pelagius.

[2] The Acts are in Mansi, ix. 173 *sqq.* There were eight sessions, the last on June 2. The Origenistic heresy seems to have been discussed at meetings of the bishops previous to May 5, which did not form part of the proceedings of the Council proper, and at one of these conferences a letter of the Emperor was read which is preserved in the chronicle of George Monachus (ed. de Boor, 630 *sqq.*). This is the result of Diekamp's investigations (*op. cit.*). Origen is mentioned in the eleventh Anathema of the Council, but the fifteen canons against Origenistic doctrines (Mansi, ix. 395 *sqq.*) were drawn up at the previous meetings, and apparently were not specially confirmed by the Council.

[3] It is known as the *Constitutum Vigilii*, and will be found in *P.L.* lxvii. *sqq.*, and *Coll. Avell., Ep.* 83.

diptychs on account of his tergiversation and because he refused to attend the Council. This was done.

The decrees of the Fifth Ecumenical Council, which condemned a Pope, as well as Theodore of Mopsuestia and works of Theodoret and Ibas, were accepted without opposition. In the west they led to the banishment of some bishops,[1] and Pelagius, who had signed the document of the Pope, was imprisoned.

Vigilius found himself alone, and once more he revoked his latest decision. In yielding to the Emperor's wishes, he may have been moved by the fact that Narses had just completed the subjugation of the Ostrogoths and that his own place was at Rome. " He chose among the different opinions which he had successively defended that which appeared most favourable to his personal interests and undoubtedly to those of his flock long deprived of its shepherd."[2] At the end of six months he addressed to the Patriarch Eutychius a letter signifying his acceptance of the decrees of the Council (December 8, A.D. 553),[3] and then prepared a formal judgment in which he refuted the arguments alleged against the condemnations of the Three Chapters (February 26, A.D. 554).[4] The Emperor showed his satisfaction by conferring benefits on the Roman see,[5] and in the following year the Pope set out for Italy. But he never saw Rome again. He died at Syracuse (June 7, A.D. 555), and his body was conveyed to Rome and buried in the Church of St. Silvester on the Via Salaria.

Pelagius had refused to follow Vigilius in his last recantation, and had written pamphlets against the Council. But he was soon to do even as Vigilius, when the Emperor, who valued his qualities, told him that he might succeed to the pontifical throne if he would accept the Council. He revised his opinions with little delay and was chosen and consecrated bishop of Rome.[6] On this occasion, Justinian assumed the right, which had been

---

[1] Like Victor Tonnennensis and Liberatus. The *Breviarium* of Liberatus, which has been often quoted in the foregoing pages, was written with polemical intention against the Three Chapters. Primasius, who had succeeded the exiled Reparatus in the see of Carthage, yielded.

[2] Duchesne, *ib.* 422.

[3] Mansi, ix. 413 *sqq.* ; *P.L.* lxix. 121 *sqq.*

[4] Mansi, ix. 457 *sqq.*

[5] By a so-called *Pragmatica*, dated August 13, 554 ; *Novellae*, App. vii. (= *Nov.* 164, ed. Zachariä).

[6] Duchesne's dates for the pontificate of Pelagius are April 16, 556 (not 555), to March 4, 561 (not 560). Cp. *op. cit.* 428. At his consecration Pelagius declared a profession of faith in which he entirely ignored the Fifth Council.

exercised by the Ostrogothic kings, of confirming elections to the Roman see.[1] The Fifth Ecumenical Council failed utterly in its main object of bringing about unity in the east, and it caused a schism in the west. Milan and Aquileia would know nothing of its decrees, and though political events, when the Lombards invaded Italy, forced Milan to resume communion with Rome, the see of Aquileia maintained its secession for more than a hundred and forty years.

It is possible that under the stress of persecution the Monophysitic faith might have expired, had it not been for the indefatigable labours of one devoted zealot, who not only kept the heresy alive, but founded a permanent Monophysitic Church. This was Jacob Baradaeus, who was ordained bishop of Edessa (about 541) by the Monophysitic bishops who were hiding at Constantinople under the protection of Theodora. Endowed with an exceptionally strong physical constitution, he spent the rest of his life in wandering through the provinces of the East, Syria, Mesopotamia, and Asia Minor, disguised as a beggar, and he derived the name Baradaeus [2] from his dress, which was made of the saddle-cloths of asses stitched together. His disguise was so effective, and his fellow-heretics were so faithful, that all the efforts of the Imperial authorities to arrest him were vain, and he lived till A.D. 578. His work was not only to confirm the Monophysites in their faith and maintain their drooping spirit, but also to ordain bishops and clergy and provide them with a secret organisation. His name has been perpetuated in that of the Jacobite Church which he founded.

§ 8. General Significance of Justinian's Policy

The Fifth Ecumenical Council differed from the four which preceded it in that, while they pronounced on issues which divided Christendom and which called for an authoritative decision of the Church, the Fifth dealt with a question which had been artificially created. Constantine, Theodosius the Great, his grandson, and Marcian had convoked ecclesiastical assemblies

---

[1] Cp. Liber Diurnus Rom. Pont., ed. Rozière (1869), lviii. p. 103 sqq.

[2] From the Arabic form al-Barādi'ā, which corresponds to the Syriac Burde'āyā. The chief sources for Jacob are the Life by John of Ephesus, Comm. c. 49 ; another Life wrongly ascribed to the same writer, ib. p. 203 sqq. ; and John Eph. Hist. ecc. Part III. B. iv. 13 sqq.

to settle successive controversies which had arisen in the natural course of theological speculation and which threatened to break up the Church into sects ; the purpose of the Council which Justinian summoned was to confirm a theological decision of his own which was incidental indeed to a vital controversy, but only incidental. His object was to repair the failure of Chalcedon and to smooth the way to reunion with the Monophysites ; and it may be said that the Three Chapters were entirely in the spirit of the orthodox theological school of his time.[1] But the question was provoked by himself ; it was not one on which the decree of a General Council was imperatively required.

The importance of this episode of ecclesiastical history lies in the claim which Justinian successfully made to the theological guidance of the Church, a claim which went far beyond the rights of control exercised by previous emperors. Zeno had indeed taken a step in this direction by his Henotikon, but the purpose of the Henotikon was to suppress controversy, not to dictate doctrine. Justinian asserted the principle that doctrinal decisions could be made by Imperial edicts. An edict imposed upon the Church the orthodoxy of the Theopaschite formula ; an edict condemned opinions of Origen ; and, though the behaviour of Pope Vigilius forced the Emperor to summon a Council, the Council did no more than confirm the two edicts which he had issued on the Three Chapters. Justinian seems to have regarded it as merely a matter of policy and expediency whether theological questions should be settled by ecclesiastical synods or by Imperial legislation. Eastern ecclesiastics acquiesced in the claims of the Emperor when they adhered to the first edict on the Three Chapters, even though they made their adhesion conditional on the attitude of Rome ; and at the synod of A.D. 536, while the assembled bishops said " We both follow and obey the apostolic throne," it was also laid down by the Patriarch that nothing should be done in the Church contrary to the will of the Emperor.[2]

[1] Cp. Loofs, op. cit. 316. In one of his laws (Nov. 132, A.D. 544) Justinian appeals to his books and edicts to prove his zeal for orthodox doctrine. His extant works (see P.G. 86) include, besides the edicts against Origen and on the Three Chapters and some minor writings, a dogmatic refutation of the Monophysite doctrine, addressed to monks of Alexandria, c. 542–543 ; and an open letter against the defenders of Theodore of Mopsuestia. See Loofs, op. cit. 310 sqq. ; W. H. Hutton, The Church of the Sixth Century, 189 sqq.

[2] Mansi, ix. 970 προσήκει μηδὲν τῶν ἐν τῇ ἁγιωτάτῃ ἐκκλησίᾳ κινουμένων παρὰ γνώμην αὐτοῦ καὶ κέλευσιν γενέσθαι.

This Caesaro-papism, as it has been called, or Erastianism, to use the word by which the same principle has been known in modern history, was the logical result of the position of the Church as a State institution.

The Three Chapters was not the last theological enterprise of Justinian. In the last years of his life he adopted the dogma of aphthartodocetism, which had been propagated, as we have seen,[1] by Julian of Halicarnassus, and had sown strife among the Monophysites of Egypt. This change of opinion is generally considered an aberration due to senility ; but when we find a learned modern theologian asserting that the aphthartodocetic dogma is a logical development of the Greek doctrine of salvation,[2] we may hesitate to take Justinian's conversion to it as a sign that his intellectual power had been enfeebled by old age. The Imperial edict in which he dictated the dogma has not been preserved. The Patriarch Eutychius firmly refused to accept it, and the Emperor, not forgetting his success in breaking the will of Vigilius, caused him to be arrested (January 22, A.D. 565). He was first sent to the Island of the Prince and then banished to a monastery at Amasea.[3] The other Patriarchs were unanimous in rejecting the Imperial dogma. Anastasius of Antioch and his bishops addressed to the Emperor a reasoned protest against the edict. Their bold remonstrances enraged Justinian, and he was preparing to deal with them, as he had dealt with Eutychius, when his death relieved the Church from the prospect of a new persecution.[4]

[1] See above, p. 375.

[2] Harnack, *History of Dogma*, iv. 238, where it is suggested that Justinian was inclined to this heresy in the early years of his reign.

[3] Eustratius, *Vita Eutychii*, c. 5. Eutychius was succeeded in the Patriarchate by John of Sirmium, who held the see for twelve and a half years, and then Eutychius was restored (A.D. 577).

[4] The sources for Justinian's heresy are : Evagrius, *H.E.* iv. 39. 40 ; Eustratius, *ib.* cc. 4, 5 ; Theophanes, A.M. 6057 (=Cramer, *Anecd.* ii. 111), whose notice is probably derived from John Malalas ; Michael Mel. *Chron.* ix. 34, who gives the text of the Antiochene document (his ultimate source was probably John of Ephesus, *H.E.* Part II.) ; John of

Nikiu, *Chron.* c. 94, p. 399 ; Nicephorus Patriarcha, *Chronogr.* p. 117, ed. de Boor. Victor Tonn., *s.a.* 566, notices the deposition of Eutychius, but does not assign the reason. There is also a letter of Nicetius, bishop of Trier, to Justinian, reproaching him with his lapse into heresy in his old age (*in ultima senectute tua*), though the bishop appears to have had no clear idea as to the nature of the heresy (*P.L.* lxviii. 378). An attempt to rescue the reputation of Justinian for unblemished orthodoxy was made by Richard Crakanthorp, who in 1616 published a pamphlet, *Justinian the Emperor defended against Cardinal Baronius*, in which he sought to invalidate the evidence (which at that time mainly consisted of Evagrius and Eustratius). In 1693 Humphrey Hody refuted his arguments in a treatise entitled *The Case of Sees Vacant by an Unjust or Uncanonical Deprivation Stated.* The thesis of Crakanthorp has been revived in modern times, with much greater ingenuity and learning, by W. H. Hutton (*op. cit.* 205 *sqq.*, and articles in *The Guardian*, August 12, 1891, April 22, 1897; cp. my articles, *ib.*, March 4, 1896, January 13, 1897). But the testimonies are too strong and circumstantial to be set aside or evaded. It may be noted that, according to Michael Mel. (*loc. cit.*), Justinian was perverted by a monk of Joppa ; and according to some he returned to the path of orthodoxy just before he died.

CHAPTER XXIII

THE LEGISLATIVE WORK OF JUSTINIAN

§ 1. *Codification of the Law*

JUSTINIAN is the only Emperor after Constantine, or at least after Julian the apostate, whose name is familiar to many who have never read a line about the history of the later Empire. He owes this fame to the great legal works which are associated with his name ; and it may be suspected that some of those who have heard of the Digest and Institutions of Justinian think of him as a jurist and are hardly aware that he was an Emperor.

Justinian's legal achievements were twofold. By new legislation he brought to completion, in several important domains of civil law, the tendencies towards simplicity and equity which had been steadily developing for many centuries. This alone would have made his name remembered in the history of European law. But his chief work did not consist in legislative improvements. It consisted in reducing to order and arranging in manageable form the enormous and unwieldy body of Roman law as it existed.[1]

Roman law, at this time, was of two kinds, which we may distinguish as statute law and jurisprudence ; the statute law consisting of the Imperial constitution, and the jurisprudence of the works of the authoritative jurists who had written in the second and third centuries. Codification of the statute law was not a novelty. There had already been three Codes, the last of which, as we saw, was issued under the auspices of Theodosius II.

---

[1] Good general accounts of the legal works of Justinian will be found in Roby's *Introduction to the* *Digest*, and in Bryce's article on Justinian in the *Dict. of Christian Biography.*

and his western colleague in A.D. 438. But a new collection, more compendious and up-to-date, was a pressing need. The book of Theodosius was bulky, and was not always at hand to consult in the courts. Many of the enactments contained in it were wholly obsolete or had suffered modification, and in the seventy years which had elapsed since its appearance, a large number of new laws had been made.

It seems almost certain that Justinian had conceived the idea of compiling a new Code before he ascended the throne, for not many months after his accession to power he issued a constitution addressed to the Senate, in which he announced the plan of a new collection of laws, edited up to date, with contradictions carefully eliminated, obsolete constitutions expunged, superfluous preambles or explanations omitted, words altered, eliminated, or added for the sake of clearness ; and appointed a commission of ten expert jurists to execute the work.[1] Of these ten, the pagan Tribonian, afterwards Quaestor, the Emperor's right hand in his great legal enterprise, and perhaps partly their inspirer, and Theophilus, professor of law at Constantinople, were the most distinguished.

The commission must have worked hard, for the Code was completed and published in little more than a year. The Imperial constitution which introduced it to the world and made it authoritative was dated on April 7, A.D. 529.[2] But the Code which then appeared, and was arranged in ten Books, has not come down to us. Five and a half years later, an amended edition was issued,[3] arranged in twelve Books and including the new constitutions of the intervening period. It is this edition which we possess, and it contains 4652 laws.

In the meantime a more original and far more difficult work had been planned and completed. This was to reduce to order and consistency, and to present in a convenient form, the admirable body of jurisprudence which had been built up in the second and third centuries, the classical period of Roman law. The great

---

[1] February 13, A.D. 528. This constitution (*Haec quae* —) is prefixed to the Code.

[2] Prefixed to Code (*Summa* —) ; addressed to the Prefect of the City. [A fragment of the *Index titulorum* of the 1st ed., found in Egypt, has been published this year by A. S. Hunt

(*Oxyrh. Papyri*, xv. p. 217 *sqq.*). It contains the Index to Bk. i., titles 11-18, but 12 and 13 are omitted. Among other interesting points it supplies the name of the Emperor who enacted i. 11. 9 : it was Anastasius.]

[3] Prefixed to Code (*Cordi nobis* —) ; addressed to the Senate.

lawyers of that age, who were licensed to give opinions and
whose "answers" carried the weight of Imperial authority,
explained and developed the rules of law which had been finally
embodied in the Perpetual Edict of Hadrian. Their opinions
(*responsa prudentium*) were scattered in many treatises, and they
often differed. On many points antagonists might produce two
opposite opinions, and on almost any the judge might be perplexed by inconsistent citations. The writings of five jurists
soon came to obtain a predominant influence. These were Gaius,
Papinian, Ulpian, Paulus, and Modestinus. The Emperor Constantine sought to diminish the practical inconvenience caused
through the disagreements of these lawyers by exalting the
authority of Papinian above Paulus and Ulpian. Valentinian III.
and Theodosius II. passed an important measure, known as the
Law of Citations, ordaining that the majority of opinions should
determine the decision of the judge, and that, if they were equally
divided, the ruling of Papinian should prevail.[1]

But the treatises of the recognised experts were so voluminous
that in practice it was very difficult to administer good law. At
most courts there was probably neither the necessary library nor
the necessary learning available. It was a crying need, in the
interests of justice, to make the opinions of the jurists easily
accessible, and the idea was conceived and carried out by
Justinian of meeting this want by "enucleating the old jurisprudence."

But one thing had to be done first. The Law of Citations
imposed upon each judge the task of examining and correcting
the opinions of the authorities when they disagreed. Plainly it
would be much more convenient and satisfactory to have all
important cases of disagreement settled once for all, so that the
judge should have one clear ruling to guide him. Accordingly
Justinian's lawyers drew up Fifty Decisions, which settled principal points of dispute.

This cleared the way for compiling an authoritative and consistent body of Jurisprudence. In the last month of A.D. 530,
Justinian authorised a commission of sixteen lawyers, under the
presidency of Tribonian, to set about the work.[2] They were to
eliminate all contradictions and omit all repetitions, and when
they had thus prepared the vast material they were to arrange

---

[1] A.D. 426, *C. Th.* i. 4. 3.   [2] *C.J.* i. 17. 1.

it in one fair work, as it were a holy temple of Justice, containing
in fifty Books the law of 1300 years. Tribonian seems to have
adopted the practical expedient of dividing the commission into
three committees, each of which digested and prepared a portion
of the material.[1] Immense as the task was, it was completed
in less than three years, and was published in December, A.D. 533.[2]
The work was known as the Digest or the Pandects.[3]

The Code and the Digest were each promulgated as an
Imperial statute. They were to comprehend the whole body
of valid law, except such Imperial constitutions as might
subsequently be issued. All the books of the jurists were
herewith rendered obsolete, as well as the Twelve Tables and the
older Codes.

During the compilation of the Digest, Tribonian and his two
most learned coadjutors, Theophilus, professor at Constantinople,
and Dorotheus, professor at Berytus, prepared and published an
official handbook of civil law for the use of students, the famous
Institutions. This manual reproduces the Commentaries of Gaius,
the great jurist of the second century, but brings that work up
to date by numerous changes, omissions, and additions. Like
the Code and Digest, it is published with all the authority of a
statute.[4]

With the publication of the Institutions and the Digest, the
Emperor announced a reform of legal studies. The education
of a student in the legal schools extended over five years.
Justinian prescribed a rearrangement of the course,[5] which was
now to be confined to his own law books, and he abolished all

---

[1] The composition of the Digest
was elucidated by F. Bluhme, *Die
Ordnung der Fragmente in den Pan-
decten-titeln*. Bluhme showed that
the arrangement of the Books was
determined by Pythagorean theories
of numbers. This was quite in the
spirit of the time. Cp. Roby, preface
to *Introduction to the Digest*.

[2] See the constitutions prefixed
to the work (*Omnem reipublicae* —,
and *Dedit nobis* —) ; and *C.J.* i. 17. 2.

[3] *Digesta* ; πανδέκται. *C.J.* i. 17.
1 § 12.

[4] See the prefixed constitution
(dated A.D. 533, November 21)
addressed *cupidae legum iuventuti*.
Gaius and the Institutions can be
conveniently compared in Gneist's

ed., in parallel columns (2nd ed.,
1880).

[5] See the constitution *Omnem*
(addressed to the professors of law,
antecessoribus). The students of each
year were distinguished by special
names : 1st year, *Dupondii* ; 2nd,
Edictales ; 3rd, *Papinianistae* ; 4th,
λύται ; 5th, προλύται. Justinian
stigmatises *dupondii* as a frivolous
and ridiculous name, and orders
that the freshmen shall henceforth
be designated *Iustiniani novi*. In
Zacharias, *Life of Severus* (ed. Kugener), there is some interesting
information about the life of law
students at Berytus. It was a
regular practice for the Edictales to
" rag " the Dupondii.

the law schools of the Empire except those of Constantinople and Berytus. This was intended to secure that the teaching should be in the hands of entirely competent persons.[1]

The Code, Digest, and Institutions form the principal parts of the Corpus Juris Civilis, on which the law of most European countries is based, and which has influenced English law, although it was never accepted in England. The fourth part of the Corpus consists of the later laws of Justinian, published after the second edition of the Code, and known as the Novels. It is perhaps surprising that the Emperor did not, in the course of the last thirty years of his reign, issue another edition of the Code, including the new constitutions. He promised to publish a collection of his Novels, but he never did so ; [2] and it was left to private jurists to collect them after his death.[3] Thus the fourth part of the Corpus has not the same official character as the other three. The Novels testify to the growing disuse of Latin as the official language. Previous Emperors, even Theodosius II., had occasionally issued constitutions in Greek ; but in the reign of Justinian, Greek became the rule and Latin the exception. Nearly all the Novels (except those intended for publication in Africa and Italy) were drawn up in Greek.[4]

Many of the laws of Justinian are concerned with administrative reforms, which have claimed our attention in other places. Here we may consider how civil jurisprudence and criminal law developed under his predecessors and were completed or modified by him.

---

[1] Const. *Omnem*, § 7 *audivimus etiam in Alexandrina splendidissima civitate et in Caesariensium et in aliis quosdam imperitos homines devagare et doctrinam discipulis adulterinam tradere.*

[2] See Const. *Cordi nobis* (prefixed to Code) : *aliam congregationem— quae novellarum nomine constitutionum significetur.* It has been conjectured that the death of Tribonian may have had something to do with the non-fulfilment of this purpose.

[3] The basis of our text is a collection of 168 Novels, of which four are duplicates, seven belong to Justin II. and Tiberius II., and four are edicts of Praetorian Prefects ; so that it contains 153 laws of Justinian. Another collection formed the basis of the Latin epitome of Julian, which

we possess (125 Novels). We have also the Authenticum, a Latin version used in the Middle Ages (134 Novels). But we know of other collections too (cp. Heimbach, *Gr.-röm. Recht*, p. 199). At the end of the first text are eleven edicts (not counted as Novels) ; and we have also some other constitutions of Justinian, derived from various sources. These additional texts will be found as Appendices I. and II. to the edition of Schoell and Kroll.

[4] Zachariä von Lingenthal attributes this change to the influence of John the Cappadocian (Appendix to his ed. of *Novellae*, pp. 6, 8). John was ignorant of Latin, and most of the laws were addressed to the Praet. Pref. of the East.

§ 2. *Civil Law*

The civil legislation of Justinian forms in many respects the logical term of the development of Roman law. The old law of the Twelve Tables had undergone profound modifications, first by the judgments of the Praetors under the influence of the *Ius gentium*, and then by Imperial statutes. We may say that this development was marked by two general features. The law was simplified on form, and it was humanised in substance. Both these processes were mainly a consequence of the Imperial expansion of Rome. The acquisition of strange territories, the subjection of foreign peoples, had led to the formation of a second system of jurisprudence, the praetorian law ; and this, which had the merit of greater elasticity, reacted upon the native civil law of Rome and eventually wrought considerable changes in it, both by mitigating some of its harsher features and by superseding some of its cumbrous forms. At later stages the process of simplification progressed, first by Caracalla's grant of Roman citizenship to all the free subjects of the Empire (in A.D. 212), and secondly, at a later time, by the disappearance of the distinction between Roman and provincial soil, whereby it became possible to simplify the law of real property. The gradual changes in the spirit of Roman law responded generally to changes in public opinion, and the chief agency in educating Roman opinion and humanising the Roman attitude to life was undoubtedly Greek thought. The spirit of the *De officiis* of Cicero illustrates how far Roman educated opinion had travelled during the last two centuries of the Republic.

The extension of Roman citizenship to all freemen in the Empire did away with the *ius Latii* and the legal distinctions appertaining to it. But between the slaves and the citizens there still remained some intermediate classes, who were less than citizens and more than slaves. There were the Latini Iuniani, slaves who had been manumitted, but through some flaw in the process had not become citizens in the full sense, having neither the right to hold public office nor to marry a free person, and being unable to make a will or to inherit under a will. There were the *dediticii*, slaves who had undergone punishment for crime and were afterwards manumitted, but who, in consequence of their old offences, did not enjoy the full rights of a citizen and could not live within a hundred miles of Rome. And there were persons *in mancipii causa* ; children whom their fathers had surrendered into slavery, in consequence of some misdemeanour which they had committed, and whose status differed from that of true slaves in that, if they were manumitted, they became not freedmen but freemen (*ingenui*). These three classes had little importance in the time of Justinian, but he finally did away with them, and thus consummated the simplification of personal status. There were now, in the eyes of the law, only two classes, citizens and slaves. Among citizens indeed the class of freedmen was still distinguished, but only by the obligations which a freedman owed to his patron, not by any civil disabilities. Formerly he could not be a senator or a magistrate, unless the restrictions were removed by Imperial favour,[1] nor could he marry a lady of senatorial family. Justinian abolished these disabilities.

In regard to slavery itself, the legislation of Justinian was also progressive. He repealed the Lex Fufia Caninia (A.D. 8), which limited the number of slaves a master might manumit, and he abolished the restrictions which the Lex Aelia Sentia had imposed on the liberation of slaves under thirty years of age. The solemn forms of manumission [2] ceased to be necessary ; any signification of the intention to manumit was legally valid.

The *patria potestas* was one of the fundamental principles which underlay the fabric of Roman law, and nothing better illustrates the influence which the gradual humanising of public opinion exercised on legislation than the limitations which were successively placed upon the authority of the paterfamilias over the persons and property of those who were under his *potestas*. One of the last severities to disappear was the right of a father to surrender his children as slaves to any one whom they had wronged, a right of which he might be tempted to avail himself if he were unable or unwilling to pay compensation. This practice (*noxae deditio*) had practically disappeared before

---

[1] Namely, by a decree granting *restitutio natalium* (which cancelled the rights of the patron), or *ius anulorum aureorum.* Justinian granted these to all freedmen, but reserved the patron's rights, *Nov.* 78.

[2] Under the Empire, till the fourth century manumission could in general only be effected by vindicta or by testament. The recognition of Christianity introduced a new form, declaration *in ecclesiis.*

the sixth century, but was still legally recognised. Justinian abolished it formally, and his observations on the subject illustrate the tendency of Roman legislation.[1] "According to the just opinion of modern society, harshness (*asperitas*) of this kind must be rejected, and this practice has fallen utterly into disuse. Who will consent to give his son, far less his daughter, into noxal servitude ? For a father will suffer, through his son, far more than the son himself, and in the case of a daughter such a thing is barred still more by consideration for her chastity."

By the harshness of early law, all property acquired by persons in *potestas* belonged to the father. This was modified by successive provisions under the Empire, and, before Justinian, the father was entitled to the usufruct of the property which his son had independently acquired. If he emancipated his son, he retained one third as absolute owner. Justinian changed this law to the advantage of the children. He gave the father a life interest in half the son's property ; but when the father died, it reverted to the son.[2]

Justinian also simplified the process of emancipation. The ancient elaborate method of emancipating persons in *potestas* by fictitious sales was still in use. The Emperor Anastasius introduced, as an alternative method, emancipation by Imperial rescript, but this did not make the process easier, though it was highly convenient when the person to be emancipated was not residing in the same place as the paterfamilias. Justinian " exploded " the old fictitious process[3] and enacted that a simple declaration of both parties in the presence of a magistrate or judge should be legally valid.

The history of marriage shows the same tendency to simplification. In early times a legal marriage between Roman citizens could be contracted in one of three ways : by a religious ceremony, which was confined to patricians (*confarreatio*) ; by a process of fictitious sale (*coemptio*) ; and by cohabitation for a year (*usus*). In each of these ways, the wife came under the power (*manus*)

---

[1] *Inst.* iv. 8 § 7.   The influence of "oriental" (Greek) law on many of Justinian's reforms is traced and emphasised in P. Collinet's valuable *Études historiques sur le droit de Justinian*, vol. i., 1912. The Syro-Roman lawbook, edited by Bruns and Sachau (1880), is of much service in elucidating this subject.

[2] *C.J.* vi. 61. 6.

[3] *Fictione pristina explosa, Inst.* i. 12 § 6. For the influence of Greek law on the simplification of form in this case and in that of adoption see Collinet, *op. cit.* 52 *sqq.*

of her husband ; this power, in fact, was the fundamental feature in the legal conception of marriage. Towards the end of the second century A.D., these old forms of contracting civil marriage had fallen into disuse.[1] In other words, *manus* was obsolete. The Romans had adopted the *matrimonium iure gentium*, which had formerly been used by those who did not possess the right of marriage with Roman citizens (*ius connubii*).[2] This union did not produce *manus*, nor did it originally give the father *potestas* over his children. It was quite informal ; consent only was required. But as it came into use among Roman citizens, it was allowed to carry with it the *patria potestas*. Divorce by consent was the logical result of marriage by consent and the disuse of *manus*. So long as *manus* had constituted the legal relation, the husband had to emancipate his wife in order to effect a divorce.

But the disuse of *manus*, which had placed the wife in the position of a daughter, did not make her legally independent (*sui iuris*). She remained either under *patria potestas* or under guardianship (*tutela*). The old theory was that a woman was not a person capable of legal action, and that if she were under neither *potestas* nor *manus* she must be legally represented by a guardian. Exceptions were made to this rule even in the time of Augustus ;[3] and the result of the growing belief that women were capable of acting for themselves was that by the fourth century perpetual guardianship of females had disappeared.

If we turn from the law of persons to the law of property, we notice similar tendencies. When the distinction between Italian and provincial soil disappeared,[4] the distinction also fell away between the full *quiritary* ownership, which applied only to Italian land, and the *bonitary* ownership granted to the actual proprietors of provincial land, of which the supreme owner was the Roman people. The curious classification of property, which had played a great part in the old law, as *res mancipi* (real property in Italy, slaves, the chief domestic animals)[5] and *res nec mancipi*, was abandoned and abolished ; and the conveyance

---

[1] *Confarreatio* survived, but was only used by families who held certain religious offices.

[2] Caracalla's law abolished, *ipso facto*, all restrictions on the *ius connubii*.

[3] Lex Iulia et Papia Poppaea, A.D. 9.

[4] *Inst.* ii. 8. 40 ; *C.J.* vii. 25 ; vii. 31.

[5] Also rural servitudes. The word *res* has of course a much wider connotation than property.

of property was simplified by the disappearance of the ancient
and cumbrous civil methods (*mancipatio* and *in iure cessio*) which
were superseded by the natural process of simple delivery (*traditio*).
Full ownership (*dominium*) could now be acquired by delivery.
It could also be acquired by long possession or *usucapio*. This
method of acquisition had formerly been inapplicable to provincial
land (because the *dominium* belonged to the Roman people),
and the praetors had introduced an equivalent institution (*longi
temporis praescriptio*), which was extended to all kinds of property. Justinian simplified the law by applying the second
method to land which could be acquired by prescription after
ten or (in some cases) twenty years, and the first method to
moveables, possession of which for three years produced full
ownership.[1]

The governing conception in the Roman jurisprudence which
concerned the family was the relationship known as *agnatio*.
This untranslatable term is defined by Roman lawyers as kinship
(*cognatio*) through males, but perhaps its scope is more clearly
explained by saying that agnates were those who were under the
patria potestas of the same person, or would have been so, if
he were alive.[2]

The most important sphere in which agnation operated was
the law of inheritance. When a man died without making a
will, his heirs at law were in the first instance those persons
(children, grandchildren, etc.) who were in his *potestas* and
whom his death automatically rendered independent (*sui iuris*).
These were called *sui heredes* and did not include sons whom he
had emancipated before his death or married daughters. If there
were no *sui heredes* the inheritance passed to the nearest agnates ;
and if these failed to the *gens*. The two most serious defects in
this system were the exclusion of sons and daughters who had
passed out of the *potestas* of the deceased before his death, and
the disqualification of cognates who were not also agnates. The

---

[1] *Inst.* ii. 6; *C.J.* vii. 31. 1; vii. 33. 12.

[2] For the benefit of readers who
are not familiar with the conception,
it may be explained that if we start
with a paterfamilias (A), a first group
of agnates is formed by his sons and
daughters, the children of his sons,
the children of the sons of his sons,
etc. This group is determined by a
common relation to A. A second
group of *agnati proximi* is constituted
by those who were in the *potestas*
of A's father ; namely, A's brothers
and sisters, the sons and daughters
of the brothers, and so on. A third
and more remote group is formed by
those who were in the potestas of
A's grandfather. And so on in
ascending scale. Adoption carried
with it inclusion among the agnates.

Practors devised expedients to remedy these hardships and to introduce new rules of succession which favoured cognation at the expense of agnation ; but it was reserved for Justinian finally to lay down a scheme of intestate succession, which prevails in most European countries to-day.[1]

By this reform the first heirs to an estate are the cognate descendants of the deceased, that is, his sons and daughters, their children, grandchildren, etc. The children inherit in equal shares ; grandchildren only come in if their parent is dead, and divide his or her share. One trace, indeed, of the agnate system remains ; adopted children count as natural.

If there are no descendants, the full brothers and sisters of the deceased, or the next nearest cognates, inherit, and dead brothers and sisters are represented by their issue, in the same way as in the former case. Failing heirs of this group, half-brothers and half-sisters have the next claim ; after this, other collaterals.[2]

In this legislation, there is no recognition of the claim of a wife or of a husband. The theory was that the wife was adequately provided for by her dowry ; but Justinian enacted that a poor widow should inherit a quarter of her husband's estate.

Nor was the law of inheritance under wills left unaltered. Hitherto if a testator failed to make any provision for his near kin, the aggrieved relatives had to seek a remedy by a process known as " complaint against an undutiful will."[3] Justinian obliged a testator to leave his children, if they were four or fewer, at least one third ; if they were more than four, at least one half of his estate ;[4] and bound him further to institute as his heirs those descendants who would be his heirs in case of an intestacy, unless he could specify some cause for disinheriting them which would appear reasonable in the eyes of the law.[5]

The jurists of Justinian also introduced a simple and final remedy for the hardship of the ancient law, by which the heir

---

[1] *Nov.* 118 ; *Nov.* 127.

[2] In the case of an intestate freedman, the patron's rights had to be considered and the law was different. His heirs were (1) natural descendants ; (2) his patron ; (3) the patron's children ; (4) the patron's collaterals.

[3] *Querela inofficiosi testamenti.*

[4] *Nov.* 18.

[5] *Nov.* 115. It may be added that Justinian also simplified the law of Legacies, and the law of Trusts, by assimilating all legacies to one another (there used to be four different kinds), and by placing legacies and trusts on much the same footing. Cp. *Inst.* ii. 20 § 2, and 23 § 12.

was made responsible for the liabilities of the deceased even if they exceeded the value of the estate which he inherited. He might of course refuse to accept the inheritance, but if he accepted it he assumed, as it were, the person of the deceased, and any property he otherwise possessed was liable for debts which the estate could not meet. Of this law, which may well be considered one of the asperities of Roman antiquity, various modifications had been devised to meet particular cases, but they were inadequate. Justinian's " benefice of inventory " solved the difficulties. The heir was required to make an inventory of the estate and complete it within two months of the decease ; if he did this, the estate alone was liable.[1]

The history of the law of divorce may be considered separately, for the legislation on this subject under the autocracy forms a remarkable and unpleasing exception to the general course of the logical and reasonable development of Roman jurisprudence. Here ecclesiastical influence was active, and the Emperors from Constantine to Justinian fluctuated between the wishes of the Church on one side, and on the other common sense and Roman tradition. The result was a confusion, no less absurd to a lawyer's sense of fitness than offensive to the reason of ordinary men. The uncertainty and vacillation which marked the Imperial attempts at compromise was aggravated by the fact that the ecclesiastics themselves had not yet arrived at a clear and definite doctrine, and were guided now, as later, not by any considerations of the earthly welfare of mankind, but by inconsistent texts in the New Testament [2] which they were at some loss to reconcile.

Roman law recognised two ways in which a marriage could be dissolved—divorce by mutual consent, and the repudiation of one spouse by the other.[3] Divorce by mutual consent was always regarded as a purely private matter and was never submitted to a legal form, and even the Christian Emperors before Justinian did not attempt to violate the spirit of the Roman law of contract by imposing any limitations. It was reserved for Justinian to prohibit it, unless the motive was to allow one of the spouses

---

[1] *Ib.* 19. 6.

[2] Matthew v. 32, against Mark x. 2-12, Luke xvi. 18. Gregory of Nazianzus expressed the general ecclesiastical disapprobation of divorce when he wrote (*Ep.* 176), " Divorce is altogether displeasing to our laws, though the laws of the Romans ordain otherwise."

[3] Divorce *bona gratia* and *repudium*.

to embrace a life of asceticism.[1] This arbitrary and rigorous
innovation was intolerable to his subjects, and after his death
his successor was assailed by numerous petitions for its repeal.
The domestic misery resulting from incompatibility of temper
was forcibly represented to him, and he restored the ancient
freedom as a concession to the frailty of human nature.[2]

One-sided divorce had been equally unfettered ; Augustus
only required that the partner who decided to dissolve the
marriage should make a formal declaration to this effect in the
presence of seven citizens. Constantine introduced a new and
despotic policy. He forbade one-sided divorce entirely except
for a very few specified reasons. A woman was only permitted
to divorce her husband, if he was found guilty of murder, poison-
ing, or the violation of tombs. If she separated herself from him
for any other reason, she forfeited her dowry and all her property
to the very bodkin of her hair, and was condemned to be deported
to an island. A man might divorce his wife for adultery, or if
she were guilty of preparing poisons, or of acting as a procuress.
If he repudiated her for any other reason he was declared incapable of contracting a second marriage.[3] This cruel law was but
slightly softened by Honorius,[4] but in the reign of Theodosius II.
reason and Roman legality prevailed for a moment. The legal
advisers of that Emperor persuaded him that in the matter of
divorce " it is harsh to depart from the governing principle of
the ancient laws," and he abolished all the restrictions and
penalties which his Christian predecessors had imposed.[5] But

---

[1] *Nov.* 117, § 10, A.D. 542. Six
years before he had confirmed the
old practice on the ground that all
ties can be dissolved, τὸ δεθὲν ἅπαν
λυτόν, *Nov.* 22, § 3.—It is interesting to read records of actual divorces.
Thus in *P. Cairo*, ii. No. 67154, we
have a contract of divorce by mutual
consent between Fl. Callinicus, a
notary, and Aurelia Cyra. They
state that they have quarrelled, they
ascribe their quarrel to a malignant
demon (σκαιοῦ δαίμονος), and agree to
separate permanently by the " written
contract of dissolution which has the
force of a *repudium*." It is agreed
that they are to have the care of
their son Anastasius in common (ἀνὰ
μέσον ἀμφοτέρων). This amicable
document is signed for the wife
(who cannot write) and by several
witnesses. It belongs to the reign of
Justinian, evidently before the law of
A.D. 542.—No. 67153 and No. 67155
are examples of one-sided divorce, in
the form of a letter of repudiation from
the husband to the wife, the former
in the year 568, the latter undated.

[2] This law of Justin is included in
the collection of Justinian's Novels :
Nov. 140, A.D. 566.

[3] *C. Th.* iii. 16. 1 (A.D. 331).

[4] *Ib.* 2 (A.D. 421). If a woman
divorced her husband for immorality
or faults that were not legally heinous,
she forfeited the *dos* and *donatio*,
and could not remarry ; a man who
divorced his wife for *culpa morum
non criminum*, might remarry after
two years. In other cases, Constantine's penalties remained in force.

[5] Theodosius, *Nov.* 12, A.D. 439.

this triumph of reason and tradition was precarious and brief. Ten years later, the same Emperor, under contrary influence, did not indeed venture to revive the stringent laws which he had abolished, but attempted a compromise between the old Roman practice and the wishes of the Church.[1] He multiplied the legitimate grounds for divorce. If a man was condemned for any one of nine or ten serious crimes, if he introduced immodest women into his home, if he attempted to take the life of his consort or chastise her like a slave, she was justified in repudiating him. If she dissolved the marriage on any other ground, she was forbidden to remarry for five years.[2] A woman, guilty of similar crimes, might be divorced, or if she sought her husband's life, or spent a night abroad without good cause, or attended public spectacles against his command. He might divorce her for adultery, but she could not divorce him. The husband who dissolved the marriage for any other than the specified reasons, was obliged to restore the dowry and the donation.

In his early legislation Justinian made no serious change in the law of Theodosius, but he added some new grounds for divorce, permitting a marriage to be dissolved if the husband proved to be impotent, or if either partner desired to embrace an ascetic life.[3] But the Emperor soon repented of the comparative liberality of these enactments, and his final law, which deals comprehensively with the whole subject, exhibits a new spirit of rigour, though it does not altogether revive the tyrannical policy of Constantine.[4] The causes for which a husband may dissolve the union and retain the dowry, and for which a wife may dissolve it and receive the dowry with the donation, are reduced in number ;[5] no release is allowed for a partner guilty of a public crime, except in the case of treason. A woman who repudiates her husband on other than the legal grounds is to be delivered to the bishop and consigned to a monastery. A man, in the same case, suffers only in his pocket. He forfeits the

---

[1] C.J. v. 17. 8, A.D. 449.

[2] Anastasius reduced this to one year, A.D. 497, ib. 9. The woman of course forfeited both dowry and donation. It may be mentioned that Justinian enacted (Nov. 97) that the amount of the donation shall be exactly equal to that of the dowry; this was due to the influence of Greek law, Collinet, op. cit. 145 sqq.

[3] C.J. v. 17. 10 and 11 ; Nov. 22 (536).

[4] Nov. 117 (542).

[5] But some new causes are added in the wife's favour ; she may dissolve the marriage if her husband is persistently and flagrantly unfaithful, if he falsely accuses her of adultery, or if he is detained in captivity in a foreign country.

dowry, the donation, and a further sum equal to one-third of
the donation. But this disparity of treatment was afterwards
altered, and the husband was also liable to incarceration in a
monastery.[1]

The general tenor of these enactments of Justinian, though
they were temporarily set aside in the eighth and ninth centuries,
remained in force throughout the later period of the Empire, and
the ecclesiastics never succeeded in bringing the civil into harmony with the canonical law which pronounced marriage indissoluble, and penalised a divorced person who married again as
guilty of adultery.

This was perhaps the only department in which the Church
exercised an influence on the civil law. It did not aim at nor
desire any change in the laws concerning slaves, for slavery was
an institution which it accepted and approved.[2] In practice, of
course, it encouraged mitigation of the slave's lot, but there it
was merely in accord with general public opinion. Enlightened
pagans had been just as emphatic in their pleas for humanity
to slaves as enlightened Christians,[3] and for the growing improve-
ment in the conditions of slavery since the days of Cicero, the
Stoics are perhaps more responsible than any other teachers.
In this connexion it may be added, though it does not concern
the civil law, that the Church happily failed to force upon the
State its unpractical policy of prohibiting the lending of money
at interest.[4] In the sphere of criminal law, as we shall now see,
it intervened effectively.

§ 3. *Criminal Law*

The criminal law of the Empire, which was chiefly based on
the legislation of Sulla, Pompey, and Augustus, had been little
altered or developed under the Principate ;[5] and the Cornelian

---

[1] *Nov.* 134, § 11 (556).
[2] For the views of the Fathers and
the Church on slavery see Carlyle
(R. W. and A. J.), *A History of the
Mediaeval Political Theory in the
West*, i. 116 *sqq.* ; ii. 117 *sqq.* A full
history of the *Roman Law of Slavery*
will be found in W. W. Buckland's
treatise with that title (1908).
[3] Take, for instance, the views
expressed by the pagan Praetextatus
in the *Saturnalia* of Macrobius (i. 11).

Dill observes (*Roman Society*, p. 136) :
" The contempt for slaves expressed
by S. Jerome and Salvianus is not
shared by the characters of Macrobius."
[4] On laws on interest see above,
Vol. I. p. 55, *n.* 1 ; Vol. II. p. 357.
[5] Roman jurisprudence did not
draw a capital distinction between
civil and criminal law. What corresponds to our criminal law came
partly under private (*privata delicta*)

laws on murder and forgery, the Pompeian law on parricide, the Julian laws on treason, adultery, violence, and peculation, were still the foundation of the law which was in force in the reign of Justinian. Such minor changes as had been made before the reign of Constantine were generally in the direction of increased severity. This tendency became more pronounced under the Christian Emperors. Two fundamental changes were introduced by these rulers by the addition of two new items to the list of *public* crimes, seduction and heresy ; but in those domains of crime which we should consider the gravest there were no important alterations.[1]

Ordinary murder,[2] for instance, was punished by banishment [3] under Justinian as under Augustus, and in the penalties for treason, arson, sorcery, forgery and kindred offences, theft and robbery in their various forms, violence, false witness, there was little change. In contrast with this conservatism, a new spirit animated Constantine and his successors in their legislation on sexual offences, and the inhuman rigour of the laws by which they attempted to suppress sexual immorality amazes a modern reader of the Codes of Theodosius and Justinian. Adultery, which in civilised countries to-day is regarded as a private wrong for which satisfaction must be obtained in the civil courts, had been elevated by Augustus to the rank of a public offence, and the injured husband who let the adulterer go free or com-

partly under public law (*publica iudicia*). See *Digest*, Bks. 47, 48 ; *Instit.* iv. 18 ; *C.J.* Bk. 9 ; *C. Th.* Bk. 9. The subject is treated exhaustively in Mommsen's *Römisches Strafrecht*.

[1] Three legislative acts may be noticed. (1) For *plagium* (which may be roughly translated " kidnapping "), the penalty before Constantine had been exile with confiscation of half the property of the condemned. Constantine made it death, *C. Th.* ix. 18. 1, but Justinian allowed this punishment only in aggravated cases (*Inst.* iv. 18). (2) Anonymous libellous publications : Constantine made the penalty death instead of deportation, *C. Th.* ix. 34, but Justinian rejected this law. (3) Arcadius (*C. Th.* ix. 14. 3) extended the law of *maiestas* (treason) to include attacks on the persons of senators, members of the

Imperial Council, and all Imperial officials. Previously only magistrates (consuls, praetors, etc.) were protected from personal violence by the law of *perduellio*.

[2] Except in the case of parricide (murder of near relatives), for which Constantine (*C. Th.* ix. 15. 1) revived the ancient punishment of the *culleus*, or sack, in which the criminal was sewn up in the society of snakes (*serpentum contuberniis misceatur*) and drowned.

[3] Originally banishment from Italy with " interdiction of fire and water." Under the Principate deportation to an island replaced this penalty. But the statement in the text applies only to freemen of the better classes ; death was inflicted not only on slaves, but also on men of the lower classes— a distinction which will be explained below.

pounded with him for the injury, was liable to the same penalty as if he had himself committed the crime. The penalty consisted in the deportation of the guilty partners to separate islands. Augustus assuredly did not err on the side of leniency, but his severity did not satisfy Constantine, who made death the penalty of adultery.[1] Perhaps this law was seldom enforced;[2] and Justinian relaxed it by condemning the guilty female to be immured in a nunnery.[3] The crime of incest, or marriage of persons within forbidden degrees, was usually punished by deportation; the Christian Emperors sought both to aggravate the penalty and to extend the prohibitions. Constantine imposed the penalty of death on marriage with a niece,[4] and forbade unions with a deceased wife's sister or a deceased husband's brother.[5] The savage legislator Theodosius I. prohibited the marriage of first cousins, and decreed for those who were guilty of this or any of the other forbidden alliances, the penalty of being burned alive and the confiscation of their property.[6] There were limits to the patience of the Roman public under the autocracy. Theodosius was not long in his grave before his son Arcadius cancelled these atrocious penalties,[7] and some years later the same Emperor rescinded the prohibition of the marriage of cousins.[8]

The abduction of a female for immoral purposes, if not accompanied by violence, was, under the Principate, regarded as a private injury which entitled the father or husband to bring an action. Constantine made the abduction of women a public crime of the most heinous kind,[9] to be punished by death in a painful form. The woman, if she consented, was liable to the same penalty as her seducer; if she attempted to resist, the lenient lawgiver only disqualified her from inheriting. If the nurse who was in charge of a girl were proved to have encouraged her to yield to a seducer, molten lead was to be poured into

---

[1] *C. Th.* ix. 7. 1, 2; ii. 36. 4. In *Inst.* iv. 18 the death penalty is erroneously ascribed to the Lex Iulia. The texts which Mommsen cites to show that this penalty had been introduced in the third century (*op. cit.* 699, *n.* 3) do not appear to be decisive.

[2] Ammianus (xxviii. 1. 16) mentions one case, but as an instance of the inhuman cruelty of Valentinian I.

[3] *Nov.* 77; 141.

[4] *C. Th.* iii. 12. 1. Claudius had permitted, and set the example of, the union of a niece with her *father's brother*.

[5] *Ib.* 2.

[6] Ambrose, *Ep.* 60; *C. Th.* iii. 12. 3 (cp. Augustine, *De civ. Dei*, xv. 16).

[7] *C. Th. ib.* (A.D. 396).

[8] *C. Th.* v. 4. 19 (A.D. 405); cp. *Instit.* i. 10. 4.

[9] See Mommsen, *op. cit.* 701-702; *C. Th.* ix. 24. 1.

her mouth and throat, to close the aperture through which the wicked suggestions had emanated. Parents who connived at abduction were punished by deportation. This astonishing law, with slight mitigation,[1] remained in force, and was extended to the seduction of women who had taken vows of chastity. Justinian made a new law on the subject, but the essential provisions were the same.[2]

Unnatural vice was pursued by the Christian monarchs with the utmost severity. Constantius imposed the death penalty on both culprits, and Theodosius the Great condemned persons guilty of this enormity to death by fire.[3] Justinian, inspired by the example of the chastisement which befell " those who formerly lived in Sodom," and firmly believing that such crimes were the immediate causes of famines, plagues, and earthquakes, was particularly active and cruel in dealing with this vice. In his laws,[4] he contented himself with imposing the penalty of death, but in practice he did not scruple to resort to extraordinary punishments. It is recorded that senators and bishops who were found guilty were shamefully mutilated, or exquisitely tortured, and paraded through the streets of the capital before their execution.[5]

The disproportion and cruelty of the punishments, which mark the legislation of the autocracy in regard to sexual crimes, and are eminently unworthy of the legal reason of Rome, were due to ecclesiastical influence and the prevalence of extravagant ascetic ideals. That these bloodthirsty laws were in accord with ecclesiastical opinion is shown by the code which a Christian

---

[1] *C. Th.* ix. 24. 2. (Julian punished the offence by banishment, Ammianus, xvi. 5. 12.)

[2] *C.J.* ix. 13. 1.

[3] *C. Th.* ix. 7. 3 and 6. In the third century the seduction of a *puer praetextatus* was punished by death (*Digest*, xlvii. 11. 1, 2). Measures, but we do not know what, were taken by the Emperor Philip to suppress this vice (*Hist. Aug.* xviii. 24. 4).

[4] *Nov.* 77 ; 141.

[5] John Malalas, xviii. p. 436 ; Procopius, *H.A.* 11, *ad fin.* ; Theodosius of Melitene, *Chron.* p. 90 τοὺς μὲν ἐκαυλοτόμησε τοῖς δὲ καλάμους ὀξεῖς ἐμβάλλεσθαι εἰς τοὺς πόρους τῶν αἰδοίων ἐκέλευσεν καὶ γυμνοὺς κατὰ

τὴν ἀγορὰν θριαμβεύεσθαι. Cp. Michael Syrus, ix. 26. The enemies of Justinian alleged that the trials were a farce, that men were condemned on the single testimony of one man or boy, who was often a slave ; and the victims were selected because they belonged to the Green Faction, or were very rich, or had given some offence to the Emperor (Procop. *loc. cit.*). No account was taken by the law of female homosexuality. Abbesses were obliged to take precautions against it in nunneries. See the *Epistle* of Paul Helladicus, abbot of Elusa (p. 21), one of the most unsavoury documents of Christian monasticism. He lived in the sixth century.

missionary, untrammelled by Roman law, is reported to have imposed on the unfortunate inhabitants of Southern Arabia.

We saw how in the reign of Justin, Christianity was established in the kingdom of the Himyarites by the efforts of the Christian king of Ethiopia. When Abram was set upon the throne, Gregentius was sent from Alexandria to be the bishop of Safar, the chief city of the Himyarites.[1] The laws which Gregentius drew up in the name of Abram are preserved. Doubts of their authenticity have been entertained, but even if they were never issued or enforced, they illustrate the kind of legislation at which the ecclesiastical spirit, unchecked, would have aimed. It is characteristic that sexual offences occupy a wholly disproportionate part of the code. Fornication was punished by a hundred stripes, the amputation of the left ear, and confiscation of property. If the crime was committed with a woman who was in the *potestas* of a man, her left breast was cut off and the male sinner was emasculated. Similar but rather severer penalties were inflicted on adulterers. Procurers were liable to amputation of the tongue. Public singers, harp-players, actors, dancers, were suppressed, and any one found practising these acts was punished by whipping and a year's hard labour. To be burned alive was the fate of a sorcerer. Severe penalties were imposed for failing to inform the public authorities of a neighbour's misconduct. On the ground of St. Paul's dictum that the man is the head of the woman, cruel punishments were meted out to women who ventured to deride men.[2]

Perhaps the greatest blot in Roman criminal law under the Empire, judged by modern ideas, was the distinction which it drew, in the apportionment of penalties, between different classes of freemen. There was one law for the rich, and another for the poor. A distinction between the honourable or respectable, and the humble or plebeian classes was legalised,[3] and different treatment was meted out in punishing criminals according to the class to which they belonged. The privileged group

---

[1] See above, p. 327.
[2] *Homeritarum Leges*, P.G. lxxxvi. 1. 581 *sqq.* One curious provision regards early marriages ; parents who do not arrange for the future marriage of their children when they are between the ages of ten and twelve are liable to a fine.

[3] *Honesti*, and *humiles* (*tenuiores*, plebeii ; εὐτελεῖς). Mommsen, *op. cit.* 1032 *sqq.* A member of the higher classes could be degraded to the lower (*reiectus in plebem*), *C. Th.* vi. 22. 1. The distinction was based on status, not on income, but it virtually discriminated the richer from the poorer.

included persons of senatorial and equestrian birth, soldiers, veterans, decurions and the children of decurions ; and on such persons milder penalties were inflicted than on their fellow-citizens of inferior status. They were, in general, exempt from the degrading and painful punishments which were originally reserved for slaves. If a man of the higher status, for instance, issued a forged document, he was deported, while the same crime committed by a poor man was punished by servitude in the mines.[1] The general principle, indeed, of this disparity of treatment was the extension of servile punishments to the free proletariate, and it appears also in the use of torture for the extraction of evidence. Under the Republic freemen could not be legally tortured, but under the Empire the question was applied to men of the lower classes as well as to slaves.[2]

The normal mode of inflicting death on freemen was decapitation by the sword. But more painful modes of execution were also prescribed for certain offences.[3] Sorcerers, for instance, were burnt alive, and deserters to the enemy incurred the same penalty, or the gallows. In some cases, as for treason, the painful death was inflicted only on people of the lower class ; [4] and in some, persons of this status were put to death while persons of higher rank got off with a sentence of deportation. The privileged classes were also exempted from the punishment of being destroyed by wild beasts in the arena. Next to death, the severest penalty was servitude in the mines for life, or for a limited period. This horrible fate was never inflicted on the better classes. They were punished by deportation to an island, or an oasis in the desert.[5]

---

[1] In many cases death was inflicted on the *humiles* where the *honesti* were only deported. See the table showing the disparity of punishments in the first half of the third century (based on the *Sententiae* of Paulus), in Mommsen, *op. cit.* 1045 *sqq.*

[2] Mommsen, 406 *sq.* In cases of treason, and magic, and forgery, indeed, any citizen might be tortured, and many instances are recorded.

[3] Such modes are often designated in the laws as *summum supplicium.* Four are recognised under the autocracy : (1) the gallows, *furca* ; (2) fire ; (3) the sack, for parricides ; this had fallen out of use but was revived by Constantine ; (4) exposure to wild beasts ; this was an alternative to (1) or (2) and could be inflicted only when there happened to be a popular spectacle immediately after the condemnation. Crucifixion was discontinued under the Christian emperors.

[4] Cp. *Digest,* xlviii. 19. 28. The milder form of banishment (*relegatio*) allowed to the condemned a choice of the place of his domicile, and did not involve disfranchisement.

[5] Penal servitude and deportation, when they involved disfranchisement, were classified as *capital* punishments. All capital punishments involved confiscation of property.

Mutilation does not appear to have been recognised as a legal penalty under the Principate, but it may sometimes have been resorted to as an extraordinary measure by the express sentence of an Emperor. It first appears in an enactment of Constantine ordaining that the tongue of an informer should be torn out by the root.[1] Leo I. condemned persons who were implicated in the murder of Proterius, patriarch of Alexandria, to excision of the tongue and deportation.[2] In the sixth century, mutilation became more common, and Justinian recognises amputation of the hands as a legal punishment in some of his later enactments. Tax-collectors who falsify their accounts and persons who copy the writings of Monophysites are threatened with this pain.[3] And we have records of the infliction of a like punishment on other criminals.[4] This practice seems to have been prompted by the rather childish idea that, if the member which sinned suffered, the punishment was fitly adjusted to the crime.[5] Amputation of the nose or tongue was frequently practised, and such penalties afterwards became a leading feature in Byzantine criminal law, and were often inflicted as a mitigation of the death penalty. When these punishments and that of blinding are pointed to as one of the barbarous and repulsive characters of Byzantine civilisation, it should not be forgotten that in the seventeenth century it was still the practice in England to lop off hands and ears.

It must be remembered that a considerable latitude was allowed to the judges (praetors, prefects, provincial governors) in passing sentences on culprits.[6] The penalties prescribed in the laws were rather directions for their guidance than hard and fast sanctions. They were expected to take into account circumstances which aggravated the guilt, and still more circumstances which extenuated it. For instance, youth, intoxication, an ethical motive were considered good reasons for mitigating

<hr/>

[1] *C. Th.* x. 10. 2; it is not quite clear whether this was to be done before or after death (strangulation on the gallows). A later law reduced the penalty to death by the sword, *ib.* 10.

[2] Theophanes, A.M. 5951.

[3] *Nov.* 17, § 8; 42, § 1. Cp. *Nov.* 134, § 13, where it is forbidden to punish theft by cutting off οἱονδήποτε μέλος.

[4] John Mal. xviii. pp. 451 (for

gambling, A.D. 429; but no physical penalty is enacted in the law of this year against gambling in *C.J.* iii. 43. 2), 483, 488.

[5] Cp. *C. Th.* x. 10. 2; and Zonaras, xiv. 7. 2, where Justinian is reported to have justified his punishment of paederasty on this principle. The same idea may have dictated the punishment of incendiaries by fire.

[6] On this subject see Mommsen, *op. cit.* 1037 *sqq.*

penalties, and women were generally treated more leniently than men.

On the whole, the Roman system, from Augustus to Justinian, of protecting society against evil - doers and correcting the delinquencies of frail humanity, can hardly arouse much admiration. It was, indeed, more reasonable and humane than the criminal law of England before its reform in the nineteenth century. Its barbaric features were due either indirectly to the institution of slavery, or to the influence of the Church in those domains which especially engaged the interest of ecclesiastics. Augustus and his successors definitely stemmed the current of tendency which in the last period of the Republic promised entirely to do away with capital punishment, but they did not introduce any new reasonable principle into the theory or practice of criminal law. Wider extension of the field of public crimes, increasing severity in the penalties, and differential treatment of citizens of the lower classes, are the most conspicuous features of the development of criminal justice under the Empire.

CHAPTER XXIV

PROCOPIUS

THROUGHOUT the fifth century there were Greek historians writing the history of their own times, and, if their writings had survived, we should possess a fairly full record of events, particularly in the East, from the accession of Arcadius to the reign of Zeno. And it would have been a consecutive record, or at least there would have been only one or two short gaps. The bitter pagan sophist Eunapius of Sardis carried down his history, composed in his old age, to A.D. 404.[1] Olympiodorus, a native of Egyptian Thebes, began his book at A.D. 407 and went down to A.D. 425.[2] The work of Priscus of Panion (near Heraclea on the Propontis) probably began about A.D. 434 and ended with the death of Leo I. Malchus, of the Syrian Philadelphia, continued Priscus, and embraced in his work either the whole or a part of the reign of Zeno.[3] But all these histories have perished. Some of the information they contained passed into later writers; for instance, Zosimus, who wrote towards the end of the fifth century, derived much of his material for the later portion of his work from Eunapius and Olympiodorus.[4]

[1] Eunapius designed his history as a continuation of that of Dexippus which ended at 270. The evidence does not point to any continuity between him and Olympiodorus, or between Olympiodorus and Priscus.

[2] Olympiodorus was a traveller and a poet. He was sent on an embassy in 412 to Donatus, a Hunnic prince of whom otherwise we know nothing.

[3] From the evidence of the excerpts and the notice of Photius, *Bibl.* 78, we should conclude that he stopped at 480, but Suidas *sub nomine* says that he went down to the reign of Anastasius. He certainly wrote after the death of Zeno, to whom he was hostile.

[4] After a brief survey of the earlier Empire, Zosimus began his fuller narrative about A.D. 270. He is the only important historian who wrote non-contemporary history in the fifth and sixth centuries, except Peter the Patrician—the diplomatist and Master of Offices—who composed a History of the Roman Empire from

But of the original texts we possess only excerpts which in many cases are mere summaries. The ecclesiastical histories written by the orthodox laymen, Socrates and Sozomen, about the middle of the century, have fared better ; we have them intact ; and fortunately they include notices of secular events rather capriciously selected.[1]

The fragments of these lost historians enable us to judge that Priscus is a greater loss than any of the rest. The long fragment on Attila and his court, of which a translation was given in an earlier chapter, shows that he was a master of narrative, and the general impression we get is that he was the ablest Roman historian between Ammian and Procopius.

Why did all these works disappear ? Some of them survived till the ninth and tenth centuries, but were doubtless extremely rare then, and no more copies were made from the one or two copies that existed. The probability is that they never had a wide circulation, and it is fair to ascribe this partly to the fact that their authors were pagans.[2] But there is another reason which may partly account for the loss of some of these historians, and may also explain the character of the excerpts which have come down. In the ninth and following centuries the Greeks were interested in the past history of the Illyrian peninsula and in the oriental wars with the Persians, which were fought on the same ground as the contemporary wars with the Moslems ; they were not interested in the history of Italy and the West. Now in the fifth century, with the exception of one or two short and unimportant episodes of hostility, there was hardly anything to tell of the oriental frontier, so that the portions of historians like Priscus and Malchus that had a living interest for readers were those which dealt with the invaders and devastators of the Balkan provinces. And so we find that the most consider-

---

Augustus to Julian. Of this we have fragments, some of which—known as the anonymous continuation of Dio Cassius—have only recently been connected with Peter's work, by C. de Boor, *Römische Kaisergeschichte*, *B.Z.* i. 13 *sqq.*, 1892.

[1] For secular history Theodoret's *Ecclesiastical History* is almost negligible ; it has hardly anything that is not in Socrates or Sozomen. The work of Philostorgius, the Eunomian, is a real loss, as the fragments show ;

the works of heretics had little chance of surviving.

[2] This is not so clear in the case of Priscus, but his friendship with the pagan Maximin establishes a presumption. The sympathies of Malchus were plainly Neoplatonic, as is shown by his treatment of Pamprepius, and his designation of Proclus as " the great Proclus."—It is curious that the aggressively pagan work of Zosimus survived.

able fragments of Priscus, preserved in the summaries and
selections that were made in the ninth and tenth centuries,
relate to the doings of the Huns, and the most considerable
fragments of Malchus to the doings of the Ostrogoths. It is, in
fact, probable that these extracts represent pretty fully the information on these topics given by both writers. On the other
hand, it is significant that the Gallic and Italian campaigns,
which Priscus must certainly have described, were passed over
by those who made the selections.[1]

That there is almost as much to tell about thirty years of
the sixth century, as there is about the whole of the fifth, is due
partly to Justinian's activity as a legislator, but chiefly to the
pen of Procopius. It was one of the glories of Justinian's age
to have produced a writer who must be accounted the most
excellent Greek historian since Polybius. Procopius was a
native of Caesarea, the metropolis of the First Palestine. He
was trained to be a jurist, and we have seen how he was appointed
in A.D. 527 councillor to Belisarius,[2] how he accompanied him
in his Persian, African, and Italian campaigns, and how he was
in Constantinople when the city was ravaged by the plague.
He was not with Belisarius in his later campaigns in the East,
and it is improbable that he revisited Italy.[3]

His writings attest that Procopius had received an excellent
literary education. There is nothing which would lead us to
suppose that he had studied either at Athens or at Alexandria,
and it seems most probable that he owed his attainments to the

[1] Perhaps the clearest illustration
of the point is that, if the works of
Procopius had been lost, we should
know a great deal about his Persian
Wars, but very little about his
Vandalic and Gothic Wars; for
Photius, in his *Bibliotheca*, gives a
long account of the former, but none
of the latter.

[2] Haury argues that he was not a
jurist (*Zur Beurteilung*, etc., p. 20),
but he is not convincing. For the
post of *consiliarius* (ξύμβουλος) cp.
C.J. i. 51. 11. Cp. Dahn, *Prokopius*,
pp. 19-20.

[3] It is indeed possible that Procopius was with Belisarius in 541,
though it seems more probable that
his place had been taken by George
(*B.P.* ii. 19. 22; cp. Haury, *ib.*).

Dahn leaves it open (*ib.* p. 30)
whether he was in Italy after 542.
Haury has argued that he went to
Italy in 546, because he relates the
events of 546-547 at greater length
than those of the other years of the
Second Italian War (*Procopiana*, i.
8-9). But this is not very convincing.
It appears probable to me that he
lived at Constantinople continuously
after his return from Italy, and there
collected from officers, ambassadors,
etc., the material which he required
for his *History*, both in the East and
in the West from 541 to 553. Haury
thinks that he wrote his *History* in
Caesarea (*ib.* 26), but it would have
been difficult for him there to have
obtained regularly first-hand and
detailed information about the war in
Italy.

professors of the university of Constantinople. It has indeed been held that he was educated at Gaza,[1] but this theory rests on no convincing external evidence, and the internal evidence of his style does not bear out the hypothesis that he ever sat at the feet of his namesake Procopius and the other sophists of Gaza. We know a good deal about that euphuistic literary school.

It may be conjectured that Procopius formed the design of writing a history of the wars, of which Belisarius was the hero, at the time of the expedition against the Vandals, and that he commenced then to keep a written record of events.[2] He had

---

[1] This theory of Haury (*op. cit.*) is closely connected with a theory as to his parentage. Haury argues that he was the son of Stephanus, a leading citizen of Caesarea, who, before A.D. 526, held the post of *astynomos* or commissioner of public works, won distinction by restoring the aqueduct which supplied the city, and in 536 was appointed proconsul of the First Palestine (Choricius, *Epithal.* p. 22; *In Arat. et Stephanum*, § 10; Justinian, *Nov.* 103, § 1; Aeneas Gaz. *Ep.* 11). Stephanus was a friend of Procopius of Gaza, and sent his son to be educated there (Procopius, *Ep.* 18). This unnamed son Haury identifies with a Procopius who married a young woman of Ascalon, wealthy and of good family; two of his fellow-students married at the same time; and Choricius wrote an (extant) epithalamion for the occasion. In the Samaritan revolt of A.D. 556, Stephanus was murdered by the rebels in his court house. His wife went to Constantinople and besought Justinian to punish the murderers. The Emperor did her justice promptly, ordering Amantius, Master of Soldiers in the East, to search them out, and they were executed (John Mal. *fr.* 48, *De ins.*). In this incident Haury finds the explanation of the revolution in the attitude of Procopius towards Justinian between 550 and 560. The theory is ingenious, but much more evidence would be needed to make it probable. It is difficult to believe that, if Procopius had been the son of such a notable civil servant as **Stephanus**, the fact would not

have been recorded. The known facts do not point to any connexion with Gaza. And it is to be observed that the theory involves *two* conjectural identifications: that of the historian with the Procopius who married the girl of Ascalon, and that of this Procopius with the son of Stephanus.

[2] The account of the First Persian War (*B.P.* i. 12-22) is so (comparatively) brief and incomplete that we may perhaps infer that he had not formed the plan of writing a history of it during its progress. The chronology of the composition of his works has been cleared up by the researches of Haury (*Procopiana*, i.). In the latter part of 545 he was writing *B.P.* i. 25. 43; *B.G.* i. 24. 32 (cp. *Procopiana*, ii. p. 5); and ii. 5. 26-27. These passages indicate that he contemplated this year as the termination of his history, and if he had then published it, it would have consisted of *B.P.* i.-ii. 28, 11; *B.V.*, except the last two pages; *B.G.* i.-iii. 15. He may have circulated what he had written among his acquaintances, but he continued to add to it from year to year, without changing what he had already written, and finally published the seven Books of the Wars, as they stand, in 550. In the same year he wrote the *Secret History*. In 553 he published the eighth and last Book of the Wars. In 560 he wrote the *De aedificiis*, as is proved by the mention of the building of the bridge over the Sangarius (v. 3. 10) which was built in 559-560 (Theoph. A.M. 6052). On this bridge cp. Anderson, *J.H.S.* xix. 66 *sq.*

certainly begun to compose his history immediately after his return from Italy with Belisarius, for he states that, as that general's councillor, he had personal knowledge of almost all the events which he is about to relate, a statement which would not be true of the later campaigns. While he is studiously careful to suppress feeling, he gives the impression, in his narrative of the early wars, that he sympathised with Justinian's military enterprises, and viewed with satisfaction the exploits of Belisarius. As to Justinian himself he is reticent; he may sometimes imply blame; he never awards praise. The sequel disillusioned him. He was disappointed by the inglorious struggles with Chosroes and Totila, and by the tedious troubles in Africa; and his attitude of critical approbation changed into one of bitter hostility towards the government. His vision of his own age as a period of unexpected glory for the Empire faded away, and was replaced by a nightmare, in which Justinian's reign appeared to him as an era of universal ruin. Seeking to explain the defeat of the early prospects of the reign, he found the causes in the general system of government and the personalities of the rulers. The defects of the Imperial administration, especially in the domain of finance, were indeed so grave, that it would have been easy to frame a formidable indictment without transcending the truth, or setting down aught in malice; but with Procopius the abuses and injustices which came to his notice worked like madness on his brain, and regarding the Emperor as the common enemy of mankind he was ready to impute the worst of motives to all his acts.

We may divine that the historian went through a mental process of this nature between A.D. 540 and 550, but we cannot believe that pure concern for the public interests is sufficient to explain the singular and almost grotesque malignity of the impeachment of Justinian and all his works, which he drew up at the end of the decade. Any writer who indulges in such an orgy of hatred as that which amazes us in the *Secret History*, exposes himself to the fair suspicion that he has personal reasons for spite. We hardly run much risk of doing an injustice to Procopius if we assume that he was a disappointed man. One who had occupied a position of intimate trust by the side of the conqueror of Africa and Italy could not fail to entertain hopes of preferment to some administrative post. But he was passed over. The influence of Belisarius, if it was exerted in his favour, did not avail, and from being a friendly admirer of his old patron he became a merciless critic.

In a book which was intended to be published and to establish a literary reputation, Procopius could not venture to say openly what was in his mind. But to an attentive reader of his narrative of the later wars there are many indications that he disapproved of the Imperial policy and the general conduct of affairs. His *History of the Wars* was divided into seven books, and the material, on the model of Appian, was arranged geographically. Two books on the Persian War brought the story down to A.D. 548, two on the Vandalic War embraced events in Africa subsequent to the conquest and reached the same date. The three books of the Gothic War terminated in A.D. 551. It was probably the final defeat of Totila in A.D. 552 that moved the author afterwards to complete his work by adding an eighth book, in which, abandoning the geographical arrangement, he not only concludes the story of the Italian War, but deals with military operations on every front from A.D. 548 to 553.

We shall presently see that in the later parts of this work the historian went as far as prudence permitted in condemning the policy of Justinian. But in A.D. 550 he secretly committed to writing a sweeping indictment of the Emperor and the late Empress, of their private lives and their public actions. It was a document which he must have preserved in his most secret hiding-place, and which he could read only to the most faithful and discreet of his friends. It could never see the light till Justinian was safely dead, and if he were succeeded by a nephew or cousin, its publication even then might be impossible. As a matter of fact we may suspect that his heirs withheld it from circulation, and that it was not published till a considerable time had elapsed. For it was unknown to the writers of the next generation, unless we suppose that they deliberately ignored it.[1]

The introduction to the *Secret History* [2] states that its object

---

[1] Some have supposed that Evagrius was acquainted with it, but the evidence is quite unconvincing. The earliest reference to the work is in Suidas (tenth century), *s.v.* Προκόπιος. He calls it the *Anecdota*.

[2] It used to be supposed that the date of composition was 559, because it was written in the thirty-second year of Justinian's régime (*H.A.* 18. 33 ; 23. 1 ; 24. 29). But it is a fundamental part of the thesis of Procopius that Justinian was the real governor (διῳκήσατο τὴν πολιτείαν)

is to supplement the *History of the Wars* by an account of things
that happened in all parts of the Empire, and to explain certain
occurrences which in that work had been barely recorded, as it
was impossible to reveal the intrigues which lay behind them.
It is hinted that so long as Theodora was alive,[1] it would have
been dangerous even to commit the truth to writing, for her
spies were ubiquitous, and discovery would have meant a miserable death. This reinforces other evidence which goes to prove
that Theodora was held in much greater fear than Justinian.

The thesis of the *Secret History*[2] is that in all the acts of his
public policy Justinian was actuated by two motives, rapacity
and an inhuman delight in evil-doing and destruction. In this
policy he was aided by Theodora, and if they appeared in
certain matters, such as religion, to pursue different ends, this
was merely a plot designed to hoodwink the public.[3] Procopius
gravely asserts that he himself and " most of us " had come to
the conclusion that the Emperor and Empress were demons

throughout the reign of Justin, and
the thirty-second year is to be
reckoned from 518, not from 527.
This was first established by Haury
(Procop. i.). On the old view it
would be impossible to explain why
Procopius should have ignored all
the material which the events between
550 and 559 would have supplied
for his purpose. Cp. also Haury,
Zur Beurteilung, p. 37. The revised
date of the *Secret History* shows that
the first lines of the last Book of the
Wars (*B.G.* iv.) were modelled on
the opening lines of *H.A.* and not
vice versa. Haury has suggested
that the author originally began
B.G. iv. with ἤδη μὲν οὖν (c. i. 3), and
afterwards added the preceding sentences for the purpose of misleading
posterity, and suggesting that *H.A.*
was the work of an imitator. Con-
versely it might be argued that the
motive was to indicate identity of
authorship.

[1] 1. 2 περιόντων ἔτι τῶν αὐτὰ εἰργα-
σμένων must mean simply Theodora
(cp. 16. 3).

[2] The book is badly arranged. A
preliminary section (1-5) is devoted
to Belisarius and the scandals connected with his private life; his
pitiful uxoriousness, his weakness,

which leads him into breach of faith,
and his military failures. The next
subject is the family and character
of Justinian (6-8), and then the
author goes on to tell the scandalous
story of Theodora's early life (9, 10).
He proceeds to characterise the
revolutionary policy of the Emperor,
and to give a summary account of
his persecutions, his avarice, and
his unjust judgments (11-14). Then
he reverts again to Theodora, and
illustrates her power, her crimes, and
her cruelties (15-17). He goes on to
review the calamities and loss of life
brought not only upon his own
subjects, but also on the barbarians
by Justinian's wars, as well as by
the pestilence, earthquakes, and inundations, for which he holds him
responsible (18); and then enters
upon a merciless criticism of his
financial administration (19 - 23).
Various classes of society—the army,
the merchants, the professions, the
proletariate—are then passed in review, and it is shown that they are
all grievously oppressed (24-26). The
last chapters are occupied with
miscellaneous instances of cruelty
and injustice (27-29), the decline of
the *cursus publicus*, and new servile
customs in court etiquette (30).
[3] 10. 14.

in human form, and he did not mean this as a figure of speech.[1]
He tells a number of anecdotes to substantiate the idea. Justinian's mother had once said that she conceived of a demon.
He had been seen in the palace at night walking about without
a head, and a clairvoyant monk had once refused to enter the
presence chamber because he saw the chief of the demons
sitting on the throne. Before her marriage, Theodora had
dreamt that she would cohabit with the prince of the devils.
Even Justinian's abstemious diet is adduced as a proof of his
non-human nature. It was a theory which did not sound so
ludicrous in the age of Procopius as in ours, and it enabled him
to enlarge the field of the Emperor's mischievous work, by
imputing to his direct agency the natural calamities like earthquakes and plagues which afflicted mankind during his reign.

In elaborating his indictment Procopius adopted two sophistic
tricks. One of these was to represent Justinian as responsible
for institutions and administrative methods which he had
inherited from his predecessors. The other was to seize upon
incidental hardships and abuses arising out of Imperial measures,
and to suggest that these were the objects at which the Emperor
had deliberately aimed. The unfairness of the particular criticisms can in many cases be proved, and in others reasonably
suspected. But it may be asked whether the book deserves
any serious consideration as an historical document, except so
far as it illustrates the intense dissatisfaction prevailing in some
circles against the government. The daemonic theory, the
pornographic story of Theodora's early career, the self-defeating
maliciousness of the whole performance discredit the work, and
have even suggested doubts whether it could have been written
at all by the sober and responsible historian of the wars.[2] The
authorship, however, is indisputable. No imitator could have
achieved the Procopian style of the *Secret History*, and a comparison with the *History of the Wars* shows that in that work
after A.D. 541 the author makes or suggests criticisms which
are found, in a more explicit and lurid form, in the libel.

For in the public *History* he sometimes used the device of

---

[1] 12. 14 *sqq.* ; 18. 1. Theodora's
influence over her husband is ascribed
to magic practices, 22. 27.

[2] L. von Ranke (*Weltgeschichte*, iv.
2. 300 *sqq.*) argued that it was not
written by Procopius, but was partly
based on a Procopian diary. The
Procopian style of the *Secret History*
is unmistakable and has been well
illustrated by Dahn, 257 *sqq.*, 416 *sqq.*

putting criticism into the mouths of foreigners. One of the prominent points in the *Secret History* is Justinian's love of innovations; he upset established order, and broke with the traditions of the past. The same character is given him in the public *History* by the Gothic ambassadors who went to the Persian Court.[1] The motive of the speech which is attributed to the Utigur envoys in A.D. 552 is to censure the policy of giving large grants of money to the trans-Danubian barbarians, which is bitterly assailed in the *Secret History*.[2] Procopius indeed criticises it directly by an irony which is hardly veiled. The Kotrigurs, he says, " receive many gifts every year from the Emperor, and, even so, crossing the Danube they overrun the Emperor's territory continually." [3] Although Justinian was here only pursuing, though perhaps on a larger scale, the inveterate practice of Roman policy, his critic speaks as if it were a new method which he had discovered for exhausting the resources of the Empire. " It is a subject of discussion," he says, " what has happened to the wealth of the Romans. Some assert that it has all passed into the hands of the barbarians, others think that the Emperor retains it locked up in many treasure chambers. When Justinian dies, supposing him to be human, or when he renounces his incarnate existence if he is the lord of the demons, survivors will learn the truth." [4]

In the *Secret History* the Emperor is arraigned as the guilty party in causing the outbreak of the second Persian War. In the published *History* the author could not say so, but goes as far as he dares by refusing to say a word in his favour. Having stated the charges made by Chosroes that Justinian had violated the treaty of A.D. 532, he adds, "Whether he was telling the truth, I cannot say." [5] On the peace of A.D. 551, which evidently excited his indignation, he resorts to the same formula. " Most of the Romans were annoyed at this treaty, not unnaturally. But whether their criticism was just or unreasonable I cannot say." [6] Nor did the historian of the Vandalic War fail to

---

[1] *B.P.* ii. 2. 6 νεωτεροποιός τε ὤν φύσει . . . μένειν τε οὐ δυνάμενος ἐν τοῖς καθεστῶσι, cp. *H.A.* 11. 1-2. See also the remark in a speech of Armenian envoys to Chosroes, *B.P.* ii. 3. 38 τί οὐκ ἐκίνησε τῶν καθεστώτων;
[2] *B.G.* iv. 19. 9 *sqq.* ; *H.A.* 11. 5. 7.
[3] *B.G.* iv. 5. 16.

[4] *H.A.* 30. 33-34, the last words of the book.
[5] *B.P.* ii. 1. 15; *H.A.* 11. 12.
[6] *B.G.* iv. 15. 13 (the author's opinion is clearly suggested *ib.* 7). His dissatisfaction with the particular favour shown by Justinian to the Persian envoy Isdigunas is not disguised, *ib.* 19, 20 ; *B.P.* ii. 28. 40-44.

suggest the same conclusion which is drawn in the *Secret History* as to the consequences of the Imperial conquest. Having recorded the victory of John, the brother of Pappus, over the Moors in A.D. 548, he terminates his story with the remark, " Thus, at last and hardly, to the survivors of the Libyans, few and very destitute, there came a period of peace." [1]

In fact, the attitude of Procopius towards the government, as it is guardedly displayed in the *History of the Wars*, is not inconsistent with the general drift of the *Secret History*, and the only reason for doubting the genuineness of the libel was the presumption that the political views in the two works were irreconcilable. It is another question whether the statements of the *Secret History* are credible. Here we must carefully distinguish between the facts which the author records, and the interpretation which he places upon them. Malice need not resort to invention. It can serve its purpose far more successfully by adhering to facts, misrepresenting motives, and suppressing circumstances which point to a different interpretation. That this was the method followed by Procopius is certain. For we find that in a large number of cases his facts are borne out by other contemporary sources,[2] while in no instance can we

---

[1] *B.V.* ii. 28. 52. Other points of comparison between the public and the *Secret History* may be noted. (1) The view of Justin's reign as virtually part of Justinian's, *B.V.* i. 9. 5 (Justin is ὑπεργήρως): *H.A.* 6. 11 ,(Justin is τυμβογέρων). (2) Pessimistic utterances as to the general situation, A.D. 541–549 ; *B.P.* ii. 21. 34 ; *B.G.* iii. 33. 1. (3) Justinian's slackness in prosecuting his wars is ascribed, in *H.A.* 18. 29, partly to his avarice and partly to his occupation with theological studies. The latter reason is plainly assigned in *B.G.* iii. 35. 11 βασιλεὺς δὲ Ἰταλίας μὲν ἐπηγγέλλετο προνοήσειν αὐτός, ἀμφὶ δὲ τὰ Χριστιανῶν δόγματα ἐκ τοῦ ἐπὶ πλεῖστον διατριβὴν εἶχεν, and is perhaps hinted at *ib.* 36. 6 ἀσχολίας οἱ ἴσως ἐπιγενομένης ἑτέρας τινὸς τὴν προθυμίαν κατέπαυσε. (The same ironical formula is employed when the Emperor failed to send money due to Gubazes at the right time, ἐπιγενομένης οἱ ἀσχολίας τινὸς, *B.P.* ii. 29. 32.) Cp. also *B.G.* iii. 32. 9. (4) The financial oppression of the government is exposed in the case of the logothete Alexander (*ib.* iii. 1. 29). More pointed is the remark that John Tzibos was created a general because he was the worst of men, and understood the art of raising money, *B.P.* ii. 15. 10. The criticism of Justinian that, though well aware of the unpopularity of Sergius in Africa, οὐδ' ὣς would he recall him, may be noted. (5) In holding up to reprobation the conduct of the second Italian War by Belisarius, the author of the libel has only to repeat (*H.A.* 5. 1) what was said in *B.G.* iii. 35. 1. Compare also the remarks, *ib.* xiii. 15-19.

[2] *E.g.* (1) The unscrupulousness of Theodora is illustrated by the episode of the Nobadae, above, p. 328 *sqq.* ; (2) the statements as to the intrigue against Amalasuntha fit into the other evidence, above, p. 165 *sqq.* ; (3) the connexion of Antonina with the episode of Silverius, cp. p. 378 ; (4) John Eph. (*Hist. ecc.* i. c. 32) confirms the information that Antonina's son Photius was a monk ; (5) the

convict him of a statement which has no basis in fact.[1] We have seen that even in the case of Theodora's career, where his charges have been thought particularly open to suspicion, there is other evidence which suggests that she was not a model of virtue in her youth. The *Secret History* therefore is a document of which the historian is entitled to avail himself, but he must remember that here the author has probably used, to a greater extent than elsewhere, material derived from gossip which he could not verify himself.

Procopius entertained the design of writing another book dealing especially with the ecclesiastical policy of the reign.[2] If the work was ever executed it is lost, but as there is no reference to it in subsequent literature, it seems most probable that it was never written. Among other things which the historian promised to relate in it was the fate of Pope Silverius, concerning which our extant records leave us in doubt as to the respective responsibilities of Vigilius and Antonina. Apart from the facts which it would have preserved to posterity, the book would have been of singular interest on account of the Laodicean attitude of the author, who, whatever may have been his general opinion of Christian revelation, was a Gallio in regard to the theological questions which agitated the Church. " I am acquainted with these controversial questions," he says somewhere, referring to the Monophysite disputes, " but I will not go into them. For I consider it a sort of insane folly to investigate the nature of God. Man cannot accurately apprehend the constitution of man, how much less that of the Deity." [3] The words imply an

---

story of Callinicus, *H.A.* 17. 2, is confirmed by Evagrius, iv. 32 ; (6) that of Priscus, *H.A.* 16. 7, by John Mal. xviii. 449, and *fr.* 46, *De ins.* : (7) that of Theodotus by John Mal. xviii. 416 ; while (8) the story of Psoes, *H.A.* 27. 14, is consistent with ecclesiastical records. (9) The laws referred to in the *H.A.* can be verified in the legal monuments of the reign ; (10) the statements about religious persecutions accord with facts ; and (11) in what is said, *H.A.* 17. 5 *sqq.*, of the attempts to repress prostitution, other evidence shows that the author is only representing facts in a light unfavourable to the policy.

[1] There is indeed an exception in

the statement, *H.A.* 22. 38, that the gold nomisma was reduced in value, which is not in accordance with the numismatic evidence. But even here it may be doubted whether Procopius had not some actual temporary or local fact in mind.

[2] This intention can be inferred from three passages in *H.A.* (1. 14 ; 11. 33 ; 26. 18), and from *B.G.* iv. 25. 13. The fulfilment of the promise in *H.A.* 17. 14, to tell the sequel of the story of two young women who had been unhappily married, may possibly have been also reserved for this book, though there is no hint that it had anything to do with ecclesiastical affairs.

[3] *B.G.* i. 3. 6.

oblique hit at the Emperor who in the *Secret History* is described as gratuitously busy about the nature of God.[1] That the book would also have been a document of some significance in the literature of toleration we may infer from a general remark which Procopius makes on Justinian's ecclesiastical policy. " Anxious to unite all men in the same opinion about Christ, he destroyed dissidents indiscriminately, and that under the pretext of piety ; for he did not think that the slaying of men was murder unless they happened to share his own religious opinions." [2]

An amazing change came to pass in the attitude of Procopius between the year in which he composed the *Secret History* and ten years later when he wrote his work on the *Buildings*, in which he bestows on the policy and acts of the Emperor superlative praise which would astonish us as coming from the author of the *History of the Wars*, even if the *Secret History* had been lost or never written. The victories of Narses had probably mitigated the pessimism into which he had fallen through the failure of Belisarius and the long series of Totila's successes ; but it is difficult to avoid the conjecture that he had received some preferment or recognition from the Emperor.[3] In the opening paragraph of the *Buildings* there is a hint at private motives of gratitude. " Subjects who have been well treated feel goodwill towards their benefactors, and may express thanks by immortalising their virtues." The author goes on to review and appreciate briefly Justinian's achievements in augmenting the size and prestige of the Empire, in imposing theological unity on its inhabitants, in ordering and classifying its laws, in strengthening its defences, and, noting particularly his indulgent treatment of conspirators, praises his general beneficence. This was a wonderful recantation of the unpublished libel, and we may doubt whether it was entirely sincere. Procopius did not take the *Secret History* out of its hiding-place and burn it, but he abstained from writing the book on ecclesiastical history which he had planned.

Wherever he was educated, Procopius had been saturated

---

[1] *H.A.* 18. 29.

[2] *Ib.* 13. 7.

[3] There is some evidence (see Suidas *sub* Προκόπιος) that he attained the rank of Illustrious, and there is a possibility that he was the Procopius who was Prefect of the City in 562 (Theophanes, A.M. 6055). But the name was a common one.

with Herodotus and Thucydides. His works are full of phrases which come from their works, and his descriptions of military operations sometimes appear to be modelled on passages in Thucydides. This fact has in modern days suggested the suspicion that some of his accounts of battles or sieges are the literary exercise of an imitator bearing little relation to what actually occurred.[1] But when we find that in some cases, which we can control, other sources bear out his accounts of operations at which he was not present (for instance, of the siege of Amida in the reign of Anastasius), we see that he did not misconceive the duty of a historian to record facts, and was able through his familiarity with Thucydides and Herodotus to choose phrases from their writings suitable to a particular case. It is remarkable that he does not seem to have read the *History* of Priscus, for, where he relates events of the fifth century, he seems to have derived his information not directly from that historian, but from intermediate writers who had used Priscus and perhaps distorted his statements.[2] He appears to have known the Syriac tongue, and it has been suggested that this knowledge recommended him to Belisarius when he selected him as his assessor in his first Persian campaigns.[3]

For his own time he derived information as to events and transactions, with which he was not in contact himself by virtue of his office on the staff of Belisarius, from people who had personal knowledge of them. It is probable that Peter, the Master of Offices, and possible that John, the nephew of Vitalian, were among his informants on Italian affairs.[4] And he seems to have lost no opportunity of making the acquaintance of ambassadors who came from foreign courts to Constantinople, and questioning them about the history of their countries.[5]

He wrote in the literary Greek which had developed in a

[1] See the tracts of Braun and Brückner, mentioned in Bibliogr. ii. 2, B, and the refutation of their suggestions by Haury, *Zur Beurt.* 1 *sqq.*—The fatalistic remarks which Procopius introduces from time to time are Herodotean.

[2] One of the intermediaries may have been Eustathius of Epiphania, who (see Evagrius, v. 24) wrote a universal history, for the latter part of which his sources were Zosimus and Priscus, whom he abbreviated.

It ended with the year 503. He was one of the principal sources of Evagrius. See further Haury's preface to his ed. of Procopius.

[3] Haury, *Zur Beurt.* p. 20. Haury thinks that he made use of Zacharias of Mytilene, and perhaps of the History of Armenia by Faustus of Byzantium in a Syriac version, *ib.* pp. 4 and 21.

[4] See above, Chap. XVIII. § 2.

[5] See above, Chap. XIX. § 8.

direct line from the classical writers of antiquity, and had hardly
been affected by the ordinary spoken language, from which it
was far removed. His prose is straightforward and unadorned ;
his only affectation is that he liked to imitate Thucydides.
For it would be unfair to describe as an affectation the avoidance
of current terms of his own day,[1] especially when they were
of Latin origin, or the introduction of them with an explanation
which is almost an apology.[2] For that was common form with
all authors who aimed at writing dignified prose. His " so-
called " is simply equivalent to our inverted commas. But he
did not conform to the technical rules which governed the
prose of the more pretentious stylists of his time. He did not
contort his sentences in order to avoid hiatus, and he ignored
the rule which had recently been coming into fashion as to the
fall of the accents in the last words of a clause. This rule was
that the last accented syllable in a clause must be preceded by
at least two unaccented syllables.[3] Thus a sentence ending with
the words *pántōn anthrópōn* would be right, but one ending
with *anthrópōn pántōn* would be wrong. This rule is observed
by Zosimus, and was strictly adopted by the two chief sophists
of the school of Gaza, Procopius and Choricius.[4] Some writers
observed it in a modified form, allowing occasional exceptions.

The history of Procopius breaks off in A.D. 552, and Agathias
of Myrina takes up the story.[5] Agathias is a much less interesting
person. By profession he was a lawyer, and his ambition was
to be a poet. He was inferior to Procopius as a historian, and

---

[1] For instance he regularly describes a bishop as ἱερεύς, not ἐπίσκοπος.
[2] Φοιδεράτοι is one of the few words of
this class that he employs *sans phrase*.
[3] Attention was drawn to it by
W. Meyer (*Der accentuirte Satzschluss*), but his conclusions have
been considerably modified by C.
Litzica (*Das Meyersche Satzschlussgesetz*), who pointed out that, in all
Greek prose writers, the majority of
sentences conform to the rule. This
is due to the nature of the language.
His conclusion is that unless the
exceptions do not exceed 10 or 11
per cent the writer was unconscious
of the rule.
[4] The fact that the historian Procopius did not observe it would not
prove that he was not educated at

Gaza, for the contemporary sophist
Aeneas of Gaza does not seem to have
adopted it. But it is an argument
against Haury's attempt to associate
him, on grounds of style, with the
Gaza school of prose.
[5] Born c. 536, he died in 582. He
probably intended to continue his
history till 565. It was continued
by his admirer, Menander, who was
trained as a lawyer, but spent his
early life as a man about town.
The fragments of Menander, whose
work terminated at 582, suggest that
he was a better historian than
Agathias. It is to be noticed that
Agathias made some use of Persian
chronicles, from which his friend
Sergius, the official interpreter, made
translations for him.

modern readers will judge him inferior as a writer, though this
would not have been the opinion of his contemporaries, to whose
taste his affected style, with its abundance of metaphors and its
preciosity, strongly appealed. His clauses carefully observed
that accentual law which Procopius had wisely neglected.

Agathias occupies a place in the history of Greek poetry
both for his own compositions and for the anthology which he
compiled of short poems by contemporary writers, including
some of his own and some of his friend Paul the Silentiary.[1]
This, like the earlier collections of Meleager and Philip, passed,
perhaps almost entire, into the Anthology of Constantine
Cephalas which has been preserved.[2] His talent was considerable, and he was a master of metrical technique in the style
which was then fashionable, and of which the best example
from the age of Justinian is the poem of Paul on the church of
St. Sophia. This technique had been elaborated in the previous
century by Nonnus of Panopolis.[3]

The *Dionysiaca* of Nonnus is the most interesting Greek poem
that was written since the days of the great Alexandrines,
Theocritus, Callimachus, and Apollonius. Published perhaps
after the middle of the fifth century,[4] it arrested the attention

[1] It was arranged in seven books
according to subject. See his Prooemium (*Anth. Gr.* iv. 3).

[2] *Anthologia Palatina* (so called
because the sole MS. is preserved
in the Palatine library of Heidelberg).
Agathias also wrote a volume of
epyllia, love stories from Greek
mythology, which he called *Daphniaca*.

[3] The Egyptians, it was said (see
next note), are mad about poetry.
And so in the fifth and sixth centuries
we have a long procession of
Egyptian poets ; Palladas, Claudian,
Synesius, Cyrus, and Nonnus ; then
Christodorus of Coptus, Colluthus,
Tryphiodorus, Julian (writer of many
epigrams in the *Anth. Gr.*) ; and
finally we have the horrible scribblings
with which Dioscorus of Aphrodito
plagued the life of a duke of the
Thebaid (*Pap. Cairo*, i. 67055,
67097, etc. ; ii. 67177-67188).

[4] The date of Nonnus is disputed.
We know that he was posterior to
Gregory of Nazianzus whom he echoes
in *Dionys.* i. 310, and wrote before
the reign of Anastasius, during which
Christodorus and Colluthus, who

were influenced by him, lived (Suidas,
sub nn.). Ludwich dates the *Dionysiaca* about 390–405 on the ground
of a passage in Eunapius, *Vit.
Proaeresii*, p. 92, who says that the
Egyptians ἐπὶ ποιητικῇ σφόδρα μαίνον-
ται. But why should this necessarily
allude to the poem of Nonnus ?
When Eunapius was writing before
405, there were at least two distinguished contemporary Egyptian poets,
Palladas and Claudian, as well as
Synesius. In two places (xvi. 321,
xx. 372) Nonnus has αἵδε πατήρ
με δίδαξε, identical with the first
words of a short poem of his fellow-
townsman Cyrus, who rose to be
Praetorian Prefect (see above, Vol. I.
p. 228). Ludwich holds that Cyrus
took them from Nonnus ; Friedländer, and those who place Nonnus
in the second half of the fifth century,
hold that Nonnus was the borrower.—
Christodorus was a prolific poet. He
wrote an epic on the Isaurian war
of Anastasius and much else, but
the only extant work is the *Ecphrasis*
of the statues in the baths of Zeuxippus, *Anth. Gr.* Book ii. The *Capture*

of all young men who were addicted to writing verse, and for the next three or four generations poets imitated his manner, and observed, some more and some less, the technical rules which had made his heroic metre seem a new revelation. Of these rules the most important were that a spondee is never admitted in the fifth foot ; that of the first four feet two at least must be dactyls, and when there are two spondees they should not be successive ; [1] that hiatus is forbidden ; and that elision is allowed only in the case of some particles and prepositions. If we add to these restrictions the fact that the caesura after the second syllable of the third foot predominates far more than in earlier poets, it is evident that the hexameters of Nonnus produce an entirely different poetical effect from those of Homer or of Apollonius. But Nonnus introduced another rule of a different kind which points to the direction in which Greek versification was to develop in later times. He strictly excludes proparoxytone words from the ends of his verses. This consideration of accent, which was a complete departure from classical tradition, was due doubtless to the influence of popular poetry ; and may be set side by side with the consideration of accent which, as we saw, was affecting Greek prose. The truth is, that in this age the Greeks had ceased to feel instinctively the difference between long and short syllables, and only those whose ear was educated by classical studies could appreciate poems written in the old metres. All vowels had the same value, and the new Christian hymnography, which was at its best in the sixth and seventh centuries,[2] took no account of quantity, but was governed by the simple rules that corresponding verses should have the same number of syllables and should have the final accent on the same syllable.

of Ilion by Tryphiodorus and the *Rape of Helen* by Colluthus are preserved. They exhibit Nonnian influence, but do not strictly observe his rules. John of Gaza, who wrote a description of a picture representing the cosmos in the winter-bath of Gaza (opened about A.D. 536), is a servile imitator of the master. — On the technique of this school of poetry see Ludwich, *Beiträge zur Kritik des Nonnus*, 1873 ; Friedländer, in *Hermes*, xlvii. 43 *sqq.* ; Tiedke, *ib.* xlix. 214 *sqq.* and l. 445 *sqq.*

[1] This is a rule to which he allows

very occasional exceptions.

[2] For the controversy on the date of Romanus, whom the admirers of hymnography consider the greatest of the Greek hymn writers, see Krumbacher, *G.B.L.*[2] 663 *sqq.* ; *Studien zu Romanos*, 1898 ; *Umarbeitungen bei Romanos*, 1879 ; *Romanos und Kyriakos*, 1901 ; C. de Boor, *Die Lebenszeit des Dichters R.*, in *B.Z.* ix. 633 *sqq.* ; P. van den Ven, *Encore Romanos le mélode*, *ib.* xii. 153 *sqq.* The last two studies seem to establish that he lived in the sixth century, not in the eighth.

By these metrical innovations the character of the epic
metre was changed and made a suitable instrument for a
Dionysiac theme. In order to achieve a whirling breathless
speed Nonnus bound it in fetters which excluded the variety
of metrical effects that the unrestricted use of spondees had
enabled the Homeric hexameter to compass.[1] His harmonious
dactyls, with the procession of long compound words which is
almost a necessary consequence of the predominance of this
foot,[2] however pleasing and effective in a short poem, become,
in a long epic like the *Dionysiaca* which has forty-eight cantos,
monotonous and wearisome.

The poem begins with the rape of Europa. The fiery birth
of the hero is not reached till the eighth book, and the proper
subject of the poem, the expedition of Dionysus to India, begins
only in the thirteenth. Such is the scale of the work. We are
carried along throughout the whole range of mythology in a
sort of corybantic dance,—a dance of words. The interest
for us lies in the unclassical, one is tempted to say romantic,
treatment of classical themes. Astraeus takes the horoscope
of Persephone for her mother.[3] We are taken aback by the
surprising modesty of Zeus when he is gazing at Semele bathing.[4]
As an example of the poet's dexterity take the verses in which
he describes the invention of the alphabet by Cadmus.[5]

> αὐτὰρ ὁ πάσῃ
> Ἑλλάδι φωνήεντα καὶ ἔμφρονα δῶρα κομίζων
> γλώσσης ὄργανα τεῦξεν ὁμόθροα, συμφυέος δὲ
> ἁρμονίης στοιχηδὸν ἐς ἄζυγα σύζυγα μίξας
> γραπτὸν ἀσιγήτοιο τύπον τορνώσατο σιγῆς.

To the peoples of Hellas he gave guerdons of speech and of thought ;
Symbols he placed in array, of the sounds which they uttered ; and
    wrought,
Mingling the yoked with the free, and setting the order of each,
The form of a speech that is soundless, a silence as vocal as speech.

The world of this poet's imagination has not the clear-cut
lines of classical art. He produces his effects by reflexions,

[1] Of every five lines of Homer,
probably four would have been
rejected by Nonnus.

[2] Thus the average number of
words in his verses is small. It has
been calculated that it is 6 to 7·2
in Homer. The great majority of
the uncommon compounds in Nonnus

are not of his own coinage. They
are to be found here and there in
earlier poets, whom he carefully
searched.

[3] vi. 58 *sqq.*

[4] vii. 265-268.

[5] iv. 259 *sqq.*

correspondences, indirections, and has a whole vocabulary of words for this purpose.[1] But he could have achieved distinction in simple pastoral poetry, as some idyllic passages show ; for instance the song with the refrain

βούτης καλὸς ὄλωλε, καλὴ δέ μιν ἔκτανε κούρη.

And occasionally he strikes off a verse which stays in the memory, like

σήμερον ἐν χθονὶ μέλπε, καὶ αὔριον ἐντὸς Ὀλύμπου.

That Nonnus was a pagan or quite indifferent to religion when he wrote the *Dionysiaca* is always taken for granted, on the ground that a believing Christian of that age would not have revelled in such a theme. But he was converted, and he composed a free paraphrase of the Gospel of St. John, which he strangely thought suitable for his dactyls. That he should have spent his extraordinary skill on such an experiment illustrates the curious defect in literary taste common to most of the poets of the age.

Of the poets of his school, all of whom are vastly inferior to the master, Paul, the poet of St. Sophia, was the most talented, and there was something to be said for employing the new hexameter in a description of the aerial creation of Justinian. But the poet whose name, though never mentioned by contemporaries, is best known to posterity is Musaeus.[2] His *Hero and Leander* caught the fancy of modern poets, more for the romance of the subject than for his treatment. The lamp of

---

[1] Such as νοθός, ἀντίτυπος, ἰσότυπος, μιμηλός, ἀντικέλευθος, ἀλλοπρόσαλλος. One of his favourite words is φειδόμενος in the sense of *forbearing, discreet, gentle* ; and adjectives in -αλέος (like φρικαλέος, σιγαλέος, ὑπναλέος), of which he has a great number, are a feature of his poetry. Another characteristic of his technique is the repetition of words, *e.g.* (xxxv. 42)

ἐπεὶ σέο μᾶλλον ὀιστῶν
μαζοὶ ὀιστεύουσιν ὀιστευτῆρες Ἐρώτων.

[2] Of his date we have no direct information, and the place of his birth is unknown. Agathias in the epigram *Anth. Gr.* v. 263 seems to be thinking of his poem. It has been guessed that he may be the Musaeus

who was a correspondent of Procopius of Gaza (*Epp.* 48). In any case he probably lived about that time. The contention of Rohde (*Der gr. Roman*, 502) that he was imitated by Achilles Tatius has been disproved by the discovery that Achilles cannot have composed his romance long after A.D. 300, as a fragment of it, written in the fourth century, was found in Egypt (*Pap. Oxyrh.* x. 1250).—The text of Musaeus is very corrupt. It is to be hoped that in the last line but one he wrote

καδ δ' Ἡρὼ τέθνηκε σὺν ὀλλυμένῳ παρακοίτη

and not καὶ διερή, as his latest editor amends. The double spondee is the one good point in the verse.

Hero gives it a certain charm, but it shows no more distinguished poetical talent than the little epics of Tryphiodorus and Colluthus, and the Nonnian metre is as little suitable to the subject.

To return from this digression, the historians like Procopius, Agathias, and Menander, who kept up the unbroken line of literary tradition and believed they wrote Attic Greek, could not be read except by highly educated people. So far had the spoken language drifted away from literary prose. For a larger public there was need of a popular history, written simply in the vulgar tongue. For this purpose John Malalas [1] of Antioch compiled, perhaps about A.D. 550, a chronicle of the history of the world, coming down to the first year of Justinian. In a new edition there was added, whether by the author or by another hand, a continuation treating Justinian's reign on a much larger scale than the reigns of his predecessors. In the earlier part of the work there is no sense of proportion, and there are many blunders. It was written down to the level of the masses, and was nicely calculated to give them what would interest them. Pages and pages are occupied with descriptions of the personal appearances of the heroes of the Trojan War. It hit the popular taste, was largely used by subsequent writers, was in a later age translated into Slavonic, and was the first of a long series of popular Byzantine chronicles.

It is an unfortunate gap in our knowledge that we have no information as to the activities of the book trade. It would be interesting to know whether the booksellers of Constantinople received regular announcements of the works produced at Alexandria, Athens, and other places, and how many copies were circulated of a book like the *Dionysiaca* of Nonnus, or the *Wars* of Procopius, or the *Chronicle* of Malalas, during the lives of their authors. We should then have some idea what these works meant for their own times.

In literature, as in law, the age of Justinian witnessed the

---

[1] Malalas is the Syriac for *rhetor*, and the author is called John Rhetor by Evagrius, who used the work in its first form. The text we possess is an abridgment, and mutilated at the end, but it can be supplemented by many excerpts and fragments, by its use in later chronicles, especially Theophanes and the *Paschal Chronicle*, and there are also fragments of the Slavonic translation. There are several difficult problems connected with Malalas which cannot be discussed here. See, for a general account, Krumbacher, *G.B.L.* 325 *sqq.*, and Bury, App. i. to Gibbon, vol. iv., where the special studies on the subject are mentioned. Cp. works of Patzig and Gleye cited below, Bibliography, ii. 2, B.

culmination of the old Graeco-Roman tradition, and at the same time the signs were quite clear that the world was turning in a new direction. While his talented lawyers were shaping the greatest creation of Rome, its jurisprudence, into a final form, Latin was being definitely abandoned for Greek as the language of the legislator and the jurist ; and from the same age which produced the best Greek historian since the time of Scipio Africanus comes the first of the popular chronicles which reflected the ignorance and superstition of the Middle Ages. It must not, however, be supposed that the old Greek tradition in literature disappeared. It was attenuated and modified in many tasteless ways, but the literary language was always learned as a second tongue, and never fell into disuse. The educated laity never ceased to read the ancient classics, and while in western Europe the writing of books was almost confined to ecclesiastics, in Greek lands the best books were generally written by laymen.

BIBLIOGRAPHY

The following lists include most of the works cited in the footnotes (though not, as a rule, articles in journals), and also some which are not cited but have been consulted.

ABBREVIATIONS USED IN FOOTNOTES AND BIBLIOGRAPHY

A.S.S.	=Acta Sanctorum.	J.H.S.	=Journal of Hellenic Studies.
B.Z.	=Byzantinische Zeitschrift.	J.R.S.	=Journal of Roman Studies.
C.I.G.	=Corpus Inscriptionum Graecarum.	M.G.H.	=Monumenta Germaniae Historica.
C.I.L.	=Corpus Inscriptionum Latinarum.	P.G.	=Migne, Patrologia Graeco-Latina.
C.J.	=Codex Justinianus.	P.L.	=Migne, Patrologia Latina.
C. Th.	=Codex Theodosianus.	P.-W.	=Pauly-Wissowa, Realencyklopädie der klassischen Altertumswissenschaft.
D. Chr. B.	=Dictionary of Christian Biography.		
E.H.R.	=English Historical Review.	R.I.S.	=Rerum Italicarum Scriptores.
F.H.G.	=Fragmenta Historicorum Graecorum.	S.B.	=Sitzungsberichte.
		Viz. Vrem.	=Vizantiiski Vremennik.

I. SOURCES

1. MONUMENTAL SOURCES

COHEN-FEUERDENT. Descriptions des monnaies frappées sous l'Empire romain. Ed. 2, vol. 8. 1880–92.

Corpus Inscriptionum Graecarum. Ed. Boeckh. 4 vols. 1828–77.

Corpus Inscriptionum Latinarum. Ed. Mommsen and others. 1863 , in progress.

DESSAU. Inscriptiones Latinae Selectae. 3 vols. 1892–1916.

ECKHEL. Doctrina Nummorum Veterum. Vol. viii. 1798.

GORI, A. F. Thesaurus veterum diptychorum consularium et ecclesiasticorum. 3 vols. 1759.

Inscriptiones Graecae (Berlin). 1873– , in progress.

LEFEBVRE. Recueil des inscriptions grecques-chrétiennes d'Égypte. 1907.

ROSSI, DE. Inscriptiones Christianae Urbis Romae. 2 vols. 1857–88.

SABATIER, J. Description générale des monnaies byzantines. Vol. i. 1862.

WROTH, W. Catalogue of the Imperial Byzantine Coins in the British Museum. 2 vols. 1908.
Catalogue of the Coins of the Vandals, Ostrogoths, etc., in the British Museum. 1911.

2. LITERARY SOURCES

A. Greek and Latin

Acta Conciliorum. See Mansi.
Acta martyrii Arethae. A.S.S. Oct. 24, x.
Acta Sanctorum Bollandiana. 1643–1894.
AENEAS OF GAZA. See Epistolographi Graeci.
AETHERIA. See Itinera Hierosol.
AGATHIAS. Historiae. (1) Ed. Niebuhr. 1828. (2) Ed. Dindorf, in Hist. Graec. Min. ii. 1871.
AGNELLUS. Liber Pontificalis. (1) Ed. Holder-Egger, in M.G.H., Script. rer. Lang. (2) Ed. Muratori, in R.I.S. i.
ANASTASIUS I. Edict for Libya Pentapolis. Ed. Zachariä von Lingenthal. Monatsberichte d. k. pr. Ak. d. Wiss. p. 134 sqq. 1879.
ANONYMUS BYZANTIUS. Περὶ στρατηγικῆς. In Griech. Kriegsschriftsteller, edd. Köchly and Rüstow, ii. 2. 1855. (Includes the Ἑρμήνεια.)
ANONYMUS VALESIANUS. Pars II. (1) Ed. Cessi, in new ed. of Muratori, R.I.S., 1913. (2) Ed. Mommsen, in Chron. Minora, i.
Anthologia Graeca. (1) Ed. Dübner. 2 vols. 1864–72. (2) Ed. Stadtmüller (incomplete). 1896–
Anthologia Latina. Edd. Bücheler and Riese. 2 parts. 1894–1906.
ANTONIUS. Vita Symeonis Stylitae. Ed. Lietzmann. 1908. (Along with German tr. of a Syriac life, and Symeon's letters, by Hilgenfeld.)
APOLLINARIS SIDONIUS. Opera. Ed. Luetjohann. 1887.
Letters, transl. by O. M. Dalton. 2 vols. 1915.
ARISTAENETUS. See Epistolographi Graeci.
ASTERIUS. Homiliae. P.G. 40.
AUGUSTINE, S. Epistulae. Ed. Goldbacher. 4 parts. 1895–1911.
Confessiones. Ed. Knöll. 1896.
De civitate Dei. Ed. Hoffmann. 2 vols. 1899, 1900.
AVITUS, ALCIMUS ECDICIUS. Opera. Ed. Peiper. 1883.

BENEDICT, S. Regula. (1) Ed. Wölfflin, 1895. (2) Ed. Butler, 1911. (Eng. tr. by Gasquet, 1908.)
Blemyomachia. See Eudocia.
BOETHIUS. Philosophiae Consolatio. (1) Ed. Peiper, 1871. (2) Edd. Stewart and Rand, with Eng. tr. (along with the Theological Tractates). 1918.

CALLINICUS. Vita Hypatii. Edd. Semin. Phil. Bonn. sodales. 1895.
CANDIDUS. Fragmenta. F.H.G. iv.
Carmen de Providentia divina. Printed among Prosper's works. P.L. 51.
CASSIODORUS SENATOR. Varia. Ed. Mommsen. 1894.
Chronicle. Chron. Minora, ii.
CEDRENUS. Historiarum Compendium. Vol. i. Ed. Bekker, 1838.
CHORICIUS. Orationes, declamationes, fragmenta. Ed. Boissonade. 1846.
Duae orationes nuptiales. Ed. Förster. 1891.
Duae in Brumalia Iustiniani et de Lydis Orationes. Ed. Förster. 1891.
Miltiadis Oratio. Ed. Förster. 1892.
In Aratium et Stephanum. Ed. Graux. In Œuvres de C. Graux, vol. ii. 1886.

Chronica Caesaraugustana. Chron. Min. ii.
Chronica Gallica. Chron. Min. ii.
Chronica Minora, saec. iv., v., vi., vii. 3 vols. Ed. Mommsen. 1892–98.
Chronicon Paschale. 2 vols. Ed. Dindorf. 1832.
CLAUDIAN. Opera. (1) Ed. Birt. 1892. (2) Ed. Koch. 1893.
Codex Justinianus. See Corp. Jur. Civ.
Codex Theodosianus. (1) Ed. Gothofredus, 6 vols., 1736–43. (2) Ed. Haenel,
    1837–44. (3) Edd. Mommsen and Meyer, 2 vols., 1905.
Collectio Avellana. Epp. Imperatorum, Pontificum, aliorum (A.D. 367–553).
    2 parts. Ed. Günther. 1805 08.
COLLUTHUS. Raptus Helenae. See Tryphiodorus.
CONSTANTINE. Vita Germani. A.S.S., July 31, vii.
CONSTANTINE PORPHYROGENNETOS. Excerpta Historica. 4 vols. (1. De
    legationibus. 2. De virtutibus et vitiis. 3. De insidiis. 4. De senten-
    tiis.) Edd. Boissevain, De Boor, Büttner-Wobst. 1903–6.
De cerimoniis. Ed. Bekker. 1829.
Consularia Constantinopolitana. Chron. Min. i.
Consularia Italica. Chron. Min. i.
CORIPPUS. Carmina. Ed. Partsch. 1879.
Corpus Juris Antejustiniani. 6 fasc. Ed. Haenel. 1835–44.
Corpus Juris Civilis. I¹². Institutiones, Digesta. Ed. Krüger. 1911. II³.
    Codex Justinianus. Ed. Krüger. 1884. III. Novellae. Edd. Schöll
    and Kroll. 1912.
COSMAS (Indicopleustes). Christian Topography. (1) In P.G. 88. (2) Ed.
    Winstedt, 1909. (Eng. tr. by M'Crindle, 1897.)
CYRIL OF SCYTHOPOLIS. Vita Cyriaci. A.S.S., Sept. 29, 147 *sqq.*
    Vita Euthymii magni. Ed. Cotelerius, in Monumenta eccl. Graecae,
    vol. iv. 1692.
    Vita Sabae. (1) Ed. Pomialovski (with the Slavonic version). 1890.
    (2) Ed. Cotelerius, in op. cit. vol. iii. 1080.
    De Theodosio abbate. See Theodore of Petrae.

DAMASCIUS. Vita Isidori. (1) Ed. Westermann (in the vol. of the Didot
    series containing Diogenes Laert.). 1878. (2) Ed. Asmus (with German
    tr. and commentary). 1911.
Διήγησις περὶ τῆς ἁγίας Σοφίας. See Scriptores Orig. Const.
DRACONTIUS. See Merobaudes.

Edictum Theoderici regis. (1) In Haenel, Corp. Jur. Antejust. (2) In Dahn's
    Könige der Germanen, iv. 45 *sqq.* The text of the Edictum Athalarici
    = Cassiodorus, Var. ix. 18, is also printed here, 125 *sqq.*
ENNODIUS Opera. Ed. Hartel. 1882.
Epistolographi Graeci. Ed. Hercher. (Includes the letters of Aeneas and
    Procopius of Gaza, of Synesius ; and also Aristaenetus.)
Epistulae Merowingici aevi. Ed. Gundlach. 1892.
Ἑρμήνεια (dictionary of tactical terms). See Anonymus Byz.
EUDOCIA (AUGUSTA). Carmina. Ed. Ludwich. 1897. (Along with Proclus,
    Claudian's Greek poems, and the Blemyomachia.)
EUGIPPIUS. Vita Severini. Ed. Mommsen. 1877.
EUNAPIUS. Vitae Sophistarum. 2 vols. Ed. Boissonade. 1822.
    Historiae fragmenta. In Constantine, Exc. hist., and F.H.G. iv.
EUSTATHIUS OF EPIPHANIA. Fragmenta. F.H.G. iv.
EUSTRATIUS. Vita Eutychii patriarchae. P.G. 86.
EVAGRIUS. Historia Ecclesiastica. Edd. Bidez and Parmentier. 1898
Expositio totius mundi et gentium. Ed. Lumbroso. 1899.

FACUNDUS OF HERMIANE.   Opera.   P.L. 67.
Fasti Consulares.   Ed. Liebenam.   1909.
Fasti Vindobonenses.   Chron. Min. i.
Fragmenta Historicorum Graecorum.   Vols. iv. and v. 1.   Ed. Müller.   1851-70.

GEORGIUS (MONACHUS).   Chronicle.   Vol. i.   Ed. De Boor.   1894.
GREGENTIUS.   Homeritarum leges, and Disputatio cum Herbano.   P.G. 86.
GREGORY I. (Pope).   Dialogi, Book ii. (Vita Benedicti).   P.L. 66.
GREGORY OF TOURS.   Opera.   Edd. Arndt and Krusch.   1885.

HESYCHIUS OF MILETUS.   Origines Constantinopolis.   F.H.G. iv.
HIEROCLES.   Synecdemus.   Ed. Burckhardt.   1893.
HIMERIUS.   Eclogae ; Declamationes.   Ed. Wernsdorf.   1790.
Historia Miscella.   Muratori, R.I.S. i.
HYDATIUS.   Chronicle.   Chron. Minora, ii.

ISIDORE OF SEVILLE.   Historia Gothorum Wandalorum Sueborum ;   and
    Chronica.   Chron. Minora, ii.
Itinera Hierosolymitana, saec. iiii.-viii.   Ed. Geyer.   1898.

JEROME, S.   Epistulae.   P.L. 22.
JOHN OF ANTIOCH.   Fragments.   In Constantine, Exc. Hist., and F.H.G. iv., v.
JOHN CHRYSOSTOM.   Opera.   13 vols.   Ed. Montfaucon.   (Editio Parisina
    altera.)   1834-39.   Montfaucon's text is also reprinted in P.G. 47-64.
JOHN OF GAZA.   Ἔκφρασις τοῦ κοσμικοῦ πίνακος τοῦ ὄντος ἐν τῷ χειμερίῳ Λουτρῷ.
    Ed. Friedländer.   1912.   (Along with Paul Silentiarius.)
JOHN THE LYDIAN.   De magistratibus.   Ed. Wünsch.   1903.
    De mensibus.   Ed. Wünsch.   1898.
    De ostentis.   Ed. Wachsmuth.   1863.
JOHN MALALAS.   Chronicle.   Ed. Bekker.   1831.
    Additional fragments of Book xviii., in Constantine,. Exc. Hist. iii.
    Fragments, in Mai, Spicilegium Romanum, ii. (at end of volume).   1839.
JOHN PHILOPONUS.   De aeternitate mundi.   Ed. Rabe.   1899.
    De opificio mundi.   Ed. Reichardt.   1897.
JORDANES.   Opera.   Ed. Mommsen.   1882.
JUSTINIAN (Emperor).   Ecclesiastical Edicts and Writings.   P.G. 86.

Laterculus regum Wandalorum et Alanorum.   Chron. Minora, iii.
Leges Visigothorum antiquiores.   Ed. Zeumer.   1894.
LEO I. (Pope).   Epistulae.   P.L. 54.
LEONTIUS OF BYZANTIUM.   Opera.   P.G. 86.
Lex Romana Wisigothorum.   Ed. Haenel.   1847.
LIBANIUS.   Opera.   Ed. Förster.   (In progress.)   1903-   .
    Epistulae.   Ed. Wolf.   1738.
Liber Diurnus.   (1) Ed. E. de Rozière.   1869.   (2) P.L. 105.
Liber Pontificalis.   Vol. i.   Ed. Duchesne.   1886.
Liber de promissionibus.   P.L. 51.
LIBERATUS.   Breviarium.   P.L. 68.

MALCHUS.   Fragmenta.   In Constantine, Exc. Hist. i., and F.H.G. iv.
MANSI.   Sacrorum Conciliorum nova et amplissima collectio.   Vols. iv.-ix.
MARCELLINUS.   Chronicle.   Chron. Minora, ii.
MARCUS (diaconus).   Vita Porphyrii Gaz.   Edd. Soc. Phil. Bonn. sodales.
    1895.   (Eng. tr. by Hill, 1913.)
MARINUS.   Vita Procli.   Ed. Boissonade.   (In the vol. of the Didot series
    containing Diogenes Laert.)   1878.

MARIUS OF AVENTICUM. Chronicle. Chron. Minora, ii.
MARIUS VICTOR. Aletheia. See Poetae Christ. Min.
MAURICE (PSEUDO-). Strategikon. Ed. Scheffer. 1664.
MAXENTIUS, JOHANNES. Opera. P.G. 86.
MENANDER. Fragmenta. F.H.G. iv., and Constantine, Exc. Hist. i.
MEROBAUDES. Reliquiae. Ed. Vollmer. 1905. (Along with Dracontius.)
MUSAEUS. Hero and Leander. Ed. Ludwich. 1912.

Narratio de Impp. domus Valentinianae et Theodosianae. Chron. Min. i.
Nestoriana. Ed. Loofs. 1905.
NICEPHORUS URANUS. Vita S. Simeonis iunioris. P.G. 86.
NICETAS OF REMESIANA. Opera. Ed. Burns, in Life and Works of N. 1905
NONNOSUS. Fragmenta. F.H.G. iv.
NONNUS. Dionysiaca. (1) Ed. Ludwich. 2 vols. 1909–11. (2) Ed. Köchly.
    2 vols. 1857–58.
Paraphrasis S. Evangelii Joannei. Ed. Scheindler. 1881.
Notitia dignitatum, (1) Ed. Seeck, 1876. (2) Ed. Böcking, with commentary,
    5 vols. and Index. 1839–53.
Notitia Galliarum. (1) Ed. Seeck, with Not. dig. (2) In Chron. Minora, i.
Notitia provinciarum et civitatum Africae. See Victor Vitensis.
Notitia urbis Constantinopolitanae. Ed. Seeck, with Not. dig.

OLYMPIODORUS. Fragmenta. F.H.G. iv.
ORIENTIUS. Carmina. Ed. Ellis. See Poet. Christ. Min.
OROSIUS. Historiae adv. Paganos. Ed. Zangemeister. 1889.

PALLADIUS. Dialogus de Vita Chrysostomi. See John Chrysostom.
    Historia Lausiaca, 2 vols. Ed. Butler. 1898–1904. (Eng. tr. by
    Lowther Clarke, 1920.)
Papyri. B.G.U. Ägyptische Urkunden aus den k. Museen zu Berlin,
    Griechische Urkunden, iii., 1903; iv., 1912.
Pap. Brit. Mus. Greek Papyri in the British Museum, iii. Edd. Kenyon and
    Bell. 1907.
Pap. Cairo. Catalogue générale des antiquités égyptiennes. Papyrus grecs
    d'époque byzantine. Ed. J. Maspéro. i., 1911; ii., 1913.
Pap. Leiden. Papyri graeci musei ant. publ. Lugduni-Batavi. Ed. C.
    Leemans. 1906.
Pap. Oxyrhyncus. The Oxyrhyncus Papyri. Edd. Grenfell and Hunt.
    i., 1898; viii., 1911; x., 1914; xiv., 1920; xv., 1922.
    Wessely. Griechische Papyrusurkunden kleineren Formats. 2 parts.
    1904–8.
Passiones vitaeque sanctorum aevi Merovingici. Ed. Krusch. 1896.
Πάτρια Κωνσταντινουπόλεως. See Scr. Orig. Const.
PAULINUS OF NOLA. Opera. (1) 2 vols. Ed. Hartel. 1894. (2) P.L. 61.
PAULINUS OF PELLA. Eucharisticos. Ed. Brandes. See Poet. Christ. Min.
PAULUS HELLADICUS. Epistula. Ed. Lundström. Anecd. Byz. e codd.
    Upsaliensibus. 1902.
PAULUS (SILENTIARIUS). Ἔκφρασις τοῦ ναοῦ τῆς ἁγίας Σοφίας. (1) Ed.
    Friedländer. See John of Gaza. (2) Ed. Bekker. 1837. (3) P.G. 86.
PELAGIUS I. (Pope). Epistulae. P.L. 69.
PETER (patricius). Fragments of his Περὶ πολιτικῆς καταστάσεως, in Constan-
    tine Porph., De cer., q.v.
PHILOSTORGIUS. Historia Ecclesiastica. Ed. Bidez. 1913.
PHOTIUS. Bibliotheca. Ed. Bekker. 1824. (Eng. tr. by Freese, vol. i., 1920.)
Poetae Christiani Minores. Including Paulinus of Petricordia, Orientius,
    Paulinus of Pella, Marius Victor, and Proba. Edd. Petschenig and
    others. 1888.

POLEMIUS SILVIUS.   Laterculus (A.D. 449).   Chron. Min. i.
POSSIDIUS.   Vita Augustini.   P.L. 32.
PRISCIAN (grammaticus).   Panegyric on Anastasius I.   In Dexippi etc.
    Historiae.   Edd. Bekker and Niebuhr.   1829.
PRISCUS.   Fragmenta.   In Constantine, Exc. Hist. i., and F.H.G. iv.
PROBA.   Cento.   Ed. Schenkl.   See Poet. Chr. Min.
PROCLUS.   Carmina.   See Eudocia.
PROCOPIUS OF CAESAREA.   Opera.   (1) 3 vols.   Ed. Haury.   1905–13.   (2)
    6 vols. (with Eng. tr.).   Ed. Dewing.   1914–   (in progress).
    La Guerra Gotica.   3 vols.   Ed. Comparetti (with Ital. tr.).   1895–98.
    Anecdota.   Ed. Orelli.   1827.
PROCOPIUS OF GAZA.   Epistulae.   See Epist. Graeci.
    Panegyric on Anastasius I.   (1) Along with Priscian, q.v.   (2) Ed. Kempen.
    1918.
PROSPER.   Opera.   P.L. 51.
    Chronicle.   Chron. Minora, i.
PRUDENTIUS.   Carmina.   Ed. Dressel.   1860.   (Eng. tr. by Morison, 1887–
    1889.)

RUFINUS.   Historia Ecclesiastica.   P.L. 21.
RUTILIUS NAMATIANUS.   De reditu suo.   Ed. Müller.   1870.

SALVIAN.   Opera.   Ed. Pauly.   1883.
Scriptores Originum Constantinopolitanarum.   (1) 2 parts.   Ed. Preger.
    1901–7.   (2) In Banduri, Imperium Orientale.   Vol. i.   1711.
Sirmondianae, Constitutiones.   At the end of Codex Theodosianus.   Ed.
    Mommsen, vol. i.
SOCRATES.   Historia Ecclesiastica.   (1) Ed. Valesius.   Oxford reprint.   1844.
    (2) P.G. 67.
SOZOMEN.   Historia Ecclesiastica.   P.G. 67.
SUIDAS.   Lexicon.   Edd. Gaisford, Bernhardy.   2 vols.   1853.
SULPICIUS SEVERUS.   Ed. Halm.   1866.
SYMMACHUS.   Opera.   Ed. Seeck.   1883.
SYNESIUS.   Opera.   P.G. 66.
    Epistulae.   See Epist. Graeci.

THEODORE (bishop of Petrae).   Vita Theodosii abbatis.   Ed. Usener.   1890.
    (With Cyril's Memoir of Theodosius.)
THEODORE LECTOR.   Historia Ecclesiastica (fragments).   P.G. 86.
THEODORET.   Historia Ecclesiastica.   Ed. Parmentier.   1911.
    Opera.   5 vols.   P.G. 80–84.
THEODOSIUS OF MELITENE.   Chronographia.   Ed. Tafel.   1859.
THEOPHANES.   Chronographia (with Latin version of Anastasius).   2 vols.   Ed.
    De Boor.   1883.
TRYPHIODORUS.   Ἅλωσις Ἰλίου.   (With Colluthus.)   Ed. Weinberger.   1896.

VEGETIUS.   Epitoma rei militaris.   Ed. Lang.   1885.
VICTOR TONNENNENSIS.   Chronicle.   In Chron. Minora, ii.
VICTOR VITENSIS.   Historia persecutionis Africanae provinciae.   Ed. Halm.
    1879.   (With an ecclesiastical Notitia provinciarum et civitatum Africae
    in reign of Huneric.)
Vita Aniani.   In Passiones vit aeque sanct. aevi Mer., q.v.
Vita Caesarii Arelatensis.   P.L. 67.
Vita Danielis (Stylitae).   Ed. Delehaye.   Analecta Boll. 32.   1913.
Vita Fulgentii.   P.L. 65.
Vita Gregentii.   Extracts.   Ed. A. Vasil'ev.   Viz. Vrem. xiv. 23 sqq.   1907.

Vita Marcelli (archimandritae). In Surius, De probatis Sanctorum historiis, vi., Dec. 29, p. 1020 *sqq.*
Vita Melaniae iunioris. Ed. Rampolla. 1905.
Vita Olympiadis. Analecta Boll. xv. 1896.

ZONARAS. Epitome historiarum. (1) Libri xiii.-xviii. Ed. Büttner-Wobst. 1897. (2) Ed. Dindorf, vol. iii. 1870.
ZOSIMUS. Historia nova. Ed. Mendelssohn. 1887.

B. *Oriental*

AGAPIUS. Universal History. Arabic text with French tr. Ed. Vasil'ev. 1909.

Chronica Minora (Syriac). 3 parts with Latin tr. Edd. Guidi, Brooks, and Chabot. 1903.
Chronicon Edessenum. Ed. Guidi. Chron. Min., *q.v.*
Collection des historiens de l'Arménie. Ed. Langlois. 2 vols. 1867–69.

ELISHA VARTABED. History of Armenia. In Coll. des hist. de l'Arménie, vol. ii.

JACOBUS SARUGENSIS. Epistle to the Himyarite Christians (Syriac). Ed. Guidi (with Ital. tr.). Atti della r. Accad. dei Lincei, vii. 1881–82.
JOHN OF BEITH-APHTHONIA. Vita Severi (Syriac). Ed. Kugener (with French tr.) 1904.
JOHN OF EPHESUS. Ecclesiastical History (Syriac).
    Part 2 (fragments). Some published by Nau in Revue de l'Orient chrétien, ii. 455 *sqq.*, 1897, and others in Comm. de B. or. ; see below.
    Part 3. (1) English version by Payne Smith, 1860. (2) German version by Schönfelder, 1862.
    Commentarii de Beatis orientalibus. Latin tr. by Van Douwen and Land. 1889.
JOHN OF NIKIU. Chronicle (Ethiopian) (1) Ed. Zotenberg (with French tr.) 1883. (2) English version by Charles. 1916.
JOSHUA STYLITES. Chronicle (Syriac). Ed. Wright (with English tr.). 1882.

LAZARUS OF PHARBI. Coll. des hist. de l'Arménie, vol. ii.

MICHAEL SYRUS. Chronicle (Syriac), vol. ii. Ed. Chabot (with French tr.). 1901.
MOSES OF CHORENE. History of Armenia. (1) French tr. Coll. des hist. de l'Arménie, vol. ii. (2) Russian tr. by Emin. 1893 (Moscow).

NESTORIUS. Le Livre d'Héraclide de Damas. Tr. Nau. 1910.
    Fragments of a Sermon. (1) In Loofs, Nestoriana. 1905. (2) P.G. 66.

TABARI. Chronicle (Arabic). German tr. of a portion, by Nöldeke (Geschichte der Perser und Araber zur Zeit der Sassaniden). 1879.

ZACHARIAS OF MITYLENE. Chronicle (Syriac). (1) English tr. by Hamilton and Brooks. 1899. (2) German tr. by Ahrens and Krüger. 1899.
ZACHARIAS SCHOLASTICUS. Vita Severi (Syriac). Ed. Kugener (with French tr.). 1903.

II. MODERN WORKS

1. GENERAL

A. *Books of Reference (Dictionaries, Encyclopaedias, etc.)*

BARDENHEWER, O. Patrologie. Ed. 3. 1910.

CABROL, F. Dictionnaire d'archéologie chrétienne et de liturgie. 1907– .
CLINTON, H. FYNES. Fasti Romani. 2 vols. 1845–50.

DAREMBERG AND SAGLIO. Dictionnaire des antiquités grecques et romaines.
    1877– .
Dictionary of Christian Antiquities. Edd. Smith and Cheetham. 2 vols.
    1875–80.
Dictionary of Christian Biography. Edd. Smith and Wace. 4 vols. 1877–87.
Dictionary of Greek and Roman Geography. Ed. Smith. 2 vols. 1873.

FABRICIUS, J. A. Bibliotheca Graeca. Ed.[4] Harles. 12 vols. and Index.
    1790–1837.
FRIEDLÄNDER, L. Roman Life and Manners (Eng. tr.). 4 vols. 1909–13.

HAUCK. Real-Encyklopädie für protestantische Theologie und Kirche. Ed. 3.
    1896–1909.

LE QUIEN, M. Oriens Christianus. 3 vols. 1740.

MAS-LATRIE, COMTE DE. Trésor de chronologie, d'histoire et de géographie.
    1889.

PAULY. Realencyklopädie der klassischen Altertumswissenschaft. Ed.
    Wissowa. 1894– (in progress).
POTTHAST, A. Bibliotheca historica medii aevi. Ed. 2. 2 vols. 1896.

RUGGIERO, E. DE. Dizionario epigraphico di antichità romane. Vols. i.– .
    1895– .

SUICERUS, J. C. Thesaurus ecclesiasticus e patribus Graecis. Ed. 2. 2 vols.
    1728.

B. *General Histories (Political and Ecclesiastical)*

BUSSELL, F. W. Constitutional Hist. of the Roman Empire (from 81 A.D. to
    1081 A.D.). 2 vols. 1910.

Cambridge Medieval History. Vols. i. and ii. Edd. Gwatkin and Whitney.
    1911–13.

DAHN, F. Die Könige der Germanen. 12 vols. 1861–1909.

FINLAY, G. History of Greece. Vol. i. 1876.

GIBBON, E. Decline and Fall of the Roman Empire. Vols. iii. and iv. Ed.
    Bury. 1909.
GIESELER, C. L. Lehrbuch der Kirchengeschichte. Ed. 4. Vol. i. 1844.

HARNACK, A.   History of Dogma (Eng. tr.).   Vol. iv.   1898.
HEFELE, C. J.   Conciliengeschichte.   Ed. 2.   Vol. ii.   1875.
HODGKIN, T.   Italy and her Invaders.   Vols. i.-iv.   Ed. 2.   1892–96.   Vol. v. 1895.

KULAKOVSKI, J.   Istoriia Vizantii.   Vols. i. and ii.   1910–12.

LEBEAU, CH.   Histoire du Bas-Empire.   Vols. v.-ix.   Ed. Saint Martin.   1826–28.

PAPARRIGOPULOS, K.   'Ιστορία τοῦ 'Ελληνικοῦ ἔθνους.   Vols. ii., iii.   Ed. 2.   1886.

RANKE, L. VON.   Weltgeschichte.   Vol. iv.   1883.
RAWLINSON, G.   The Seventh Great Oriental Monarchy.   1876.

SEECK, O.   Geschichte des Untergangs der antiken Welt.   Vols. i.-vi.   1895– .

TILLEMONT, L. S. DE LE NAIN DE.   Histoire des Empereurs.   Vols. v., vi.
1732–39 (Venice).
Mémoires pour servir à l'histoire ecclésiastique des six premiers siècles.
Vols. x.-xvi.   1732 (Venice).

USPENSKI, TH. J.   Istoriia Vizantiiskoi.   Vol. i.   1912.

YOUNG, G. F.   East and West through Fifteen Centuries.   Vol. ii.   1916.

2. SPECIAL

A. On Political and Ecclesiastical History

ADONTS, N.   Armeniia v epokhu Iustiniana.   1908.
ASDOURIAN, P.   Die politischen Beziehungen zwischen Armenien und Rom
(190 B.C.–A.D. 428).   1911.
AUDOLLENT.   Carthage romaine 146 B.C.–A.D. 698.   1901–4.

BABUT, E. CH.   Le Concile de Turin.   1904.
BARTH, W.   Kaiser Zeno.   1894.
BAYNES, N.   Rome and Armenia in the Fourth Century.   E.H.R. xxv.   Oct.
1910.
BESSE, J. M.   Les Moines d'Orient antérieurs au concile de Chalcédoine (451).
1900.
BETHUNE-BAKER, J.   Nestorius and his Teaching.   1908.
BINDING, C.   Das burgundisch-romanische Königreich (443–532).   Vol. i.   1868.
BLASEL, C.   Die Wanderzuge der Langobarden.   1909.
BROCKHOFF, W.   Studien zur Geschichte der Stadt Ephesos (4th to 15th cent.).
1905.
BROOKS, E. W.   The Emperor Zenon and the Isaurians.   E.H.R. viii.   April
1893.

CAGNAT, R.   L'Armée romaine d'Afrique.   1913.
CHAMICH, M.   History of Armenia.   Eng. tr. by Avdall.   Vol. i.   1827.

DELBRÜCK, H.   Geschichte der Kriegskunst.   Vol. ii.   1901.
DIEHL, CH.   L'Afrique byzantine.   1896.
Justinien et la civilisation byzantine au vie siècle.   1901.
Figures byzantines.   1e série.   1906.
Théodora, impératrice de Byzance.   N.D.

DILL, S.   Roman Society in the Last Century of the Western Empire.   1898.
DUCHESNE, L.   Églises séparees.   1896.
   Histoire ancienne de l'Église.   Vol. iii.   1910.
   Vigile et Pélage.   Revue des questions historiques, vol. xxxvi.   1884.
DUMOULIN, M.   Le Gouvernement de Théodoric et la domination des Ostrogoths
   en Italie.   Rev. Hist.   106.   1902.

FREEMAN, E. A.   Western Europe in the Fifth Century.   1904.
FUSTEL DE COULANGES.   Histoire des institutions politiques de l'ancienne
   France.   1875.

GASQUET, A.   L'Empire byzantin et la monarchie franque.   1888.
GEFFCKEN, J.   Der Ausgang des griechisch—römischen Heidentums.   1920.
GELZER, H.   Kosmas der Indienfahrer.   Jahrbb. f. protestantische Theologie.
   ix. 105 sqq.   1883.
GÉNIER, FR. R.   Vie de Saint Euthyme le Grand.   1909.
GREGOROVIUS, F.   History of the City of Rome in the Middle Ages (tr. by A.
   Hamilton).   Vols. i. and ii.   1895.
   Geschichte der Stadt Athen im Mittelalter.   Vol. i.   1889.
   Athenais.   1882.
GRISAR, H.   History of Rome and the Popes in the Middle Ages (Eng. tr.).
   Vols. i.-iii.   1911-12.
GSELL, S.   Les Monuments antiques de l'Algérie.   2 vols.   1901.
GÜLDENPENNING, A.   Geschichte des oströmischen Reiches unter den Kaisern
   Arcadius und Theodosius II.   1885.
GÜTERBOCK, K.   Byzanz und Persien in ihren diplomatisch-völkerrechtlichen
   Beziehungen im Zeitalter Justinians.   1906.

HARTMANN, L. M.   Geschichte Italiens im Mittelalter.   Vol. i.   1897.
HAVERFIELD, F.   The Romanization of Roman Britain.   Ed. 3.   1915.
HERTZBERG, G. F.   Geschichte Griechenlands seit dem Absterben des antiken
   Lebens.   Part i.   1876.
   Geschichte Griechenlands unter der Herrschaft der Römer.   Part iii.   1875.
HEYD, W.   Geschichte des Levantehandels im Mittelalter.   Vol. i.   1879.
HIRTH, F.   China and the Roman Orient.   1885.
HOLM, A.   Geschichte Siciliens im Altertum.   Vol. iii.   1898.
HOLMES, T. S.   The Christian Church in Gaul.   1911.
HOLMES, W. G.   The Age of Justinian and Theodora.   2 vols.   1905-7.
HOWORTH, H. H.   The Avars.   Journal Asiatic Soc.   III. ser   Vol. i.   1889.
HUART, C.   Histoire des Arabes.   Vol. i.   1912.
HUTTON, W. H.   The Church of the Sixth Century.   1897.

JÖRS, P.   Die Reichspolitik Kaiser Justinians.   1893.
JUNG, J.   Römer und Romanen in den Donauländern.   1887.
JUNGHANS, W.   Histoire critique des règnes de Childerich et de Chlodowech
   (Fr. tr. by Monod).   1879.

KALLIGAS, P.   Μελέται καὶ λόγοι.   1882.
KELLER, R.   Stilicho.   1884.
KHVOSTOV, M.   Istoriia vostochnoi torgovli greko-rimskago Egipta.   1907.
KÖRBS, O.   Untersuchungen zur ostgotischen Geschichte.   I.   1913.
KULAKOVSKI, J.   Proshloe Tavridy.   Ed. 2.   1914.
KURTH, G.   Histoire poétique des Mérovingiens.   1893.

LABOURT, J.   Le Christianisme dans l'empire perse sous la dynastie sassanide.
   1904.

LEUTHOLD, H. Untersuchungen zur ostgotischen Geschichte der Jahre 535–537. 1908.

LOEWE, R. Die Reste der Germanen am schwarzen Meere. 1896.

LOOFS, F. Leontius von Byzanz. 1887.
Nestorius and his Place in the History of Christian Doctrine. 1914.
Leitfaden zum Studium der Dogmengeschichte. Ed. 4. 1906.

LOT, F. Les Migrations saxonnes en Gaule et en grande Bretagne. Revue historique, 119. May 1915.

MARIN, ABBÉ. Les Moines de Constantinople (330–898). 1897.

MARQUART, J. Die Chronologie der alttürkischen Inschriften. 1898.

MARTROYE, F. L'Occident à l'époque byzantine. Goths et Vandales. 1904. Genséric. 1907.

MERTEN, E. De bello Persico ab Anastasio gesto. Comm. philol. Jenenses vii. fasc. poster. 1906.

MILNE, J. G. History of Egypt under Roman Rule. 1898.

NAU, F. Nestorius d'après les sources orientales. 1911.

NÉMÄTI, K. Die historisch-geographischen Beweise der Hiungnu = Hun Identität. 1910.

OMAN, C. W. C. History of the Art of War. 1898.

PAUE, B. I Barbari o Bizantini in Sicilia. 1011.

PARGOIRE, J. L'Église byzantine de 527 à 847. Ed. 2. 1905.

PETRIE, W. M. F. Migrations. Journ. of Anthr. Inst. xxxvi. 1906.

PFEILSCHIFTER, G. Der Ostgotenkönig Theoderich der Grosse und die katholische Kirche. (Kirchengeschichtliche Studien, edd. Knöpfler, Schrörs, Sdralek, vol. iii.) 1896.

PUECH, A. St. Jean Chrysostome et les mœurs de son temps. 1891.

REMÉNYI, A. Zur Geschichte der Donauflotilla. 1888.

ROSE, A. Kaiser Anastasius I. 1882.

RÜGAMER, P. W. Leontius von Byzanz. 1894.

ŠAFAŘÍK, P. J. Slawische Alterthümer (tr. by Wuttke). 2 vols. 1843–44.

SAGOT, F. La Bretagne romaine. 1911.

SCALA, R. VON. Die wichtigsten Beziehungen des Orientes zum Occidente in Mittelalter und Neuzeit. 1887.

SCHMIDT, L. Geschichte der deutschen Stämme. Vol. i.– (in progress). 1904–
Geschichte der Wandalen. 1901.

SCHULTZE, V. Konstantinopel. 1913.
Geschichte des Untergangs des griechisch-römischen Heidenthums. 2 vols. 1887–92.

SIEVERS, G. R. Studien zur Geschichte der römischen Kaiser. 1870.

SUNDWALL, J. Weströmische Studien. 1915.
Abhandlungen zur Geschichte des ausgehenden Römertums. 1919.

TOMASCHEK, W. Die Goten in Taurien. 1881.

TOURNEBIZE, F. Histoire politique et religieuse de l'Arménie. 1901.

TOUTAIN, J. Les Cités romaines de la Tunisie. 1896.

VASIL'EV, A. A. Lektsii po istorii Vizantii. Vol. i. 1917.

VOGT, E. Die politischen Bestrebungen Stilichos. 1870.

WESTBERG, F.   Zur Wanderung der Langobarden.   (In Zapiski imp. Ak.
    Nauk, vi. No. 5.)   1904.

ZEILLER, J.   Les Origines chrétiennes dans les provinces danubiennes de
    l'empire romain.   1918.

B. Criticism of Sources

ANGUS, S.   Sources of the first Ten Books of Augustine's De Civitate Dei.   1906.
ASMUS, J. B.   Zur Rekonstruktion von Damascius' Leben Isidorus.   B.Z. xviii.,
    xix.   1909–10.
AULER, A.   De fide Procopii Caes. in secundo bello Persico Iustiniani I. imp.
    enarrando.   1876.

BATIFFOL, P.   Quaestiones Philostorgianae.   1891.
BAUER, M.   Asterios, Bischof von Amaseia.   1911.
BAUMSTARK, R.   Das Alter der Peregrinatio Aetheriae.   Oriens Christianus,
    N.S. i.   1911.
BAUR, CHR.   St. Jean Chrysostome et ses œuvres.   1907.
BIDEZ, J.   La Tradition manuscrite de Sozomène.   1908.
BOOR, C. DE.   Suidas und die Konstantinsche Exzerptsammlung.   B.Z. 21, 23.
    1912–14.
BRAUN, H.   Procopius Caesariensis quatenus imitatus sit Thucydidem.   1885.
    Die Nachahmung Herodots durch Prokop.   1894.
BRÜCKNER, M.   Zur Beurteilung des Geschichtsschreibers Prokopius von
    Caesarea.   1896.
BURY, J. B.   The Notitia Dignitatum.   J.R.S. x.   1922.

CIPOLLA, C.   Ricerche intorno all' "Anonimus Valesianus II."   (Bull. del-
    l' Istituto Italiano, No. ii.)   1892.
CREES, J. H. E.   Claudian as an Historical Authority.   1908.

DAHN, F.   Procopius von Cäsarea.   1865.
    Paulus Diaconus.   I. Abth.   1876.

FÖRSTER, J. W.   Quaestiones Vegetianae.   1895.
FRANKE, G.   Quaestiones Agathianae.   1914.

GEPPERT, F.   Die Quellen des Kirchenhistorikers Socrates Scholasticus.   1898.
GLEYE, C. E.   Beiträge zur Johannesfrage.   B.Z. v. 422 sqq.   1896.
GÜNTHER, K.   Theodoret von Cyrus.   1913.

HAURY, J.   Procopiana [i.].   1891.
    Procopiana, ii.   1893.
    Zur Beurteilung des Geschichtsschreibers Procopius von Caesarea.   1897.
HEINEMANN, M.   Quaestiones Zonareae, i.   1895.
HEUSSI, K.   Untersuchungen zu Nilus dem Asketen.   1917.

JACOBI, R.   Die Quelle der Langobardengeschichte des Paulus Diaconus.   1877.
JEEP, L.   Quellenuntersuchungen zu den griechischen Kirchenhistorikern.
    1884.

LUNDSTRÖM, V.   Prolegomena in Eunapii Vitas.   1897.

MILLER, E.   Théodore le lecteur et Jean d'Égée.   Revue arch., 26, 273 sqq. and
    396 sqq.   1873.

PANCHENKO, B. O tainoi istorii Prokopiia. 1897.
PATZIG, E. Unerkannt und unbekannt-gebliebene Malalas-Fragmente. 1891.
    Johannes Antiochenus und Johannes Malalas. 1892.
SARRAZIN, V. De Theodoro Lectore. In Comm. Phil. Jenenses. 1881.
SAUERBREI, P. De fontibus Zonarae quaestiones selectae. In Comm. Phil.
    Jenenses. 1881.
SCHOO, G. Die Quellen des Kirchenhistorikers Sozomenos. 1911.
SEECK, O. Die Briefe des Libanius, zeitlich geordnet. 1906.
SHESTAKOV, S. P. Kandid Isavriiskii. In Lietopis' ist.-phil. obshchestva, of
    Odessa. IV. (Viz. otd. ii.). 1894.
    O znachenii Slavianskago perovoda khroniki Ioanna Malaly. Viz. Vrem.
    i., ii. 1894, 1895.
SOTIRIADIS, G. Zur Kritik von Johannes von Antiochia. 1887.

C. Laws, Institutions, Administration, etc.

ACCARIAS, Ç. Précis de droit romain. 2 vols. 1886–91.
ALIVISATOS, H. S. Die kirchliche Gesetzgebung des Kaisers Justinian I. 1913.
ANDREADES, A. M. Ἱστορία τῆς Ἑλληνικῆς δημοσίας Οἰκονομίας. I. 1918.
    Περὶ τοῦ πληθυσμοῦ καὶ τοῦ πλούτου τῆς Κωνσταντινουπόλεως. 1918.
    Reproduced in French with additions and improvements in Metron.
    Vol. i. No. 2, 1920.
    Περὶ νομίσματος καὶ τῆς κτητικῆς δυνάμεως τῶν πολυτίμων μετάλλων κατὰ
    τοὺς Βυζαντινοὺς χρόνους. 1918.
    Le Montant du Budget de l'empire byzantin. Revue des études grecques,
    xxxiv. No. 156. 1921.
AUSSARESSES, F. L'Armée byzantine à la fin du viᵉ siècle. 1909.

BARUT, CH. La Garde impériale et le corps d'officiers de l'armée romaine aux
    ivᵉ et vᵉ siècles. Revue historique 114, 116. 1914–16.
BENJAMIN, C. De Iustiniani imp. aetate quaestiones militares. 1892.
BILLETER, G. Geschichte des Zinsfusses . . . bis auf Justinian. 1898.
BOAK, A. E. R. The Master of Offices in the Later Roman and Byzantine
    Empires. 1919.
BORGHESI, B. Les Préfets du prétoire. Ed. Cuq. 2 parts (=vol. x. of Œuvres
    complètes). 1897.
BRUNNER, H. Deutsche Rechtsgeschichte. Vol. i. Ed. 2. 1906.
BURY, J. B. The Constitution of the Later Roman Empire. 1910.

CARETTE, E. Les Assemblées provinciales de la Gaule romaine. 1895.
COLLINET, P. Études historiques sur le droit de Justinien. Vol. i. 1912.

DIEHL, CH. Études sur l'administration byzantine dans l'exarchat de Ravenne.
    1888.

ELLISSEN, O. A. Der Senat im oströmischen Reiche. 1881.

GEBHARDT, E. Das Verpflegungswesen von Rom und Constantinopel in der
    späteren Kaiserzeit. 1881.
GELZER, M. Studien zur byzantinischen Verwaltung Ägyptens. 1909.
GROSSE, R. Römische Militärgeschichte von Gallienus bis zum Beginn der
    byzantinischen Themenverfassung. 1920.
    Das römisch-byzantinische Marschlager vom 4.–10. Jahrhundert. B.Z.
    xxii. 1912.
    Die Rangordnung der römischen Armee des 4.–6. Jahrhunderts. Klio,
    xv. 1915.

HARTMANN, L. M.   Untersuchungen zur Geschichte der byzantinischen Verwaltung in Italien (540–750).   1889.

HIS, R.   Die Domänen der römischen Kaiserzeit.   1896.

HUDEMANN, E. E.   Geschichte des römischen Postwesens während der Kaiserzeit.   1878.

KARLOWA.   Römische Rechtsgeschichte.   Vol. i.   1885.

KOCH, P.   Die byzantinischen Beamtentitel von 400 bis 700.   1903.

LÉCRIVAIN, CH.   Le Sénat romain depuis Dioclétien à Rome et à Constantinople.   1888.

LEO, F.   Die capitatio plebeia und die capitatio humana.   1900.

MARQUARDT, J.   Römische Staatsverwaltung.   3 vols.   1887.

MASPÉRO, J.   Organisation militaire de l'Égypte byzantine.   1912.
Φοιδεράτοι et Στρατιῶται dans l'armée byzantine au viᵉ siècle.   B.Z. 21. 1912.

MITTEIS, L.   Reichsrecht und Volksrecht in den östlichen Provinzen des römischen Kaiserreichs.   1891.

MOMMSEN, TH.   Römisches Staatsrecht.   3 vols.   1887.
Römisches Strafrecht.   1899.

MONNIER, H.   Études de droit byzantin.   Nouvelle Revue historique de droit, xvi.

MÜLLER, A.   Das Heer Justinians.   Philologus, lxxi.   1912.

PIGANIOL, A.   L'Impôt de capitation sous le Bas-empire romain.   1916.

REID, J. S.   The Municipalities of the Roman Empire.   1913.

ROBY, H. J.   Introduction to Justinian's Digest.   1884.

ROSTOWZEW, M.   Studien zur Geschichte des römischen Kolonates.   1910.

SEECK, Die Schatzungsordnung Diocletians.   Zeitschrift für Social- und Wirtschaftsgeschichte, iv.   1896.

STEIN, E.   Studien zur Geschichte des byzantinischen Reiches.   1919.
Ein Kapitel vom persischen und vom byzantinischen Staate.   Byz.-neugriechische Jahrbücher, i.   1920.

STÖCKLE, A.   Spätrömische und byzantinische Zünfte.   1911.

WALTZING, J. P.   Étude historique sur les corporations professionnelles chez les Romains depuis les origines jusqu'à la chute de l'Empire d'occident. 4 vols.   1895–1900.

ZACHARIÄ VON LINGENTHAL, K. E.   Geschichte des griechisch-römischen Rechts.   Ed. 3.   1892.

D. Chronology

ANDREEV, J.   Konstantinopol'skie Patriarkhi ot vremeni Khalkidonskago sobora do Photiia.   1895.

DULAURIER, E.   Recherches sur la chronologie arménienne, i.   1859.

GELZER, H.   Sextus Iulius Africanus und die byzantinische Chronographie. 2 parts.   1880–98.

MURALT, E. DE.   Essai de chronographie byzantine, 395 à 1057.   1855.

BIBLIOGRAPHY 451

E. *Geography, Topography, Maps*

ANDERSON, J. G. C.   Asia Minor (in Murray's series of Handy Classical Maps). 1903.
   The Road-System of Eastern Asia Minor.   J.H.S. xvii.   1897.

BANDURI, A.   Imperium orientale.   Vol. ii.   1711.
BIELIAEV, D. TH.   Byzantina (in Russian).   Books i., ii.   1891–93.   Book iii., in Zapiski klass. otd. imp. russkago arkheol. obshchestva, iv.   1907. Khram Bogoroditsy Khalkopratiiskoi v Konstantinopolie.   In Lietopis' ist.-phil. Obshchestva, Viz. otdiel 1, of Odessa.   1892.

CHAPOT, V.   La Frontière de l'Euphrate, de Pompée à la conquête arabe.   1907.
CLUVERIUS, P.   Italia Antiqua.   2 vols.   1624.
COLUCCI, G.   Antichità picene.   Vol. vii.   1790.

DETHIER, P. A.   Der Bosphor und Constantinopel.   Ed. 2.   1876.
DUBOIS DE MONTPÉREUX, F.   Voyage autour du Caucase.   6 vols.   1839–43.
DUCANGE, C. DU FRESNE.   Constantinopolis Christiana.   1729 (Venice).

EBERSOLT, J.   Le Grand Palais de Constantinople.   1910.
EVANS, A. J.   Antiquarian Researches in Illyricum.   4 parts.   Archaeologia, xlviii., xlix.   1883–85.

FORCHHEIMER, P., and STRZYGOWSKI, J.   Die byzantinischen Wasserbehälter von Constantinopel.   1893.

GROSVENOR, E. A.   Constantinople.   2 vols.   1895.
GYLLIUS, P.   De Constantinopoleos topographia libri iv.   1632.
   De Bosporo Thracio libri iii.   1632.

JIREČEK, C.   Die Heerstrasse von Belgrad nach Constantinopel und die Balkanpässe.   1877. .
JORDAN, H.   Topographie der Stadt Rom im Alterthum.   2 vols. (vol. i. part 3, by Hülsen).   1871–1907.

KIEPERT, H.   Formae urbis Romae antiquae.   1912.
   Formae orbis antiqui.   1894–

LABARTE, J.   Le Palais impérial de Constantinople et ses abords.   1861.
LECLERCQ, G.   Art. Byzance, in Cabrol, Dict.   See above, II. 1, A.

MILLER, K.   Itineraria Romana.   1916.
MILLINGEN, A. VAN.   Byzantine Constantinople.   1899.
MORDTMANN, DR.   Esquisse topographique de Constantinople (and plan). 1892.

NISSEN, H.   Italische Landeskunde.   2 vols.   1883–1902.

OBERHUMMER, E.   Constantinopolis.   1899.

PARGOIRE, J.   Hiéria.   Izv. russk. arkh. Inst. v Kplie, iv.   1899.   Les SS. Mamas de Cple.   *Ib.* ix.   1904.
   Rufinianes.   B.Z. viii. 1899.   À propos de Boradion.   *Ib.* xii.   1903.
PASPATES, A. G.   Τὰ Βυζαντινὰ Ἀνάκτορα.   1885.   Eng. tr. by Metcalfe, 1893.

RAMSAY, W. M.   Historical Geography of Asia Minor.   1890.
Cities and Bishoprics of Phrygia.   2 vols.   1895–97.

SACHAU, E.   Reise in Syrien und Mesopotamien.   1883.

TAFEL, L. F.   De Thessalonica eiusque agro.   1839.
De via militari Romanorum Egnatia.   1842.
TAFRALI, O.   Topographie de Thessalonique.   1913.
TISSOT, CH. J.   Géographie comparée de la province romaine d'Afrique.   2 vols.
and atlas.   1884–88.

F. Art

AINALOV, D. V.   Ellinisticheskiia osnovy vizantiiskago iskusstva.   1900.
ANTONIADES, G. M.   Ἔκφρασις τῆς ἁγίας Σοφίας.   3 vols.   1907–9.

BERTAUX, É.   L'Art dans l'Italie méridionale.   Vol. i.   1904.

DALTON, O. M.   Byzantine Art and Archaeology.   1911.
DELBRÜCK, R.   Porträts byzantinischer Kaiserinnen.   Mitth. d. k. d. arch.
Inst., Röm. Abt. xxviii.   1913.
DIEHL, CH.   Manuel d'art byzantin.   1910.

FRESHFIELD, E. H.   Cellae Trichorae.   2 vols.   1913–18.

GEORGE, W. S.   The Church of Saint Eirene at Constantinople.   1913.

HÉBRARD, E., and ZEILLER, J.   Spalato, le palais de Dioclétien.   1912.
HEISENBERG, A.   Grabeskirche [Jerusalem] und Apostelkirche [Konstantinopel].
2 vols.   1908.

JACKSON, T. G.   Byzantine and Romanesque Architecture.   2 vols.   1913.

KONDAKOV, N.   Histoire de l'art byzantin.   2 vols.   1886–91.
Vizantiiskiia tserkvi i pamiatniki.   1886.
KRAUS, F. X.   Geschichte der christlichen Kunst.   2 vols. in 5 parts.   1895–
1908.

LETHABY, W., and SWAINSON, H.   Sancta Sophia.   1894.

MEYER, W.   Zwei antike Elfenbeintafel der k. Staats-Bibliothek in München.
Abh. der k. Bayerischen Akad. der Wiss., xv.   1881.
MILLINGEN, A. VAN.   Byzantine Churches in Constantinople.   1912.

PASPATES, A. G.   Βυζαντιναί Μελέται.   1877.

RICHTER, J. P., and TAYLOR, A. C.   Golden Age of Classic Christian Art.   1904.
RIVOIRA, G. T.   Lombardic Architecture.   (Eng. tr. by Rushforth.)   2 vols.
1910.

SALZENBERG.   Altchristliche Baudenkmale von Constantinopel.   1854.
STRZYGOWSKI, J.   Orient oder Rom.   1901.

TEXIER, C., and PULLAN, R.   Byzantine Architecture.   1864.

WILPERT, J. Die römischen Mosaïken und Malereien der kirchlichen Bauten vom iv. bis xiii. Jahrhundert (mit 300 farbigen Tafeln und 542 Text-bildern). 4 vols. 1916.

WULFF, O. Altchristliche und byzantinische Kunst. I. Die altchr. Kunst. 1918.

G. *Literature*

BAUMGARTEN, F. De Christodoro poeta Thebano. 1881.

CHRIST, W. Geschichte der griechischen Litteratur. Ed. 2. 1890.

EBERT, A. Allgemeine Geschichte der Litteratur des Mittelalters im Abend-lande. Vol. i. 1889.

KRUMBACHER, K. Geschichte der byzantinischen Litteratur. Ed. 2. 1897

LITZICA, C. Das Meyersche Satzschlussgesetz. 1898.

MANITIUS, M. Geschichte der christlich-lateinischen Poesie. 1891.
Geschichte der lateinischen Literatur des Mittelalters. Part i. 1911.
MEYER, W. Der accentuirte Satzschluss in der griechischen Prosa vom iv. bis xvi. Jahrh. 1891.

PETER, H. Die geschichtliche Litteratur über die römische Kaiserzeit bis Theodosius I. und ihre Quellen. 2 vols. 1897.

ROHDE, E. Der griechische Roman und seine Vorläufer. Ed. 2. 1900.

SANDYS, J. E. History of Classical Scholarship. Vol. i. 1903.
SEITZ, K. Die Schule von Gaza. 1892.

TEUFFEL, W. S. Geschichte der römischen Litteratur. Ed. 4. 1882.

WHITTAKER, T. The Neoplatonists. Ed. 2. 1918.
WILAMOWITZ-MÖLLENDORFF, U. VON. Die Hymnen des Proklos und Synesios. (S.B. pr. Ak. d. Wiss.) 1907.

INDEX

I.

ENGLISH (AND LATIN)

INDEX

II.

GREEK

THE END

A CATALOGUE OF SELECTED DOVER BOOKS
IN ALL FIELDS OF INTEREST

A CATALOGUE OF SELECTED DOVER BOOKS
IN ALL FIELDS OF INTEREST

AMERICA'S OLD MASTERS, James T. Flexner. Four men emerged unexpectedly from provincial 18th century America to leadership in European art: Benjamin West, J. S. Copley, C. R. Peale, Gilbert Stuart. Brilliant coverage of lives and contributions. Revised, 1967 edition. 69 plates. 365pp. of text.

21806-6 Paperbound $3.00

FIRST FLOWERS OF OUR WILDERNESS: AMERICAN PAINTING, THE COLONIAL PERIOD, James T. Flexner. Painters, and regional painting traditions from earliest Colonial times up to the emergence of Copley, West and Peale Sr., Foster, Gustavus Hesselius, Feke, John Smibert and many anonymous painters in the primitive manner. Engaging presentation, with 162 illustrations. xxii + 368pp.

22180-6 Paperbound $3.50

THE LIGHT OF DISTANT SKIES: AMERICAN PAINTING, 1760-1835, James T. Flexner. The great generation of early American painters goes to Europe to learn and to teach: West, Copley, Gilbert Stuart and others. Allston, Trumbull, Morse; also contemporary American painters—primitives, derivatives, academics—who remained in America. 102 illustrations. xiii + 306pp.

22179-2 Paperbound $3.00

A HISTORY OF THE RISE AND PROGRESS OF THE ARTS OF DESIGN IN THE UNITED STATES, William Dunlap. Much the richest mine of information on early American painters, sculptors, architects, engravers, miniaturists, etc. The only source of information for scores of artists, the major primary source for many others. Unabridged reprint of rare original 1834 edition, with new introduction by James T. Flexner, and 394 new illustrations. Edited by Rita Weiss. 6⅝ x 9⅝.

21695-0, 21696-9, 21697-7 Three volumes, Paperbound $13.50

EPOCHS OF CHINESE AND JAPANESE ART, Ernest F. Fenollosa. From primitive Chinese art to the 20th century, thorough history, explanation of every important art period and form, including Japanese woodcuts; main stress on China and Japan, but Tibet, Korea also included. Still unexcelled for its detailed, rich coverage of cultural background, aesthetic elements, diffusion studies, particularly of the historical period. 2nd, 1913 edition. 242 illustrations. lii + 439pp. of text.

20364-6, 20365-4 Two volumes, Paperbound $6.00

THE GENTLE ART OF MAKING ENEMIES, James A. M. Whistler. Greatest wit of his day deflates Oscar Wilde, Ruskin, Swinburne; strikes back at inane critics, exhibitions, art journalism; aesthetics of impressionist revolution in most striking form. Highly readable classic by great painter. Reproduction of edition designed by Whistler. Introduction by Alfred Werner. xxxvi + 334pp.

21875-9 Paperbound $2.50

POEMS OF ANNE BRADSTREET, edited with an introduction by Robert Hutchinson. A new selection of poems by America's first poet and perhaps the first significant woman poet in the English language. 48 poems display her development in works of considerable variety—love poems, domestic poems, religious meditations, formal elegies, "quaternions," etc. Notes, bibliography. viii + 222pp.

22160-1 Paperbound $2.00

THREE GOTHIC NOVELS: THE CASTLE OF OTRANTO BY HORACE WALPOLE; VATHEK BY WILLIAM BECKFORD; THE VAMPYRE BY JOHN POLIDORI, WITH FRAGMENT OF A NOVEL BY LORD BYRON, edited by E. F. Bleiler. The first Gothic novel, by Walpole; the finest Oriental tale in English, by Beckford; powerful Romantic supernatural story in versions by Polidori and Byron. All extremely important in history of literature; all still exciting, packed with supernatural thrills, ghosts, haunted castles, magic, etc. xl + 291pp.

21232-7 Paperbound $2.50

THE BEST TALES OF HOFFMANN, E. T. A. Hoffmann. 10 of Hoffmann's most important stories, in modern re-editings of standard translations: Nutcracker and the King of Mice, Signor Formica, Automata, The Sandman, Rath Krespel, The Golden Flowerpot, Master Martin the Cooper, The Mines of Falun, The King's Betrothed, A New Year's Eve Adventure. 7 illustrations by Hoffmann. Edited by E. F. Bleiler. xxxix + 419pp. 21793-0 Paperbound $3.00

GHOST AND HORROR STORIES OF AMBROSE BIERCE, Ambrose Bierce. 23 strikingly modern stories of the horrors latent in the human mind: The Eyes of the Panther, The Damned Thing, An Occurrence at Owl Creek Bridge, An Inhabitant of Carcosa, etc., plus the dream-essay, Visions of the Night. Edited by E. F. Bleiler. xxii + 199pp. 20767-6 Paperbound $1.50

BEST GHOST STORIES OF J. S. LEFANU, J. Sheridan LeFanu. Finest stories by Victorian master often considered greatest supernatural writer of all. Carmilla, Green Tea, The Haunted Baronet, The Familiar, and 12 others. Most never before available in the U. S. A. Edited by E. F. Bleiler. 8 illustrations from Victorian publications. xvii + 467pp. 20415-4 Paperbound $3.00

MATHEMATICAL FOUNDATIONS OF INFORMATION THEORY, A. I. Khinchin. Comprehensive introduction to work of Shannon, McMillan, Feinstein and Khinchin, placing these investigations on a rigorous mathematical basis. Covers entropy concept in probability theory, uniqueness theorem, Shannon's inequality, ergodic sources, the E property, martingale concept, noise, Feinstein's fundamental lemma, Shannon's first and second theorems. Translated by R. A. Silverman and M. D. Friedman. iii + 120pp. 60434-9 Paperbound $1.75

SEVEN SCIENCE FICTION NOVELS, H. G. Wells. The standard collection of the great novels. Complete, unabridged. *First Men in the Moon, Island of Dr. Moreau, War of the Worlds, Food of the Gods, Invisible Man, Time Machine, In the Days of the Comet.* Not only science fiction fans, but every educated person owes it to himself to read these novels. 1015pp 20264-X Clothbound $5.00

AGAINST THE GRAIN (A REBOURS), Joris K. Huysmans. Filled with weird images, evidences of a bizarre imagination, exotic experiments with hallucinatory drugs, rich tastes and smells and the diversions of its sybarite hero Duc Jean des Esseintes, this classic novel pushed 19th-century literary decadence to its limits. Full unabridged edition. Do not confuse this with abridged editions generally sold. Introduction by Havelock Ellis. xlix + 206pp. 22190-3 Paperbound $2.00

VARIORUM SHAKESPEARE: HAMLET. Edited by Horace H. Furness; a landmark of American scholarship. Exhaustive footnotes and appendices treat all doubtful words and phrases, as well as suggested critical emendations throughout the play's history. First volume contains editor's own text, collated with all Quartos and Folios. Second volume contains full first Quarto, translations of Shakespeare's sources (Belleforest, and Saxo Grammaticus), Der Bestrafte Brudermord, and many essays on critical and historical points of interest by major authorities of past and present. Includes details of staging and costuming over the years. By far the best edition available for serious students of Shakespeare. Total of xx + 905pp.
21004-9, 21005-7, 2 volumes, Paperbound $7.00

A LIFE OF WILLIAM SHAKESPEARE, Sir Sidney Lee. This is the standard life of Shakespeare, summarizing everything known about Shakespeare and his plays. Incredibly rich in material, broad in coverage, clear and judicious, it has served thousands as the best introduction to Shakespeare. 1931 edition. 9 plates. xxix + 792pp. (USO) 21967-4 Paperbound $3.75

MASTERS OF THE DRAMA, John Gassner. Most comprehensive history of the drama in print, covering every tradition from Greeks to modern Europe and America, including India, Far East, etc. Covers more than 800 dramatists, 2000 plays, with biographical material, plot summaries, theatre history, criticism, etc. "Best of its kind in English," New Republic. 77 illustrations. xxii + 890pp.
20100-7 Clothbound $8.50

THE EVOLUTION OF THE ENGLISH LANGUAGE, George McKnight. The growth of English, from the 14th century to the present. Unusual, non-technical account presents basic information in very interesting form: sound shifts, change in grammar and syntax, vocabulary growth, similar topics. Abundantly illustrated with quotations. Formerly Modern English in the Making. xii + 590pp.
21932-1 Paperbound $3.50

AN ETYMOLOGICAL DICTIONARY OF MODERN ENGLISH, Ernest Weekley. Fullest, richest work of its sort, by foremost British lexicographer. Detailed word histories, including many colloquial and archaic words; extensive quotations. Do not confuse this with the Concise Etymological Dictionary, which is much abridged. Total of xxvii + 830pp. 6½ x 9¼.
21873-2, 21874-0 Two volumes, Paperbound $6.00

FLATLAND: A ROMANCE OF MANY DIMENSIONS, E. A. Abbott. Classic of science-fiction explores ramifications of life in a two-dimensional world, and what happens when a three-dimensional being intrudes. Amusing reading, but also useful as introduction to thought about hyperspace. Introduction by Banesh Hoffmann. 16 illustrations. xx + 103pp. 20001-9 Paperbound $1.00

MATHEMATICAL PUZZLES FOR BEGINNERS AND ENTHUSIASTS, Geoffrey Mott-Smith. 189 puzzles from easy to difficult—involving arithmetic, logic, algebra, properties of digits, probability, etc.—for enjoyment and mental stimulus. Explanation of mathematical principles behind the puzzles. 135 illustrations. viii + 248pp.
20198-8 Paperbound $1.75

PAPER FOLDING FOR BEGINNERS, William D. Murray and Francis J. Rigney. Easiest book on the market, clearest instructions on making interesting, beautiful origami. Sail boats, cups, roosters, frogs that move legs, bonbon boxes, standing birds, etc. 40 projects; more than 275 diagrams and photographs. 94pp.
20713-7 Paperbound $1.00

TRICKS AND GAMES ON THE POOL TABLE, Fred Herrmann. 79 tricks and games— some solitaires, some for two or more players, some competitive games—to entertain you between formal games. Mystifying shots and throws, unusual caroms, tricks involving such props as cork, coins, a hat, etc. Formerly *Fun on the Pool Table*. 77 figures. 95pp.
21814-7 Paperbound $1.00

HAND SHADOWS TO BE THROWN UPON THE WALL: A SERIES OF NOVEL AND AMUSING FIGURES FORMED BY THE HAND, Henry Bursill. Delightful picturebook from great-grandfather's day shows how to make 18 different hand shadows: a bird that flies, duck that quacks, dog that wags his tail, camel, goose, deer, boy, turtle, etc. Only book of its sort. vi + 33pp. 6½ x 9¼. 21779-5 Paperbound $1.00

WHITTLING AND WOODCARVING, E. J. Tangerman. 18th printing of best book on market. "If you can cut a potato you can carve" toys and puzzles, chains, chessmen, caricatures, masks, frames, woodcut blocks, surface patterns, much more. Information on tools, woods, techniques. Also goes into serious wood sculpture from Middle Ages to present, East and West. 464 photos, figures. x + 293pp.
20965-2 Paperbound $2.00

HISTORY OF PHILOSOPHY, Julián Marias. Possibly the clearest, most easily followed, best planned, most useful one-volume history of philosophy on the market; neither skimpy nor overfull. Full details on system of every major philosopher and dozens of less important thinkers from pre-Socratics up to Existentialism and later. Strong on many European figures usually omitted. Has gone through dozens of editions in Europe. 1966 edition, translated by Stanley Appelbaum and Clarence Strowbridge. xviii + 505pp. 21739-6 Paperbound $3.00

YOGA: A SCIENTIFIC EVALUATION, Kovoor T. Behanan. Scientific but non-technical study of physiological results of yoga exercises; done under auspices of Yale U. Relations to Indian thought, to psychoanalysis, etc. 16 photos. xxiii + 270pp.
20505-3 Paperbound $2.50

Prices subject to change without notice.
Available at your book dealer or write for free catalogue to Dept. GI, Dover Publications, Inc., 180 Varick St., N. Y., N. Y. 10014. Dover publishes more than 150 books each year on science, elementary and advanced mathematics, biology, music, art, literary history, social sciences and other areas.